The Rise in Unemployment

*Edited by C. R. Bean, P. R. G. Layard
and S. J. Nickell*

Basil Blackwell

This paperback version first published by Basil Blackwell Ltd, 1987

Basil Blackwell Ltd
108 Cowley Road, Oxford OX4 1JF, UK

Basil Blackwell Inc.
432 Park Avenue South, Suite 1503
New York, NY 10016, USA

British Library Cataloguing in Publication Data

The Rise in unemployment.
1. Unemployment   2. Labor economics
I. Bean, Charles R.   II. Layard, Richard
III. Nickell, Stephen
331.13'7   HD5707.5

ISBN 0-631-15419-1

Library of Congress Cataloging in Publication Data

The Rise in unemployment.

Includes indexes.
1. Unemployment.   I. Bean, C. R. (Charles R.),
1953–   . II. Layard, P. R. G. (P. Richard G.)
III. Nickell, S. J.
HD5707.5.R57   1987   331.13'7   87-699
ISBN 0-631-15419-1 (pbk.)

Printed in Great Britain by
T. J. Press Ltd, Padstow

Contents

Editors' Introduction   vii

The Rise in Unemployment: A Multi-Country Study
    C. R. BEAN, P. R. G. LAYARD and S. J. NICKELL   1

Unemployment: Getting the Questions Right   R. M. SOLOW   23

Aggregate Supply and Demand Factors in OECD Unemployment: An Update
    M. BRUNO   35

Wages Policy and Unemployment in Australia   R. G. GREGORY   53

Labour Supply as a Signal for Real-Wage Adjustment; Austria 1968−83
    K. PICHELMANN and M. WAGNER   75

A Discussion of Belgian Unemployment Combining Traditional Concepts and
Disequilibrium Economics   H. R SNEESSENS and J. H. DRÈZE   89

Unemployment in Britain   P. R. G. LAYARD and S. J. NICKELL   121

Why Have Unemployment Rates in Canada and the United States Diverged?
    O. ASHENFELTER and D. CARD   171

The Rise of Unemployment in France   E. MALINVAUD   197

The Nature and Causes of Unemployment in the Federal Republic of Germany
since the 1970s: An Empirical Investigation   W. FRANZ and H. KÖNIG   219

Aggregate Unemployment in Italy: 1960−83
    F. MODIGLIANI, F. PADOA SCHIOPPA and N. ROSSI   245

Trends in Unemployment, Wages and Productivity: The Case of Japan
    K. HAMADA and Y. KUROSAKA   275

Unemployment in the Netherlands   W. DRIEHUIS   297

Spanish Industrial Unemployment: Some Explanatory Factors
    J. J. DOLADO, J. L. MALO DE MOLINA and A. ZABALZA   313

Data Appendices   335

Author Index   375

Subject Index   379

Introduction

The rise of unemployment in Europe is one of the main economic problems of our time. It is also not easy to explain. Though unemployment has risen in most countries, the size of the increase differs greatly. There is much to be learned from a simultaneous attempt to explain the experience of different countries.

A conference on the topic of rising unemployment was therefore held at the White House Conference Centre, Chelwood Gate, Sussex, England, on 27–31 May 1985. This special issue of *Economica* contains the proceedings of that conference.

The bulk of the volume contains detailed studies of the unemployment experience of most of the major developed economies. In addition, there is a keynote address by Robert Solow and two multi-country studies: one by Michael Bruno and a second by the Editors, which seeks to draw together a few of the strands that emerged over the course of the conference.

The conference would not have been possible without generous financial assistance from the Commission of the European Communities (DG V), the Economic and Social Research Council, the Department of Employment, and Her Majesty's Treasury. We are also grateful to all the participants and discussants at the conference who helped to make it a success.

The London School of Economics   CHARLES BEAN
                                                    RICHARD LAYARD
                                                    STEPHEN NICKELL

The Rise in Unemployment: A Multi-country Study

By C. R. BEAN and P. R. G. LAYARD

The London School of Economics

S. J. NICKELL

Oxford Institute of Economics and Statistics

INTRODUCTION

One of the most remarkable features of recent economic history has been the remorseless rise in unemployment throughout the industrialized countries. However, while the trend to higher unemployment is universal, the experience of individual countries also differs widely. The increase is especially marked within the European Community, where unemployment rates rival those reached in the interwar years. By contrast, in the Scandinavian countries and Japan unemployment is lower and has risen very much less. Experience in the United States lies somewhere between these extremes, and in the last few years unemployment there has fallen sharply.

This picture is documented for 19 OECD countries in Table 1. Unemployment rates in 1984 exceeded 10 per cent of the workforce in Belgium, Canada, Italy, Netherlands, Spain and the United Kingdom, with Australia, France and even the virtuous German economy not far behind. At the other end of

TABLE 1

OECD STANDARDIZED UNEMPLOYMENT RATES, 1956–1984
(period average)

	1956–66 (%)	1967–74 (%)	1975–79 (%)	1980–83 (%)	1984 (%)
Australia	2·2	2·1	5·5	7·2	8·9
Austria	2·4	1·5	1·9	3·0	3·8
Belgium	2·6	2·6	7·0	11·5	14·0
Canada	4·9	5·2	7·5	9·4	11·2
Denmark	2·3	1·3	6·5	9·9	n.a.
Finland	1·6	2·5	5·1	5·4	6·1
France	1·5	2·5	4·9	7·5	9·7
Germany	1·4	1·1	3·5	5·4	8·6
Ireland	5·4	5·6	7·0	9·7	n.a.
Italy	6·5	5·6	6·8	8·6	10·2
Japan	1·7	1·3	2·0	2·3	2·7
Netherlands	1·2	2·2	5·3	9·9	14·0
New Zealand	0·1	0·3	1·0	3·6	n.a.
Norway	2·3	1·7	1·9	2·4	3·0
Spain	2·1	2·7	5·8	14·6	20·1
Sweden	1·7	2·2	1·9	2·8	3·1
Switzerland	0·1	0·0	0·4	0·5	1·2
United Kingdom	2·5	3·4	5·8	10·9	13·2
United States	5·0	4·6	6·9	8·4	7·4

Sources: All except Denmark, Ireland and New Zealand: OECD *Economic Outlook*; Denmark, Ireland and New Zealand; Grubb (1984).

the spectrum, Austria, Japan, Norway, Sweden and Switzerland were still experiencing unemployment rates around the 3 per cent mark, although even these modest levels represent a marked deterioration compared with their performance earlier in the postwar era.

One popular explanation that is sometimes advanced to explain the rise in unemployment is that it is primarily a consequence of rapid labour force growth with the supply of jobs lagging behind the demand for them. While it is true that female participation has risen in many countries, particularly among married women, as attitudes towards the role of women in the economy and society have altered,[1] nevertheless the growth in the labour force in recent years has not in general been markedly faster than in the 1960s, as Table 2 amply demonstrates. While discouraged worker effects may render the exact interpretation of these figures open to question, they do weigh heavily against the view that rapid labour supply growth is at the root of the unemployment problem.

But if labour force growth is not the culprit, what is? The widespread upward trend in unemployment rates suggests that there may be common factors at work. Much of the debate, at both an academic and a political level, has focused on the role of real wages. One view is that much of the current unemployment is the result of an excessively high level of real wages. The commodity and oil price shocks of the 1970s necessitated a fall in real consumption wages to restore equilibrium in the labour market, but this adjustment took place only slowly. The result was a period of prolonged 'classical' unemployment. The converse of this view is that aggregate demand has been too low and that the unemployment is therefore 'Keynesian' in nature. The

TABLE 2

OECD LABOUR FORCE AVERAGE GROWTH RATES, 1961–1984

(per cent per annum)

	1961–71	1977–82	1977–82	1982–84
Australia	2·8[a]	2·0	1·5	1·5
Austria	−1·2[a]	0·0	1·7	0·9
Belgium	0·7	0·8	0·7	0·4[b]
Canada	2·8	3·3	2·6	1·8
Denmark	1·3[a]	0·9	1·2	1·2[b]
Finland	0·3	1·5	1·2	0·9
France	0·9	1·0	0·7	0·2
Germany	0·2	−0·3	0·7	−0·1
Ireland	0·3	0·8	2·0	1·0[b]
Italy	−0·7	0·9	0·8	1·0
Japan	1·3	0·8	1·2	1·3
Netherlands	1·1	0·4	2·5	1·6[b]
New Zealand	2·2	2·3	1·0	1·7[b]
Norway	1·0	2·3	1·5	0·8
Spain	0·8	0·3	0·2	0·3
Sweden	0·8[a]	0·9	0·9	0·4
Switzerland	1·2	−1·3	0·7	−0·9[b]
United Kingdom	0·0	0·7	0·4	0·6
United States	1·8	2·5	2·1	1·5

Source: OECD Labour Force Statistics.
[a] Australia from 1964, Austria from 1968, Denmark from 1960, Sweden from 1962.
[b] 1982–83.

demand deficiency in turn is largely attributed to a shift in government priorities, away from maintaining full employment and towards containing inflation, which has resulted in the widespread adoption of contractionary monetary and, outside the United States, contractionary fiscal policies.

There are two problems with this general line of approach. The first is the artificial dichotomy between explanations relying on excessively high real wages and those relying on deficient aggregate demand, which stems from the assumption that firms are price-takers. While the assumption of perfect competition is often a convenient fiction, it is here distinctly misleading. Within such an environment the 'Keynesian' explanation can be rationalized only if prices do not clear the product market, yet it is difficult to see what impediments could prevent opportunities for gains from trade being realised, except perhaps in the very short run. In reality, however, prices are set by firms in markets that are less than fully competitive. Under imperfect competition firms can be optimizing in their pricing and employment decisions, yet the demand for labour will depend on both the level of real product wages and the level of real aggregate demand. This approach underlies a number of papers in this volume.

The second problem, emphasized in Solow's opening address to the conference, is that an explanation of current unemployment levels in terms of an excessive level of real wages is at best incomplete since it fails to explain the exogenous factors that have brought real wages to their present level. Only in the Soviet bloc countries can the real wage be considered exogenous. In OECD countries it is an endogenous variable, which is the outcome of the process by which nominal wages are set in the labour market and prices are set in the product market. These in turn will reflect a variety of factors such as the generosity of unemployment benefits, trade union strength, skill mismatch and the like. Similarly, the assertion that the way to reduce unemployment is to reduce real wages—as advanced for instance by the current British Chancellor of the Exchequer—is vacuous unless it details how such a reduction in labour costs is to be brought about.

I. A THEORETICAL FRAMEWORK FOR ANALYSIS

In order to shed further light on the data in Table 1, we present for each country estimates of a simple structural macroeconomic model centred on the labour market. The model assumes an imperfectly competitive environment and is spelt out in much greater detail in the Layard–Nickell paper on the United Kingdom in this volume. Here, therefore, we shall simply provide an outline of the theoretical structure, and refer the reader to that paper for a fuller discussion of the optimization problem and aggregation assumptions underlying the model. The paper on Spain by Dolado, Malo and Zabalza utilizes an identical theoretical structure, and the model in the paper on Italy by Modigliani, Padoa Schioppa and Rossi, although differing in details, is very similar in philosophy. In schematic form, the model consists of the following four equations:

Labour demand

$$(1) \qquad \frac{N}{K} = f^1 \left(\frac{W}{P}, A, \sigma \right)$$
$$\qquad\qquad\qquad - \quad ? \quad +$$

Price-setting

$$(2) \quad \frac{P}{W} = f^2 \left(\underset{-}{\frac{K}{L}}, A, \underset{?}{\sigma}, \underset{+}{\frac{W}{W^r}} \right)$$

Wage-setting

$$(3) \quad \frac{W}{P} = f^3 \left(\underset{+}{\frac{N}{L}}, \underset{+}{\frac{K}{L}}, \underset{?}{A}, \underset{-}{\frac{P}{P^e}}, \underset{+}{Z^s} \right)$$

Aggregate demand

$$(4) \quad \sigma = f^4 \left(\underset{+}{\frac{M}{P}}, \underset{+}{\frac{eP^*}{P}}, \underset{+}{Z^D} \right)$$

where

N = employment
L = the labour force
K = the capital stock
W = hourly labour cost (including employment taxes)
P = the GDP deflator
A = an index of technical progress
σ = an index of real aggregate demand (relative to potential output)
M = the money stock
eP^* = the level of competitors' prices in domestic currency
Z^s = a set of wage push factors (e.g. benefit levels)
Z^D = a set of demand shift factors (e.g. fiscal variables)

An 'e' superscript denotes an expected variable. In the absence of wage and price surprises, the model solves for the employment rate (N/L), demand (σ), the real wage (W/P) and the price level (P) as functions of the capital-labour ratio (K/L), technical progress (A), the money stock (M), competitors' prices (eP^*) and the supply demand shift variables (Z^s, Z^D), which are all treated as exogenous. Since σ is demand relative to potential, real balances and the demand shift variables also should be measured relative to potential.

Our focus is on the first three equations, which describe the supply side of the model, and especially on the employment and wage equations. The derivation of these equations is as follows. First, the firm decides on a pricing strategy. Once the firm has set its price, output is determined by demand, which depends on the price of its output relative to its competitors' output and the level of real demand in the economy as a whole. Employment is then determined through the production technology, which is assumed to exhibit constant returns to scale and to be separable in value added and raw materials. (The empirical results suggest that the latter assumption is approximately satisfied for most countries.) If prices are set as a mark-up, $\nu(\sigma)$, on marginal cost, then it follows immediately that the marginal product of labour is equal to the product of this same mark-up and the real wage.[2] So under perfect competition, or under imperfect competition with a constant elasticity demand curve, the price mark-up on marginal cost is independent of demand and the employment–capital ratio depends only on the real wage ($f_\sigma^1 = 0$).[3] At the other extreme, however, if prices are set as a mark-up on normal cost, independent of demand σ, then the mark-up on marginal cost, $\nu(\sigma)$, must be decreasing in demand since marginal costs are increasing. So the marginal product of labour must be decreasing in demand for a fixed real wage, and thus employment must be increasing in σ ($f_\sigma^1 > 0$). So if there is any element of normal cost pricing behaviour in the economy, we must expect the employment–capital ratio to depend on both demand and the real wage as in (1).

The price equation (2) then follows immediately from the general pricing rule that prices are some mark-up on marginal cost where output is eliminated from marginal cost by setting it equal to the firm's demand. It is worth noting that the net impact of demand on prices is a combination of the upward pressure exerted by increasing marginal cost and the downward pressure exerted by the falling marginal cost mark-up. Under perfect competition the latter effect is absent and $f_\sigma^2 > 0$, whereas under normal cost pricing the two effects exactly cancel and prices do not vary with the state of the cycle ($f_\sigma^2 = 0$). Finally, the presence of the wage surprise (W/W^e) in (2) allows for the fact that some prices may have to be set before the outcome of wage negotiations is known.

The wage equation (3) encompasses four possible mechanisms by which wages may be set: (i) supply and demand in a competitive market; (ii) firms; (iii) unions; and (iv) bargaining between firms and unions.

If $f_{K/L}^3 = f_A^3 = 0$, then (3) is simply a labour supply curve relating the proportion of the labour force who are willing to work with the real wage and a set of shift factors which might include taxes, relative import prices and any other variables affecting search intensity and willingness to work, such as the size and availability of unemployment benefit.

The class of models in which firms set wages include those of the efficiency wage type (surveyed in Stiglitz, 1984, and Johnson and Layard, 1986). These models have the property that, for one reason or another, an increase in the wage paid generates a benefit to the firm that partially offsets the cost. For instance, increasing wages might reduce quits (Pencavel, 1972; Weiss, 1980), reduce vacancies (Jackman, Layard and Pissarides, 1984) or increase work effort (Shapiro and Stiglitz, 1984). In all these models the wage is set to equate marginal benefit to marginal cost, and in general will reflect the attractiveness of outside opportunities, including alternative wages, the unemployment rate and benefit levels.

In the monopoly union model (Dunlop, 1944) unions and firms bargain over wages knowing that employment will be determined according to the labour demand schedule (1), and this is taken account of when they evaluate their welfare and profit functions. If union welfare depends on both the level of wages and the employment rate of its members, the final level of real wages will depend on all the variables in the firm's labour demand function, the employment rate and the shift variables Z^s, which might now include proxies for relative bargaining strength. However, such an equation would, in the aggregate, be under-identified, so (3) also substitutes out σ from the bargaining solution using the labour demand function. Alternatively, it could be regarded

6 BEAN, LAYARD and NICKELL

as a structural relation if unions and firms bargain in the light of the 'normal' level of demand. (For further discussion of union or bargaining models of wage determination, see Layard and Nickell, 1985a.)[4]

Equations (1) and (3) can be used to eliminate the real wage and give the employment rate in terms of its proximate determinants:

$$(5) \quad \frac{N}{L} = g^1\left(\frac{K}{L}, A, \frac{P}{P^e}, \sigma, Z^s\right).$$

Equations (2) and (3) can also be combined to eliminate the real wage:

$$(6) \quad \frac{N}{L} = g^2\left(\frac{N}{L}, A, \frac{P}{P^e}, \frac{W}{W^e}, \sigma, Z^s\right).$$

If there are no surprises, (5) and (6) solve jointly for the 'natural' rate of unemployment in terms of the capital–labour ratio, technical progress and the shift variables. However, in the empirical work that follows we shall not estimate the price equation (2) and instead shall concentrate on an appraisal of the relative importance of demand and supply shift factors as proximate causes of the rise in unemployment.

II. Empirical Results

Our comparative approach owes a great deal to the work of Bruno and Sachs (1985) and Newell and Symons (1986), both of which report and compare wage and employment equations for a number of OECD countries.

The data set for Spain is unfortunately incomplete but otherwise our estimates cover the remaining 18 countries whose unemployment history is described in Table 1. The data are annual and the sample period runs from 1953 to 1983.[5] Our aim has been to estimate a common specification across all countries. Obviously there are likely to be special factors operating in many of the countries whose incorporation would enhance the explanatory power of the model, and a more comprehensive search over the dynamic specification for individual countries might also prove fruitful. However, it is precisely a discussion of those specific factors that constitutes the aim of the various country papers that make up the bulk of this volume. Further, by maintaining the same general specification across all countries, we hope to demonstrate both the robustness of the model and its usefulness as a general framework. It also makes clearer the *differences* in structure between countries, which are the concern of Section IV.

Turning now to the shift factors Z^s in the wage equation, we include first the variables defining the total wedge θ between the consumption wage and the product wage:

$$(7) \quad \theta = t_1 + t_2 + t_3 + S_M \log(P_M/P)/(1+S_M)$$

where

t_1 = the employment tax rate
t_2 = the income tax rate
t_3 = the consumption tax rate
S_M = the share of imports in value added
P_M = the price of imports in domestic currency

For most countries the restriction that the tax rates and the import price term enter with the same coefficient is not rejected statistically.

Second, we want variables reflecting unemployment benefit levels, search intensity, etc. The effect of the level and duration of unemployment benefit on unemployment is, of course, a contentious issue. However, deriving series that adequately capture the multi-dimensional complexity of the benefit system for all 18 countries is a truly Herculean task which is well beyond the scope of this exercise. As an alternative, we therefore adopted the expediency of including a variable designed to capture the outward shift in the unemployment-vacancy relationship that has occurred in many countries. Specifically, we estimated for each country the relationship

$$(8) \qquad \Delta U = \gamma_0 + \gamma_1 \Delta V + \gamma_2 \Delta U_{-1} + \gamma_3 U_{-1} + \gamma_4 V_{-1} + \gamma_5 t + \gamma_6 t^2$$

where

$U = 1 - N/L =$ the unemployment rate
$V =$ the vacancy rate
$\Delta =$ the difference operator

The linear and quadratic time trends capture this outward shift in the unemployment-vacancy relationship and reflect the increasing generosity of the unemployment benefit system and other changes in labour market structure, while the remaining terms capture the dynamics in the relationship associated with the business cycle. We then constructed[6] a variable

$$(9) \qquad \phi = (\gamma_5 t + \gamma_6 t^2)/\gamma_3$$

which gives (subject to a constant and a change of sign) the equilibrium unemployment rate associated with a given vacancy rate as a 'catch-all' variable for these factors. We shall refer to ϕ as the 'search' variable, although, of course, it may reflect a number of factors entirely unrelated to the search intensity of the unemployed.

Finally, we also tried including a measure of strike activity and, for those countries when it was available, a time series of the unionization rate as proxies for bargaining strength. However, in general we were unable to obtain significant effects from these variables, and they are omitted from the results reported below. In other work (Layard and Nickell, 1985b) we have been able to obtain significant effects for a number of countries using the union/non-union mark-up as well as strikes data, but such information is not readily available for all 18 countries studied here.

Turning now to the demand shift variables (Z^D), in previous applications of this model we have usually used cyclically and inflation-corrected budget deficits as a measure of domestic fiscal impact. This is not readily available for all the countries in the sample.[7] Instead, we simply enter the level of government spending and the tax wedge separately. To capture foreign demand we use GDP in the rest of the OECD: i.e. for each country we subtract its own GDP from total OECD GDP.

In previous applications we have also usually implicitly substituted out σ using (4), including our demand variables directly in the employment and price equations. However, this is rather profligate with degrees of freedom, as we have four demand variables (government spending, the tax wedge, foreign output, and competitiveness),[8] which doubles up to eight if lags are allowed for. Since the effect of these variables is only via their effect on aggregate demand, we constructed a single index of aggregate demand by regressing (the logarithm of) GDP on (the logarithm of) each of these four variables, current and lagged, and a lagged dependent variable, and then taking the predicted value of this regression as a measure of σ. Since σ represents demand relative to potential output, GDP, government spending and foreign output were all first normalized on the capital stock as a proxy for the size of the economy.[9] Thus our σ variable is a particular linear combination of the exogenous demand factors.[10]

Capital accumulation and technical progress is likely to lead to shorter working weeks and may affect participation. However, given the definition of the labour force, it is reasonable to suggest that they do not affect the equilibrium unemployment rate, and our estimates are constrained to satisfy this requirement. Technical progress is here proxied by a simple linear and quadratic time trend (this seems to work as well as an index of total factor productivity). We also need to dynamize the system to allow for lags. After a little experimentation with the dynamic specification, we settled on the following (log-linear) representation of equations (1) and (3):

$$(10a) \quad \Delta \log N = \alpha_0 + \alpha_1 \log\left(\frac{N_{-1}}{K}\right) + \alpha_2 \log\left(\frac{W}{P}\right) + \alpha_3\sigma + \alpha_4\Delta \log N_{-1}$$
$$+ \alpha_5 t + \alpha_6 t^2$$

$$(10b) \quad \Delta \log\left(\frac{W}{P}\right) = \beta_0 + \left(\frac{\beta_1}{\alpha_2}\right)\left\{\alpha_1 \log\left(\frac{L}{K}\right) + \alpha_2 \log\left(\frac{W}{P}\right)_{-1} + \alpha_5 t + \alpha_6 t^2\right\}$$
$$+ \beta_2 \log\left(\frac{L}{N}\right) + \beta_3\theta + \beta_4\phi.$$

The term in braces is a sort of 'error correction' term, and the coefficient restrictions ensure neutrality with respect to the capital stock and technical progress. We tried proxying price 'surprises' in (10b) by $\Delta^2 \log P$, but for most countries this was insignificant. Under rational expectations, the price 'surprise' should be white noise and orthogonal to the information set. If all the exogenous variables are included in this information set, then its omission should not bias the remaining coefficients.

Table 3 presents maximum likelihood estimates of the parameters of system (10) for each country and their standard errors.[11] For brevity, the constants and technical progress terms are omitted. We also report the long-run wage elasticity $(-\alpha_2/\alpha_1)$ and its associated standard error.

For most countries the estimates are fairly sensible. Wages have a depressing effect on employment in all countries except the United States, and their effect is generally quite well defined with most of the long-run elasticities somewhere between one-half and unity in absolute value. The finding of a 'perverse' response for the United States accords with a certain amount of other research (e.g. Bruno and Sachs, 1985, p. 173) and may account for the common assertion that real wages have little impact on employment. Table 3 reports an alternative estimate for the United States including lagged real wages and replacing the

TABLE 3

ESTIMATES OF LABOUR DEMAND AND WAGE-SETTING EQUATIONS (10)

Independent variables Parameter	Labour demand					Wage-setting			
	Lagged employment α_1	Wage α_2	Demand α_3	Lagged change in employment α_4	Long-run wage elasticity $-\alpha_2/\alpha_1$	Lagged wage β_1	Unemployment β_2	Wedge β_3	Search β_4
Australia	-1·43 (0·41)	-0·44 (0·07)	-0·37 (0·33)	0·54 (0·43)	-0·28 (0·10)	-0·03 (0·32)	-2·77 (1·0)	0·48 (0·55)	-1·71 (2·2)
Austria	-0·44 (0·10)	-0·32 (0·07)	0·32 (0·13)	0·03 (0·22)	-0·50 (0·12)	-0·48 (0·22)	-10·2 (3·2)	-1·18 (0·45)	-7·89 (4·4)
Belgium	-0·24 (0·12)	-0·21 (0·04)	0·54 (0·22)	0·08 (0·30)	-0·87 (0·47)	-0·07 (0·11)	-2·28 (0·48)	0·24 (0·11)	-1·68 (0·50)
Canada	-0·83 (0·30)	-0·35 (0·11)	0·60 (0·08)	0·23 (0·25)	-0·42 (0·20)	-0·19 (0·16)	-0·79 (0·47)	0·28 (0·24)	0·12 (0·18)
Denmark	-0·74 (0·18)	-0·45 (0·15)	0·39 (0·11)	0·07 (0·22)	-0·61 (0·12)	-0·19 (0·07)	-0·49 (0·15)	-0·22 (0·10)	-0·13 (0·10)
Finland	-0·68 (0·22)	-0·48 (0·10)	0·47 (0·19)	0·36 (0·16)	-0·71 (0·16)	-0·70 (0·19)	-2·10 (0·70)	0·17 (0·21)	-0·59 (0·90)
France	-0·28 (0·08)	-0·17 (0·05)	0·14 (0·11)	0·22 (0·21)	-0·62 (0·15)	-0·39 (0·09)	-2·93 (0·82)	0·20 (0·08)	-2·17 (1·5)
Germany	-0·64 (0·30)	-0·53 (0·15)	0·46 (0·34)	0·51 (0·29)	-0·47 (0·29)	-0·05 (0·24)	-3·31 (0·76)	-0·42 (0·50)	-4·28 (1·5)
Ireland[a]	-0·29 (0·09)	-0·30 (0·07)	0·25 (0·07)	0·50 (0·29)	-1·03 (0·20)	-0·51 (0·23)	-2·83 (0·54)	0·70 (0·25)	0·17 (0·15)
Italy[a]	-0·35 (0·17)	-0·13 (0·05)	0·10 (0·13)	0·14 (0·34)	-0·37 (0·08)	-0·46 (0·17)	0·03 (0·83)	-0·15 (0·20)	0·45 (0·38)
Japan	-0·35 (0·07)	-0·36 (0·07)	-0·01 (0·02)	-0·43 (0·19)	-1·02 (0·05)	1·29 (0·53)	-41·0 (8·6)	-0·92 (0·83)	-42·7 (12·0)
Netherlands	-0·10 (0·12)	-0·11 (0·10)	0·21 (0·23)	0·31 (0·69)	-1·15 (1·05)	-0·36 (0·15)	-0·77 (0·61)	0·15 (0·29)	-0·25 (0·86)
New Zealand	-1·03 (0·16)	-0·23 (0·07)	0·19 (0·07)	0·13 (0·22)	-0·23 (0·06)	-0·45 (0·13)	-0·84 (0·88)	0·02 (0·23)	0·00 (0·50)
Norway	-0·93 (0·29)	-0·18 (0·06)	0·39 (0·15)	0·78 (0·29)	-0·14 (0·07)	-0·55 (0·19)	-5·93 (2·1)	-0·13 (0·13)	1·97 (5·5)
Sweden	-0·84 (0·18)	-0·55 (0·12)	-0·17 (0·25)	0·85 (0·47)	-0·66 (0·11)	-0·97 (0·40)	-7·77 (2·0)	0·48 (0·21)	-9·64 (4·4)
Switzerland	-0·88 (0·13)	-0·83 (0·09)	0·55 (0·14)	0·79 (0·22)	-0·94 (0·09)	-0·44 (0·23)	-23·3 (3·9)	-0·63 (0·48)	-3·78 (3·3)
United Kingdom	-0·63 (0·13)	-0·40 (0·20)	0·50 (0·07)	0·45 (0·20)	-0·63 (0·20)	-0·03 (0·19)	-0·53 (0·46)	0·04 (0·10)	-0·23 (0·72)
United States	-0·59 (0·15)	0·92 (0·28)	0·51 (0·12)	-0·09 (0·23)	1·57 (0·31)	-1·15 (0·24)	0·38 (0·19)	0·38 (0·14)	0·96 (0·45)
United States[b]	-1·28 (0·34)	-0·61 (0·19)	0·19 (0·13)	0·42 (0·27)	-0·48 (0·17)	-0·16 (0·17)	-0·28 (0·21)	0·33 (0·14)	0·92 (0·39)

Notes: Asymptotic standard errors in parentheses.
[a] Search variable is a simple time trend ($\times -0.001$).
[b] With lagged wage and split time trends (see text).

quadratic time trend by split time trends starting in 1975 and 1980. While this produces a negative effect of wages on employment, we remain somewhat unhappy with the data mining necessary to unearth it.[12] Nevertheless, we use these estimates in what follows. It appears that a crucial ingredient is the use of lagged rather than current real wages. This may reflect institutional differences in the labour market, but we conjecture that it may be a consequence of the fact that, of all the countries studied, the United States is the nearest to a closed economy. If the marginal propensity to consume out of wages is higher than that out of profits, an increase in real wages will boost demand, and this may be swamping the direct negative effect on labour demand. In the other 17 countries, which are rather more open, this effect is likely to be much less pronounced. Demand has a positive effect on employment (α_3) everywhere except Australia, Japan and Sweden, and in these cases the negative effect is insignificant.

Turning to the wage equation, unemployment has a depressing effect on real wages (β_2) everywhere except Italy, where there is a quite insignificant positive effect, and the basic estimates for the United States, where the interpretation is in any case open to question. The estimates for Japan are slightly peculiar since there is a positive 'error correction' coefficient (β_1). This does not imply that the estimates are dynamically unstable, however, since there is a very powerful unemployment term that offsets it. In general, the estimates of β_1 and β_2 are strongly negatively correlated and these slightly strange estimates for Japan are therefore likely to represent sampling error. The wedge variable is positively signed for two-thirds of the countries (β_3) and the sign of the search variable (β_4) conforms with prior expectations (negative) for a similar proportion of the countries in the sample.

III. Accounting for the Rise in Unemployment

We shall now use the empirical results to investigate the proximate causes of the rise in unemployment using the empirical counterpart of equation (5). Equations (10a) and (10b) may be combined to give

$$(11) \quad (\delta_0 + \delta_1 B + \delta_2 B^2 + \delta_3 B^3) \log N = (\alpha_2 \beta_0 - \alpha_0 \beta_1) + (\alpha_1 \beta_1 + \alpha_2 \beta_2) \log L$$
$$+ (1 + \beta_1) \Delta (\alpha_5 t + \alpha_6 t^2 - \alpha_1 \log K)$$
$$+ \alpha_3 \{1 - (1 + \beta_1) B\} \sigma + \alpha_2 \beta_3 \theta + \alpha_2 \beta_4 \phi$$

where

$$\delta_0 = 1 + \alpha_2 \beta_2$$
$$\delta_1 = -(2 + \alpha_1 + \alpha_4 + \beta_1)$$
$$\delta_2 = (1 + \beta_1)(1 + \alpha_1 + \alpha_4) + \alpha_4$$
$$\delta_3 = -\alpha_4(1 + \beta_1)$$

and B is the backward shift operator.[13] This gives the level of employment conditional on the labour force, capital stock, technical progress, demand, taxes, relative import prices and search intensity. It can then be used to derive the predicted behaviour of the unemployment rate over the sample period.

Some of the countries display quite long and complex dynamics. In order to sidestep this and present the results in an easily digestible manner, we focus on the effects of changes in the independent variables over a long time period, utilizing the long-run coefficients generated by equation (11). However, to make some allowance for sluggish adjustment the independent variables are first appropriately lagged using the mean lag of the filter $(\delta_0 + \delta_1 B + \delta_2 B^2 + \delta_3 B^3)^{-1}$ as a criterion (see Table 6).

Table 4 gives the results of a historical breakdown of the causes of the rise in the unemployment rate between 1956–66 and 1980–83 using this procedure. Thus, for Australia the mean lag is 1·07 years and the effect of changes in search intensity on the unemployment rate is calculated as $-\alpha_2 \beta_4 (\phi_{79-82} - \phi_{55-65})/(\delta_0 + \delta_1 + \delta_2 + \delta_3)$, where ϕ_{79-82} is the average value of the search variable over the period 1979–82. Although our philosophy has been to avoid searching widely over specifications in pursuit of the most favourable results, there are a number of countries in Table 3 with perverse signs for the effect on wages of the wedge (β_3) and the search variable (β_4). Rather than present a breakdown of the rise in unemployment with possibly nonsensical numbers, we have re-estimated the model for these countries setting the relevant coefficients to zero. For most countries this does not result in a significant deterioration in fit (Austria and the United States are the chief exceptions). These constrained estimates, presented in Table 5, were then used in the compilation of Table 4 rather than the unrestricted estimates.

These estimates are for the most part fairly sensible and confirm the importance of demand in the rise in unemployment, especially in the European

TABLE 4

BREAKDOWN OF THE CHANGE IN UNEMPLOYMENT, 1956–66 TO 1980–83
(percentage points)

	Taxes	Import prices	Search	Demand	Total	Actual
Australia	2·56	−0·03	2·44	−0·28	4·69	4·98
Austria	—	—	—	0·09	0·09	0·57
Belgium	1·41	−0·04	5·28	2·53	9·15	8·93
Canada	1·34	0·02	—	4·59	5·95	4·56
Denmark	—	—	0·00	5·40	5·40	7·56
Finland	1·02	0·13	1·04	1·48	3·66	3·79
France	0·46	−0·04	3·27	2·39	6·08	5·98
Germany	—	—	3·68	−0·03	3·65	4·02
Ireland	3·73	−0·38	—	2·29	5·65	4·33
Italy	1·12	−0·02	—	−1·68	−0·58	2·09
Japan	—	—	0·59	0·06	0·65	0·63
Netherlands	2·93	−1·38	−3·41	9·68	7·84	8·77
New Zealand	0·08	0·01	0·00	2·28	2·38	3·48
Norway	—	—	—	0·50	0·50	0·11
Sweden	1·70	0·12	−0·47	−0·49	0·85	1·04
Switzerland	—	—	0·18	0·29	0·48	0·41
United Kingdom	2·06	−0·05	2·25	5·33	9·60	8·33
United States	1·30	0·19	—	0·48	1·97	3·35

Note: Australia, Belgium, Canada, Denmark, France and New Zealand: independent variables lagged once; Italy, Netherlands, United Kingdom, United States: independent variables lagged twice.

TABLE 5

RESTRICTED LABOUR DEMAND AND WAGE-SETTING EQUATIONS (10)

Independent variables Parameter	Labour demand					Wage-setting			
	Lagged employment α_1	Wage α_2	Demand α_3	Lagged change in employment α_4	Long-run wage elasticity $-\alpha_2/\alpha_1$	Lagged wage β_1	Unemployment β_2	Wedge β_3	Search β_4
Austria	-0·37 (0·09)	-0·21 (0·07)	0·34 (0·11)	-0·01 (0·19)	-0·56 (0·09)	0·03 (0·03)	-2·09 (0·62)	—	—
Canada	-0·89 (0·23)	-0·38 (0·10)	0·63 (0·08)	0·27 (0·23)	-0·43 (0·19)	-0·19 (0·14)	-0·94 (0·42)	0·14 (0·12)	—
Denmark	-0·74 (0·02)	-0·50 (0·16)	0·33 (0·13)	0·16 (0·24)	-0·68 (0·12)	-0·23 (0·10)	-0·45 (0·20)	—	0·00 (0·10)
Germany	-0·66 (0·30)	-0·58 (0·15)	0·47 (0·34)	0·52 (0·30)	-0·87 (0·39)	0·07 (0·11)	-3·02 (0·61)	—	-3·32 (0·78)
Ireland	-0·35 (0·08)	-0·32 (0·07)	0·25 (0·07)	0·62 (0·28)	-0·93 (0·17)	-0·44 (0·21)	-2·53 (0·49)	0·51 (0·18)	—
Italy	-0·30 (0·21)	-0·11 (0·08)	-0·05 (0·12)	0·17 (0·35)	-0·38 (0·09)	-0·47 (0·18)	0·24 (0·71)	0·05 (0·14)	—
Japan	-0·35 (0·07)	-0·37 (0·07)	-0·03 (0·04)	-0·43 (0·17)	-1·06 (0·05)	0·44 (0·33)	-25·4 (5·5)	—	-20·8 (6·7)
Norway	-1·26 (0·34)	-0·29 (0·08)	0·53 (0·19)	1·11 (0·35)	-0·23 (0·07)	-0·78 (0·20)	-8·38 (2·1)	—	—
Switzerland	-0·91 (0·13)	-0·83 (0·09)	0·59 (0·16)	0·84 (0·28)	-0·92 (0·08)	-0·33 (0·21)	-26·8 (3·1)	—	-6·46 (3·9)
United States[b]	-1·17 (0·28)	-1·24 (0·26)	0·25 (0·14)	0·34 (0·25)	-1·06 (0·15)	-0·66 (0·08)	-0·05 (0·16)	0·07 (0·06)	—

Notes: See Table 3.

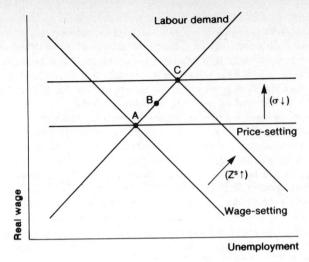

FIGURE 1.   Perfect competition.

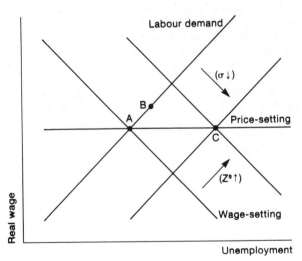

FIGURE 2.   Normal cost pricing.

Community. However, in most cases there is also a significant contribution from reduced search intensity (recall that this will pick up the effect of unemployment benefits, etc.) and a higher tax burden. Import prices play a small role overall, although they have a significant effect in the immediate aftermath of the commodity price boom of the early 1970s and the two oil shocks.

How do these results tie up with those of Bruno in this volume? First, it is helpful to recast the story told in his Figure 2 in our framework. In Figures 1 and 2 we have drawn the employment, price and wage equations (1), (2) and (3) in unemployment–real-wage space, assuming that wage and price expectations are fulfilled. A supply shock, such as the oil price hike, shifts the wage function to the right. If we hold the level of real demand, σ, constant, the economy will move from the initial equilibrium A along the labour demand curve to a point such as B, where there is (unanticipated) inflation in wages and consumer prices. This extra inflation ensures that the realized real wage is lower than that bargained for in the labour market and higher than that implicit in the planned price-setting behaviour of firms.

In order to reach a new equilibrium in which expectations are fulfilled, real demand must fall. This can happen both automatically, as a result of the real balance effect and a decline in competitiveness, and autonomously, as a result of changes in fiscal and monetary policy. However, the effect on employment depends crucially on the pricing strategy of firms. Figures 1 and 2 present the two polar cases of perfect competition and normal cost pricing, respectively. Under perfect competition the price function shifts upwards (recall that $f_\sigma^1 = 0$ and $f_\sigma^2 > 0$ under competitive pricing) and a new equilibrium is established at C with higher real wages and higher unemployment. Under normal cost pricing the labour demand function shifts rightwards (recall that $f_\sigma^1 > 0$ and $f_\sigma^2 = 0$ in this case) and the new equilibrium is at C with unchanged real wages but higher unemployment.

The 'wage gap' methodology of Bruno (see also Bruno–Sachs) starts by calculating the difference between actual wage and the full employment marginal product of labour. If the economy is deemed to be at full employment initially, then this gap is given by the excess of the current wage, say at B or C in Figure 1, over the full employment wage at A. Bruno finds that the wage gap rose during the latter half of the 1970s, but since 1980 has been declining in most countries. Given our finding that demand has a positive effect on employment in most countries, this suggests that we may be observing something closer to the normal cost pricing case portrayed in Figure 2 than the competitive case of Figure 1.

Bruno's decomposition of the rise in unemployment in terms of the wage gap and aggregate demand (his Table 8) seems to support our own findings that lack of demand has been a proximate cause of the rise in unemployment. However, statistical quibbles aside, there is an important methodological difference between the two approaches, stemming from the fact that the wage gap is an endogenous variable which in general will be affected by the level of real demand. Thus, suppose the economy is at the final equilibrium C in Figures 1 and 2 and the government undertakes a fiscal or monetary expansion, reversing the previous contraction in demand. In the competitive case of Figure 1, this produces a downward shift in the price function and takes the economy to a temporary equilibrium like B, where there is a fall in the wage gap and unanticipated inflation. By contrast, in the normal cost pricing case of Figure 2, the labour demand function shifts leftwards and again at the new temporary equilibrium B there is unanticipated inflation—but now there is a *rise* in the wage gap. Because demand has an indirect effect via the wage gap as well as a direct effect, that portion of the rise in unemployment which is attributed to demand will be different in the two approaches.

It is perhaps also worth adding a note of caution on the policy implications to be drawn from Bruno's Table 8 and our own Table 4. The fact that demand may have played a role in the rise of unemployment does not necessarily imply that this can be entirely reversed by expansionary fiscal or monetary policy, other than in the short run. The model of equations (1)-(4) possesses a 'natural' level of real demand as well as a 'natural' level of unemployment, or NAIRU. This 'natural' level of demand is obtained by solving equations (5) and (6) for σ assuming that expectations are fulfilled. Attempts to raise σ above (below) this level will raise (lower) employment only so long as the wage and price expectations of firms and workers differ from the levels actually realized. In that sense the model of equations (1)-(4) has much in common with equilibrium business cycle models of the Friedman–Lucas variety. Only if an expansion of demand has a minimal effect on wages and/or prices, as in disequilibrium models of the Barro–Grossman–Malinvaud fix-price type, can unemployment be permanently reduced.

The ad hoc rigidity of wages and prices in disequilibrium models is one of their least satisfactory features in anything other than the very short-run. An alternative approach taken by Driehuis, Malinvaud and especially Sneessens and Dreze, is to focus on limited short-run substitution possibilities between labour and capital as the source of disequilibrium, rather than wage and price rigidity *per se*. In the model of Sneessens and Dreze, wages and prices are flexible and respond to economic conditions, but real wages do not directly affect employment because the capital–labour ratio is fixed in the short-run. Labour demand is, in essence, determined by either the capital stock or the demand for domestically produced goods, whichever is the smaller, and Keynesian, Classical and Repressed Inflation regimes can arise as in the first generation fix-price disequilibrium models. However the differences between the disequilibrium approach and the model which appears in this paper and a number of the other contributions to this volume are less pronounced than they appear. Factor proportions are flexible in the Sneessens–Dreze model in the medium/long-run and such factors as benefit levels, union power, mismatch, etc. will play a central role in determining the equilibrium level of unemployment. Conversely the sluggish adjustment evidenced by the lags in the labour demand equations in Table 3 could be rationalized as representing short-run behaviour in disequilibrium as well as equilibrium behaviour with convex adjustment costs. Rather the differences are primarily in emphasis: the Sneessens–Dreze disequilibrium model focuses on the short-run, whereas the Layard–Nickell imperfect competition approach is directed more closely at medium term issues. In both models expansionary fiscal or monetary policy may be able to affect the level of unemployment temporarily, but should not affect the equilibrium unemployment rate.

There is, however, another way in which an expansion in demand could permanently lower the level of unemployment, and that is through hysteresis effects. If the current NAIRU depends on past levels of unemployment, then demand management will be able to affect the future NAIRU's. While a rigorous theoretical framework for such hysteresis effects has yet to be spelt out, one can suggest a variety of ways in which they might arise: the 'discouraged worker' effect leads marginal workers to quit the labour force; the human capital of the unemployed may depreciate rapidly, making it difficult to find a suitable job match; the unemployed lose workplace contacts which are the source of information on new jobs for many workers; finally, firms may use unemployment experience as a screening device for identifying low productivity workers. In the paper on the United Kingdom in this volume we find that unemployment excluding the long-term unemployed performs better in wage equations than the overall unemployment rate which lends some credence to the idea of a state-dependent NAIRU.[14] This possibility is explored in much greater depth in the paper on Australia by Gregory. He shows that overtime/short-time data are a much better explanation of wage behaviour than unemployment, and cites social survey evidence to support the argument that it is conditions inside the firm rather than outside that matter. If this dichotomy between insiders and outsiders can be shown to generalize to other countries, it must surely have important implications for both macroeconomic theory and policy. Clearly this is an area where further research is warranted.

IV. THE ROLE OF INSTITUTIONS: A COMPARATIVE ASSESSMENT

The empirical results of Sections II and III suggest that this approach provides a useful analytical framework. However, the cross-country differences in the coefficient estimates appearing in Table 3 indicate that the heterogeneity in unemployment experience manifested in Table 1 arises not only from a differing contribution by the exogenous variables—demand, taxes, import prices, search intensity and so forth—but also as a result of differences in structure. In this section we shall try to relate this cross-country variation in labour market behaviour to institutional factors.

Recently a number of writers (Cameron, 1982; McCallum, 1983, 1984; Tarantelli, 1982; Bruno and Sachs, 1985) have focused especially on the effect of 'corporatism' on macroeconomic performance. Corporatism is identified as a mode of social organization in which groups rather than individuals wield power and transact affairs. In the context of labour markets, several structural characteristics have been used as indicators of corporatism. These are: whether negotiations take place at a national or local level; the power of national vis-à-vis local labour organizations; the extent of employer co-ordination; and the power of local union stewards. Nations are deemed to be corporatist if wage bargaining is highly centralized, wage agreements do not have to be ratified at a local level, employers are organized, and local union officials have limited influence. Bruno and Sachs report a corporatism rank ordering of 17 of our 18 countries (Ireland is not included) based on these criteria. This index is reported in Table 6. The ranking is intuitively plausible, with Austria, Germany, The Netherlands and the Scandinavian economies being classified as most corporatist, the United States and Canada as least corporatist, and Japan and the remaining European economies somewhere in between.

Most of the authors cited above relate indices of corporatism to overall measures of macroeconomic performance such as unemployment and inflation (and especially their sum—the so-called 'misery index'). However, these reflect not only the underlying structure of the economy, but also macroeconomic policy choices. We shall be particularly concerned with relating various parameters describing the functioning of the labour market per se to the degree of corporatism.[15] Corporatism could be associated with a number of features of the labour market. If there is greater consensus in corporatist economies, then disequilibrium may be eliminated more rapidly. This is reflected in the coefficient on unemployment in the wage equation, β_2, which gives the short-

TABLE 6

CORPORATISM RANKING, UNIONIZATION RATE AND LABOUR MARKET
MEAN LAG

	Corporatism ranking	Unionization rate (%)	Mean lag (years)
Australia	15	46·1	1·07
Austria	1	52·6	0·14
Belgium	9	68·0	0·55
Canada	16	28·3	1·52
Denmark	7	52·9	1·76
Finland	8	43·4	0·12
France	13	20·0	0·60
Germany	2	31·8	0·34
Ireland	—	—	0·24
Italy	14	32·3	2·70
Japan	10	22·6	−0·04
Netherlands	3	35·5	2·26
New Zealand	11	36·7	0·75
Norway	4·5	64·2	0·02
Sweden	4·5	70·1	−0·13
Switzerland	6	29·4	−0·12
United Kingdom	12	45·5	2·64
United States	17	28·2	3·56

Source: Bruno and Sachs (1985, Table 11.3) and Table 3 above.

run effect on wages of a perceived disequilibrium in the labour market. One
might also be interested in the long-run effect of unemployment on wages,
$-\beta_2/\beta_1$, and in the sluggishness of adjustment to that long-run equilibrium,
which is measured here by the mean lag, $-(1+\beta_1)/\beta_1$. Finally, real-wage
resistance to increases in taxes and import prices might be expected to be less
pronounced in economies that are corporatist and exhibit a high degree of
consensus. The short-run effect of tax and import price shocks is given by the
coefficient on the wedge, β_3, and the long-run effect is given by $-\beta_3/\beta_1$.

All of these coefficients relate to the characteristics of the wage equation
per se. More generally, the degree of corporatism may influence not only
wage-setting behaviour but also employment directly. In terms of the labour
market as a whole, a sensible question to ask is how quickly the effects of a
temporary shock to employment or wages are eradicated from the system. An
efficiently functioning labour market will presumably ensure that the effects
of a transitory shock are short-lived. Equation (11) gives the dynamic equation
relating employment to a wage (tax, import prices or search) shock, and the
mean lag in the response is given by

(12) $\quad -(\delta_1+2\delta_2+3\delta_3)/(\delta_0+\delta_1+\delta_2+\delta_3)$

$\qquad = (\alpha_4\beta_1 - \alpha_1\beta_1 - 2\alpha_1\beta_1)/(\alpha_1\beta_1 + \alpha_2\beta_2).$

This is also the mean lag between an employment (demand) shock and the
wage, and therefore provides a single summary statistic of the efficiency of
the labour market as a whole. Table 6 also includes the mean lag for each
country in the sample, based on the estimates of Table 3.

Because the measure of corporatism is qualitative rather than quantitative, non-parametric methods are needed to assess the degree of association between the various coefficients and the corporatism ranking in Table 6. In each case we have computed the coefficient in question and then ranked the countries in the order, most responsive/shortest mean lag to least responsive/longest mean lag.[16] Table 7 gives the value of Kendall's tie-adjusted τ statistic (Kendall, 1970) between each of these rankings and the corporatism ranking.[17] For comparison, we have also included the τ statistics for the association between the degree of corporatism and the average level of unemployment over 1980–83 and with the change in the average level of unemployment between 1956–66 and 1980–83 in the table.

The results support the idea that the functioning of the labour market is related to the degree of corporatism. Wages in the more corporatist economies display a greater response to unemployment in both the long and (especially) the short run. Even more pronounced is the association with the response to changes in the wedge between consumer and product wages, with the effect of changes in taxes or import prices on the wage, and hence on unemployment levels, being significantly smaller in corporatist economies. Finally, adjustment, not only of wages but especially of the labour market as a whole, is faster in corporatist environments. In comparison, the association with the average level

TABLE 7

ASSOCIATION WITH CORPORATISM INDEX (KENDALL'S τ)

		Partial τ	
	τ	With corporatism, controlling for unionization	With unionization, controlling for corporatism
Short-run effect of unemployment on wage (β_2)	0·391	0·391	−0·061
Long-run effect of unemployment on wage ($-\beta_2/\beta_1$)	0·199	0·186	0·018
Short-run effect on wage of tax and import price wedge (β_3)	−0·435	−0·478	0·231
Long-run effect on wage of tax and import price wedge ($-\beta_3/\beta_1$)	−0·524	−0·530	0·113
Speed of adjustment in wage equation $\{(1+\beta_1)/\beta_1\}$	0·258	0·197	0·206
Overall speed of adjustment of employment $\{(\delta_1+2\delta_2+3\delta_3)/(\delta_0+\delta_1+\delta_2+\delta_3)\}$	0·406	0·377	0·067
Average level of unemployment, 1980–83	0·244	0·268	−0·123
Change in average level of unemployment between 1956–66 and 1980–83	0·125	0·149	−0·100

Note: 1 per cent significance level = 0·426, 5 per cent significance level = 0·309, 10 per cent significance level = 0·250.

of unemployment since the start of the 1980s, and more especially with the rise in unemployment since the 1950s and 1960s, is rather weak. Thus, more corporatist economies may possess labour markets that function more efficiently in the face of shocks, but this does not imply that their unemployment experience has necessarily been less unpleasant. For that, one needs to look at both the shocks that have impinged on the economy and the response of governments, in both their demand management and their tax policies.

It could be objected that corporatism matters only in economies that are already highly unionized. A perfectly competitive labour market should also function efficiently, while high unionization without a corporatist consensus is the worst of all worlds. Table 7 therefore also includes values of Kendall's partial τ statistic,[18] conditional on the unionization rate (given in Table 6). It can be seen that the correlation coefficients are hardly altered by controlling for the degree of unionization. The converse of this is that the unionization rate has very little effect on the efficiency of the labour market or its responsiveness to shocks once the degree of corporatism has been controlled for (again, see Table 7). Of course, the unionization rate may mean different things in different countries, and may not be a good guide to the relative importance of unions in the wage-setting process. Nevertheless, the results are not very supportive of the notion that unions *per se* inhibit the efficient functioning of the labour market.

Concluding Remarks

Unemployment has risen markedly in most of the OECD countries during the past decade or so. Is this the result of supply or demand factors? Our answer is that it is six of one and half a dozen of the other. The estimated wage and employment equations confirm the view that for most countries both demand and the level of real wages affect employment. The decline in demand, relative to potential, seems to have been an important proximate cause of the rise in unemployment, especially in the European Community. However, it is clear that supply-side factors have also played a significant role. This is a broad conclusion that seems to be shared by many of the authors who have contributed to this volume, even if the details are often different.

The evidence also seems to support the notion that structural differences in labour markets can be related to national differences in institutional and social characteristics. In particular, wages seem to be more responsive to labour market disequilibrium and less responsive to tax and import price shocks, and the labour market as a whole seems to adjust more quickly in economies that are more corporatist in nature. However, our analysis of international differences in labour market performance is perforce very crude. The impact of different modes of labour market organization across the developed countries can be fully appreciated only by reading the various country papers which reveal a rich variety of customs and institutions. An unanswered question is the extent to which these institutional arrangements are themselves a response to the economic environment.

Although institutional characteristics seem to be important in explaining differences in labour market behaviour, it appears that more corporatist economies have not necessarily fared better with respect to the rise in unemployment. There is, however, some suggestion that the overall level of unemployment is lower in these countries, perhaps because there is more 'disguised' unemployment. In order to explain international differences in unemployment performance, therefore, one also needs to look at both the external shocks impinging on the economy and the stance of government policy. The latter includes not only the macroeconomic impact of fiscal and monetary policy, but also the microeconomic effects of the tax and benefit system and of labour market policy.

ACKNOWLEDGEMENTS

This paper is largely the work of Charlie Bean who must therefore take the blame for errors. Statistical advice from Jan Magnus is gratefully acknowledged.

APPENDIX: DATA SOURCES

N Total employment (including armed forces). *Source*: OECD *Labour Force Statistics*.

U Standardized unemployment rate. *Source*: OECD *Economic Outlook* (various) and Grubb (1984).

L Labour force; defined as $N/(1-U)$.

K Capital stock; calculated from investment data by perpetual inventory assuming a depreciation rate of 5 per cent per annum and no trend in the capital-output ratio between 1950 and 1974. *Source*: OECD *National Accounts*.

W Labour costs; calculated as $W_H(\hat{H}/H)^{0.25}(1+t_1)$, where W_H is hourly earnings in manufacturing, H is average weekly hours and $\hat{H}$ is a proxy for normal hours, obtained as the fitted value from a regression of $(H-4)$ on a constant and trend. *Source*: OECD *General Statistics*; OECD *Main Economic Indicators*; and International Labour Office (ILO) *Yearbook of Labour Statistics*.

P GDP deflator at market prices. *Source*: OECD *National Accounts*.

P_M Import price deflator. *Source*: OECD *National Accounts*.

S_M Share of imports in GDP. *Source*: OECD *National Accounts*.

t_1 Employment taxes on firms; ratio of employers' contributions to social security and pensions to the wage bill. *Source*: OECD *National Accounts*; ILO *The Costs of Social Security*.

t_2 Tax rate on household income; household contributions to social security and direct taxes as a proportion of receipts. *Source*: UN and OECD *National Accounts*.

t_3 Indirect tax rate; calculated as indirect taxes (net of subsidies) as a proportion of consumers' expenditure. *Source*: OECD *National Accounts*.

Data for government expenditure and GDP used to construct σ (see text) are also taken from OECD *National Accounts*. The data set is described in Grubb (1984).

NOTES

1. See for instance the special issue of the *Journal of Labour Economics*, (January 1985).
2. This follows the fact that marginal cost is always equal to the wage divided by the marginal product of labour.
3. In general, demand will have the same qualitative effect on employment as it has on the elasticity of demand. It is sometimes suggested that the elasticity of demand rises in booms, which would lead to $f_\sigma^1 > 0$, but $f_\sigma^1 < 0$ is a logical possibility.
4. Note that this model does not encompass efficient contracting models of the McDonald-Solow (1981) variety. In these models firms and unions bargain over both wages and employment. Equation (3) will still describe wage-setting behaviour, but the employment function (1) now also depends on outside opportunities, including the shift variables Z^s.
5. For the Netherlands, estimation over the full sample yields a root almost on the unit circle—the system mean lag is 22 years! This appears to be associated with some parameter instability

at the very start of the period. The sample for the Netherlands omits the first two observations and runs from 1955 to 1983.
6. For a number of countries vacancy data are available only over a sub-sample. For these countries (8) was estimated over this sub-sample and the resulting coefficient estimates were used to construct ϕ over the full sample. For Ireland and Italy no vacancy data are available and ϕ is a simple linear trend for these countries.
7. Its appropriateness as a measure of fiscal impact is in any case open to question (see Buiter, 1985).
8. Real balances are not available for all countries and were generally insignificant for those countries where data were available.
9. The capital stock series are constructed from investment data so as to ensure no trend in the capital–output ratio between 1950 and 1974. Hence, our measure of demand relative to potential is approximately trendless over this period. We also constructed a measure of potential output along the lines of our previous work and used this as a normalizing factor. It made little difference to the results.
10. Strictly speaking, current competitiveness is, of course, endogenous and we could either estimate the complete model in equations (1)–(4) or else substitute out current competitiveness, replacing it by all the other exogenous variables in the system. The first is beyond the scope of this introductory paper, although we intend to pursue it in the future. The second is rather profligate with degrees of freedom, and our approach is likely to perform better in small samples. (Recall that our objective is to obtain a measure of σ that is largely independent of the error in the employment and price equations.)
11. The standard errors are not strictly valid since σ is a generated regressor. Pagan (1984) provides a comprehensive discussion of the use of generated regressors.
12. Layard and Nickell (1985b) report a significant negative wage elasticity using a slightly different specification, as do Newell and Symons (1986). Both of these papers use lagged real wages in their employment equation for the United States.
13. For the United States, $\delta_0 = 1$, $\delta_1 = \alpha_2\beta_2 - (2 + \alpha_1 + \alpha_4 + \beta_1)$, and (10) becomes

$$(\delta_0 + \delta_1 B + \delta_2 B^2 + \delta_3 B^3) \log N = (\alpha_2\beta_0 - \alpha_0\beta_1) + (\alpha_1\beta_1 + \alpha_2\beta_2) \log L_{-1}$$
$$+ \Delta(\alpha_5 t + \alpha_6 t^2 - \alpha_1 \log K)$$
$$+ \alpha_3\{1 - (1 + \beta_1)B\}\sigma + \alpha_2\beta_3\theta_{-1} + \alpha_2\beta_4\phi_{-1}.$$

14. Such hysteresis effects might also be modelled by entering the change rather than the level of unemployment in the wage equation. However, for most of the countries in our sample the change in unemployment is insignificant when added to equation (10b). It may be that such an effect is too subtle to be modelled in such a simple way.
15. McCallum (1984) also relates the degree of real-wage rigidity in the Phillips curve to the level of corporatism.
16. With respect to the wage–unemployment trade-off, Japan and Italy, both of whom display perverse estimated trade-offs, are ranked top and bottom, respectively.
17. Kendall's τ ranges between plus and minus unity like an ordinary correlation coefficient.
18. The distribution of partial τ is not known. It is, however, asymptotically equivalent to the distribution of τ when the controlled-for ranking is independent of the other two rankings. See Kendall (1970) and Moran (1951).

REFERENCES

BRUNO, M. and SACHS, J. (1985). *The Economics of Worldwide Stagflation*. Oxford: Basil Blackwell.

BUITER, W. H. (1985). A guide to government debt and deficits. *Economic Policy*, **1**, 13–61.

CAMERON, D. R. (1982). Social democracy, corporatism, and labor quiescence: the representation of economic interest in advanced capitalist society. Paper presented at the conference on Governability and Legitimacy in Western European Democracies, Stanford University.

DUNLOP, J. T. (1944). *Wage Detrmination Under Trade Unions*. New York: Macmillan.

GRUBB, D. (1984). The OECD data set. London School of Economics, Centre for Labour Economics, Working Paper no. 615.

JACKMAN, R. A., LAYARD, P. R. G. and PISSARIDES, C. (1984). On vacancies. London School of Economics, Centre for Labour Economics, Discussion Paper no. 165.

JOHNSON, G. and LAYARD, P. R. G. (1986). The natural rate of unemployment and labor market policy. In O. Ashenfelter and P. R. G. Layard (eds), *Handbook of Labor Economics*. Amsterdam: North-Holland.

KENDALL, M. G. (1970). *Rank Correlation Methods.* London: Charles Griffin.

LAYARD, P. R. G. and NICKELL, S. J. (1985a). The causes of British unemployment. *National Institute Economic Review,* **111,** 62–85.

—— (1985b). Unemployment, real wages and aggregate demand in Europe, Japan and the US. *Journal of Monetary Economics,* Supplement, 143–202.

McCALLUM, J. (1983). Inflation and social consensus in the seventies. *Economic Journal,* **93,** 784–805.

—— (1984). Unemployment in the OECD countries in the 1980s. Unpublished paper, University of Quebec (mimeo).

McDONALD, I. and SOLOW, R. M. (1981). Wage bargaining and employment. *American Economic Review,* **71,** 896–908.

MORAN, P. A. P. (1951). Partial and multiple rank correlation. *Biometrika,* **38,** 26.

NEWELL, A. and SYMONS, J. S. V. (1986). Wages and employment in the OECD countries. *Economic Journal* (forthcoming).

PAGAN, A. R. (1984). Econometric issues in the analysis of regressions with generated regressors. *International Economic Review,* **25,** 221–48.

PENCAVEL, J. H. (1982). Wages, specific training, and labor turnover in US manufacturing industries. *International Economic Review,* **13,** 53–64.

SHAPIRO, C. and STIGLITZ, J. E. (1984). Equilibrium unemployment as a worker discipline device. *American Economic Review,* **74,** 433–44.

STIGLITZ, J. E. (1984). Theories of wage rigidity. Paper presented at the conference of Keynes's Economic Legacy, Delaware.

TARANTELLI, E. (1982). The economics of neocorporatism. Chapter 1 of unpublished book. Rome: Bank of Italy.

WEISS, A. (1980). Job queues and layoffs in labour markets with flexible wages. *Journal of Political Economy,* **88,** 526–38.

Unemployment: Getting the Questions Right

By ROBERT M. SOLOW

Massachusetts Institute of Technology

In my opinion, the form and conception of this conference exemplifies the right instinct for modern macroeconomics. There is a fact, a big unmistakable unsubtle fact: essentially everywhere in the modern industrial capitalist world, unemployment rates are much higher than they used to be two or three decades ago. Why is that? If macroeconomics is good for anything, it ought to be able to understand and explain that fact. We should be able to produce a fairly convincing analytical account of the occurrence and persistence of unusually high unemployment rates.

You might think that to be a mere commonplace. To what other sort of end would anyone organize a conference? My experience, however, is that most high-powered academic conferences are stimulated by purely technical developments, or—less often—by ideological or political promotion, rather than by the need to deal with an outstanding fact. I do not blame anyone for this state of affairs. We may not be blessed with many significant observations too big to be quibbled over. And technical innovations do need to be thrashed out by experts. Anyway, it is good to be faced by a brute fact that needs explanation. It is what macroeconomics ought to be about.

I compliment the organizers also on a second aspect of the agenda: the country-by-country organization of the papers. We can all hope to learn something from cross-country comparisons. One of the few good ways we have to test analytical ideas is to see whether they can make sense of international differences in outcomes by appealing to international differences in institutional structure and historical environment. The right place to start is within each country separately, studied by someone who knows the peculiarities of its history and its data.

You might think that this too ought to be obvious. But in fact the usual approach is just the opposite. More often than not we fail to take institutional differences seriously. One model is supposed to apply everywhere and always. Each country is just a point on a cross-section regression, or one among several essentially identical regressions, leaving only grumblers to worry about what is exogenous and what is endogenous, and whether simple parametrizations do justice to real differences in the way the economic mechanism functions in one place or another.

I have no way of knowing whether this organized effort will get anywhere in explaining high unemployment, but it seems to be set up to give itself the best chance.

For better or worse, probably for the better, theoretical and empirical work are closely intertwined in macroeconomics. Scratch a macro-theorist and you find a casual econometrician. Scratch a macro-econometrician and you find a casual theorist. Usually you do not have to scratch very hard. Thus, the discussion of the issues central to the conference has already hardened into certain characteristic forms. There are questions already lying on the table that the individual country papers will be trying to answer. I suspect that some of these questions are badly or carelessly posed. Answers to badly posed questions usually have corresponding problems of their own.

Perhaps I had better say what I mean by a badly posed question: I mean that it is hard to imagine a plausible theoretical framework in which the question makes sense, or in which any answer can sensibly and unambiguously be interpreted. So I propose to raise and discuss some theoretical issues suggested by the form that the analytical debate has already taken.

For example, if past performance is any sort of a guide, many of the papers at this conference will be preoccupied with the relation between real wage rates and employment, and more particularly with the question of whether unemployment rates in Europe are currently unusually high mainly because 'real wages are too high'. I want to argue that much of this argument lacks an acceptable theoretical framework (or makes sense only in a theoretical framework that many of those who make the argument would not really wish to accept). It is not my intention to prejudge the answer, but rather to clarify the question. To be specific, I want to propose that the useful questions are better phrased in terms of nominal wage behaviour even when the desired answers relate to real wages. There is no implication here that anyone 'cares' about the nominal wage. The point is rather the old one that groups of workers and employers cannot bargain over the real wage.

The second issue I want to nominate for discussion is more of an old chestnut and is usually taken as essentially settled in current research and policy analysis. it has to do with the 'natural rate of unemployment'. I do not want to question what appears to be a robust finding of recent research on the Phillips curve: that the term that is usually identified as either a forward-looking 'expected rate of inflation' or a backward-looking carrier of 'inertial inflation' enters with a coefficient very near to one. I shall not even ask why that was not so during a sample period running from 1950 to the mid-1960s and what one is to make of that fact, if it is a fact. But I do want to suggest that the usual, if casual, interpretation of the 'natural rate' has very little basis either in theory or in data analysis. In a sense, it is not clear what we are talking about when we talk about the natural rate.

Finally, I want to say a word about the concept of 'involuntary unemployment' because I think that there has been a loss of analytical clarity in recent years. There is no real intellectual difficulty here, only a kind of careless backsliding into vagueness. One needs to be reminded only because otherwise the lack of clarity tends to affect other aspects of the ongoing discussion.

I. REAL AND NOMINAL WAGES

What does it mean to say that high unemployment is caused by high real wages? Are not real wage rates and unemployment both endogenous variables in any reasonable picture of a modern capitalist economy? The father of the contemporary discussion of this question is probably Edmond Malinvaud, and he, characteristically, is completely clear about what is required for this manner of speaking to make analytical sense, and about the possibility that the requirements will not be meant in any concrete instance:

> The subject (i.e. why unemployment may result from inappropriate real wages) would not arise if the evolution of real wages was strictly determined by the growth

process and had no autonomy with respect to other determinants of this process. But some of the questions now raised precisely assume such an autonomy, and I shall take it to exist, even though I easily recognize that the evolution of real wages is mostly induced.   Malinvaud, 1982, p.1]

When might an analytical observer find it useful to treat an economy's real wage as given? I suppose the simplest case would be that of an economy whose internal prices are largely determined in international markets via a fixed exchange rate and whose nominal wages are imposed on it by a more or less omnipotent trade union movement or perhaps a government agency. The wage-setting agency has to be more than omnipotent: it has to be in a sense arbitrary. If there is a structural equation—a sort of 'deep structure' or reaction function—underlying the behaviour of nominal wages, then the real wage is endogenous after all. If, for instance, the union or wage board cares about unemployment (has a Phillips curve in its head), then it is no longer meaningful to say whether the real wage causes unemployment or unemployment causes the real wage. We have to adopt the right procedure, which is to look for the true exogenous variables.

Another story I have heard tells of an economy in which prices are exogenous and nominal wage rates are tightly and fully indexed. Then the real wage is not only exogenous but more or less constant, except for bias built into the indexing formula. This may have been the case for some periods in some European economies—Italy, for example. It seems unlikely, however, that the real wage will stay constant for ever. There must be some endogeneity somewhere, if only through wage drift, and the right strategy is to bring it into the open.

There may be other stories that lead to predetermined prices and nominal wages, and therefore to predetermined real wages. They all seem pretty special, which is not to deny that they may be true from time to time and place to place. But I imagine that the general theoretical picture in the minds of most macroeconomists is rather different. Let me try to reconstruct it in static terms, trying not to be so specific as to evoke disagreement on particular points.

Usually both the real wage and the level of employment are endogenous variables. A well specified aggregative model will have some exogenous variables as well. It will also have an equilibrium concept, perhaps more than one, each appropriate to a particular 'length of run'. The model will map each possible configuration of the exogenous variables into an equilibrium configuration of the endogenous variables. If one of the equilibrium conditions of the model says 'Employment (or demand for labour) equals supply of labour', that equation should be omitted or suspended. Otherwise the model is not suitable for studying the problem of unemployment, at least not for the length of run under consideration.

This set-up can be exemplified in terms of the simplest version of the model in the back of everyone's mind. Imagine an economy consisting of a fixed number of firms, identical except that each is the sole producer of a slightly differentiated product. The demand function facing the ith firm is $A(\ldots, \ldots)D(p_i/p)$. Here A is an aggregate demand factor. It is written as a function of unspecified variables to indicate that it depends on one or more exogenous policy variables, such as tax rates and the money supply. A may also be a function of some endogenous variables—the real money supply, for

example. The multiplicative form has the symmetric implication that any
change in aggregate demand shifts the demand curve facing each firm in the
same proportion and isoelastically. The fraction of aggregate demand flowing
to each firm falls as the ratio of its price to the appropriately defined price
index rises. The demand curves are identical from firm to firm. In a moment
I will make the same assumption about the technology. Thus, in symmetric
equilibrium, each $p_i = p$.

These monopolistically competitive firms set their own prices as profit-
maximizers. They are, however, price-takers in the labour market, where they
face the common nominal wage w. All I need from the common technology
is a common demand function for labour, denoted $N\{w, AD(p_i/p)\}$. The wage
is inserted as an argument of this function to allow informally for substitution
possibilities, so the partial derivatives are negative and positive, respectively.
I am fudging here about capital and other inputs, but that is only to avoid
unnecessary complications. In the standard short-run case, when labour is the
only variable input, the demand for labour is $F^{-1}\{AD(p_i/p)\}$, where $y_i = F(N_i)$
is the short-run production function.

The ith firm chooses p_i to maximize its profit $p_i AD(p_i/p) -
wN\{w, AD(p_i/p)\}$, ignoring of course the effect of its own decision on p. In
a symmetric Nash equilibrium in prices, therefore, $(1 - j^{-1})/N_2 = w/p$, where
j is the elasticity of $D(\cdot)$ evaluated at $p_i/p = 1$, taken to be positive and
assumed for the usual reason to exceed unity. The employment offered by the
representative firm is simply $N\{w, AD(1)\}$. Obviously there are loose ends to
be tied up, but this is enough to make the main point. In this model the
exogenous variables are the nominal wage and whatever exogenous factors
determine the level of aggregate demand. There are two equations to
determine the endogenous variables: the common price p, and the level of
employment N.

For a finger exercise, take the case already mentioned, where labour is the
only variable input. In addition, specify $A = A(M, p) = M/p$: aggregate
demand is given by the quantity theory of money with constant velocity, set
equal to one by choice of monetary unit. The two equations of the model
become:

(1) $kF'(N) = w/p$

and

(2) $F(N) = (M/p)D(1) = (M/w)(w/p)D(1)$

where

$k = 1 - j^{-1}$.

In what follows, I am going to assume that k is more or less constant, or,
more precisely, that variations in the elasticity of demand along the demand
curve are not so large as to undermine simple qualitative presumptions. If
they were, that would only strengthen the larger case I am trying to make.

Equation (1) defines a negatively sloped curve in the plane of w/p and N.
It looks like the 'demand curve for labour'. It does, in fact, say that the wage

equals the marginal revenue product of labour. It would be the ordinary demand curve for labour *if w and p were exogenous to the representative firm.* Suppose, as in Figure 1, that the economy were at point A, to the left of the vertical corresponding to the supply of labour. It would be tempting to say that unemployment of the amount $N^s - N_0$ occurs because the real wage is too high. But the causal statement is fundamentally misleading. In the model, firms do not 'face' the real wage w/p: they face the nominal wage w, and they *choose* the real wage by choosing p. There is no point in wishing that w/p were at the level corresponding to full employment because w/p is not available for wishing: wishing should be reserved for exogenous variables or for parameters, and, at least in this model, w/p is endogenous.

The correct way to read the figure is different. From (1) and (2) it is clear that the two exogenous variables M and w affect the outcome only through the single exogenous factor M/w, the money supply in wage units. Substitution of (1) into (2) yields:

$$(3) \qquad kD(1)(M/w) = F(N)/F'(N).$$

Thus, N is an increasing function of M/w. Then (1) says that w/p must be a decreasing function of M/w. In the figure, then, the economy traverses from north-west to south-east along the curve as M/w rises. The meaningful causal statement is that, at point A, unemployment occurs because the money supply is too low and/or the nominal wage is too high. That is what I meant earlier by the remark that the focus should be on the nominal wage even if the real wage is higher than its full-employment level. If the nominal wage were lower than it is at A, the price level would be lower too, but not by so much as to keep the real wage from being lower and employment from being higher. (Please note: these are statements about 'lower' and 'higher'—'falling' and 'rising' are a much more complicated dynamic story.)

It goes without saying that a serious macro-model would add a lot of complications. I shall mention only some of the more important possibilities.

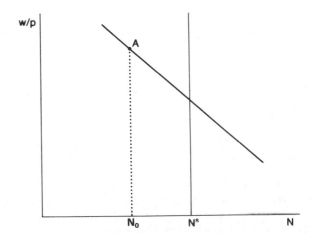

FIGURE 1. An equilibrium locus.

First of all, the two key simplifying assumptions—that aggregate demand is governed by a childishly simple quantity theory, and that employment is determined uniquely by the level of output—combined to reduce the effective number of exogenous variables to one, the money supply in wage units. A model of aggregate demand complex enough to interpret the real world would certainly involve a considerably larger number of exogenous variables: fiscal policy variables, open-economy variables, and probably others. For example, as soon as there are two variables, the real wage–employment plane is covered by a family of equilibrium loci, each describing how the equilibrium point varies with one of the exogenous factors for prescribed setting of the others. Questions of policy mix arise, and multiple causation will be the rule. Full employment may be achievable with a range of real wage rates. Statements about the real wage being 'too high' will have to be qualified still further.

A secondary easy finger exercise will clarify the situation. Suppose now that the capital stock is fixed in the short run, but there is another variable factor—imported raw materials, say, whose domestic currency price is constant throughout, and can thus be suppressed. Shephard's Lemma applied to the capital-restricted cost function gives the conditional demand function for labour, $N(w, y)$. Let this have the form $w^{-a}y^b$, as for a Cobb–Douglas technology, or a valid local approximation to almost any smooth technology. Here y will be replaced by $AD(1) = A$ in symmetric equilibrium; a and b are positive constants and the unit cost curve is locally falling or rising according as $b < 1$ or $b > 1$.

For simplicity, if no one will laugh, I hold to the quantity theory specification, $A = M/p = (M/w)(w/p)$. Then it is easy to solve the model; i.e. write down the mapping from the exogenous variables (M, w) to the endogenous variables $(N, w/p)$:

(4) $N = (k/b)(M/w)$

and

(5) $w/p = (k/b)^{1/b} w^{(a+b-1)/b} M^{(1-b)/b}$.

Thus the money supply and the nominal wage determine the price of goods and the level of output, and therefore the level of employment and the real wage. Output and employment are no longer uniquely related on account of the second variable factor.

Now fix M and treat w as a parameter to get the representation:

(6) $w/p = (k/b)M^{b/a}N^{(1-a-b)/b}$

Assuming that $a + b > 1$, this defines a family of negatively sloped curves in the real-wage–employment plane, as in Figure 2. Two of the curves are drawn, with $M_1 > M_0$. (Changes in the domestic price of raw materials will shift the whole family of curves.)

Suppose that $M = M_0$, and the nominal wage is such as to put the economy at point A. It is certainly correct to say that a lower nominal wage would lead to a lower real wage and would achieve full employment at B. In that sense the real wage is too high. It is equally true, however, that full employment is

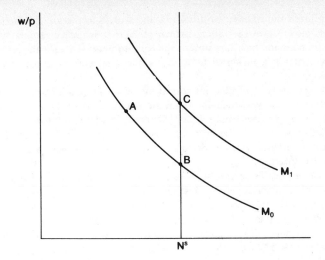

FIGURE 2. A family of equilibrium loci.

achievable at C with a larger money supply (read: aggregate demand), a higher nominal wage and the same real wage, or even a slightly higher one. Rational discussion of the choice requires both a more complete and sensible model than the sketch I have used and serious attention to the dynamics of wages, prices and employment. It is certainly inadequate, however, just to say that the real wage is too high, as if the real wage were 'everywhere and always' an exogenous variable.

Substitution possibilities in production offer still other variations on the basic theme. If persistent under-utilization and unemployment reduces investment and the stock of capital, then an equilibrium locus, like that in the diagram, may shift to the left, lowering the real wage corresponding to full employment.

Mention of capital accumulation is a reminder that up until now the discussion has been confined to the short run, with a fixed number of firms. A short-run equilibrium—a point on (one of) the equilibrium locus (loci)— could yield positive or negative profits for each identical firm. A natural longer-run equilibrium concept could be Chamberlinian: positive or negative profits evoke entry or exit, until the number of firms is such that equilibrium profits are zero. If firms typically operate along U-shaped cost curves, entry of optimum-sized firms could even be the vehicle by which investment occurs.

But then a quite remarkable configuration can easily arise. A long-run equilibrium locus, analogous to the short-run curve in the figure, can turn out to be positively sloped. A model along these general lines can be constructed with the following property: with a fixed number of firms, exogenous variations in aggregate demand cause employment and the real wage to move in opposite directions, one rising while the other falls; but variations in aggregate demand sustained long enough for entry and exit to eliminate profits will trace out a long-run equilibrium locus along which employment and real wages rise and fall together. The underlying idea is that higher aggregate demand induces both an increased number of firms and an increase in the size of each firm. As firms move down the falling branch of their U-shaped cost curves, with competition eliminating pure profits, the equilibrium real wage can easily rise. That is certainly a powerful blow to simplistic statements about 'classical unemployment'.

It seems pretty clear that this sort of model could be adapted to describe an open economy in which the domestic market is shared by foreign and domestic firms. That will make it more likely that higher real wages—or, better still, relative wages—will be associated with domestic unemployment. But the range of exogenous variables driving the real or relative wage will be correspondingly enlarged.

My object in this section was not a particular explanation of the recent shift to higher unemployment rates. But I hope to have made a case that one of the currently popular ways of asking and answering the question is improperly formulated and therefore unlikely to lead to clear thinking. The proper strategy is to focus on the exogenous variables (and of course on the equilibrium conditions themselves). Whatever one may believe about the nominal wage, the real wage is unlikely to be exogenous, except under special circumstances.

II. The Natural Rate of Unemployment

Milton Friedman, it will be remembered, originally defined the 'natural rate of unemployment' as the unemployment rate 'ground out by the Walrasian equations', or words to that effect. The concept, or a concept going under that name, has become firmly established in the literature. But I doubt that many of those who use the concept would accept Friedman's definition, or would imagine econometric estimates of the 'natural rate' to be estimates of a component of Walrasian equilibrium, or would regard the Walrasian model as a valid representation of anything that a macroeconomist would be much interested in.

In practical terms, the 'natural rate' these days figures in two ways. It might appear as a NAIRU, an unemployment rate below which the economy can not stay without accelerating inflation. Or—in models that contain an 'expected inflation' or 'inertial inflation' term on the right-hand side with a coefficient of unity—it occurs as the unemployment rate compatible with a rate of inflation that does not deviate from the expected or inertial rate. This shift of meaning is important because it diminishes the temptation to ascribe optimality properties to the natural rate as one might automatically do with a Walrasian concept.

There is a minor ambiguity about the first—the NAIRU—definition. It is compatible with the idea of a long-run Phillips curve that slopes downward everywhere, but has a vertical asymptote at the left, at a positive unemployment rate, precisely the NAIRU. The second definition, however, insists on a vertical long-run Phillips curve, and defines the long run to be a state in which the actual and expected (or inertial) inflation rates are equal.

In recent years the vertical Phillips curve interpretation of the natural rate has come to dominate the literature. There seem to be two reasons for this. First, econometric Phillips curves estimated from post-965 sample periods routinely produce near-unit coefficients on the expectational or inertial variable, so the empirical basis is there. The second reason is purely theoretical: if we imagine two otherwise identical economies, fully adjusted to different rates of inflation (and money supply growth, say), we see no reason for them to have different real outcomes. This is why, way back in 1969, I described the vertical long-run Phillips curve story as 'hard not to believe'. It does, however, put quite a lot of strain on the notion of 'fully adjusted'.

This version of the natural rate of unemployment also has one very uncomfortable implication that seems not to have been directly faced in the literature. Later on, in another connection, I am going to refer to some recent estimates of the natural rate in several OECD countries. One of these puts the current natural rate at 8·0 per cent in the Federal Republic of Germany and at 2·4 per cent in Austria. One might be prepared to agree that there would eventually be accelerating inflation in Germany if the unemployment rate were held below 8·0 per cent for a long time, and in Austria if the unemployment rate were held below 2·4 per cent for a long time. Would anyone, however, accept the symmetrical proposition: that there would eventually be accelerating deflation in Germany if the unemployment rate were above 8·0 per cent for a long time, and in Austria if the unemployment rate were to exceed 2·4 per cent for a long time? Somehow one doubts it. Yet that is an implication of the whole apparatus.

The easy dodge will not work. One is tempted to say, Oh, well, so the natural rate is a bit fuzzy, an interval rather than a point, and there is a band in which the Phillips curve slopes down, even in the long run. The trouble is that, if the band is very narrow, the discomfort remains: would one believe that Austria would have accelerating deflation if the unemployment rate were sustained at 2·6 per cent? If the band is fairly wide, however, then, in effect, the long-run Phillips curve is not vertical and one can talk about trade-offs within that 'fairly wide' zone.

If there is a natural rate of unemployment, then it is clearly important for policy purposes to know what it is. It would make a lot of difference to policy whether the high unemployment rates we are here to discuss occur because the natural rate is very high or because current unemployment is far above the natural rate. Of course, there are estimates of the natural rate, and this conference will undoubtedly produce more.

Estimates of the natural rate in the NAIRU tradition tend to emphasize changes in the composition of the labour force by demographic or skill category, obstacles to mobility, the size of unemployment insurance benefits, and such factors. In the vertical Phillips curve tradition, however, the estimated natural rate arises from the Phillips curve itself if the coefficient on the inertial-expectational variable is unity: one simply equates the current and expected inflation rates and solves for the implied natural rate of unemployment (which will then be a function of any other right-hand side variables). That is nowadays the common procedure.

A mild paradox arises here. Those who estimate the natural rate in this way occasionally go on to discuss events or policies that might possibly change the natural rate. When they do, they normally talk about the factors I mentioned earlier as figuring in the NAIRU tradition. But those factors have played no role in the estimation. It seems like rather a bold leap, calling for more justification than it gets. One can always *define* the unemployment rate to be below the natural rate whenever inflation is accelerating. But then it is vacuous to say that inflation is accelerating because unemployment is below the natural rate.

The main point I want to make about estimates of the natural rate is rather different. For concreteness I turn to a recent Working Paper of the OECD Economics and Statistics Department (Coe and Gagliardi, 1985). I emphasize that I am not being critical of this paper, which seems to be an excellent and exceptionally thoughtful example of the genre: it is the genre I want to question.

The paper produces vertical Phillips curve estimates of the natural rate for nine or ten countries, and for three or four sub-intervals of the period since 1961 or 1967. Their Phillips curves are not really vertical because changes in unit labour costs need not be passed one-for-one into changes in domestic prices, with changes in import costs accounting for the difference. But the numbers seem to allow the point I want to make. As already mentioned, the current (early 1980s) natural rates range from 2·3 and 2·4 per cent in Japan and Austria to 8·0 per cent in Germany and 9·0 per cent in France. (Surprisingly, I guess, the estimate for the UK, which was 7·3 per cent in 1976-80, falls to 5·9 per cent in 1981-83; but there is a variant, with a different treatment of import prices, that gives a figure of 9·6 per cent for 1981-83. The alternative treatment of import prices gives more sensible-looking results for the United States too, but my argument does not depend on such details. Coe and Gagliardi are, however, calling attention to a neglected aspect of the NAIRU in an open economy.)

The country papers at this conference will very likely emerge with estimates of the natural rate that vary widely from place to place. Can we rationalize those differences in terms of labour market institutions and other factors in a convincing way? It is hardly enough to allow that there are unspecified 'differences' between countries: the differences have to be quantitatively adequate to the task.

It is even more striking that the estimated natural rates within countries vary widely from sub-period to sub-period. The estimate for Germany goes from 1·6 to 8·0 per cent in ten years; that for France goes from 3·3 to 9·0 per cent in five years; that for the UK, from 2·6 to 7·2 per cent between 1967-70 and 1971-75. Can those dramatic changes be rationalized in a satisfactory way?

Coe and Gagliardi take note of the possibility that the apparent 'natural rate' may be closely related to observed past rates of unemployment. They perform an interesting experiment; but my interpretation of the outcome is utterly different from theirs. They enter the unemployment rate in the Phillips curve as a deviation from its own four-year (occasionally eight-year moving average. Here is their summary:

> In the case of Australia the improvement relative to the equation with just the unemployment rate is dramatic. As well as improving the explanatory power of the equation, the coefficient estimates on both the activity variable and the inflation rate become significantly different from zero, and the coefficient on the inflation term corresponds more closely to *a priori* beliefs. For the United Kingdom there is a marginal improvement in the equation. For the other countries, incorporating a natural rate specified in this way makes little difference to the estimation results and hence the more straigthforward specification ... is maintained.
>
> [Coe and Gagliardi, 1985]

I take this as saying that the data do not prefer the conventional, natural rate, specification to the one that looks at lagged unemployment rates. But the implications of those two alternative hypotheses differ radically. The lag interpretation says that there is yet another way to bring down the currently effective 'natural rate': just have low unemployment for a while. That would seem to be front-page news. It is hardly a natural-rate story at all.

The proper conclusion is not that the vertical long-run Phillips curve version of the natural-rate hypothesis is wrong. I would suggest instead that the empirical basis for that story is at best flimsy. A natural rate that hops around from one triennium to another under the influence of unspecified forces, *including past unemployment rates*, is not 'natural' at all. 'Epiphenomenal' would be a better adjective; look it up.

III. INVOLUNTARY UNEMPLOYMENT

A year or two ago I had a memorable conversation with a few of my teaching colleagues in macroeconomics. We are discussing the coverage of the course we teach together: what must all of our graduate students, whatever their specialities, know about macroeconomics? I offered the (casual) opinion that we could leave out any treatment of the supply of labour, on the grounds that one can assume the supply of labour to be inelastically given and constant in the short to medium run without losing anything of significance to macroeconomics. One of my colleagues objected that that was impossible. I asked why. Because then one could not explain fluctuations in employment. I explained that I thought employment could be a lot smaller than the supply of labour. The look I got in return could have signified amusement, disbelief, pity and—maybe?—the dawning of a new idea, in unknown proportions. I would rather not know.

Someone once defined an economist as a parrot trained to repeat 'Supply and demand, supply and demand'. There are many worse things you could teach a parrot to say—and we hear them every day—but I want to suggest that, in the case of the labour market, our preoccupation with price-mediated market-clearing as the 'natural' equilibrium condition may be a serious error.

For example, it is often argued that individual unemployed workers could accept lower-skill, lower-paid jobs than they are used to, because such jobs are usually available. Since they do not do so, their 'unemployment' should be regarded as 'voluntary'. (I think I once pointed out that, by this standard, all the American soldiers who were killed in Vietnam could be counted as suicides since they could have deserted, emigrated to Canada or shot themselves in the foot, but did not.) The key point here is that the notion of 'involuntary unemployment' is not metaphysical or psychological; it has little or nothing to do with free will. From the economist's point of view, there is involuntary unemployment whenever, for any substantial number of workers, the marginal (consumption) value of leisure is less than the going real wage in occupations for which they are qualified. That definition covers underemployment as well as total unemployment, and it covers both the skilled mechanic who does not take work as a sweeper and the one who does. It has empirical content.

There is a valid and important question of why workers who are involuntarily unemployed do not actively bid for jobs by nominal wage-cutting.

It is an equally interesting observation that employers do not usually encourage such behaviour. Economic theory is not without useful answers to that question: there are asymmetric information theories, efficiency-wage theories, relative-wage theories, bargaining theories, fairness theories, insider–outsider theories. Research has come to no firm conclusion yet; and the problem of empirical discrimination has not even been touched. International comparison may play an important part here.

Any interesting and useful solution to that riddle will almost certainly involve an equilibrium concept broader, or at least different from, price-mediated market-clearing. (I say 'almost' to allow for the possibility that slowly self-correcting disequilibrium may turn out to be a better idea.) That will mean taking seriously the problem of modelling the strategy sets actually seen by firms and workers as available to them, and their criteria of choice. In neither respect, it seems to me, has economic theory yet done justice to the institutional and affective complexity of the labour market. The conventional assumptions seem particularly implausible and unappealing there.

Once one starts down that line, other interesting possibilities open up. We are all used to the idea that non-cooperative games can have inefficient equilibrium points. The example of Nash equilibrium has, of course, been studied in detail. In such cases it is natural to ask if there are better allocations that are cooperatively attainable, and what mechanisms could most effectively achieve them. That is what the theory of economic policy is presumably about. I do not think it will prove useful simply to turn macroeconomics into game theory; but I think it will be useful to incorporate some game-theoretic habits of thought into the way we do macroeconomic theory. Keynes's idea that anything that could be accomplished by wage deflation could be accomplished more quickly and less stressfully by monetary expansion is, right or wrong, an example of the sort of thing that needs to be done, a bit more formally and on a broader front.

REFERENCES

COE, DAVID T. and GAGLIARDI, FRANCESCO (1985). *Nominal Wage Determination in Ten OECD Countries.* OECD Economics and Statistics Department Working Paper no. 19, March. Paris: OECD.

MALINVAUD, EDMOND (1982). Wages and unemployment. *Economic Journal,* **92,** 1–12.

Aggregate Supply and Demand Factors in OECD Unemployment: An Update

By Michael Bruno

Hebrew University of Jerusalem

Introduction

Unemployment in the OECD countries has continued to rise to unprecedented levels. The EEC countries, which on average ended the turbulent 1970s with an unemployment rate of close to 7 per cent, are now, in the mid-1980s, approaching an 11 per cent level. The United States is virtually the only country for which the changes in unemployment during the 1970s have not been systematically upward and for which the 1984 rate was, more or less, back to where it had been both ten years and five years earlier (see Figure 1).

The reasons for the sustained increase in unemployment during the 1970s as well as the possible reasons for differences in patterns across industrial countries have been studied, but question marks undoubtedly remain. Our own emphasis in an earlier study has been on the combination of the great supply shocks of the previous decade and the contractionary macro-policy response of most OECD countries to these shocks, as well as on the more recent policy coordination problem between the United States and Europe. With a few more years that have elapsed, and quite a few percentage points of additional unemployment, there is obviously room for both an update and a reappraisal.[1]

Starting from a fairly conventional aggregate supply (AS) and aggregate demand (AD) macro-framework, an increase in unemployment may come

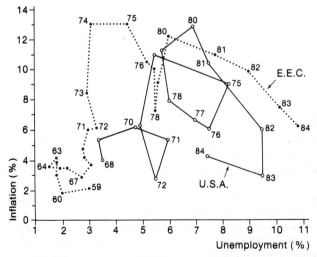

FIGURE 1. EEC inflation and unemployment, 1959–84, and US inflation and unemployment, 1968–84.

about as a result of a leftward shift of either the AS curve or the AD curve, or a combination thereof (see Figure 2). The first 'pure' case of a supply shock brings about both unemployment and inflation and is generally understood to have characterized the period both immediately before and after the first oil shock (1973–74), the extent of resulting stagflation in various countries depending on the extent of real-wage rigidity. Such shift from south-west to north-east in the unemployment–inflation framework (see Figure 1) has also characterized the second oil shock (1979–80). An added leftward bias of the AS curve in the 1970s may have been caused by the depressive effect of the profit squeeze on capital accumulation. All of these have imparted a 'classical' element to the unemployment which has certainly not been present in earlier, cyclical unemployment episodes. However, even the developments immediately following the two oil shocks cannot be understood without paying explicit regard to contractionary forces coming from leftward shifts in the AD schedules of countries (see Figure 2).

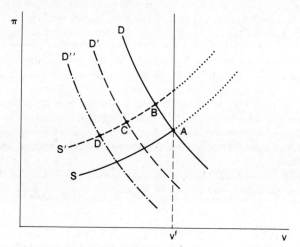

FIGURE 2.   AD and AS framework for individual economy: π = final goods terms-of-trade; v = GDP.

The period immediately following the first oil shock (1974–77) certainly looks more like a conventional north-west-to-south-east movement down a short-run Phillips curve (see Figure 1). In terms of the story for the 1970s, this could be explained as a combination of the depressing effect of oil and raw material prices on real income, the anti-inflationary response of macro-policy to the first oil shock, and the interaction of depressed world markets on export demand in the individual countries. A similar story, with some variations, could still be told for 1980–81. From that phase onwards the differential movement of unemployment in the United States and Europe has become a central issue which requires analysis in its own right.

In the coming sections I shall take up the main issues pertaining to the role of AS and AD factors in the rise of unemployment. Section I reconsiders the concept of the real-wage gap, and applies alternative measures to the data up to, and including, 1983. The general finding is that, by the end of the period considered, wage gaps for most countries recorded have come down from their peak levels in 1979-81, but are still sizeable on average in Europe. Section II takes up the role of the profit squeeze. We find that, while profits have played a very important role in the investment slowdown, the main reason for the profit squeeze has come from depressed demand conditions and less from the direct effect of high real wages. While the slowdown in capital growth may provide an eventual constraint on rapid growth in the manufacturing sector, it is unlikely to be an obstacle to expansion at the present moment owing to excess capacity.

Section III takes a summary overview of the demand for labour in the manufacturing sector, applying a neoclassical demand curve for labour with some Keynesian AD elements superimposed on it. Section IV reconsiders the overall unemployment performance of countries in terms of the basic underlying AS and AD components, reinforcing the argument that the more recent rise in unemployment is primarily an AD contraction phenomenon. The final section discusses the dilemma of individual country expansion and reconfirms the argument that there is a serious policy coordination problem between the United States and Europe in which the large US deficit, coupled with monetary restraint and the European fear of renewed inflation, have simultaneously provided the conditions for rapid US expansion and the sluggishness of revival in Europe. The policy proposals recently put forward,[2] calling for coordinated, more active, expansion in Europe with some incomes policy hedges, thus receive added support.

I. THE RISE AND GRADUAL FALL OF WAGE GAPS

Several studies have produced evidence that, for a number of countries during the 1970s at least, an important supply factor has been a persistent excess of real-wage levels above the marginal product of labour at full employment.[3] It is therefore important to update and reconsider the evidence from the vantage point of the mid-1980s.

Assume a well-behaved production function in terms of value added: $V = F(L, K; t)$; and suppose that one can measure the marginal product at full employment (L^f), $F_L(L^f, K; t)$. Under output-market-clearing and competitive firms, $(W/P_v)^f = F_L(L^f, K; t)$ is the level of product wage at which labour demand will equal L^f. The wage gap, w^x, is the percentage deviation of the actual product wage W/P_v over $(W/P_v)^f$; or, in log-linear approximation, $w^x = (w - p_v) - (w - p_v)^f$.

The notion that the marginal product of labour may mean something in the aggregate or that the aggregate demand for labour may depend on the real wage is, of course, controversial, mainly because of the competitive assumption implied for firms. We here proceed under the supposition that, like many artefacts in applied macroeconomics, the notion of a wage gap could, under certain circumstances and with some caveats, perform a useful diagnostic function. When based on a sub-sector like manufacturing, it may be less controversial than otherwise, since for most economies this is a highly tradable industry and one that is reasonably competitive.[4]

Under a CES production function with elasticity of substitution σ between L and K, the elasticity of demand for labour with respect to the product wage is σ/s_k, where s_k is the capital share in value added. Thus, a log-linear approximation of the employment shortfall in the short run (i.e. at *given* capital stock,[5]) arising from a positive wage gap is given by

$$(1) \qquad l^d - l^f = -(\sigma/s_k)w^x \qquad\qquad (l^d = l^f \text{ when } w^x = 0).$$

The main problem of measurement lies in estimating the marginal product of labour at full employment. In principle, one could estimate the production technology directly and calculate F_L for l^f. Such estimates must usually assume market-clearing on a year-to-year basis, which is obviously problematic. The alternative procedure followed here is to suggest a range of estimates of w^x under alternative assumptions from which, it is argued, a general picture none the less emerges.

The simplest assumption for calculating w^x is the Cobb–Douglas technology ($\sigma = 1$), for which the marginal product moves parallel to the average product and the problem then boils down to measuring the gap between $(w - p_v)$ and the trend of the average product at full employment $(v^f - l^f)$, namely, a corrected relative wage share measure, normalized by some base-year benchmark. Table 1 gives this first measure for 12 OECD countries taking the

TABLE 1

WAGE GAPS, 12 OECD COUNTRIES, 1965–1983, UNADJUSTED
(percentages over 1965–1969 average)

	1965	1970	1973	1976	1979	1981	1982	1983	Country weights[a]
USA	1·2	−1·3	3·1	0·6	4·0	5·0	5·3	4·9	28·9
Canada	−1·7	1·5	−1·4	4·6	0·9	1·5	1·8	2·0	3·1
Japan	2·3	4·1	9·8	21·5	24·1	23·4	20·2	16·4	20·6
Europe									
UK	−1·5	1·5	3·1	8·1	9·3	14·3	13·9	13·9	11·0
Belgium	0·4	1·7	18·7	32·7	33·0	31·9	24·2	—	1·6
Denmark	−2·4	2·6	8·5	14·3	16·1	13·1	9·5	4·1	0·8
France	0·3	−3·8	−0·3	4·9	2·6	2·7	4·1	—	8·9
Germany	1·7	1·9	8·0	14·0	14·6	17·1	13·3	9·6	12·6
Italy	3·8	4·2	10·9	17·8	9·6	6·5	4·8	2·9	8·4
Neth.	2·1	0·2	−2·2	−1·5	−6·5	−16·1	−20·4	—	1·8
Norway	−3·2	−3·4	0·6	17·4	19·4	8·8	7·1	6·4	0·7
Sweden	3·4	−2·2	−7·4	3·3	−3·9	−7·6	−11·4	14·6	1·6
Mean (weighted)	1·2	1·7	5·3	10·1	10·7	11·1	9·7	—	100·0
Partial mean[b]	1·3	1·4	5·8	10·5	11·4	12·1	10·6	8·8	
Mean, 8 countries[c]									
$\sigma = 1$	1·0	0·6	4·7	9·1	10·7	11·7	10·5	—	
$\sigma = 0·7$	0·9	0·7	4·9	9·1	10·3	11·1	9·8	—	
$\sigma = 0·5$	0·8	0·9	5·3	9·0	9·8	10·3	8·9	—	

[a] Relative size, based on 1975 manufacturing employment levels (percentages).
[b] Weighted mean of nine countries for which 1983 observations are recorded.
[c] Weighted mean of eight countries (for which capital stock numbers exist) under alternative CES assumptions (countries excluded are Belgium, Denmark, Italy and the Netherlands).

benchmark for $w^x (= w - p_v - (v^f - l^f))$ to be 0 on average during the period 1965–69 and taking the average growth rates of $v - l$ during 1960–73 and 1973–85 to represent the respective 'full-employment' trend $(v^f - l^f)$.[6]

The findings, based on the simplest measure of the gap, suggest that, after a rise in the gap in the early 1970s and a very sharp rise during the first oil shock, to a weighted average of 11 per cent by the end of the decade, there was a gradual fall in most countries from about 1980 onward. The move in a downward direction seems to have become more marked during 1982–83. The table also underscores the fact that there are sharp differences among countries, both for the peak years and for the deceleration. The United States and Canada, importantly, show very little variation during the oil shock, and only the Netherlands and Sweden were the exception to an otherwise real-wage-resistant Europe.[7] The UK and Belgium stand out as two countries with large remaining gaps by the end of the period. Japan's 1979 figure, one can argue, is misleading, since the reference period, 1965–69, probably did not reflect an equilibrium in its labour market.[8] Anyway, it shows substantial reduction after 1979.

We consider two major sensitivity tests for the basic measure used in Table 1, one having to do with the technology and the other with the hypothetical measure of $v^f - l^f$ during the recent unemployment years.

The first argument against findings based on the simple measure of w^x comes from the assumed unitary elasticity of substitution. We know that, when $\sigma < 1$, a rise in real wages will also result in a rising labour share in value-added, which would have nothing to do with disequilibrium. The sharpness of the rise in w^x in the mid-1970s and its subsequent fall towards the early 1980s would cast doubt on such explanation, but it is none the less important to see how sensitive this result is to the size of σ. Various recent studies of the production function for manufacturing across countries suggest the assumption of Harrod-neutral technical progress and a range of estimates of σ between 0·5 and 1, with an average of about 0·7.[9]

We recalculated $v^f - l^f$ on the two alternative assumptions, $\sigma = 0·5$ and $\sigma = 0·7$, using the approximation formula[10]

$$(2) \qquad v_l = (v - l) + \{(1 - \sigma)/\sigma\}\{s_k/(1 - s_k)\}(k - v)$$

and again applying it to the trend between the 'peak' years 1960, 1973 and 1983.

The above approximation obviously requires a knowledge of capital stock figures, which were available for only eight of the countries in question. The last three lines of Table 1 give a summary average estimate for these eight countries (Belgium, Denmark, Italy and the Netherlands are excluded here) for the three assumptions on σ, from which we can see that the 1979 and 1981 peak estimates of w^x are only slightly modified. There is a somewhat larger difference in the subsequent years—the smaller is σ, the larger is the estimated reduction in the gap by 1982. There are, of course, differences for individual countries (these data are not reproduced here), but the general result holds on average.

The second sensitivity test involves an alternative estimate for $v^f - l^f$ which attempts to correct for the effect of the unemployment level and changes thereof on full-employment productivity growth. The method used[11] was to run for each country a regression of labour productivity on unemployment, the current and lagged change in unemployment and time, with a time shift factor after 1975:

$$(3) \qquad v - l = \alpha_0 + \alpha_1 t + \alpha_2 t_{7583} + \alpha_3 U_t + \alpha_4 \Delta U_t + \alpha_5 \Delta U_{t-1}.$$

Generally, as one would expect, $\alpha_3 > 0$ and α_4, $\alpha_5 < 0$ (the regressions are not reproduced here).

By setting $U_t = \Delta U_t = \Delta U_{t-1} = 0$ in the estimated equation, we get an estimate of $v^f - l^f$ which was used instead of the simple trend, again normalized to zero in 1965–69.

The resulting adjusted estimates are given in Table 2. It is interesting to note that, on the whole, the previous general finding remains intact, concerning both the size of the increase in 1976 and the gradual fall after 1979. The two extreme cases, Belgium and the UK, now look even worse, and it seems that France too is in much worse shape once the correction for unemployment is made. We note that the weighted mean for Europe, when Belgium and the UK are excluded, shows a lower peak but only a very mild slowdown.

An important question that arises relates to the sources of these changes in the measured wage gap. At least a partial answer is provided by a breakdown of changes in the wage gap ($\dot{w}^x$) into the parts attributable to the real consumption wage ($\dot{w}_c$), the changes in relative consumption to product prices ($\dot{p}_c - \dot{p}_v$), where the latter include changes in relative import prices, and the assumed productivity trend ($\dot{v}^f - \dot{l}^f$).

Table 3 provides a breakdown of $\dot{w}^x$ by sub-period (using the basic measure of Table 1), using the identity

$$(4) \qquad \dot{w}^x = \dot{w}_c + (\dot{p}_c - \dot{p}_v) - (\dot{v}^f - \dot{l}^f).$$

TABLE 2

ADJUSTED WAGE GAPS, 12 OECD COUNTRIES, 1965–1983
(percentages over 1965–1969 average)

	1965	1970	1973	1976	1979	1981	1982	1983
USA	0·2	0·1	6·0	2·9	6·8	8·1	8·6	8·4
Canada	−1·9	1·9	−0·5	3·3	0·8	2·2	2·9	3·5
Japan	2·2	4·3	10·1	18·2	20·7	19·8	16·6	12·7
Europe								
UK	−2·0	2·2	4·6	11·0	16·4	24·1	25·0	26·4
Belgium	2·1	−0·8	13·6	30·2	37·2	40·7	35·2	—
Denmark	−2·3	2·5	8·1	13·0	17·6	16·4	13·7	9·2
France	0·0	−3·4	−0·4	7·9	10·7	14·3	17·4	—
Germany	2·0	1·5	7·2	13·0	15·3	19·1	15·9	12·9
Italy	2·3	6·4	15·4	19·5	11·8	9·1	7·6	5·9
Neth.	2·8	1·0	−4·4	−6·7	−11·7	−21·3	−25·7	—
Norway	−2·5	−4·3	−1·3	13·9	17·3	7·7	6·4	6·2
Sweden	2·7	−1·1	−5·2	3·7	−1·6	−4·0	−7·1	−9·6
Mean (weighted)[a]	0·8	1·6	6·6	10·5	12·6	14·0	13·1	—
Partial mean[b]	0·8	2·2	7·4	10·8	12·8	14·2	13·0	11·6
Mean, Europe	0·7	1·4	5·9	12·3	13·3	15·8	14·9	—
Mean, Europe, Excl. UK and Belgium	1·5	1·2	5·9	11·9	11·2	12·0	11·3	—

[a] Weighted by 1975 employment levels.
[b] Mean of nine countries for which 1983 observations are recorded.

TABLE 3
DECOMPOSITION OF CHANGES IN THE WAGE GAP, 1964–1983
(annual percentage rates of change)

	1964–70				1970–74				1974–78				1978–80				1980–83			
	$\dot{w}^x$	$\dot{w}_c$	$\dot{p}_c - \dot{p}_0$	$-(\dot{v}^f - \dot{l}^f)$	$\dot{w}^x$	$\dot{w}_c$	$\dot{p}_c - \dot{p}_0$	$-(\dot{v}^f - \dot{l}^f)$	$\dot{w}^x$	$\dot{w}_c$	$\dot{p}_c - \dot{p}_0$	$-(\dot{v}^f - \dot{l}^f)$	$\dot{w}^x$	$\dot{w}_c$	$\dot{p}_c - \dot{p}_0$	$-(\dot{v}^f - \dot{l}^f)$	$\dot{w}^x$	$\dot{w}_c$	$\dot{p}_c - \dot{p}_0$	$-(\dot{v}^f - \dot{l}^f)$
USA	-0·8	1·5	1·2	-3·5	0·9	1·1	2·9	-3·1	-0·1	2·0	-0·1	-1·9	1·7	-1·5	5·3	-1·9	-0·2	0·6	1·1	-1·9
Canada	0·9	3·4	2·1	-4·7	-0·9	3·4	-0·4	-3·9	1·2	2·1	0·5	-1·5	-2·0	0·5	-1·0	-1·5	1·1	1·8	0·8	-1·5
Japan	0·4	8·6	2·1	-10·4	2·8	8·9	3·4	-9·5	1·9	2·3	6·2	-6·7	1·5	0·7	7·3	-6·7	-3·0	2·1	1·4	-6·7
Europe																				
UK	0·6	3·8	1·0	-4·3	2·2	5·0	1·0	-3·8	-2·2	2·3	-1·9	-2·6	4·2	5·0	1·9	-2·6	1·4	2·7	1·3	-2·6
France	-0·6	4·3	0·8	-5·8	1·9	5·6	1·8	-5·5	0·0	4·4	0·1	-4·5	0·0	2·6	1·9	-4·5	0·0	2·0	1·7	-4·5
Germany	0·5	6·3	-0·2	-5·5	2·3	7·0	0·6	-5·3	0·8	5·2	-0·2	-4·1	0·8	3·4	1·5	-4·1	-2·1	0·5	1·4	-4·1
Italy	-0·7	6·9	-0·4	-7·3	2·3	9·3	-0·6	-5·3	-0·4	4·0	-1·2	-3·2	-3·3	0·3	-0·4	-3·2	-0·7	2·9	-0·4	-3·2
Neth.	-0·6	7·2	-0·4	-7·4	0·4	8·0	-0·7	-6·9	-1·9	3·2	-0·4	-4·7	-2·9	1·1	0·6	-4·7	-4·5	-0·3	0·6	-4·7
Norway	0·0	5·1	-0·7	-7·4	2·0	5·8	0·0	-3·8	4·4	4·7	1·8	-2·1	4·4	0·1	-2·5	-2·1	-2·2	-0·8	0·7	-2·1
Sweden	-1·3	5·2	-0·2	-6·4	-0·1	5·5	-0·2	-5·4	0·4	4·1	-1·0	-2·7	-2·8	-0·9	0·8	-2·7	-2·6	-0·8	0·8	-2·7
Belgium	0·3	7·3	-0·1	-6·9	4·8	12·4	-0·5	-7·1	2·7	8·3	0·4	-6·0	1·0	5·6	1·2	-6·0	-4·8	-0·9	1·8	-6·0
Denmark	0·9	5·5	2·0	-6·5	2·6	7·1	1·4	-5·9	-0·1	2·7	0·8	-3·6	1·6	0·3	5·0	-3·6	-3·9	-0·6	0·3	-3·6
Mean (weighted)[a]	0·1	4·9	1·0	-6·0	1·8	5·5	1·8	-5·4	0·3	3·1	0·9	-3·7	1·0	1·1	3·6	-3·7	-1·1	1·4	1·1	-3·7

[a] Weighted by 1975 employment level.

The table suggests that real-wage moderation has attenuated the effect of real import prices (as reflected in $\dot{p}_c - \dot{p}_v$) on w^x in the second oil shock (see 1978–80, unlike 1970–74). The deceleration of relative import prices in 1980–83 is the main explanatory factor behind the concomitant fall in w^x. We shall come back to the role of this negative supply shock in Section V.

II. The Role of the Profit Squeeze

The general picture that emerges from the data shown in the last section suggests that, during the depression years of the early 1980s, the wage gap has most probably been reduced in all but two or three countries. What this implies is that, at given capital stock levels (provided the estimated wage gap is applicable to the whole economy, and not only to the manufacturing sector), the demand for labour would come closer to maintenance of full employment. The emphasis on the word *given* is important, because both the labour force and the capital stock normally grow at some balanced rate from which we have abstracted so far. The point is that, when the capital stock levels depart from their previous growth paths, this could be an additional argument for a gap between labour demand and full employment, quite apart from Keynesian arguments to which we turn later. A fall in investment demand could be linked to a profit squeeze, which, in itself, may have been caused by an increase in the price of other factors of production (material inputs and labour), by depressed demand conditions, or (as in fact was the case) by a combination of both.

In the absence of full-fledged investment demand functions based on a q-measure of rationally expected profits, we here apply a rather simple-minded approach in which capital stock growth is expressed as a function of past profits (a three-year average is used in the data below) and the real rate of interest. The real rate of profit, in turn, is expressed as a function of the real product wage (based on the factor price frontier) and a measure of demand pressure.

Let r denote the logarithm of the real rate of profit (where profits are deflated by GDP prices and the capital stock by investment goods prices) and w_v the logarithm of the product wage. A log-linear approximation of the factor price frontier (FPF) can be written in the form

$$(5) \qquad r = a_0 + a_1(w_v - \lambda t) + a_2 d$$

where a_1 should equal minus the ratio of the labour and capital shares, and λ is the labour-augmenting technical progress parameter (for the case of Harrod-neutral technical progress, which is assumed here).

For deviations from the FPF arising from short-term demand fluctuations, we add a term $a_2 d$ to equation (5) and also allow for a drop in productivity growth after 1974 by adding a slope dummy (D7582) to the equation for estimation. The regression equation and the estimates for eight countries are given in Table 4. For the d variable a proxy was used in the form of the ratio of manufacturing output over its ten-year moving average.[12]

For all countries, the a_1 coefficient comes out negative, as expected, though in the case of France and Italy it is statistically insignificant. As to its relative size, the average for the eight countries, 1·62, seems reasonable as it implies

TABLE 4

RATE OF PROFIT EQUATIONS FOR MANUFACTURING,
EIGHT COUNTRIES, 1965-1982[a]

$$(r = a_0 + a_1 w_v + a_2 d + a_3 t + a_4 D_{7582})$$

Country	a_0	a_1	a_2	a_3	a_4	ρ	$\bar{R}^2$	DW
USA	2·88	−3·41	2·37	0·12	−0·05	0·57	0·90	1·87
	(0·22)	(1·26)	(0·44)	(0·05)	(0·02)	(0·30)		
Canada	−5·15	−2·28	2·96	0·15	−0·10	−0·03	0·84	1·65
	(2·94)	(1·06)	(0·50)	(0·05)	(0·04)	(0·48)		
Japan	4·48	−0·61	1·88	0·07	—	—	0·97	1·70
	(0·51)	(0·14)	(0·01)	(0·01)				
UK	0·87	−1·75	2·08	0·06	—	0·63	0·94	1·63
	(0·76)	(0·59)	(0·50)	(0·03)		(0·24)		
France	1·10	−0·21	3·48	0·04	—	—	0·78	1·97
	(0·66)	(0·67)	(0·53)	(0·04)				
Germany	1·51	−1·06	1·70	0·07	−0·01	0·43	0·95	1·73
	(0·35)	(0·46)	(0·27)	(0·03)	(0·01)	(0·31)		
Italy	4·33	−0·44	3·08	0·07	—	0·65	0·78	1·38
	(1·36)	(0·35)	(0·41)	(0·02)		(0·24)		
Sweden	12·48	−3·17	6·65	0·22	−0·07	—	0·95	2·23
	(3·08)	(0·82)	(0·81)	(0·05)	(0·04)			

[a] Numbers in brackets are standard errors.
Sources: Real rate of profit = r, calculated from operating surplus over capital stock in manufacturing, corrected for relative GDP to investment goods prices—all from OECD data (Chan-Lee and Sutch, 1985); real product wage = w_v, nominal wage in manufacturing, BLS data deflated by GDP prices—OECD; demand proxy = d, manufacturing output divided by ten-year moving average—OECD data.

a labour share of 0·62. The average elasticity for the d coefficient (a_2) is 3·02. The implied technical progress coefficients can be got from the ratio $-a_3/a_1$ (corrected by the slope a_4 after 1974) for the various countries. Running a cross-section regression for the first differences of all countries (with country intercept dummies) gives a lower coefficient for the wage elasticity (−0·82 with s.e. 0·27) and about the same for the output coefficient (2·69 with s.e. 0·19); the $\bar{R}^2$ for the overall regression (136 observations) is 0·62.

Next, consider the relationship between investment and profits. A glance at the average data by sub-period suggests that the slowdown in capital accumulation both across countries and over time is correlated with the extent of the profit squeeze. A cross-section regression of period averages for the rate of change of the capital stock with the average rate of profit and the real rate of interest gives the following two alternative regressions for a linear or logarithmic specification (the data are four-period averages for eight countries, i.e. 32 observations):

(6) $\quad \dot{k} = (\text{country dummies}) + 0·467R - 0·098i_r, \quad \bar{R}^2 = 0·81$
$\qquad\qquad\quad (0·062) \quad (0·137)$

(6)′ $\quad \ln(\dot{k}) = (\text{country dummies}) + 1·101r + 0·077\{\ln(1 + i_r)\} \quad \bar{R}^2 = 0·64$
$\qquad\qquad\qquad (0·272) \quad (0·081)$

Both equations show a very strong effect of the profit rate and an insignificant effect of the real rate of interest. The economic reasoning behind the former could be via the effect of present profit rates on the expectations of future profits or else may be a result of financing constraints on firms, which enhances investment from retained earnings when the latter increase, Whichever the channel, it is obviously a strong relationship. It is further borne out by individual country regressions given in Table 5. These are based on annual data and a logarithmic specification (with the exception of the UK, in which only the linear form gave significant results). There the profit variable ($\bar{r}$) stands for the log average profit rate for the last three years.

Table 5 shows the elasticity of capital stock growth with respect to profits to be highly significant in almost all cases (the United States is a possible exception), the average value being 1·46. The coefficient for the real interest rate is significantly negative in only three cases.[13] (Only one case with a significantly positive coefficient, France, makes no economic sense.)

Writing the investment equation in the form

(7) $\quad \ln \dot{k} = b_0 + b_1 \bar{r} + b_2 i_r$

and substituting for $\bar{r}$ from r in equation (5), we can express the growth in the capital stock as a function of the real product wage (level), the demand variable (d) and the real interest rate (leaving out time shifts):

(8) $\quad \ln \dot{k} = b_0 + b_1 a_0 - b_1 a_1 w + b_1 a_2 d - b_2 i_r$.

Looking at the size of the implied elasticities and the actual change in the underlying variables, one major conclusion emerges—the real wage could not but have a relatively small direct role in the slowdown of capital accumulation, while the output contraction (from the demand side) played the dominant role in the profit squeeze and the resulting contraction in investment.

TABLE 5

INVESTMENT EQUATIONS FOR MANUFACTURING, EIGHT COUNTRIES, 1965–1982

$(\ln \dot{k} = b_0 + b_1 \bar{r} + b_2 i_r)$

Country	b_0	b_1	b_2	ρ	$\bar{R}^2$	DW
USA	−0·90	0·79	−9·00	0·61	0·55	1·83
	(1·46)	(0·50)	(3·15)	(0·21)		
Canada	−1·30	1·07	2·95	0·55	0·60	1·29
	(1·23)	(0·47)	(3·06)	(0·23)		
Japan	−4·47	2·00	0·62	0·33	0·88	1·74
(1967–82)	(0·89)	(0·27)	(1·42)	(0·29)		
UK[a]	1·14	0·20	−0·77	−0·89	0·62	2·37
	(0·42)	(0·04)	(5·06)	(0·16)		
France	−1·57	1·13	10·60	—	0·65	1·82
	(0·68)	(0·25)	(2·41)			
Germany	−7·72	3·22	−0·47	0·64	0·91	1·32
	(1·41)	(0·51)	(6·03)	(0·21)		
Italy	−3·86	1·83	−6·29	0·85	0·78	1·70
	(2·74)	(0·96)	(2·00)	(0·14)		
Sweden	−1·81	1·45	−12·45	—	0·56	1·32
	(0·72)	(0·33)	(5·50)			

[a] The regression for the UK is linear in $\dot{k}$ and $\bar{r}$.

Source: $\bar{r} =$ log of three-year mean rate of profit, OECD Economic Outlook (rate of operating surplus over capital stock); $i_r =$ log (1 + real rate of interest), where real rate equals nominal rate minus rate of consumer price inflation, IMF; $\dot{k} =$ percentage rate of change, real capital stock, OECD.

The product of the average a_1 (1·6) and the average b_1 (1·5) gives an elasticity of 2·4. A permanent increase in w_v of 5 per cent over its equilibrium level would thus imply a fall in $\hat{k}$ of 12 per cent.[14] We know from Section I that in the mid-1970 s there were temporary increases of w_v which on average were twice that, but by the beginning of the 1980s the gap for most countries had already come down substantially. At the same time, the rate of growth of the capital stock was cut to less than half its rate over the decade for most European countries for which data are recorded here. The total elasticity for the d variable, on the other hand $(b_1 a_2)$, amounts to 4·5, and the relative fall in its level over the period was of the order of 20 per cent, thus being capable of 'explaining' drops of up to 90 per cent in $\hat{k}$.

This general assessment of the relative importance of the two factors (as well as a minute role for the real rate of interest) also emerges when an analysis of components is carried out by individual country (not reproduced here). We may thus conclude that, while the profit squeeze probably played an important role in the investment slowdown, for most countries and for most of the time, high real wages played only a small direct role in the latter. Indirectly, of course, the contractionary bias of macroeconomic policy was probably related to wage rigidity (fear of inflation), but this is another matter to which we shall return. First, we take a summary overview of the factors affecting employment in manufacturing.

III. An Analysis of the Demand For Labour in Manufacturing

To take a summary view of the factors affecting employment in manufacturing, we modify the conventional demand curve for labour by assuming gradual adjustment $(l - l_{-1} = \beta(l^d - l_{-1}))$ as well as a short-run role for aggregate demand factors. For the latter three variables were used: the government deficit (d_f, corrected for full employment and inflation), deviations from the trend in world trade (d_w), and the real money stock (m, lagged). For most countries there is a considerable positive correlation between the fiscal and monetary variables, and only for the United States, where the two conflicted, did the monetary variable play an important separate role. (M_2 was used and the world trade variable was not included.) The log-linear equation that was fitted for most countries (see Table 6) is the following:

$$(9) \qquad l - k_{-1} = c_0 + c_1(l_{-1} - k_{-1}) + c_2 w_v + c_3 d_f + c_4 d_w + c_5 t + c_6 D_{7582}.$$

We note that, with the exception of the United States and Canada, all other countries show significant negative coefficients for the product wage variable. The 'long-run' elasticity (but at given capital stock) of labour demand varies from about $\frac{1}{2}$ for Belgium and Norway to 2 and above for Japan, Denmark, France and the Netherlands (these values are obtained by dividing c_2 by $1 - c_1$). The implied elasticity of substitution can be obtained by multiplication of these values by the share of capital which for most countries is of the order $\frac{1}{3}$ (somewhat higher for Japan). The world trade variable is significantly positive in most cases, as is the deficit variable for those countries for which data could be included.

The direct role attributed to aggregate demand in these regressions is certainly not negligible, and if we add the indirect role working through the

TABLE 6
DEMAND FOR LABOUR IN MANUFACTURING, 1961–1982, ELEVEN COUNTRIES

$$(l - k_{-1} = c_0 + c_1(l_{-1} - k_{-1}) + c_2 w_v + c_3 d_f + c_4 d_w + [c'_4 m] + c_5 t + c_6 D_{7582})$$

Country	c_1	c_2	c_3	$c_4[c'_4]$	c_5	c_6	DH[a]	SE
USA	0·34	0·17	1·16	[0·61]	−0·06	0·02	−0·84	0·0023
	(0·13)	(0·30)	(0·80)	(0·10)	(0·01)	(0·05)		
Canada	1·12	−0·29	1·19	0·50	0·02	−0·014	−1·34	0·0037
	(0·16)	(0·25)	(0·55)	(0·18)	(0·01)	(0·010)		
Japan	0·62	−1·03	1·41	0·24	0·07	−0·02	−0·35	0·0033
	(0·20)	(0·35)	(0·73)	(0·16)	(0·03)	(0·01)		
UK	0·41	−0·59	0·46	0·26	−0·00	−0·022	1·41	0·0039
	(0·17)	(0·21)	(0·26)	(0·19)	(0·01)	(0·005)		
Belgium[b]	0·45	−0·25	—	0·53	0·015	−0·024	−0·01	0·0018
	(0·12)	(0·24)		(0·09)	(0·005)	(0·006)		
Denmark[b]	0·41	−1·20	—	0·61	0·08	−0·04	−1·88	0·0027
	(0·12)	(0·24)		(0·13)	(0·02)	(0·01)		
France	0·71	−0·57	0·67	0·23	0·017	−0·011	−1·40	0·0014
	(0·11)	(0·12)	(0·39)	(0·08)	(0·009)	(0·003)		
Germany	1·00	−0·64	1·98	0·70	0·044	−0·012	1·59	0·0026
	(0·18)	(0·22)	(0·74)	(0·16)	(0·021)	(0·008)		
Italy[c]	0·25*	−0·76	−0·00	0·20	0·026	−0·04	1·30	0·0034
	(0·23)	(0·28)	(0·00)	(0·18)	(0·20)	(0·02)		
Neth.[b]	0·76	−0·40	—	0·28	0·019	−0·015	−0·169	0·0026
	(0·10)	(0·17)		(0·09)	(0·010)	(0·009)		
Norway[b]	0·79	−0·104	—	0·035	0·004	−0·008	1·17	0·0027
	(0·17)	(0·056)		(0·098)	(0·003)	(0·005)		

[a] Durbin H-coefficient.
[b] For these four countries there are no capital stock or deficit data in the regression.
[c] 1965–82.

Data in brackets are standard errors of coefficients.

Sources: l = (log) man-hours in manufacturing, BLS data; k = capital stock, see Table 3; w_v = product wage, see Table 3; d_w = deviations from world trade trend, see Layard and Nickell (1984); m = log of real money stock, IMF; d_f = inflation-corrected structural deficit, EEC data.

investment slowdown it is quite sizeable. In the way we have specified the model, it is constrained to show constant returns to scale in labour and capital; and thus any factor accounting for a 1 per cent cut in the rate of change of k also, *ceteris paribus*, indirectly accounts for the same in terms of the rate of change in man-hours. At the same time, the fact that the slowdown in demand played a direct role in the regression provides evidence that by the end of that period (after considerable demand slowdown) there was probably no capacity constraint. This is also borne out by direct measurements of capacity utilization (see European Community business surveys quoted in *European Economy*, 1983, and in Layard *et al.*, 1984).

IV. AN ANALYSIS OF OVERALL UNEMPLOYMENT

So far, the analysis has dealt only with the manufacturing sector. There are obvious advantages to a consideration of that sector, both for analytical reasons (a neoclassical labour demand framework is more defensible for this sector, at least in a typical European open-economy context) and because such data as product wages and capital input are more readily available. We do not, at the moment, have a satisfactory aggregate macroeconomic model formally combining demand and supply factors in a way that could be used for econometric estimation of labour demand, especially in an imperfectly competitive setting. In the absence thereof, we make do with an *ad hoc* formulation, which follows the logic of the preceding discussion and could also be given justification on the basis of a gradual adjustment to aggregate demand and aggregate supply within a disequilibrium setting.[15]

We write down a reduced form in which unemployment is expressed as a function of the lagged real-wage gap, and the aggregate demand factors with two lags for each. The more distant lags could be rationalized on the basis of delayed effects working either on the aggregate demand schedule or via profitability and capital investment on the aggregate supply side. It is in that 'hybrid' sense that the results of Table 7 should be interpreted.

Table 7 presents unemployment regressions for eight countries. Only in the case of the United States do both the monetary and fiscal variables appear (without the world trade variable). In the case of the other countries, the addition of a fiscal variable did not make any significant difference and the lagged real-money stock variables seemed to do all of the action on the domestic demand side.[16] Note that the signs of coefficients are, in most cases, the 'right' ones,[17] although they are not always significant at the 1 per cent level.

Because of the statistical problems that are attached to this type of single-equation estimation for each country, there is some advantage to also taking an overall cross-section view of the rise in unemployment using the same

TABLE 7

UNEMPLOYMENT EQUATIONS FOR EIGHT COUNTRIES, 1962–1982

$$(U = h_0 + h_1 w^x_{-1} + h_2 w^x_{-2} + h_3 m_{-1} + h_4 m_{-2} + h_5 d_w + h_6 d_{w-1} (+ h'_5 d_{f-1} + h'_6 d_{f-2}) + \text{time shift}^a)$$

Country	h_1	h_2	h_3	h_4	$h_5[h'_5]$	$h_6[h'_6]$	DW	SE
USA	20·11	−1·44	−4·95	−11·05	[−0·27]	[−0·05]	1·76	0·051
	(4·06)	(4·89)	(1·66)	(1·67)	(0·11)	(0·11)		
Canada	20·34	8·52	2·31	−7·58	−7·01	1·02	1·99	0·069
	(7·32)	(8·47)	(3·01)	(2·68)	(5·57)	(5·25)		
Japan	2·46	1·44	0·26	0·01	−2·02	−0·83	2·49	0·035
	(0·70)	(0·76)	(0·45)	(0·34)	(0·48)	(0·62)		
UK	8·48	13·77	−3·27	−1·48	−10·03	−4·25	1·88	0·087
	(6·20)	(7·51)	(3·62)	(2·95)	(5·05)	(4·72)		
Belgium	3·67	7·32	−3·62	0·89	−11·76	−10·63	1·77	0·045
	(2·63)	(2·92)	(1·97)	(1·71)	(2·03)	(2·02)		
Denmark	1·70	45·03	−10·03	13·49	−17·12	−1·27	1·91	0·109
	(14·53)	(15·38)	(4·99)	(4·66)	(5·66)	(9·50)		
France	1·70	−5·91	−3·20	2·42	−2·38	−3·82	2·00	0·047
	(2·53)	(2·76)	(1·58)	(1·38)	(1·33)	(1·50)		
Germany	7·75	3·62	−4·83	−5·58	−7·27	−3·79	1·70	0·124
	(3·99)	(4·03)	(1·97)	(2·39)	(3·06)	(2·55)		

[a] The regressions include separate time shift factors for the period 1962–74 and 1975–82 and were run using AR_1.

Sources: Unemployment = U, OECD standardized unemployment data: Wage gap = w^x. See Table 1; Real-money balances = m, IMF data; for Canada and the USA, M2 (of the USA) was used; Government deficit = d_f, see Table 6; World trade = d_w see Table 6.

underlying model. The following is the resulting regression (20 years ×8 countries = 160 observations) of first differences:

$$(10) \quad \Delta U = 0.32 + 6.84\Delta w^x_{-1} + 7.47\Delta w^x_{-2} - 5.75\Delta m_{-1} + 0.61\Delta m_{-2}$$
$$\quad\quad (0.08)(2.30) \quad\quad (2.37) \quad\quad (1.08) \quad\quad (1.00)$$
$$\quad\quad -9.56\Delta d_w - 6.26\Delta d_{w-1} \quad\quad \bar{R}^2 = 0.51$$
$$\quad\quad (1.57) \quad\quad (1.71)$$

With the exception of the second lag on money (which could be left out), all coefficients have the right sign and are highly significant (numbers in brackets are standard errors of coefficients). The assumption underlying (10)— that the elasticities are the same across countries—is, of course, problematic, but it is reassuring to find such a strong overall qualitative result. If one adds dummy variables for countries and/or each time period, none of these dummies comes out significant, and the overall regression is not improved.

The average quantitative implications that could be read into the regression is that, for each 1 per cent rise (fall) in the wage gap, the unemployment rate rises (falls) by 0.15 per cent within two years, while for each 1 per cent drop in the rate of growth in real money stock unemployment rises by 0.06 per cent after a year.

Consider, for example, the average drop in real-money growth between 1974–78 and 1978–82, which was about 4 per cent in annual average terms. The regression would thus attribute an annual average rise of 0.24 per cent in the unemployment rate to this factor alone in the last period.[18]

TABLE 8

ADJUSTED ACCOUNTING FOR THE RISE IN UNEMPLOYMENT SINCE 1965–1969

	1970–74	1974–78	1978–82	1982	1970–74	1974–78	1978–82	1982
	USA				Belgium			
Total	1.7	3.5	3.7	5.8	0.3	4.5	8.1	10.8
Adj. wage gap	−0.1	0.1	−0.1	0.0	0.7	3.4	5.6	12.2
Aggregate demand	1.5	3.2	4.0	5.7	−0.2	1.3	2.3	−1.3
	Canada				Denmark			
Total	1.9	3.7	4.4	7.0	0.6	8.0	8.2	10.2
Adj. wage gap	0.4	0.1	0.3	0.4	2.5	7.8	11.0	6.3
Aggregate demand	1.5	3.4	4.3	6.2	−1.5	−0.5	−2.4	4.6
	Japan				France			
Total	0.1	0.8	1.0	1.1	0.7	2.6	4.8	5.9
Adj. wage gap	0.3	0.9	1.1	1.1	−0.2	0.6	1.4	1.6
Aggregate demand	−0.2	−0.1	0.0	0.9	2.0	2.0	3.3	4.3
	UK				Germany			
Total	0.9	3.1	6.1	9.5	0.2	2.7	3.3	5.3
Adj. wage gap	0.6	2.5	3.7	5.5	0.3	1.2	1.7	1.9
Aggregate demand	0.3	0.8	2.0	3.9	−0.1	1.4	1.6	3.4

Table 8 gives a summary analysis of the analogous regressions that were based on the adjusted wage gap measure (these regressions are not reported here). It indicates the role of the major factors accounting for the increase in unemployment in each country. For each period the average cumulative change in the average unemployment rate since 1965-69 is given, as well as the estimated role of the adjusted wage gap (with its two lags) and the sum total of the aggregate demand factors. The table reinforces the earlier finding that wages played an important role mainly in the mid-1970s and primarily for three of the countries recorded (the UK, Belgium and Denmark), and that its relative importance for most countries diminished during the last sub-period, 1978-82, where most of the *incremental* increase in unemployment can be attributed to aggregate demand shifts (substract the second column of Table 8 from the third or fourth column). However, by 1982 the average remaining effect of the wage factor was still high for the five European countries recorded in this table.

V. INFLATION, EXHANGE RATES AND THE COORDINATION PROBLEM

The discussion so for has highlighted the dominant role of contractionary macro-policy in the recent further rise of unemployment in Europe. The same framework is also consistent with the concomitant fall in unemployment in the United States, given the extensive fiscal expansion in that country since 1981. We conclude the discussion by noting that it is the combination of fiscal expansion and monetary contraction in the United States that, at least in part, may indirectly account for the reluctance to expand in Europe on account of sluggish inflation deceleration. The causal link is provided by exchange rate developments during the same period.

The rise in real interest rates and net capital flows into the United States account for the large dollar appreciation since the beginning of 1981 (of the order of 50 per cent nominal and 38 per cent in real terms). This has had a dramatic effect on the relative import price developments in the United States as compared to Europe, which, we would argue, is the dominant reason for the differential inflation performance on the two sides of the Atlantic (see Figure 1).[19] The evidence for this is so striking that it is hard to understand why it often gets overlooked.

In Table 9 the two sets of numbers for annual rates of change in import prices and consumer prices for the United States and the average for the EEC

TABLE 9

MOVEMENTS IN IMPORT AND CONSUMER PRICES: USA AND EEC

	1981	1982	1983	1984
Import prices:				
USA	5·5	−1·6	−3·7	0·3
EEC	15·6	7·1	4·2	8·5
Consumer prices:				
USA	10·4	6·2	3·2	4·3
EEC	11·1	9·8	7·5	6·3

countries since 1980. A simple reduced-form inflation equation for the years 1961-80 (based on a pooled regression prepared two years ago) gives a fairly close post-sample prediction of 1982-84 developments for both the United States and the EEC. It considers the inflation rate as a sum of lagged inflation (with a coefficient of 0·66) and current import price change (with a coefficient of 0·18) along with a capacity term which is ignored here. This gives the predicted rates of 7·1, 3·9, 2·7 for the United States during 1982-84 and 9·0, 7·6, 6·9 for EEC. The predicted mean inflation during 1982-84 is 4·6 and 7·8, respectively, while the actual rates were 4·6 and 7·9—not a bad fit, on the average.

The real depreciation of European currencies relative to the dollar thus explains why inflation slowed down so much less rapidly on the European continent. It may also help to explain why Europe as a whole was reluctant to expand and instead adopted contractionary macro-policies until very recently. These helped to support the slowdown in inflation, but at a formidable cost in terms of unemployment. Each country by itself will not expand because it risks running into balance of payments problems and added pressure on its exchange rate (with inflationary consequences), and for all countries to expand simultaneously requires more coordination than seems politically feasible, especially since the United States must agree to cut its own fiscal deficit *pari passu*. A turn-around in change rates, such as occurred in 1985, could of course alleviate some of the pressure. On the other hand, too rapid expansion in the OECD countries as a whole would risk the possibility that relative prices of industrial raw materials will rise again, but it is a trade-off worth considering.

ACKNOWLEDGEMENTS

I am indebted to Carlos Bachrach for very able research assistance, much of which was performed with the help of the DRI system. I also wish to thank Andrew Abel, Robert Gordon, Jeffrey Sachs and the Editors for valuable comments on an earlier draft.

NOTES

1. See Bruno and Sachs (1985). The period covered in that study extended only up to 1981, for which the coverage in terms of data for individual countries was still incomplete. It is worth pointing out that between 1981 and 1985 the number of unemployed in Europe increased by almost 50 per cent!
2. See, for example, Layard *et al.* (1984).
3. See Sachs (1979), Bruno and Sachs (1985), Artus (1984), Lipschitz and Schadler (1984), McCallum (1984), and OECD *Economic Outlook*, miscellaneous issues.
4. Note that, as long as marginal revenues of firms move with prices (i.e. there is a constant 'degree of monopoly'), the notion of a wage gap could still remain valid even under monopolistic competition.
5. The importance of this caveat will be further clarified below.
6. While 1960 and 1973 probably represented cyclical peaks, 1983, which is the last observation in our data, is obviously not. The alternative followed in Bruno and Sachs (1985) took 1979 to be a cyclical peak and extrapolated through that year. Both procedures are problematic, and an alternative trend measure of $v^f - l^f$ after 1973 is given in Table 2.
7. See Bruno and Sachs (1985) for an extensive discussion of the difference between nominal and real-wage rigidity. French data on the low wage gap shown here may be misleading (see the discussion in Bruno and Sachs and also Table 2).
8. See Lipschitz and Schadler (1984) for discussion of this point.
9. See Artus (1984), McCallum (1984), Sneessens (1984).
10. If l' is the (log) labour input in intensity units, we have

$$(v-l')=\{s_k/(1-s_k)\}(k-v).$$

But for CES, $v_{l'}=\sigma^{-1}(v-l')$, and thus:

$$v_l=(v-l)-(v-l')+v_{l'}=(v-l)+\{(1-\sigma)/\sigma\}\{s_k/(1-s_k)\}(k-v).$$ Q.E.D.

Under Hicks-neutrality, we would similarly get

$$v_l=(v-l)+\{(1-\sigma)/\sigma\}s_k(k-l).$$

Here the correction would be larger, since $k-l$ changed by more than $(k-v)$.

11. See Bruno and Sachs (1985, Chapter 9).
12. This procedure was followed in a recent OECD memo. We also experimented with monetary, fiscal and world-trade variables to represent aggregate demand (see below). For some countries the unemployment rate, as well as its first difference, using two-stage least squares for w_v, serves the same purpose. Broadly similar results are obtained, but d seems a better aggregate proxy for all countries. For the basis of adding a demand variable to the FPF see Bruno (1984); there, the ratio of hours worked to employment level was used as a proxy for d, which also works reasonably well.
13. The limited role of interest rates may be due to the fact that they are much more volatile than profits (see Ueda and Yoshikawa, 1986).
14. The average product of $a_1 b_1$ (rather than the product of the averages) is 2·22. The highest product of $a_1 b_1$ by half the wage gap in 1976 (see Table 1), from among the eight countries recorded, is 0.24 for Germany, with all other countries far below that.
15. See Bruno and Sachs (1985, Chapter 10).
16. We have no explanation as to why the fiscal variable seems to perform better in the manufacturing labour demand equation and the monetary variable works better here.
17. Only one of the 16 coefficients of the wage gap is significantly negative, for the case of the regression for France which is suspect anyway (see discussion below). Most of the coefficients on the demand variables are negative as expected.
18. The 'world trade' factor here appears separately, although it too could ultimately, in a world model, be attributed to 'domestic' contraction in all countries combined. Its implied response coefficient of 0·16 'explains' a rise in unemployment of 0·4 per cent annually during 1974–78 and 0·3 per cent during 1978–82.
19. The drop in world relative commodity prices is the dominant factor in the overall inflation slowdown, while exchange rates have respectively enhanced or weakened their effect. For cross-section analyses of inflation in the OECD countries emphasizing the key role of import prices and exchange rates, see Bruno (1980), and Beckerman and Jenkinson (1984); see also Gordon (1977).

REFERENCES

ARTUS, J. A. (1984). The disequilibrium real wage hypothesis: an empirical evaluation. *IMF Staff Papers*, **31**, 249–302.

BECKERMAN, W. and JENKINSON, T. (1984). Commodity prices, import prices and the inflation slowdown: a pooled cross-country time series analysis. Unpublished paper, Balliol College, Oxford.

BRUNO, M. (1980). Import prices and stagflation in the industrial countries: a cross-section analysis. *Economic Journal*, **90**, 479–92.

—— (1984). Raw materials, profits and the productivity slowdown. *Quarterly Journal of Economics*, **99**, 1–29.

—— and SACHS, J. (1985). *Economics of Worldwide Stagflation*. Cambridge, Massachusetts: Harvard University Press.

CHAN-LEE, J. H. and SUTCH, H. (1985). Profits and rates of return in OECD countries. OECD Economics and Statistics Department Working Paper no. 20.

GORDON, R. J. (1977). World inflation and monetary accommodation in eight countries. *Brookings Papers on Economic Activity*, no. 2, 409–68.

LAYARD, R., BASEVI, G., BLANCHARD, O., BUITER, W. and DORNBUSCH, R. (1984). Report of the CEPS macroeconomic Policy Group-Europe: the case for unsustainable growth. *ECE Economic Papers*, 31.

—— and NICKELL, S. (1984). Unemployment and real wages in Europe, Japan and the US. Centre for Labour Economics, LSE, Working Paper no. 677.

LIPSCHITZ, L., and SCHADLER, S. M. (1984). Relative prices, real wages and macroeconomic policies: some evidence from manufacturing in Japan and the UK *IMF Staff Papers*, **31**, 303–38.

MALINVAUD, E. (1980). *Profitability and Unemployment*, Cambridge: Cambridge University Press.

McCALLUM, J. (1984). Wage gaps, factor shares, and real wages. Unpublished paper, University of Quebec.

SACHS, J. (1979). Wages, profits and macroeconomic adjustment: a comparative study. *Brookings Papers on Economic Activity, no.* 2 269–319.

SNEESSENS, H. (1984). Keynesian vs classical unemployment in western economies: an attempt at evaluation. Unpublished paper, Lille.

UEDA, K. and YOSHIKAWA, H. (1986). Financial volatility and the q theory of investment. *Economica*, forthcoming.

Wages Policy and Unemployment in Australia

By R. G. Gregory

Australian National University

Introduction

It is generally accepted among Australian economists that high rates of growth of wages at various times over the last decade have made the achievement of full employment and lower rates of inflation more difficult. Fear of a further acceleration of wage growth has also been a policy constraint. It is when one attempts to go further that considerable disagreement becomes evident. From a labour market viewpoint, there does not seem to be a consensus as to the answers to the two broad questions that should be addressed. First, how important are wage changes relative to other factors that depress employment and add to the inflation rate? Second, how does government policy impinge on the process that generates wage changes? To do justice to both of these in a paper as short as this one is difficult, so I shall focus most of the paper on the second question.

The relationships between government policy and wage changes are particularly important at this time. For most of the last decade, successive governments have operated a national wages policy, which to a large degree has been based on the indexation of wages for past price changes. The latest experiment, the Prices and Incomes Accord, is the centrepiece of the current government's employment and inflation policy, and, after almost two years of wide community and media support, the key principles upon which it is based are suddenly being questioned.[1]

Our prime endeavour, therefore, will be to build up sufficient understanding of the wage determination process so that some evaluation can be made as to the effectiveness of these national wage policies. This turns out to be a remarkably difficult task which generates considerable concern in our mind that the data may not be sufficiently rich to serve as a basis for sound judgments. It does appear, however, that the effect of a given level of unemployment upon wage changes has consistently weakened over the last decade. Why this should be so is a major unresolved puzzle. I offer a loosely constructed theory that is consistent with the facts, but it is by no means the only possible explanation.

Section I provides a description of wage-setting in Australia and some key facts of the economy. In Section II the statistical analysis of wage changes focuses on two competing theories: one is the Phillips curve approach, and the other stresses that wage outcomes may be, to a significant degree, independent of the level of unemployment and may depend instead on utilization rates of labour within the firm. Section III considers the efficacy of incomes policies in Australia. Some final comments are offered in Section IV.

I. Some Background Facts

Unemployment

Table 1 provides data as to the performance of the economy. The large reduction in the average rate of growth of non-farm output and employment since 1974–75 is immediately obvious. Labour productivity growth has also slowed down in per capita terms, and on a per-hour basis.

Unemployment has continued to increase throughout the last decade, reaching a peak of around 10 per cent in 1983. This unemployment rate is more than five times the average of the decade 1964–65 to 1973–74. Currently, unemployment appears to have stabilized at about 8·5 per cent. As in most countries, there is a heavy concentration of unemployment upon young people.

The duration of measured unemployment is currently very long and has increased at a faster rate than the number of unemployed (Table 2). In August 1966 the average duration of unemployment, all persons (incomplete spells), was three weeks: it is currently 49 weeks (Household Survey data).

A special feature of the Australian system of unemployment benefits is that they are paid as long as the recipient is actively seeking work. Benefits are subject to an income test, which is applied on a family basis, and are not earnings-related. The rate of unemployment benefits increased quite considerably during the early to mid-1970s (Table 2).

Over the decade 1964–65 to 1973–74 the average take-up rate of unemployment benefits was around 30 per cent, but sometimes was as low as 20 per cent of those seeking full-time work. As unemployment has increased, so has the take-up rate. Currently the total number of benefit recipients exceeds by about 6 percentage points the number of unemployed seeking full-time work as measured by the Labour Force (Household) Survey.

TABLE 1

SELECTED ECONOMIC INDICATORS, 1964/65–1973/74; 1974/75–1983/84
(per cent per annum)

Annual rate of growth	1964/65–1973/74	1974/75–1983/84
Gross domestic product (non-farm)	5·5[b]	2·5[a]
Employment		
Persons: Total	2·8	0·9
Male	1·9	0·4
Female	4·9	1·9
Hours: Total	2·3[c]	0·2[d]
Male	2·0	−0·1
Female	3·5	0·8
Labour productivity		
Per person	2·6	1·6
Per hour	3·4	2·3
Nominal wages[e]	8·4	11·1
Consumer prices	4·6	10·0
Real wages	3·8	1·1

[a] 1979–80 constant price estimates.
[b] 1966–67 constant price estimates.
[c] Hours worked for 1965–66; earlier data not available.
[d] February 1984 hours data adjusted because of holiday period.
[e] Average weekly earnings per employed male unit.
Sources: The Labour Force, ABS, Cat. no. 6203.0 (various issues); quarterly estimates of National Income and Expenditure, 1984(III), ABS, Cat. no. 5206.0; historical series of estimates of National Income and Expenditure, Australia, ABS, Cat. no. 5207.0; average weekly earnings, ABS, Cat. no. 6302.0.

TABLE 2
UNEMPLOYMENT, DURATION, PROPORTION OF BENEFIT RECIPIENTS AMONG THE UNEMPLOYED SEEKING FULL-TIME WORK AND THE AVERAGE LEVEL OF UNEMPLOYMENT BENEFITS AS A PROPORTION OF AFTER-TAX EARNINGS

Year	Unemployment rate (August) (%)	Ave. duration of unemployment[a] (incomplete spells) (weeks)	Take-up rate of unemployment benefits[b] (%)	Unemployment duration 6 months or more (% of unemployed)	Unemployment benefits as a proportion of estimated A.W.E.		
					Single persons <18 years[c]	21+ years[d]	Married persons[e]
1966–67	1·6	3	28	13	13	21	28
1967–68	1·7	10	28	13	12	20	27
1968–69	1·6	7	26	9	14	23	29
1969–70	1·5	7	20	6	13	21	27
1970–71	1·4	7	21	7	12	19	24
1971–72	1·7	10	30	6	19	29	33
1972–73	2·5	10	36	9	47	33	44
1973–74	1·9	7	40	10	49	34	47
1974–75	2·4	13	61	4	55	39	51
1975–76	4·6	19	83	16	48	40	49
1976–77	4·7	22	84	25	43	41	44
1977–78	5·7	28	83	30	39	41	50
1978–79	6·2	30	90	35	27	38	49
1979–80	5·8	35	92	38	34	35	51
1980–81	5·9	33	95	40	30	32	47
1981–82	5·6	35	94	37	28	32	50
1982–83	6·7	44	101	39	27	33	48
1983–84	9·9	49	106	53	28	39	48

[a] Mean unemployment duration of those seeking full-time work: ABS, The Labour Force, Cat. no. 6203.0.
[b] Average number of beneficiaries: Department of Social Security Annual Reports (various issues). Average number of unemployed seeking full-time work: ABS, The Labour Force, Cat. no. 6203.0 (average of February, May, August, November).
[c] Potential earnings assumed to be half average weekly earnings per employed male unit and then adjusted for taxes paid.
[d] Potential earnings assumed to be three-quarters of average weekly earnings per employed male unit and then adjusted for taxes paid.
[e] Potential earnings assumed to be average weekly earnings per employed male unit and then adjusted for taxes paid.

The nature of our unemployment experience appears to be very similar to that of other countries. The probability of leaving unemployment is much lower among those who have been long unemployed than among those who have been unemployed for a short time (Table 3). At August 1984 new benefit recipients left the benefit rolls at a rate of 24 per cent in the first month; those receiving unemployment benefits for more than three years were leaving at about 3 per cent a month.

TABLE 3

CHARACTERISTICS OF UNEMPLOYMENT DURATION, AUGUST 1984

Period	Proportion of unem- ployed	Probability of leaving per month	Expected completed spells for a new group of unemployed persons (%)	Allocation of unemployment among an outflow group[a] (%)
0 < 3 weeks	8	0·24	17	1
3 weeks < 3 months	20	0·18	29	5
4 < 6 months	16	0·17	23	12
7 < 12 months	20	0·12	16	26
1 < 2 years	20	0·09	9	30
2 < 3 years	9	0·05	2	11
3 years and over	7	0·03	2	17

[a] Total weeks of unemployment experienced by those leaving unemployment allocated to spells of different lengths (%).
Source: Quarterly Survey of Unemployment Benefit Recipients, Department of Social Security, Canberra.

Most unemployment spells tend to be relatively short. In the three months to August 1984, 17 per cent of the inflow group terminated their unemployment spell within three weeks and another 29 per cent would terminate between four weeks and three months. About 13 per cent of an inflow group could expect to be unemployed more than a year.

Wage changes and the institutional structure

Until recently, it was widely believed that there was a well defined and a stable relationship between (a) nominal wage increases and unemployment and (b) unemployment and the excess supply of labour.

The first doubts about these relationships began to arise in Australia in response to the wage increases of the 1973–75 period. In the third quarter of 1974, wage increases were proceeding at an annual rate of about 30 per cent (Figure 1), and yet unemployment of between 2 and 3 per cent was high relative to the past. Unemployment duration was almost three times that of 1966, and yet employers were reporting record shortages of labour. Obviously something new was happening in the labour market.

The partial economic recovery of 1979–82 again raised questions about the relationship between wage changes and unemployment. During this period normal rates of employment growth returned to Australia, unemployment stabilized at about 5·5–6·0 per cent, and yet at these record rates of high unemployment there was an acceleration first of nominal wage inflation and then of real-wage growth. Neither the nominal nor the real-wage outcomes were expected at unemployment rates that were three times the average of the 1960s.

There is extensive wage regulation in Australia. Almost all wages consist of an award, and usually an overaward payment. Awards are minimum rates of pay for the job and are legally binding. There are thousands of job classifications, each with its own award payments—professors, plumbers, stenographers, storemen and packers, etc. The awards are set by a system of state and federal tribunals, either by ratifying private agreements between unions and employers or by arbitrating between the parties. The federal tribunals are part of the Australian Conciliation and Arbitration Commission (the Commission). The Commission sets national award wage levels which are usually followed quite quickly by consistent decisions by the state tribunals. Overaward payments allow flexibility in pay structures between employees and are paid in response to private agreements between employees and employers.

There has been a long debate in Australia as to whether the Commission affects the rate of growth of nominal or real wages at the macro-level, or merely acts as a veil for market forces. The literature is extensive, and there does not seem to be a clear answer (see Kirby, 1981a; Phipps, 1981; Dornbusch and Fischer, 1984; Mitchell, 1984). Presumably the power of the Commission varies from period to period.[2]

At various times, the Commission has attempted to operate an incomes policy for those under its direct or indirect jurisdiction, about 90 per cent of wage and salary earners. Between April 1975 and June 1981, in response to broad agreement among the government, employer associations and trade unions, the Commission operated a national wage system that, on a quarterly or half-yearly basis, provided wage indexation for past price increases. For most of the early period there was full indexation for price changes, but increasingly the degree of indexation was marginally adjusted to less than 100 per cent.

Between April 1975 and June 1980 almost all wage increases originated in Commission decisions, and as a result there was a close association of price and wage increases.[3] It was only from June 1980 that wage increases began to run consistently ahead of award increases, and the Commission's control over wage outcomes began to weaken. The system finally broke down in June 1981 and was replaced by a combination of collective agreements and Commission-initiated judgments.

There have been two subsequent experiments with an incomes policy using the Commission. In December 1982 the Liberal Country Party government introduced a wage freeze for 12 months. The incoming Labour government reduced the wage freeze to six months and then introduced full wage indexation, again through the Commission. Full wage indexation has continued to this day.

The significance of these experiments for our statistical analysis of wage changes is illustrated in Figure 1. If we assume that the wage increases during *all* the indexation or pay freeze periods are not market outcomes, and add to

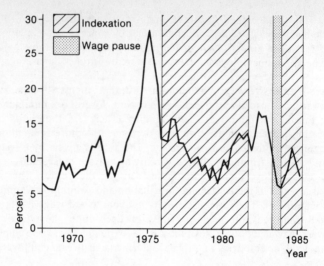

FIGURE 1.   Rate of change of average weekly earnings (percent change on year earlier).

that assumption the inability of previous researchers, to date, to explain satisfactorily the wage explosion of 1973-74, then it becomes obvious that, in the absence of understanding the exact links between the Commission's decisions and free market outcomes, there is a distinct lack of data observations upon which to estimate a wage equation. In the light of this history it is perhaps to be expected that wage outcomes since 1973 will be difficult to explain.

In attempting to understand the processes leading to wage changes we adopted the following research strategy. First, we operate on the assumption that the Commission is a veil and does not itself affect economic outcomes. This procedure is often adopted in Australian wage equations (Kirby, 1981b; Dornbusch and Fischer, 1984). Then we reconsider the situation and attempt to discover whether the Commission's policies have had any effect.[4]

II. Empirical Results

The Phillips curve: wage increases and unemployment

Table 4 presents a number of estimated wage equations. The data are seasonally adjusted and the dependent variable is the proportionate rate of change, from one quarter to the next, of average weekly earnings per employed male unit. The first equation is a simple expectations-augmented Phillips curve fitted to quarterly data from 1966(IV) to 1982(IV). Price expectations are measured by the quarterly rate of change of consumer prices, lagged five quarters. The equation also includes a dummy variable for 1974(III) when nominal wages were growing at an annual rate exceeding 30 per cent.

Many writers have shown that this simple type of equation was successful for earlier periods (Kirby, 1981a). Over this data period the unemployment variable is insignificant and the explanatory power of the regression is very

TABLE 4

WAGE EQUATIONS: QUARTERLY RATE OF CHANGE OF AVERAGE WEEKLY EARNINGS, 1966(IV)–1982(IV)

Equation no.	Constant	Un	Vac	O/T	Time	D.V.	P^e	P_1^e	P_2^e	R^2	DW
(1)	2·183 (5·90)	−0·027 (0·27)				7·865 (5·77)	0·303 (1·82)			0·39	1·97
(2)	2·331 (7·22)	−0·875 (4·25)			0·095 (4·57)	6·893 (5·74)	0·346 (2·40)			0·54	2·53
(3)	2·403 (5·96)	−0·192 (1·19)				7·720 (5·69)		0·419 (2·24)	0·763 (1·99)	0·39	2·05
(4)	2·239 (6·29)	−0·858 (4·11)			0·101 (4·33)	6·892 (5·71)		0·295 (1·77)	0·135 (0·37)	0·53	2·55
(5)	2·270 (5·75)		−0·003 (0·56)			7·747 (5·69)	0·310 (2·14)			0·39	1·97
(6)	2·581 (7·27)		−0·032 (4·02)		0·762 (4·31)	6·603 (5·33)	0·672 (0·48)			0·53	2·48
(7)	−2·481 (1·68)			3·458 (3·18)		7·017 (5·52)	0·598 (3·78)			0·47	2·39

Notes: Data are seasonally adjusted.

Un = unemployment rate, s.a.

Vac = vacancies divided by the labour force, s.a.

O/T = overtime hours worked

D.V. = dummy variable: 1974(III) = 1

P^e = quarterly rate of change of the consumer price index, lagged five quarters.

$P_1^e = P^e$, 1966(IV)–1978(II).

$P_2^e = P^e$, 1978(III)–1982(IV).

low, an R^2 of 0·39. The price expectation coefficient is not quite statistically significant and a good deal less than unity.

If a time trend is added to the equation, then the results improve considerably (equation (2)). The unemployment coefficient becomes significant and the time trend is also significant. The R^2 increases to 0·54. The coefficient attached to the price expectations term becomes significant at conventional levels but is a very low number, 0·34. Although the statistical results are now more satisfactory, the equation does not contribute a great deal to our economic understanding of wage changes. There are two problems.

First, the price expectations coefficient is too low. If inflation were to increase by 5–10 percentage points, equation (2) would suggest that only $1\frac{1}{2}$ percentage points would be added to the rate of increase of nominal wages.

Second, what economic effect is the time trend capturing? Why is it that over two decades, and after taking account of the other variables in the equation, the time trend has added 5 percentage points to the quarterly rate of nominal wage increases? Why is it that the unemployment term is insignificant unless a time trend is included?

There are a number of paths that could be followed in seeking an answer to these questions. Staying with the assumption that the Commission's decisions are a reflection of market forces, these paths point in two broad directions: (1) those paths that stay within the terrain of the simple Phillips curve and seek better measures of the excess demand for labour and price expectations, and (2) those paths that seek to use different theories to explain wage changes. We begin by staying within the Phillips curve country; then, in the next section, we consider different models of wage determination.

Price expectations. There seems to be a close negative association between the time trend and the price expectations coefficient. Whenever the time trend is included in any of our regressions, the price expectation coefficient falls. Most Australian Phillips curves measure price expectations as we do, as a weighted sum of past price changes. Perhaps past price changes with fixed weights are no longer an adequate indication of the community's expectations of future price increases, and perhaps over the last two decades the expectations coefficient has drifted upwards?

Figure 2 presents a direct measure of price expectations constructed from a quarterly survey undertaken for the Institute of Applied Economic and Social Research of the University of Melbourne. In this survey about 2000 respondents are asked whether they expect prices to rise, fall or stay the same over the next 12 months. A further question asks those respondents who expect a price change to express a percentage estimate. The series is available from 1973 onwards.

The arithmetic mean of expected inflation constructed from this survey is given as the broken line. The unbroken line is the actual rate of inflation. The expected and actual rates of inflation are fairly well correlated, although since 1977 the expected rate of inflation has been continually above the actual rate. This series, therefore, might suggest that since 1977 past price changes, and even future price changes, have been a poor indicator of price expectations.

There does, however, seem to be some problems with this expectation series.[5] Over the last 12 months the inflation rate has been the lowest for over

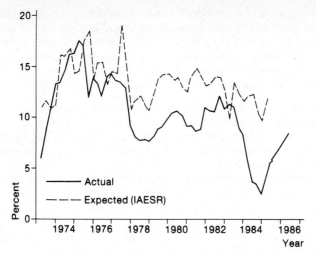

FIGURE 2.   Inflation expectations *v.* actuals, 1973–1986.
Sources: Price expectations: Institute of Applied Economic and Social Research, University of Melbourne; CPI: ABS Consumer Price Index, Cat. no. 6401.0.

a decade, and official forecasts suggest that it will remain low at least for the next 12 months. The Melbourne Institute series, however, appears to indicate that over the next year people are expecting inflation rates of 11–12 per cent, well above the current rate of 4–6 per cent. It is a little disturbing therefore that, although expectations as to the inflation rate are falling, the rate of decline is very slow.

Since the expectations and actual series were similar during the 1974–76 period, we spliced the expectation series on to the actual price series and used this synthetic series in the regressions. The statistical results were not improved.

We also experimented with a range of other price expectation variables and allowed the coefficients to vary across time periods. Again, the results were not really satisfactory in that the unemployment variable generally remained insignificant. The inclusion of a time trend, however, generally produced a significant unemployment coefficient, whichever price expectations term was used. The time trend dominated the price expectation variable, reducing the size of the coefficient and resulting in a loss of statistical significance.

As an example of these experiments, consider equations (3) and (4) of Table 4. Equation (3) excludes the time trend but includes a price expectations term that has been divided into two periods. Both price expectations coefficients are statistically significant, and, as expected, the coefficient for the second period is larger. This result is consistent with the rapid increase in nominal wages during 1980 and 1981. The coefficient attached to the unemployment variable, however, is insignificant. When a time trend is added (equation (4)), both price expectation coefficients fall in size and become statistically insignificant at conventional levels. The unemployment coefficient becomes statistically significant.

Obviously, there are a large number of permutations and combinations that may be tried to measure price expectations, and on *a priori* grounds it seems reasonable to believe that the process generating price expectations should have changed over the period. Presumably, one should keep searching, although the experience generated by the specifications that we have tried do not lead us to feel confident as to the outcome.[6]

Unemployment and the excess supply of labour. It is a characteristic of all the regressions that we tried that without a time trend the unemployment coefficient is always statistically insignificant. It is quite possible, therefore, that the time trend effect is capturing a changing relationship between unemployment and wage changes. It has been increasingly argued, over the last three years, that the natural rate of unemployment in Australia is now about 7 per cent (Simes and Richardson, 1985; Gregory and Smith, 1985; Trivedi and Baker, 1982).

Why should unemployment have become a less effective curb on wage increases? There is no evidence that the rate of unemployment *overstates* the true rate of unemployed resources. Indeed, all the evidence suggests the opposite (Stricker and Sheehan, 1981). There seems to be a large number of people, not measured by the official unemployment statistics, who are only too willing to accept employment at current wages when the rate of job creation increases.

There is some evidence of a greater degree of mismatching in the labour market, but the effect of this on the unemployment rate is probably very small. Consider, for example, the relationship between unemployment and vacancies (Figure 3). Any change in this relationship, however, is clearly of second-order

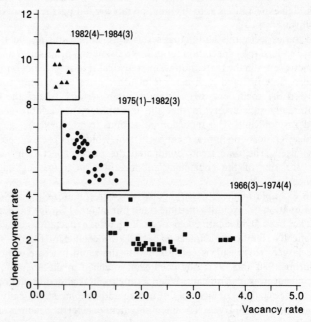

FIGURE 3.   The unemployment–vacancy relationship.

importance relative to the very large increase in unemployment and the very large reduction in vacancies. Accordingly, there does not appear to be any excess demand for labour that might explain the wage acceleration of 1979–80.[7]

The broad result, that labour shortages have not been a constraint operating on the economy for more than a decade, is confirmed by other data. The Bank of New South Wales and the Confederation of Australian Industry conduct a survey of manufacturers that includes the question, 'What single factor, if any, is most limiting your ability to increase production?'

In Figure 4 we plot the percentage of respondents who replied that labour was the most limiting factor acting as a constraint on production. It is evident that there have been three periods of acute labour shortages since 1960: the years 1965, 1970 and 1973. There is no evidence of a comparable shortage since 1975. It is unlikely, therefore, that a shifting unemployment–vacancy relationship is behind the time trend effect in the wage equation. This of course is easily checked by including vacancies in the wage equation (Table 4). Although the time trend effect is now a little smaller, it still remains an important variable. Without the time trend the vacancy coefficient is insignificant.

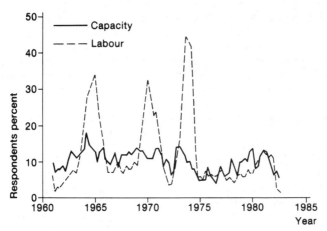

FIGURE 4.   Constraints on manufacturing production, 1960–1984.
Source: Survey of Industrial Trends in Australia, Confederation of Australian Industry and Bank of New South Wales.

To conclude, it is obvious that the simple Phillips curve does not do a good job at explaining the wage determination process. Before we look to see whether the difficulties are caused by the wage-indexation periods, we consider a recent theory of wage determination that has been subject to some debate in Australia.

An alternative theory: wage increases and labour utilization rates within the firm

Background and results. Recent writings in Australia (Gregory, 1982; Gregory and Smith, 1985) and abroad (Solow, 1980; Hall, 1980; Okun, 1981) have begun to suggest that perhaps it is the labour utilization rate within the *firm* that is particularly important for wage negotiations, rather than the labour utilization rate within the economy. These writings stress that most employed people stay with firms a long time and build up firm specific human capital and that, as a result, wage variations should be seen in the context of a long-term relationship between firms and workers. Under these conditions, rules of fairness and equity for sharing productivity growth among the employed workforce are developed and the existence of idle labour outside the firm may not exert a great deal of direct influence on wage growth.

During the 1950s and 1960s the labour utilization rates within the average firm and within the economy as a whole moved closely together, and it appeared that wage increases were related to unemployment when in fact they may have been determined by labour utilization rates within the firm. Since the late 1970s the two utilization rates have diverged, and we suggest that it is this divergence that has caused the displacement of the Phillips curve. If wage increases are related to the labour utilization rate within the firm, then the wage–labour utilization relationship has not shifted.

The basic idea is that not all resources adapt at the same rate to a long period of subdued output growth. If the recession is a long one, as it was between 1975 and 1979, then labour and capital employed within the firm will tend to get placed back at their full utilization rates while labour in the economy as a whole may remain at a low utilization rate; i.e. unemployment may be high. As *employed* labour and capital approach their normal utilization rates within the firm, normal conditions with regard to wage negotiations tend to reapply without regard to the unemployed. It is at this stage that the implicit contracts between employer and employee begin to deliver normal rates of real-wage increases independent of the state of the labour market outside the firm.

One reason why labour resources outside firms may fail to exert much direct influence upon the wage negotiation process is that the unemployed and employed are very different types of labour which are not close substitutes. Unemployed labour, for example, tends to be young, unskilled and inexperienced in firm-specific capital.

Perhaps the contrast between the two groups may be brought out best by considering job tenure data. In Australia the employed labour force can expect a completed job tenure with their current employer, in the current geographical location, of about 12 years. Furthermore, about 20 per cent of the employed labour force can expect a job tenure of more than 20 years with their current employer. For most of the employed workforce, therefore, their dominating workforce experience relates to employment with a particular firm, during which time they build up firm-specific capital. There appears to have been no significant change in average job tenures over the last decade (Table 5). By contrast, most of the unemployed either had not had a job, or their last job was of very short tenure (Gregory, 1982).

Further indirect evidence of this separation of the employed and unemployed can be seen in attitudinal data. Since 1975 the Morgan Gallup Poll has collected opinions as to job security and the ability of the employed to find another job (Table 5).[8] Between 1975 and 1979 the unemployment rate increased from 4·6 to 5·8 per cent, and during this period more than half of employed persons interviewed believed that unemployment would continue to increase. The proportion of the employed who regarded their job as safe, however, was quite high and, *more importantly*, tended to increase marginally.

TABLE 5

UNEMPLOYMENT AND OPINIONS AS TO JOB PROSPECTS AMONG THE EMPLOYED, VARIOUS YEARS, 1975–1984

	1975	1976	1977	1978	1979	1980	1982	1983	1984
Proportion of employed respondents									
Present job safe	76	78	82	79	77	73	74	79	82
Chance of unemployment	21	17	15	19	20	23	22	18	17
Proportion of employed respondents who believe they could find a new job									
Quickly	57	57	55	50	54	50	52	51	61
May take longer	33	33	35	41	36	39	39	41	33
Future job prospects of those who believe there is a chance of being unemployed									
Could find a new job quickly	n.a.	41	n.a.	36	34	39	37[a]	n.a.	44
May take longer	n.a.	52	n.a.	58	59	53	55[a]	n.a.	50
Unemployment rate (August)	4·6	4·7	5·7	6·2	5·8	5·9	6·7	9·9	8·6
Unemployment duration (incomplete spells) (Weeks)	13	18	21	26	28	32	33	42	46
Those who left a job during the year as a proportion of those employed the following February	16	n.a.	n.a.	11	14	16	14	14	n.a.
Those who were laid off (or fired) from their first job during the year, as a proportion of those employed the following February	6·4	n.a.	n.a.	6·4	5·7	n.a.	8·2	6·3	n.a.
Proportion of those employed with job tenure greater than 3 years	53	n.a.	n.a.	53	54	52	53	55	n.a.
Proportion of those with tenure over 3 years that left a job	12	n.a.	n.a.	n.a.	n.a.	n.a.	n.a.	13	n.a.

[a] 1981.

Source: Morgan Gallup Poll. Labour Mobility Cat. no. 6209 (various issues)

Between 1979 and 1984 the unemployment rate increased from 5·8 to 8·6 per cent, and again the proportion of the employed who regarded their job as safe increased. A close inspection of these data suggests that, at the onset of each recession, the proportion of the employed who regard their job as safe falls initially but soon returns to something like the previous level. Not only do most employed people experience long job tenure, but they also *expect* long tenure.

The Morgan Gallup Poll also asked those who thought that their job was safe whether they thought they could find a new job quickly. Over the decade when the average duration of unemployed has increased from about 12 to 45 weeks, the proportion of the employed who believed that they could find a new job quickly has not changed significantly. Indeed, in 1984 this proportion was higher than ever before. There appears to be a clear difference between the attitudes of the employed and the picture of the economy as presented by the statistics of the level and duration (incomplete spells) of unemployment.

This separation can be illustrated a number of other ways. We have also included in Table 5 information as to the number of individuals who have left a job each year and the number of individuals fired or laid off, as a proportion of the stock of employed and unemployed. Very few individuals appear to *lose* their job in our society and the number affected does not appear to increase with the unemployment rate. If the number of individuals who left their first job during 1975 because they were laid off is expressed as a ratio of total employment at February 1976, the ratio is 6·4 per cent; eight years later, when the unemployment rate had doubled, the ratio is 6·2 per cent. Consequently, because this ratio is so small and varies so little, it is not surprising that so many of the employed labour force believe their job to be safe and that this belief does not vary significantly with unemployment.[9] This result supports the conjecture that it is economic conditions within the firm that affect wage claims, rather than the unemployment rate in the economy at large.

To provide a simple test of this hypothesis, we replace the unemployment rate in the wage equation by the level of overtime hours worked (Table 4).[10] The results appear to be satisfactory. The overtime variable is statistically significant and the price expectation coefficient, although considerably less than unity, is also statistically significant. The equation performs much better than the unemployment equation, which excludes the time trend, but it is not superior to the equations that include it. When a time trend is added to the equations that include internal labour utilization rates, the results are not improved and the time trend is not statistically significant.[11]

To conclude, the dislocation between the labour utilization rate in the economy as a whole and the utilization rates of labour within the firm is illustrated in Figure 5. Before 1975 these two labour utilization rates moved together. Since 1975, however, the utilization rate of employed labour has tended to go back towards the average of the pre-1974 levels whereas the utilization rate of the labour force as a whole has not adjusted. At 1979 and 1980, when unemployment was 5 per cent, the average level of factory overtime had returned to close to previous long-run and normal levels. For the employed labour force, therefore, economic conditions within a firm during 1979 and 1980 did not appear to be that different from a decade ago when full employment in the economy as a whole prevailed. If we define 1·4 hours as a normal

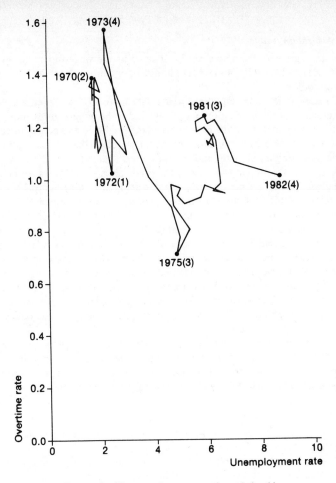

FIGURE 5. The unemployment-overtime relationship.

rate of overtime, then the equilibrium unemployment rate has moved up from about 1·7 per cent for 1970 to 2·4 per cent for the 1970–74 period and to about 5·8 per cent for the 1979–82 period.[12]

This dislocation between the two labour utilization rates has important implications for the likelihood of the economy being able to return to low unemployment rates in the future. Whenever there is a long recession there may be a ratchet effect operating as each unemployment increase tends to create economic conditions that make it difficult to return to full employment.

While the model may explain the outcomes of the last decade, there appears to be a problem of asymmetry in the description. The loosely formulated model explains the shift to the right in the relationship but does not offer any mechanism—short of government intervention to directly affect the relationship between unemployment and wage changes between the firm and its employees—to shift wage negotiations back to the left.

III. Incomes Policies

The Australian results

To what degree are the above results affected by the wage indexation period of 1975(II) and 1981(II), and what light do our equations throw on the efficacy of these policies?

First, we fit the wage equations to the data up to 1975 and then we predict the outcomes of the indexation period. We judge the impact of the indexation policy from an analysis of the gaps between the predicted and actual outcomes. These results were not very satisfactory, so we fitted the wage equations to the data before and after the indexation period (Table 6).

A four-quarter moving average of the predicted and actual wage outcomes during the indexation period are presented in Figures 6(a) and 6(b). Figure 6(a) refers to the predictions from the Phillips curve and Figure 6(b) refers to the predictions from the alternative theory. For both sets of predictions indexation appears to hold wages up at the beginning of the period, but within two years its effectiveness as a policy of wage constraint is evident (see the shaded area). In both instances the constraint of wage indexation at the end of the period appears to offset the early effect of the policy when wage increases were higher than expected. Furthermore, the rapid increase of wages at the end of the period, which leads to the collapse of indexation, does not appear to involve a catch-up phase where the constraint delivered by the policy over the last few years is undone.

These results suggest that, although the process of wage increases is not well identified, the judgment that the indexation policy kept nominal wage increases at lower levels than otherwise and that there was not a serious re-entry problem is not affected by the choice among these two models.

An international comparison

A difficulty encountered when working with Australian quarterly data is that individual coefficients change considerably when the data period or the equation specification is altered. This characteristic of wage equations generates a large degree of scepticism as to our ability to understand in detail the process of wage changes.

It may be useful, therefore, to place Australian wage changes in a broader setting and compare the Australian wage outcomes with those of other countries. To do this we took the annual rate of change of hourly manufacturing wages of six countries[13] and weighted them by Australian trade shares. This series is compared with the Australian wage series (Figure 7). A number of features stand out.

First, the two series are very similar. Wage increases build up to a peak in 1974-75, then moderate until there is a mild acceleration of wage changes around 1979-82, after which the rate of change of wages begins to fall. Second, the Australian wage series appears to be less constrained in an upwards direction. This outcome may be the result of the arbitration system, which delivers wage increases very quickly to all wage-earners. Third, the similarity of the two series encourages one to suggest, perhaps heroically, that the rate of change of nominal wages of our trading partners could serve as a counterfactual history against which to test the efficiency of Australian wage policy. If

TABLE 6

WAGE EQUATIONS: QUARTERLY RATE OF CHANGE OF AVERAGE WEEKLY EARNINGS
(various sub-periods)

Period	Constant	Un	O/T	Time	D.V.	P^e	R^2	DW
1966(IV)–1975(II)								
(1)	0·869	0·152			8·400	1·241	0·57	1·97
	(1·09)	(0·52)			(6·36)	(2·51)		
(2)	1·462	−0·675		0·100	7·405	0·734	0·70	2·46
	(2·16)	(2·08)		(3·82)	(6·55)	(1·70)		
(3)	−0·843		1·761		8·397	1·113	0·59	2·04
	(0·53)		(1·35)		(6·55)	(2·26)		
1966(IV)–1975(II), 1981(III)–1982(IV)								
(4)	1·806	−0·213			8·644	1·082	0·55	1·87
	(4·59)	(1·24)			(6·73)	(2·93)		
(5)	2·223	−0·911		0·093	7·696	0·588	0·67	2·40
	(6·22)	(3·80)		(3·71)	(6·78)	(1·70)		
(6)	−1·248		2·348		8·424	0·743	0·59	2·04
	(0·83)		(1·99)		(6·76)	(3·22)		

Notation: as in Table 4.

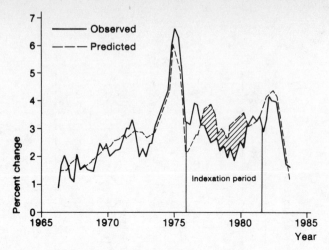

FIGURE 6(a).   Observed and predicted average weekly earnings using pre- and post-indexation
unemployment data (moving average).

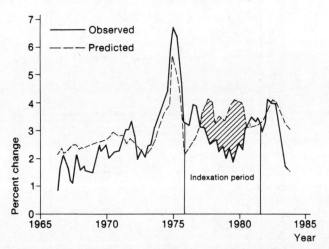

FIGURE 6(b).   Observed and predicted average weekly earnings using pre- and post-indexation
overtime (moving average).

this is done the same story emerges as earlier. During the first two years of
wage indexation the rate of decline of wage increases was slower in Australia;
after 1978 Australian wage increases were lower than the average of our six
large trading partners. Perhaps these divergences were the result of indexation.

The conclusions as to the efficacy of the indexation policy is the same
whether the experience of foreign countries or predictions from the Australian
wage equations are used as the norm. After the indexation period, however,
the results differ. On the basis of the international comparison there may be
evidence of a rebound. We tend, however, to attribute this to the same properties
of our arbitration system that led to the greater wage explosion in 1974–75

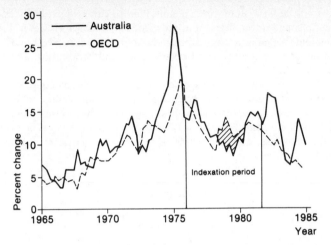

FIGURE 7.   Annual rate of change of earnings: OECD hourly manufacturing wages v. Australian
Average Weekly Earnings.

rather than to the aftermath of indexation. A period of accelerating wage increases overseas tends to be magnified in Australia.

These remarks are obviously only exploratory, and a fuller story would look at changes in unemployment rates across countries, changes in exchange rates and so on. Nevertheless, the similarity of nominal wage experience between Australia and our trading partners suggests that this may be a fruitful area of research.

IV. CONCLUDING REMARKS

Our understanding of the processes that generate real and nominal wage changes in the Australian economy is not very good. It is fairly clear that the wage equations presented in Tables 5 and 6 are not very satisfactory. The fit to the data is not very good, and the price coefficients seem unreasonably low and change from period to period. The best equations on statistical grounds include an influential time trend. Given the role that wages may play in determining inflation and unemployment, this is a very unsatisfactory state of affairs.

Yet there are a number of positive results. Until three or four years ago it was widely believed that the natural rate of unemployment was around 2 per cent, and a number of published articles emphasized the stability of the Phillips curve and of the price expectations process (Kirby, 1981a, 1981b). There have been large changes since then which seem to be well documented. Within the class of models built on the concept of a natural rate of unemployment, it has become clear that the natural rate of unemployment has increased and that a simple Phillips curve, which does not account for this change, is unstable. Unemployment does not seem to affect wage changes unless a time trend is included in the regression.

There have also been attempts to specify wage equations which rely on a different theoretical basis. These equations, which stress labour utilization rates within the firm, dominate a simple Phillips curve which includes price expectations and unemployment as independent variables. However, they do not dominate a Phillips curve that includes a time trend. As yet, however, we do not understand at all what effects the time trend is capturing. The search has only just begun.

Until a clearer idea of the wage determination process emerges, it will not be possible to be certain as to the efficiency of wage indexation policies. The range of experiments reported here, however, suggest that, overall, the 1975-81 indexation experiments kept the rate of growth of nominal wages below levels that might have been expected. These gains were not lost in a subsequent wage rebound.

ACKNOWLEDGMENT

My thanks to Vivian Ho for her excellent research assistance.

NOTES

1. A current problem, for example, is whether wages should be fully indexed for price increases flowing from the recent large devaluation of the Australian dollar. The government has responded by arguing for partial indexation and is thus placing the Accord in jeopardy.
2. Before reaching a legally binding judgment, the Commission conducts hearings at which the three parties—the government, employees and unions—present evidence and arguments as to an appropriate judgment.
3. There is, however, evidence of an increase of overaward payments in 1978 that has yet to be adequately explained.
4. Many wage equations recognize the existence of the Commission by including award payments as an independent variable. With this specification, labour market pressure determines overaward payments, the earnings drift. This is not an ideal research strategy. After all, the Commission's decisions also need to be explained, and including award payments in the wage equation is, in a sense, avoiding the problem of the determination of wage changes.
5. There are considerable difficulties encountered when using a direct measure of price expectations. For example, what should be done about the outlying observations which appear to be unreasonable forecasts? Some people in the survey, for example, forecast 100 per cent inflation. It is also not clear whether arithmetic means are a better measure of inflationary expectations than medians. It is difficult to know what to make of this series since it does not extend back beyond 1973. It could, for example, be subject to an upward bias. If the series is biased upwards, however, it would need to be explained why this bias increased around 1978.
6. To give some idea of the variability of the price expectations coefficient, consider the following. Kirby (1981a) shows that for his data, and for the 1966-78 period, there is little evidence of instability of the Phillips curve. The price coefficient is usually estimated to be around 1·4. Phipps (1981) generates similar results for a similar period. Dornbusch and Fischer (1984) produce results with a unit coefficient on the price term. For our data period, 1966-82, the price coefficients are always less than unity.
7. Earlier investigations (Hughes, 1975; Harper, 1980; Trivedi and Baker, 1982) have measured a slight outward shift in the Beveridge curve, perhaps adding one, and at the most two, percentage points to the unemployment rate. But over the last few years vacancies have been so low, and so far outside the previous range of experience, that it would be difficult to detect any further shifts with a reasonable degree of reliability. The outward shift is 'explained' in terms of immigration flows, unemployment benefit increases and a Stoikov index of structural change. There seems little doubt that the curve has shifted outwards, but it is by no means certain why the change has occurred.
8. Adrian Pagan drew my attention to these data. He used them to support a similar argument to that developed here in his comments upon the Gregory-Smith and Dornbusch-Fischer controversy at the Brookings-Centre for Economic Policy Research Conference on the Australian Economy (Pagan, 1985).
9. If the number of layoffs by firms increases with the unemployment rate, then this relationship must be generated, to a significant degree, by an increased incidence of being fired falling upon a relatively constant proportion of the labour force. Of course, once the unemployment rate has stabilized at a new high level, it is even not clear that the number of firings and layoffs by firms will be higher than if the unemployment rate had stabilized at a lower level.

10. The Treasury also include overtime hours worked in the wage equation and note the changing relationship between overtime hours worked and the utilization rate of labour in the economy as a whole (Simes and Richardson, 1985).

11. The dependent variable of the equations in Tables 5 and 6 and that of our earlier work (Gregory and Smith, 1985) is average weekly earnings, so the possibility arises of a spurious correlation between earnings and the labour utilization rates within the firm. Dawkins and Wooden (1985) have subjected our model to a more thorough empirical analysis. They make the following adjustments:

—overtime hours worked is replaced by deviations of average hours worked around trend;
—average weekly earnings is replaced by average earnings per hour worked;
—labour productivity growth is added to the equations.

They find that their equations outperform the Phillips curve and our equations, but they conclude: 'This paper supports the underlying hypotheses of Gregory and Smith (1985), adding strength to the view that *to understand the process of wage inflation at the macro-level we must examine the utilization of labour at the micro level of the firm*' (Dawkins and Wooden, 1985, p. 520).

12. A similar dislocation seems to be occurring between the rate of capacity utilization within the firm and the rate of utilization of labour within the economy. During 1981, 45 per cent of respondents to the survey of manufacturers indicated that their rate of capacity utilization was satisfactory. This was the second highest rate of capacity utilization over the last 12 years. The unemployment rate was 5·5 per cent. In 1970, when 45 per cent of respondents reported a satisfactory rate of capacity utilization, the level of unemployment was 1·6 per cent.

13. The six countries were: USA, Canada, UK, France, Germany and Italy. Jonson *et al.* (1974) is one of the few Australian articles to emphasize the similarity of the Australian and overseas experiences.

REFERENCES

DAWKINS, P. and WOODEN, M. (1985). Labour utilization and wage inflation in Australia: an empirical examination. *Economic Record*, **61**, 516–21.

DORNBUSCH, R. and FISCHER, S. (1984). The Australian macro-economy. In R. E. Caves and L. B. Krause (eds), *The Australian Economy: A View From the North*, Brookings Survey of the Australian Economy. Sydney: George Allen and Unwin.

GREGORY, R. G. (1982). Work and welfare in the years ahead. *Australian Economic Papers*, **21**, 219–43.

—— (1983). The slide into mass unemployment: labour market theories, facts and policies. Annual Lecture, Academy of the Social Sciences, Australia.

—— and SMITH, R. E. (1985). Inflation and job creation policies in Australia, in Argy. V and Nevile J. (eds) *Inflation and Unemployment; Theory, Experience and Policy Making*, George Allen & Unwin London.

HALL, R. E. (1980). Employment fluctuations and wage rigidity. *Brookings Papers on Economic Activity*, **1**, 91–123.

HARPER, I. (1980). The relationship between unemployment and unfilled vacancies in Australia: 1952–78. *Economic Record*, **56**, 231–43.

HUGHES, B. (1975). The U-V displacement. *Australian Bulletin of Labour*, **1**, 1–23.

ISAAC, J. E. (1981). Equity and wage determination. *Australian Bulletin of Labour*, 7, 205–18.

JONSON, P. D., MAHAR, K. D., THOMPSON, G. L. (1974). Earnings and award wages in Australia. *Australian Economic Papers*, **22**, 80–98.

KIRBY, M. (1981a). An investigation of the specification and stability of the Australian aggregate wage equation. *Economic Record*, **57**, 35–46.

—— (1981b). A variable expectations co-efficient model of the Australian Phillips curve. *Australian Economic Papers*, **20**, 351–8.

MITCHELL, D. (1984). The Australian labor market. In R. E. Caves and L. B. Krause (eds), *The Australian Economy: A View from the North*, Brookings Survey of Australian Economy. Sydney: George Allen and Unwin.

OKUN, A. (1981). *Prices and Quantities: A Macroeconomic Analysis.* Washington, DC: Brookings Institution.

PAGAN, A. (1985). Comment. In Papers arising from 'The Brookings Survey of the Australian Economy', Discussion Paper no. B5, Centre for Economic Policy Research, Australian National University, 1–17.

PHIPPS, A. J. (1981). The impact of wage indexation on wage inflation in Australia. *Australian Economic Papers*, **20**, 333–50.

SIMES, R. M. and RICHARDSON, C. J. (1985). Wage determination in Australia. Paper presented to 14th Conference of Economists, New South Wales, May.

SOLOW, R. (1980). On theories of unemployment. *American Economic Review*, 70, 1-9.

STRICKER, P. and SHEEHAN, P. (1981). Hidden unemployment: the Australian experience. Institute of Applied Economic and Social Research, Melbourne.

TREASURY (1981). *The NIF-10 Model of the Australian Economy*. Canberra: Australian Government Publishing Service.

TRIVEDI, P. K. and BAKER, G. M. (1982). Equilibrium unemployment in Australia: concepts and measurement. Discussion Paper no. 59, Centre for Economic Policy Research, Australian National University.

Labour Surplus as a Signal for Real-wage Adjustment: Austria, 1968-1984

By KARL PICHELMANN and MICHAEL WAGNER

Institute for Advanced Studies, Vienna, and Institute for Economic and Social Research, Vienna

INTRODUCTION

Unemployment figures for Austria have been running well below the OECD average since the late 1960s. In fact, before 1981 there was hardly any unemployment problem in Austria. In 1982 and 1983 unemployment rates doubled. Since then the upward movement has slowed down; but there are no indications that Austrian unemployment could drop substantially below the 5 per cent level during the second half of the 1980s (see Figure 1).

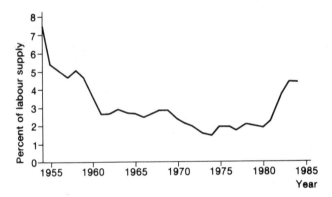

FIGURE 1. Rate of unemployment, Austria, 1954–1984. *Source*: IHS-Datenbank.

The absence of any long-term trend of increasing unemployment in Austria during the 1970s attracted interest from economists of quite different persuasions. Some argued that it proved the case for supply-side policies (Haberler, 1982), while others took it as a 'real-world' analogue to the prescriptive models proposed by economists like Malinvaud (1982) or Meade (1983).

A similar dualistic grouping of views has emerged from discussions on the recent departure of the Austrian economy from its full employment path. Supply-side economists suggest that Austria's experience after the second oil price shock fits Olson's (1982) hypothesis of 'institutional sclerosis', which runs as follows: during the long period of stability (prolonged by the successful weathering of the first OPEC episode), the Austrian economy lost its capacity to respond swiftly to a changing environment. This applies particularly to the labour markets, where trade unions seem to have become less flexible in their collective bargaining strategies (Flanagan *et al.*, 1983).

This 'sclerosis' hypothesis has met with scepticism from those who point to the fact that Austrian fiscal policies underwent a major change at the beginning of the 1980s. The central government is no longer willing to run up budget deficits large enough to cover deflationary gaps, whatever their size (owing to world trade conditions or union wage demands) might be. There is a limit on current budget deficits now, where there was none during the 1970s. Moreover, this budget constraint has become binding, pushing the Austrian economy below full employment.

Before taking up various threads of this debate on the causes of rising unemployment in Austria, it might be useful to review some of the data to be considered (see Table 1).

TABLE 1

AVERAGE ANNUAL RATES OF GROWTH

	1964–74 (%)	1974–84 (%)
Working-age population	0·2	0·8
Labour force	−0·1	0·2
Self-employed	−4·1	−2·0
Labour supply, total	1·1	0·6
Labour supply of migrant workers	24·0	−4·1
Employment	1·2	0·3
Hours of work	−0·7	−0·6
Productivity	4·3	2·5
Real GDP	4·7	2·2
Real capital stock	3·4	3·0
Real product wage	5·2	2·9
CPI	5·0	5·7
Average rates over the period		
Participation rate	72·9	71·3
Rate of unemployment	2·3	2·7

Source: IHS-Datenbank.

I. LABOUR MARKET TRENDS

Over the decade 1974–84, real GDP grew at an average rate of 2·2 per cent. This was sufficient to ensure the net creation of new jobs at an annual rate of 0·3 per cent (with annual productivity increases per man-hour of 2·5 per cent). However, as Figure 2 shows, the expansion of the workforce fell short of the growth of labour supply, and the rate of unemployment rose (Pichelmann, 1985).

For the problem at hand, it seems worthwhile to note that, at least in the short run, variations in the Austrian labour supply (and its components) are large relative to variations in the unemployment rate. Some more detailed figures illustrate the case. In 1983 the Austrian labour supply was 16·9 per cent larger than in 1970. This growth, substantial by European standards, resulted from divergent trends of its components during this period. The working-age population grew (10 per cent), whereas the participation rate dropped, from 72·2 to 69·5 per cent; this brought about an expansion of the labour force by 6 per cent. At the same time, the share of self-employed persons

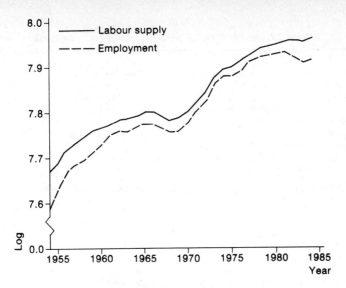

FIGURE 2.   Log labour supply, log employment, Austria, 1954–1984 (size of labour supply in 1984: 2,875 million persons). *Source*: IHS-Datenbank.

in the labour force declined sharply, from about 22 per cent in 1970 to about 14 per cent in 1983. This accounts for the increase of labour supply, the migrant worker component of which fluctuated sharply. At its historic maximum, in 1973, the share of guest workers was 8·6 per cent; by 1983 it had dropped to 5·4 per cent.

The implications of this supply-side flexibility on the Austrian labour market for the rate of observed unemployment are nicely borne out by a simple *ceteris paribus* calculation. Had the number of migrant workers in 1983 been kept at the 1973 level, then the rate of unemployment would have been 7 per cent rather than 4·5 per cent.

Foreign workers are the most conspicuous of the flexible components of Austrian labour supply, but they are not the only such component. During slumps participation rates drop, whereas the share of self-employed people decreases at a significantly slower pace. Though available Austrian time-series estimates of these effects are not very robust (as is the case with time-series evidence on labour supply in many other countries), the results of Christl (1982) indicate that there is a substantial discouraged worker effect in Austria.

The substantial supply-side flexibility (see Table 2) could not prevent the emergence of unemployment. The inflow into the unemployment register rose by 70 per cent between 1980 and 1984. The stock of unemployed more than doubled in the same period. The total annual length of unemployment per person increased from 83 days in 1980 to 108 days in 1984. Approximately one in six unemployed persons is registered for more than six months per year (Wagner, 1985a). Of those long-term unemployed, roughly three-quarters receive unemployment benefits below the minimum standard of living (as defined by the pension system). The replacement ratio (proportion of benefits

TABLE 2

STRUCTURE OF UNEMPLOYMENT, AUSTRIA, 1980–1984

	1980	1984
Inflow	243,000	414,000
Stock	56,000	125,000
Annual duration per person (days)	83	108
Share in inflow (%)		
Women	43	37
Age group below 25 years	29	33
Long-term unemployed (more than six months	8	16
of completed spells of unemployment)		

Replacement ratio (for fiscal year 1983) for the 'median unemployed'[a] (%)

	Exclusive tax rebates	Inclusive tax rebates
No family allowances	53.5	67·9
Two family allowances	68·7	80·8

Median unemployed with respect to post tax earnings and length of annual unemployment. The replacement ratio is defined as proportion of benefits (with or without tax rebates) to past net earnings.
Source: Projects TRANSFER and ARBEITSLOS (Institute for Economic and Social Research, Vienna, 1984).

to past earnings) for the single 'median unemployed' was 67·9 per cent (inclusive tax rebates) in 1983 (Fischer and Wagner, 1985).

Even if these unemployment data do not seem to be extreme by OECD standards, they do create substantial problems for the management of the economy; for the design of Austrian policy-making rests on 'full employment' insurance underwritten by the federal government, as is somewhat more fully explained in the next section.

II. THE MACROECONOMIC SETTING

During the early 1970s a consensus on the appropriate conduct of macroeconomic policy emerged among the most influential institutions involved; i.e. between the federal government, the trade unions, the employers' association and the (to a great extent nationalized) banking system. The underlying model can roughly be sketched as a sequence of interventions. (For more details see Wagner, 1985b).

Exchange rate policies

To start with, the central bank aims at stabilizing the real exchange rate of the Austrian shilling against a trade-weighted basket of currencies. It does not set itself targets for either the level of interest rates or the growth of monetary aggregates. The sole objective is to neutralize the domestic impact of the difference in price rises at home and abroad. From this perspective, Austrian policy-makers, in particular the trade unions, are willing to take the blame for inflationary spurts being 'home-made'. Such accelerations of price increases, however, tend not to last very long; for the unions and the employers' associations aim at nominal wage contracts which achieve target real wages at as low a rate of nominal increases as seems feasible.

Wage formation

The federation of the (highly concentrated and centralized) Austrian trade unions sets wage guidelines. Though these are never officially announced, all unions tend to move in line, with the metal workers opening the 'wage rounds'. The level of target wages is set in real terms. Unions ask for full compensation of cost-of-living (COLA) increases, but there are no formal COLA-clauses in collective bargaining agreements, which generally cover a 12-month period.

When determining the target level of real wage increases, the unions and the representatives of the employers' associations take account of past labour productivity growth and of the current general labour market condition. Both sides give the same justifications for doing so. First, labour productivity growth serves as a guideline for the fair division of the social product between wages and profits. Second, the general labour market conditions provide an indicator on the current trade-off between job security and wage increases; unions and employers are anxious not to 'price themselves out of jobs and markets', particularly in view of the openness of the Austrian economy. (For a time-series model on this behavior, see Kunst and Winckler, 1984.)

Incomes policy and the 'full employment insurance'

The federal government takes a rather favourable view of the wage formation process between unions and employers' associations. It considers itself a third partner in a neo-corporatist arrangement, in which exchange rate and incomes policies are designed to keep inflation down without distorting (on average) either Austria's international competitiveness or the balance between domestic demand and supply. In return for the unions' and employers' submission to (implicit) incomes policy guidelines, the government has to guarantee full employment.

To do so, it has to treat the current account and budget deficits as the two 'residuals' of macroeconomic adjustment to shocks and persistent imbalances that threaten the full employment position of the Austrian economy. This is, indeed, what happened during the 1970s. Since 1981, however, the government has occasionally stepped back from its promise of a purely accommodating fiscal policy. The short-term effect of this turn-around in fiscal policies has been a rise in unemployment. In the long run this could induce a transition to a new macroeconomic policy regime, in which the central government could no longer expect to solve the inflation problem within an incomes policy framework because the other two partners of the corporatist arrangement would feel let down by the government's new fiscal course.

The causes of unemployment and the wage flexibility issue

Most Austrian economists tend to agree that the rise of unemployment from 1981 to 1983 resulted from a deflationary gap, which, contrary to previous years, was not covered totally by budget deficits. It was the 'internal fiscal balance' rather than the 'external trade balance' that became a binding constraint, pushing output growth below its full employment path. This view is well supported by experiments with macroeconometric models (Wagner, 1985b).

Even if one accepts the main thrust of this demand-side explanation, and we are inclined to do so, there is still scope for research on the wage flexibility issue, an issue that has attracted much interest in internationally comparative studies, and which tends to put Austria into the 'very flexible' group (Grubb *et al.*, 1982, 1983). More specifically, it makes sense to ask two questions:

1. How sensitive is the Austrian wage formation process to changes of 'general labour market conditions'?
2. Would a greater degree of wage flexibility have made a difference with respect to the recent rise of unemployment?

Both questions will be dealt with in the next section, which makes use of a simple two-equation framework.

III. DEMAND FOR LABOUR

Macroeconomic explanations of unemployment (such as the difference between demand and supply on labour markets) find it difficult to provide reliable time-series estimates for labour supply equations. We have encountered the same difficulty for Austria, but we feel that the problems involved should nevertheless be borne in mind (rather than 'neutralized' by a suitable set of assumptions). There are in particular two salient features of Austrian data on labour supply that deserve attention, even if they cannot be captured in a single waterproof equation: first, the aggregate supply of labour is *not* inelastic with respect to either real wages or unemployment ('discouraged worker effect'); second, the labour supply is not determined by market forces only. (In particular, the administrative regulation of early retirement schemes and of migrant workers substantially affects observed variations in supply.)

Supply costs of labour demand adjustment

These observations on the supply side of the Austrian labour market have some immediate implications for modelling the demand-for-labour equation: Austrian firms operate, at the same time, in a bargaining framework and under conditions of monopolistic competition on the labour market. The firms have to 'take' wages for the various types of employees, but they cannot automatically satisfy all of their demand for labour at the going rate. They incur additional costs for recruiting personnel from 'outside' the current labour supply. Conversely, if firms want to cut down their workforce, they have to make side-payments (e.g. golden handshakes) to the employees affected.

Such additional costs of hiring and firing entail an adjustment process in the demand-for-labour equation: the firm is in equilibrium at every time, but this position is not necessarily the long-run equilibrium.

Real-wage elasticity and the speed of adjustment at given levels of output

A demand-for-labour equation, meeting this requirement and fitting Austrian data quite well (Maurer and Pichelmann, 1983), follows immediately from the maximizing behaviour of a representative firm characterized by a CES production function (with labour and capital as inputs). Optimality conditions require

(1) $\qquad N^*H = \alpha\{(1+t_1)/P\}^{-\beta} y\, e^{-\gamma t}$

where N^* represents the number of employees, H the hours worked, W the hourly wages, t_1 the social security contribution borne by the employer, and Y output.

The adjustment process, caused by the costs of hiring and firing, is captured by the following equation:

(2) $N_t/N_{t-1} = (N_t^*/N_{t-1})^\delta,$ $\delta > 0$

with N^* denoting the long-term and N the short-term equilibrium of the firm.

A straightforward empirical specification of this model is

(3) $\log N_t - \log N_{t-1} = \delta \log \alpha + \delta \log (Y_t/H_t N_{t-1})$

$$- \delta\beta \log\{W(1+t_1)/P\}_t - \delta\gamma t$$

with the same notation as above. In practice, we use the trend value of hours rather than actual hours worked in this equation.

This demand-for-labour equation yields estimates pertinent to the task set:

1. an estimate for the adjustment coefficient, and thus for the divergence of the short- and long-run equilibrium positions, that firms take when facing shocks; and
2. an estimate for the elasticity of employment with respect to the real wage at given levels of output.

The real-wage elasticity of employment in the context of induced substitution with other factors of production has attracted some interest among Austrian unionists. (How do wages affect the choice of production techniques?) Of course, one would wish explicitly to take account of real interest rates when dealing with this problem. Various experiments to do so have, however, failed to yield significant estimates for Austria. (For similar negative results, see Newell and Symons, 1985.)

Since this first employment equation takes output as exogenously given, it does not answer the question of how real wages affect employment through output adjustment. Hence, a second employment equation is needed.

The employment–capital ratio as a function of real wages

Most suitable for our purpose is the employment equation recently tested by Newell and Symons (1985) for various OECD countries. They estimate the employment–capital ratio as a function of real product wages and labour-augmenting technical progress, under the condition of a given path of capital accumulation:

(4) $\log (N/K)_t = \alpha \log (N_{t-1}/K_t) + \beta \log (N_{t-2}/K_t)$

$$+ \gamma \log (W(1+t_1)/P)_t + \delta \log A_t$$

with the same notation as above and with K representing capital and A labour-augmenting technical progress.

The theoretical background provided by Newell and Symons for this equation is compatible with ours. (For a detailed discussion of the results of their specification search and the differences to other approaches, see Newell and Symons, 1985.) Thus, re-estimating their equation (see Table 4) provides us with three results: the 'gross' real-wage elasticity for Austria; a benchmark for 'flexibility' comparisons with other OECD countries; and an additional estimate of the speed of employment adjustment in Austria.

Empirical results

Tables 3 and 4 give the estimation results for the period 1966–84. All coefficients take the expected signs and are of a reasonable order of magnitude, but not all of them are significant.

Both demand-for-labour equations yield adjustment coefficients which indicate that employment reacts slowly to shocks in Austria: the coefficient on the lagged labour–capital ratio is about 1·3, which puts Austria into the top league of OECD countries exhibiting sluggish employment adjustment

TABLE 3

EMPLOYMENT EQUATION 1, AUSTRIA, 1967–1984

Dependent variable	$\log N_t - \log N_{t-1}$
Independent variables	
Constant	3·545 (8·3)
$\log\left[\dfrac{Y_t}{TH_t N_{t-1}}\right]$	0·342 (7·4)
$\log\left[\dfrac{W(1+t_1)}{P}\right]$	−0·097 (2·4)
t	−0·0068 (5·9)
s.e.	0·0055
DW	2·82
Real-wage elasticity	−0·28

Notes: $\log[(Y_t/TH_t)/N_{t-1}]$ and $\log\,[\{W(1+t_1)\}/P]_t$ are treated as endogenous.
t-ratios in parentheses.

TABLE 4

EMPLOYMENT EQUATION 2, AUSTRIA, 1966–1984

Dependent variable	$\log\left[\dfrac{N}{K}\right]_t$
Independent variables	
$\log\left[\dfrac{N_{t-1}}{K_t}\right]$	1·348 (5·1)
$\log\left[\dfrac{N_{t-2}}{K_t}\right]$	−0·460 (1·6)
$\log\left[\dfrac{W(1+t_1)}{P}\right]_t$	−0·082 (1·8)
$\log A_t$	−0·012 (1·8)
D7184 · $\log A_t$	0·005 (1·6)
s.e.	0·0103
DW	1·59
Real-wage elasticity	−0·74

Notes: $\log[\{W(1+t_1)\}/P]_t$ is treated as endogenous. t-ratios in parentheses.

D7184: 0 for 1966–70, 1 for 1971–84.

(compare Newell and Symons, 1985, Table 6a). This is supported by the estimate of +0·34 for the adjustment coefficient in the other labour demand equation (Table 3); within a year, firms adjust their workforce by only one-third of the difference between their short- and long-run equilibrium positions.

The 'gross' real wage elasticity is −0·74. This indicates that Austrian unions are faced with a substantial trade-off between jobs and pay rises. For every 1 per cent of wage increases, they are threatened with the loss of $\frac{3}{4}$ per cent in employment. As is to be expected, the 'substitution' wage elasticity is much smaller: only −0·28. (These values are quite within the range of OECD experience: Symons and Layard 1984.)

These results support the view that the degree of real-wage flexibility should be of concern to the partners in the Austrian corporatist arrangement. It raises the question (to be discussed in the next section), which variables provide the signals for trade unions to adjust their target real wages?

IV. Signals for Wage Adjustment

Given the Austrian corporatist framework, a model of the wage formation process must capture the following elements of the collective bargaining process: (1) unions ask (and get) full compensation for (expected) rises of the consumer price level; (2) Austrian unions favour high rates of GDP growth, and thus are willing to let real wage increases fall behind productivity growth (as long as firms keep real capital formation in line with expanding profits); (3) unions take 'general labour market conditions' into consideration.

Whereas the 'cost of living' and the 'productivity' variables can be dealt with in a straightforward manner, the 'general labour market condition' argument poses a greater problem. In principle, the obvious candidate to be chosen as indicator would be the rate of (registered) unemployment. This would lead to an expectations augmented Phillips curve (Wörgötter, 1975; Stiassny, 1985).

However, in the Austrian case the rate of unemployment is a non-starter for several reasons. Throughout the 1970s the government tried hard to prevent any potential increase of unemployment from actually surfacing. This was done partly by taking a strongly expansionary fiscal stance and partly by exerting a downward pressure on labour supply by administrative means. (The number of work permissions for migrant workers was curtailed whenever there was the threat of visible labour market slack building up.) Thus, measured rates of unemployment are an inadequate proxy variable for underlying labour market conditions. (This view is supported by time-series models of the Austrian labour market: see Neusser, 1986.)

It is, rather, the utilization of labour *within* the firms that matters for the federation of unions when it comes to formulating wage guidelines. Above-average levels of utilization indicate a high degree of job security and increase the chance of promotion to better paid jobs for those already employed. Conversely, if the existing workforce is underutilized, then there is always the threat that union members may be downgraded if not made redundant.

There are two measures of labour utilization (within the firm) that are fairly standard in wage equations: (1) vacancies and (2) the deviation of the hours actually worked from standard hours of work. Both variables have the disadvantage that they mirror rather badly the worsening of labour market conditions below a certain floor. Thus, it might be helpful to add a third variable: the difference between the short-term and long-term employment equilibrium of the economy.

This measure is useful in several respects. It lends itself to symmetrical interpretations for periods of booms and slumps. If the short-run equilibrium is below its long-run level, then there is a 'notional labour shortage'; i.e., firms will adjust their labour force by drawing in additional workers from 'outside' (which is a costly and time-consuming process). Conversely, if firms underutilize their employees, then they face a 'notional labour surplus' (even though the firm has achieved, at every point of time, its short-term equilibrium). In this sense the 'notional surplus/shortage' is an indicator of whether firms will hire or fire people, and of how strong this tendency is relative to the size of the workforce.

Empirical results

The Austrian framework of wage formation is captured by the following equation:

(5) $\quad \log W_t - \log W_{t-1} = \alpha \log(PC_t/PC_{t-1}) + \beta \log (HPR_{t-1}/HPR_{t-2})$

$$+\gamma\{(N^*_{t-1} - N_{t-2})/N_{t-2}\}$$

where W denotes nominal wages, PC consumer prices, N^* and N the long- and short-term equilibrium of employment, respectively, and HPR hourly productivity.

The results for this equation are shown in the first column of Table 5. As is to be expected from our discussion of the Austrian framework of collective bargaining, the coefficient on consumer prices is highly significant and takes the value 1. The productivity term is at 0·65 (significant), implying that unions ask to be compensated for only two-thirds of lagged labour productivity increases. The 'notional surplus/shortage' coefficient takes the correct sign, is significant, and is of a reasonable order of magnitude.

TABLE 5

WAGE EQUATIONS, AUSTRIA, 1968-1984

Dependent variable: $\log W_t - \log W_{t-1}$				
Independent variables	(1)	(2)	(3)	(4)
$\log PC_t - \log PC_{t-1}$	1·073 (5·9)	1·548 (6·4)	0·934 (4·3)	1·091 (5·8)
$\log HPR_{t-1} - \log HPR_{t-2}$	0·652 (2·9)	0·803 (3·1)	0·232 (0·9)	0·863 (3·0)
$\dfrac{N^*_{t-1} - N_{t-2}}{N_{t-2}}$	0·317 (2·1)	—	—	—
U_t	—	−0·009 (2·1)	—	—
V_t	—	—	0·022 (2·2)	—
$CU_t - CU_{t-1}$	—	—	—	−0·005 (1·5)
s.e.	0·0199	0·028	0·0186	0·0238
DW	1·46	1·81	1·66	1·48

Notes: $\log PC_t - PC_{t-1}$ is treated as endogenous in equations (1)-(4).
U_t is treated as endogenous in equation (2), V_t in equation (3).
t-ratios in parentheses.

This specification of Austrian wage formation seems to be superior to either an augmented Phillips curve, a 'vacancy' or an 'overtime' approach; this is at least what columns (2), (3) and (4) of Table 5 would suggest. Substituting an unemployment term for the 'notional surplus/shortage' variable pushes the price coefficient up to an unrealisticly high level; Austrian unions just do not ask for an 150 per cent compensation for cost-of-living rises. With a nonlinear inclusion of the U-term, the productivity term becomes insignificant. (For a detailed specification search within a Phillips curve approach for Austria see Stiassny, 1985.)

The use of the vacancy variable does not yield sensible results, either. The productivity term becomes insignificant and too small. In the 'overtime' version of the wage equation, the coefficient on the 'deviation from trend hours' variable takes the wrong sign and is not significant. Though we have unsuccessfully experimented with other specifications of the 'overtime' approach, we do not want to suggest that further work along the lines of Gregory (1985) or Mendis and Muellbauer (1984) could not produce valuable results for Austria. At present, however, we prefer relying on the 'notional surplus/shortage' approach.

An exercise in wage flexibility

In order to evaluate how much the existing real-wage flexibility falls short of the degree necessary to ensure full employment, we have run an experiment to determine how the hypothetical time series of real wages (which would generate full employment via the employment equation (4)) compares to the actual values.

For the years 1981–84 the two series (actual values in brackets) are, in percentages: $-6\cdot2(+2\cdot3)$, $-7\cdot1(-1\cdot4)$, $+10\cdot8(+1\cdot9)$, $+5\cdot3(0\cdot0)$. Though the hypothetical trajectory of real wages is more volatile than the actual time path, both end up at the same *level* or real wages for 1984. Thus, Austrian unions could have achieved full employment (i.e. a rate of unemployment of 2 per cent at the given supply of labour) without a permanent loss in real wages.

From the point of view of policy-making, however, such an exercise does not take us very far. Unions, as organizations in which leadership has to seek broad support among members, do not have the option to seek 'optimality' in a mechanical way. Two consecutive years of real-wage cuts of between 6 and 7 per cent (as is suggested by the hypothetical trajectory) is beyond the degree of flexibility that one could expect realistically from a large trade union.

V. CONCLUSIONS

1. The Austrian labour market exhibits the following features:

(a) Labour supply is highly elastic with respect to demand in the short run.

(b) Firms adjust their workforce rather slowly to shocks (demand failures or cost-push factors). Their demand-for-labour function, nevertheless, exhibits a significant (gross) real (product) wage elasticity of about $-0\cdot74$.

(c) Unions do not suffer from money wage illusion. They ask for a (less than 100 per cent) compensation for productivity growth, and they take the degree of labour utilization into account. The best way to capture this 'general labour market condition' argument in a wage equation is by way of including the 'notional surplus/shortage' variable, (i.e. the difference between long- and short-term employment equilibria).

2. During the 1970s the highly expansionary fiscal policies of the Austrian government kept the economy on the full employment path; budget deficits were always tailored to the need of compensating a potential deflationary gap, resulting from a slowdown of world trade growth. Unemployment figures started to rise after the federal government decided to set limits on the size of the current budget deficit. This constraint pushed the economy below its level of full employment growth. A higher degree of (real-) wage flexibility on part of the parties involved in collective bargaining could have cushioned the impact of the less expansionary course of fiscal policies. However, it is unlikely that such a high degree of flexibility is feasible within the political and organizational framework of neocorporatist incomes policies, which has served Austria so well in fighting inflation.

ACKNOWLEDGMENTS

We are grateful to Charles Bean, Wolfgang Franz, David Grubb, Richard Layard and Steve Nickell for valuable comments and criticism.

REFERENCES

CHRISTL, J. (1982). An econometric model of labor supply. *Empirica*, 10, 155-73.

FISCHER, G. and WAGNER, M. (1985). Gestaffelte Einkommenstransfers. Die Verteilungswirkung der österreichischen Arbeitslosenversicherung. *Wirtschaft und Gesellschaft*, 11, 231-42.

FLANAGAN, R. J., SOSKJE, D. W. and ULMAN, L. (1983). *Unionism, Economic Stabilization, and Incomes Policies*. Washington: Brookings Institution.

GREGORY, R. (1985). Wage policy and unemployment. Unpublished paper, Austrian National University.

GRUBB, D., JACKMAN, R. and LAYARD, R. (1982). Causes of the current stagflation. *Review of Economic Studies*, 49, 707-31.

—— (1983). Wage rigidity and unemployment in OECD countries. *European Economic Review*, 21, 11-40.

HABERLER, G. (1982). Austria's economic development after the two world wars; a mirror picture of the world economy. In S. W. Arndt (ed), *The Political Economy of Austria*, pp. 61-75. Washington: American Enterprise Institute.

KUNST, R. and WINCKLER, G. (1984). The influence of wage rate variations on the level of employment with and without an exogenous interest rate. Discussion paper. Vienna: IHS.

LAYARD, R. and NICKELL, S. J. (1984). Unemployment and real wages in Europe, Japan, and the US. Working Paper no. 677. London: LSE Centre of Labour Economics.

MALINVAUD, E. (1982). Wages and unemployment. *Economic Journal*, 92, 1-13.

MAURER, J. and PICHELMANN, K. (1983), Makroökonomische Effekte einer Wochenarbeitszeitverkürzung. Discussion paper. Vienna: IHS.

MEADE, J. (1983). A new Keynesian approach of full employment. *Lloyds Bank Review*, 150, 1-18.

MENDIS, L. and MUELLBAUER, J. (1984). British manufacturing productivity 1955-1983: measurement problems, oil shocks and Thatcher effects. Discussion paper no. 32. London: Centre for Economic and Policy Research.

NEUSSER, K. (1986). Time-series representations of the Austrian labour market. *Weltwirtscheftliches Archiv*, forthcoming.

NEWELL, A. and SYMONS, J. S. V. (1985). Wages and Employment in the OECD countries. Discussion Paper no. 219. London: LSE, Centre for Labour Economics.

OLSON, M. (1982). *The Rise and Decline of Nations. Economic Growth, Stagflation and Social Rigidities*. New Haven and London: Yale University Press.

PICHELMANN, K. (1985). The Austrian economy in the mid-eighties: assessment and outlook. LINK Fall Meeting, Madrid.

PICHELMANN, K. and WAGNER, M. (1984). Full employment at all cost: Austrian employment and labour market policy since the late 1970s. In K. Gerlach et al. (eds), Public Policy to Combat Unemployment in a Period of Economic Stagnation, pp. 65-85. Frankfurt: Campus.

STIASSNY, A. (1985). The Austrian Phillips curve reconsidered. Empirica, 12, 43-66.

SYMONDS, J. and LAYARD, R. (1984). Neoclassical demand for labour functions for six major economies. Economic Journal, 94, 788-99.

WAGNER, M. (1985a). Die Risken steigender Arbeitlosigkeit. Österreich in den achtziger Jahren. Journal für Sozialforschung, 25, 151-7.

—— (1985b). Nachfrageorientierte Beschäftigungssicherung. Die österreichische Variante des Keynesianismus 1974/84. In F. Buttler et al. (eds.), Staat und Beschäftigung, pp. 73-87. Nuremberg: IAB.

WÖRGÖTTER, A. (1975). Lohn- und Preisgleichungen für Österreich. Empirica, 1, 57-77.

A Discussion of Belgian Unemployment, Combining Traditional Concepts and Disequilibrium Econometrics

By Henri R. Sneessens and Jacques H. Drèze

Faculté Libre des Sciences Economiques de Lille and CORE, Université Catholique de Louvain

The sorest ill that Heaven hath
Sent on this lower world in wrath—
Unemployment (to call it by its name)
Waged war on economics,
Sparing no country from the plague.
They died not all, but all were sick.
No jobs were left;
So hope and therefore joy were dead.
Richard the Lion-hearted council held and said:
'Let us all turn eyes within
And ferret out the hidden sin.'
Himself let no one spare nor flatter,
But make clean conscience in the matter.
'I Yield myself', concluded he;
'And yet I think, in equity,
Each should confess his sins with me.'
Belgians, confessing in their turn,
Thus spoke in tones of deep concern:
'We have little to say
That you do not know anyway.
Without claiming to be exhaustive
We put a few facts in perspective.
Then turn to summarizing
Scanty results on manufacturing.
Next we illustrate a methodology
That was pioneered in our country.
By way of conclusions
We share our interrogations.'

I. Factual Perspective

With a GDP of less than $100 billion and exports of more than $60 billion, Belgium comes perhaps closer than any other country to being a 'small open economy'. Consequently, trends in world trade and export performance have a major impact on domestic activity, whereas the impact of domestic fiscal policy is damped by import leakages. Table 1 presents a few figures confirming these observations.

The rise in Belgian unemployment since 1974 has been appalling. Figure 1 compares the unemployment rate in Belgium with that of the European Community (EC9) since 1960. It displays clearly the sharper take-off of Belgian unemployment since 1974.

Additional facts about employment and unemployment over the period 1974–83 are collected in Table 2. The salient features are as follows.

TABLE 1

GDP, BELGIUM 1975-83, AT 1980 PRICES

	% of GDP, 1975	% change, 1975-80	% change, 1980-83	% change, 1975-83	% of GDP, 1983
Private consumption	63	17	−1	16	63
Public consumption	18	18	0	18	18
Gross fixed investment	22	9	−22	−15	16
Exports	47	48	7	58	63
Imports	48	50	−3	45	60
GDP	100	15	0	15	100
Public deficit	6	67	32	119	14

Source: OECD National Accounts (1984).

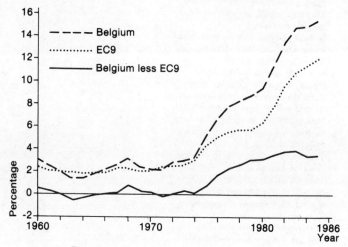

FIGURE 1. Unemployment rate, Belgium, 1960-84.

1. Male employment has gone down by 10 per cent while female employment has gone up by 3 per cent; the sharper increase in female unemployment is thus due to the increase in active population.
2. The increase in female employment is equal to the number of women in special employment programmes; otherwise, there are offsetting movements in public employment (+69,200) and private employment (−71,000) of women.
3. The decline in private employment (15·3 per cent altogether) is concentrated (up to 88 per cent) in manufacturing, where the decline is staggering: 29·8 per cent!

The evolution of total employment (private and public) in five sectors is given in Figure 2.

Another useful piece of information concerns hours worked and the evolution of labour inputs in man-hours. In the manufacturing sector, average hours went down by 11 per cent in 10 years (1973-83), so that labour inputs

TABLE 2

BELGIAN POPULATION AND EMPLOYMENT, BY SEX AND STATUS, 1974–83

	Men			Women			Total		
	1974 ('000)	1974–83 ('000)	1974–83 (%)	1974 ('000)	1974–83 ('000)	1974–83 (%)	1974 ('000)	1974–83 ('000)	1974–83 (%)
(1) Population of working age (men: 15–64, women: 15–59)	3103·1	+225·9	+7·3	2827·6	+199·8	+7·3	5930·7	+425·7	7·2
(2) Active population	2625·1	−45·9	−1·8	1354·2	+279·9	+20·7	3979·3	+233·0	+5·9
(3) Participation rates	84·6		−7·1	47·9		+6·1	67·1		−0·8
(4) Early retirements	0	+99·8		0	+26·4		0	+126·2	
(5) Unemployment	45·7	+207·1		51·2	+241·1		96·9	+448·2	
(6) Unemployment rates	1·7		+8·1	3·8		+14·1	2·4		+10·5
(7) Total employment	2579·4	−253·0	−9·8	1302·9	+38·9	+3·0	3882·3	−214·1	−5·5
(8) of which: special programmes	7·6	+35·4		1·4	+40·5		9·0	+75·9	
(9) Public servants	537·4	+57·9	+10·8	262·0	+109·7	+41·9	799·4	+167·6	+21·0
(10) Self-employed	405·8	9·1	−2·2	228·5	+1·5	+0·7	634·3	7·6	1·2
(11) Wage-earners	1636·0	−301·6	−18·4	812·5	72·5	−8·9	2448·5	−374·1	−15·3
(12) of which: manufacturing	805·2	−213·7	−26·5	295·9	−114·8	−38·8	1101·1	−328·5	−29·8

Source: Official statistics and calculations at ECOS and IRES, Université Catholique de Louvain.

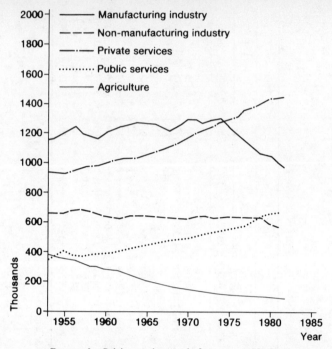

FIGURE 2.   Belgian employment in five sectors, 1953–81.

went down by 37·3 per cent.[1] Taking into account a 15 per cent increase in value added at constant prices, the apparent increase in gross hourly productivity is nearly 85 per cent. In services, average hours went down by 9 per cent and gross hourly productivity went up by 27 per cent.

That enormous apparent increase in gross hourly productivity in manufacturing accounts for much of the differential rise in Belgian unemployment; it is one of the main facts to be explained if anything is to be learned from the rise in Belgian unemployment.

A broader picture of the Belgian economy is given by Figure 3, which presents time-series for the income share of labour, unemployment, budget deficits and balance of payments deficits. The striking (though not unexpected) aspect of these series is the concomitant break in trends in the early 1970s. At that time Belgium underwent a deep and swift transformation: the country, previously one of relatively stable prices and labour share, with low unemployment and low deficits, thereafter came to be characterized by significant inflation, including real wage inflation, high unemployment and sizeable deficits.

The percentage change in real wages for the period 1971–80 amounts to 57 per cent for Belgium as against 37 per cent for the rest of the European Community (EC9). The third and fourth columns of Table 3 give the income share of labour in 1971 and 1980. The picture emerging from the table is by no means clear-cut. There is a mild suggestion that real wages rose more rapidly in countries where the income share of labour was initially lower, and

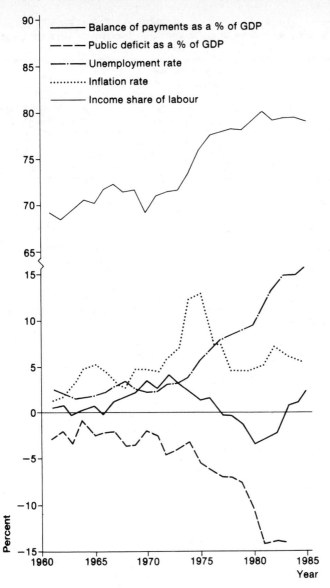

FIGURE 3. The Belgian economy, 1961-84.

typically rose quickly enough there to bring about, by 1980, a labour share exceeding the average (with Italy and Denmark the more obvious exceptions). The more solid fact, in so far as Belgium is concerned, is the exceptionally high rate of increase of real wages in the 1970s—a fact that one would like to explain, and the consequences of which one would like to evaluate.

A similar picture of rapid transition from balanced growth to pronounced disequilibrium is conveyed by Figure 4. This figure, which is discussed at

TABLE 3

GROWTH RATES OF REAL WAGES AND INCOME SHARES OF LABOUR,
1971–80

	Growth of real compensation per employee, total economy, 1971–80		Adjusted share of labour income total economy		
	Ave. rate	Cumulative percentage	1971	1980	1980–71
Belgium	4·6	57	70·9	79	8·1
Japan	4·2	51	73·4	80·6	7·2
France	4·1	49	70·9	75·7	4·8
Italy	3·4	40	80·7	81·7	1
EC9	**3·2**	**37**	**74·6**	**76·3**	**1·7**
W. Germany	3·1	36	73·2	73	−0·2
Netherlands	2·8	32	74·2	73·9	−0·3
UK	2·3	26	73·2	75·4	2·2
Denmark	1·4	15	79·4	79·4	0
USA	1·0	11	74·1	74·1	0

Source: European Economy (1984, Tables 23 and 24). The deflator of compensation per employee is the consumer price index.

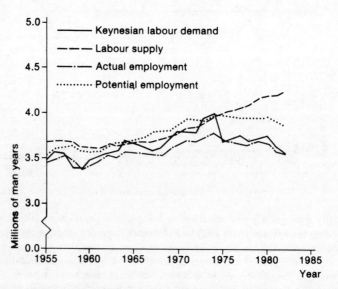

FIGURE 4.   Labour supply (*LS*), potential employment (*LP*), Keynesian labour demand (*LK*) and actual employment (*LT*), Belgium, 1955–82.

greater length in Section IV, presents estimates of labour supply (LS), 'potential employment' (LP—defined as the employment corresponding to the desired utilization of productive capacities) and 'Keynesian labour demand' (LK—defined as the employment needed to meet effective demand for domestic output). Three distinct time periods stand out clearly on that figure: 1955-62, 1963-74 and 1975 onward. In the first subperiod, structural unemployment was progressively eliminated by industrialization in Flanders—see Leroy (1962). The development of new industrial activities there had by 1963 led to a situation of near equilibrium ($LS \simeq LP \simeq LK$). That situation prevailed until 1974. The 'golden sixties' give an almost perfect picture of balanced growth: the three series move on parallel trends, with cyclical fluctuations superimposed on the demand series (LK). Since 1975, however, the three series diverge markedly: labour supply keeps growing (owing to the growth of female population and participation rates); potential employment stagnates until 1979 and then falls off (owing to the decline in investment), and Keynesian labour demand declines sharply in 1975 and again in 1981 (owing to insufficient effective demand). The behaviour of LP and LK is also influenced by labour-saving investment and technological progress (see below).

On the policy side, three points seem worth mentioning.

1. Ever since unemployment became a major issue in the mid-1970s, Belgium has actively developed a number of special programmes: early retirement, apprenticeships for the young, the fully subsidized hiring of unemployed persons in non-profit organizations, etc. Without these programmes, the unemployment rate would be another 5 percentage points higher (Table 2, rows (4), (5) and (8)).
2. Until 1981, Belgium tried to maintain the stability of its exchange rate vis-à-vis the German mark and Dutch guilder; by 1981 a substantial current deficit had developed. In February 1982 the Belgian franc devalued by 8 per cent. This measure was accompanied by an incomes policy which has been continued until now. Whereas almost all wages and salaries had previously been fully indexed, the government has imposed real wage reductions of some 2 to 3 per cent per year since then.
3. Business investments have for many years benefited from interest rate subsidies. Over the past three years, tax advantages have been granted to individuals investing in stocks and to individuals or institutions subscribing new equity issues.

II. Some Tightrope Exercises over Manufacturing

In this section, we report briefly on three empirical studies of the Belgian manufacturing sector, which hopefully bear some relevance to the decline of employment there. Our reports are brief because these studies proceed from a very thin data base; their results are suggestive, but not conducive to precise quantitative conclusions. Accordingly, we simply quote a few relevant results, with a minimum of explanations.

d'Alcantara (1983) has estimated a seven-sector model of the Belgian economy, with a putty-clay vintage production model for each sector. There are four inputs (capital, labour, energy and materials). The model is estimated from 14 annual observations (1963-76). As of 1977, the estimated output elasticity of manufacturing labour demand was 2·5 times higher when computed for scrapping old equipment than when computed for new investment. In other words, when replacing old equipment by new at unchanged capacity, three out of every five workers concerned could be dispensed with. The loss of some 150,000 jobs in manufacturing from 1973 to 1977 is explained by d'Alcantara as the net outcome of 'destroying' 340,000 jobs by scrapping old equipment, while 'creating' 190,000 jobs through new investment (of which some 135,000 correspond to modernization and some 55,000 correspond only to capacity expansion).

Lambert (1984) has estimated a streamlined model of the Belgian manufacturing sector, defined by aggregation of micro-markets in disequilibrium. On specific micro-markets, transactions correspond to the minimum of supply and demand. Assuming lognormality of the distribution over micro-markets of the ratio of supply to demand, one obtains an approximate expression for aggregate transactions as a CES function of aggregate supply and aggregate demand. The exponent of the CES function can be estimated from business survey data, namely from the proportion of firms reporting excess supply of goods and or excess demand for labour.

The model is estimated from 18 annual observations (1963–80). The estimation results permit a decomposition of the observed decline in manufacturing employment from 1974 to 1980 (namely, 23·5 per cent) into four components: the change in frictional unemployment (negligible), the change in demand (accounting for 4·5 out of 23·5 per cent), the change in the stock of capital (negligible), and the substitution of capital for labour induced by relative prices (accounting for 19 out of 23·5 per cent).

A related approach is followed by Gérard and Vanden Berghe (1984) in their analysis of manufacturing investment. These authors recognize that at any point in time some firms operate on competitive product markets and gear investment to a desired capital stock reflecting relative prices, whereas other firms operate on imperfectly competitive product markets and gear investment to a desired capital stock reflecting effective demand. An aggregation procedure comparable to that of Lambert (1984) leads again to an approximate expression for the desired stock of capital as a CES function of two expressions, one of which involves relative prices and the other effective demand. Estimates of the parameters of that expression imply estimates of the elasticity of desired capital with respect to relative prices (here, the ratio of the cost of capital to the price of output) and with respect to effective demand (here, actual output). These two elasticities vary over time. The former is positively related to the proportion of firms constrained by sales expectations; the latter, negatively related. Estimates derived from annual observations for the period 1956–82 (without reliance on business survey data) suggest a rapidly growing influence of effective demand on investment after 1974. Tentative as it may still be, that finding is worth keeping in mind when speculating about the determinants of investment.

When considering the share of exports in the final demand for Belgian manufactures, it is also important to treat exports endogenously, and to investigate the influence on exports of domestic costs and production capacities. Bauwens and d'Alcantara (1983) have estimated a two-equation model (price and quantities) for Belgian exports of manufactures. Their results are consistent with an elasticity of export quantities with respect to domestic production capacities equal to unity and suggest an elasticity of the value of exports with respect to domestic wages of the order of -0.3. As for export prices, they seem to be determined largely by world prices (elasticity 0.8) and less so by domestic costs (elasticity 0.2).

Before drawing a tentative conclusion from the material collected in this section, we wish to introduce an additional bit of evidence. It concerns the number of (blue and white-collar) workers laid off as a result of their employers' bankruptcy. The exact coverage of the statistic is not entirely clear; bankruptcies involving less than 20 employees are not included, and there may be other omissions. On the other hand, some of the bankrupt firms continued under new ownership (typically with a much smaller workforce). Be that as it may, it is striking to find an annual average (1976–83) of at least 30,000 workers laid off because of bankruptcy. It was noted in Table 2 that, over the period 1974–83, an average of 37,400 jobs a year were destroyed in the private sector. The rate of attrition suggested by bankruptcies is thus not far from the actual overall rate!

We conclude that all the findings reported in this section are consistent with, and give empirical content to, the frequently heard diagnostic that the Belgian manufacturing sector was choked by the *combination* of domestic labour costs growing faster than those of competitors and effective demand slackening off in a context of world recession. That *combination* was particularly damaging for two reasons. First, high costs and low output resulted in a severe loss of profitability, leading some firms to scrap capacity and lay off workers, while other firms simply went bankrupt. Second, slack demand at the world level prevented Belgian producers from passing on wage costs into prices and enabled foreign competitors to take over the market share thus abandoned. (From 1975 to 1979, wholesale prices of manufactures showed no trend, whereas retail and service prices went up 40 per cent.)

If one adds the observation that those firms that survived could do so only thanks to major gains in productivity, one has come a long way towards explaining the exceptional increase in apparent gross labour productivity of Belgian manufacturing industries. It would be hazardous to attempt to impute the overall increase back to individual causes, as there was much interaction. But it seems clear that wage behaviour has played a significant role; without that additional complication, the impact of the recession on manufacturing employment (down by 29.8 per cent from 1974 to 1983) would have been less severe. The differential rise of unemployment in Belgium relative to EC9 since 1974 corresponds to some 10 per cent of the employment in manufacturing; with a differential rise in real wages of some 20 percentage points in Belgium relative to EC9 over the period 1971–80, a moderate wage elasticity of employment of -0.5 would account for the differential rise in unemployment.

III. A Macroeconomic Rationing Model

This section is devoted to the presentation and estimation of a two-market macroeconomic rationing (or disequilibrium) model of the Belgian economy. The background is thus a Barro-Grossman-Benassy-Malinvaud model, i.e. a situation in which price and wage adjustments are not sufficient to clear the goods and labour markets at each moment of time, so that employment can be, broadly speaking, determined by a sales constraint (Keynesian unemployment), by a capacity constraint (classical unemployment), or by a labour supply constraint (repressed inflation and underconsumption).[2] The model that will be developed rests on previous work on Belgian data by Sneessens (1981, 1983) and Lambert (1984). The first subsection below will be devoted to the discussion of production constraints. These are the cornerstone of the model, around which the rest is organized. The first part of the model describes the determination of production and employment, given the production constraints just mentioned. The second part describes the formation of prices and wages. Prices are represented by a mark-up on costs, plus a positive demand pressure effect. Wages are determined by productivity gains plus a negative unemployment effect. These specifications are rather crude, and we do not claim that they reflect a fully satisfactory theory of price and wage formation. Rather, they reflect minimal influences taken into account in most empirical studies. The simplicity of these specifications is convenient to bring out the properties of the whole model, which are considered in the second subsection below. We pay special attention to the inflation–unemployment trade-off and to the meaning of the non-inflationary rate of unemployment ($NIRU$) in a quantity rationing model. Empirical results are presented in Section IV.

Production constraints

Traditional macroeconomic models typically contain production relationships appearing indirectly in the form of factor demand functions. In a rationing context, production constraints will furthermore be used to determine the highest production level at which firms can reasonably aim, given the availability of production factors (capital and labour) and the prevailing production technology. The determination of these upper bounds on production is crucial for the distinction between the three regimes alluded to above, namely Keynesian unemployment, classical unemployment and repressed inflation. These upper bounds can be modelled in several ways. We shall use an extended version of the Leontief–Cobb–Douglas model already used in Sneessens (1981).

Optimal factor proportions (or technical coefficients) are chosen so as to minimize production costs. Let us assume that changing these technical coefficients is costly. When these costs are high, transitory stimuli (such as a sales constraint) will not induce a firm to modify its production technique. Consequently, labour and capital appear as complementary inputs in the short run although they are substitutes in the longer run. This seems realistic enough.

If long-run cost considerations only are taken into account and temporary disturbances such as sales constraints are neglected, a Cobb–Douglas production function is readily shown to imply a capital–labour ratio that remains proportional to relative labour costs:

(1) $$\ln \frac{K}{L} = C_0 + \Theta(\Lambda) \ln \frac{W}{V}$$

where W and V stand for labour and capital usage costs, respectively, and Λ is the lag operator. The lag polynomial function $\Theta(\Lambda)$ represents the slow adjustment of the capital–labour ratio to relative cost changes. By substitution into the Cobb–Douglas function itself, one can derive expressions for the output-labour and output-capital ratios:

(2)
$$\begin{cases} \ln \dfrac{Y}{L} = C_1 + a_1(t) + (1 - a_2)\Theta(\Lambda) \ln \dfrac{W}{V} \\[4mm] \ln \dfrac{Y}{K} = C_2 + a_1(t) - a_2\Theta(\Lambda) \ln \dfrac{W}{V} \end{cases}$$

where $a_1(t)$ allows for exogenous technical progress and a_2 is the coefficient of labour in the Cobb-Douglas function. Constant returns to scale are implicitly assumed. Equation (2) can be written more compactly as

(3)
$$\begin{cases} \dfrac{Y}{L} = A\left(t, \dfrac{W}{V}\right) \\[4mm] \dfrac{Y}{K} = B\left(t, \dfrac{W}{V}\right). \end{cases}$$

In the very short run, the technical coefficients A and B are fairly rigid, as in a Leontief production model. The limits imposed on production by the availability of production factors are $A \times LS$ and $B \times KA$, where LS and KA stand for the supply of labour and the available capital stock, respectively. *Repressed inflation* occurs when the labour constraint is operative, *classical unemployment* when the capital constraint is operative. *Keynesian unemployment* occurs when the demand for goods remains below these two upper bounds, so that the production level is determined by the demand for goods.

When production capacities are fully utilized, the production level is $YP \equiv B \times KA$. The corresponding 'potential' employment level is $LP = A^{-1} \times YP = A^{-1} \times B \times KA$. After substitution for A and B and first-differencing, one obtains

(4) $\Delta \ln LP = -\Theta(\Lambda)(\Delta \ln W - \Delta \ln V) + \Delta \ln KA.$

The rate of growth of potential employment is equal to minus the rate of growth of relative labour costs plus the investment rate ($\Delta \ln KA \simeq I/KA$). Notice that the lag polynomial $\Theta(\Lambda)$ implies that the effects of a wage change will be slow to appear, while the effects of changes in the investment rate are more immediate. Figure 5 reproduces the evolution of the two series $\Theta(\Lambda)(\Delta \ln W - \Delta \ln V)$ and $\Delta \ln KA$ from 1955 to 1982. The values of the lag polynomial are those obtained by ML estimation (see Section IV). The potential employment level declines whenever the investment rate falls below the rate of growth of relative labour costs, that is, whenever the rate of growth of the economy does not induce the creation of enough new jobs to replace those lost by productivity gains. This situation has been observed in every year since 1975, except for 1979. The investment slack has become especially important in 1981-82. It is responsible for the fall in the potential employment level indicated in Figure 4.

Potential employment is not a constraint that can be relaxed overnight through wage adjustments. Technical adjustment costs imply that changes in relative factor costs are only progressively translated into capital-labour substitution. It is even likely that the adjustment to a wage fall is slower than the

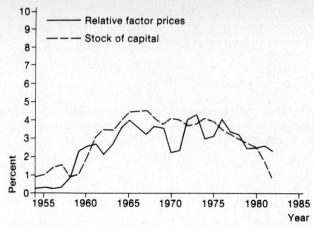

FIGURE 5.   Rates of change in the stock of capital and relative factor prices.

adjustment to a rise, because there is little incentive to get rid of capital-intensive equipment once it has been paid for. More precisely, wage moderation in the short run is likely to have a larger impact on the demand for goods than on supply and potential employment. This point has already been stressed forcefully by Malinvaud (1982).

Properties of the model

Our definition in the previous section of the Keynesian, classical and inflation regimes applies to individual firms only. What we observe at the aggregate level is a time-varying mixture of the three regimes. This point has been illustrated by Muellbauer (1978) and Malinvaud (1980). It is taken into account by aggregating explicitly over 'micro-markets', as in Lambert (1984). For expository reasons, we first consider an homogeneous economy and analyse each polar case separately; that is, we proceed as though all firms were always at the same time in the same regime. The consequences of aggregation and of structural imbalances are then reintroduced.

Specification details will not be given until Section IV. Moreover, because investment is kept exogenous, we take as given throughout this subsection the technical coefficients A and B. This places us in a short-run perspective.

Keynesian unemployment. The relevant set of equations is reproduced in Table 4. Suffixes D and S denote demanded and supplied quantities respectively; suffix T denotes transacted quantities. Total final demand FD is defined as private consumption plus an exogenous component that includes public expenditures, investment and exports. Private consumption demand is determined by total disposable income DI. The demand for imports MD is the usual function of total final demand and relative prices. The difference between FD and MD defines the demand for domestic goods YD which, together with other variables such as the previous employment level (not shown), determines the demand for labour. As we are by assumption in a situation of generalized excess supply, transactions on both the goods and the labour markets are

TABLE 4

DETERMINATION OF MACROECONOMIC AGGREGATES IN A PURE
KEYNESIAN REGIME ($YD < YP$, $LD < LS$)

Demand for goods:	$\begin{cases} FD = CD(DI) + EXO \\ MD = MD(FD, PF, PM) \\ YD = FD - MD \end{cases}$	
Demand for labour:	$LD = L(YD)$	
Transacted quantities:	$\begin{cases} CT = CD, \ MT = MD, \ YT = YD \\ LT = LD \end{cases}$	
Wages and prices:	$\begin{cases} W = \omega_0 (LD/LS)^{\omega_1} A^e P^e \\ P = e^{\pi_0} APC^e \\ \text{where } APC = A^{-1}W + B^{-1}V \end{cases}$	$\omega_0, \omega_1 \geqslant 0$ $\pi_0 \geqslant 0$

determined by the demand side. The wage equation simply says that the expected real wage rate is proportional to the expected productivity of labour. With an elasticity of real wage demands to productivity gains equal to one (as assumed), the proportionality factor is merely the share of total value added claimed by labour. That share is here inversely related to the unemployment rate. The last equation defines the price of value-added by a mark-up on expected average production costs APC. Coefficient π_0 represents the share of total value-added that firms claim over and above interest and depreciation. It is equal to the mark-up rate. It corresponds to pure profits and/or to a margin for incomplete utilization of factors (labour hoarding, excess capacity).

The basic properties of the real part of the model are well known. For given wages and prices, the levels of output and employment are determined by final demand. To increase employment, one must increase either the exogenous component of final demand or consumption demand. Under reasonable assumptions, higher real wages imply more consumption demand.

The price equation in Table 4 embodies an assumption of downward price rigidity: the excess supply of goods does not lead to price decreases. Consequently, prices are entirely determined by costs and the only form of inflation is 'cost-push'. Aside from exogenous shocks, a systematic inflationary bias may or may not be present, depending upon the presence or absence of excessive income claims relative to value added. This is most easily seen by looking at a stationary perfect foresight equilibrium.

With correct expectations, the price equation can indeed be rewritten (using the approximation $e^{-\pi_0} \simeq 1 - \pi_0$) as

$$1 = \pi_0 + A^{-1} \frac{W}{P} + B^{-1} \frac{V}{P};$$

that is, total value added is divided into three parts: mark-up π_0, labour income $A^{-1}(W/P)$, and capital income $B^{-1}(V/P)$. Let us assume a fixed capital share κ_0, as if capital usage costs were perfectly indexed on the price of value added. The share of total value-added left for labour is then simply

$$(5) \qquad A^{-1} \frac{W}{P} = 1 - \pi_0 - \kappa_0.$$

The desired labour share is in turn obtained from the wage equation as[3]

(6) $A^{-1}\dfrac{W}{P} = \omega_0 - \omega_1\, UR.$

Coefficient ω_0 thus represents the share of total value added that would be claimed by workers in a zero unemployment economy.

The income claims represented by equations (5)-(6) include a single *endogenous* influence, namely, that of unemployment on wages. Accordingly, any inflationary bias arising from conflicting income claims can be corrected only through unemployment, a crude specification made popular by the discussion of 'non-inflationary rates of unemployment' (*NIRU*). The *NIRU* is in our case the unemployment rate that reconciles (5) and (6):

(7) $NIRU = \dfrac{1}{\omega_1}(\pi_0 + \kappa_0 + \omega_0 - 1) \underset{\text{def}}{=} \dfrac{1}{\omega_1} DG$

where DG stands for 'distributive gap', i.e. the relative excess of income claims over value added. The *NIRU* is proportional to the 'distributive gap', with a factor of proportionality equal to the reciprocal of the elasticity of wages with respect to unemployment. In other words, a Keynesian equilibrium with stationarity of both prices and quantities implies an employment level $LS(1 - NIRU)$ uniquely determined by the sum of income claims $(\pi_0 + \kappa_0 + \omega_0)$ and the elasticity ω_1. With $\omega_1 \simeq 0\cdot4$ (see empirical results, Section IV), a discrepancy of four percentage points would imply a *NIRU* of 10 per cent! Notice, though, that the *NIRU* should be lowered by the extent to which firms lower $(\pi_0 + \kappa_0)$ when demand is slack. This is not modelled here. Finally, an oil shock with full indexation of wages on consumer prices is in this setting equivalent to an increase in ω_0, hence in the *NIRU*.

Needless to say, a perfect-foresight stationary Keynesian equilibrium can exist if and only if the *NIRU* defined in (7) is feasible, i.e. if it is non-negative *and* larger than the rate of unemployment that would prevail if all production capacities were utilized. Otherwise, the economy would end up in either repressed inflation or classical unemployment.

Classical unemployment. The relevant equations are reproduced in Table 5.

TABLE 5

DETERMINATION OF MACROECONOMIC AGGREGATES IN A PURE CLASSICAL
UNEMPLOYMENT REGIME
$(LD < LS, YD > YS)$

Demand for goods:	Same as in Table 4
Demand for labour:	$LD = L(YP) = L'(KA)$
Transacted quantities:	$\begin{cases} LT = LD \\ YT = Y(KA) \\ MT = MD + M(YD/YT) \\ CT = CD \end{cases}$
Wages and prices:	$\begin{cases} W = \omega_0(LD/LS)^{\omega_1}A^e P^e \\ P = e^{\pi_0}(YD/YT)^{\pi_1}APC^e \\ \text{where } APC = A^{-1}W + B^{-1}V \end{cases}$

The goods demand equations remain unchanged. Labour demand and employment are now determined by the availability of capital rather than the demand for goods. The availability of capital determines production, which falls short of the demand for goods.[4] Total imports are therefore the sum of 'structural' imports MD plus a positive component representing the spillover from the domestic goods market $(M(YD/YT) \geq 0)$. Despite the shortage of domestic goods, we still assume that the demand for consumption goods is not rationed $(CT = CD)$. Implicitly, this means that the shortage of production capacities is fully compensated by a combination of increased imports, higher factor utilization rates (overtime working, for example) and inventory decumulation, although the latter effects are not explicitly modelled here. (Pure rationing could also appear in the form of delivery lags; it seemed wiser not to overemphasize their role in an annual macro-model.)

The wage equation remains unchanged. The price equation includes a positive effect of demand pressure on the mark-up rate. This asymmetric treatment of excess demand versus excess supply amounts to assuming that prices are more flexible upwards than downwards.

Again, the properties of the real part of the model are well known. Output and employment are determined by production capacities—which in turn depend upon available physical capital and real wages. Demand management does not affect output and employment except via investment. Real wages affect employment via capital–labour substitution and investment levels.

Demand pressures affect prices, which are assumed flexible upwards. Accordingly, there are now two sources of inflation: cost-push and demand-pull. With excess demand for output, demand-pull introduces a systematic inflationary bias. Price stability accordingly requires an offsetting trend in costs. The rate of classical unemployment introduces a downward bias in wages, to be considered jointly with the income claims.

In this framework, the NIRU is a meaningless concept, but one can define a 'non-inflationary rate of excess demand', or NIRED, to express conveniently the single endogenous influence on prices and wages.

The properties of the perfect-foresight stationary classical unemployment equilibrium are derived in exactly the same fashion as for the Keynesian regime. In this case, however, the unemployment rate is fully determined by production capacities. At given technical coefficients, this unemployment rate measures the capital gap' (CG), i.e. the shortage of production capacities relatively to the capacity required to eliminate unemployment:

$$CG = \frac{LS - L(YP)}{LS} = 1 - \frac{L(YP)}{LS}.$$

From the price and wage equations we obtain, respectively,

(8) $A^{-1}\dfrac{W}{P} = 1 - \pi_0 - \pi_1 \ln \dfrac{YD}{YT} - \kappa_0$

and

(9) $A^{-1}\dfrac{W}{P} = \omega_0 - \omega_1 CG.$

Combining these two results and solving for the rate of excess demand, $RED = (YD - YT)/YT \simeq \ln YD/YT$, yields the 'non-inflationary rate of excess demand':

(10) $NIRED = \dfrac{1}{\pi_1}(\omega_1 CG - DG)$.

It is a positive function of the capital gap (owing to the negative effect of CG on wage claims) and a negative function of the distributive gap $DG = (\pi_0 + \kappa_0 + \omega_0 - 1)$. Inflation will develop if and only if $RED > NIRED$. This can be avoided by adequate demand management policies. The RED thus becomes the relevant policy indicator in the classical regime, a role played by UR in a Keynesian regime.

The stationary classical unemployment equilibrium described by (10) will of course obtain if and only if $NIRED \geq 0$ and $CG \geq 0$. Given (7), the first condition can also be recast as $CG \geq NIRU$. There is otherwise no stationary classical unemployment equilibrium.

Repressed inflation. The relevant equations are similar to those of the classical regime, except for the production and employment levels, which are now constrained by the availability of labour rather than capital ($LT = LS$, $YT = Y(LS)$). Demand pressures are now positive on both the goods and the labour markets.

A stationary 'repressed inflation' equilibrium[5] will not exist unless the distributive gap DG and the capital gap CG are both negative. The first condition would imply weak income claims ($\omega_0 + \pi_0 + \kappa_0 < 1$); the second would imply a potential employment level larger than the supply of labour. If these two conditions are not satisfied, price adjustment will progressively lead to either Keynesian or classical unemployment, depending on the values of DG and CG.

Aggregation. We now abandon the fiction of an homogeneous economy in favour of an explicit aggregation over micro-markets. This procedure calls for specifying a joint frequency distribution over the demand for goods, the supply of labour and the availability of production capacities. Simple assumptions (see Lambert, 1984) lead to an employment equation where the aggregate employment level is a CES function of the aggregate concepts $L(YD)$, $L(YP)$ and LS used so far. This CES function thus replaces the usual 'min' condition. More formally, we have

(11) $LT = \{L(YD)^{-\rho} + L(YP)^{-\rho} + LS^{-\rho}\}^{-1/\rho}, \qquad \rho \geq 0$

where ρ is linked to the correlations between the values across micro-markets of the demand for goods, the availability of production capacities and the supply of labour. The lower the value of ρ, the lower the correlation between these values and thus the more important the mismatch between the distribution of these three quantities across micro-markets. Note that this simple formulation makes impossible the distinction between labour mismatch and capacity mismatch. Such a distinction would require the use of a different exponent for each aggregate variable appearing in (11).

We define as the 'structural unemployment rate at equilibrium' ($SURE$) the unemployment rate that would be observed in a situation of macroeconomic equilibrium, i.e. for $L(YD) = L(YP) = LS$. Given (11), one obtains

(12) $\quad SURE = \dfrac{LS - LT}{LS} = 1 - 3^{-1/\rho}.$

It is a negative function of ρ. For $\rho \to \infty$, $SURE \to 0$, structural imbalances disappear, and equation (11) boils down to the usual min condition.

An immediate implication of (11) is that the elasticities of employment with respect to $L(YD)$, $L(YP)$ and LS are all less than unity and correspond to the proportions of firms or micro-markets in each regime (denoted ϕ_K, ϕ_C and ϕ_I, respectively):

(13) $\quad \eta_{LT \cdot L(YD)} = \left\{ \dfrac{LT}{L(YD)} \right\}^{\rho} = \phi_K$

$\qquad \eta_{LT \cdot L(YP)} = \left\{ \dfrac{LT}{L(YP)} \right\}^{\rho} = \phi_C$

$\qquad \eta_{LT \cdot LS} = \left(\dfrac{LT}{LS} \right)^{\rho} = \phi_I.$

The elasticities of aggregate employment to the wage rate or to the demand for domestic goods will thus be a weighted average of the elasticities in each pure regime, with weights ϕ_K, ϕ_C and ϕ_I, respectively. With respect to the wage rate, we have

(14) $\quad \eta_{LT \cdot w} = \phi_K \eta_{L(YD) \cdot w} + \phi_C \eta_{L(YP) \cdot w} + \phi_I \eta_{LS \cdot w}.$
$\qquad\qquad\qquad +\qquad\qquad\quad -\qquad\qquad\quad ?$

As for the demand for domestic goods, we may reasonably assume that it has no short-term effect on production capacities or on labour supply. The elasticity of aggregate employment to YD is then simply

(15) $\quad \eta_{LT \cdot YD} = \phi_K \eta_{L(YD) \cdot YD}.$

Because all three regimes are simultaneously present, inflationary pressures are again a mixture of cost-push and demand-pull, as in the classical unemployment regime. The endogenous influences on wages and prices are now twofold, namely, unemployment UR (which moderates wages) and demand pressures RED. They operate against the background of income claims DG and classical unemployment CG. Price stability again requires that demand-pull inflationary pressures be exactly offset by cost-push deflationary pressures. The stationary equilibrium relationship between the rates of unemployment and excess demand is given by the wage and price equations. With perfect foresight we obtain—say from (10), written in terms of observed rates,

(16) $\quad UR = \dfrac{1}{\omega_1}(DG + \pi_1 RED).$

To determine the $NIRU$ and the $NIRED$, we need a second relationship between these two variables. It is given by the employment equation (11). The latter can be rewritten as

$$1 = \left\{ \dfrac{L(YD)}{LT} \right\}^{-\rho} + \left\{ \dfrac{L(YP)}{LS} \dfrac{LS}{LT} \right\}^{-\rho} + \left(\dfrac{LS}{LT} \right)^{-\rho}$$
$$= (1 + RED)^{-\rho} + (1 - CG)^{-\rho}(1 - UR)^{\rho} + (1 - UR)^{\rho}$$

where we use the definitions

$$CG = \frac{LS - L(YP)}{LS} \quad \text{and} \quad RED = \frac{YD - YT}{YT} = \frac{L(YD) - LT}{LT}$$

(with given technical coefficients and no labour hoarding). Simply rearranging the terms leads to

(17) $(1 - UR)^{\rho} = \dfrac{1 - (1 + RED)^{-\rho}}{1 + (1 - CG)^{-\rho}}.$

Equations (16) and (17) are reproduced in Figure 6. The positively sloped linear function PP' is (16), the negatively sloped nonlinear function LL' is (17). The effects of changes in the parameters DG, CG and ρ are indicated by dashed curves. When ρ decreases and goes to zero (growing mismatch), the negatively sloped curve becomes steeper and steeper; in the limit ($\rho = 0$), it becomes vertical at $UR = 1$. At the other end, when ρ goes to infinity, the curvature of the function increases until it becomes a right angle with vertex at CG on the horizontal axis. The employment equation (11) then boils down to the 'min' condition used in the previous subsections. The intersection of the functions depicted in Figure 6 determines the stationary equilibrium of the economy. The $NIRU$ is seen to be a positive function of the capital gap CG, of the distributive gap DG and of the degree of mismatch $(1/\rho)$. The $NIRED$ is positively affected by the capital gap and the degree of mismatch, negatively affected by the distributive gap. This is summarized in Table 6.

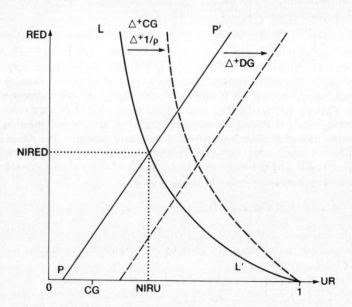

FIGURE 6. Determination of the stationary equilibrium (equations (16) and (17)).

TABLE 6
EFFECTS OF INCREASES IN DG, CG AND $(1/\rho)$ ON THE
UNEMPLOYMENT AND EXCESS DEMAND RATES AND ON
REGIME PROPORTIONS

	UR	RED	ϕ_K	ϕ_C	ϕ_I
Distributive gap (DG)	+	−	+	−	−
Capital gap (CG)	+	+	−	+	−
Mismatch $(1/\rho)$	+	+	0	0	0

The table also indicates the effects of DG, CG and $1/\rho$ on the proportion of firms in each regime. The signs of these effects follow from the definitions of ϕ_K, ϕ_C and ϕ_I given in (13):

$$\phi_K = \left\{ \frac{L(YD)}{LT} \right\}^{-1/\rho} = (1 + RED)^{-\rho}$$

$$\phi_C = \left\{ \frac{L(YP)}{LT} \right\}^{-1/\rho} = (1 - UR)(1 - CG)^{-\rho}$$

$$\phi_I = \left\{ \frac{LS}{LT} \right\}^{-1/\rho} = (1 - UR)^{\rho}$$

with $\phi_K + \phi_C + \phi_I = 1$.

The LL' and PP' curves depicted in Figure 6 only describe stationary equilibrium conditions. In the very short run, the economy can be off these two curves and in either one of the four regions they delineate. The slow adjustment of labour to its equilibrium value (the so-called labour hoarding phenomenon) is responsible for deviations from LL'; the sluggishness of wage and price expectations or adjustments is responsible for deviations from PP'. The rate of change of employment is positive above LL', negative below; the rate of inflation is positive (or more generally larger than its expected value) above PP' and negative below. Traditional fix-price models completely disregard the PP' curve and proceed as if any point on LL' could be reached by adequate demand management policies. This amounts to assuming that, in the very short run, wage-price stickiness enables demand management policies to produce any desired deviation from PP'.

IV. EMPIRICAL RESULTS

We have six equations to estimate: the two technical relationships (2), the consumption function, the import and employment equations, the wage and price equations. Ideally, one would like to estimate all these equations jointly by $FIML$, in order to take account in an efficient way of simultaneity and of the many cross-equation restrictions. Because of the strong nonlinearities involved and of the danger of not being able to control effectively an iterative optimization procedure involving all the parameters at once, we used instead a sequential block-by-block limited information procedure. This means (1) joint *ML* estimation of the two technical relationships; (2) OLS estimation of the consumption function; (3) joint *ML* estimation of the import and employment equations (this joint estimation is motivated by the presence in both equations of the unobserved variable *YD*, the demand for domestic goods defined as (observed) total final demand minus (unobserved) structural imports—see p. S100 above; (4) instrumental variable estimation of the wage and price equations.

This sequential estimation procedure implies that the values of the technical coefficients *A* and *B* used in estimating the employment and the price equations are those obtained in step (1) from the estimation of the technical relationships. Similarly, the values of the excess demand indicator ln $YD/YT^* \simeq RED$ used in estimating the price equation are the values previously derived from the estimation of the import and employment equations. The results of this sequential estimation procedure are reproduced in Table 7. We first discuss each equation separately; these comments are numbered (1)–(16), and those that are specific to our approach are italicized. We then turn to the implied values of the *NIRU* and *NIRED*.

Technical coefficients (equations (1) and (2))

1. The *observed* productivities of labour and capital are not in general equal to the *technical* productivities. This discrepancy is taken into account by using two indicators of factor utilization, *DUL* and *DUC*. The former is based on partial unemployment figures, the latter on business surveys in the manufacturing sector. The values of the coefficients of these variables should not be given too much economic significance, except to note that a coefficient of *DUC* smaller than unity may indicate that the fluctuations in the rate of capital utilization as reported by firms in the manufacturing sector overestimate the fluctuations at the aggregate level.

2. The coefficients of the trend variables t and t' indicate that the rate of exogenous technical progress has decreased from 2·2 per cent before 1974 to 0·9 per cent afterwards.

3. The values of the relative factor costs lag polynomial function were generated recursively, according to

$$\left\{\Theta(\Lambda)\ln\frac{W}{V}\right\}_t \equiv \frac{1-\theta}{1-\theta\Lambda}\ln\left(\frac{W}{V}\right)_t$$

$$\equiv (1-\theta)\ln\left(\frac{W}{V}\right)_t + \theta\left\{\Theta(\Lambda)\ln\frac{W}{V}\right\}_{t-1}.$$

The starting value $\{\Theta(\Lambda)\ln W/V\}_{t=0}$ was set at 5·45, close to the 1953 value of ln W/V. This restriction was not rejected by a *LR* test. A value of θ equal to 0·73 means that only 27 per cent of the change in the optimal technical coefficients *A* and *B* implied by a change in relative factor costs is realized within a year.

4. In all this, we assumed the capital usage cost *V* to be proportional to the price of investment goods *PI*, which amounts to assuming, *inter alia*, a constant long-term real interest rate. More elaborate specifications, based on the observed nominal interest rate minus a weighted average of current and past inflation rates, proved unsuccessful.

Consumption function (equation (3))

5. We postulate a constant elasticity of private consumption CT to household disposable income DI. The static specification is written as

$$(18) \qquad CT = e^{c_0 + c_1 UR}(DI^e)^{c_2}$$

where DI^e stands for expected disposable income and coefficient c_1 allows for an effect of unemployment on consumption. The dynamic specification is in the form of an error correction mechanism. Simple rearrangements of (18)

TABLE 7

ESTIMATED EQUATIONS

(Standard errors in parentheses; estimated variables denoted $\tilde{\ }$)

(1) $\quad \ln \dfrac{YT}{LT} = 2\cdot58 + 0\cdot022t - 0\cdot013t' + 0\cdot55 \dfrac{0\cdot27}{1 - 0\cdot73\Lambda} \ln \dfrac{W}{PI} + 0\cdot06 \ln DUL$

$\qquad\qquad (0\cdot27)\,(0\cdot002)\ \ (0\cdot001)\ \ (0\cdot05) \qquad\qquad\qquad\qquad (0\cdot04)$

$\qquad\qquad$ s.e.e. $= 0\cdot0075 \qquad\qquad DW = 2\cdot00 \qquad\qquad$ sample $= 1954\text{–}82$

(2) $\quad \ln \dfrac{YT}{KA} = 1\cdot55 + 0\cdot022t - 0\cdot013t' - 0\cdot45 \dfrac{0\cdot27}{1 - 0\cdot73\Lambda} \ln \dfrac{W}{PI} + 0\cdot25 \ln DUC$

$\qquad\qquad (0\cdot27)\,(0\cdot002)\ \ (0\cdot001)\ \ (0\cdot05) \qquad\qquad\qquad\qquad (0\cdot06)$

$\qquad\qquad$ s.e.e. $= 0\cdot0149 \qquad\qquad DW = 2\cdot00 \qquad\qquad$ sample $= 1964\text{–}82$

Notes to equations (1) *and* (2): Correlation between the residuals of equations (1) and (2): $0\cdot71$

$\qquad t' = 0$ before 1974 $(t = 22)$, $t' = t - 22$ afterwards

(3) $\quad \Delta \ln CT = 0\cdot28 + 0\cdot22 UR - 0\cdot76 \Delta UR + 0\cdot013 \Delta \ln PC$

$\qquad\qquad\quad (0\cdot15)\,(0\cdot17) \qquad (0\cdot30) \qquad\quad (0\cdot10)$

$\qquad\qquad\qquad + 0\cdot46\Delta \ln DI + 0\cdot42 \ln DI_{-1} - 0\cdot47 \ln CT_{-1}$

$\qquad\qquad\qquad\quad (0\cdot14) \qquad\qquad (0\cdot13) \qquad\quad 0\cdot15)$

$\qquad\qquad$ s.e.e. $= 0\cdot0087 \qquad\qquad DW = 2\cdot00 \qquad\qquad$ sample $= 1954\text{–}82$

(4) $\quad \ln MT = -2\cdot08 + 1\cdot14 \ln FD - 0\cdot28 \ln PM^* + 0\cdot69 \ln PF^* + 1\cdot79 \ln \dfrac{\widetilde{YD}}{YT^*}$

$\qquad\qquad\quad (0\cdot0008)\,(0\cdot00004)\ (0\cdot01) \qquad\quad (0\cdot0002) \qquad (0\cdot24)$

$\qquad\qquad$ s.e.e. $= 0\cdot0173 \qquad\qquad DW = 2\cdot13 \qquad\qquad$ sample $= 1955\text{–}82$

where $\ln PM^* \equiv (0\cdot70 + 0\cdot20 \Lambda + 0\cdot10 \Lambda^2) \ln PM$

$\qquad\quad \ln PF^* \equiv (0\cdot15 + 0\cdot25 \Lambda + 0\cdot60 \Lambda^2) \ln PF$

(5) $\quad LT = \{L(YD)^{-\rho} + L(YP)^{-\rho} + LS^{-\rho}\}^{-1/\rho}$

$\qquad\quad \ln L(YD) \equiv 0\cdot014 + 0\cdot73\{-\ln \tilde{A} + (0\cdot96 \ln YD + 0\cdot04 \ln \widetilde{YP})\} + 0\cdot27 \ln LT_{-1}$

$\qquad\qquad\quad (0\cdot004)\,(0\cdot01) \qquad\qquad (0\cdot05) \qquad\quad (0\cdot05) \qquad\qquad (0\cdot01)$

$\qquad\quad \ln L(YP) \equiv 0\cdot023 + 0\cdot73(-\ln \tilde{A} + \ln \widetilde{YP}) + 0\cdot27 \ln LT_{-1}$

$\qquad\qquad\quad (0\cdot000)\,(0\cdot01) \qquad\qquad (0\cdot01)$

$\qquad\quad LS \equiv LT + U$

$\qquad\quad \rho \equiv (0\cdot0065 + 0\cdot0012t)^{-1}$

$\qquad\qquad\quad (0\cdot001)\ \ (0\cdot000005)$

$\qquad\qquad$ s.e.e. $= 0\cdot004 \qquad\qquad DW = 2\cdot28 \qquad\qquad$ sample $= 1955\text{–}82$

TABLE 7—continued

(6) $\Delta \ln W = 1\cdot31 \, \Delta \ln P - 0\cdot004 - 0\cdot11 \, UR$
     $\quad\quad\quad (0\cdot22) \quad\quad (0\cdot13) \; (0\cdot50)$

$$+0\cdot55 \, \Delta \ln \frac{YT}{LT} + 0\cdot04 \left\{ \ln \left(\frac{YT}{LT} \right)_{-1} - \ln \left(\frac{W}{P} \right)_{-1} \right\}$$

$\quad\quad\quad\quad (0\cdot30) \quad\quad\quad\quad (0\cdot27)$

s.e.e. $= 0\cdot0126$ $\quad\quad\quad DW = 1\cdot70$ $\quad\quad\quad$ sample $= 1956\text{-}82$

(6') $\Delta \ln WN = 0\cdot91 \, \Delta \ln PC - 0\cdot092 - 0\cdot43 \, UR$
     $\quad\quad\quad\;\; (0\cdot17) \quad\quad\quad\;\; (0\cdot095)\,(0\cdot15)$

$$+0\cdot48 \, \Delta \ln \frac{YT}{LT} + 0\cdot17 \left\{ \ln \left(\frac{YT}{LT} \right)_{-1} - \ln \left(\frac{WN}{PC} \right)_{-1} \right\}$$

$\quad\quad (0\cdot25) \quad\quad\quad\quad (0\cdot15)$

s.e.e. $= 0\cdot0166$ $\quad\quad\quad DW = 2\cdot01$ $\quad\quad\quad$ sample $= 1956\text{-}82$

Instruments: $t, t', DUL, DUC, \ln \left(\dfrac{\widetilde{YD}}{YT^*} \right)_{-1}, \Delta \ln \left(\dfrac{YT}{LT} \right)_{-1}, \left(\dfrac{0\cdot27}{1-0\cdot73 \, \Lambda} \ln \dfrac{W}{PI} \right)_{-1}$

(7) $\Delta \ln P = 0\cdot038 + 1\cdot04 \ln \left(\dfrac{\widetilde{YD}}{YT^*} \right) - 0\cdot54 \, \Delta \ln \left(\dfrac{\widetilde{YD}}{YT^*} \right)$
     $\quad\quad\;\; (0\cdot064)\,(0\cdot50) \quad\quad\quad\quad (0\cdot33)$

$$+0\cdot63 \, \Delta \ln APC - 0\cdot27 \, \Delta^2 \ln APC + 0\cdot41 (\ln APC_{-1} - \ln P_{-1})$$

$\quad\quad (0\cdot17) \quad\quad\quad\quad (0\cdot16) \quad\quad\quad\quad 0\cdot28)$

s.e.e. $= 0\cdot010$ $\quad\quad\quad DW = 1\cdot70$ $\quad\quad\quad$ sample $= 1956\text{-}82$

$APC \equiv (\tilde{A}^{-1} W + \tilde{B}^{-1} 0\cdot20 \, PI)$
$\quad\quad\quad\quad (0\cdot06)$

Instruments: $t, t', DUL, DUC, \ln \left(\dfrac{\widetilde{YD}}{YT^*} \right)_{-1}, \ln \left(\dfrac{YT}{LT} \right)_{-1}, \left(\dfrac{0\cdot27}{1-0\cdot73\Lambda} \ln \dfrac{W}{PI} \right)_{-1}, \Delta \ln P_{-1}$

lead to

(19) $\Delta \ln CT = c_1 UR + c_2 \, \Delta \ln DI^e + (c_0 + c_2 \ln DI_{-1} - \ln CT_{-1}).$

In words a change in CT may result from an abnormal unemployment rate, from an expected change in disposable income, or from a previous discrepancy between desired and realized values. Let us now assume that only a fraction $\delta_2 \leqslant 1$ of such a discrepancy is corrected in the subsequent period. Let us furthermore define $\Delta \ln DI^e$ as $(\delta_0 \Delta \ln DI + \delta_1 \Delta \ln DI_{-1})$ and generalize $c_1 UR$ to $(c_{10} UR + c_{11} UR_{-1})$. Equation (19) then becomes

(20) $\Delta \ln CT = c_0 \delta_2 + (c_{10} + c_{11}) UR - c_{11} \Delta UR$

$\quad\quad\quad + c_2 (\delta_0 + \delta_1) \Delta \ln DI - c_1 \delta_1 \Delta^2 \ln DI$

$\quad\quad\quad + \delta_2 (c_2 \ln DI_{-1} - \ln CT_{-1})$

6. With δ_1 set equal to zero. OLS stimation of (20) yields an elasticity of aggregate consumption to disposable income of $c_2 = 0\cdot90$ in the long run and $\delta_0 c_2 = 0\cdot46$ in the short run. The interpretation of the unemployment rate effect is unclear; the effect appears strongly negative in the short run, but positive in the long run. When added as an explanatory variable, the inflation rate appears insignificant.

Imports (equation (4))

7. The structural demand for imports *MD* (excluding energy, which is left exogenous) is specified as a log-linear function of total final demand (less public consumption and energy imports)*FD*, import prices *PM* and domestic prices *PF*. That is,

$$\ln \widetilde{MD} \underset{\text{def}}{=} -2\cdot08 + 1\cdot14 \ln FD - 0\cdot28 \ln PM^* + 0\cdot69 \ln PF^*.$$

8. *As there are always some domestic 'micro-markets' in excess demand, observed imports will always be larger than or equal to the structural demand MD. The discrepancy between the two is a function of the importance of domestic production shortages, measured by* $\ln YD/YT^* \simeq RED \geqslant 0$, *where YT* is the production level that could be reached with currently available inputs and a normal input utilization rate, after correction for the hoarding of labour.*

9. The dynamics of the price effects turned out to be poorly defined. The weights given to past and current values were fixed at what seemed to be reasonable values in view of the unconstrained estimation results. These restrictions decrease the log-likelihood from 175 to 171 but leave the other parameter estimates basically unchanged. The elasticity of imports to final demand prices is (in absolute value) about twice their elasticity to import prices themselves. The bundles of goods involved are perhaps different; or changes in *PM* may have repercussions on *PF*, so that their impact is split among the two variables.

10. *The elasticity of imports to total final demand is not very far from unity and substantially below that obtained with traditional methods, i.e. when demand pressure effects are not modelled explicitly but are simply replaced by a term (most often insignificant) involving the degree of capacity utilization. The demand pressure coefficient is here significant and implies that a 1 percentage point increase in the excess demand for domestic goods increases imports by 1·79 per cent. With imports representing about 50 per cent of GDP in the 1970s, about 90 per cent of any excess demand for goods is immediately compensated by additional imports.*

Figure 7 reproduces the ratio of total imports to structural imports (MT/MD) and of domestic demand to normal domestic supply—given available inputs— (YD/YT*) from 1955 to 1982. These two demand pressure indicators are always larger than one, thereby indicating that there always subsists a certain proportion of firms in the classical and inflation regimes which are constrained by capacity and labour shortages respectively rather than sales. That proportion, however, becomes especially weak in 1958 and after 1980, when the proportion of firms in the Keynesian regime becomes more important (77 per cent in 1982).

Employment equation (equation (5))

11. The employment equation has the form suggested in (11). Variable $\tilde{A}$ is the technical productivity of labour as estimated from equation (1). That is,

$$\ln \tilde{A} \underset{\text{def}}{=} 2\cdot58 + 0\cdot022t - 0\cdot013t' + 0\cdot55\Theta(\Lambda) \ln \frac{W}{V}.$$

The potential and past employment levels appearing in the Keynesian labour demand function *L*(*YD*) represent the effects of adjustment costs and the ensuing hoarding of labour during recessions. The interpretation of LT_{-1} in

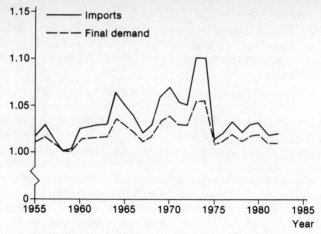

FIGURE 7.   Indicators of tension in the Belgian economy, 1955–82: imports (MT/MD) and final
demand (YD/ YT*).

$L(YP)$ is similar. *The short-run elasticity of the Keynesian demand for labour*
$L(YD)$ *to demand for domestic goods is estimated at*

$$\frac{\partial \ln L(YD)}{\partial \ln YD} = (0\cdot96)(0\cdot73) = 0\cdot70.$$

*The short-run elasticity of actual employment can be substantially lower and
depends on the proportion of firms in the Keynesian regime* ϕ_K:

$$\frac{\partial \ln YT}{\partial \ln YD} = \phi_K \frac{\partial \ln L(YD)}{\partial \ln YD}.$$

A typical value of ϕ_K *is* $0\cdot55$, *which would imply a short-run elasticity equal to* $0\cdot39$.

12. *The mismatch parameter* ρ *is represented as an inverse linear function
of time. The values of* ρ_0 *and* ρ_1 *indicate a regular and significant increase in
structural imbalances. As a consequence, the structural unemployment rate at
equilibrium* ($SURE$) *has risen from* $1\cdot39$ *per cent in 1955 to* $4\cdot5$ *per cent in 1982.*

13. *The values of the Keynesian labour demand LK and of the potential
employment level LP are reproduced in Figure 4. They are obtained from* $L(YD)$
and $L(YP)$, *respectively, after deduction of the labour hoarding effect (no lagged
employment effect). Both series remained fairly close to the supply of labour LS
throughout the 1960s and early 1970s. In 1975 the Keynesian demand for labour
collapsed; it has never recovered since. After 1975, the decline in the investment
rate (see Figure 5) caused the stagnation, and then the decline of potential
employment. In 1982 the capital gap (i.e. the discrepancy between the supply of
labour and the potential employment level in percentage points) reached about
9 per cent.*

14. The dramatic fall in the Keynesian demand for labour in 1975 resulted
mainly from the collapse of the demand for domestic goods, enhanced by the
effects of productivity gains (see Table 8). The change in the demand for
domestic goods was itself the result of a similar change in total final demand

TABLE 8

ANALYSIS OF THE CHANGES IN THE KEYNESIAN DEMAND FOR LABOUR
AND ITS DETERMINANTS AFTER 1975
(PERCENTAGE POINTS)

	1975	1976	1981	1982
Growth in Keynesian demand for labour	−8·0	+0·7	−3·0	−1·8
of which: wages	−2·8	−3·3	−2·4	−2·2
demand for domestic goods	−5·2	+4·0	−0·6	+0·4
Growth in final demand	−4·4	+7·3	−1·3	+1·2
of which: consumption	+1·2	+4·9	−0·1	+1·3
government spending	+4·8	+3·9	+1·2	−1·5
investment:				
fixed capital	−2·1	+2·8	−16·4	−0·8
total investment	−14·1	+7·1	−17·0	−1·5
exports	−9·4	+11·8	+3·3	+3·4
Growth in imports demand	−2·8	+15·4	−1·1	+3·2
of which: final demand	−7·0	+9·3	−1·9	+1·9
prices	+4·2	+6·1	+0·8	+1·3

arising from lower investments and lower exports. By 1976 investments and exports had both recovered, and they produced a strong increase of total final demand. The rise in the demand for domestic goods turned out to be much weaker, however, while the demand for imports rose strongly, with 40 per cent of the increase owing to a significant loss of competitiveness. The years 1981–82 witnessed again an important decrease in investment. This time, however, exports remained steady and there was no additional loss of competitiveness.

Wage equation (equations (6)-(6'))

15. The dynamic structure of the wage equation is similar to that of the consumption function (see above). The wage equation can be written in terms of either labour costs or net labour income per employee. In the former case, the dependent variable is defined as the wage cost per employee, including employers' social security contributions, and the relevant price index is the price of value added. In the latter case, the dependent variable is the net wage rate, after deduction for direct taxes and employees' social security contributions, and the relevant price index is the price of consumption goods. In both cases the observed productivity of labour proved to have a larger explanatory power than the technical concept derived from equation (1). The sign of the unemployment rate coefficient is negative, as expected, albeit not significantly different from zero in the labour cost formulation. In the latter case, also, the coefficient of the inflation rate at 1·31 is larger than (although not significantly different from) unity. This is the sort of result one would expect in the face of an oil shock with wage demands indexed on the price of consumption goods rather than the price of value added. From the estimates of equation (6) and (6'), one can retrieve the values of ω_0 and ω_1 mentioned in Tables 4 and 5. One obtains from (6) $\hat{\omega}_0 = 0·90$, $\hat{\omega}_1 = 0·11$ and from equation (6') $\hat{\omega}_0 = 0·58$, $\hat{\omega}_1 = 0·43$. One must be aware however, of the extremely poor precision of these estimates. Further work is obviously needed on this point.

Price equation (equation (7))

16. The dynamic structure is again similar to that of the consumption function. The specification imposes that, in the long run, cost increases are fully passed on to prices. This restriction is not rejected by the data. When freely estimated, the long-run elasticity of prices to average production costs turns out to be 0·97 and not significantly different from unity. The capital usage cost is approximated by a constant α times the price index of investment goods, PI. This amounts to assuming that the sum of the depreciation and real interest rates (corrected for taxation) remains constant at α. The latter is estimated at 0·20. It follows that $\hat{\kappa}_0 \simeq \hat{\alpha}(KA/YP) \simeq 0\cdot4$. One notices the strong and significant demand pressure effect, implying that the mark-up on costs increases by one percentage point for every 1 per cent increase in excess demand. The constant term and the error correction coefficient imply a normal mark-up rate equal to $\hat{\pi}_0 = 0\cdot038/0\cdot4 = 9\cdot5$ per cent, which seems quite reasonable (but again is subject to a high standard error).

Estimates of the NIRU and NIRED

The 1973, 1975 and 1982 estimated values of the $NIRU$ and the $NIRED$ are reproduced in Table 9. Each of these three years corresponds to a turning point in the economic developments between 1970 and 1985. 1973 is the last year with rapid growth and one-digit inflation; 1975 coincides with the trough of the recession consecutive to the first oil shock; 1982, the last year covered by our data, is also the starting point of a strict incomes policy.

The values of the capital gap CG and of the mismatch parameter ρ used to compute the $NIRU$ and the $NIRED$ and reported in Table 9 are those obtained from the estimation of the econometric model. This is not the case however for the values of the distributive gap DG. The extremely poor precision of the parameter estimates underlying DG (especially ω_0 and κ_0), and the crude specification whereby ω_0 and π_0 are constant through time, call for the use of extraneous information. It seemed reasonable to us to assume a widening of the distributive gap from 0 per cent in 1973 to 4 per cent in 1975, as a result of the first oil shock. The distributive gap may have been reduced towards zero again in 1982 as a result of the strict incomes policy.

From Table 9, we draw the following conclusions.

1. The estimated decline in ρ (an inverse function of time, as an approximation) entails a growing mismatch (whether due to the labour market or to the production facilities and product mix), and hence a steadily growing 'structural unemployment rate at equilibrium' ($SURE$).
2. The assumption made about the distributive gap is very important: the difference in the estimated value of the $NIRU$ is 5·1 per cent in 1975 and 2·6 per cent in 1982. If $DG = 4$ per cent is indeed more plausible for 1975 and $DG = 0$ is more plausible for 1982, one would estimate that the $NIRU$ has not changed much between 1975 and 1982, remaining at the embarrassing level of 10–11 per cent.
3. The factors behind the $NIRU$ in 1974–75 and in 1982 are quite different. The main difference comes from the 'capital gap'—the insufficient number of working posts—which accounts for 4·7 percentage points in the 1982 estimate of the $NIRU$ ($10\cdot8 - 6\cdot1 = 4\cdot7$). The observed level of unemploy-

TABLE 9

ESTIMATES OF THE NON-INFLATIONARY UNEMPLOYMENT RATE (*NIRU*) AND NON-INFLATIONARY RATE OF EXCESS DEMAND (*NIRED*).

	Distributive gap, *DG* (%)	Capital gap, *CG* (%)	Mismatch *ρ*	Equilibrium structural unemployment rate, *SURE* (%)	Non-inflationary unemployment rate, *NIRU* (%)	Non-inflationary rate of excess demand, *NIRED* (%)	Unemployment rate, *UR* (%)	Rate of excess demand, *RED* (%)
1973	0·00	−0·41	31·8	3·4	4·5	1·9	3·8	5·6
1975	4·00	0·30	29·6	3·6	10·1	0·3	7·5	0·8
Variant	*0·00*	0·30	29·6	3·6	5·0	2·1		
1982	0·00	8·77	23·8	4·5	10·8	4·5	16·0	1·0
Variant 1	0·00	*0·00*	23·8	4·5	6·1	2·5		
Variant 2	4·00	8·77	23·8	4·5	13·4	1·7		

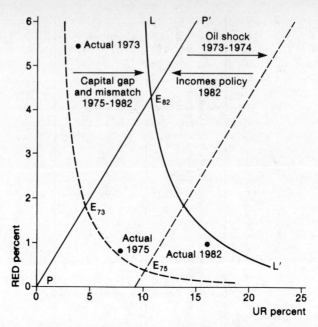

FIGURE 8.   Actual and non-inflationary values of *UR* and *RED* in Belgium, 1973, 1975 and 1982.

ment for 1982 could be decomposed as follows:

	(%)
Total unemployment	16·0
due to: the capital gap	4·7
structural mismatch	4·5
need to offset potential demand pressures	1·6
insufficient demand	5·2

An important conclusion is that *stronger demand could reduce unemployment* (in 1982) *by 5 per cent without inflationary pressure*, so long as the 'distributive gap' *DG* remains close to zero. Another important conclusion is that *creation of additional capacity* (*to eliminate the capital gap*) *and better adjustment of supply to demand* (*to eliminate structural mismatch*) *would be needed to reduce unemployment* (*and the NIRU*) *below 11 per cent*.

The results of Table 9 are portrayed in Figure 8. The figure reproduces the positions in 1973, 1975 and 1982 of the two curves *LL'* and *PP'*, the intersection of which determines the *NIRU* and the *NIRED*. The 1982 curves are represented by continuous lines. The points E_{73}, E_{75} and E_{82} describe the values of the *NIRU* and the *NIRED* in 1973, 1975 and 1982, respectively.

V. CONCLUDING REMARKS

We embarked on this confession with the modest aims of (1) seeking an explanation for the differential rate of growth of Belgian real wages in the

1970s; (2) seeking an explanation for the dramatic decline in employment and increase in gross apparent labour productivity of the Belgian manufacturing sector over the past decade; and (3) summarizing what we had learned from the estimation of quantity rationing models.

On the first point, we note that our price and wage equations, crude as their specification may be, track the sample data quite accurately without revealing residual anomalies in the 1970s. At the same time, several coefficients of these equations are estimated with low precision. The equations reflect the interdependence of prices, wages, productivity and employment; caution is needed in drawing conclusions about causal or dynamic structures.

Are the mechanisms of price and wage formation in Belgium apt to create an inflationary spiral? The *estimation* of our equation for the price of value added yields a unitary long-run elasticity to average production costs, and a unitary short-run elasticity to demand pressures. The *estimation* of our wage equation suggest a short-run elasticity of nominal wage costs to prices (of either value added or consumption) close to, and possibly exceeding, unity. Also, the *specification* of our wage equation imposes a unitary long-run elasticity to gross average productivity, which itself is positively related to real wages. In such a model, exogenous inflationary pressures through wages (an oil shock, with full indexation of wages on consumption prices) or prices (a temporarily excessive level of final demand) may easily result in an inflationary spiral. The record of the 1970s confirms that danger, and suggests an alarming sensitivity of the Belgian economy to inflationary tendencies. The manufacturing sector, with its heavy dependence on export sales, bears the brunt of that sensitivity.

On the second and third questions, we reach parallel conclusions: *it is difficult to separate out the respective influences of factor prices (real wages) and effective demand in accounting for the inadequate performance of Belgian employment since 1974. The only safe conclusion is that both aspects matter.*

Looking at history through the filter of quantity rationing models, we feel that the concepts of 'potential employment' and 'Keynesian labour demand' provide a convincing (to us) interpretation, which is still grossly incomplete. These concepts are helpful to portray the supply side and demand side of the economy. It seems definitely useful to evaluate by how much output and employment could be boosted without either additional investment or the high rates of capacity utilization suspected of 'rekindling inflation'. Expressing these evaluations in terms of 'non-inflationary rates' of unemployment and excess demand is also helpful. As a corollary, one evaluates how many new working posts should be made available (through investment, additional shifts or work-sharing, in order of decreasing contributions to potential output) along the road to full employment to bridge the 'capital gap'. Hopefully, this combination of traditional and disequilibrium concepts may help bridge 'intellectual gap' as well.

At the same time, one must be careful not to interpret the spread between labour supply (or potential employment) and Keynesian labour demand as being 'due' to insufficient demand. In a country that exports more than one-third of its value added and competes with imports for another third, excess supply may simply reflect excessive, though non-increasing, costs—either marginal (quantity-setting firms) or average (price-setting firms). Thus, *a part of what is commonly labelled 'Keynesian unemployment' may well be the consequence of a real-wage problem.* And that part could be significant in Belgium.

Similarly, one must be careful not to interpret the spread between labour supply and potential employment as being 'due' to factor prices (real wages). When potential employment corresponds to full use of given facilities, and varies over time through scrapping and/or new investments, *one must reckon with the decisive influence of demand expectations on scrapping and investment decisions.* Then, *a part of what is commonly labelled 'classical unemployment' may well be the consequence of an effective demand problem*—and that part could be significant in Belgium.

We must accordingly conclude that an analysis of the employment problem which does not treat exports and investment endogenously is grossly inadequate. If, as suggested by Bauwens and d'Alcantara (1983), the elasticity of exports with respect to domestic production capacity is three times as high as the elasticity with respect to domestic wages, then a better understanding of the investment process deserves first priority on the research agenda. Given the complexity of the problem, it would seem imperative to rely on more disaggregated data, using all available sources of information.

There is an additional reason why such a research strategy commends itself. A number of authors have stressed the growing extent to which labour is now regarded as fixed factor—a remark that is particularly applicable to Europe, and even more so to Belgium. New hirings and new fixed investments are then best viewed as a joint decision, and should be analysed as such—even though the choice of techniques (factor proportions) deserves separate attention.

There is an element of paradox here, since the model of Section IV suggests instead a quite rapid adjustment of employment to desired levels, as if labour were in fact a variable factor. However, the 'investment' aspect of hiring decisions is much less significant in periods of growth (1963–74) than in periods of stagnation, or high uncertainty about future growth rates (today). Again, that aspect may affect less significantly layoffs (as in the period 1975–83) than new hirings (today?).

Needless to say, the care needed to interpret the result of our disequilibrium econometrics is equally appropriate when interpreting traditional concepts, like the *NIRU* (see in particular our comments about Table 9).

A related question left unanswered in this confession came up in the first part of Section III: Is the elasticity of employment with respect to real wages the same in case of wage increases and wage decreases? Or could it be that the relationship of employment to real wages is 'kinky', in a small open economy like Belgium, with a higher elasticity of employment to wage increases than to wage cuts? What prompts us to repeat this interrogation is the feeling that employment in the Belgian manufacturing sector is unlikely to grow, in response to the incomes policy of the 1980s, at a rate comparable to that at which it fell in response (partially at least) to the differential growth of real wages in the 1970s.

There is again an element of paradox here, since contractual and legal measures have attempted to protect labour from easy dismissals. These measures have clearly been of limited effectiveness in the manufacturing sector. One type of situation when they are bound to be ineffective is of course bankruptcy—a phenomenon of quantitative significance, as revealed above, but seldom modelled explicitly in econom(etr)ics. A realistic model of investment decisions should thus treat scrapping and new investment separately, and should consider financial constraints explicitly. A combination of traditional and disequilibrium concepts is also appropriate in that area.

ACKNOWLEDGMENTS

We wish to acknowledge gratefully the collaboration of Robert Leroy and Serge Wibaut in collecting and organizing data, of Fati Mehta in estimating the model of Section IV, and of Yves Leruth in preparing auxiliary computations. Responsibility for all the views expressed or omitted here is our own. We also acknowledge the financial support of the Belgian government under Projet d'Action Concertée, no. 80/85-12.

NOTES

1. Indeed, $70 \cdot 2 \times 0 \cdot 89 = 62 \cdot 5$. The figures in this paragraph come from Sonnet (1985).
2. For the sake of simplicity, we shall not make explicit the distinction between the repressed inflation and underconsumption regimes, although this distinction will be taken into account in estimation via the labour hoarding phenomenon.
3. We use the approximations $\omega_0(LD/LS)^{\omega_1} \simeq e^{\omega_0 - 1} e^{-\omega_1 UR} \simeq \omega_0 - \omega_1 UR$.
4. Notice however that, because of employment adjustment costs, the observed employment and production levels may also be influenced by past employment and production levels; i.e. LT and YT do not necessarily coincide exactly in the short run with the potential levels of LP and YP defined earlier.
5. The now well-established terminology 'repressed inflation' may seem inappropriate in our case, as all three regimes can actually witness inflation or deflation, depending on the values of the parameters and of starting conditions. We use it only to mean 'generalized excess demand'.

REFERENCES

BAUWENS, L. and D'ALCANTARA, G. (1983). An export model for the Belgian industry. *European Economic Review*, 22, 265–76.

D'ALCANTARA, G. (1983). *SERENA: A Macroeconomic Sectoral Regional and National Accounting Econometric Model for the Belgian Economy.* Leuven: Katholieke Universiteit Leuven.

EUROPEAN ECONOMY (1984). *Annual Economic Report 1984–85.* Strasbourg: EEC.

GÉRARD, M. and VANDEN BERGHE, C. (1984). Econometric analysis of sectoral investment in Belgium (1956–1982). *Recherches Economiques de Louvain*, 50, 89–118.

LAMBERT, J. P. (1984). *Disequilibrium macro-models based on business survey data: Theory and estimation for the Belgian manufacturing sector.* Unpublished doctoral dissertation, Louvain-la-Neuve, Université Catholique de Louvain; to be published by Cambridge University Press.

LEROY, R. (1962). *Signification du Chômage Belge.* Brussels: Office Belge Pour l'Accroissement de la Productivité.

MALINVAUD, E. (1980). Macroeconomic rationing of employment. In E. Malinvaud and J. P. Fitoussi (eds), *Unemployment in Western Countries.* London: MacMillan.

—— (1982). Wages and unemployment. *Economic Journal*, 92, 1–12.

MUELLBAUER, J. (1978). Macrotheory vs. macroeconometrics: the treatment of disequilibrium in macromodels. Discussion Paper no. 59, Birkbeck College, London.

SNEESSENS, H. (1981). *Theory and Estimation of Macroeconomic Rationing Models.* Berlin: Springer-Verlag.

—— (1983). A macroeconomic rationing model of the Belgian economy. *European Economic Review*, 20, 193–215.

SONNET, A. (1985). Valeur ajoutée, contenu en emplois et en travail. *Service de Conjoncture.* Louvain-la-Neuve: IRES.

Keynesian AD   Classical supply side.

Layard imperfectly competitive mkts
         where supply & demand side
                    policies are imp.

      natural rate of U.

      firms demand for labour will
      depend on bth the real product
         wage & the real level of AD

                        ↓

                  see Dawson - for
                       Notru.

         p146

Compromises bth the demand &
         Supply influences affecting U&
      inflation

Unemployment in Britain

By Richard Layard and Stephen Nickell

The London School of Economics, and Oxford University

Male unemployment in Britain has risen from around 2 per cent in the 1950s to around 17 per cent in 1985 (see Figure 1). (The figures are for male unemployment because there is no consistent series for women.[1]) Even more remarkably, unemployment has fallen in only three years out of the last twenty (1973, 1978 and 1979).

To account for this, we need a model that explains both changes in the natural (or non-accelerating inflation) rate of unemployment (NAIRU) and deviations from it. We use a three-equation supply-side model, centred on the labour market. This has two main features. The first concerns the determination of employment in the short run. The labour demand function that we use cuts through the fruitless debate now raging (especially in Europe) as to whether current unemployment is 'classical' or 'Keynesian'. According to the 'classical' view, employment is too high because real wages are too high. According to the 'Keynesian' view, real wages are not binding, and unemployment is high because the product market does not clear—with prices too high relative to nominal demand. The whole debate is set in the framework of perfect competition. Yet in perfect competition prices are set by impersonal forces, and it is not clear what could possibly stop prices clearing the market. It is much more reasonable to think of prices as being set by imperfectly competitive firms, existing prices being the best they can think of, given the demand they face. In this context, firms' demand for labour will depend on both the real product wage and the level of real aggregate demand. This is the demand function we estimate, and it conforms both to common sense and to the data.

However, this does not imply that employment can be made to grow without limit by pumping up real demand. For in the medium term, when price surprises are eliminated, our model determines three variables (employment, real wages and real demand) on the basis of three equations (an employment equation, a price equation and a wage equation). Thus in the medium term there is a 'natural' level of employment and, corresponding to this, a 'natural' level of real aggregate demand.

The second key feature of our model concerns the medium-term determination of unemployment. In the medium term the planned mark-up of wages over prices in wage settlements must be consistent with the mark-up of prices over wage costs in employers' pricing behaviour. For if wage-setters try to set real product wages higher than is consistent with employers' pricing behaviour, this generates ever-increasing inflation. Thus the key to understanding unemployment in the medium term is the behaviour of wage-setters. If events occur that push them towards too-high real wages, then unemployment has to rise to offset these influences. We shall call these influences 'wage pressure variables' or 'push factors,' and they are clearly crucial in understanding unemployment. The variables here include the social security system, employment protection legislation, mismatch between unemployment and vacancies, union power, taxation, and real import prices.

To understand the actual course of unemployment, we have to operate in the short term, where employment is determined by both aggregate demand and real wages. Since real wages in turn depend on the 'push factors', unemployment depends on aggregate demand and on the 'push factors'. The prime purpose of this paper is to explain the course of unemployment in terms of these two groups of factors. In other words, we attempt to decompose the growth of unemployment into its originating causes. We also show how the push factors have affected the natural rate of unemployment.

A second purpose of the paper is to look closely at dynamics. In particular, we want to look at the joint movement of real wages and unemployment in response to shocks both to demand and to supply (i.e. to shocks adding to aggregate demand or to wage pressure).

We begin in Section I by reviewing the facts about unemployment, as well as the various wage pressure variables and the forces affecting real aggregate demand. In Section II we describe our model and in Section III we discuss its empirical counterpart.[2] In Section IV we estimate it on annual data and use it to perform the decomposition of the causes of increased unemployment.[3] In Section V we estimate the model on quarterly data, using the results to illuminate the dynamics of unemployment and real wages. Our conclusions are given in Section VI.

I. TRENDS IN UNEMPLOYMENT AND IN CAUSAL FACTORS

Unemployment

We have already shown the rise in aggregate male unemployment. This is due hardly at all to changes in the age structure of the labour force: unemployment

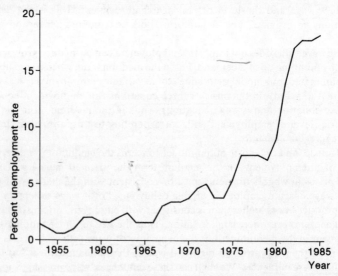

FIGURE 1.   Male unemployment rate (mid-year), pre-1982 definition, 1953–1985. (*Source*: Data Appendix at the end of volume.)

has risen extremely sharply in all age groups. This emerges from Table 1. As the table shows, unemployment has risen rather more than average among those aged 18–19. (People younger than this have been protected by a guaranteed offer of a place on a public programme for school-leavers, operative in 1979 and after.[4]) But the striking point is the broad uniformity of the proportional rise in unemployment among all age groups.

Unemployment in Britain often lasts a very long time, and the main mechanism by which unemployment has risen is an increase in its duration. This is brought out clearly in Table 2. In fact, the flow into unemployment is not much higher than in the early 1970s and the numbers who have been unemployed for *under* six months are now somewhat lower than in 1981. As we shall argue later, this provides some clue as to why wage inflation is not falling as much as one might expect, given the high current level of total unemployment.

Even today, unemployment is basically a matter affecting manual workers and low-skilled non-manual workers, such as shop assistants. Taking the 1982 figures for men, 83 per cent of the unemployed were manual workers, compared with only 61 per cent of the labour force. The unemployment rate for semi-

TABLE 1

MALE UNEMPLOYMENT RATE, BY AGE, 1975-1984
(percentages)

	Under 18	18–19	20–24	25–34	35–44	45–54	55–59	All
1975	13·8	9·6	6·8	4·8	4·1	3·7	3·7	5·4
1980	21·0	13·8	11·2	7·3	5·8	5·6	6·6	8·2
1984	25·6	29·1	22·6	15·0	11·5	11·5	17·3	15·8

Note: Annual averages of January, April, July and October for 1980 and 1984; July only for 1975. The series is not strictly comparable pre- and post-1982, and changes in the 1983 budget reduced the numbers claiming benefit, particularly, but not exclusively, those aged over 60.
Source: Department of Employment *Gazette*.

TABLE 2

MALE UNEMPLOYMENT BY DURATION, 1965-69 TO 1984
(thousands)

	<2 weeks	2–26 weeks	26–52 weeks	52+ weeks	Average uncompleted duration of current spells (months)
1965–69	62	171	47	60	7·25
1970–74	88	278	81	120	7·95
1975–79	97	470	161	223	8·91
1980	104	603	189	289	9·60
1981	114	890	440	467	9·40
1982	101	837	475	818	11·53
1983	122	773	431	902	13·23
1984	121	724	399	953	15·85

Source: Department of Employment *Gazette*; Johnson and Layard (1986).

and unskilled workers was 22 per cent, compared with 5 per cent for non-manual workers.[5]

We turn now to the various possible causes of unemployment. We shall start with the medium-term causes—that is, the various push factors that may have tended to generate pressure for 'too-high' real labour costs. First, there are influences that might tend to reduce the effective supply of labour from the measured labour force. These fall under three headings: (1) unemployment benefit and social security, (2) mismatch between the unemployed and the available vacancies, and (3) employment protection legislation.

Unemployment benefits and social security

On this first point we have evidence on the ratio of unemployment benefits to net income in work—that is, of the 'replacement ratio' (ρ). In the Data Appendix at the end of this book we give the most reasonable index that we have of this. It shows a sharp rise from the late 1950s to the late 1960s with no trend since then. Unless the lags are very long, changes in the value of benefits do not seem to be a major explanation of the unemployment trend.

But there have been other changes in the benefit system. The tests for eligibility were steadily weakened from the 1960s (Layard, 1982, p. 43). In addition, there may have been changes in public attitudes to 'living off the state'. These things can never be quantified. But one possible way of trying to get some insight is to look at the movement of unemployment at given vacancies. As we shall argue, the matter is more complicated than that, but let us first look at the basic data on vacancies and unemployment. This is shown in Figure 2.[6] As can been seen, there have been two basic changes since the 1960s.

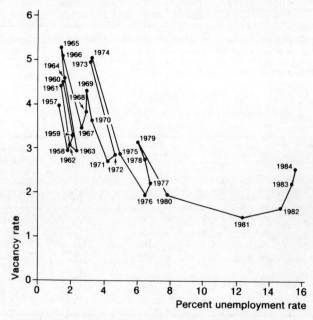

FIGURE 2.   Vacancies and male unemployment. (*Source*: Jackman, Layard and Pissarides, 1984.)

Misuseful

Vacancies have fallen dramatically, and unemployment at given vacancies has risen dramatically. The latter phenomenon (i.e. the shift of the U/V curve) can be summarized in the following relationship:[7]

$$\log U = -1\cdot71 + 0\cdot387 \log U_{-1} - 0\cdot549 \log V + 0\cdot0603\,MM$$
$$\qquad\quad (4\cdot9)\qquad\qquad (4\cdot7)\qquad\quad (0\cdot9)$$
$$+\,0\cdot023t + 0\cdot00023t^2$$
$$(2\cdot1)\quad (0\cdot7)$$

where U is the male unemployment rate, V is the vacancy rate and MM is mismatch. Mismatch is measured indirectly by the turbulence in the economy, as indicated by the absolute annual change in the proportion of employees working in production industries. (There is no effect from lagged unemployment beyond the first lag.)

Mismatch

How are we to interpret the shift of the U/V curve? The rise in unemployment at given vacancies is certainly striking, with only a very little of it explained by changes in mismatch. We have better measures of mismatch for the period since 1962, based on the lack of congruence between vacancies and unemployment across sectors. Table 3 shows, for occupational groups, regions and industries, the index $\frac{1}{2}\sum |u_i/u - v_i/v|$ where u_i/u is the share of the sector in total unemployment and v_i/v is the share in total vacancies. The table shows no upward trend in mismatch, even in the 1960s. We are thus confident that increased mismatch is not an important part of the explanation for increased unemployment.

Employment protection

But can the whole shift of the U/V curve legitimately be attributed to a decrease in the willingness of unemployed workers to accept the available jobs? Clearly not. An equally possible explanation is that, owing to tighter employment protection laws, employers have been less willing to fill the available jobs from among the unemployed workers.[8] This second explanation is discussed at length in Jackman, Layard and Pissarides (1984). There are two basic points. First, employment protection laws should decrease the level of turnover in the economy. This has indeed fallen considerably since the late 1960s, but would of itself tend to shift the U/V curve inwards. Second, employment protection laws would, at a given level of turnover, tend to shift the U/V curve outward. Thus the net effect of employment protection on the U/V curve is uncertain. We are therefore inclined to attribute a substantial part of the U/V shift to a decrease in the willingness of workers to accept work. However, we make no guess as to proportions, and we simply attribute the shift of the U/V curve to decreased 'search intensity' (s) on the part of both workers and firms. Using the previous equation, s is computed as

$$s = \frac{-0\cdot023t - 0\cdot00023t^2}{1 - 0\cdot387}.$$

Union power

This is as far as we are able to take influences affecting the availability of suitable workers to employers. We turn now to other influences that might

TABLE 3

MORE STRUCTURAL UNEMPLOYMENT? BRITAIN, 1962-1982

	Mismatch of unemployment and vacancies			
	By occupation (24/18)	By region (10/11)	By region and occupation (198)	By industry (24)
1962	0·43	0·33		
1963	0·39	0·34		0·24
1964	0·42	0·38		0·24
1965	0·41	0·34		0·24
1966	0·42	0·28		0·23
1967	0·37	0·28		0·23
1968	0·38	0·30		0·27
1969	0·39	0·28		0·28
1970	0·38	0·24		0·25
1971	0·37	0·28		0·23
1972	0·37	0·34		0·21
1973	0·40	0·33		0·23
1974	0·41	0·32	0·49	0·23
1975	0·43	0·20	0·48	0·23
1976	0·38	0·17	0·42	0·19
1977	0·35	0·20	0·40	0·19
1978	0·35	0·25	0·42	0·18
1979	0·35	0·28	0·44	0·18
1980	0·37	0·27	0·44	0·23
1981	0·41	0·21	0·44	0·32
1982	0·37	0·21	0·41	0·30

Notes:
(i) The mismatch index is $\frac{1}{2} \sum |u_i/u - v_i/v|$.
(ii) Number in brackets indicate number of cells.
(iii) Before 1966 only 10 regions were identified (East Midlands and West Midlands were not separated); afterwards, 11. Also, definitions of present South-East and East Anglia regions differed. The break is not serious, however. The occupational index is based on totally different classifications before and after 1973; this is a serious break.
(iv) All vacancies are classified by industry but some unemployed are unidentified by industry and are omitted. (Unemployed unidentified by occupation are included in the 'miscellaneous' category.) In August 1981 684,117 people, or 24·1 per cent of total unemployed, were unclassified.
Source: (All data are annual averages unless indicated below.)
Occupation: 1962-73: September data from *British Labour Statistics, Historical Abstract* and *British Labour Statistics Year Books*. (Male and female are summed.)
1974-82: Department of Employment Gazette.
Region; 1962-82: unemployment from *Monthly Digest of Statistics*. 1982-82; vacancies from Department of Employment *Gazette*, but for Northern Ireland from *Annual Abstract of Statistics*.

Region by occupation: Department of Employment *Gazette*.

Industry: Department of Employment *Gazette*.

Employment data: Department of Employment *Gazette*.

tend to raise real labour costs and thus reduce employment.[9] The most obvious of these is union power. Trade union membership as a percentage of employed workers rose substantially from 1970 to 1980, since when it has fallen. The series is shown in Figure 3. However, we doubt whether this is the best index of union power. As an alternative, one can construct an index of the mark-up of wages set by collective bargaining over other wages. This is obtained by running for every year an industry cross-section of earnings on a number of factors including union coverage.[10] The series then consists of the union

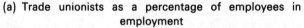

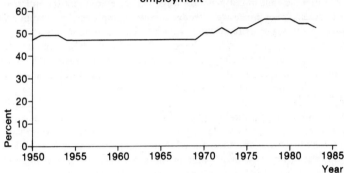

(a) Trade unionists as a percentage of employees in employment

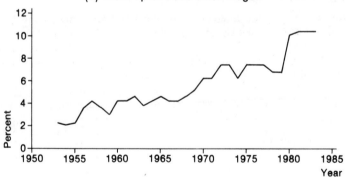

(b) Mark-up of trade union wages

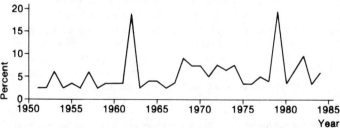

(c) Workers involved in industrial conflicts as a percentage of employees in employment

FIGURE 3. Union power, 1950-1984. (*Source*: Data Appendix at end of volume.)

coverage coefficient for each year. This is also shown in Figure 3 and rises sharply after the Paris events of 1968, as one might expect, and again (more surprisingly) after Mrs Thatcher's advent to power. A final index of interest is the number of workers involved in industrial disputes. This also shows a rise in the early 1970s. Clearly, none of the indices is totally exogenous, but we feel that the union mark-up variable (U_p) comes nearer than any other to reflecting the element in union behaviour that is affecting unemployment rather than being affected by it. This is the one we use.

Taxation and relative import prices

Other influences that might generate wage pressure are taxation and relative import prices. These introduce a 'wedge' between employers' real labour costs (relative to the GDP deflator) and workers' real take-home pay (relative to consumer prices).[11] But in our analysis employers' real labour costs are determined essentially by the pricing policy of firms.[12] Thus, increases in the 'wedge' must be borne by labour. If increases in the wedge generate wage pressure, they must therefore cause offsetting unemployment.

Figure 4 shows the various elements of the wedge. There have been striking increases in both employers' taxes (t_1) and employees' taxes (t_2). Increases in indirect taxes (t_3) have been much less. The behaviour of real import prices weighted by the share of imports in GDP has been uneven—down until 1972, then up, down, up and down. Some of the movements of import prices (but not all) are mirrored in the course of unemployment.

Productivity downturn

We turn now to a rather different line of thought. If productivity growth falls off, it seems possible that wage-setters will aim at unduly high real wages in line with former trends. This might reflect the behaviour of unions, or even of employers wishing to motivate their workforces (see for example Grubb, Jackman and Layard, 1983; Johnson and Layard, 1986).

In Figure 5, therefore, we look at trends in the growth of the capital-labour force ratio and of technical progress (assumed labour-augmenting). As is well known, both these growth rates fell sharply in the mid-1970s.

Previous unemployment

Another theory of wage pressure asserts that high rates of unemployment in the past tend to reduce the skills and work habits of the labour force, and thus to reduce effective labour supply. If lagged unemployment were important in the wage equation, this would make the short-term natural rate of unemployment a function of recent unemployment. It would also make the medium-term natural rate much more sensitive to the other push variables we have examined.[13] We therefore look hard for the effects of lagged unemployment terms in explaining wage behaviour. As it turns out, our attempt to establish this hysteresis effect is not notably successful, although there is some evidence for it in our quarterly wage equation. This brings us to two explanations of increased unemployment to which we give little credence.

Labour force

There are those who believe that unemployment has gone up because of an increase in the labour force. This seems most unlikely. As Figure 6 shows, the

(a) Employer's tax rate (t_1)

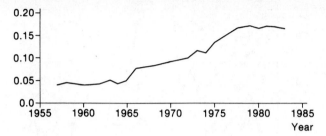

(b) Employee's tax rate (t_2)

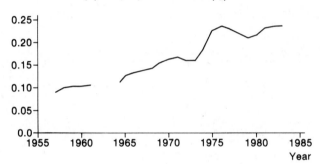

(c) Indirect tax rate (t_3)

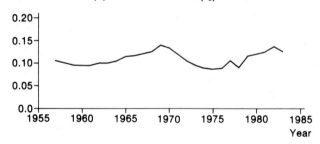

(d) Log real import prices weighted by import share (1972=0)

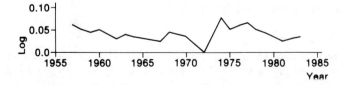

FIGURE 4.   The wedge. (*Source*: Data Appendix at end of volume.)

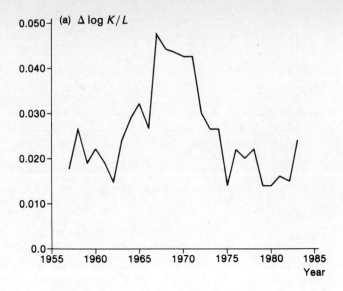

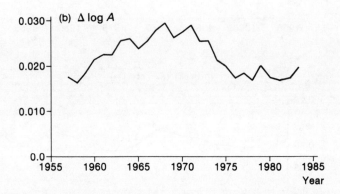

FIGURE 5.   Δlog K/L and Δlog A, 1957–1983. (*Source*: Data Appendix at end of volume.)

labour force grew at least as sharply between 1950 and 1966 as between its 1971 trough and 1980. Between 1980 and 1983 it was fairly stable, and has now begun growing again. So it is difficult to suppose that the rise in unemployment is due to the increase in labour force.

Physical capacity

Others think that recent unemployment can be explained simply by a lack of physical capacity to employ the labour force. Fortunately, in Britain the Confederation of British Industries regularly asks its members, 'Is your output over the next four months likely to be limited by lack of physical capacity?' The replies are shown in Figure 7, together with the percentage of firms not

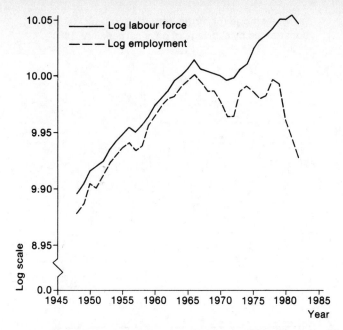

FIGURE 6.   Log labour force and log employment, with the unemployment rate as the difference, 1948–1983. (*Source*: Data Appendix at end of volume.)

reporting that they were working below capacity. These figures show that until recently physical capacity has been anything but a limiting feature. In any case, there are clearly possibilities of shiftwork in factories, shops and elsewhere, which make it inherently unlikely that physical capacity could be a major limit on employment.

Real labour costs

So much for the medium-term forces affecting unemployment (the push factors). We can now turn briefly to the short-run factors affecting the level of employment (relative to capital)—i.e. to real wages and aggregate demand.

As Figure 8 shows, there is a close log-linear relation between employment (relative to capital) and real labour cost. However, there are still divergences that can be explained in part by aggregate demand factors.

Aggregate demand factors

Figure 9(a) shows the demand-weighted government deficit, adjusted for deviations of output from potential and for inflation.[14] This variable shows a severe contraction from 1979 onwards.

The other aggregate demand variables charted in Figure 9 are world trade (net of a quintic trend) and competitiveness, measured by world manufacturing export prices relative to the final expenditure deflator. This too has taken a beating in recent years.

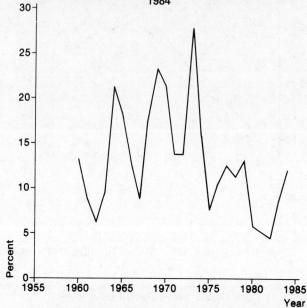

(a) Percentage of firms reporting output to be constrained by shortage of physical capacity, 1960–1984

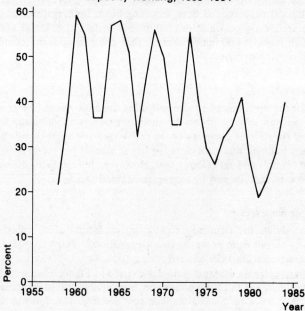

(b) Percentage of firms not reporting below-capacity working, 1958–1984

FIGURE 7. Capacity constraints on British firms. (*Source*: Confederation of British Industries, *Industrial Trends Survey.*)

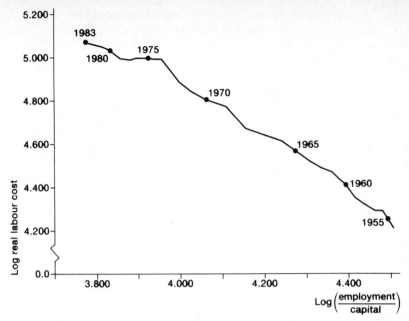

FIGURE 8.   Real labour cost and the employment–capital ratio, 1954–1982. (*Source*: Data Appendix at end of volume.)

II. THE MODEL

Our model relates to an economy with price-setting firms. It comprises both the demand and supply influences affecting unemployment and inflation. But the demand side is handled by a simple reduced form, whereas the supply side is modelled in greater detail. The model comprises equations for the employment, pricing and output decisions of the firm, as well as for wage-setting behaviour in the labour market. These equations determine the level of unemployment, for given values of the real exchange rate. Since the real exchange rate has such an effect on wage pressure (p. S128) above) we can determine the long-run level of unemployment only by including a trade balance equation determining the level of competitiveness in the long run.

The overall model is set out on p. S141 below, followed by a discussion of its working. The impatient reader may wish to go straight there. But first we have to derive the rationale behind each relationship.

Employment, prices and the supply of output

Suppose the economy consists of a number (n) of identical imperfectly competitive firms. Each firm's final output is produced by a production function in which inputs (i.e. materials) are separable from capital and labour. We impose this restriction because it increases the efficiency of our estimates and does not appear to violate the data. Hence the ith firm's production of value added is determined by its capital (K_i) and its labour (N_i). In each period, the firm uses the capital stock with which it begins the period: any investment undertaken during the period only influences the capital stock for next period.

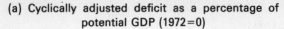

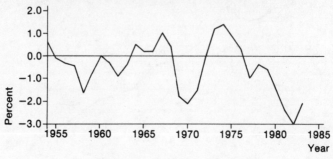

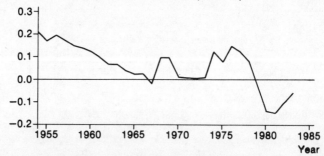

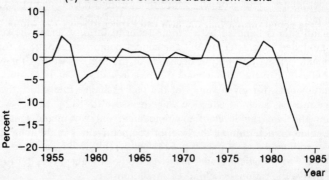

FIGURE 9.   Demand variables, 1957–1983. (*Source*: Data Appendix at end of volume.)

Production involves some fixed set-up costs,[15] but thereafter the ith firm's output is produced at constant returns to scale. Technical progress (A) is assumed to be labour-augmenting (for which we later find some empirical support), with the firm's output depending on K_i and AN_i. Hence, given constant returns to scale, value-added output, Y_i, is given by

$$(1) \qquad Y_i = \psi\left(\frac{AN_i}{K_i}\right) K_i \qquad\qquad (\psi' > 0,\ \psi'' < 0).$$

This relation can also be inverted to give the amount of labour required to produce a given output:

$$(2) \qquad N_i = f\left(\frac{Y_i}{K_i}\right)\frac{K_i}{A} \qquad\qquad\qquad (f = \psi^{-1}, f', f'' > 0).$$

It follows, for future reference, that

$$(3) \qquad \psi'\left(\frac{AN_i}{K_i}\right) = 1\Big/f'\left(\frac{Y_i}{K_i}\right).$$

In other words, the marginal product of labour equals the reciprocal of the marginal cost of output measured in terms of labour. Any of the previous three equations is an equally valid description of the production process.

We come now to the behaviour of the firm. For the purposes of this exposition, we suppose that the firm sets prices, produces output, and fixes employment one period in advance, all on the basis of its expectation of the demand for its output (Y_i^e). If its demand forecast is wrong, the difference between production and sales is absorbed by inventories. In practice, of course, hours of work can also be varied almost instantaneously in order to make some adjustments to output when demand is revealed. Such a model is described in Nickell (1985) but requires a more complicated analysis; the resulting empirical model is, however, exactly the same as that given here. In our present model, then, output is equal to expected demand; that is, $Y_i = Y_i^e$.

In order to choose a price and thus determine its output and employment, the firm must forecast demand, and this is done as follows. If all the labour and capital in the economy were to be fully employed, each individual firm would produce $1/n$ of the total 'potential' output of the economy, i.e., $\psi(AL/K)K/n$, where L is the labour force and K is the aggregate capital stock. But the actual output that the firm can expect to sell (Y_i^e) will be less than that, since expected aggregate demand is only a fraction (σ^e) of total 'potential' output. The firm's expected sales will also depend on the firm's relative price (P_i/P^e) where P_i is the (value-added) output price and P^e is the expected aggregate (value-added) price level. So we can write the firm's expected demand, and thus its output, as

$$(4) \qquad Y_i = D\left(\frac{P_i}{P^e}, \sigma^e\right)\psi\left(\frac{AL}{K}\right)\frac{K}{n}.$$

The firm now has to choose its price. We can specify a completely general pricing rule in which (P_i) is a mark-up (v) on expected marginal costs. Using (2), this gives us the *pricing rule*

$$(5) \qquad P_i = vMC_i = v\frac{W}{A}f'\left(\frac{Y_i}{K_i}\right)$$

where W is the cost per worker including employment taxes.[16]

If the firm maximizes short-run profit, then the mark-up, v, is $(1 - 1/\eta)^{-1}$ where η is the elasticity of demand facing the firm. This, of course, includes the perfect competition case where $v = 1$. If v is constant, the mark up of prices on *wages* (as opposed to *marginal* cost) rises when output rises because marginal costs are increasing as the marginal product of labour falls.[17] There is, however, a great deal of evidence for many industries which suggests that the mark-up of value-added prices on *wages* is very unresponsive to, or even independent of, demand fluctuations (normal cost pricing).[18] This implies that the mark-up on *marginal cost*, v, is decreasing with demand.[19] So, in general, we suppose that

$$v = v(\sigma^e) \qquad\qquad (v' \le 0).$$

We can now move to the level of the aggregate economy by noting that $P = P_i$, $K = nK_i$, $N = nN_i$, $Y = nY_i$. So in aggregate, (3), (4) and (5) become

(6a) $\psi'\left(\dfrac{AN}{K}\right) = 1/f'\left(\dfrac{Y}{K}\right)$ Production function

(6b) $Y = D\left(\dfrac{P}{P^e}, \sigma^e\right)\psi\left(\dfrac{AL}{K}\right)K$ Expected output demand

(6c) $P = v(\sigma^e)\dfrac{W}{A}f'\left(\dfrac{Y}{K}\right)$ Pricing rule.

Note that Y is output supplied and appears on the left-hand side of (6b) because output supply is set equal to expected demand.

These equations are fairly standard blocks in most macroeconomic models. However, for the purposes of practical implementation it is convenient to have a more streamlined model in which these three equations are reduced to two, neither of which includes output. One of these equations is for prices and one for employment.

We first amalgamate equations (6b) and (6c) to obtain the equation for prices as a function of wages and expected product demand. This gives a fairly standard *price equation*

(7) $\dfrac{P}{W} = g^1\left(\sigma^e, \dfrac{L}{K}, A, \dfrac{P}{P^e}\right).$
                    ? + ? −

Since $v' < 0$, the impact of σ is strictly indeterminate, because a rise in σ reduces the mark-up of prices over marginal cost but at the same time the real marginal labour requirement rises. However, in this context the most extreme form of behaviour that has ever been proposed is the normal cost pricing hypothesis where demand has no effect. All other hypotheses generate a positive relationship, and so we would expect $g_1^1 \ge 0$. Note also the fact that, if prices turn out to be higher than expected $(P > P^e)$, this is automatically associated with a fall in the mark-up of prices on wages.

For our employment equation, the most natural relation is that obtained by using (6a) to eliminate output from (6c). This yields

(8) $\psi'\left(\dfrac{AN}{K}\right) = v(\sigma^e)\dfrac{W}{PA}.$

Thus, the marginal product of labour is equal to the product of the real wage in efficiency units, W/PA, and the price mark-up on marginal cost, $v(\sigma^e)$. This is a very interesting equation in at least two senses. First, it is the natural generalization of the perfect competition result ($v = 1$). In particular, it demonstrates that the *ceteris paribus* real-wage elasticity of employment is unaffected by conditions in the product market. Second, it illustrates the crucial role of the price mark-up on marginal cost in determining employment. If, when demand increases, prices do not rise as much as marginal cost, then employment must rise (since $v' < 0$).

The marginal productivity condition, (8), thus generates an *employment equation* of the form

$$(9) \qquad \frac{N}{K} = \frac{1}{A} g^2 \left(\underset{-}{\frac{W}{PA}}, \underset{+}{\sigma^e} \right).$$

To many people this is an unfamiliar equation. One question that arises is how (in the short run, with K, A fixed) real wages can vary while expected demand, σ^e, is unchanged. The answer is that P/P^e may vary, and this will affect real wages through equation (7).

Let us consider an example of this. Suppose that a firm strikes an unexpectedly poor wage bargain but its expectation concerning aggregate prices remains unchanged. Then it will certainly raise prices and cut production, although prices will not rise by as much as wages because it does not wish to lose out too much *vis-à-vis* its competitors. But all firms are in an identical position. All prices respond in the same way, and so actual prices turn out to be higher than expected but the price mark-up on wages has declined. Furthermore, all firms produce less and employ fewer workers as a consequence of these events although σ^e remains unchanged. So we have a rise in real wages, and employment falls exactly as predicted by equation (9).

As an alternative to the employment equation (9) derived above, we can consider two other possible employment equations, one of which excludes the real wage, W/PA, and the other of which excludes demand, σ^e. To obtain the former we simply use demand (6b) to replace output in the production function (6a). This would give

$$\frac{N}{K} = g^3 \left(\sigma^e, \frac{L}{K}, A, \frac{P}{P^e} \right)$$

which is, in many ways, less appealing than (9), at least as far as empirical implementation is concerned. Its advocates (see, for example, Carlin and Soskice, 1985) are generally those who believe that the marginal product of labour is constant, so that (8) and (9) are actually invalid. But our empirical work gives such strong support for the presence of real-wage effects in (9) that we are convinced that real marginal cost does indeed rise.[20]

In the third possible employment relation, expected demand (σ^e) does not appear. To obtain this we have to combine all three equations (6a), (6b) and (6c), or (which is equivalent) to use (7) to eliminate σ^e from (9). This gives

$$\frac{N}{K} = g^4 \left(\frac{W}{PA}, \frac{L}{K}, A, \frac{P}{P^e} \right).$$

Clearly, this procedure will fail in the special case where there is exactly normal cost pricing, and hence σ^e does not appear in (7). But even if there is nearly (but not exactly) normal cost pricing, an equation with only real wages is not likely to be robust. We therefore strongly prefer the simplicity and generality of equation (9) to the alternative employment relations.

The determination of demand, σ

Our demand variable, σ, represents demand relative to total potential output and can be thought of as being solved out of a standard, open-economy, IS-LM system. It is therefore a function of government fiscal and monetary policy instruments, x_d, an index of world economic activity, Y^*, and an index of price competitiveness, $P^*/\bar{P}$, the ratio of the world price of output in domestic currency to the price of domestic output. It is also worth noting that, when specifying the firm's demand in equation (4), we chose as the relative price the ratio of the firm's price to the aggregate domestic price level. In an open economy it is more natural to suppose that the appropriate normalizing price is some weighted average of domestic and world prices. Our formulation is, however, perfectly satisfactory, since we absorb the domestic to world price ratio into σ. To summarize, therefore, σ may be written as

$$(10) \qquad \sigma = \sigma\left(x_d, Y^*, \frac{P^*}{\bar{P}}\right).$$

Wage determination

We turn next to wage formation. Initially, we suppose that prices are correctly foreseen, so there is no discrepancy between the real wage that agents intend to bring about as a result of their activities and the real wage that actually occurs.

We can imagine real wages being determined by four possible mechanisms; (1) supply and demand (i.e. by impersonal forces); (2) firms; (3) unions; (4) bargaining between firms and unions. Any of the last three can give rise to involuntary unemployment (see Johnson and Layard, 1986). It does not require unions to produce 'real-wage resistance'.

It is highly probable that all four mechanisms are used in various sectors of the economy. It is important, therefore, that our estimated model of wage determination is sufficiently general to encompass all types of model. In fact, this is not as difficult as it seems, because all the models have broadly similar implications. In order to see how this comes about, let us start with the standard model of competitive wage determination.

The demand for labour is given by (9), and we can write the supply of labour, conditional on the labour force, as

$$(11) \qquad N = g^s\left(\frac{W}{P}, Z^s\right)L$$

where g^s is the proportion of the labour force prepared to work at the real wage W/P. Z^s is a set of variables that influence labour supply given the real wage. Remember that the real wage is defined as hourly labour costs divided by value-added prices, and so Z^s must incorporate all elements of the wedge between this and the real consumption wage (see p. S128 above and n. 11). So Z^s includes taxes as well as relative import prices and any other variables affecting the search intensity and willingness of the unemployed to work, such as the size and availability of unemployment benefit. Equating supply and demand in the labour market generates an equilibrium real-wage function of the form

(12) $\qquad \dfrac{W}{P} = h^1 \left(\sigma^e, A, \dfrac{K}{L}, Z^s \right).$
$\qquad\qquad\quad + \quad ? \quad +$

The real wage is influenced by the variables that affect the supply and demand for labour, with K/L being the key variable explaining the secular rise in the real wage over time. This is, of course, a reduced-form equation relative to the labour market.

Now suppose firms set wages. There are numerous models of firms' wage-setting behaviour, many of which are summarized in Johnson and Layard (1986) and Stiglitz (1986). A typical group of such models is the efficiency wage type. These have the property that, for one reason or another, an increase in the wage paid generates a benefit to the firm, which partially offsets the direct cost. For example, increasing wages relative to some externally given level[21] reduces quitting (Pencavel, 1972), or reduces vacancies (Jackman, Layard and Pissarides, 1984), or raises employees' work effort (Shapiro and Stiglitz, 1984). The firm thus sets the wage to equate the marginal benefit to the direct marginal cost. This generates a wage function which may be thought of as a pseudo-supply price relationship. The wages set depend on outside opportunities, which would include some alternative wage level as well as the outside employment rate and Z^s variables, such as the unemployment benefit levels.

One possibility is that the wage-setting equation requires the wage set to be proportional to the expected outside wage. In that case, in the absence of expectational errors, the natural rate of unemployment is determined in a very simple way. When the wage-setting equations are averaged across all firms, the average level of wages would not appear in the resulting relationship. Instead, the equation determines the employment rate as a function of the Z^s variables. This is in the spirit of the traditional augmented Phillips curve. However, it is better to allow for the possibility that the wages set are not proportional to the expected outside wage. There will then, in fully anticipated equilibrium, be a long-run relationship between the prevailing real wage, the employment rate and the Z^s variables. Eliminating the employment rate via the labour demand function would lead to a reduced-form real wage function much the same as that in (12).

Similar conclusions follow from union or bargaining models of wage determination, which are discussed fully in Layard and Nickell (1985a). There are strong grounds for believing that, even in the presence of unions, employers fix employment, taking the wage as given (see Oswald, 1986; Oswald and Turnbull, 1985). Thus, in bargaining, unions and firms compute their welfare and expected profit functions, knowing that this is how employment will be determined. The expected profit function of the ith firm will depend on all the variables entering its profit equation (especially W_i/P, σ^e, A, K/L and

K_i). The welfare function of the union will depend on W_i/P, on any other determinants of employment (as above), on any wedges between real labour costs and real take-home pay (taxes and import prices), and on the alternative opportunities open to union members who do not get work in the firm. The outside opportunities will be affected by the outside wage (W/P), the general level of employment (N/L) and the level of wellbeing of those who are unemployed.

Thus, the final level of the real wage settled for (W_i/P) will depend on σ, K, A, K/L, N/L, W/P and the whole set of supply-side variables (Z^s).[22] It will also, of course, depend on the degree of union strength (U_p). Taking the equilibrium relationship (with $W_i = W$) gives us (provided W_i is not proportional to W) a structural real-wage equation:

$$(13) \quad \frac{W}{P} = h^2 \left(\sigma^e, A, \frac{K}{L}, \frac{N}{L}, Z^s, U_p \right).$$
$$? \quad + \; + \; + \; + \; +$$

This differs from (11) in that it is a structural equation yet includes demand-side variables (σ, A, K/L). It differs from the reduced-form equation (12) in that it includes employment. It is thus the most general wage equation and forms the basis of our approach to estimation.

However, a number of minor adjustments must be made to this formulation. First, we expect the impact of the demand variable, σ^e, to be relatively minor since it mainly reflects short-run fluctuations and firms would be reluctant to allow short-run demand shifts to influence longer term wage agreements, especially if they are using normal cost pricing. We therefore omit σ^e from our wage model.[23] Second, as we have already noted, one of the elements of Z^s is the real price of imports $P_m/\bar{P}$ where P_m is the price of imports and $\bar{P}$ is the price of domestic output. This may be rewritten as $(P_m/P^*)(P^*/\bar{P})$ where the first term may be thought of as the exogenous world terms of trade between importables and world output and the second term represents endogenous price competitiveness. We may thus separate the wage pressure variables Z^s and U_p into all the exogenous factors, which we simply term Z, and the price competitiveness $P^*/\bar{P}$. Finally, our wage derivation in fact relates to the intended real wage W/P^e. If we wish to explain the actual real wage, W/P, then we must clearly include P/P^e as an explanatory variable taking a negative sign. If prices rise faster than expected, real wages will turn out lower than were bargained for.

The upshot of this discussion is a real-wage equation of the form

$$(14) \quad \frac{W}{P} = h^3 \left(A, \frac{K}{L}, \frac{N}{L}, Z, \frac{P^*}{\bar{P}}, \frac{P}{P^e} \right).$$
$$+ \; + \; + \; + \; -$$

Note that an improvement in competitveness leads to an increase in the real price of imports, a consequent rise in wage pressure, and a rise in the real wage.

The long-run determination of competitiveness, $P^*/\bar{P}$

We assume that competitiveness is determined in the long run by the condition that the balance of trade is zero. This suggests an equation of the form

(15) $\quad P^*/\bar{P} = h^4(\sigma, Y^*, Z^c)$
$\qquad\qquad\quad +\ \ -$

where Z^c represents exogenous factors including the value of oil production.

The model in operation

We are now in a position to discuss the workings of the model as a whole, but in order to do so it is convenient to set out our equations *en bloc*, starting with the supply side. This consists of four equations (already derived) for employment, prices, wages and output:

(9) $\quad \dfrac{N}{L} = g^2\left(\dfrac{W}{PA}, \sigma^e\right)\dfrac{K}{AL} \qquad$ Employment
$\qquad\qquad\quad -\quad \geq 0$

(7) $\quad \dfrac{P}{W} = g^1\left(\sigma^e, \dfrac{K}{L}, A, \dfrac{P}{P^e}\right) \qquad$ Prices
$\qquad\qquad\quad \geq 0\ -\ ?\ -$

(14) $\quad \dfrac{W}{P} = h^3\left(A, \dfrac{K}{L}, \dfrac{N}{L}, Z, \dfrac{P^*}{\bar{P}}, \dfrac{P}{P^e}\right) \qquad$ Wages
$\qquad\qquad\qquad +\ +\ +\ +\ +\ -$

(6b) $\quad Y = D\left(\dfrac{P}{P^e}, \sigma^e\right)\psi\left(\dfrac{AL}{K}\right)K \qquad$ Output
$\qquad\qquad\quad\ -\ \ +\qquad +$

We can now look at *actual product demand* and how this relates to supply. Actual aggregate sales are[24]

(16) $\quad Y^d = D(1, \sigma)\psi\left(\dfrac{AL}{K}\right)K \qquad$ Aggregate sales

where

(10) $\quad \sigma = \sigma\left(x_d, Y^*, \dfrac{P^*}{P}\right).$
$\qquad\qquad\ +\quad +$

If $P = P^e$ and $\sigma = \sigma^e$, then actual output, given by (6b), equals aggregate sales. Otherwise the difference is made up by changes in inventories by an amount equal to $(Y - Y^d)$.

Finally, there is a relation determining the long-run level of competitiveness, given by

(15) $\quad P^*/\bar{P} = h^4(\sigma, Y^*, Z^c).$
$\qquad\qquad\quad +\ -$

The first three equations (for employment, prices and wages) are the key to understanding unemployment, both in the long run and the short run.

(i) *Long-run analysis.* Let us take the productive capacity of the economy (K, L, A), the level of competitiveness, $P^*/\bar{P}$, and the degree of wage pressure, Z, as given. Then the supply side of this model tells us the level of output (Y), employment (N), the real wage (W/P) and the price surprise (P/P^e) generated by any given level of expected demand. It therefore follows that there is a particular level of demand that will generate no price surprise $(P/P^e = 1)$. Furthermore, this 'long run' feasible level of demand is determined along with employment and the real wage, simply by setting $P = P^e$ in the key supply equations (9), (7) and (14). This is a very classical result from what looks like a very non-classical model. It must, however, be emphasized that large numbers of individuals may be voluntarily unemployed, since wage determination is not based on market-clearing.

Clearly, if wage pressure (Z) increases, this will make things worse, by making it more difficult for firms to provide the real wages that wage-bargainers would like. Only higher unemployment will force wage-bargainers back into line.

By contrast, a loss of competitiveness will make it easier for firms to meet the real-wage targets of wage-bargainers. Thus it would be possible, even in the absence of price surprises, to get rising employment if this were accompanied by a loss of competitiveness (shades of the United States in the recent past). Demand (σ) would need to expand to generate the extra employment. How long such a loss of competitiveness could be sustained would, however, depend on the underlying forces determining the real exchange rate. In the very long run, (15) would come into play and pin down the real level of activity in the economy.

To understand the dynamics of the system we can now perform two experiments. First, we shall examine what happens when there is a real demand shock (which must in its nature be temporary). Second, we shall examine a supply shock, looking at both its short-run and long-run effects.

(ii) *A short-run demand shock.* What happens if demand is pushed above its natural rate? According to the price equation, real wages cannot rise unless prices are higher than expected. But according to the wage equation, real wages will have to be higher if output and employment rise, unless prices are higher than expected. Thus, the only way in which the behaviour of price-setters and wage-setters can be reconciled is by prices running ahead of expectations. This is what makes both price-setters and wage-setters happy with their mark-up even though at prevailing levels of employment both sides could not be happy if they realized what was happening.

In this situation do real wages rise or fall? This depends mainly on the slope of the pricing relationship. Here we shall make two polar assumptions. First, we shall assume normal cost pricing. So demand (σ) has no effect on pricing and a strong effect on employment. Then we shall assume perfect competition, so that σ has a strong effect on the real wage and no direct effect on employment.

The two cases are illustrated in Figure 10. Initially we are at the natural level of σ, with $P = P^e$. The economy is at A. Now σ rises.

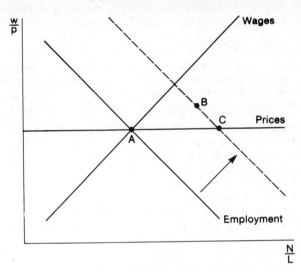

(a) Normal cost pricing

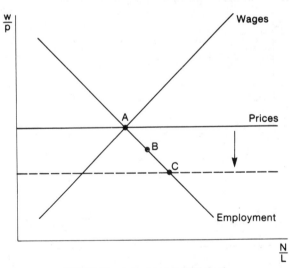

(b) Competitive pricing

FIGURE 10. A short-run demand shock.

If we have normal cost pricing, the real wage must rise; for as prices rise above their expected levels, firms reduce the mark-up of prices on wages. It is true that this also induces wage-bargainers to reduce the mark-up of wages on prices. But this is not enough to reduce the real wage because of the tighter labour market. The new disequilibrium observation is at *B*. Thus this model is consistent with the common claim that real wages rise in demand-led booms.

By contrast, if we have competitive pricing, the real wage has to fall; for this is the only way in which employment can rise, as at *B*. Thus, one clear test of pricing models is the behaviour of real wages in relation to demand shocks.

Of course, if at the same time as demand rises there is a supply-side improvement in wage behaviour, then prices need not run ahead of expectations. In the present case we should need a fall in the wage equation till it went through point *C*. Such a shift could come from a reduction of any of the 'push factors' including, as we have said, a fall in competitiveness.

(iii) *A supply shock: short-run and long-run.* We can now look at the effect of an exogenous increase in wage pressure, brought about, for example, by a rise in relative import prices such as occurred in the 1970s. If in the short run real demand remains unchanged, then there must be positive price surprises, typically brought about by rising inflation. In terms of Figure 11, as wage pressure rises the wage function moves to the left and we move from the equilibrium point *A* up the labour demand curve to a point such as *B*. As before, the new point must be above the price function and below the wage function, because of positive price surprises. Because the demand-for-labour schedule is fixed, the rise in wage pressure produces a fall in employment, and a rise in real wages. This fall in employment is decidedly classical in the sense that the rise in wage pressure has succeeded in raising real wages and opening up a 'wage gap' (see Bruno's paper in this volume).

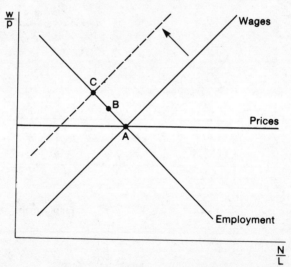

FIGURE 11. An increase in wage pressure (real demand fixed).

However, this is not the end of the story. In order to stabilize inflation at the new higher level of wage pressure, real demand must fall. This could happen endogenously or by a policy reaction. Endogenous mechanisms might include reduced consumption arising from higher inflation, higher real interest rates associated with lower real balances, losses of competitiveness (from the same source) and falls in the real value of cash-limited government expenditure.

In any event, let us suppose that, somehow or other, demand (σ) has
adjusted down to the level appropriate to the new level of wage pressure.
What happens to real wages? To examine this we present two diagrams
corresponding to the two extremes of firm behaviour, normal cost pricing in
Figure 12(a) and competitive pricing in Figure 12(b). As a consequence of the
increase in wage push we have a fall in the equilibrium level of employment

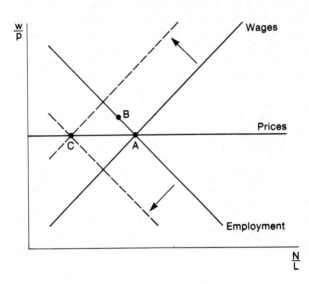

(a) Normal cost pricing

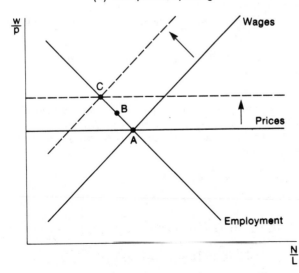

(b) Competitive pricing

FIGURE 12.   An increase in wage pressure: the new equilibrium.

and a correspondng fall in the level of real demand consistent with stable inflation. But under competitive pricing we have a rise in the real wage whereas under normal cost pricing there is no such rise. This is hardly surprising, for under normal cost pricing real wages are fixed, independently of demand, by the pricing policies of firms. Under competitive pricing, however, real wages must rise if lower employment is to be generated, and this happens naturally as lower demand leads to a lower mark-up of prices on wages since prices are rising with marginal cost. What happens in this 'second phase' thus depends crucially on firms' pricing behaviour. Under competitive pricing, unemployment remains 'classical'. The labour demand schedule is fixed, and real wages and the 'wage gap' increase further. Under normal cost pricing, however, unemployment now begins to look more 'Keynesian'. As demand is reduced, employment falls further from B to C, but the real wage falls and the 'wage gap' is closed. This provides an explanation of the continuing rise in European unemployment in the 1980s while the 'wage gap' is falling (see Bruno, this volume, and Gordon, 1985). It must, however, be emphasized that it is the rise in wage pressure that is the ultimate cause of the fall in employment, whichever form of pricing behaviour is assumed. The fall in demand has to come about in order to stabilize inflation, and the real wage outcome is entirely a secondary matter in the macroeconomic context.

To summarize, it should now be clear why we have unemployment. Very crudely, firms try to achieve a certain mark-up of prices on wages as part of their pricing strategy. On the other hand, workers try to achieve a certain mark-up of wages on prices in wage bargaining. If they are inconsistent, then in the short run they may be realigned by surprises. But in the long run these must be ruled out, and unemployment is the key mechanism that reduces the workers' aspirations, with the concomitant fall in demand possibly also reducing the aspirations of the firms. In the competitive economy the aspirations of firms do not come into it; but as soon as we move away from perfect competition in both labour and product markets there is a 'battle of the mark-ups', and, in the long run, it is unemployment that provides the resolution.

III. The Empirical Framework

As we have already noted in the previous section, in order to investigate unemployment in both the short and the long run, all we require is the employment equation (9), the price equation (7), the wage equation (14) and the competitiveness equation (15). In this section, therefore, we set out our empirical versions of these four equations and discuss how they may be utilized to analyse unemployment.

The employment equation

The dynamic version of (9) which we estimate has the form

$$(17) \quad \log N = \alpha_0 + \alpha_1 \log N_{-1} + \alpha_2 \log N_{-2} + \alpha_3 \log \left(\frac{W}{P} \right)_{-1} + \alpha_4 \sigma^e$$

$$+ \alpha_5 \log A + (1 - \alpha_1 - \alpha_2) \log K,$$

$$(\alpha_3 < 0, \ \alpha_4 > 0, \ 1 - \alpha_1 - \alpha_2 > 0)$$

where N = employment, W = hourly labour cost, P = value-added prices, σ^e = expected real demand relative to potential output, A = labour-augmenting technical progress and K = capital.

Three points are worth noting. First, dynamics may arise via adjustment costs and aggregation in the usual way. Second, it is clear from the form of (9) that the impact of technical progress is related to that of capital and the real wage. In fact, the restriction is

(18) $\alpha_5 = -\alpha_3 - (1 - \alpha_1 - \alpha_2)$.

So technical progress will have no impact on employment if the long-run wage elasticity of the demand for labour is unity. Third, in order to estimate our model we must specify how we measure real demand relative to potential output, σ. This is specified as a linear combination of price competitiveness, $P^*/\bar{P}$, the adjusted fiscal deficit relative to GDP, AD, and detrended world trade, WT. We tried including long-term real interest rates but with no success.

Thus we have

(19) $\sigma = \log \dfrac{P^*}{\bar{P}} + \alpha_{41} AD + \alpha_{42} WT$

where we take care of the fact that we have expected demand in our equation by using actual values and instrumenting in the usual way (see Wickens, 1982, for example).

The price equation

If there is some degree of sluggishness in price adjustment, then we have a simple dynamic version of (7) of the form

(20) $\log P = \log \ W + \beta_0 + \beta_1 \log \left(\dfrac{P}{W}\right)_{-1} + \beta_2 \sigma^e + \beta_3 \log \dfrac{K}{L}$

$+ \beta_4 \log A + \bar{\beta}_5 (\log \ P - \log P^e)$.

In order to deal with the last term, note that, if we take expectations of (20) and subtract, we obtain

$\log P - \log P^e = \log \ W - \log W^e + \bar{\beta}_5 (\log \ P - \log P^e)$

where we assume that K/L and A are known in advance. Hence we may replace $\log P - \log P^e$ by $(\log \ W - \log W^e)/(1 - \bar{\beta}_5)$, which we model by a distributed lag on $\Delta^2 \log W$. Thus we estimate an equation of the form

(21) $\log \left(\dfrac{P}{W}\right) = \beta_0 + \beta_1 \log \left(\dfrac{P}{W}\right)_{-1} + \beta_2 \sigma^e + \beta_3 \log \dfrac{K}{L} + \beta_4 \log A$

$+ \beta_5 \Delta^2 \log W + \beta_6 \Delta^2 \log \ W_{-1}, \qquad (\beta_2 > 0; \ \beta_3, \ \beta_5, \ \beta_6 < 0).$

In addition, the derivation of the price and employment equations ensures that there are some cross-equation restrictions which essentially follow from the production function constraint (6a). These are

(22) $\beta_3/(1 - \beta_1) = (1 - \alpha_1 - \alpha_2)/\alpha_3; \ \beta_4/(1 - \beta_1) = -(1 - \alpha_1 - \alpha_2)/\alpha_3 - 1$

and a proof may be found in Layard and Nickell (1985b).

The wage equation

The wage equation is based on equation (14) and has the form

$$(23) \quad \log \frac{W}{P} = \gamma_0 + \log \frac{P^e}{P} + \gamma_1 U + \gamma_2 \log \frac{K}{L} + \gamma_3 \log A + Z + \gamma_4 \nu \log \frac{P_m}{\bar{P}},$$

$$(\gamma_1 < 0, \ \gamma_2, \ \gamma_4 > 0)$$

where U = unemployment rate $\simeq -\log N/L$, and ν = share of imports in GDP. We exclude the real price of imports, $P_m/\bar{P}$, from Z because it is endogenous, so Z now includes mismatch (MM), the replacement rate (ρ), an index of union power (U_P), the labour tax rate on employers (t_1), the income tax rate (t_2), the indirect tax rate (t_3), and a dummy for incomes policy (IPD). These variables are all described in the Introduction, so we may write Z as

$$(24) \quad Z = \gamma_{31} MM + \gamma_{32}\rho + \gamma_{33} U_p + \gamma_{34} t_1 + \gamma_{35} t_2 + \gamma_{36} t_3 + \gamma_{37} IPD,$$

$$(\gamma_{31}, \ \gamma_{32}, \ \gamma_{33}, \ \gamma_{34}, \ \gamma_{35}, \ \gamma_{36} > 0, \ \gamma_{37} < 0)$$

Although (23) does not look much like a standard Phillips curve equation, it is, in fact, very closely related, as our discussion in Layard and Nickell (1985a) makes clear.

In our empirical work, we use a number of different variants of equation (23), as we shall see. In particular, we replace U successively by $\log U$, $\log V$ (the vacancy rate) and U_s (the short-term unemployment rate), and we also include $\nu \log (P_m/\bar{P})$. The reasons for this are discussed with the results.

The competitveness equation

In order to determine the long-run level of competitiveness given by equation (15), we estimate an equation explaining the trade balance as a proportion of potential GDP (B/Y^P). The actual equation used is

$$(25) \quad \frac{B}{Y^P} = \delta_0 + \delta_1 \nu \log \left(\frac{P^*}{\bar{P}}\right)_{-1} + \delta_2 \nu \log \left(\frac{P_m}{P^*}\right)_{-1}$$

$$+ \delta_3 \sigma_{-1} + \delta_4 OIL_{-1} + \delta_5 WT, \qquad (\delta_1 > 0, \ \delta_3 < 0, \ \delta_4, \ \delta_5 > 0).$$

where P_m/P^* is the price of imports relative to world prices in domestic currency and OIL is the real value of oil production (nominal value divided by $\bar{P}$). Setting $B/Y^P = 0$ then gives the long-run equilibrium level of competitiveness.

The analysis of unemployment

In order to use these equations to analyse the changes in unemployment, we proceed as follows. First, to account for the medium-term changes in unemployment, we combine the employment function (17) and wage function (23) to obtain an unemployment function of the form

$$(26) \quad (1 - \alpha_1 - \alpha_2 + \alpha_3 \gamma_1) U = -(\alpha_0 + \alpha_3 \gamma_0) - (1 - \alpha_1 - \alpha_2 + \alpha_3 \gamma_2) \log \frac{K}{L}$$

$$- (\alpha_3 \gamma_3 + \alpha_5) \log A - \alpha_3 \log \left(\frac{P}{P^e}\right) - \alpha_3 Z - \alpha_3 \gamma_4 \nu \log \left(\frac{P_m}{\bar{P}}\right) - \alpha_4 \sigma.$$

where we have used the long-run solutions to the two equations. This equation determines the unemployment rate conditional on the demand index σ and the level of competitiveness, $P^*/\bar{P}$. As the equation makes clear, in the long run the unemployment rate could be affected by the capital–labour force ratio but not by the size of the labour force (for any given K/L). However, in the light of history it does not seem reasonable to think of the capital–labour force ratio as an important determinant of unemployment *in the long run*. If long-run 'neutrality' holds with respect to K/L and $\log A$, we would have to find

(27a) $\quad \gamma_2 = -(1 - \alpha_1 - \alpha_2)/\alpha_3$

(27b) $\quad \gamma_3 = -\alpha_5/\alpha_3.$

In other words, wage behaviour would have to be such that, when K/L or A alters the demand price for labour, the actual wage changes in the same proportion.

The second use of the model is to compute the natural rate of unemployment and the effect upon it of the Z variables. For this purpose we set $P = P^e$ and $W = W^e$. In practice, we compute two versions of the natural rate, one conditional on the actual level of price competitiveness, $P^*/\bar{P}$, and an unconditional version assuming zero trade balance. The former may be obtained by noting that the employment equation and the price equation together imply

$$(28) \quad (1 - \alpha_1 - \alpha_2)U = -\alpha_o\left(-\frac{\alpha_3\beta_0}{1-\beta_1}\right) - \left(1 - \alpha_1 - \alpha_2 - \frac{\alpha_3\beta_3}{1-\beta_1}\right)\log\frac{K}{L}$$
$$-\left(\alpha_4 - \frac{\alpha_3\beta_2}{1-\beta_1}\right)\sigma - \left(\alpha_5 - \frac{\alpha_3\beta_4}{1-\beta_1}\right)\log A.$$

Notice that the restrictions (18) and (22) imply that the coefficients on both $\log K/L$ and $\log A$ are zero. So long-run 'neutrality' in this equation is a consequence of the production function constraint. Next we eliminate σ between (26) and (28) and, given K/L and A neutrality, obtain

$$(29) \quad U = \text{constant} + \frac{\{\alpha_4(1-\beta_1) - \alpha_3\beta_2\}(Z + \gamma_4\nu\log P_m/\bar{P})}{\beta_2(1 - \alpha_1 - \alpha_2 + \alpha_3\gamma_1) - \alpha_4\gamma_1(1-\beta_1)}$$

which emphasizes the crucial role of the wage pressure variables.

To obtain the zero-trade-balance natural rate, we note that under this condition (25) implies that

$$(30) \quad \delta_1\nu\log\left(\frac{P^*}{\bar{P}}\right) = -\delta_0 - \delta_2\nu\log\left(\frac{P_m}{P^*}\right) - \delta_3\sigma - \delta_4 OIL - \delta_5 WT.$$

If we now write

$$(31) \quad \nu\log\frac{P_m}{\bar{P}} = \nu\log\frac{P_m}{P^*} + \nu\log\frac{P^*}{\bar{P}}$$

we can use (28), (30) and (31) to eliminate $\nu\log P_m/\bar{P}$ from (29) to obtain

$$(32) \quad U = \frac{\Delta\{\alpha_4(1-\beta_1) - \alpha_3\beta_3\}}{\Delta - \gamma_4\delta_3(1 - \alpha_1 - \alpha_2)(1-\beta_1)}$$
$$\times\left\{Z - \frac{\delta_4\gamma_4}{\delta_1}OIL - \frac{\delta_5\gamma_4}{\delta_1}WT + \frac{(\delta_1-\delta_2)}{\delta_1}\gamma_4\nu\log\frac{P_m}{P^*}\right\}$$

where $\Delta = \beta_2(1 - \alpha_1 - \alpha_2 + \alpha_3\gamma_1) - \alpha_4\gamma_1(1-\beta_1) > 0.$

Note that both oil and positive deviations in world trade from trend will tend to reduce the natural rate because they tend to improve the terms of trade (lower competitiveness).

IV. ACCOUNTING FOR UNEMPLOYMENT GROWTH (USING ANNUAL DATA)[25]

We now estimate the model based on equations (17), (21), (23) and (25) with appropriate lags introduced as suggested by the data. The first three equations are estimated simultaneously, with the cross-equation restrictions (22) and (27) imposed.

Labour demand

Estimates of the labour demand equation corresponding to (17) are presented in Table 4. The long-run unit capital ˙stock elasticity is imposed and the *t*-statistic (0·3) is based on a Wald test of this hypothesis. To test the validity of the separability assumption which enables us to use value-added prices, we first include, as separate variables, wages relative to final output prices ($W/\bar{P}$)

TABLE 4

LABOUR DEMAND EQUATION, 1954–1983

Independent variables	Dependent variable log N
Constant	2·57 (4·9)
log N_{-1}	1·057 (8·2)
log N_{-2}	−0·361 (2·6)
log K	0·304 ($t = 0·3$)
log $(W/P)_{-1}$	−0·285 (4·9)
*log $(P^*/\bar{P})$⎫	0·0667 (3·2)
*AD ⎬ σ	0·718 (3·6)
WT ⎭	0·0686 (1·9)
s.e.	0·0077
DW	2·23
LM (autocorrelation χ^2 (2))	2·20
Parameter stability χ^2 (7)	5·12
Wage elasticity	0·94
Capital stock elasticity	1·0

Notes:
(i) Asymptotic absolute *t*-ratios in parentheses.
(ii) The parameter estimates are generated by nonlinear 3SLS (TSP 4·0) and refer to the labour demand equation corresponding to the wage equation, Model 1. Additional instruments include lags on the endogenous variables. Not surprisingly, the labour demand equations corresponding to Models 2 and 3 are very similar and are not reported here. The autocorrelation and parameter stability statistics refer to unrestricted instrumental variables estimates of the same equation since these are not to be found in TSP.
(iii) The demand index, σ, is given by $\sigma = \log (P^*/\bar{P}) + 10·76AD + 1·028 WT$.
Variables:
N = aggregate employment, K = aggregate capital stock, W = labour costs, P = value-added deflator, AD = adjusted deficit-potential GDP, P^* = world price of manufacturers (pounds), $\bar{P}$ = TFE deflator at factor cost, WT = deviation of world trade from trend.

and import prices relative to final output prices $(P_m/\bar{P})$, weighted by the share of imports in value added (ν). The coefficients were almost identical $(t = 0.04)$. The long-run wage elasticity is -0.93. If technical progress is labour-augmenting, the technical progress coefficient should be around -0.07 (see equation (18)). In fact, it turns out to be very close to this, but it is so near zero that its contribution to the model is negligible. It is therefore simply omitted. The demand side variables make a significant positive contribution to labour demand, and if they are omitted the real-wage coefficient is both smaller and less well determined. Their strength also indicates that a simple competitive model, where only K and W/P would appear, is not an adequate representation of the data.

Prices

Turning now to the price equation based on (21), the results are reported in Table 5. The equation is very simple, with the price surprise terms being captured by second differences in the wage. Demand shows up as having a significant but small positive impact on prices, which is consistent with the strong showing of the same variables in the employment equation. We also investigated the consequences of including an additional variable capturing the effective tax rate on profits including investment incentives and the like (t_4). The idea here is that firms will allow some erosion of pre-tax profit margins if they are more generously treated on the tax front. The variable used is based on that described in Beath (1979).[26] As can be seen, it appears to show up quite well in the equation with the expected sign.

TABLE 5
PRICE EQUATION, 1954–1983

	Dependent variable	
Independent variable	$\log (P/W)$	$\log (P/W)$
Constant	-4.18 (4.2)	-4.47 (4.5)
$\log (P/W)_{-1}$	0.544 (5.0)	0.514 (4.7)
*$\Delta^2 \log W$	-0.336 (4.2)	-0.318 (4.1)
$\Delta^2 \log W_{-1}$	-0.242 (3.8)	-0.210 (3.3)
*σ	0.0381 (2.1)	0.0371 (2.1)
$\log (K/L)$	-0.486 ($t=0.1$)	-0.518 ($t=0.4$)
t_4		0.0318 (1.1)
s.e.	0.015	0.0155
DW	2.27	1.71
LM (autocorrelation χ^2 (2))	5.37	4.83
Parameter stability χ^2 (5)	1.18	7.70 $(\chi^2$ (6))
(sample split 1968)		

Notes:
(i) Asymptotic absolute t-ratios in parentheses.
(ii) See note (ii), Table 4.
Variables not recorded in Table 4:
L = labour force; σ = the demand index, given in Table 4, note (iii); $t_4 = (1-\tau)^{-1}$ where τ = effective rate of tax on profits.

Wage behaviour

Turning to wage behaviour, we consider three different models. First (Model 1) we estimate equation (23)—see Table 6, column (1). In comparison with (23), a number of differences may be observed. First, $\log P^e - \log P$ is omitted. This is not a consequence of any prior judgment concerning its place in the equation; it simply follows from the fact that, in spite of innumerable attempts, we were unable to model this term in a satisfactory manner. We tried modelling P^e explicitly, using fitted values from a subsidiary regression. We tried approximating $\log P^e - \log P$ by any number of different formulations of past wages, prices, etc.[27] We had absolutely no success, in the sense that the results were often incorrectly signed, generally of negligible significance, and made no contribution of any value to the equation. We therefore consigned the term to the equation error (see Minford, 1983, for a similar result). This, of course, has consequences for estimation, in the sense that any variable that is included in the equation which represents a current-dated shock will be correlated with this error. As a consequence, all such variables are treated as endogenous, and, with the exception of predetermined variables such as K/L, only lagged variables are used as instruments in this context.

TABLE 6

WAGE EQUATION, 1954–1983

	Dependent variable: $\log (W/P)$		
		Equation number:	
	Model 1	Model 2	Model 3
Constant	8·41 (9.0)	9·31 (106·5)	8·50 (9·9)
*$\log U$	−0·0621 (4·4)		
*$\log V$		0·0357 (3·8)	
*U_s			−2·47 (4·2)
MM	0·039 (3·3)	0·0144 (1·88)	0·0350 (3·6)
*ρ	0·182 (1·5)		0·142 (1·2)
*$\nu \log P_m/\bar{P}$	0·499 (2·5)	0·268 (2·5)	0·685 (3·3)
*$\Delta(\nu \log P_m/\bar{P})$	0·419 (2·0)	0·619 (3·2)	0·196 (0·9)
*U_p	0·0853 (4·1)	0·0506 (3·8)	0·0775 (4·1)
*t_1	0·179 (0·9)		0·156 (0·9)
IPD	−0·0214 (1·7)	−0·0177 (1·5)	−0·197 (1·6)
$\log (K/L)$	1·07 ($t = 1·03$)	1·07 ($t = 1·3$)	1·07 ($t = 0·9$)
s.e.	0·0145	0·0167	0·0147
DW	1·66	1·67	1·47
LM (autocorrelation χ^2 (2))	3·73	4·75	5·91
Parameter stability χ^2 (7) (sample split, 1968)	0·92	9·81	18·32 (χ^2 (8))

Notes:
 (i) Asymptotic absolute t-ratios in parentheses.
 (ii) See note (ii), Table 4.
Variables not reported in Tables 4 and 5;
$U_p = \log$ union mark-up; $\rho = $ replacement ratio; $MM = $ the *absolute* change in the proportion of employees in the production sector; $IPD = $ incomes policy dummy ($=1,1976+7$; zero, elsewhere); $U = $ male unemployment rate; $V = $ vacancy rate; $U_s = $ short-term unemployment rate, i.e. proportion of the labour force unemployed for less than 26 weeks.

These points bear emphasis. We have *not* simply omitted a relevant variable. What we have done is to estimate consistently the parameters of the equation, which *includes* log P^e − log P. The only thing we have not done is to estimate the coefficient on log P^e − log P. In any event, the variable is· zero in the long-run equilibrium and will clearly make no contribution to the secular trends in unemployment in which we are particularly interested.

Turning now to the variables that are included, a key point is that, instead of U, the equation contains log U. This appears because it is a more robust formulation, but it does of course, have very serious consequences. In essence, it says that, when it comes to holding down wages, it is proportional and not absolute increases in unemployment that are important. This may not look to be a very significant difference, but its ramifications are serious. In particular, the *absolute* consequences for the natural rate of any exogenous changes will tend to be bigger if we start from a higher initial level of unemployment. This is, of course, entirely consistent with the hypothesis that the short-term unemployed exert greater downward pressure on wages than the long-term unemployed. As unemployment rises, the short-term proportion falls and the unemployment effect has the concave shape characteristic of the log function. For reasons already explained, we also looked for effects from lagged unemployment terms, but could find none. (However, see the quarterly model of the next section.)

Turning to the effects of the push variables, the replacement ratio appears with the correct sign and is relatively well determined. The union mark-up variable also shows up clearly. This variable seems to us to represent a good *ex post* measure of union activity which will reflect fluctuations in the autonomous use of power. For example, it rises strongly in the period 1968–72. This contrasts with the alternative variable that is sometimes favoured, namely union density. This seems to us to have a very limited theoretical pedigree as well as appearing to be highly unrobust once the sample period is extended beyond 1979. In fact, our experiments with this variable indicate that it is empirically more or less useless as a measure of union power.

The mismatch variable is another case where a proxy is required, and here we simply use the *absolute* change in the proportion of employees in the production sector. This appears to work rather well. Looking next at the tax variables, the point to note is that the only one that is included is the labour tax rate on employers, the others being completely insignificant. The other element of the wedge between the net consumption wage and the real wage in terms of value added is the real price of imports. Here we have a positive long-run effect, reinforcing a similarly signed short-run effect.

Turning to the productivity variable (K/L), we imposed a coefficient equal to the inverse of the wage elasticity of labour demand. This was done for reasons explained earlier, but, as we can see from the t-statistic, this restriction in no sense violates the data. We had no success in our attempt to capture the wage effects of productivity slowdowns using Δ^2 log K/L terms. In fact, we tried many variations on this theme, looking at the rate of change of productivity growth over various time horizons and testing for asymmetries (e.g. the variable has an impact only if it is negative). We also included an incomes policy dummy for the years 1976–77, although we recognize that this is an inappropriate procedure for dealing with incomes policies. (Pudney, 1983, for example, allows systematically for the strength of the policy by comparing the norm with the wage that would have resulted in its absence.)

Finally, it is worth commenting on the dynamic structure of the equation, which is somewhat spartan. Of course, the combination of a very short time series and a rather large number of regressors precludes extensive dynamics, although it should be noted that there is no evidence that the lagged dependent variable should be included (coefficient $= 0 \cdot 10$ $(0 \cdot 4)$).

The problem with this equation is that it may not fully capture the effects of changes in the availability of social security. The value of benefits is by no means the only relevant variable here, since ease of access to benefits is also very important. Employment protection may also affect the perceived shortage of labour and thus affect wage pressure. To capture the effect of all these influences, we can use as a variable the shift of the U/V curves as measured by the 'search intensity' variable(s) described on p. S125 above.

One approach would be simply to incorporate this in equation (23) as one of the push variables (Z). However, given the trended nature of the variable, this is not very satisfactory. A preferable approach is to estimate equation (23) with vacancies (V), rather than unemployment (U), as the pressure-of-demand variable. One can then eliminate vacancies (V) from the equation, replacing it by unemployment (U), search intensity (s) and mismatch (MM), using the long-run relation

(33) $\log U = -2 \cdot 79 - 0 \cdot 896 \log V + 0 \cdot 098 MM - s$

derived on p. S125.

The wage equation including vacancies (V) is shown in column (2) of Table 6. As we might expect, the replacement ratio effect drops out since the inclusion of vacancies in place of unemployment takes account of this effect already. But the equation is generally somewhat less satisfactory than the unemployment version, providing a considerably weaker explanation of the data. The employers' tax rate also disappears.

Our third approach to wage behaviour is motivated by an attempt to understand why wage pressure has not fallen in recent years as much as one might expect, given our high levels of unemployment. One obvious fact is that since 1981 the whole increase in unemployment has been of people unemployed for over six months. Could it be that such people exert very little downward pressure on wages? There is evidence from the Department of Health and Social Security Cohort Study of the Unemployed that long-term unemployed people spend less time and money searching for work than the short-term unemployed. They also make fewer job applications. It therefore seems quite likely that they exert less downward pressure on wages than the short-term unemployed. This would be reinforced if there was any tendency for downward pressure on wages to be exerted especially by increasing inflows into unemployment. We therefore estimate equations in which we include both the long-term unemployed (over six months) as a proportion of the labour force (U_L) and the total unemployment rate (U). These turn out to have almost exactly equal and opposite signs $(t = 0 \cdot 5)$, indicating that we can simply use the short-term unemployment rate. This we do in column (3) of Table 6. Otherwise the equation is fairly similar to the equation in the first column, although it explains the data less well.

To close this third model, we have an equation for the long-term unemployment proportion (U_L/U), of the form

$$(34) \quad \frac{U_L}{U} = 0\cdot159 + 0\cdot466\left(\frac{U_L}{U}\right)_{-1} \quad 0\cdot689\,U + 3\cdot89\,U_{-1} - 2\cdot15\,U_{-2}$$

$$(2\cdot5) \qquad\qquad (1\cdot0) \quad\quad (3\cdot9) \qquad (2\cdot1)$$

$$(OLS, 1955\text{-}83).$$

This yields a long-run relation between the short-term unemployment rate (U_S) and the total rate, of the form

$$(35) \quad U_S = 0\cdot702\,U - 1\cdot968\,U^2$$

which has the concave structure picked up by the log transformation of U in the first equation.

Trade balance

In order to compute our long-run natural rate estimates, we require a trade balance equation, and one based on (25) is reported in Table 7. It differs from (25) in so far as world trade deviations are omitted because we obtained no significant estimate of their contribution. Otherwise the variables are sensibly signed, but the explanatory power of the equation is not strong.

TABLE 7

TRADE BALANCE EQUATION, 1954-1983

	Dependent variable B/Y^P
Constant	41·68 (2·6)
$\nu \log (P^*/\bar{P})_{-1}$	361·03 (2·7)
$\nu \log (P_m/P^*)_{-1}$	135·84 (1·4)
σ_{-1}	−39·82 (2·3)
OIL_{-1}	24·67 (1·4)
s.e.	10·46
DW	1·56
LM (autocorrelation χ^2 (2))	4·12
Parameter stability χ^2 (4) (sample split, 1968)	4·41

Note:
Asymptotic t-ratios in parentheses.
Variables not reported in Tables 4, 5 and 6:
B/Y^P = (value of exports—value of imports)/nominal potential;
GDP, OIL = real value of North Sea Oil production in terms of output prices.

Accounting for postwar unemployment growth

We can now use these estimates to account for postwar unemployment growth. Using Model 1, the empirical equivalent to equation (26) is

$$(36) \quad U + 0\cdot0579 \log U = \text{constant} - 0\cdot22\sigma + 0\cdot029\,MM + 0\cdot17\rho$$

$$+ 0\cdot47(\nu \log P_m/\bar{P}) + 0\cdot39\Delta(\nu \log P_m/\bar{P})$$

$$+ 0\cdot080\,U_P + 0\cdot17t_1 - 0\cdot096\,IPD.$$

Note that we have retained $\Delta(\nu \log P_m/\bar{P})$ even in the 'long run' because it exhibits such strong long-period trends.

Our first step is to analyse the changes in unemployment conditional on the actual values of the demand variable σ. In order to do this while coping with the nonlinearity inherent in the log U term, we divide up the sample into four periods: 1956-66, 1967-74, 1975-79, 1980-83. We then consider average values of the variables over these periods and look at changes from one period to the next. This gives us, from (36),

$$\left(1+\frac{0\cdot0579}{\bar{U}}\right)\Delta U = \Delta \text{ (right-hand side)}$$

where $\bar{U}$ is set at the average level of U *across the two periods being considered.* The next question concerns the dating of the changes on the right-hand side. Here we take the demand variables at the current date (e.g. we consider $\sigma(67\text{-}74) - \sigma(56\text{-}66)$); but for all the other variables we have taken a two-year lag (e.g. we have $t_1(65\text{-}72) - t_1(54\text{-}64)$). Because the real wage has a one-year lag in the labour demand equation, this generates a natural one-year delay; and, given the compression of the lags in the employment equation inherent in the long-run solution, we felt that two years was appropriate for these more structural changes, particularly as their impact on wages has probably been artificially compressed in our estimation of the wage model. It is also worth noting that the first long period, 1956-66, was selected because it exhibits practically no change in inflation. We can, therefore, consider its average unemployment rate as being close to its long-run natural level. This serves as a baseline for our natural rate investigations.

For reference purposes it is useful to set down the actual changes in the relevant variables over these periods, and this we do in Table 8. Noteworthy

TABLE 8

CHANGES IN THE AVERAGE VALUES OF SELECTED VARIABLES, 1954-1981

	1954-64 to 1965-72	1965-72 to 1973-77	1973-77 to 1978-81
Employers' labour taxes (t_1)	0·045	0·049	0·042
Benefit replacement ratio (ρ)	0·097	−0·011	−0·0088
Log union mark-up (U_p)	0·45	0·32	0·16
$\nu \log (P_m/\bar{P})$	−0·040	0·052	−0·012
$\Delta\{\nu \log (P_m/\bar{P})\}$	0·0024	0·020	−0·024
MM	0·17	0·15	0·27
UV shift factor (s)	−0·48	−0·36	−0·27
Log (K/L)	0·28	0·21	0·085
Technical progress (log A)	0·26	0·18	0·077
Oil production (OIL)	—	0·10	0·55

	1956-66 to 1967-74	1967-74 to 1975-79	1975-79 to 1980-83
Model 1	−0·017	−0·054	−0·477

are the powerful increases in labour taxes, the large changes in the union mark-up over the earlier periods, the considerable fluctuations in real import prices, and the close correlation between technical progress and the capital-labour force ratio.

Once we have considered the contributions of various factors to the actual change in unemployment, we can then set $\Delta^2 \log W = 0$ in the first price equation in Table 5 and use this in conjunction with the employment equation and (36) to eliminate σ and obtain the equation for the natural rate conditional on real import prices (equation (29)). This gives

$$(37) \quad 0 \cdot 26 U^* + 0 \cdot 0579 \log U^* = \text{constant} + 0 \cdot 029 MM + 0 \cdot 17\rho$$
$$+ 0 \cdot 47\nu \log P_m/\bar{P} + 0 \cdot 39\Delta (\nu \log P_m/\bar{P})$$
$$+ 0 \cdot 08 U_P + 0 \cdot 17 t_1 - 0 \cdot 196 IPD.$$

Perhaps more interesting is the equation for the natural rate conditional on balanced trade (equation (32)), which may be obtained by setting $B = 0$ in the trade balance equation of Table 7 and then using it and the other equations to eliminate competitiveness, $(P^*/\bar{P})$, from (37). The final equation thus has the form

$$(38) \quad 0 \cdot 44 U^* + 0 \cdot 0579 \log U^* = \text{constant} + 0 \cdot 029 MM + 0 \cdot 17\rho + 0 \cdot 08 U_P$$
$$+ 0 \cdot 17 t_1 - 0 \cdot 196 IPD + 0 \cdot 29\nu \log P_m/P^*$$
$$+ 0 \cdot 24\Delta \nu \log P_m/P^* - 0 \cdot 032 OIL$$
$$- 0 \cdot 027\Delta OIL.$$

Two points are worth noting. First, a rise in both the level and rate of growth of the world price ratio between UK imports and world manufacturers raises the natural rate, because it increases wage pressure. On the other hand, increasing oil production lowers the natural rate, because it reduces wage pressure via the real exchange rate. Demand can thereby be increased without adverse inflationary consequences.

We shall use both equations (37) and (38) to generate natural rate series by estimating changes between the four periods mentioned above and assuming that, on average, unemployment was at the natural rate during the first period. First, however, we present, in Table 9, a breakdown of the changes in unemployment over the postwar period as generated by equation (36) (Model 1). The overall degree of explanation seems quite satisfactory, so let us turn to the actual numbers. The changes between the first two periods are dominated by the rise in employers' labour taxes, the rise in the benefit replacement ratio and the rise in union power or militancy. 'Demand' factors play an insignificant role but there are some gains arising from the continuing improvement in the terms of trade.

Employers' labour taxes and unions again figure strongly in the second-to third-period unemployment change, but here there is a very powerful effect owing to the dramatic rise in real import prices in 1973–74. The final and largest increase is completely dominated by 'demand' factors although some other factors are by no means insignificant, in particular the beneficial effect of the fall in the real price of imports brought about in the main by the appreciation of the pound.

TABLE 9

BREAKDOWN OF THE CHANGE IN UNEMPLOMENT RATE (MALE), 1956-1983
(Basis, Table 6, Model 1)
(percentage points)

	1956-66 to 1967-74	1967-74 to 1975-79	1975-79 to 1980-83
Employers' labour taxes (t_1)	0·25	0·38	0·44
Benefit replacement ratio (ρ)	0·54	−0·09	−0·10
Union (U_p)	1·18	1·17	0·80
Real import prices ($P_m/\bar{P}$)	−0·58	1·47	−0·93
divided into			
(P_m/P^*) and ($P^*/\bar{P}$)	(−0·35 −0·23)	(2·40 −0·93)	(−0·15 −0·77)
Mismatch (MM)	0·16	0·20	0·49
Demand factors (σ)	0·12	0·54	6·56
Incomes policy (IPD)	—	−0·36	0·49
Total	1·67	3·31	7·75
Actual change	1·82	3·01	7·00

Note:
P_m/P^* is the international 'terms of trade' between UK imports and world manufacturers, both priced in dollars, and $P^*/\bar{P}$ is output price competitiveness.

Let us now consider the natural rate sequences reported in Table 10. The sequence based on given real import prices was, on average, above the actual rate throughout the period 1967-79 but moved to around 3 percentage points below it by 1980-83. The 'longer-term' natural rate based on trade balance reveals a similar story, although by 1980-83 it was around 4 percentage points below the actual rate. In two cases out of three, this pattern is consistent with the changes in inflation, the exception being the period from 1975-79, when wage inflation came down and yet the natural rate was considerably above the actual rate.

This is an interesting result, suggesting that there were other forces at work during this period. The obvious one is the incomes policy, and, although we have tried to capture its effect by using dummies, it seems likely that its impact was, in fact, rather greater than the coefficients on these dummies would

TABLE 10

ESTIMATED 'NATURAL' RATE OF UNEMPLOYMENT, MALES, 1956-1983
(Basis, Table 6, Model 1) (percentages)

	1956-66	1967-74	1975-79	1980-83
'Natural' unemployment rate (a) (conditional on given real import prices)	1·96	4·02	8·20	10·47
'Natural' unemployment rate (b) (conditional on trade balance)	1·96	4·19	7·63	9·07
Actual unemployment rate	1·96	3·78	6·79	13·79

suggest. In any event, some forces were at work during this period which enabled inflation to come down without unemployment having to rise above its equilibrium level, at least as generated by the structural factors that we have considered. However, it is worth noting that, if we exclude 1976 and 1977, when the incomes policy was dramatically successful, then wage inflation rose somewhat over the remainder of the period.

In order to see the full contributions to the natural rate increase of the push factors set out in Table 9, we must remember that their impact is larger than shown in that table. This follows from the fact that, when a push factor, such as the benefit replacement ratio, moves adversely, it not only has a direct impact on unemployment but also serves to reduce the level of demand (σ) consistent with unchanging inflation. In order to see these effects, we have set out a breakdown of changes in the natural rate (given balanced trade) in Table 11. Notice the importance of the surge in raw material prices in the 1973–74 period and the important role of oil in *reducing* the natural rate in the last period. The union effect is quite large in all three periods, and this reflects two factors; the continuing increase in wage pressure delivered by the wage-bargaining institutions in Britain, and the fact that the absolute employment effects of any given increase in wage pressure are themselves tending to rise because of the concave shape of the unemployment effect on wages.

TABLE 11

BREAKDOWN OF CHANGES IN THE NATURAL RATE (b) GIVEN IN TABLE 10

	1956–66 to 1967–74	1967–74 to 1975–79	1975–79 to 1980–83
Employers' labour taxes (t_1)	0·29	0·51	0·69
Benefit replacement rate (1)	0·64	−0·12	−0·15
Unions (U_p)	1·40	1·58	1·25
Oil production (*OIL*)	—	−0·32	−1·73
UK import/world manufactures, price ratio (P_m/P^*)	−0·29	2·02	−0·17
Mismatch (*MM*)	0·19	0·27	0·77
Incomes policy (*IPD*)	—	−0·50	0·78
Total	2·23	3·44	1·44

In addition to analysing natural rates, we can also look at the amounts by which demand would have had to change in order to remain consistent with unchanging inflation. The numbers here for the three successive shifts are −0·071, −0·140 and −0·076, and these may be compared with the actual demand changes reported in the last row of Table 8, namely −0·017, −0·054 and −0·477. So we see that for the first two changes (1956–66 to 1967–74, and 1967–74 to 1975–79), the actual 'demand' reductions were lower than those required for unchanging inflation. As a consequence, of course, inflation rose on average over the whole period and actual unemployment was, on average, below the natural rate. But when we go from 1975–79 to 1980–83, we see that 'demand' actually fell by more than five times what was required for unchanging inflation, with the obvious consequences. Of this remarkable fall in demand, about 46 per cent was due to fiscal policy, 42 per cent to competitiveness and 12 per cent to world trade.

Turning now to Model 2, we find that the UV shift factor (search intensity, s), not surprisingly, plays an important role contributing some 2 percentage points to the rise in unemployment, given demand. In this model, neither employment taxes nor the replacement ratio show up at all, and the role of the union variable is strongly attenuated. Aside from this, the structure of the results is not altered a great deal and the same is true of the natural rate estimates (for further details see Layard and Nickell, 1985a). In some respects, of course, this model is less satisfactory than the previous one, since we are picking up the impact of unobservable variables (workers' search intensity and employment protection legislation) by simple trends. The corresponding wage equation is also a good deal less satisfactory in terms of data explanation.

Finally, the Model 3 results, containing the short-term unemployment rate, are very similar to those of Model 1, although the general fit is less good. The implications of the wage equation in this model are, however, rather profound. In essence, it tells us that, if we reduce unemployment using a policy targeted at the long-run unemployed, its impact on wages will be negligible.

To sum up this section, we have presented our estimates of the causes of the secular rise in unemployment in the postwar period. One point must be remembered. All the numbers in these tables are based on estimated equations, where many of the coefficients are not determined with any degree of precision; the same therefore applies to the numbers in the tables. Nevertheless, we feel that this approach is a valuable one and indicates the direction in which to proceed.

V. Dynamics of Unemployment and Real Wages (Using Quarterly Data)

We now present a quarterly version of our model and use it to investigate the dynamics of wages, prices and unemployment. Aside from the dynamic structure, the model we estimate is more or less identical to Model 1 of the previous section. The equations are independently estimated, with the parameter restrictions being carried over from the labour demand equation.

Table 12 presents the labour demand equation. As with the other quarterly equations that follow, we present the equation in differences and levels. This enables one to read off the long-run effects simply by dividing through by the coefficient on the level of the lagged dependent variable (e.g. 0·0324 in this case). Not surprisingly, the long-run effects are similar to those generated by the annual model, although the wage elasticity is slightly larger at 1·19. The only essential long-run difference is our inability to find a level world trade effect in the present model.

The short-run dynamics, on the other hand, are completely different, and in this case are not really satisfactory because the speed of adjustment is very slow. The level employment coefficient is 0·0324, which is tantamount to a lagged dependent variable coefficient of 0·968. This suggests that we are having trouble in actually explaining the level of employment, with the equation being dominated by its dynamic properties. The estimates imply that any shock that hits labour demand will take an excessively long time to filter through the

TABLE 12

LABOUR DEMAND EQUATION, QUARTERLY, 1957(I)–1983(IV)

Independent variables	Dependent variable $\Delta \log N$
Constant	0·261 (2·5)
$\Delta \log N_{-4}$	0·142 (1·5)
$\log N_{-1}$	−0·0324 (2·4)
$\log K$	0·0324
$\log (W/P)_{-1}$	−0·0385 (2·7)
$\Delta_4 \log (W/P)_{-1}$	0·0284 (1·6)
AD_{-1}	0·126 (2·1)
$\log (P^*/\bar{P})_{-1}$	0·0136 (1·8)
$\Delta_4 WT$	0·0374 (3·4)
s.e.	0·00500
$\bar{R}^2$	0·496
DW	1·85
LM (autocorrelation χ^2 (4))	6·46 (5% = 9·48)
Parameter stability $F(16, 97)$ (sample split, 1979(IV))	1·64 (5% = 1·8)
Wage elasticity (long-run)	−1·19
Capital stock elasticity	1·0

Notes:

(i) Asymptotic absolute t-ratios in parentheses; seasonal dummies were also included.

(ii) There are no current endogenous variables on the right, so estimation is by OLS.

(iii) On the basis of this equation, the demand index, σ, is defined as $\sigma = \log (P^*/\bar{P}) + 9 \cdot 26AD$. $\Delta_4 WT$ is not part of the index because it only represents a transient effect.

system, given that it takes about five years to complete half of its long-run impact on employment.

Why we obtain this result is not clear. However, given the much faster adjustment that emerges in the UK manufacturing sector for a similar kind of equation (see Symons, 1985, for example), we suspect that it arises because of the problems of trying to aggregate over different sectors, including the public sector, with very different employment adjustment paths.

Turning now to the price equation in Table 13, we come up against a similar kind of problem, with the equation being unable to explain adequately the level of the price/wage mark-up on a quarterly basis. There is, however, a strong wage-surprise effect, confirming the annual result, and we seem to have pinned down some quite precise dynamics, even if the long-run effects are rather weak.

The wage equation is far more satisfactory, in the sense that we are clearly able to explain the level of the real wage as it emerges from wage bargaining. The equation compares quite well with its annual counterpart, although there are a number of important differences. In particular, there is now a large price-surprise effect (which we have constrained to be unity—see note v to Table 14) and a strong negative effect of the current change in unemployment.

Many of the long-run effects on real wages seem to be rather bigger than in the annual model, including both the Z effect and the unemployment effect.

TABLE 13

PRICE EQUATION, QUARTERLY, 1957(I)–1983(IV)

Independent variables	Dependent variable $\Delta \log (P/W)$
Constant	$-0\cdot883$ (1·9)
$\Delta \log (P/W)_{-2}$	$0\cdot224$ (3·1)
$\Delta \log (P/W)_{-4}$	$0\cdot131$ (1·9)
$\log (P/W)_{-1}$	$-0\cdot110$ (1·8)
*$\log W^e - \log W)$	$0\cdot685$ (5·0)
$\log (K/L)$	$-0\cdot0925$
σ_{-1}	$0\cdot0202$ (1·6)
t_4	$0\cdot0583$ (1·5)
s.e.	$0\cdot020$
$\bar{R}^2$	$0\cdot572$
DW	$2\cdot19$
LM (autocorrelation χ^2 (4))	$9\cdot10$ (5% $=9\cdot48$)
Parameter stability $F(16, 99)$ (sample split, 1979(IV))	$1\cdot11$ (5% $=1\cdot8$)

Notes:
   (i) Asymptotic *t*-ratios in parentheses; seasonal dummies were also included.
   (ii) Starred variables are treated as endogenous. Estimation is by instrumental variables. Instruments comprise ΔP_m^*, ΔP_{m-1}^*, $\log G$, $\log G_{-1}$, $\log T$, $\log T_{-1}$; $P_m^* =$ world price of manufacturing exports in dollars, $\bar{G} =$ real government expenditure, $T = t_1 + t_2 + t_3$.
   (iii) The coefficient on $\log (K/L)$ is restricted so that its long-run value is $8\cdot406$, the inverse of the long-run wage elasticity of labour demand.
   (iv) Log W^e is based on the fitted value from the time series regression

$$\Delta \log W = -0\cdot0406 \, \Delta \log W_{-1} + 0\cdot2436 \, \Delta \log W_{-2} + 0\cdot2091 \, \Delta \log W_{-3}$$
$$(0\cdot52) \qquad\qquad (3\cdot2) \qquad\qquad\quad (2\cdot8)$$

$$+ 0\cdot5879 \, \Delta \log W_{t-4}.$$
$$(7\cdot8)$$

Note that there is no constant and the sum of the coefficient is unity. Thus we have imposed long-run neutrality with respect to inflation. This does not significantly violate the data.

However, this makes little difference to the breakdown of the causes of unemployment (owing to offsetting effects) as we can see by looking at the annual version of equation (36). This has the form

$$U + 0\cdot111 \log U = \text{constant} - 0\cdot42\sigma + 1\cdot18\rho + 0\cdot72\Delta \log P_m/P$$
$$+ 0\cdot195 U_P + 3\cdot16\Delta t_1$$

where note that the very much larger coefficients on the right-hand side are offset by the bigger coefficient on log U. The resulting breakdown of unemployment changes, therefore, exhibits much the same broad pattern as in Table 9.

   Our main purpose, however, in estimating a quarterly model is to see if we can capture the short-run wage–price dynamics. We illustrate these by looking at the separate consequences of a demand shock and a wage shock. A wage shock is induced by anything that causes wages to rise relative to GDP prices, and therefore includes those shifts that are commonly termed 'supply shocks', such as a rise in oil prices.

TABLE 14

WAGE EQUATION, QUARTERLY, 1957(I)–1983(IV)

Independent variables	Dependent variable $\Delta \log (W/P)$
Constant	2·764 (3·8)
$\Delta \log (W/P)_{-1}$	−0·235 (1·9)
$\Delta \log (W/P)_{-2}$	−0·132 (1·2)
$\Delta \log (W/P)_{-3}$	−0·103 (1·2)
$\log (W/P)_{-1}$	−0·387 (3·7)
*$(\log P^e - \log P)$	1·0 ($t = 1·08$)
$\log (K/L)$	0·325
$\log U_{-1}$	−0·0312 (3·3)
*$(\Delta \log U)$	−0·0743 (1·7)
$\Delta \log (P_m/\bar{P})_{-2}$	0·181 (1·8)
Δt_1	0·973 (4·0)
U_{p-1}	0·0574 (3·1)
ρ_{-1}	0·369 (3·7)
s.e.	0·0207
$\bar{R}^2$	0·48
DW	2·03
LM (autocorrelation χ^2 (4))	6·32 (5% = 9·5)
Parameter stability $F(16, 94)$	1·12 (5% = 1·8)
(sample split, 1979(IV))	

Notes:

(i) Asymptotic t-ratios in parentheses; seasonal dummies were also included.

(ii) Starred variables are treated as endogenous. Estimation is by instrumental variables. Instruments are as in the price equation except that $\log T$, $\log T_{-1}$ are not included.

(iii) The coefficient on $\log (K/L)$ is restricted so that its long-run value is 0·8406, the inverse of the long-run wage elasticity of labour demand.

(iv) $\log P^e$ is based on the fitted value from the time series regression

$$\Delta \log P = 0·0283 \, \Delta \log P_{-1} + 0·6785 \, \Delta \log P_{-2} + 0·3156 \, \Delta \log P_{-3}$$
$$\quad\;\; (\;0·29) \qquad\qquad (7·5) \qquad\qquad (3·5)$$

$$- \; 0·0224 \, \Delta \log P_{-4}.$$
$$\;\; (\;0·24)$$

As with the wage regression, we have imposed long-run inflation neutrality.

(v) The coefficient on $\log P^e/P$ is set at unity. In unrestricted form it is greater than unity, and the t-ratio represents a test of this restriction.

In Table 15 we show the consequences of a one-period (one-quarter) demand shock which is roughly equivalent to a shift in the budget deficit equivalent to 1 per cent of GDP. The unemployment effect is very long and drawn-out for reasons we have already mentioned, and it seems to be leading to a permanent rise in inflation of just over $\frac{1}{2}$ per cent. The real-wage dynamics are most interesting. The first-period reduction arises because the immediate acceleration in prices leads wage-setters to underestimate price rises. This effect wears off immediately, however, and the real wage rises quite strongly after the first quarter as the labour market becomes more buoyant. The persistently higher employment is consistent with the long period of higher real wages only because of the imperfect competition nature of the model. The first and third columns taken together are, of course, inconsistent with a perfectly competitive labour demand curve, although they are consistent with

164   LAYARD and NICKELL

TABLE 15

CONSEQUENCES OF DEMAND AND WAGE SHOCK

Quarter	Percentage point difference in U	Percentage point difference in the annual rate of price inflation	Percentage difference in real wages
(a) Temporary demand shock			
1	−0·13	0·25	−0·06
2	−0·12	0·27	0·03
3	−0·12	0·38	0·13
4	−0·11	0·44	0·16
8	−0·11	0·53	0·12
12	−0·08	0·61	0·07
16	−0·05	0·60	0·07
(b) Temporary increase in wage pressure			
1	0·0	3·1	6·9
2	0·07	2·3	3·5
3	0·10	3·1	3·2
4	0·13	4·6	0·6
8	0·49	5·6	1·3
12	0·48	5·1	−0·16
16	0·39	3·7	−0·78

Note: All differences are measured by comparison with the no-shock case.

the known consequences of demand shocks as they emerge in simulation of all the UK macro-models (see Andrews *et al.*, 1985, Table 3).

In Table 15 we also show the consequences of a temporary increase in wage pressure (10 per cent for one quarter) such as could have been caused by a supply shock. The upshot is a period of stagflation as the pressure on wages generates inflation and raises the real wage, thus raising unemployment. The slackness in the labour market eventually starts to lower the real wage, but it is clear that it takes a long time for the inflationary pressure to disappear from the system, and the overall rise in inflation is going to be around $3\frac{1}{2}$ per cent.

VI. CONCLUSIONS

Causes of increased unemployment

To summarize, we can begin with our conclusions about increased unemployment (based on Section IV). Clearly, there are a number of levels at which this question can be answered. At one level we can take the employment function and combine it with the wage equation to get employment as a function of demand factors and 'push' factors. This exercise yields the important information that most of the rise in unemployment since 1979 is due to falls in demand.[28] Turning to the various push factors, we can divide them into factors tending to push up product wages and factors that would tend to reduce net take-home pay at given product wages. We begin with the former.

(i) *Benefits*. Our model finds a direct impact of benefit changes of about 0·4 percentage points of unemployment since the late 1950s, corresponding to a benefit elasticity at the sample mean of around 0·7. This contrasts with the results reported in Minford (1983), who finds a benefit elasticity of about 4. This is hardly surprising, given that real benefits and union density are the only trended variables in his wage equation.[29] Our results here are of the same order of magnitude as the cross-section estimates reported in Nickell (1979a) and Lancaster (1979), although they are fractionally higher than those estimated by Narendranathan, Nickell and Stern (1985).[30] This last study, however, uses data from 1978, when unemployment was particularly high relative to the sample average. Under these circumstances one might expect to find that measured benefit effects are somewhat smaller.

In addition to the direct effect of benefits, unemployment may have risen somewhat because unemployment benefit has become less harshly administered, and people are more willing to live off the state. Some evidence in support of decreased intensity of search comes from the massive rise in unemployment at given vacancies.

(ii) *Employment protection.* However, the shift of the U/V curve may also be due in part to the growth of employment protection, making employers less willing to fill vacancies except with superior candidates. When we take the shift of the U/V curve as an index of the combined effect of social security and employment protection, we attribute around 3 per cent of the extra unemployment to these two sources.

(iii) *Mismatch of unemployment and vacancies, and structural unemployment.* The increase of unemployment is not importantly due to an increased mismatch between unemployment and vacancies, our estimate being around 1 percentage point. There has been no major increase in the rate at which jobs shift from one industry to another, leaving pockets of unemployment in declining industries or regions. Nor has there been any obvious increase in the mismatch between the pattern of unemployment and vacancies, by industry, region or occupation.

(iv) *Lagged unemployment.* We have some evidence that past unemployment tends to raise unemployment today, but only in our quarterly model.

(v) *Union militancy.* We use as an indicator of union militancy the mark-up of union over non-union wages. This has risen, and the corresponding increase in unemployment is of the order of 3 percentage points, given demand, with the effect on the natural rate being somewhat higher. However, unions may also play a role in preventing the full adjustment of real wages to external changes, discussed later.

We now turn to factors that (for given real labour costs to employers) would tend to reduce real take-home pay.

(vi) *Income taxes and indirect taxes.* We found little evidence that these had any impact on unemployment.

(vii) *Employers' taxes on labour.* Employers' 'taxes' on labour have risen by 13 points, and this may have increased unemployment by around 1·4 percentage points.

(viii) *Relative import prices.* These raised unemployment by around 1·5 percentage points in the mid-1970s, but are not now causing problems. The main reason for the latter fact is that the onset of UK oil production raised the balanced trade real exchange rate, reducing wage pressure.

(ix) *The productivity slowdown.* Slower capital accumulation in the 1970s and 1980s reduced the warranted real wage, but we found no evidence that the actual wage failed to respond.

(x) *Technical progress.* Technical progress slowed down in the 1970s, but we find no important role for this variable.

(xi) *Technological unemployment and capital shortage.* There is no evidence that the technology embodied in the capital stock is limiting employment. Technical progress and capital accumulation have always caused dislocation, but there is no evidence that this is greater now than in the past.

(xii) *Public employment.* This is an important area which we have not fully examined.

(xiii) *Incomes policy.* We have not studied incomes policy closely. But our analysis makes clear that this should be seen as a microeconomic policy, aimed at reducing the NAIRU.

Most of our conclusions on the decomposition of the growth in unemployment are necessarily tentative. This is less true of our conclusions about real-wage/unemployment dynamics in Section V. These are that a positive demand shock will, except in the very first quarter, raise the real wage and reduce unemployment. A positive supply shock (meaning a temporary increase in wage pressure) will also raise real wages but will increase unemployment. These two basic patterns are possible because of our assumption of imperfect competition. They cannot coexist under perfect competition. The obvious fact of their coexistence is strong evidence in support of our approach.

ACKNOWLEDGMENTS

We are most grateful to Paul Kong and Andy Murfin for help on the project. We are also grateful to the Economic and Social Research Council and the Esmee Fairbairn Charitable Trust for financial assistance.

NOTES

1. The series relates to men without work registered as seeking work at public employment offices. Until the last three years such registration was a condition for receiving any form of unemployment benefit, but this condition has now been dropped and numbers unemployed now refer to those seeking benefit. These numbers in the last three years have been adjusted on to the earlier basis. Women's entitlement to benefits has grown substantially over the last 20 years and the series of women registered for work does not therefore give a good measure of trends in female job-seeking. Even now, many unemployed women are not entitled to benefit. As regards the *level* of female joblessness, the following US-style survey results hold for 1981. Census: Men 11·4, Women 7·4; General Household Survey: Men 11·1, Women 9·4; Labour Force Survey: Men 9·9, Women 8·8.
2. This draws heavily on the presentation in Layard and Nickell (1985b). The model is similar to that in Blanchard (1985), and we are very grateful to him for encouraging us to think along these lines.
3. These are an update of the results in Layard and Nickell (1985a).
4. The original scheme was known as the Youth Opportunities Programme (YOP). In 1979 a six-month place was guaranteed from Easter onwards for those leaving school the previous summer. For those leaving school in 1979 onwards, a place was guaranteed from Christmas. Followng on the youth riots (summer 1981), this was succeeded in summer 1983 by the Youth

Training Scheme. A one-year place on this is guaranteed from six weeks after leaving school and includes 13 weeks of off-the-job training. The guarantee is not a legal right but a statement of intent. In practice, sufficient places have been forthcoming.

5. General Household Survey. Data kindly supplied by Office of Population Censuses and Surveys.

6. Instead of looking at vacancies, we can also look at the percentage of manufacturing firms replying to the Confederation of British Industries that their output is likely to be limited by shortages of (a) skilled labour and (b) other labour. The picture is very similar to that in Figure 2.

7. 1954–83, IV estimation with log V_{-1} as instrument for log V. We also experimented with the more flexible functional form where V is replaced by $(V-\beta)$. β was not well determined, but (more relevant here) the trend in the equation was more or less invariant with respect to β.

8. There have been three main changes. The Redundancy Payments Act 1965 introduced statutory payments when a worker is made redundant, a part of which is a direct cost to the employer. The Industrial Relations Act 1971 established legal rights against unfair dismissal. The Employment Protection Act 1975 extended the periods of notice required before a termination. Employment protection has been studied in some detail in both Nickell (1979b) and Nickell (1982), with mixed results. The impact on unemployment is not clear-cut. If it becomes more difficult or expensive for firms to reduce employment, this will reduce flows into unemployment; but, by making employers more choosy, it will also increase unemployment duration. Both these effects were detected in Nickell (1982), but the net impact was in the direction of unemployment reduction. This result is, however, very tentative, since the variable used to capture the legislation (numbers of Industrial Tribunal cases) is clearly rather weak. Survey evidence is also ambiguous (see Jackman, Layard and Pissarides, 1984).

9. Our model assumes that employment always occurs on the labour demand curve.

10. See Layard, Metcalf and Nickell (1978, Table 5). The index estimated there has for purposes of Figure 3 been scaled down proportionately in all years so that the estimated mark-up in 1976 is equal to the best available estimate of the level of mark-up in that year (in Stewart, 1983). In regressions the log of the untransformed variable has been used.

11. As a matter of accounting, the following relationship approximately holds where $\bar{p}=\log$ producer prices, $p=\log$ value added prices, $\bar{w}=\log$ wages, $p_m=\log$ import prices, $t_1=$ employers' taxes, $t_2=$ employees' taxes, $t_3=$ indirect taxes, $\nu=$ share of imports in GDP.

$$(1+\nu)\bar{p} = p + \nu p_m + \text{constant}.$$

Hence

$$\bar{p} - p = \nu(p_m - \bar{p}) + \text{constant}$$

and

$$(\bar{w}+t_1-p)-(\bar{w}-t_2-\bar{p}-t_3)=\bar{p}-p+t_1+t_2+t_3=\nu(p_m-\bar{p})+t_1+t_2+t_3+\text{constant}.$$

12. We assume separability of raw materials from capital and labour, so that the GDP deflator is a mark-up on wages determined by K/L and A.

13. Suppose that real wages are fixed by firms' pricing behaviour at $(W/P)^*$, and that the wage equation is

$$\frac{W}{P} = a_0 - a_1 U + a_2 U_{-1} + a_3 Z, \qquad\qquad (a_1, a_2 > 0)$$

where Z is a push factor. Then the short-run natural rate is

$$\bar{U} = \frac{1}{a_1}\left\{ a_0 - \left(\frac{W}{P}\right)^* + a_2 U_{-1} + a_3 Z \right\}.$$

The medium-term natural rate is

$$U^* = \frac{1}{a_1 - a_2}\left\{ a_0\left(\frac{W}{P}\right)^* + a_3 Z \right\}.$$

14. Its construction is described in the Data Appendix at the end of this book.

15. In the *very* long run the set-up cost and the zero profit condition determine the number of firms. Our measures of K_i and N_i should strictly exclude the set-up cost, but we have ignored this point.

16. Our measure of cost is hourly cost. This is because we assume that, for the economy as a whole, a fall in hours per worker also involves an equiproportional fall in hours per unit of capital. Hence the marginal product of a man-hour depends on the capital-labour ratio—or, equivalently, on the output-capital ratio—as in equation (5).

17. Good evidence in favour of short-run diminishing returns to labour comes from inventory behaviour. If marginal cost were constant, there is no reason why firms should wish to smooth their production over time.
18. See, for example, Sawyer (1983).
19. This is perfectly consistent with short-run profit maximization if the elasticity of demand is increasing with demand itself. Otherwise, normal cost pricing can be viewed as average profit maximization over the cycle where, for a variety of possible reasons, firms find it difficult or costly to adjust prices every time demand shifts (see Domberger, 1979, for example). Finally, of course, normal cost pricing is optimal if marginal costs are constant. Given the compelling evidence against this proposition, we do not find this a persuasive argument.
20. See also earlier n. 17 about inventory behaviour.
21. This externally given level may simply be the employees' estimate of the alternative wage, adjusted for the probability of finding alternative employment, or it may include some element of what is deemed to be a 'fair' wage.
22. For a more formal exposition, see Nickell (1985).
23. This is quite consistent with the data; see Layard and Nickell (1985a).
24. This is because the actual demand facing each firm is

$$Y_i^d = D\left(\frac{P_i}{P}, \sigma\right) \psi\left(\frac{AL}{K}\right) \frac{K}{n}.$$

25. The results in this section differ from those in Layard and Nickell (1985a) because we have improved the data in a number of respects (see Data Appendix at the end of this book).
26. In fact, $t_4 = (1 - \tau)^{-1}$ where τ is the effective tax rate. The idea here is that firms set prices in order to maintain post-tax profits as a constant share (β) of value added. So if π represents profits, we have

$$(1 - \tau)\pi = \beta PY$$

or

$$(1 - \tau)(PY - WN) = \beta PY$$

or

$$P = \frac{WN}{Y}\left(1 - \frac{\beta}{1 - \tau}\right)^{-1}$$

or

$$\log \frac{P}{W} \simeq \beta\left(\frac{1}{1 - \tau}\right) + \text{productivity}.$$

So β is the coefficient on t_4.
27. We also tried using the National Institute Economic Review's forecasts of inflation.
28. Less than a quarter of this demand effect was 'needed' if inflation was to be held stable given the increase in the push factors.
29. See also Nickell's review of Minford in the *Economic Journal* (Nickell, 1984).
30. Note that cross-section results measure the 'supply' shift. The total effect (after the interaction of supply and demand) should be less.

REFERENCES

ANDREWS, M. J., BELL, D. N. F., FISHER, P. G., WALLIS, K. F. and WHITELY, J. D. (1985). Models of the UK Economy and the Real Wage-Employment Debate. *National Institute Economic Review*, 112, 41-52.

BEATH, J. (1979). Target profits, cost expectations and the incidence of the corporate income tax. *Review of Economic Studies*, 46, 513-26.

BLANCHARD, O. (1985). Monopolistic competition, small menu costs and real effects of nominal money. Unpublished paper, Massachusetts Institute of Technology (mimeo).

CARLIN, W., and SOSKICE, D. (1985). Real wages, unemployment, international competitiveness and inflation; a framework for analysing closed and open economies. Unpublished paper, University College, Oxford (mimeo).

DOMBERGER, S. (1979). Price adjustment and market structure. *Economic Journal*, 89, 96-108.

GORDON, R. J. (1985). Wage-price dynamics and the manufacturing output gap in Europe, Japan and North America. Paper presented at a conference on The Causes of Unemployment, sponsored by the Swedish Employers' Organization, September, Northwestern University (mimeo).

GRUBB, D., JACKMAN, R. A. and LAYARD, P. R. G. (1983). Wage rigidity and unemployment in OECD countries. *European Economic Review*, **21**, 11-41.

HENRY, B. and WREN-LEWIS, S. (1984). The aggregate labour market in the UK: some experiments with rational expectations models. In P. Malgrange and P. Muet (eds), *Contemporary Macroeconomic Modelling*. Oxford: Basil Blackwell.

JACKMAN, R., LAYARD, P. R. G. and PISSARIDES, C. (1984). On vacancies. London School of Economics, Centre for Labour Economics, Discussion Paper no. 165 (revised).

JOHNSON, G. and LAYARD, R. (1986). The natural rate of unemployment: explanation and policy. In O. Ashenfelter and R. Layard (eds), *Handbook of Labor Economics*. Amsterdam: North-Holland.

KING, M. (1975). The United Kingdom profits crisis: myth or reality. *Economic Journal*, **85**, 33-54.

LANCASTER, T. (1979). Econometric methods for the duration of unemployment. *Econometrica*, **47**, 939-56.

LAYARD, R. (1982). *More Jobs Less Inflation*. London: Grant McIntyre.

——, METCALF, D. and NICKELL, S. (1978). The effects of collective bargaining on relative wages. In A. Shorrocks and W. Krelle (eds.), *The Economics of Income Distribution* (1978) and *British Journal of Industrial Relations*, **56**, 287-303.

—— and NICKELL, S. (1985a). The causes of British unemployment. *National Institute Economic Review*, **111**, 62-85.

—— (1985b). Unemployment, real wages and aggregate demand in Europe, Japan and the US. *Journal of Monetary Economics*, Supplement: Carnegie-Rochester Public Policy Conference, no. 23.

MINFORD, P. (1983). Labour market equilibrium in an open economy. *Oxford Economic Papers*, **35** (Supplement), 207-44.

NARENDRANATHAN, W., NICKELL, S. and STERN, J. (1985). Unemployment benefits revisited. *Economic Journal*, **95**, 307-29.

NICKELL, S. J. (1979a). The effect of unemployment and related benefits on the duration of unemployment. *Economic Journal*, **89**, 34-49.

—— (1979b). 'Unemployment and the structure of labour costs. *Journal of Monetary Economics*, Supplement: Carnegie-Rochester Public Policy Conference, no. 11.

—— (1982). The determinants of equilibrium unemployment in Britain. *Economic Journal*, **92**, 555-75.

—— (1984). Review of *Unemployment: Cause and Cure*, by P. Minford with D. Davies, M. Peel and A. Sprague. *Economic Journal*, **94**, 946-53.

—— (1985). Unemployment and the real wage. Paper presented at a conference on The Causes of Unemployment, sponsored by the Swedish Employers Organization, September, Institute of Economics and Statistics, University of Oxford (mimeo).

OSWALD, A. (1986). Unemployment insurance and labour contracts under asymmetric information: theory and facts. *American Economic Review*, forthcoming.

—— and TURNBULL, P. (1985). Pay and employment determination in Britain: what are labour contracts really like? London School of Economics, Centre for Labour Economics, Discussion paper no. 212.

PENCAVEL, J. H. (1972). Wages, specific training, and labour turnover in US manufacturing industries. *International Economic Review*, **13**, 53-64.

PUDNEY, S. (1983). Earnings equations and incomes policy. Unpublished paper, London School of Economics (mimeo).

SARGAN, J. D. (1964). Wages and prices in the UK. In P. E. Hart, G. Mills and J. K. Whittaker (eds), *Econometric Analysis for National Economic Planning*. New York: Macmillan.

SAWYER, M. (1983). Business pricing and inflation. London: Macmillan Press.

SHAPIRO, C. and STIGLITZ, J. (1984). Equilibrium unemployment as a worker discipline device. *American Economic Review*, **74**, 433-44.

STEWART, M. (1983). Relative earnings and individual union membership in the UK. *Economica*, **50**, 111-26.

STIGLITZ, J. E. (1986). Theories of wage rigidity. In J. L. Butkiewicz, K. J. Koford and J. B. Miller, *Keynes' Economic Legacy*, New York, Praeger.

SYMONS, J. (1985). Relative prices and the demand for labour in British manufacturing. *Economica*, **52**, 37-50.

WICKENS, M. (1982). The efficient estimation of econometric models with rational expectations. *Review of Economic Studies*, **49**, 55-67.

Why Have Unemployment Rates in Canada and the United States Diverged?

By Orley Ashenfelter and David Card

Princeton University

Introduction

At the same time that unemployment has disappeared from public policy discussions in the United States, it has become the major focus of discussion in Europe and elsewhere. It is not hard to explain the difference in public interest. European unemployment rates are at postwar highs and seem to be stuck at current levels. By contrast, the US unemployment rate is high by postwar standards, but it has declined considerably in the last four years to the point where there is now clear evidence of labour shortages in some parts of the country.

Even more remarkable than the comparison of recent US and European experiences is the comparison of recent US and Canadian experiences. Throughout the postwar period, US and Canadian unemployment rates moved in tandem. Figure 1 displays this relationship graphically by plotting the Canadian unemployment rate on the vertical axis against the US rate on the horizontal axis.[1] This historical link between unemployment rates in the two countries seems to have ended in 1982. During the past three years, Canadian unemployment rates have been some three percentage points higher than their US counterparts, and this gap shows no sign of diminishing.[2]

A variety of explanations has been offered for the disparity between US and European economic performance in the past decade.[3] Many of these explanations revolve around rigidities in the labour market attributable to government intervention or other institutional features.[4] It seems apparent that simple structural explanations for the divergence between US and European labour market performance ought to be equally useful in explaining the US and Canadian divergence, and indeed, we have heard many of the same explanations offered. Our purpose in this paper is to examine the relationship between US and Canadian unemployment for the light it sheds on any of these explanations.

From a practical viewpoint, a comparison of US and Canadian labour market indicators is relatively straightforward, since both countries use the same methods to measure these indicators.[5] A direct comparison of US and European indicators, on the other hand, is complicated by differences in survey instruments and even in the underlying concept of unemployment.[6]

Our goal is to explore the data for the light they shed on a series of hypotheses that attribute the divergence in unemployment rates to structural rigidities in the labour market. Before examining these hypotheses in detail, however, we examine the extent to which the unemployment gap between Canada and the United States is either a secular phenomenon or a result of differential business cycle movements in the two countries. As Figure 1 suggests, we find no evidence of an unemployment gap prior to 1981. Furthermore, the

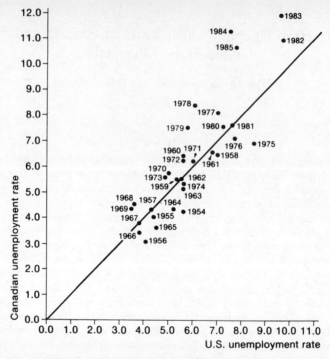

FIGURE 1.   US and Canadian unemployment rates, 1954–1984.

unemployment gap in 1983 and 1984 is not easily explained by movements in relative output during the period. While Canadian output recovered from the 1982 recession at a rate consistent with historical patterns, Canadian employment lagged far behind, opening up an *employment* gap which in 1983 and 1984 explained most of the difference in unemployment rates between Canada and the United States.

This unprecedented increase in productivity is remarkably similar to employment and output changes observed in many European countries during the last decade. In Section II we explore primarily mechanical explanations for the shortfall of Canadian employment growth. We first explore the extent to which the divergence in unemployment rates between the United States and Canada may be attributed to changes in the demographic composition of employment. We then consider the possibility that differences in the industrial composition of the two nations, coupled with underlying differences in industrial growth rates, may explain differences in employment growth.

In Section III we turn to arguments about structural rigidity in the labour market. It is often argued that structural barriers discourage employment growth, either by preventing the flow of workers to new jobs, or by raising the costs of hiring new workers. Looking first at direct government intervention in the labour market, we compare the unemployment insurance and minimum wage laws in Canada and the United States and how they have changed over the past two decades. We then examine the extent of unionization in the two countries and relative changes in union coverage since 1960. Our goal is to explore the possibility that the labour market may have become more or less encumbered by non-competitive barriers in either of these two countries.

In Section IV we examine the postwar history of real-wage movements in the United States and Canada, and the correlation between relative employment growth and relative wage rates. In some analyses unsustainable rates of real-wage growth force down the profitability of employment and lead to higher unemployment. Direct examination of profits data is difficult, but it is straightforward to analyse the course of labour costs between the United States and Canada and to test this candidate explanation for the divergence in employment rates.

The conclusions from our structural analysis of the US and Canadian labour markets are unenlightening. We find no evidence that minimum wage or unemployment insurance provisions have changed sharply in Canada relative to the United States. In both countries, minimum wages have declined recently relative to average hourly earnings. Both countries increased the generosity of their unemployment insurance plans in the early 1970s and both have recently taken steps to reduce unemployment benefits (broadly defined). The only structural aspect of the labour market that has changed substantially in Canada relative to the United States is the extent of unionization. This change has occurred gradually over the past 15 years, however, with relatively little change since 1980.

Our investigation of wage behaviour is similarly unenlightening. Historically, relative wage growth and relative employment growth between Canada and the United States have been *positively* correlated. The short-run relationship between wages and employment in each country is likewise inconsistent with the hypothesis that wage increases prevent employment growth. In any case, however, wages in Canada relative to their US counterparts have fallen dramatically since the mid-1970s with the depreciation of the Canadian exchange rate. We have been singularly unsuccessful in documenting structural differences in the US and Canadian labour markets that can explain the recent divergence in unemployment rates between the two countries.

I. An Analysis of Recent Movements in Unemployment

Table 1 presents some basic time-series data on the US and Canadian labour markets.[7] At this broad level, the labour markets of the two countries are very similar, in terms of both labour force participation rates and unemployment rates. Labour force participation rates were lower in Canada in the 1950s but caught up to US rates by 1975. In the late 1970s Canadian unemployment rates were slightly higher than those in the United States. In 1980 and 1981, however, unemployment rates were about equal in the United States and Canada.

Our analysis is motivated by the sharply higher unemployment rates in Canada after 1982. Table 2 presents a simple regression analysis of the problem. In column (1) we present the least squares regression of the Canadian unemployment rate on the US rate, using data from 1955 to 1981. Over this period Canadian unemployment rates moved more or less point-for-point with US

TABLE 1

LABOUR FORCE, EMPLOYMENT AND UNEMPLOYMENT, CANADA AND THE UNITED STATES, 1954-1984

	Canada				United States			
	Labour force participation rate (%) (1)	Labour force (2)	Employment (3)	Unemployment rate (4)	Labour force participation rate (%) (1)	Labour force (2)	Employment (3)	Unemployment rate (4)
1954	54·5	5,567	5,334	4·2	58·8	63,692	60,119	5·6
1955	54·5	5,682	5,457	4·0	59·3	64,991	62,156	4·4
1956	55·1	5,863	5,682	3·1	60·0	66,542	63,799	4·1
1957	55·6	6,101	5,820	4·3	59·6	66,951	64,074	4·3
1958	55·5	6,205	5,804	6·5	59·5	67,674	63,044	6·8
1959	55·4	6,315	5,971	5·5	59·3	68,352	64,623	5·5
1960	55·8	6,485	6,068	6·4	59·4	69,643	65,767	5·5
1961	56·2	6,568	6,138	6·6	59·3	70,439	65,733	6·7
1962	55·9	6,663	6,301	5·5	58·8	70,611	66,695	5·5
1963	55·9	6,797	6,452	5·1	58·7	71,809	67,755	5·6
1964	56·2	6,989	6,688	4·3	58·7	73,077	69,299	5·2
1965	56·5	7,202	6,943	3·6	58·9	74,433	71,079	4·5
1966	57·3	7,493	7,242	3·4	59·2	75,749	72,884	3·8
1967	57·6	7,747	7,451	3·8	59·6	77,345	74,372	3·8
1968	57·6	7,951	7,593	4·5	59·6	78,707	75,908	3·6
1969	57·9	8,194	7,831	4·4	60·1	80,706	77,875	3·5
1970	57·8	8,395	7,919	5·7	60·4	82,800	78,672	4·9
1971	58·1	8,639	8,103	6·2	60·2	84,377	79,352	5·9
1972	58·6	8,897	8,344	5·2	60·4	87,019	82,139	5·6
1973	59·7	9,276	8,761	5·5	60·8	89,410	85,051	4·9
1974	60·5	9,639	9,125	5·3	61·3	91,967	86,789	5·6
1975	61·1	9,974	9,284	6·9	61·2	93,788	85,841	8·5
1976	61·1	10,203	9,477	7·1	61·6	96,152	88,751	7·7
1977	61·6	10,501·	9,651	8·1	62·3	98,981	92,015	7·1
1978	62·7	10,895	9,987	8·3	63·2	102,234	96,048	6·1
1979	63·4	11,231	10,395	7·4	63·7	104,960	98,824	5·8
1980	64·1	11,573	10,708	7·5	63·8	106,974	99,303	7·1
1981	64·8	11,904	11,006	7·6	63·9	108,668	100,394	7·6
1982	64·1	11,958	10,644	11·0	64·0	110,238	99,525	9·7
1983	64·4	12,182	10,734	11·9	64·4	111,515	100,823	9·6
1984	64·8	12,400	11,000	11·3	64·4	113,521	104,999	7·5

Note: Labour force, employment and unemployment data pertain to the civilian non-institutional population, aged 15 and over in Canada; 16 and over in the United States. Canadian data for 1954-65 are adjusted for comparability with the revised Canadian Labor Force Survey. US data represent annual averages of seasonally adjusted monthly data from *Citibase*. Canadian data are taken from Statistics Canada, *Historical Labor Force Statistics* 1974 and 1983 editions.

TABLE 2

RELATIONSHIP BETWEEN ANNUAL CANADIAN AND US
UNEMPLOYMENT RATES, 1955-1984[a]

	Dependent variable: Canadian unemployment rate (%)					
	1955–1981			1955–1984		
	(1)	(2)	(3)	(4)	(5)	(6)
(1) Constant	0·52	0·00	−0·09	0·82	−1·17	−0·05
	(0·62)	—	(0·53)	(0·71)	(0·48)	(0·53)
(2) US unemployment	0·93	0·51	0·52	0·87	0·66	0·55
rate	(0·13)	(0·11)	(0·12)	(0·13)	(0·11)	(0·10)
(3) Linear trend	—	—	0·03	—	—	0·03
			(0·02)			(0·02)
(4) Lagged Canadian	—	0·51	0·52	—	0·59	0·40
unemployment rate		(0·11)	(0·12)		(0·09)	(0·10)
(5) Post-1981	—	—	—	2·76	—	1·57
intercept shift				(0·68)		(0·51)
(6) Standard error	0·86	0·63	0·62	0·88	0·70	0·58

[a] OLS standard errors reported. Equations without lagged dependent variable exhibit strong residual serial correlation.

rates. An examination of the data in Figure 1 suggests that Canadian unemployment rates typically responded to changes in US rates with a lag. In column (2) of Table 2 we include lagged Canadian unemployment as an additional explanatory variable. The fit of this simple equation is remarkably good. Typically, a 1 point increase in US unemployment rates brings about a 0·5 point increase in Canadian rates within the year, and a 0·9 point increase within three years. Column (3) shows that, allowing for this partial adjustment mechanism, there is only a negligible upward trend in Canadian unemployment rates relative to US rates prior to 1982.

Column (4) of the table extends the regression in column (1) to the post-1982 period, with the addition of an intercept shift. The regression indicates a 2·8 per cent increase in Canadian unemployment rates after 1981 that is unexplained by contemporaneous US movements. Allowing for partial adjustment, the conclusion is very similar.[8] While there is no indication of an emerging unemployment gap prior to 1981, Canadian unemployment rates after 1982 are some 2·5–3 per cent higher than expected.

This simple analysis suggests that the post-1982 unemployment gap is neither a secular phenomenon nor a result of the timing relationship between US and Canadian unemployment. In order to pursue the timing issue more formally, and also to explore the contribution of output demand to relative unemployment, we estimated a quarterly autoregressive forecasting model for the North American economy as a whole, taking as jointly dependent variables the levels of real GNP (output), employment and unemployment in the United States and Canada.[9] In the data, this model has a simple recursive structure in which the level of US output is determined only by its own lagged values. This recursive structure makes it relatively easy to form forecasts of US employment and unemployment, and Canadian output, employment and

176 ASHENFELTER and CARD

unemployment, conditional on starting values of each of these variables in
1981 and the sequence of realized US output from 1981 to 1984.[10] We can
then decompose movements in employment and unemployment in each
country, and the unemployment gap between Canada and the United States,
into components explained by the movement of US output during 1982–84,
and unexplained components. Since the 'explained components' correspond
to conditional expectations, the forecast errors should be close to zero if there
has been no structural change in the link between US output and the other
variables. Large and systematic forecast errors indicate a breakdown in this
linkage.

The average annual prediction errors, or 'unexplained' components of US
employment and unemployment, and Canadian output, employment and
unemployment, are presented in Table 3. The unexplained components of US
employment and unemployment are relatively small. In 1984 US unemployment was approximately one percentage point lower than expected, conditional
on actual US output. About one-half of this unexpected reduction in
US unemployment corresponded to extra employment: the remainder is
attributable to labour force movements.[11]

In Canada, on the other hand, the prediction errors are large and systematic.
Canadian real GNP was about 3·5 per cent lower than expected in 1982,
controlling for the simultaneous contraction in US output. Historically, output
shocks in the United States translate into contemporaneous Canadian shocks
with an elasticity of about one-half. In 1982 the large external shock to
Canadian output was reinforced by a domestic shock of about the same order
of magnitude.[12]

TABLE 3

PREDICTION ERRORS FOR CANADIAN GNP AND US AND CANADIAN
EMPLOYMENT AND UNEMPLOYMENT, CONDITIONAL ON ACTUAL US GNP[A]
(annual average of quarterly values)

	United States		Canada		
	Employment (%)	Unemployment Rate[b]	Real GNP (%)	Employment (%)	Unemployment Rate[b]
1982	0·1	−0·1	−3·4	−2·8	1·5
1983	0·0	−0·5	−2·2	−3·5	2·3
1984	0·5	−1·2	−1·9	−3·9	2·7

[a] Predictions based on a fourth-order vector-autoregressive representation of seasonally adjusted
quarterly data. The model is estimated with data from 1956 to 1981, and is used to predict US
employment and unemployment, and Canadian GNP, employment and unemployment for 1982–
84, conditional on 1981 starting values and realized US real GNP.
[b] Expressed as percentage points of unemployment. The unemployment rate is defined as the
difference between the logarithms of the labour force and employment.

During 1983 and 1984 Canadian GNP continued to be lower than predicted
on the basis of US output, but the gap was shrinking. Based on historical
evidence, domestic shocks to Canadian output decay at a rate of about 70 per
cent per year, holding constant US output.[13] The post-1982 pattern of prediction
errors for Canadian GNP is consistent with a large domestic shock to GNP

in 1982 and relatively small domestic shocks after that. There is no evidence of an increasing gap in aggregate demand during 1983 and 1984.

In the Canadian labour market, however, prediction errors based on realized US GNP actually increased in magnitude during 1983 and 1984. Employment was 2·8 per cent less than predicted in 1982, 3·5 per cent less in 1983, and 3·9 per cent less in 1984. Unemployment was higher than predicted in all three years, although the loss in employment was larger than the gain in unemployment in each case, reflecting an unpredicted contraction of the Canadian labour force.

Table 4 summarizes the decomposition of the Canadian–US unemployment gap into components attributable to movements in US output, and unexplained components. The table makes clear that the unemployment gap is not a result of predictable lags in the response of the Canadian labour market to the US business cycle.

TABLE 4

ACTUAL AND PREDICTED UNEMPLOYMENT
IN CANADA AND THE UNITED STATES[a]
(annual averages of quarterly values)

	Canadian unemployment minus US unemployment[a]		
	Actual (%)	Predicted (%)	Residual (%)
1982	1·5	−1·0	1·6
1983	2·5	−0·3	2·8
1984	4·2	0·3	3·9

[a] See notes to Table 3.

The increasing magnitude of the Canadian employment and unemployment prediction errors in Table 3, together with the declining output prediction errors, suggest that an output-based explanation of the unemployment gap is incomplete. To investigate the possibility of a breakdown of the labour market-output relationship in Canada after 1982, we performed a second simulation of Canadian employment and unemployment, conditional on 1981 starting conditions and realized *Canadian* GNP. Again, the predictions have the interpretation of conditional expectations, given 1981 conditions and the entire sequence of Canadian GNP.[14] The results of the simulations are summarized in Table 5. Conditional on output, Canadian employment was 1·8 per cent less than expected in 1982, 2·4 per cent less than expected in 1983, and 3·3 per cent less than expected in 1984. At the same time, unemployment was 1 per cent higher than predicted in 1982, 2·2 per cent higher in 1983, and 3·4 per cent higher in 1984. The gap between employment growth and output growth in Canada, and the corresponding increases in unemployment, explain most of the unpredicted unemployment in Canada in Table 3 and most of the unemployment gap between Canada and the United States in 1983 and 1984.

On the basis of this evidence, we conclude that traditional demand-side determinants of output and employment are not a major source of the unemployment gap between Canada and the United States. Output was relatively

TABLE 5

PREDICTION ERRORS FOR
CANADIAN EMPLOYMENT AND
UNEMPLOYMENT, CONDITIONAL ON
ACTUAL CANADIAN GNP[a]
(annual averages of quarterly values)

	Canadian employment (%)	Canadian unemployment rate[b]
1982	−1·8	1·0
1983	−2·4	2·2
1984	−3·3	3·4

[a] Predictions based on a fourth-order vector-autoregressive representation of seasonally adjusted quarterly data. The model is estimated with data from 1956 to 1981, and is used to predict employment and unemployment conditional on 1981 starting values and realized Canadian real GNP.
[b] Expressed as percentage points of unemployment. The unemployment rate is defined as the difference between the logarithms of the labour force and unemployment.

depressed in Canada in 1982, but has recovered predictably since then. The unemployment gap, by comparison, widened in 1983 and 1984, and continued in 1985. In the remainder of the paper, we examine conditions within the US and Candian labour markets that may potentially explain the relative lack of employment growth in Canada.[15]

II. DEMOGRAPHIC AND INDUSTRIAL COMPOSITION OF LABOUR MARKETS IN CANADA AND THE UNITED STATES

In this section we briefly summarize the demographic and industry structures of the US and Canadian labour markets. Table 6 presents the shares of various age and sex groups in employment, unemployment and the labour force in Canada and the United States. The table also summarizes trends in these shares during the last two decades, and the shares as of 1983.

The table illustrates several points. First, the demographic structure of these two countries' labour forces is very similar. There is no evidence that Canadian unemployment rates are higher because of a greater concentration of high-unemployment groups. Second, a disproportionate share of unemployment is concentrated among young workers in both countries. Third, the pool of employed workers has become relatively older in Canada. The employment shares of 15 to 24-year-olds were below their long-run averages in both countries in 1983, but by a wider margin in Canada. While this may account for an upward trend in relative productivity in Canada, the changes are too small and too gradual to explain the rapid increase in Canadian productivity after 1982.

TABLE 6
DEMOGRAPHIC COMPONENTS OF EMPLOYMENT AND UNEMPLOYMENT, CANADA AND UNITED STATES

	Canada									United States								
	% of labour force			% of employment			% of unemployment			% of labour force			% of employment			% of unemployment		
	Mean	Trend	1983	Mean	Trend	1983	Mean	Trend	1983	Mean	Trend	1983	Mean	Trend	1983	Mean	Trend	1983
(1) Men 15–24	14·2	0·0	12·6	13·3	−0·1	11·1	26·5	−0·1	23·8	12·4	0·1	11·6	11·5	0·0	10·4	25·2	0·0	22·1
(2) Men 25–54	40·4	−0·4	38·2	41·3	−0·3	39·2	26·9	−0·2	30·8	37·9	−0·3	36·9	38·7	−0·3	37·5	22·9	0·5	31·4
(3) Men 55 and older	8·9	−0·2	7·4	9·1	−0·2	7·8	6·4	−0·4	4·5	9·9	−0·2	8·0	10·1	−0·2	8·4	5·5	−0·2	4·7
(4) Women 15–24	11·7	0·1	11·3	11·1	0·0	10·6	18·6	0·2	16·2	10·3	0·1	10·1	9·6	0·1	9·5	21·8	−0·3	16·7
(5) Women 25–54	21·3	0·6	26·7	21·4	0·6	27·3	19·3	0·6	22·4	23·7	0·4	27·9	23·9	0·4	28·5	21·2	0·1	22·3
(6) Women 55 and older	3·7	0·0	3·7	3·8	0·0	3·9	2·3	0·0	2·2	5·9	−0·1	5·4	6·0	0·0	5·7	3·4	−0·1	2·7

Note:
Based on quarterly unadjusted data, 1966–83. Trends are expressed as percentage points per year, and are estimated from a linear regression on constant, trend and seasonal factors. Values shown for 1983 represent annual averages.

TABLE 7

RELATIVE GROWTH RATES OF EMPLOYMENT IN CANADA AND THE UNITED STATES BY INDUSTRY, 1964-1984[a]

	Mining		Manufacturing		Construction		Transportation, Public utilities	
	Can.	USA	Can.	USA	Can.	USA	Can.	USA
(1) % of total employment (average), 1961-84	1.9	1.0	23.9	26.0	5.7	5.0	10.2	6.2
(2) % change in employment, 1964-69	10.0	-2.3	12.9	16.7	14.0	15.5	9.4	12.4
(3) % change in employment, 1969-74	11.0	12.5	9.5	-0.4	17.7	12.7	15.7	6.4
(4) % change in employment, 1974-79	14.4	37.5	2.0	4.8	4.5	10.7	7.2	8.7
(5) % change in employment, 1979-84	-2.7	4.2	-12.5	-6.9	-4.3	-3.3	0.8	0.6

	Trade		Finance, insurance, Real estate		Services[b]		Government[b]		Total[c]	
	Can.	USA	Can.	USA	Can.	USA	Can.	USA	Can.	USA
(1) % of total employment (average), 1961-84	16.9	21.7	5.1	5.3	28.4	17.3	7.1	17.5	100.0	100.0
(2) % change in employment, 1964-69	23.8	20.9	29.2	20.6	39.3	29.0	19.4	27.2	21.5	20.8
(3) % change in employment, 1969-74	27.4	15.6	35.3	18.1	22.5	20.4	31.9	16.2	19.7	11.2
(4) % change in employment, 1974-79	12.5	18.8	23.9	19.9	20.5	27.3	11.9	12.6	11.8	14.9
(5) % change in employment, 1979-84	7.2	7.9	10.2	13.9	15.5	20.7	7.1	0.1	4.1	4.8

[a] Data are based on annual averages of seasonally adjusted data. US data are taken from Citibase. Canadian data are taken from Cansim (1961-83) and the Bank of Canada Review (1983-84). Canadian employment series are spliced at March 1983 to reflect the revision of the Establishment Survey. Growth rates represent actual percentage changes (rather than changes in logarithms).

[b] In Canada, service employment includes education and health service workers employed by provincial and local governments. These workers are classified as government workers in the United States.

[c] Total non-agricultural employment. Canadian non-agricultural employment includes forestry workers (who made up less than 1 per cent of non-agricultural employment in 1984). In the United States forestry workers are classified as agricultural workers.

Table 7 presents the industry composition of employment in Canada and the United States and compares five-year employment growth rates in the two countries by industry. Employment shares and growth rates by industry are fairly similar. At this level of aggregation, there is no indication that Canadian employment is more heavily concentrated in slow-growth industries. The last two columns of the table give the aggregate employment growth rates for both countries by five-year intervals. According to these data, Canadian growth rates were about the same as US rates for 1964–69 and 1979–84, and were significantly higher than US rates over the 10-year period 1969–79. By an absolute comparison, then, Canadian employment growth performed as well as or better than US growth during the past two decades. An absolute comparison is misleading, however, because of the higher labour force growth rate in Canada. Equal employment growth rates in the United States and Canada from 1979 to 1984 actually lead to an increase in relative unemployment of 2·3 per cent. The lack of employment growth in Canada in the 1980s is better interpreted as a *relative* shortfall than an absolute one.

Our comparison of the demographic and industry structure of the United States and Canada leads us to an important conclusion: these structures are remarkably similar. Consequently, the recent divergence between the aggregate unemployment rates in the two countries cannot be attributed in any simple way to differences in demographic or industrial structure. It follows that alternative, less mechanical, explanations for the divergence in unemployment rates are worth examining, and we turn to those next.

III. Labour Market Rigidities in Canada and the United States

The similarity of the industrial and demographic structures of the Canadian and US labour markets deepens the puzzle of the recent unemployment divergence between the two countries. One explanation for the European–US divergence is the widely discussed 'Eurosclerosis' hypothesis. According to this hypothesis, employment costs have increased rapidly in Europe relative to the United States as a result of government intervention in the labour market, social welfare policies and trade union policies. Government and union regulations on hiring and firing decisions, and social policies that discourage worker mobility, are said to lead to unemployment, resulting mainly from failure to absorb new labour market entrants.

This 'regulatory rigidity' hypothesis is rarely spelled out in a way that encourages empirical examination, and we are unaware of any serious analysis of it. A simple hypothesis, however, is to associate some level of structural or 'regulatory' unemployment with the extent of regulation in each country. If the 'regulatory rigidity' hypothesis is to explain the recent divergence of US and Canadian unemployment rates, two conditions must be met. First, measures of labour market rigidity must be roughly similar in the United States and Canada throughout the 1960s and 1970s, in order to explain the similarity of unemployment in the two countries during this period. Second, there must be a sharp increase in 'rigidity' in 1981 or 1982.

In what follows we select three straightforward measures of labour market regulation for examination. The first is an index of the minimum wage rate, which is often alleged to operate as a barrier to the employment of younger workers. The second is an indication of the generosity of the unemployment insurance benefit system, which is often alleged to cause workers to prolong their unemployment spells and to cause employers to initiate too many temporary layoffs. The third is the extent of unionization of the labour force. We are aware that there are many other rigidities in the labour market, including government- and non-government-induced rigidities. Most of these are difficult to quantify, however, and we leave our attempts to do so to further research.

Minimum wage regulation

Table 8 indicates our measures of the statutory minimum wage rate in the United States and Canada and their levels since 1966. It is conventional to use the ratio of the minimum wage to some aggregate wage rate as an index of the effective minimum wage. We have selected average hourly earnings in manufacturing as a benchmark in each country. Minimum wages vary by province in Canada, and we have used a labour force weighted average of provincial relative minimum wage rates to form a national index. In the United States there is a uniform federal minimum wage, but coverage of employment by minimum wage statutes is not universal. Traditionally, the ratio of the minimum wage to average wages is multiplied by the fraction of covered employment to obtain an effective minimum. It is clear from the table that, as conventionally measured, the minimum wage is typically higher in Canada than in the United States. Without the coverage adjustment, however, the relative minimums in the two countries are very similar. Since 1980 the effective minimum has apparently declined in both countries by about the same percentage amount. There is no evidence of an increase in minimum wage regulation in Canada, either in absolute terms or relative to the United States.

Unemployment benefits

Tables 9a and 9b provide a history of information on unemployment benefits in the United States and Canada since 1966. We present three measures of the generosity of unemployment insurance benefits. The first of these is the aggregate replacement rate, which measures the ratio of average unemployment benefits to average earnings.[16] We have calculated both a gross replacement rate and a net replacement rate, which adjusts for the differing tax treatment of benefits in the United States and Canada. There have been some changes in relative replacement rates in the past two decades. In 1972, for example, revisions in the Unemployment Insurance Act in Canada increased benefits dramatically in that country relative to the United States. Since the late 1970s gross and net replacement rates have remained more or less constant in the United States and Canada, although net rates are apparently lower in Canada.

A second measure of the generosity of the unemployment insurance system is the average duration of benefit spells. During the 1970s, benefit spells in both Canada and the United States averaged about 15 weeks. The duration of benefits is highly sensitive to economic conditions, and durations were longer in the United States in 1975 and 1976, and longer in Canada in 1978 and 1979, reflecting the relative strengths of cyclical downturns in the two countries. In 1980 and 1981, benefit spells were about of equal length in the two countries.

MINIMUM WAGE RATES, COVERAGE, AND COVERAGE-WEIGHTED MINIMUM WAGES, CANADA AND UNITED STATES, 1966–1984

	Canada[a]				United States[b]		
	Actual minimum (male workers)			Weighted relative minimum	Actual minimum	Proportion of Non-supervisory workers covered	Coverage-weighted relative minimum
	Nova Scotia	Ontario	Quebec				
1966	1·08	1·00	0·75	0·41	1·25	0·63	0·30
1967	1·10	1·00	1·04	0·43	1·25	0·75	0·35
1968	1·14	1·00	1·08	0·43	1·40	0·73	0·35
1969	1·19	1·30	1·25	0·46	1·60	0·78	0·41
1970	1·25	1·35	1·32	0·45	1·60	0·78	0·39
1971	1·33	1·61	1·44	0·46	1·60	0·78	0·36
1972	1·45	1·65	1·58	0·46	1·60	0·78	0·34
1973	1·60	1·79	1·73	0·46	1·60	0·78	0·32
1974	1·72	2·06	2·00	0·47	1·87	0·81	0·36
1975	2·24	2·35	2·49	0·48	2·10	0·83	0·37
1976	2·50	2·60	2·84	0·47	2·30	0·85	0·39
1977	2·75	2·65	3·08	0·45	2·30	0·87	0·37
1978	2·75	2·65	3·27	0·43	2·65	0·78	0·35
1979	2·81	3·00	3·42	0·42	2·90	0·78	0·35
1980	2·81	3·00	3·61	0·40	3·10	0·78	0·34
1981	3·08	3·28	3·84	0·38	3·35	0·79	0·34
1982	3·41	3·50	4·00	0·36	3·35	0·80	0·32
1983	3·75	3·50	4·00	0·35	3·35	0·80	0·31
1984	3·75	3·83	4·00	0·35	3·35	0·80	0·30

[a] Minimum wage rates are taken from *Labour Standards in Canada*. The weighted relative minimum wage represents a labour-force-weighted average of relative minimum wage rates by province and sex. For each province, the minimum wage is expressed as a fraction of average hourly earnings in manufacturing. Minimum wages cover essentially all workers in all provinces for the years in this table. Data for 1966–70 were provided by R. Swidinsky. Data for 1971–84 represent the author's calculations.

[b] Actual minimum wage data are taken from the *Social Security Bulletin Annual Statistical Supplement* (1983). Coverage data are taken from *Minimum Wage and Maximum Hours Standards Under the Fair Labor Standards Act* (various issues). Coverage data for 1982, 1983 and 1984 represent extrapolations. The coverage-weighted minimum wage is the product of the coverage ratio and the actual minimum, divided by average hourly earnings of production workers in manufacturing, excluding overtime.

TABLE 9a

COVERAGE, BENEFITS, AND DURATION OF UNEMPLOYMENT INSURANCE, CANADA, 1966-1984[a]

	Proportion of labour force covered	Ave. weekly benefit	Ave. weekly earnings	Gross replacement rate	Tax adjustment[b]	Net replacement rate	Ave. duration of benefit claims[c]	Ave. no. of UI recipients per unemployed worker[d]
1966	0·61	24	96	0·25	1·25	0·31	—	0·92
1967	0·62	25	103	0·24	1·25	0·30	—	0·90
1968	0·64	27	110	0·24	1·25	0·30	—	0·89
1969	0·66	32	118	0·27	1·25	0·34	—	0·84
1970	0·67	35	127	0·28	1·25	0·35	—	0·80
1971	0·67	39	138	0·28	1·25	0·35	—	0·81
1972	0·89	62	149	0·42	1·00	0·42	13·5	1·06
1973	0·90	68	160	0·43	1·00	0·43	14·4	1·10
1974	0·90	75	178	0·42	1·00	0·42	13·1	1·06
1975	0·90	85	203	0·42	1·00	0·42	14·2	1·04
1976	0·91	93	228	0·41	1·00	0·41	14·6	0·96
1977	0·90	101	250	0·40	1·00	0·40	15·0	0·88
1978	0·89	110	265	0·42	1·00	0·42	15·9	0·88
1979	0·89	109	288	0·38	1·00	0·38	16·0	0·85
1980	0·89	121	317	0·38	1·00	0·38	15·2	0·81
1981	0·89	130	355	0·37	1·00	0·37	14·8	0·79
1982	0·89	145	391	0·37	1·00	0·37	17·0	0·88
1983	0·89	155	420	0·37	1·00	0·37	21·2	0·88
1984	0·89	162	444	0·36	1·00	0·36	19·2	0·85

[a] The proportion of the labour force covered represents the sum of insured employment and unemployment, divided by the labour force. Data on insured employment and unemployment are taken from Statistics Canada, *Statistical Report on the Operation of the Unemployment Insurance Act* (various issues). Data on average benefits and average duration of benefits are taken from Statistics Canada, *Social Security National Programs*, Vol. 2 (1984), and Riddell (1980). Average weekly earnings are for production workers on private payrolls, from *Employment, Earnings and Hours*.
[b] Calculated on the assumption that the marginal tax rate for a typical UI recipient is 20 per cent on earned income. UI benefits were untaxed prior to 1972. From 1972 to 1979 they were taxed as ordinary income. After 1979, UI recipients with annual net income in excess of $20,670 (1·5 times maximum insurable earnings) were forced to reimburse 30 per cent of the benefits that made up the excess.
[c] Measured by dividing total benefit weeks paid by the number of initial claims.
[d] Measured by dividing total benefit weeks paid by 52 times the average number of unemployed workers.

TABLE 9b

COVERAGE, BENEFITS, AND DURATION OF UNEMPLOYMENT INSURANCE, UNITED STATES, 1966-1984[a]

	Proportion of labour force covered	Ave. weekly benefit	Ave. weekly earnings	Gross replacement rate	Tax adjustment	Net replacement rate	Ave. duration of benefit claims[c]	Ave. no. of UI recipients per unemployed worker[d]
1966	0·65	40	99	0·40	1·25	0·50	11·2	0·31
1967	0·66	41	102	0·40	1·25	0·50	11·4	0·34
1968	0·66	43	108	0·40	1·25	0·50	11·6	0·33
1969	0·67	46	115	0·40	1·25	0·50	11·4	0·33
1970	0·66	50	120	0·42	1·25	0·50	12·3	0·37
1971	0·67	54	127	0·43	1·25	0·53	14·4	0·36
1972	0·75	56	137	0·41	1·25	0·54	14·0	0·32
1973	0·76	59	145	0·41	1·25	0·51	13·4	0·31
1974	0·77	64	155	0·41	1·25	0·51	12·7	0·36
1975	0·76	70	164	0·43	1·25	0·51	15·7	0·43
1976	0·77	75	175	0·43	1·25	0·54	14·9	0·33
1977	0·80	79	189	0·42	1·25	0·54	14·2	0·31
1978	0·88	83	204	0·41	1·25	0·53	13·3	0·31
1979	0·89	90	220	0·41	1·25	0·51	13·1	0·33
1980	0·90	99	235	0·42	1·25	0·53	14·9	0·38
1981	0·90	106	255	0·42	1·25	0·53	14·5	0·32
1982	0·89	119	267	0·45	1·25	0·56	15·9	0·33
1983	0·88	123	281	0·44	1·25	0·55	17·5	0·31
1984	0·88	123	294	0·42	1·25	0·53	14·8	0·25

[a] The proportion of employees covered represents insured employment divided by total employment. Insured employment is taken from the *Handbook of Unemployment Insurance Financial Data 1938–76*, and *Monthly Labor Review* (various issues). Data on average weekly benefits and average duration are from the same source. Average weekly earnings are for all production workers on private payrolls.
[b] Calculated on the assumption that the marginal tax rate for a typical UI recipient is 20 per cent on earned income and 0 on UI benefits. In 1979 UI benefits became taxable at one-half the recipient's normal tax rate, for recipients whose adjusted gross income exceeded $20,000 ($30,000 for married taxpayers filing jointly).
[c] Measured by dividing total benefit weeks paid by the number of initial claims. Benefit weeks pertain to state unemployment insurance system only.
[d] Measured by dividing total benefit weeks paid by 52 times the average number of unemployed workers. Benefit weeks pertain to state unemployment insurance system only.

In 1982 and 1983 benefit spells increased in both countries in response to the downturn in economic activity. The increase was greater in Canada, although the relative increase is roughly consistent with historical patterns and the relative increase in unemployment rates in Canada. Evidence on the duration of benefits does not suggest that the Canadian unemployment insurance system is significantly more generous than the US system, or that there was a radical change in either system in the 1980s.

A third measure of the generosity of the unemployment insurance system is the ratio of benefit recipients to the number of unemployed workers. In contrast to the previous two measures, which characterize unemployment benefits for those workers who actually receive benefits, the ratio of recipients to unemployed workers summarizes the probability of obtaining benefits, conditional on becoming unemployed. For both Canada and the United States, we calculated the probability of receiving benefits by dividing the average weekly number of benefit recipients by the average weekly total of unemployed workers.

The last columns in Tables 9a and 9b present this number for Canada and the United States respectively. The comparison is quite remarkable. In spite of the fact that coverage of employed workers by the unemployment insurance system is approximately the same in the two countries, a given level of unemployment generates about three times as many beneficiaries in Canada as in the United States. Some caution is required in interpreting these numbers, since the US beneficiary count only includes recipients of state unemployment insurance benefits, and the United States also operates unemployment insurance schemes for veterans, federal workers and railroad workers outside of the state system. In the 1970s, only 80 per cent of average weekly insured unemployment was covered by state programmes; this number increased to 90 per cent in 1978 with revisions in US law. Nevertheless, eligibility criteria for unemployment insurance are apparently stricter in the United States, with the result that the average ratio of benefit recipients to unemployed workers is only about 0·3 in the United States, compared with about 0·9 in Canada.

The time series variation in US benefits per unemployed worker is procyclical, reflecting cyclical movements in the fraction of unemployed workers who are eligible for benefits.[17] As noted by Burtless (1983), the fraction of unemployed workers in the United States receiving benefits has fallen in the last five years (controlling for business cycle conditions). A similar decline in the ratio of beneficiaries to unemployed workers is apparent in Canada after the 1979 revision to the unemployment insurance system there. The ratio increased in Canada in 1982, however, so that in 1984 the relative fraction of benefit recipients to unemployed workers in Canada as against the United States was as high as its level in 1973.

The fact that unemployed workers are more likely to receive benefits in Canada than in the United States is an important difference between the countries, and the only major difference in their unemployment systems that we have found. This difference has existed for at least the past 20 years, however, and seems incapable of explaining a *recent* divergence in unemployment rates. It may none the less account for the relatively slower adjustment to cyclical shocks in Canada. The evidence in Section I above, however, suggests that the recent unemployment divergence is not purely an adjustment phenomenon.

Union coverage

Table 10 presents time-series information on the extent of union coverage in the United States and Canada. The entries for 1950, 1960, 1964 and 1970 indicate relative stability in union coverage over that period, with a small decline in US coverage during the 1960s. During the 1970s, however, union coverage ratios diverged rapidly, with union coverage increasing some 4 or 5 percentage points in Canada and decreasing by about the same amount in the United States. After 1980, information on US union coverage is irregular. Coverage measures from the Current Population Survey, which became available in 1973, stopped in 1981 and then resumed in 1984, are roughly in agreement with coverage ratios estimated indirectly from union membership. By 1984 these data suggest that union coverage was twice as high in Canada as in the United States.[18] While this is an important difference between the two economies, the gap in union coverage emerged in the early 1970s, and remained relatively constant during the 1980s. Union membership rates by themselves, therefore, cannot explain divergent unemployment rates *after* 1981.

TABLE 10

UNION MEMBERSHIP AS A PERCENTAGE OF NON-AGRICULTURAL
EMPLOYMENT, CANADA AND THE UNITED STATES, 1950–1984

| | Union membership as a percentage of non-agricultural payroll measured from union records[a] | | Union membership as a percentage of wage and salary workers measured from household survey[b] |
	Canada	USA	USA
1950	30·1	31·5	—
1960	32·3	31·4	—
1964	29·4	28·9	—
1970	33·6	27·3	—
1971	33·6	27·0	—
1972	34·6	26·4	—
1973	36·1	25·8	23·6
1974	35·8	25·8	23·2
1975	36·9	25·3	22·3
1976	37·3	24·7	23·4
1977	38·2	24·8	23·4
1978	39·0	23·6	22·7
1979	—	—	23·8
1980	37·6	24·8[c]	22·7
1981	37·4	—	21·2
1982	39·0	22·1[c]	—
1983	40·0	—	—
1984	39·6	—	19·1[d]

[a] Calculated as the ratio of estimated union membership to employment of non-agricultural payrolls. The BLS discontinued its estimates of union membership in 1980. No Canadian estimate is available for 1979.
[b] Estimated from Current Population Survey. Data for 1973–81 are from Kokkelenberg and Sockell (1985). CPS discontinued its union membership questions during 1982 and 1983. The CPS survey includes employee associations after 1976.
[c] The 1982 figure for union membership in the United States was estimated by the Bureau of National Affairs. The 1980 and 1982 membership figures include membership in employee associations. The 1978 estimate of union membership as a percentage of non-agricultural employment including association membership is 26·2 per cent.
[d] Estimate from September 1984 CPS.

Our conclusion from this analysis of minimum wage laws, unemployment insurance provisions and union coverage rates is straightforward. There is no direct evidence that changes in any of these institutional features can explain the unemployment gap in Canada after 1981. Each of these features doubtless contributes to the level of structural unemployment in each country. However, it is difficult to isolate a dramatic change in any of these features that corresponds to the timing of the unemployment gap.

IV. WAGE RIGIDITY AND EMPLOYMENT

An alternative interpretation of the hypothesis linking the regulation of labour markets to unemployment attributes the causation to wage rigidity. In this view, economic shocks that require wage decreases to restore labour market equilibrium are prohibited from working their way through the economic system by labour market regulations. According to these notions, wage rigidity is the cause of unemployment, and unemployment has increased recently because of a sequence of economy-wide shocks.

It is, of course, difficult to test this hypothesis directly when the economic shocks in question are not empirically identified, but two different aspects of this hypothesis are testable by using the comparison of wage behaviour in the United States and Canada. If it is relative wage rigidity that has caused Canadian employment to grow more slowly than the Canadian labour force relative to that of the United States, then it seems that a comparison of the time-series path of wage behaviour in the two countries is called for. Alternatively, the relative wage rigidity explanation for the divergence in unemployment presumes a causal relationship between an exogenously determined real wage and the employment level. We also subject this hypothesis to test in the two countries.

The path of real wage rates

Figure 2 portrays the history of the real wage rate in Canada relative to that of the United States since 1964. The wage series is the ratio of real average hourly earnings in manufacturing in the two countries adjusted for the real exchange rate.[19] This series provides an indication of what it costs in US dollars to buy an hour of Canadian labour relative to the cost of buying an hour of US labour, and is perhaps a useful measure of movements in relative labour costs to producers. As the figure indicates, the cost of Canadian labour increased relative to the cost of US labor continuously until the mid-1970s. After a sharp fall in the relative cost of Canadian labour in the 1977–80 period, this index remained relatively stable at around the value of $1 \cdot 0$ in subsequent periods.

These data certainly do not provide any evidence that relative wage rigidity is a major source of the divergence in Canadian and US unemployment rates. First, there has been no substantial increase in the cost of Canadian labour relative to the cost of US labour in the post-1981 period. Second, the period 1964–74, which coincided with higher rates of growth of employment in Canada than in the United States, also coincided with continued greater growth in Canadian real wage rates. Thus, treating exogenous real-wage growth as a causal source of employment changes is entirely contradictory with the facts.

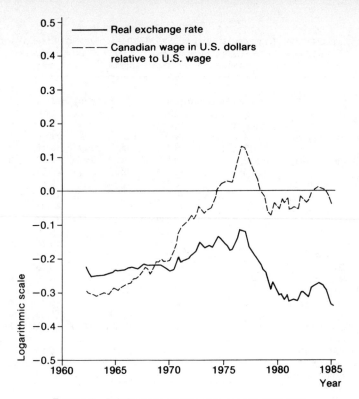

FIGURE 2.   Relative wages and the exchange rate, 1965–1983.

Although the current equality in US and Canadian employment growth is
consistent with the current stability in the US–Canadian wage ratio, the history
of relative wage growth in the two countries in earlier periods implies a positive rather than negative relation between employment growth and wage
growth.

Effects of the real wage on employment

More direct tests of the role of real wages in determining employment are
contained in Table 11. Columns (1) and (4) of the table indicate that employment may be well described as a (weakly) damped second-order autoregressive
process in both countries. Innovations in Canadian employment display somewhat greater variability than in the United States, but the rate of change of
employment is less persistent in Canada.

Causality tests of employment by the real wage are reported in row (10)
of the table. There is marginal evidence of causality from real-wage rates to
employment in both the United States and Canada. The sums of the coefficients
on the real-wage variables in the regressions reported in Table 11, however,
indicate a positive, but effectively negligible, long-run relationship between
real wage rates and employment in both the United States and Canada.[20] In

TABLE 11

AUTOREGRESSIVE REPRESENTATIONS OF MANUFACTURING EMPLOYMENT:
QUARTERLY DATA, CANADA AND THE UNITED STATES, 1962-1984
(standard errors in parentheses)

	Canadian employment			US employment			Canada –USA
	(1)	(2)	(3)	(4)	(5)	(6)	(7)
(1) Employment	1·34	1·50	1·40	1·63	1·70	1·56	1·36
$(t-1)$	(0·10)	(0·11)	(0·10)	(0·08)	(0·11)	(0·11)	(0·11)
(2) Employment	−0·38	−0·93	−0·89	−0·70	−0·87	−0·80	−0·91
$(t-2)$	(0·10)	(0·19)	(0·17)	(0·08)	(0·22)	(0·21)	(0·18)
(3) Employment	—	0·52	0·55	—	0·12	0·18	0·69
$(t-3)$		(0·20)	(0·18)		(0·22)	(0·21)	(0·18)
(4) Employment	—	−0·13	−0·12	—	−0·02	−0·04	−0·26
$(t-4)$		(0·12)	(0·11)		(0·11)	(0·10)	(0·12)
(5) Real wage	—	—	−0·12	—	—	0·09	0·11
$(t-1)$			(0·19)			(0·16)	(0·17)
(6) Real wage	—	—	0·19	—	—	−0·07	0·20
$(t-2)$			(0·28)			(0·25)	(0·25)
(7) Real wage	—	—	−0·31	—	—	0·30	−0·14
$(t-3)$			(0·28)			(0·24)	(0·25)
(8) Real wage	—	—	0·34	—	—	−0·42	−0·09
$(t-4)$			(0·19)			(0·16)	(0·16)
(9) Standard error	0·014	0·014	0·013	0·010	0·010	0·010	0·023
(10) Probability value of exclusion test for 4 lagged values of real wages	—	—	0·04	—	—	0·15	0·12

[a] Seasonally adjusted data (all variables in logarithms). The wage rate represents average hourly
earnings of hourly-rated workers in Canada; production workers in the United States. Regressions
include a linear trend and quarterly dummy variables.
[b] Canadian and US employment regressions are estimated jointly in a two-step procedure. Correlation of the first-stage residuals from Canadian and US equations is 0·40. The probability value
of an F-test for equality of the US and Canadian coefficients is 0·02.
[c] All variables in difference form. The probability value for an F-test that all US and Canadian
variables enter with equal and opposite coefficients is 0·11.

sum, we find no evidence that real wage rates have been a factor in employment
determination in either country.

The last column of Table 11 provides a more direct test of whether
movements in the relative wage of Canadian v. US workers have been a causal
factor determining relative employment movements in the two countries. Here
we simply difference the dynamic employment equations in the two countries
and compute the regression of relative employment on relative real wage rates
directly. This specification has the attractive feature that it differences out
unobservable error components in employment demand that are common to
both countries. To the extent that input prices and productivity shocks are
similar between the two countries, mis-specification in the demand equation
of one country or the other is eliminated.

A test for coefficient equality between lagged US and Canadian variables shows that these restrictions are not easily rejected. Consequently, the differenced employment regression provides a powerful test of the role of relative wages in the determination of relative employment. The results are the same as when the test are performed for each country separately: there is no evidence that relative employment and relative wage rates are negatively related.

V. Conclusions

We began our investigation with the puzzle set out in Figure 1: Why has the unemployment rate in Canada increased so substantially relative to the unemployment rate in the United States? This question is all the more interesting because, as we have shown, the demographic and industrial composition of the two economies are remarkably similar. It seems that simple mechanical hypotheses cannot explain the basic puzzle.

It is also evident, however, that the increase in Canadian unemployment relative to US unemployment cannot be fully attributed to output movements. We find that the gap between actual and predicted Canadian output, based on US output, has fallen dramatically since 1982 while the unemployment gap has widened. We also find that unemployment in Canada was 2 to 3 percentage points higher in 1983 and 1984 than predicted by Canadian output. Some caution is nevertheless required in interpreting post-1980 movements in employment and output in Canada, since the magnitude of the 1982 contraction was unprecedented in Canadian post-war history.[21]

We have investigated a variety of hypothesis to explain the slow growth of employment in Canada after 1982. These hypotheses refer to rigidities in the labour market, which raise employers' costs and restrict the flow of workers between sectors. The evidence does not support the notion that the growth in relative unemployment in Canada is due to differences in the regulation of the labour market in the two countries. Minimum wage laws and unemployment benefits are fairly similar in Canada and the United States, and neither has changed relative to the other in the last decade. Unionization rates have increased in Canada relative to the United States since 1970; most of this divergence occurred before 1980, however, and does not seem to have created an unemployment gap prior to 1980.

Finally, the hypothesis that differential real wage rates are a major determinant of relative employment in the United States and Canada is soundly rejected by the data. In the time-series data, real wage rates have been essentially uncorrelated with employment movements within each country and between the two countries.

ACKNOWLEDGMENTS

We are grateful to Ruth Beck for research assistance and to Robert Swidinsky for generously supplying his minimum-wage data for Canada. We have benefited from comments from Joe Altonji, Pierre Fortin, John McCallum, Douglas Purvis, and seminar participants at Queen's University and the Canadian Department of Finance.

APPENDIX

TABLE A1

MACROECONOMIC INDICATORS FOR CANADA

	Monetary statistics[a]			Real expenditure statistics (1972 $ billions)				
	Change in nominal M1	Change in nominal M2	90-day T-bill rate	Government expenditure	Private fixed investment	Consumption	Net exports	GNP
1973	14·5	14·7	5·4	23·5	20·6	63·9	−1·7	107·8
1974	9·3	20·5	7·8	24·5	21·7	67·2	−4·9	111·7
1975	14·0	15·2	7·4	25·5	22·5	70·6	−5·7	113·0
1976	8·0	13·0	8·9	25·5	23·8	75·2	−6·0	119·6
1977	8·5	14·3	7·4	26·2	23·7	77·0	−4·6	122·0
1978	10·1	11·1	8·6	26·5	23·7	79·0	−3·1	126·3
1979	6·9	15·7	11·6	26·4	25·8	80·6	−4·5	130·4
1980	6·4	18·9	12·8	26·5	26·8	81·4	−3·0	131·8
1981	3·6	15·2	17·8	27·2	28·6	82·8	−3·6	136·1
1982	0·7	9·3	13·8	27·5	25·3	81·1	0·0	130·1
1983	10·2	5·7	9·3	27·5	23·8	83·7	−0·5	134·4
1984	3·2	4·4	11·1	28·5	23·7	86·8	1·2	141·1

[a] Based on annual averages of weekly money supply statistics.

TABLE A2

MACROECONOMIC INDICATORS FOR THE UNITED STATES

	Monetary statistics[a]			Real expenditure statistics (1972 $ billions)				
	Change in nominal M1	Change in nominal M2	90-day T-bill rate	Government expenditure	Private fixed investment	Consumption	Net exports	GNP
1973	7·3	9·9	7·0	253·3	200·4	767·9	15·5	1254·3
1974	5·0	6·1	7·9	260·3	183·9	762·8	27·8	1246·3
1975	4·6	9·3	5·8	265·2	161·5	779·4	32·2	1231·6
1976	5·7	13·0	5·0	265·2	176·7	823·1	25·4	1298·2
1977	13·7	12·7	5·3	269·2	200·9	864·3	22·0	1369·7
1978	2·5	8·5	7·2	274·6	220·7	903·2	24·0	1438·6
1979	7·7	8·2	10·0	278·3	229·1	927·6	37·2	1479·4
1980	6·3	8·1	11·5	284·3	212·9	931·8	50·3	1475·0
1981	7·1	9·5	14·0	287·0	219·6	950·5	43·8	1512·2
1982	6·5	9·4	10·7	292·7	204·7	963·3	29·7	1480·0
1983	11·3	12·3	8·6	291·9	224·6	1009·2	12·6	1534·7
1984	6·9	7·9	9·6	302·2	265·5	1062·6	-15·5	1639·0

[a] Based on annual averages of weekly money supply statistics.

NOTES

1. For display purposes, we have superimposed the 45° line on Figure 1. The slope of a regression line (fit to pre-1982 data) is 0·93.
2. 1985 unemployment rates in the United States and Canada were 7·2 and 10·5 per cent respectively.
3. For an academic analysis of these disparities, see Bruno, this volume.
4. The current situation stands in dramatic contrast to the 1950s and 1960s. In those years unemployment rates were significantly higher in the United States than in Europe, and many economists apparently concluded that the happy state of affairs in Europe was to be attributed to the *more* interventionist government policies towards the labour market in Europe.
5. Both countries use a rotating monthly household survey to measure unemployment and employment, and use the same definition of unemployment. The establishment surveys in each country, which measure industry employment and average hourly earnings, are also very similar.
6. Some of these differences are discussed in Bureau of Labor Statistics (1978).
7. Consistent historical labour force statistics are not available for Canada prior to 1966. We have adjusted 1954–65 data for comparability with the revised labour force survey used after 1975.
8. The steady-state impact of the intercept shift in column (6) is 2·6 percentage points.
9. The model was estimated on seasonally adjusted data from 1956 to 1981 with four lags of each dependent variable, quarterly dummy variables, a linear trend, and a trend shift variable taking effect in first quarter 1974.
10. As an illustration, consider the problem of forming conditional forecasts of a variable y, given the actual values of a variable x from t to $t+j$, and a recursive forecasting model:

$$x_s = ax_{s-1} + u_s$$
$$y_s = by_{s-1} + cx_{s-1} + v_s.$$

Let P denote the least-squares projection operator, given the above information. Then

$$P(y_s) = bP(y_{s-1}) + cx_{s-1} + P(v_s).$$

Since v_s is a forecast error, it is uncorrelated with x_{s-j}. Since y does not Granger-cause x, v_s is also uncorrelated with x_{s+j}. Therefore $P(v_s) = ru_s$ where r is a population regression coefficient. Using the forecast equation for x_s,

$$P(y_s) = bP(y_{s-1}) + rx_s + (c - ar)x_{s-1}.$$

The coefficients of this equation correspond to the coefficients of a regression of y_s on x_s and x_{s-1}. Given a starting value for y, this equation can be iterated forward in time to obtain the required conditional forecasts.
11. For convenience, we have defined the unemployment rate as the difference in logarithms of the labour force and employment. By definition, then, the difference in employment and unemployment represents movements in the labour force.
12. There is reasonable evidence that the 1982 monetary contraction in Canada was larger than the US contraction. Historical data on money supplies, interest rates and the components of GNP are recorded in appendix Tables A1 and A2.
13. In annual data, the logarithm of Canadian real GNP (Y_t^c) has approximately the following time-series representation:

$$Y_t^c = 0·91 Y_{t-1}^c - 0·22 Y_{t-2}^c + 0·56\xi_t^a + \xi_t^c,$$

where ξ_t^a is the current innovation (forecast error) in US GNP, and ξ_t^c represents an orthogonal domestic output shock.
14. This interpretation follows from the fact that Canadian employment and unemployment do not appear to Granger-cause Canadian output.
15. It is worth reiterating that productivity per employed worker (as measured by GNP and aggregate employment) actually increased sharply in Canada relative to the United States after 1982. Thus, 'low productivity' is not an explanation for relatively low employment growth in Canada. Hours per worker in Canada have not changed substantially since 1981.
16. The ratio of average benefits to average earnings may differ from the average ratio of benefits to earnings if, for example, low-wage workers are more likely to receive benefits. Presumably, this bias is about equal in the two countries.
17. One factor affecting the ratio of recipients to unemployed workers is the duration of unemployment spells. Unemployment benefits are denied for the first two weeks of an unemployment spell in Canada, and for an average of about the first week of unemployment in the United States. If average duration increases, the fraction of potentially eligible unemployed workers

increases. This phenomenon cannot explain higher beneficiary ratios in Canada as compared with the United States over the past decade since unemployment duration (as measured by the mean length of interrupted spells) is about equal in the two countries, controlling for cyclical conditions.

18. An examination of unionization rates by industry in the early 1980s suggests that union coverage rates are higher in Canada in most industries, including manufacturing (46 per cent in Canada *v.* 36 per cent in the United States) and services and public administration (36 per cent *v.* 22 per cent).

19. The real exchange rate is the ratio of consumer price indexes, multiplied by the nominal exchange rate.

20. For the United States, the sum of four lagged real-wage coefficients is 0·08 (with a standard error of 0·07). For Canada, the sum of four lagged real-wage coefficients is 0·09 (with a standard error of 0·04). The sums of coefficients are essentially the same when four lagged values of consumer prices are also included in the regressions. The finding that short-run wage movements are only weakly correlated with employment movements in the United States is well known: see Geary and Kennan (1982), Ashenfelter and Card (1982), and Symons and Layard (1984).

21. Annual employment and real GNP both fell in 1982 for the first time in Canadian post-war history. By comparison, the 1982 recession in the United States was the same order of magnitude as the 1974–75 recession.

REFERENCES

ASHENFELTER, ORLEY and CARD, D. (1982). Time series representations of economic variables and alternative models of the labor market. *Review of Economic Studies*, **49**, (supplement), 761–82.

BUREAU OF LABOR STATISTICS (1978). International comparisons of unemployment. Bureau of Labor Statistics Bulletin No. 1979. Washington: US Government Printing Office.

BURTLESS, GARY (1983). Why is insured unemployment so low? *Brookings Papers on Economic Activity*, Vol. 1, pp. 225–49.

GEARY, P. T. and KENNAN, J. (1982). The employment–real-wage relationship: an international study. *Journal of Political Economy*, **90**, 854–71.

KOKELENBERG, EDWARD C. and SOCKELL, D. R. (1985). Union membership in the United States, 1973–1981. *Industrial and Labor Relations Review*, **38**, 497–543.

RIDDELL, W. CRAIG (1980). Unanticipated Inflation, and Unemployment in Canada, Ontario, and Newfoundland. Economic Council of Canada Working Paper No. 182.

SYMONS, JAMES and LAYARD, R. (1984). Neoclassical demand for labor functions for six major economies. *Economic Journal*, **94**, 788–99.

The Rise of Unemployment in France

By E. MALINVAUD

Institut National de la Statistique et des Études Économiques

Whereas the French unemployment rate had remained less than 2 per cent throughout the postwar years up to 1967, it has since increased, having been pushed by an irresistible trend, to 2·7 per cent in 1972, 4·1 per cent in 1975, 5·2 per cent in 1978, 7·3 per cent in 1981 and 9·7 per cent in 1984 (annual averages, ILO definitions). The size of the labour force had hardly increased before 1962; during the past 20 years its growth has been slowly accelerating but has remained moderate (0·8 per cent per annum between 1975 and 1982). On the other hand, employment increased steadily from 1962 up to the first oil shock, but has been roughly constant since then (see Figure 1).

My survey of the analysis of these features and of their explanation will follow traditional lines. It will first consider the evolution of the labour force, as well as changes in the volume, structure and nature of the supply of labour. The second section, dealing with the demand for labour, will pay particular attention to changes in the economic and institutional environment of firms. Section III will examine what can be said about a possible increase in frictional

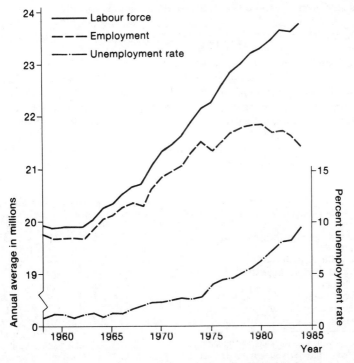

FIGURE 1.   Labour force, France, 1958–1984: employment and the unemployment rate.

unemployment and a possible increasing mismatch between the respective structures of the labour supply and the demand for labour. Section IV will try to identify the origins of the malfunctioning and to allocate responsibilities.

This paper will remain mainly descriptive, empirical and qualitative rather than econometric. Such an approach is proper at the exploratory stage of the analysis of a complex phenomenon, when the main concern is not to overlook any of the factors that may have been important. Accepting a particular specification from the beginning would probably imply neglect of quite relevant features.

Moreover, my preferred specification is unfamiliar enough for its presentation to require a good deal of explanation that would divert attention from the study of the phenomenon itself. This specification has much in common with the one presented in this volume by H. Sneessens and J. Drèze; but it must go more deeply into the analysis of some medium-term determinants, particularly those of the evolution of productive capacity, capital intensity and labour productivity. Actually, the proper specification for the analysis of the medium-term rise in unemployment is not yet quite precise in my mind and still requires preliminary econometric work on particular blocks of the full model.

This methodological choice does not mean that conclusions will be postponed to subsequent work. Indeed, I shall behave like a devoted Bayesian and have no shame in giving my subjective probabilities. For substantiating them, I shall draw in particular from the econometric work done by others, and shall even present a few econometric equations.

I. THE LABOUR FORCE

Two main factors explain the acceleration of the increase of the French labour force since 1962: the evolution of the population of working age, and the increasing participation of adult women in the labour force (see Table 1). On the other hand, net immigration, which had been particularly important in the 1960s, became negligible during the mid-1970s. The impact of decreased

TABLE 1

GROWTH OF LABOUR PRODUCTIVITY, FRANCE, 1963–1984
(thousands of people)

Source of changes	Annual average change between censuses				
	1954–62	1962–68	1968–75	1975–82	1982–84[b]
Pure demographic factor[a]	20	132	170	201	208
Immigration	66	136	58	10	—
Changes in participation:					
People aged less than 25	−20	−64	−61	−40	−90
Adult men	−3	−5	−2	−14	−11
Adult women	−3	−25	113	156	95
People aged 55 and more	−32	−84	−79	−71	−179
Total	28	140	203	242	23

[a] Change of labour force that would have been observed if net immigration had been nill and if detailed participation rates by sex and age had not changed.
[b] Estimates from the labour force survey.

participation by young people, who are remaining in the education system longer, and older ones, who are retiring earlier, has been significant throughout the postwar period.

In comparison with its long-term trend, the population of working age has increased particularly rapidly in the 1970s and 1980s, both because of the influx of people born during the postwar baby boom, which was sustained in France up to the middle of the 1960s, and because of an exceptionally low number of old people leaving the working age group—those reaching age 65 in 1980 belonged to the small cohort born in 1915 during the First World War.

Female labour supply deserves particular attention. Its increase became rapid only after 1967, precisely when labour market conditions began to deteriorate and when the fertility rate declined. This coincidence has of course no causal meaning. In particular, women participated more and more frequently in the labour force, however many children they had; the participation rate of married women aged 25-44 with two children increased from 30 per cent in 1968 to 60 per cent in 1982. At present, the working behaviour of French women is analogous to that of American women, except that on average they work longer hours. In Western Europe, only Scandinavia has higher female activity.

The main explanation of this dramatic change of behaviour is of course cultural, and is linked with the diffussion of education. The events of spring 1968 revealed and promoted new values and attitudes which downgraded the attachment of women to their homes. But economists must wonder whether some economic factors did not also play a role.

It was a shift in the composition of the demand for labour, by industry and by profession, that permitted this huge entry of female labour (see Section III below). As a result, the prospects for women finding jobs did not deteriorate much more than the prospects for men. The female unemployment rate increased from 4·5 to 13·7 per cent between 1968 and 1984, whereas the male unemployment rate increased from 1·7 to 8·7 per cent.

During the years 1968-84, a number of changes in the economic environment shifted the terms of the choice between home work and paid work. The shortening of the work week made life less difficult for employed women with a family; the increase of real wages made wage-earning more attractive, while the husbands' increasing exposure to the risk of unemployment made it more necessary; changes in family allowances shifted the trade-off in favour of employment; even the improvement in unemployment insurance may explain why some women entered into or remained in the labour force whereas they would not have done so otherwise.

I shall not attempt to evaluate the impact of all these changes on the evolution of the female labour force. Even in the United States, where a large amount of econometric work has been devoted to this issue, the evaluation of their impact is notoriously imprecise. In France the econometrics of the labour market is much less advanced.[1] I shall just broadly describe these various changes and note that they all acted against a preference to stay at home.

The average work week for full-time wage-earners had remained between 45·5 and 46 hours from 1956 to 1967. Since then it has decreased, to 42·1 hours in 1975 and 39·1 hours in 1984. Simultaneously, part-time work, which was quite limited in the 1960s, slowly spread in the 1970s. According to the

Labour Force Survey, the proportion of women that were employed part-time (among those employed) is estimated at 13 per cent in 1971, 15 per cent in 1975, 19 per cent in 1982 and 21 per cent in 1984. (Approximately 2 per cent of this increase from 1971 seems to be due to changes in definitions.)

Between 1962 and 1967 the average hourly real wage (for men and women) had increased at an annual rate of 3·2 per cent; the rate jumped to 5·4 per cent over 1968–74, then declined, to 3·3 per cent in 1977–78 and 2·1 per cent over 1979–83. If anything, this increase benefited women slightly more than men; the average annual earnings of full-time female 'employés' was 24 per cent less than for men in the 1960s, but only 21 per cent less in 1978.

In the immediate postwar period family allowances were notoriously important in France; a significant role was played by the single-earner allowance given to families in which the mother was not in paid work. Progressively, the family allowances, and particularly the single-earner allowance, became relatively less significant; this trend was reinforced after 1967, ceasing only in the late 1970s.

In 1968 unemployment insurance coverage was still rather low in France by comparison with some other developed countries. It has improved progressively since then, and has been particularly high by international standards since 1978, notwithstanding a small reduction in the last few years. A suitable indicator is the ratio of the average compensation received by unemployed people to the average wage of employed wage and salary-earners: this amounted to about 12 per cent in the late 1960s, 23 per cent in 1975, and 34 per cent in 1982. It declined to 25 per cent in 1984.

Some of the preceding changes may also have acted on the working behaviour of groups other than adult women. But the overall impact is likely to have been small. Almost all adult men were already in the labour force and a large majority of school-leavers were entering it. On the other hand, the decrease in the rate of participation of old people in the labour force has been so rapid that one can hardly imagine it any faster; for instance, for men aged 60–64 the rate was 66 per cent in 1968, 54 per cent in 1975, 39 per cent in 1982 and 32 per cent in 1984.

One must also be aware that some government policies had the direct result of slowing down the increase of the labour force. These concerned extended schooling for young people without a job (in particular the so-called 'stagiaires' and various inducements to early retirement, from the age of 55 in some cases. Partly as a result of these policies, the decline in the activity rates of young and old people since 1975 has been much stronger than had been anticipated by the extrapolation of previous trends in behaviour. From 1975 to 1982 the difference amounts to an annual net flow of 44,000 people more leaving the labour force.[2] the 'traitement social du chômage' in 1982–83 also acted in this direction.

II. The Demand for Labour

During 1973–84, whereas the labour force was steadily increasing, employment remained almost stagnant, slowly increasing at first, then slowly decreasing. Table 2 shows that this global stability was the result of contrasting movements. Between 1973 and 1984 employment increased by 2·1 million people in services,

TABLE 2

EMPLOYMENT IN FRANCE, BY SECTOR, 1963-1984[a]

(thousands)

	1963	1969	1973	1979	1984
Agriculture	3,760	2,910	2,330	1,930	1,680
Industry	5,640	5,710	6,070	5,730	5,180
Building	1,670	1,970	1,980	1,820	1,580
Transport, trades and services	5,380	6,270	6,810	7,860	8,140
Financial institutions and government	3,410	3,730	4,110	4,490	4,850
Total	19,860	20,590	21,300	21,830	21,430

[a] The selected years (except for 1984) may be considered as peak years of the business cycle.

broadly defined, but decreased by almost as much in agriculture, industry and building (at rates of, respectively, 3·0, 1·4 and 2·1 per cent per annum).

This stability of employment is of course due mainly to the slow rate of growth of output. Indeed, whereas the French economy experienced some decline in the rate of growth of labour productivity, this decline appears moderate in comparison to what happened in some other industrial countries. Table 3 gives a few relevant figures in this respect. These concern production per man-hour, but the picture would be roughly the same for production per man-year since the reduction of the length of work has been about steady since 1967.

Some analysts of French economic trends have argued that the decline in labour productivity could be fully explained in manufacturing, and largely explained for the whole economy, by two factors only; (1) the business cycle, which was responsible for a less intensive use of labour within firms in 1979 and 1984 than in the peak years 1963, 1969 and 1973, and (2) a less favourable evolution of productive capital; whereas investment had been previously accelerating, inducing a continuous shift in the composition of capital towards recent and more modern equipment, it slowed down after 1973 so that the average age of capital increased; moreover, the average length of use of equipment during the year was significantly reduced during the last decade. On these points, see Cette and Joly (1984), Dubois (1985) and Raoul and Rouchet (1980).

TABLE 3

GROWTH OF LABOUR PRODUCTIVITY, FRANCE, 1963-1984

(value added, in constant prices, per man-hour)

	Annual rates (%)			
	1963–69	1969–73	1973–79	1979–84
Industry	6·1	6·2	5·2	4·2
Global (except financial institutions and government)	5·7	6·2	4·1	3·5

Source: Dubois (1985).

Clearly, the stagnation of employment since 1973 is, above all, the result of the depression of the demand facing French firms. This assertion is commonly accepted by analysts of economic trends but is disputed by some theoreticians. I shall discuss later the econometrics of the demand for labour, but at this stage I note two facts that agree with the predominance of demand factors. First, the rise of unemployment is a general phenomenon in the world economy, along with a sluggishness of aggregate demand, while for other factors contributing to the explanation of unemployment national specificities seem to be important. Second, the rise of French unemployment was forecast with econometric models that are quite imprecise for anything but the formation of aggregate demand (Malinvaud, 1984, p. 111).

Depressed demand was of course a reflection of a world-wide phenomenon. Confronted with it, however, the French economy could have fared a little better from the viewpoint of employment (or again, still worse). Hence, we must consider in turn the two following questions: (1) Why wasn't the level of demand facing French firms somewhat higher? (2) This demand being what it was, why didn't French firms employ more labour in order to meet it?

The demand for goods

The first question raises two further sub-questions concerning, respectively, French domestic demand policy and French competitiveness.

During the first phase of the depression, from 1974 to 1978, economic policy underwent several phases of stop–go but was on the whole mildly stimulatory. Real interest rates were very low, credit rationing moderate, and budgetary policy about neutral. (Public administrations had a surplus of 0·9 per cent of GDP in 1973 and a deficit of 1·9 per cent GDP in 1978, but Chouraqui and Price (1983) show that this change is fully explained by automatic stabilizers.) Investments in public utilities (nuclear electricity generation and telecommunications), moreover, were strongly stimulated by public policy.

During the 1980s, on the contrary, economic policy became rather restrictive. Real interest rates jumped up and the autonomous stimulation given by the 1981 budget did not compensate for the restrictive effects of budgets in other years, 1979–80 and 1984 in particular. (The deficit of public administrations went up, however, to 2·8 per cent of GDP.)

Could demand policy have been a bit less restrictive in recent years? I shall leave the question unanswered here, but I must note that policy-makers definitely felt constrained by the international environment and by public perception of what sound public finances ought to be. Although real interest rates were substantial in France (around 5 per cent for bonds), they did not go as high as in other countries. Public opinion was sensitive to the existence of a public deficit and apparently was unimpressed by the situation elsewhere in the world, where public deficits are usually larger and public debts much heavier. Finally, an unsustainable balance of payments deficit was experienced in the years 1980–83.

As far as competitiveness goes, the various indicators do not all tell the same story. Indeed, it is basically difficult to evaluate changes of competitiveness for an economy that opened so quickly to foreign trade (the ratio of imports of manufactured goods to the home demand for these goods increased from 10 per cent at the beginning of 1963 to 26 per cent in 1974 and 47 per cent in 1984).

The broad facts can, however, be described by comparing the evolution of labour costs and prices in international currency to those of competitors. One then sees an unfavourable evolution during the 1970s, preceded and followed by favourable periods. Between 1967 and 1970, as a consequence in particular of the devaluation of the franc in 1969, relative labour costs adjusted for exchange rate movements declined by about 10 per cent; prices of exports of competitors relative to French export prices increased by about as much. But during the 1970s French relative labour costs increased by 15 per cent, and, whereas relative export prices seem to have declined by another 10 per cent (according to unit values derived from international trade statistics), import prices decreased much more with respect to domestic production prices (by more than 20 per cent between 1970 and 1980). On the other hand, by 1983 relative labour costs had come back to their 1970 level, relative export prices had declined by another 15 per cent, and relative import prices had stopped decreasing.

These facts about competitiveness indicators agree with the evolution of import penetration, as measured by the ratio of imports of manufactured goods to the domestic absorption of these goods. Import penetration indeed slowed down after a lag as a consequence of the favourable change that occurred before 1970 and after 1980. But the evolution of the share of the French export market in OECD exports raises an important question. Whereas this share increased from 1968 to 1973, it has been progressively declining since 1979 in value terms and has remained roughly constant in volume. Of course, the lag on the export side should be longer than for import penetration; it may, moreover, be noted that France exports mainly to Europe, where demand has recently been more sluggish than in the world as a whole. But the inability of French firms to benefit much up to now from the recent favourable shift of labour costs and production prices in international currency is worth noting; in 1982–83 it could be attributed to the fact that demand was more depressed abroad than in France, but that explanation can no longer hold in 1984. The present mediocre performance of the French market share may be related to the pronounced decline in profitability in the early 1980s, about which more will be said later.

An inappropriate response

We must now analyse why, confronted with a depressed demand for their goods and with an excess supply of labour during the last ten years, French firms did not shift their input combination more in favour of labour and did not seize more opportunities to sell and produce. But before doing so, it may be enlightening to speculate on what an appropriate response of the French economy could have been.

Let us then assume that the new configuration of disequilibria faced in the late 1970s and the 1980s had been perfectly forecast. Let us take as given world demand, exchange rates and autonomous domestic demand. Let us, moreover, assume that priority has been given to minimizing un-employment over this decade and a half. What, then, should have been done?

The answer of course depends on one's views about what generates the medium-term development of an economy in disequilibrium. It is not the place for me to display my own views, which are somewhat electric but roughly similar to those entertained by most analysts of current economic trends. I hope, then, that the following answer will be accepted by most readers, and later I shall try to discuss the econometric evidence that could substantiate at least part of it.

The appropriate fictitious programme can be described by three main actions. First, one should have stopped the substitution of capital for labour, more precisely the part of it that did not result from the introduction of new and more productive techniques. Second, one should have favoured flexibility in labour management and labour remuneration, although at the cost of valuable social objectives other than employment. Such improved flexibility would have induced firms both to seize market opportunities, even when they were suspected to be temporary, and to use unqualified labour more often for equipment upkeep, improved service to customers and the like. Third, one should have maintained profitability because it would have appeared both directly and indirectly necessary: directly, because firms will pay little attention to currently occurring opportunities if profitability is low; indirectly, because, faced with an uncertain future, they will not install new capacity or replace old unless this is likely to be rewarding. Later, when capacity margins are not available, market opportunities will again be missed.

Against the background of this fictitious programme, let us consider the evolution of the past ten years. We shall then realize that the French economy was quite slow to adapt to the new conditions within which it had to operate. Indeed, it is only quite recently that the need for adaptation was understood. Previous trends were maintained for too long, and this conflicted with the objective of minimizing unemployment.

Let us start with profitability, although its development is the consequence of other factors to be discussed later on. In Malinvaud (1983) I evaluated the net profit rate of non-financial corporations as having been equal to 6·8 per cent on average between 1962 and 1972. It then went down to 4·4 per cent in 1976-77, up to 5·3 per cent in 1978-79, down to a minimum of 1·9 per cent in 1981 (revised figure), and up again to 2·7 per cent in 1983 and 1984. But this should be compared with the real interest rate, which was 3·1 per cent on average during 1962-72, went down to quite low levels during the following years (1·3 per cent in 1979), and up again in the 1980s (4·2 and 5·1 per cent, respectively, in 1981 and 1984). So before 1980 rising inflation protected the pure profit rate (excess of the profit rate over the real interest rate) and prevented it from declining. The situation has completely changed since 1980.

Confronted with these profitability conditions, with increased business uncertainty and with progressively more pessimistic prospects for the future expansion of demand, firms slowed down the building of new capacity, first in manufacturing, more recently in trades and services. The average rate of capacity utilization in manufacturing declined somewhat from the high level reached in the early 1970s but was never really depressed; the average of 83·1 per cent for the years 1974-79 was almost exactly on the same level as that for 1965-68 (83·0 per cent) and the average for 1980-83 was hardly lower (82·3 per cent). This means that the increasing under-utilization of human resources was not accompanied by a similar under-utilization of productive capacities. There is an increasing mismatch between the two. This may also mean that firms were not very strongly pushed to increase their market share abroad or to maintain their market share at home, since a good proportion of them did not really experience idle capacity. We shall come back to this point.

The substitution of capital for labour had been a necessity in the early 1960s, when the labour market was very tight; it was still to be recommended during the fast expansion of the early 1970s. But it seems to have gone on since then, notwithstanding the mounting labour surplus. The explanation is probably to be found not only in the evolution of relative prices, as ordinarily measured, but also in the fact that labour has become more like a fixed factor of production, with recruitment often considered to be an irreversible decision.

The relative cost of labour with respect to capital increased markedly up to the middle 1970s, then remained roughly constant up to 1982; with the present high real interest rates and the recent stagnation of real labour costs, the relative cost of labour with respect to capital is now tending to fall. (The series shows rather large fluctuations, but the trend annual rate of increase may be estimated at roughly 10 per cent from 1963 to 1975.) It is clear that price stimuli strongly favoured labour-saving after labour had ceased to be a scarce production factor. The reversal of the previous trend is still too recent to have had a significant impact on labour requirements.

Even for a Frenchman, it is difficult to form a firm evaluation about the role of non-price obstacles to recruitment. These obstacles arise not only as a result of the laws and regulations themselves, but also from their method of application and more generally from public attitudes concerning labour management. They are mainly the difficulties and high costs involved in dismissing a newly recruited labour force. (The view that dismissal is practically infeasible in France is, however, very far from the truth.) In fact, managers have more and more expressed the view that good businessmen should carefully control the size of their labour force, keeping it as close as possible to the medium-term minimum requirement, even if this implies that one will occasionally miss some opportunities for extra sales. Of course, new forms of labour use developed as a consequence: firms hiring temporary workers extended their activities, and short-duration labour contracts became more and more common, notwithstanding the rather meticulous legislation concerning these forms of employment.

Since in most cases this trend towards making labour a fixed factor of production is tantamount to an increase in the user cost of labour, it could have been compensated by a decrease in the usual measure of the 'product wage', more precisely in the labour cost per unit of output divided by the GDP price. But the evolution of the latter was rather different, with in particular a rapid increase between 1973 and 1979; taking 1973 as the base year, the index was 94 in 1963, 96 in 1969, 100 in 1973, 111 in 1979, 112 in 1983 and 110 in 1984.

Another form of the reduced flexibility came from the minimum wage legislation. The minimum wage had been progressively less binding during most of the 1960s but was greatly raised in 1968 and thereafter. As an indicator, one may consider the ratio between the earnings of an adult worker paid at the minimum wage and the average wage of a manual worker; it was 0·53 in

1959, 0·46 in 1967, 0·57 in 1973, 0·60 in 1979 and 0·63 in 1983. As Martin (1983) has shown, the impact of this evolution should not be overestimated (see also OECD, 1984, Chapter V). However, it certainly played some negative role, in particular against youth employment.

An econometric assessment

In order to gauge the respective influence on the demand for labour of the various factors that have been discussed, a quantitative assessment would be required. One does not expect it to be easy, considering the complexity of the relationship to be tackled, the fact that our interest here is mainly in medium-term phenomena, and the fact that the econometrics of the demand for labour in other countries has few really conclusive results to offer, beyond the dominant importance of the demand for goods. Attention will therefore concentrate on the main question, to what extent is the stagnation of employment since 1973 due to an inappropriate structure of prices and wages?

Let us first note that the model now used for the discussion of medium-term economic policy at the Commissariat du Plan still stresses the income effect of wage changes. The results presented by Catinat and Maurice (1984) show in particular that, starting in 1983, a higher rate of increase of labour remuneration rates would lead to higher employment during the five following years, although it would induce lower investment and a larger trade deficit. Negative effects of excessive wages at a five-year horizon could then come only from a deterioration of competitiveness, which would force the government to adopt more restrictive demand management.

This model is no proof, of course, if it is biased towards Keynesianism. But one should note that other macroeconometric models of the French economy give less weight to profitability considerations and are typically still more Keynesian. More importantly, one must note that direct econometric attempts at evaluating the effect of labour costs on employment find it to be small.

Working on annual data for the period 1957–74 and fitting a simultaneous model of demand for the two main factors, labour and capital, Villa *et al.* (1980) have identified a small negative effect of labour cost on employment (elasticity 0·05). But this case seems to be unique. For instance, a number of regressions and statistical tests have been tried in Artus (1985), working with quarterly data for the years 1963–83; causality tests on the role of real wage on employment find it to be non-significant.

The specifications to be used in the present work must of course be strictly defined with respect to the phenomenon to be measured. As Figure 2 suggests, one may consider determinants that are located more or less upstream in the chain of causation. Two specifications have been tried here on annual data for the years 1963–84: one concerning the most proximate causes (arrows at the bottom of Figure 2), the other aiming at a fuller grasp of the medium-term role of prices and remuneration rates on the demand for labour.[3] The results are on the whole disappointing.

The first regression aims at detecting whether, given output and capital, flexible wages or high profitability leads to high employment. The results are negative for both factors, in so far as the coefficients of the two corresponding variables have the wrong signs with respect to the hypothesis to be tested.

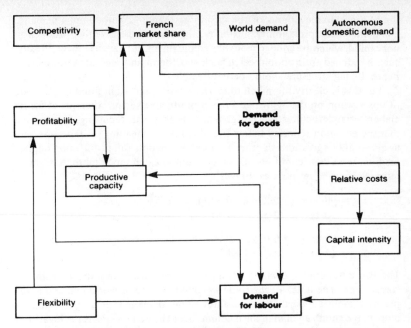

FIGURE 2. Demand for goods and demand for labour; a few determinants.

Flexibility is represented by a proxy whose effect should be in the opposite direction, the ratio φ_t of the minimum wage to the average wage rate; its coefficient is found to be positive (and just significant). The profitability measure π_t, taken from Malinvaud (1983) updated, is, on the contrary, found to have a negative and significant coefficient. I obtain the following, where n_t is the logarithm of employment;

$$(1) \qquad n_t = 0\cdot73n_{t-1} + 0\cdot39y_t - 0\cdot12k_t - 0\cdot27h_t + 0\cdot05z_{1t}$$
$$ (7\cdot1) \quad\; (-) \quad\; (-) \quad\; (-) \quad\; (1\cdot0)$$
$$ + 0\cdot07z_{2t} + 0\cdot04\varphi_t - 0\cdot13\pi_t + f_t.$$
$$ (2\cdot4) \quad\; (2\cdot0) \quad\; (3\cdot1)$$

In this regression the coefficients of the logarithms of output (y_t), capital (k_t) and hours (h_t) have been constrained to agree with a constant-returns-to-scale Cobb–Douglas production function with a $0\cdot3$ coefficient for capital in order to improve the fit. An unconstrained regression is no more favourable to the hypothesis to be tested. The exogenous variables z_{1t} and z_{2t}, which denote, respectively, the rate of capacity utilization in industry and the proportion of industrial firms constrained by labour shortages, have been introduced to capture short-term business conditions. The variable f_t is a split-time trend with a break at 1973. It corresponds to an annual rate of technical progress of $4\cdot1$ and $2\cdot4$ per cent over 1963–73 and 1973–84, respectively. The t-statistics are given in brackets. The Durbin–Watson statistic is $2\cdot24$.

The second regression aims at fitting a kind of reduced form, in which employment would be directly related to its fundamental determinants appearing at the extreme origins of the arrows of Figure 2: autonomous demand, competitiveness, profitability, flexibility and relative costs. Neither production nor capital, which are endogeneous like employment, appear any longer. Ideally, such a reduced form should catch both short-term and medium-term effects; hence, its lag structure should be left flexible.

But this is clearly too much to expect from a regression fitted on 22 years of observation on the aggregate French productive sector: attempts at fitting elaborate lag structures did not give any result worth reporting. This means that the equation reported below is ambiguous in meaning, in the same way as are similar regressions of other authors. Whereas its full justification implies medium-term considerations, it cannot claim to catch much more than short-term effects. The result is as follows:

$$(2) \qquad n_t = -0 \cdot 03 n_{t-1} + 0 \cdot 20 dd_t - 0 \cdot 13 dd_{t-1} + 0 \cdot 17 wd_t$$
$$\qquad\qquad (0 \cdot 1) \qquad (2 \cdot 5) \qquad (2 \cdot 5) \qquad\quad (6 \cdot 3)$$

$$\qquad\qquad + 0 \cdot 05 \gamma_t \quad + 0 \cdot 01 \omega_t \quad - 0 \cdot 09 \varphi_t \quad - 0 \cdot 16 \pi_t + f_t^*.$$
$$\qquad\qquad (2 \cdot 5) \qquad (0 \cdot 7) \qquad (1 \cdot 7) \qquad\quad (2 \cdot 1)$$

The two autonomous demand variables are significant and appear with the correct sign. The index of the trade-weighted volume of world demand (wd_t) plays an important part. Domestic autonomous demand is also significant, but more in the short run than in the medium run. (The variable dd_t is the logarithm of the sum of government demand, social transfers to households, investment of the main large public enterprises, and investment in housing by households.) The long-run elasticity of employment to autonomous demand appears to be roughly one-quarter, which must be considered too small. Another variable, the overall rate of taxes and social security contributions, was added in some regression runs, but turned out to have a very small t-value and the wrong sign. Finally, the linear trend f_t^* imparts a reduction of $1 \cdot 4$ per cent per annum, which cannot account fully for technical progress and the reduction of the work week. All this reinforces the view that medium-term effects are reflected only partially in equation (2). The Durbin–Watson statistic is $2 \cdot 52$.

The main point of interest here concerns the price variables. Competitiveness γ_t, as measured by relative unit labour costs, is found to be significant and to play the expected role, but with a small elasticity. Flexibility of wages, measured by the same inverse proxy φ_t as in regression (1), here has a coefficient of the expected sign and an almost satisfactory t-statistic. On the contrary, the profitability variable π_t has the same wrong sign and apparent statistical significance as in regression (1). Finally, the logarithm of the relative cost of labour with respect to capital ω_t appears with a very small coefficient (of the wrong sign) and is not significant.

These rather disappointing results reinforce my personal prior belief, which is shared by many others and gives a dominant role in Figure 2 to the causal chain running from world demand and autonomous domestic demand to the demand for goods, then to the demand for labour. Each one of the other factors appears by comparison to be marginal.

This, however, cannot mean that the structure of prices and wage rates has no effect. The role of competitiveness has been identified above. Profitability and the relative cost of labour with respect to capital are certainly also important, but their effects are probably too slow to be easily detectable by regressions of the type reported here. More detailed econometric work is required; recent studies in investment behaviour have indeed tended to identify, much more often than earlier ones, the impact of profits on investment.

This is why I maintain that an inappropriate evolution of relative prices and real costs since 1973 is a subsidiary factor explaining why the French demand for labour has grown so slowly. Unfortunately, we cannot be more precise and give a reliable measure of its impact.

III. THE LABOUR MARKET

The rise of unemployment has been the main factor behind the changes that occurred in the functioning of the labour market. All changes will not be described here. Attention will focus on those that might reveal special forces reacting on unemployment, accelerating or retarding it.

The question of whether, and by how much, frictional unemployment increased is particularly relevant, both for the explanation of the unemployment and for its welfare implications. The definition of frictional unemployment is admittedly conventional; it will not be made precise here. Various aspects of frictional unemployment will be considered in turn.

First comes the question of how the mismatch between the supply of and demand for labour evolved. This may be considered by region, by industry, by age–sex, by qualifications. A full discussion of labour market mismatch would be quite lengthy and drawing firm conclusions would be difficult, but it does not seem to be a major factor in explaining the rise of unemployment.

When the mismatch is measured by disparities between specific unemployment rates, a typical pattern emerges: relative disparities decreased, absolute differences increased. This is apparent for instance in the figures given above for female and male unemployment rates; the ratio between the two decreased from 2·7 in 1968 to 1·6 in 1984, but the difference increased from 2·8 to 5·0 percentage points. The same pattern appears for youth v. adult unemployment and for regional disparities: the inter-decile ratio of the unemployment rates in the 'départements' decreased from 2·6 to 1·7 between the two population censuses of 1968 and 1982, but the corresponding difference increased from 1·6 to 4·2 percentage points (the first and ninth deciles being, respectively, 1·0 and 2·6 in 1968, 6·5 and 10·7 in 1982). Similarly, between 1968 and 1975 the ratio between the rates applying to male manual workers and higher staff ('cadres supérieurs') decreased from 3 to 2, whereas the difference increased from 1·3 to 1·8 percentage points. (The evolution of disparities between qualifications was, however, different after 1975, as we shall see later.)

What should be concluded from such a pattern with respect to the trend of frictional unemployment is difficult to say. I tend to see the pattern essentially as being induced by the shift towards a general situation of excess supply of labour. This excess appears in all sectors, however defined, of the labour market, so that all unemployment rates increase. But a general situation of excess supply reduces the incentive to geographical mobility and leads employers to be more selective in their recruitment, so that the increase in unemployment is more important for those groups that are traditionally less in demand.

Another way of testing for an increasing mismatch consists in looking at the data on registered unemployment u_{it} and registered vacancies v_{it} for various groups i and dates t. If u_t and v_t are the corresponding totals for all groups, the index

$$(3) \qquad d_t = \sum_i \left| \frac{u_{it}}{u_t} - \frac{v_{it}}{v_t} \right|$$

may be taken as an indicator of the degree of mismatch. For the 22 French administrative regions, the indicator oscillates around 0·30 with no trend. Particularly high values are observed in March 1974 (0·37) and March 1983 (0·39), and particularly low values in March 1975, 1976 and 1977 (0·24 or 0·25); for March 1984 and 1985 the figures are 0·32 and 0·31. A similar calculation for the 42 main profession groups can be made only for recent years; the March figures for 1979–84 read as follows: 0·55, 0·65, 0·59, 0·50, 0·48 and 0·55.

Looking at productive operations, one does not find special reasons to believe in an increase in structural reorientation, and therefore in an increasing mismatch between a quickly changing demand for labour and a more slowly evolving supply of labour. Discrepancies between the growth rates of various industries roughly kept the same importance. The variance between the rates of capacity utilization in various industries was even significantly higher in the late 1960s than in the early 1980s. The average yearly rates of change of employment in 54 detailed manufacturing industries were considered for the three periods 1970–73, 1973–79 and 1979–84. The standard deviation between these industrial rates was quite stable: 2·38, 2·43 and 2·35 per cent in the three periods.

All things considered, the idea of an increasing structural mismatch cannot be sustained, except perhaps as a consequence of the lack of flexibility of relative wages (of young or unqualified workers), about which more will be said later.

The second question is whether the individual behaviour of workers is responsible for part of the increase in search time before an unemployed worker accepts a new job or exits the labour force. With this question in mind, one can look at data about labour mobility and wonder about the role of unemployment compensation.

Labour mobility had been definitely increasing in the 1960s; but it seems to have decreased somewhat recently. Among employed men who were employed five years before, the proportion of those no longer working in the same establishment was evaluated at 21 per cent in 1964, 34 per cent in 1970 and 33 per cent in 1977. The same statistics, but referring to 12 months before, give 11 per cent in 1977 and only 8 per cent in 1984. Similarly, 6·4 per cent of the labour force of 1968 was not living in the same region six years earlier. The corresponding proportion (but referring to the residence seven years earlier) was 8·9 per cent in 1975 and 8·3 per cent in 1982.

The interpretation of this trend, however, is not clear with respect to the question at issue. I tend to see it mainly as evidence of a deterioration of employment prospects: employed workers move little nowadays because they can not find better jobs; indeed, the proportion of employed workers looking for another job increased from 2·1 per cent in 1963 to 2·9 per cent in 1973 and 4·3 per cent in 1983 (4·7 in 1984); also, the number of people who entered registered unemployment by voluntarily quitting their job decreased from 438,000 in 1976 to 284,000 in 1984. One should not forget that mobility has always been low in France (a sociological feature that the imperfections of the housing market reinforce); but its recent evolution can hardly be taken as evidence of an exogenous change in workers' behaviour.

To assess whether greater unemployment compensation is responsible for a significant part of the increase in search time remains difficult. Econometric studies concerning the consequences of unemployment insurance in other countries have not yet resulted in firm conclusions, even for the partial equilibrium question that concerns us here. Perhaps the most relevant study in this respect was provided by Clark and Summers (1982), working on a sample of Americans. They show that better unemployment insurance indeed inflates the number of unemployed people because of both an increase in search time and increased labour force participation, a consequence that was mentioned in the first section of this paper. However, these effects appeared to be fairly small. The results of Narendranathan et al. (1985), working on a sample of Englishmen, seems to lead to the same qualitative conclusion.

What about France, where unemployment compensation has quite significantly improved in the 1970s (as shown by the figures given in Section I), and where it seems to be now particularly high in comparison with other countries? (According to UNO (1982), such a level of compensation as the present one in France is much higher than the one provided in the United States.)

One is tempted to relate this high compensation to the fact that long unemployment spells are particularly important in France. (In 1983, 43 per cent of unemployed French people were in this situation for more that a year; the corresponding proportion was 36 per cent in the UK and 13 per cent in the United States.) Unfortunately for the analyst, long-unemployment duration seems to be a tradition in France, and is certainly related to low labour mobility. Whereas the average length of uncompleted unemployment spells was 14·5 months in March 1984, it was already about 8·5 months from 1970 to 1972 when the labour market was still fairly tight and unemployment compensation much lower.

The third question is whether the increased 'dualism' prevailing in the French labour market induced a rise of frictional unemployment and generated a phenomenon that is well known in developing countries and is formalized by the Harris–Todaro theory.

Dualism has always existed in the French economy, as in all others; but since the middle 1970s it seems to be definitely increasing in the labour market. Two features of this evolution appear in the statistics.

In the first place, unemployment now increases much more slowly for highly qualified labour than for ordinary wage-earners. For instance, the rate of unemployment of male manual workers increased by 80 per cent between 1975 and 1982 and by another 40 per cent between 1982 and 1984, whereas the rate for male 'cadres supérieurs et professions libérales', although only half the size in 1975, increased by only 30 per cent between 1975 and 1982 and seems to have slightly decreased since then.[4] This evolution may be related to the substitution of capital for labour, which was discussed in Section II, and to changes in the structures of wages. Not only did the increase in minimum wage make poorly qualified workers more costly, but salaries to higher staff and technicians increased significantly less than average wages; between 1975 and 1982 the average real annual salary of a 'cadre supérieur' is estimated to have decreased by 8 per cent, whereas the average real annual wage of a manual worker has increased by 10 per cent. In other words, the labour market seems to have been less constrained for qualified than for unqualified labour.

In the second place, faced with the rigidity of normal labour contracts, employers often hired workers only temporarily and tended to offer contracts for a limited and preagreed duration. These two types of employment concern only a small minority of the employed labour force (about 3 per cent, but 10 per cent for workers under 25), but they reinforce the dualism of the labour market since a number of workers find only jobs of this kind and are recurrently unemployed. Indeed, among the 2·67 million workers who shifted from employment to registered unemployment at some date during 1984, 56 per cent held (up to this date) an interim or limited-duration contract; the corresponding proportion was 31 per cent in 1976. Knowing this situation, most unemployed people quite understandably take such contracts only for lack of a better alternative and after having prolonged their search for a permanent contract.

Another consequence of the dualism and lack of flexibility of the French labour market is the particular importance of youth unemployment. According to the recent OECD (1984) study, the ratio between the rates of unemployment of young and adult workers was higher in France in 1983 than in any other of the countries under examination; it had increased from 2·3 to 3·6 between 1970 and 1980.

It is worth noting that this evolution of youth unemployment had very little impact on the relative wage of young workers, contrary to what was observed in other countries. One cannot help thinking that this feature, as well as the stickiness of real wages in the lower half of the qualification scale, has something to do with the high minimum wage that was maintained during this period of unemployment.

The conclusion of this discussion is that frictional unemployment has quite probably increased in the French economy, but only because of the increase in unemployment compensation and the increased dualism of the labour market, *not* because of an increasing mismatch between the geographical and industrial structures of labour demand and supply. Hence, the increase in frictional unemployment can be only moderate.

One should like to be able to quantify this increase. The idea naturally comes to mind of looking at the 'Beveridge curve', relating the vacancy rate to the unemployment rate. An outward shift of this curve might be taken as evidence of increased frictions on the labour market and could provide a basis for a measure of a corresponding component of unemployment growth. Unfortunately, in the French case this examination of the Beveridge curve is disappointing.

It should first be said that French statistics on vacancies are poor. They concern only those vacancies that were reported at labour exchange offices; and the number of these offices greatly increased, particularly between 1967 and 1974, so that the evolution of reported vacancies is misleading. French statisticians have therefore taken to looking at the ratio of reported vacancies to the number of job applicants at the same labour exchange office.

Figure 3 plots the logarithm of the ratio v/u so defined against the logarithm of unemployment rate u (independently measured) for the years 1960–84. Clearly, the curve shifted rightwards (by about 2·5 percentage points of unemployment) between 1967 to 1972. But such a large shift, occurring early in the period of rising unemployment, simply suggests better prospecting of vacancies by labour exchange offices, which were indeed explicitly given this mission. This being the case, I consider that Figure 3 tells us nothing useful.

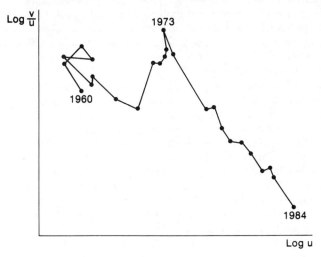

FIGURE 3.   Unemployment-vacancy relationship.

IV. The Macroeconomic Phenomenon

The three preceding sections took a partial equilibrium viewpoint (some would prefer to say 'partial disequilibrium'). The discussion did not consider only proximate causes, but it never claimed to cover all the macroeconomic inter-dependencies. This must now be rectified.

Clearly, however, some of the preceding conclusions stand and they will not be re-examined. Two of them will simply be stated. The rise of unemployment is first and foremost due to international conditions: a long period of stagflation, disorder and depression at the world level, and an inability of Western Europe to maintain its competitiveness and to organize the coordination of economic policies of its various members. But it is also due to an inadequate policy response in France. Faced with the prospect of mounting unemployment, public opinion and governments did not want to sacrifice other objectives in order to contain it; or perhaps they did not want to recognize this unpleasant prospect and did not understand what the real trade-offs were.

But a theme has been occurring repeatedly in the previous discussion and deserves more attention, namely that the system of relative prices and wages performed poorly and did not induce the necessary substitution and adaptation.

Since prices and wages were not fully controlled, we must ask why their development was not better suited to the prevailing situation.

Before considering this aspect of the macroeconomic phenomenon, however, I should like to express some reservation about the attitude of many economists who see in it the alpha and omega of any explanation of disequilibrium unemployment. Fitting Phillips curves tells nothing in itself about the causes or even the measure of this unemployment. Indeed, there is no compelling reason for accepting the identification, proposed by M. Friedman, of the frictional unemployment rate with the NAIRU (non-accelerating inflation unemployment rate). Acknowledging the frequent conflict between the two objectives of employment and disinflation does not require an acceptance of this identification. The dynamics of prices and wages is much more complex than is assumed when the identification is accepted; moreover, these dynamics are often perturbed by forces that the economist can only regard as exogenous but nevertheless must recognize.

With this reservation in mind, however, we must seriously consider the main feature that made the price vector inappropriate, namely a too-rapidly increasing average real wage rate during the 1970s. This increase in real wages resulted in a significant increase in the real average labour cost per unit of output. The increase occurred mainly between 1972 and 1976 and amounted to 8 per cent in four years; but the movement was reversed only in 1983, when real-unit labour costs at last began to fall. (A small decrease had taken place in 1978 and 1979, but was nullified by the second oil shock; the 1981–82 level exceed the 1976 level by 1 per cent.) This increase was almost equal to the deterioration of the terms of trade (8 per cent between 1972 and 1976, 11 per cent between 1972 and 1981).

It is surprising that it was so long before the rise in unemployment produced a visible impact on the evolution of real wages. We may seek an explanation in the results of econometric studies on wage and price formation. Such studies are now quite numerous for France; moreover, they have recently been the object of a very serious scrutiny into their robustness with respect to details of the specification or sample period.

The four-equation model fitted by Feroldi and Meunier (1984) serves the present purpose well. The four endogenous variables are the rates of increase of the hourly wage rate ($\dot{w}$), the manufacturing industry production price ($\dot{p}_i$), the services production price, and the consumer price ($\dot{p}_c$). The model was fitted by instrumental variables on quarterly data for the years 1966–81, with dummy variables for the second and third quarters of both 1968 and 1974. The wage equation and the industrial price equation are reported below;

(4) $\dot{w}_t = 0\cdot4 + \sum\limits_{\tau=0}^{4} b_\tau \dot{p}_{c,t-\tau} - 0\cdot5\hat{u}_t + \sum\limits_{\tau=0} d_\tau \dot{a}_{t-\tau}$

(5) $\dot{p}_{it} = 0\cdot3\dot{p}_{i,t-1} + 0\cdot3(\dot{w}_t - \dot{z}_t) + 0\cdot1\dot{p}_{et} + 0\cdot1\dot{p}_{a,t-2} + 0\cdot08\dot{p}_{mt} - 0\cdot2\,c\dot{m}_t.$

The following exogenous variables appear:

$\hat{u}$ logarithm of the ratio between the number of men aged 25–49 registered as unemployed, and the number of job vacancies

$\dot{a}$ rate of increase of hourly labour productivity

$\dot{z}$ rate of change of employers' social security contributions minus trend rate of growth of labour productivity in industry

$\dot{p}_e$ rate of increase of energy prices

$\dot{p}_a$ rate of increase of agricultural prices

$\dot{p}_m$ rate of increase of prices of industrial imports

$c\dot{m}$ change in unused capacity margins

All coefficients are statistically significant at conventional levels, except the constant of the wage equation. The sum of the coefficients b_r is equal to 1·2 and that of d_r to 0·5.

The general form of these equations is fairly robust. In particular, the Phillips phenomenon, here represented by the variable $\hat{u}$, appears in all specifications and is not weaker in France than in other countries. However, the productivity variable is not always found to be significant in the wage equation; neither is the capacity margin variable in the industrial price equation. Conversely, some regressors not present in equation (5) are sometimes significant in other formulations of the industrial price equation: the cost-to-price ratio, the rate of investment in industry, a competitiveness variable (price of industrial imports divided by industrial unit cost).

Equation (4) would imply even more than a full indexation of wages to consumer prices. Other econometric estimates of the wage equation over the same period generally give somewhat lower coefficients to consumer prices, but in no case is the hypothesis of full indexation rejected by statistical tests.

If, as is the case for equation (4), no regressor represents government wage decisions, in particular concerning the legal minimum wage or the wage rate in large public corporations, large positive residuals, often hidden by *ad hoc* dummy variables, appear in 1968, again in 1974–75, and in 1981–82. *Per contra*, extrapolation of the equation to 1983–84 gives higher wage increases than were observed.

These results suggest that two factors were responsible for the apparent sluggishness of the French real wage rate in the period from the late 1960s to the early 1980s. The first one was a high and quick *de facto* indexation of wages to the cost of living. If the dynamic of the wage–price system was not unstable it is because of the price equations; a wage push, for instance, induced some reduction of profit margins. This indexation of wages was probably related to the prevailing public attitude that placed unique emphasis on equity when considering wage questions.

Second, special events in recent French history played a role in this apparent lack of responsiveness of real wages to the rise of unemployment. We saw that large positive residuals appear in the wage equation in 1968, again in 1974–75, and in 1981–82. I need not insist on the fact that 1968 was the time of the May students' and workers' uprising that shook the whole French society and ended with large wage concessions. The period 1974–75 was the beginning of the Giscard d'Estaing presidency, when the new President attempted to install social peace. Similarly, 1981–82 followed the change to a socialist government which raised the minimum wage and decided full wage compensation for the reduction of the legal duration of the working week.

Wage indexation, and the former bias of public policies towards wage increases, have somewhat similar roots in the French common ideological core. If excessive real wages are taken to have some responsibility for the present size of unemployment, as I think it does, we can say that some of the unemployed are now paying the price for what had to be done in order to maintain the cohesion of French society, and to teach an unwilling public economics.

The same kind of socio-political explanation applies to the two other major features that characterized the French system of prices and remuneration rates: a lack of flexibility of relative wages in the lower half of the scale, and, until recently, a bias of economic policy towards inflation. Nothing more will be said about the first feature, since it was discussed above and is related directly to some of the decisions that explain excessive real wages. But the second feature deserves a few additional comments before I finish.

The acceleration of inflation, which occurred before and after the first oil shock and again after the second one, helped to alleviate for a time the burden of classical unemployment. The deterioration of real profit margins did not mean (until recently) an equivalent deterioration of profitability, because of the capital gains realized by indebted firms and because of low real interest rates. According to the estimates I made in Malinvaud (1983), the net profit rate, computed without taking these capital gains into account, was about 5 per cent from 1962 to 1972, then stayed around 2 per cent from 1974 to 1979. When capital gains resulting from the decrease in the real value of debts are accounted for, the corrected net profit rate amounts on average to 6·8 per cent from 1962 to 1972 and to 5·3 per cent from 1974 to 1979. Simultaneously, the average real interest rate declined from 3·1 per cent during the first period to 1·1 per cent during the second. Thanks to the acceleration of inflation, a margin of more than 4 per cent of the (corrected) profit rate over the interest rate was thus realized between the two oil shocks.

If we accept the argument presented in Bruno and Sachs (1985), a low profitability has some responsibility for poor productivity performance and thus feeds upon itself. *Per contra*, the fact that profitability was maintained in France longer than elsewhere by the acceleration of inflation may explain why the decline in productivity growth rates there was quite moderate.

As is well known, profitability radically deteriorated from 1980 to 1982 and real interest rates leapt. Now that inflation is receding, the risk of a strong push in the classical component of unemployment is quite real. It was, however, obvious enough to cause the 'politique de rigueur' with its strict controls and guidelines on wage rates. Feroldi and Meunier (1984) show that, indeed, significant negative residuals appear in the French wage equation since the second half of 1982; the national accounts also show a substantial improvement of industrial profit margins in 1983 and 1984.

The socio-political background of French macroeconomic policy is thus in full revision. But depressing factors acting on both demand and profitability are still so strong that employment prospects have not yet improved significantly.

ACKNOWLEDGMENTS

This article benefited from useful comments or contributions by P. Dubois, P. Mazodier, J.-P. Puig, C. Thelot and from the discussions at the Chelwood Gate Conference.

NOTES

1. See however Lollivier (1984), Bourguignon (1985) and Riboud (1986).
2. See Marc and Marchand (1984).
3. Assistance was provided by J.-P. Caffet and J.-P. Puig. Regressions (1) and (2) concern employment in non-financial non-governmental activities ("branches marchandes").
4. The phenomenon was noted in Méraud (1984), who gives other data about it. It also appears in unemployment rates by educational level.

REFERENCES

ARTUS, P. (1985). Salaire réel et emploi. Unpublished paper, INSEE (mimeo).

BOURGUIGNON, F. (1985). Women's participation and taxation in France, in Blundell, R. ed. *Applied Labor Economics*, Oxford University Press.

BRUNO, M. and SACHS, J. (1985). *Economics of Worldwide Stagflation*. Oxford: Basil Blackwell.

CATINAT, M. and MAURICE, J. (1984). Analyse quantitative d'une stratégie pour l'emploi. *Revue économique*, **35**, 1007-90.

CETTE, G. and JOLY, P. (1984). La productivité industrielle en crise, une interprétation. *Economie et Statistique*, no. 166, 3-24.

CHOURAQUI, J.-C. and PRICE, R. W. R. (1983). Public sector deficits: problems and economic policy implications. *OECD Occasional Studies*, June.

CLARK, K. B. and SUMMERS, L. H. (1982). Unemployment insurance and labor market transitions. In M. N. Baily (ed.), *Workers, Jobs and Inflation*. Washington: Brookings Institution.

DUBOIS, P. (1985). Ruptures de croissance et progrès technique. *Economie et Statistique*, no. 181, 3-31.

FEROLDI, M. and MEUNIER, F. (1984). Une maquette d'étude de la boucle prix-salaires, and La boucle prix-salaire et l'inflation depuis 1970. *Economie et statistique*, no. 169, 45-59.

LOLLIVIER, S. (1984). Revenu offert, prétentions salariales et activité des femmes mariées: un modèle d'analyse. *Economie et Statistique*, no. 167, 3-15.

MALINVAUD, E. (1983). Analyse macroéconomique des déséquilibres: la France des vingt dernières années. In E. Malinvaud, *Essais sur la théorie du chômage*. Paris: Calmann-Lévy.

—— (1984). *Mass Unemployment*. Oxford; Basil Blackwell.

MARC, N. and MARCHAND, O. (1984). La population active de 1975 à 1982: les facteurs d'une forte croissance. *Economie et Statistique*, no. 171-2, 5-23.

MARTIN, J. P. (1983). Effets du salaire minimum sur le marché du travail des jeunes en Amérique et en France. OCDE, *Etudes spéciales*, June, 51-73.

MÉRAUD J. (1984). Productivité, croissance, emploi. Report to the Conseil Economique et Social, Paris.

NARENDRANATHAN, W., NICKELL, S. and STERN, J. (1985). Unemployment benefits revisited. *Economic Journal*, **95**, 307-329.

OECD (1984). *Employment Outlook*, September. Paris; OECD.

RAOUL, E. and ROUCHET, J. (1980). Utilisation des équipements et fléchissement de la productivité depuis 1974. *Economie et Statistique*, no. 127, 39-53.

RIBOUD, M. (1986). Women in the labour force in France. *Journal of Labor Economics*, forthcoming.

UNO (1982). *The Economic Situation in Europe in 1981*, Section 1, (iii), (c). Economic Commission for Europe.

VILLA, P., MUET, P.-A. and BOUTILLIER, M. (1980). Une estimation simultanée des demandes d'investissement et de travail. *Annales de l'INSEE*, **38-9**, 237-258.

The Nature and Causes of Unemployment in the Federal Republic of Germany since the 1970s: An Empirical Investigation

By Wolfgang Franz and Heinz König

University of Stuttgart and University of Mannheim

The leading economic problem of our time is the high and persistent level of unemployment. As of early 1985, there are no signs that the severity of unemployment will weaken within the near future.

This paper discusses first some basic developments of labour supply and labour demand in the Federal Republic of Germany (FRG)—the composition of the labour supply and the structure of the labour demand for persons and hours worked, as well as the dynamics of the unemployment pool. The next section reviews very briefly some empirical findings explaining the rise in the NAIRU where we make the distinction between the 'no-shock' and the actual NAIRU. Following suggestions put by the organizers of the conference, we then elaborate on the employment function. In the empirically oriented literature most employment functions use labour services, i.e. total hours worked, as the dependent variable, thus assuming homogeneity of labour demand with respect to jobs and working hours. In the German political arena, however, the distinction between persons employed and hours worked is particularly important. First, it figures in the employment aims of labour unions, who request reductions in weekly working hours in order to induce higher manning. Second, the distinction arises in the context of overtime work, for it has been suggested that the reduction in overtime to standard working hours could create more than 1 million new jobs in Germany. We present some estimated labour demand functions, which take into account these two dimensions of labour demand (jobs and hours) and which are used to elaborate on the direction and magnitude of the employment effects of reductions in wage costs and increases in overtime premia.

I. The Anatomy of Unemployment in the FRG

This section attempts to shed some light on trends, structures and dynamics of unemployment in the Federal Republic of Germany in order to provide a basis for the analysis in the subsequent sections.

As a first reference, we present in Figure 1 the official time series of the labour force and employed persons. Except for the mild recession in 1967/68, the FRG experienced virtually no unemployment until 1973. During 1960–73 the average rate of unemployment amounted to 0·88 per cent (excluding 1967 and 1968, with a rate of 2·1 and 1·5 per cent, respectively). The labour market was characterized by excess demand which was partly reduced by the immigration of foreign workers. Employment of 'guest-workers' increased from 280,000 in 1960 to 2·6 million in 1973, i.e. from a share of 1·3 per cent in total employment to about 10 per cent.[1] In principle, foreign workers served as a

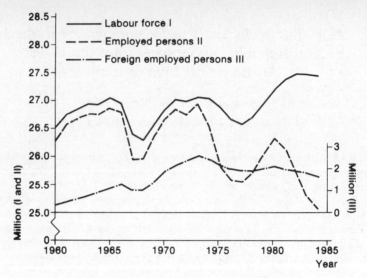

FIGURE 1.   Labour force and employment, 1960–1984.

sort of buffer stock during the recession in 1967/68: their number decreased from 1·3 million in September 1966 to 904,000 in January 1968 and, thereafter, reached its pre-recession level in June 1969.

Unemployment became a severe problem in 1973. The German economy was hit by the first oil price shock at the beginning of a recession, in contrast to the second oil price shock, which occurred in the midst of an upswing.

Labour market conditions have worsened since 1981. While the average unemployment rate during 1974–80 amounted to 4 per cent, the respective figure for 1981–84 is 7·8 per cent, with a maximum of 10·4 per cent in February 1983.[2] As can be seen from Figure 1, both decreasing employment and an increasing labour force contributed to the rise in unemployment. It is therefore worth examining both sides in greater detail.

Trend and structure of labour supply and labour demand

Supply of labour by age, sex, marital status and citizenship. During 1970–84, the total FRG labour force increased by more than 600,000 persons, i.e., by 2·3 per cent. Part of this increase arose from higher participation rates of women, and part was the consequence of changes in the proportion of guest-workers in the total labour force.

Table 1 provides data on labour force participation rates by age, sex, marital status and citizenship from 1972 to 1983.[3] For German citizens the participation rates of males aged 25–55 remained fairly constant over time, whereas those of teenagers and elderly men decreased sharply. With the exception of teenagers, participation rates of single females were higher than those of married women but these differences narrowed slightly owing to the increase in labour supply of married women. In a similar fashion to male participation rates, those of single female teenagers dropped dramatically, whereas those of single females aged 25–55 did not change substantially. The notable

TABLE 1

LABOUR FORCE PARTICIPATION RATES, BY AGE, SEX, CITIZENSHIP AND MARITAL STATUS, 1972–1983[a]

| Age group | Males | | | | Females | | | | | | | | | | | |
| | | | | | Total | | | | Single | | | | Married | | | |
	1972	1975	1980	1983	1972	1975	1980	1983	1972	1975	1980	1983	1972	1975	1980	1983
Germans																
15–20	61·3	56·6	48·4	45·8	60·0	50·7	41·6	39·2	60·2	50·2	41·0	38·7	57·3	59·9	61·5	60·7
20–25	83·0	79·6	81·6	80·0	66·4	68·5	72·1	71·5	79·8	74·8	76·8	75·7	56·7	62·2	64·3	62·6
25–30	92·5	89·7	90·9	88·0	51·7	55·8	62·8	64·4	85·7	81·8	84·8	81·3	45·3	49·8	55·1	56·9
30–35	98·1	97·3	97·4	95·8	46·9	50·1	55·9	58·3	90·1	86·4	88·3	89·0	41·9	45·7	50·6	52·1
35–40	98·6	98·2	98·4	97·0	47·4	49·0	54·9	59·8	89·0	90·3	90·5	89·7	42·7	44·7	50·2	55·1
40–45	98·3	97·9	98·0	97·4	49·2	50·0	54·2	58·9	89·0	89·1	88·3	88·4	43·9	45·3	50·0	54·2
45–50	96·6	96·6	96·6	96·3	50·4	50·8	51·8	54·6	88·7	89·4	88·0	83·2	43·6	44·6	47·0	50·5
50–55	93·9	92·9	93·3	92·9	46·3	47·2	46·9	47·4	85·7	85·1	86·7	80·3	39·8	40·1	41·1	43·0
55–60	86·0	85·6	82·1	80·8	35·9	38·3	38·4	39·8	77·4	77·5	77·1	73·8	29·5	31·6	31·5	34·6
60–65	68·4	58·0	43·6	39·4	17·4	16·4	12·8	12·4	39·6	35·5	25·9	23·3	14·5	14·0	11·0	10·9
65+	15·0	10·9	7·4	6·4	5·7	4·4	3·0	2·8	11·8	9·1	6·5	6·6	6·3	5·0	3·2	3·4
15–65	87·8	85·3	83·8	81·4	46·7	47·3	49·7	50·5	71·1	64·2	60·7	58·8	40·4	42·4	45·4	46·8
Total[b]	57·2	56·2	57·9	59·1	30·1	30·3	32·3	34·5	25·7	25·1	29·1	31·0	36·7	37·8	39·7	41·7
Non-Germans																
15–20	81·3	66·8	48·9	50·2	68·2	49·6	38·4	31·2	70·7	49·8	38·8	31·8	62·2	48·7	35·6	23·8
35–40	99·1	98·1	98·1	96·4	71·5	66·9	60·9	56·0	98·5	96·8	94·9	90·6	67·7	64·3	56·9	53·0
15–65	95·6	93·4	90·6	87·8	68·9	63·4	57·2	53·8	83·3	69·0	61·3	51·7	64·4	61·2	54·9	53·5
Total[b]	76·3	67·9	64·2	63·2	49·2	42·7	37·9	36·7	30·7	19·1	17·5	16·8	63·6	60·5	54·2	53·0

[a] Percentages of each group specified in the table.
[b] Percentages of all age groups (including less than 15 years)
Source: Statistiches Bundesamt.

exception to this pattern was married women: all age groups of married women between 15–60 experienced an increase in labour supply. This is most obvious for married women aged 35–40, with the participation rate increasing from 42·7 to 55·1 per cent over a decade.

Several factors are responsible for this pattern (Franz, 1985a). Within the past two decades, demand for higher education has increased, so reducing the labour force participation rates of teenagers and young adults. The demand for higher education by young females has induced a supply shift in subsequent years since these women have wanted to benefit from their investment in human capital. Changes in family formation, i.e. fertility, marriage and dissolution, may also have affected labour market behavior. More highly educated women tend to have fewer children and participate more. In addition, fewer women than before are getting married, the age at marriage has increased, and divorce has become more widespread. Changes in fertility rates indicate this development; in the space of 20 years fertility rates have decreased to nearly one-half. A major problem for the labour market in the 1980s is the tremendous inflow of new entrants aged 18–25 resulting from the baby boom in the mid-1960s.

In addition, over the past decade foreign workers did not re-migrate to their home countries to the extent that they did in the 1967/68 recession. Since employment of EEC workers is not under government control (because of the freedom of movement for labour within the Common Market), only the immigration of guest-workers from non-EEC countries may be considered as a goal of employment policy. A stop to the immigration of these foreigners was ordered in 1973, but, on the other hand, the decline in labour supply of this group was comparatively moderate owing to the new laws enacted in 1978 and 1979 which guarantee a claim for a longer residence permit depending on the worker's previous stay in Germany.

Summing up, and neglecting some changes in reported unemployment arising from changes in institutional regulations,[4] the rise in the labour force during the period 1970–83 was brought about mainly by females aged 25–45 and 15–25 (an additional 1 million and 0·2 million persons, respectively), whereas the number of males aged 15–65 remained constant. Both higher participation rates and a growth in the size of the population of working age contributed to the higher supply of labour.

Demand for labour: the nature and development of jobs. With respect to the demand for labour, two dimensions have to be considered: the number of jobs offered, and number of hours worked. First we examine the demand for labour measured in persons. This definition requires information on employed persons and vacancies. For the latter, however, data are available only for vacancies registered at the labour office, and this differs from the number of actual job offers in several ways. Most importantly, only a fraction of new hires is managed by the intervention of the labour office. This fraction is not constant over time but fluctuates around a declining trend. Owing to these data limitations, we focus on the number of employed persons.

Table 2 gives information on the number of employed persons and their sectoral distribution. Focusing on the time period from 1973 (i.e. at the outset of the first OPEC oil price rise) to 1983, we observe a decline of 1·7 million

TABLE 2

SECTORAL DISTRIBUTION OF EMPLOYED PERSONS, 1970–1983
(thousand persons)

Period	Total	Agriculture	Energy	Mfg sector	Construction	Trade traffic	Services	Govt	Others[b]
1970–74	26,658	2036	533	9891	2307	4910	3061	3240	679
1975–79	25,679	1612	504	8964	1986	4862	3321	3693	737
1980–83	25,749	1398	505	8592	1984	4859	3623	3969	820
Change in jobs, 1973–83									
Numbers	−1723	−553	−13	−1737	−459	−284	+535	+638	+150
Percentages[a]	−6·42	−28·74	−2·52	−17·61	−19·57	−5·66	+17·13	+18·95	+21·52

[a] As a fraction of jobs in each sector of 1973
[b] Including private households, non-profit organizations, etc.
Source: Sachverständigenrat zur Begutachtung der gesamwirtschaftlichen Entwicklung, calculations by the authors.

employed persons in the German economy. The bulk is attributable to the manufacturing sector, whereas the service and government sectors experienced a steady increase in the number of employed persons.

It is often argued that the decrease in employment is classical, i.e. is caused by too high real-wage costs (e.g. Giersch, 1983). Table 3 therefore presents some information on real-unit labour costs. Two measures of productivity growth are used: actual and trend productivity growth. Figures are deflated by output prices rather than by cost of living indices. Both measures seem to support the view that the reduction in employment during 1974–77 may be caused by 'classical' factors: the total increase in real-unit labour costs 1970–74 amounts to 7·8 per cent (using trend productivity growth) in the entire economy, which was partially reversed by a fall of 6·1 per cent during the period 1975–83. Comparing the development of jobs (Table 2) and real-unit labour costs over 1970–83, we observe a 12 per cent increase of costs and a 22 per cent decrease of jobs in the manufacturing sector. In the service sector the direction of these developments is reversed but the ratio remains the same: a 12 per cent decrease of costs and a 22 per cent increase of jobs. Of course, this is not to say that there always exists a unique relationship between both variables, as can be easily checked by examining other sectors.

Turning to the number of hours worked as the other dimension of labour demand, Table 4 attempts to disentangle the supply and the demand components. A first glance reveals that the reduction of yearly hours worked is due mainly to a longer vacation period, whereas negotiated weekly work hours decline only moderately. For overtime and short-time work (columns (6) and (8)) we observe a substantial reduction and increase, respectively, during 1970–83. But even in periods of severe recession there still exists a considerable amount of overtime work on average. This may be due partly to the fact that firms facing a transitory push in product demand prefer to switch to overtime work rather than hire new workers, because institutional regulations make it difficult to fire employees. In addition, even for permanent demand increases, it might be the result of rational economic behaviour, i.e., due to the fact that marginal labour costs of overtime work are lower than discounted marginal fixed and variable labour costs of new jobs.

The unemployment pool

We shall next examine the unemployment pool and the dynamics of unemployment. The age and sex structure of unemployment is presented in Table 5, which conveys internationally well-known results: females suffer more from unemployment than males, and, moreover, young adults and the elderly share a major burden compared with persons aged 35–55. Since 1981 the unemployment rate of foreigners has exceeded the German rate to a substantial extent, their rate being 14·2 per cent in 1983. Finally, the structure of unemployment displays the disadvantage of low-skilled workers and those without work experience.

It is common knowledge that such figures are of limited interest. What they represent is a snapshot at a particular moment in time, which can be very misleading. They mask the large flows of people who change their labour force status or who enter and leave unemployment during the course of a time interval (for details see Franz, 1982; and Evans, Franz and Martin, 1984).

TABLE 3

ANNUAL GROWTH RATES OF REAL UNIT WAGE COSTS, BY SECTOR[a]

(per cent)

Period	Total		Agriculture		Energy		Mfg sector		Construction		Trade traffic		Services		Govt		Other	
	I	II	I	II	I	II	I	II	I	II	I	II	I	II	I	II	I	II
1970–74	1·79	1·57	4·00	5·30	1·65	2·01	2·47	1·92	2·24	2·22	2·48	1·93	0·57	0·39	0·22	0·31	0·12	0·15
1975–79	−0·57	−0·42	−0·86	−2·14	−0·78	−0·73	0·43	0·75	−1·11	−0·72	−1·67	−1·37	−0·67	−0·52	−0·11	−0·20	−0·08	−0·11
1980–83	−0·70	−0·99	0·68	1·75	−0·74	−1·95	0·22	−0·35	0·12	0·03	0·38	−0·03	−2·64	−2·82	−0·17	−0·16	−0·11	−0·08
Change 1978–83	−2·20	−2·45	8·88	15·34	−7·18	−4·95	6·04	5·59	1·41	−2·05	2·09	2·13	−12·58	−13·82	−0·51	0·05	−0·13	−0·19

[a] Defined as $\hat{w} - \hat{p} - \hat{\pi}$, where W = nominal gross labour income (including employer's contribution to social security), P = output price (1976 = 100), π = productivity per non-self-employed (deflated by output prices, 1976 = 100); columns I and II differ in that they use actual productivity growth $\hat{\pi}$ (I) and trend productivity growth (II), defined as:

$$\pi_t^T = 0 \cdot 25 \ (0 \cdot 5\hat{\pi}_{t-2} + \hat{\pi}_{t-1} + \hat{\pi}_t + \hat{\pi}_{t+1} + 0 \cdot 5\hat{\pi}_{t+2})$$

Source: *Sachverständigenrat zur Begutachtung der gesamtwirtschaftlichen Entwicklung;* calculation by the authors.

TABLE 4

COMPONENTS OF YEARLY WORKED HOURS PER WORKER, 1979–1984

Period	Yearly worked hours per worker[a] (1)	Potential work-days per year[b] (2)	Vacation days per year (3)	Negotiated weekly worked hours (4)	Negotiated hours per year[c] (5)	Overtime worked hours per year (6)	Reduction in yearly worked in hours due to	
							Illness (7)	Short-time work[d] (8)
1970–74	1830	249·9	22·41	41·05	1868	133	107	63
1975–79	1735	250·5	25·36	40·23	1812	97	102	73
1980–84	1682	250·4	28·54	40·05	1778	75	92	79

[a] Col. (1) = col. (5) + col. (6) − col. (7) − col. (8).
[b] Actual days minus holidays.
[c] Col. (5) = {col. (2) − col. (3)} × col. (4)/5.
[d] Owing to business fluctuations, bad weather, strikes and part-time work.
Source: Mitteilungen aus der Arbeitsmarkt- und Berufsforschung, 1985.

TABLE 5

UNEMPLOYMENT RATES, BY AGE AND SEX, 1970–1983 (SEPTEMBER)[a]

Period	Under 20 yrs		20–25		25–35		35–45		45–55		55–60		60–65		Total		M+F
	M	F	M	F	M	F	M	F	M	F	M	F	M	F	M	F	
1970–74	1·0	1·6	0·9	1·5	0·7	1·6	0·6	1·4	0·7	1·3	1·2	1·8	2·6	1·8	0·8	1·5	1·1
1975–79	3·1	5·3	4·3	6·5	3·0	6·3	2·1	4·1	2·2	4·2	3·8	6·8	6·1	6·3	2·9	5·4	3·8
1980–83	5·6	7·9	7·6	9·9	5·6	9·5	3·7	5·6	3·7	5·8	6·7	9·1	9·7	9·6	5·1	7·8	6·1

[a] Percentage of labour force (census data).
Source: K. Ermann. *Arbeitsmarktstatistische Zahlen in Zeitreihenform, Jahreszahlen für die Bundesrepublik Deutschland, 1984; Beiträge zur Arbeitsmarkt- und Berufsforschung,* 1984.

Since the key elements of these dynamics of unemployment are the transitions from one state to another and the length of stay in these states, Figure 2 displays the development of these components over 1970–84, and Table 6 for 1977, provides information about the risk of becoming unemployed, the duration of unemployment and recurrent spells of unemployment. The data show that youths face a higher risk of unemployment than adults and that the risk is unevenly dispersed to the disadvantage of females. In marked contrast to these findings is the increase in duration of unemployment with age, whereas the number of recurrent spells does not vary substantially among all groups. Moreover, there is some evidence that unemployment is highly concentrated. One measure of concentration is the contribution to the total number of months of unemployment made by long spells. A survey of outflows from the unemployment register in May/June 1981 indicates that those who were unemployed

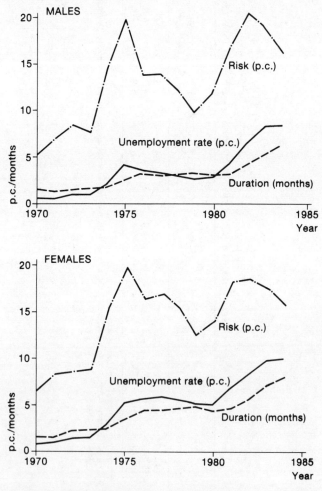

FIGURE 2.   The unemployment rate and its components by sex, 1970–1984.

TABLE 6

THE DYNAMICS OF UNEMPLOYMENT, BY AGE AND SEX, 1977

	Age group					
	15–19		35–44		60–65	
Dimension	Male	Female	Male	Female	Male	Female
Risk of becoming unemployed (per annum)[a]	15·2	24·7	5·6	10·3	6·7	8·8
Complete duration of unemployment[b]	2·05	2·34	3·50	4·11	9·88	7·74
Multiple spells of unemployment[c]	1,270	1,185	1,325	1,220	1,095	1,180

[a] Percentages.
[b] Months.
[c] Number of spells in 1977.
Source: Cramer and Werner (1984, p. 116).

for six months or more accounted for 49 per cent of all months of unemployment among teenagers and 68 per cent among adults aged 25 years and over[5] (Cramer and Werner, 1984, p. 121).

A more detailed analysis of the incidence of unemployment requires adequate information on the structure of the employed, which is rarely available. Therefore we shall elaborate further only on the duration of unemployment. In addition to some results mentioned already, Table 7 displays an uneven structure of duration, to the disadvantage of foreigners and those unemployed without completed vocational training or with a university degree. The latter observation may indicate that young adults without work experience and/or with too high reservation wages face greater difficulties in finding a job.

It is often argued that one important reason for the increasing share of low-skilled workers in unemployment is the more than-proportional growth in the wages of lower qualified workers. (This was a major target of labour union policy, especially during the 1970s.) It has been shown, however, that the unweighted structure of wage rates has not changed substantially (Brasche *et al.*, 1984). This approach might be misleading owing to shifts in the share of workers belonging to different wage groups. In order to set out the evidence in greater detail, we calculate the following general measure of the wage structure:

$$(1) \qquad WS = \frac{a_i w_i - a_j w_j}{\bar{w}}.$$

WS compares the development of two wage groups (w_i and w_j) relative to their weighted average ($\bar{w}$) where the weights (a_i and a_j) are the share of workers receiving the wage rates w_i and w_j, respectively. Hence, the time path of WS may be due to (a) changes in the differences between two wage groups, w_i and w_j, respectively, and/or (b) changes in share of workers a_i and a_j. A growing share of labour in group i will therefore, *ceteris paribus*, increase WS. Wage groups used are:[6]

WS_1 = male workers, wage groups I and II
WS_2 = male salaried employees, salary groups II and IV

TABLE 7

COMPLETE DURATION OF UNEMPLOYMENT BY SEX, AGE, CITIZENSHIP,
VOCATIONAL TRAINING AND ENTITLEMENT TO UNEMPLOYMENT BENEFITS[a]
(months)

Structure	1982	1983	1984
Sex			
Male	5·2	7·0	7·7
Female	6·7	7·6	8·3
Age group			
less than 20 years	4·5	5·4	5·2
20–25 years	5·2	6·2	6·5
25–30 years	5·9	7·2	7·9
30–35 years	6·1	7·6	8·5
35–40 years	6·2	7·5	8·4
40–45 years	6·3	7·7	8·8
45–50 years	6·2	7·8	9·2
50–55 years	7·3	8·6	9·9
55–60 years	9·2	10·1	11·3
60–65 years	13·3	14·3	15·7
Nationality			
German	6·0	7·2	7·9
Foreign	6·7	7·6	8·5
Education/training			
Without completed vocational training	6·5	7·9	8·9
With completed vocational training	5·6	6·6	7·2
—Apprenticeship training	5·2	6·6	7·1
—University degree	6·4	7·7	8·0
Receiving unemployment benefits:			
—Arbeitslosengeld	5·5	5·9	5·5
—Arbeitslosenhilfe	12·0	13·3	14·5
Not entitled to unemployment benefits	11·0	9·8	8·9
Total	6·0	7·2	7·9

[a] Complete duration of unemployment of persons who left the unemployment register in May/June 1982, 1983 and 1984, respectively.
Source: *Bundesanstalt für Arbeit, Amtliche Nachrichten 32,* 1984.

WS_3 = female workers, wage groups I and III
WS_4 = female salaried employees, salary groups III and V
WS_5 = all females, i.e., weighted average of WS_3 and WS_4
WS_6 = all males, i.e., weighted average of WS_1 and WS_2
WS_7 = weighted average WS_j, $j = 1, \ldots, 4$.

Table 8 displays the results of these calculations. The general impression given by WS_7 is that there exists a tendency to a greater dispersion in the wage and salary structure. This finding is caused by the greater dispersion for males and salaried females, whereas the wage structure of female workers remains roughly constant. This pattern concerns mainly low-skilled workers and might partly explain their higher unemployment as long as these wage increases are not accompanied by a rise in marginal productivity.

TABLE 8
WAGE STRUCTURE, BY SEX AND QALIFICATIONS[a]

Time period	WS_1	WS_2	WS_3	WS_4	WS_5	WS_6	WS_7
1964–68	44·80	20·33	−40·33	23·05	−22·77	38·42	20·23
1969–73	42·59	26·80	−40·54	31·26	−18·96	38·17	21·25
1974–78	46·94	34·79	−41·31	37·65	−14·27	43·18	26·29
1979–83	50·18	39·20	−41.02	40·51	−10·47	46·53	29·85

[a] See text for definitions.
Source: *Statistisches Bundesamt*, calculations by the authors.

Hidden unemployment

In Germany, officially announced unemployment consists of those persons who register themselves as such at the labour office. These data therefore fail to include:

1. discouraged workers who withdraw from the labour force or persons who search for a job without consulting the labour office and who do not hold a claim to unemployment compensation;
2. foreign workers who involuntarily re-migrate to their non-EEC home countries;
3. short-time workers;
4. persons who are on training programmes financed by the labour office and who would have been unemployed otherwise.

Table 9 attempts to give a rough impression on the degree of underutilization of labour (see Franz, 1985b, for more details). The outcome of these attempts to obtain a broader measure of joblessness is summarized in cols (9) and (10). Beginning in 1974, the correction results in considerably higher 'unemployment' than that officially announced.

II. VOLUNTARY AND MISMATCH UNEMPLOYMENT

In this section we elaborate on the question of whether a non-negligible part of German unemployment can be properly explained by the benefits of the unemployment insurance system and/or by structural unemployment.

The unemployment insurance system and its effect on the duration of unemployment: a Markov model

Job search theories suggest that unemployment compensation adds to the duration of unemployment for those who become unemployed and are eligible for compensation. Among other factors, such as inducing more quits and higher labour force participation, the main argument is that the unemployment insurance (UI) system lowers search costs.

There are no data available allowing us to analyse the effects of unemployment compensation schemes on duration, taking into account the state of the unemployed person before the spell, his personal characteristics, and the process of job-matching. Labour office statistics report twice a year on the duration of incomplete spells. Figures on the complete duration of a spell are calculated only for some selective time periods by the Bundesanstalt für Arbeit.

TABLE 9

OFFICIAL UNEMPLOYMENT AND UNDERUTILIZATION OF LABOUR

	Official unemployment[a]		Net discouraged workers[a] ('000)	Unemployed persons in training programmes[b] ('000)	Induced re-migration of non-EEC workers[d] ('000)	Export of unemployment[a,c]	Short-time workers[a] ('000)	Underutilization of labour	
	Unemployed persons ('000)	Unemployment rates						Persons not employed[e]	Underutilization rate[f]
Year									
(1)	(2)	(3)	(4)	(5)	(6)	(7)	(8)	(9)	(10)
1970	149	0·7	—	10	—	—	10	162	0·8
1971	185	0·8	—	16	—	—	86	230	1·0
1972	246	1·1	—	18	6	5	76	294	1·3
1973	273	1·2	—	18	18	11	44	317	1·4
1974	582	2·6	177	20	83	59	292	935	4·1
1975	1074	4·7	490	38	176	168	773	2028	8·6
1976	1060	4·6	518	30	163	215	277	1915	8·0
1977	1030	4·5	501	33	160	200	231	1841	7·8
1978	993	4·3	498	43	152	198	191	1796	7·5
1979	876	3·8	421	49	123	172	88	1547	6·5
1980	889	3·8	420	55	135	155	137	1565	6·5
1981	1272	5·5	650	66	130	160	347	2264	9·4
1982	1833	7·6	950	78	125	150	606	3213	12·7
1983	2263	9·2	1170	86	120	145	675	3889	15·0

[a] Averages per year.
[b] 1970/80, December; 1983, September.
[c] Calculated under the assumption that the foreigner would have stayed for one additional year had there been no adverse labour market conditions in Germany.
[d] Sum of all quarters.
[e] Col. (9) = col. (2) + col. (4) + col. (5) + col. (7) + col. (8)/3.
[f] Col. (10) = col. (9)/{col.(2)/col. (3)} × 100 + col. (4) + col. (5) + col. (7)} × 100.

As figures in Table 7 indicate, the effect of an entitlement on duration is not straightforward. People not, or no longer, entitled to unemployment benefits have a longer duration than those entitled to *Arbeitslosengeld*.[7] On the other hand, those holding a claim to *Arbeitslosenhilfe* leave unemployment after a considerably longer period compared with those entitled to *Arbeitslosengeld*.

For these groups we have information only about stocks and inflows on to the register. In order to get some idea about the average duration of a complete spell, we use a Markov approach to estimate the transition probability of an unemployed person registering at the beginning of period t and remaining in this state over the next j periods (for details see König, 1978).

Denoting by Z_{t-j} the inflow of unemployed persons during the period $t-j$, and by $U_{t,j}$ the stock of unemployed at the beginning of period t with a spell of j periods, the stock of unemployed is given by

$$(2) \qquad U_t = \sum_{j=1}^{\infty} U_{t,j} = \sum_{j=1}^{\infty} \left(\prod_{\tau=0}^{j} w_{t-\tau, j-\tau} \right) Z_{t-j},$$

with w as the corresponding transition probability.[8]

More revealing than these transition probabilities is the expected duration of a complete spell, calculated as

$$(3) \qquad E(d) = E(U_t / Z_t) = \sum_{j=1}^{24} \prod_{\tau=0}^{j} w_{t-\tau, j-\tau}.$$

Compared with the respective figures by the Institut für Arbeitsmarkt-und Berufsforschung (see Table 7), we note a close correspondence: for total male unemployment in May/June our estimate in 1982 is 5·5 (5·2), in 1983 6·6 (7·0) and in 1984 6·4 (7·7); the corresponding figures for female unemployment are 6·6 (6·7) in 1982, 8·0 (7·6) in 1983 and 8·2 (8·3) in 1984.

Figures 3 and 4 show the effects of both oil crises and the recessions thereafter on the duration of unemployment. Although the duration of a spell of unemployment for those males eligible for compensation is shorter than for those not so entitled, the picture is not as clear-cut as one would expect on the basis of job search models. Since the end of 1982 the duration of the former group has been less than the duration of the group not entitled (owing to the announced reduction in unemployment compensation starting at the beginning of 1982?) and, for females, has been lower since the middle of 1974. Intuitively, one might explain this particular pattern of the duration of female unemployment, especially for those not entitled to compensation, in terms of the increase in the demand for part-time work, the different composition of both groups with respect to marital status, age and so on. However, it seems to us too speculative to pursue these arguments further without additional information about those characteristics.

Structural unemployment

One way of testing the hypotheses of structural unemployment is to consult data on the regional and occupational mismatch between unemployed persons and vacancies (neglecting the deficiencies of both data sets). As a measure of mismatch, we use

$$(4) \qquad \sum_i |u_i - v_i|$$

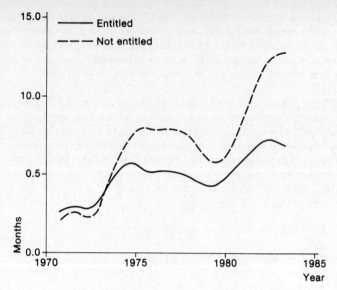

FIGURE 3.   Duration of female unemployment.

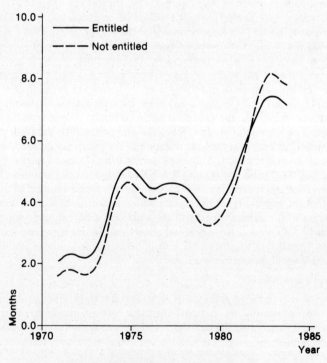

FIGURE 4.   Duration of male unemployment.

where u_i refers to the proportion of the unemployed in region i and v_i to the corresponding proportion of vacancies. This series is computed for 141 regions during 1976–83. For occupational mismatch, regions are replaced by 327 occupational groups of unemployed and vacancies. Figure 5 shows the time series of both variables. Although the regional imbalances are somewhat higher since 1978, indicating some evidence for regional mismatch, the data do not support the hypothesis that the jump in overall unemployment rates since 1981/82 can be explained on these grounds. Occupational mismatch series remain fairly constant between 1976 and 1982 and even drop in 1983. Consequently, on the basis of these figures, it seems hard to argue that the high level of unemployment during the 1980s is caused primarily by structural shifts in the demand for labour not accompanied by corresponding changes in supply patterns.

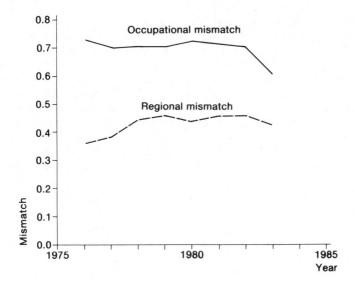

FIGURE 5.   Regional and occupational mismatch (see text for definitions).

III. The Rise of the NAIRU in Germany

As a further step towards an understanding of the rise in unemployment, we present some evidence on why that rate of unemployment that is consistent with stable inflation and inflationary expectations (NAIRU) has increased. A more satisfactory and ambitious approach is to derive full equilibrium estimates of the NAIRU. However, this is beyond of the scope of our paper, so we very briefly examine a Phillips curve framework presented elsewhere (Franz, 1983, 1985b).

As is well-known, one approach is to set up a wage and price equation. Following Gordon (1982), both equations are then condensed to a reduced-form equation for inflation. For quarterly data from 1966(I) to 1983(IV), we obtain (t-values in brackets):

(5) $\hat{p} = 1\cdot4470 + 0\cdot7754\hat{p}^*_{-4} - 0\cdot3802\,UR + 0\cdot0877\,AL\,(2,8)\hat{q}$
        $(3\cdot8)\quad\;\;(7\cdot5)\qquad\quad(3\cdot9)\qquad\qquad(2\cdot4)$

$\qquad\quad -26\cdot2919\,AL(2,8)g + 0\cdot0221\,AL\,(2,8)\hat{c}\qquad\qquad\bar{R}^2 = 0\cdot8704$
$\qquad\quad\;\;(4\cdot0)\qquad\qquad\;\;(2\cdot0)$

where $\hat{p}$ denotes the rate of inflation of consumer prices calculated as a four-quarter overlapping change. The expected rate of inflation $\hat{p}^*$ is modelled by an AR (1)-process according to the autocorrelation function of the actual rates. It is lagged four quarters since a lag of only one quarter would imply that the dependent and the right-hand variable contains three one-quarter changes in common, leading the coefficient of $\hat{p}^*$ to be upward-biased and to absorb much of the explanation that may be properly attributable to other variables.[9] UR denotes the actual unemployment rate, $\hat{q}$ the (weighted) rate of growth of real raw material and agricultural product prices, and $\hat{c}$ the rate of growth of the real user cost of capital. $AL\,(i,j)x$ denotes a polynomial distributed lag with degree i and a lag length j (Almon estimator) of the variable x with the coefficient giving the sum of the weights and the associated t-ratio of the sum. The variable g is a measure of the modernity of the capital stock minus $0\cdot66$, the maximum value of the sample period. This variable has been identified as one of the sources of the productivity slowdown in Germany; it serves as an indicator for the quality and technical standard of the capital stock, and, by representing its influence in this way, the role that the increasing average age of the capital stock has played in causing shifts of the NAIRU can be tentatively tested. It should be stressed that the approach and the construction of the variables is subject to several imperfections discussed at some length in Franz (1985b). The results may be summarized as follows.

1. The coefficient associated with $\hat{p}^*_{-4}$ is below unity, indicating that the NAIRU is not independent of inflation.[10] In what follows we assume that a 3 per cent (non-accelerating) inflation rate is seen as tolerable.

2. If the degree of modernity is restricted to the highest level of the sample period (i.e. $g = 0$), the value of the 'no-shock NAIRU' amounts to $2\cdot0$ per cent. By 'no-shock' we mean a situation where real user costs and material prices (including agricultural products) remain constant. The argument is that exogenous shocks to real user costs and material prices should not be offset by demand management. This 2 per cent NAIRU would be the no-shock NAIRU for the 1980s if no deterioration of the capital stock occurred. The actual NAIRU is higher owing to user cost and material price shocks.

3. However, between 1966 and 1973 the degree of modernity dropped and a more appropriate figure may be calculated for a no-shock NAIRU given the 1973 vintage structure of capital equipment. This calculation hypothetically erases the breakdown in investment after 1973 and yields a no-shock NAIRU of $4\cdot1$ per cent. Two examples may illustrate what this $4\cdot1$ per cent figure indicates. If, in an economic upswing, investment increases such that the level of modernity prevailing in 1973 is reached, then unemployment can be reduced to $4\cdot1$ per cent without facing accelerating inflation ('home-made' inflation corrected for exogenous shocks). On the other hand, if

economic policy fails to stimulate investment, no improvement of the modernity of the capital stock would be achieved and the 1983 NAIRU would amount to 8·9 per cent. This value corresponds to the 8·0 per cent estimate by Coe and Gagliardi (1985) for the period 1981–83. We consider this estimate, however, of minor importance for economic policy, since an economic recovery is likely to be combined with higher investment activity and, hence, with an increase in modernity. Consequently the NAIRU would fall.

In short the empirical findings suggest a shift of the NAIRU, caused to some extent by exogenous shocks such as the spurt in raw materials prices and the deterioration of the capital stock, reinforced by the reduction in investment after the first OPEC oil price rise (OPEC I). Correcting for these shocks, reversing the decline in modernity of the capital stock (to the pre-OPEC I level) and allowing for a 3 per cent tolerable and stable inflation rate, the NAIRU amounts to about 4 per cent in 1983. Compared with the 1960s, this implies an increase of 2 percentage points.

III. Labour Demand: Are Real Wages Too High for Full Employment?

It is often argued that real labour costs are too high in the FRG for full employment to be secured. As early as 1976, the Council of Economic Advisers was convinced that the main obstacle to full employment was excessively high real wages. This argument, put forward in subsequent reports by the Council and in academia, was also favoured by Giersch (e.g. 1983). Giersch argues that real-wage increases higher than the rise in employment-neutral labour productivity are primarily responsible for the increase in unemployment. The econometric evidence, as far as it exists, is based mostly upon regressions of changes in employment and corresponding changes in real wages (see Lehment, 1982; Kirkpatrick, 1982; Roth, 1982).[11] In this section we shall extend the analysis to incorporate overtime premia and labour utilization rates.

First, we present some estimates of a 'textbook' version of an employment function, based upon seasonally unadjusted data for the period 1964–83. We then discuss some problems related to the use of aggregate employment versus the number of full-time jobs *and* working hours as factor inputs. The preceding discussion about the different patterns in the structure of the labour supply suggests an elaborate model with different categories of labour. However, we shall restrict our analysis to the estimation of separate demand functions for full-time jobs and working hours, keeping in mind the usual caveats with regard to the assumption of homogeneity of labour inputs (as well as other factor inputs).

Our point of departure is a textbook version of a firm in a neoclassical world minimizing its production costs subject to a production function

(6) $Y = F(K, L, M)$, $F_i > 0$, $F_{ij} < 0$, $i, j = 1, 2, 3$

where Y denotes real value added, K is the capital stock, L is employment measured in actual working man-hours, and M is the real value of raw material imports.

Assuming that, for a 'representative' firm, output prices are exogenously determined, cost minimization leads to the well-known factor demand equations with optimal factor inputs depending upon relative prices.

Following the usual approach, adjustment costs and expectations are modelled by a distributed lag function of the Nadiri–Rosen type. The estimation of these interrelated factor demand equations, based upon a flexible form of a cost function such as the trans-log, proved to be unsuccessful without a more detailed breakdown of capital expenditures and a disaggregation of labour demand by sex and quality. This being beyond the scope of this study, we restricted our efforts to the estimation of an employment function, disregarding the possible simultaneous equation bias thereby introduced.

Table 10 presents OLS and IV estimates[12] for such an employment function, with L_t denoting actual quarterly man-hours, w_t real wage costs, c_t real user costs of capital (for details see König, 1976), q_t real prices of raw materials and Y_t real value added (corrected for the real value of raw material imports), deflated by the price index of value added. Except for user costs of capital, parameter estimates seem quite satisfactory in a statistical sense, implying a long-run elasticity of real wages of about $-1\cdot0$ and a value added elasticity of $1\cdot07$ with a mean lag of $3\cdot2$ quarters (IV estimates).

In spite of these 'plausible' results, we do not want to follow this avenue of research by introducing additional factors like the tax wedge or by splitting

TABLE 10

LABOUR DEMAND EQUATIONS: AGGREGATE EMPLOYMENT
(EFFECTIVE HOURS WORKED), 1964–1984

	(1)	(2)	(3)	(4)
Constant	1·952	1·551	1·430	1·450
	(3·0)	(2·3)	(2·1)	(2·1)
S_1	−0·110	−0·078	−0·115	−0·119
	(17·3)	(3·8)	(15·5)	(5·9)
S_2	−0·017	−0·013	−0·018	−0·018
	(5·3)	(3·5)	(5·1)	(4·5)
S_3	−0·130	−0·107	−0·135	−0·139
	(20·8)	(6·2)	(4·3)	(8·1)
ln w_t	−0·227	−0·261	−0·233	−0·229
	(6·0)	(6·2)	(4·3)	(4·3)
ln c_t	0·015	0·007	−0·003	−0·002
	(1·0)	(0·5)	(0·1)	(0·1)
ln q_t	−0·042	−0·043	−0·040	−0·039
	(3·8)	(3·9)	(3·3)	(3·2)
ln y_t	0·233	0·283	0·253	0·247
	(5·7)	(5·6)	(4·0)	(3·7)
ln L_{t-1}	0·724	0·533	0·764	0·787
	(10·8)	(4·1)	(10·5)	(6·2)
ln L_{t-2}	—	0·209	—	−0·026
		(1·7)		(10·2)
$\bar{R}^2$	0·980	0·981	0·979	0·978
DW	1·981	1·782	1·976	2·003

Notes:
(1) and (2), OLS estimates.
(3) and (4), IV estimates.

up (expected) demand into different components. Far more important, in our mind, especially in the context of the German institutional setup and labour legislation, seems a distinction of employment in working hours and jobs. As is well-known, firms facing a temporary reduction (rise) in the demand for labour that is quasi-fixed, in the sense of costs of hiring, productivity evaluation, firing or training, have at least two options: a reduction (increase) of utilization rates of labour with corresponding wage adjustment, or a layoff (hire) of workers. As has been shown in previous sections, even during a long recession German firms are still producing with overtime work, not least caused by severe restrictions on firing.

In the following we assume that a (representative) cost-minimizing firm faces a Cobb-Douglas technology with the number of jobs N, working hours h and capital stock K as inputs.[13] Working hours are split into standard hours, $\bar{h}$, i.e. negotiated working hours per week taking into account vacations and other legally determined reductions in working time, and overtime work, $h - \bar{h}$, with $h > \bar{h}$. Analogously, direct wage costs consist of two elements: the negotiated wage rate $\bar{w}$, and the effective wage rate w, including both negotiated and voluntarily paid overtime premiums. Total wage costs are defined as:

$$(7) \qquad W(N, h) = \{w(\cdot)(h - \bar{h})N + \bar{w}\bar{h}N\}^{\delta}$$

with the first term on the right-hand side denoting total overtime costs and the second term, 'normal' wage costs. Two properties of this specification have to be stressed. (1) It is assumed that, when $h > \bar{h}$, all labour is employed in overtime work. Needless to say, on a firm level this is a quite unrealistic assumption. In a macroeconomic context, however, there is no way to distinguish between those categories of labour working or not working overtime.[14] (2) Instead of defining wage costs as a simple linear function of the respective variables, we allow for a nonlinear relationship, for the following reasons. First, the terms in the braces of equation (7) cover only gross labour income, including social security contributions. They do not include fixed or quasi-fixed labour costs for hiring and firing, training costs and so forth. Owing to the fact that there exists only scattered information for those costs, we try to capture these effects on labour demand by allowing for nonlinearity. Second, in a more formal sense, one may regard the nonlinear specification of (7) as a general model admitting a test of linearity.

Empirical evidence suggests that the overtime premium, apart from negotiated rates, depends upon the number of overtime hours worked, voluntary firm-specific arrangements, the specific industry group, prevailing labour market conditions, the degree of unionization and, naturally, special characteristics of overtime work. Being unable to take into account firm and industry-specific variables in the macroeconomic context, we allow for these determinants by a time trend and use the following specification:

$$(8) \qquad w - \bar{w} = a + b(h - \bar{h}) + cz + dt$$

where z denotes the degree of unionization and t a linear time trend.

Cost minimization requires:

$$(9) \qquad \min_{K,N,H} \{rK + W(N, h)\}$$

subject to

(10) $Y = K^{\alpha} N^{\beta} h^{\gamma}$

and the corresponding restrictions (7) and (8).

First-order conditions imply the conditional demand functions

(11) $h = \dfrac{\gamma(w - \bar{w})\bar{h}}{\beta A(x) - (2\beta - \gamma)w + \beta\bar{w}}$

with $A(x) = a + cz + dt$ and

(12) $N = Br^{\alpha/\rho} Y^{1/\rho} \{\overline{wh} + w(h - \bar{h})\}^{-\delta\alpha/\rho} h^{-\gamma/\rho}$

with $B = (\beta/\alpha\delta)^{\alpha/\rho}$ and $\rho = \alpha\delta + \beta$.

It may be noted that, owing to the nonlinear cost function, the demand equations for jobs and hours worked are not simple. As in other studies on quasi-fixed labor costs, the nonlinear restrictions produce inconclusive signs (see e.g. Hart, 1984), and the effect of changes of an explanatory variable depends upon the magnitude of the relevant parameters. An interior solution requires that $\beta < \gamma$. For a unique solution for N and h, it is necessary that

(13) $w + b(h - \bar{h})\beta - \gamma\left\{ w - \dfrac{(w - \bar{w})}{w} \cdot \dfrac{\bar{h}}{h} \right\} > 0.$

This restriction has been tested at the sample mean, and the left-hand side of (13) is significantly greater than zero.[15]

Taking logs of (12) and introducing stochastic terms into equation (8), (11) and (12) can be estimated with appropriate simultaneous nonlinear methods. In the following study a two-step procedure has been used. The endogenous variable h in equation (8) has been regressed on all exogenous variables and replaced by its predicted value. Parameters are then estimated by full information maximum likelihood (FIML). The term $\{\overline{wh} + w(h - \bar{h})\}$ has been approximated by the effective wage costs per full-time worker owing to the fact that appropriate data for overtime premia are not available.

Table 11 presents parameter estimates for quarterly, seasonally unadjusted data of the manufacturing sector for the period 1964–83.[16] Coefficients show signs theoretically expected. The scale elasticity is numerically smaller than

TABLE 11

FIML ESTIMATES

Parameters	Estimates	t-values
α	0·121	1·95
β	0·328	5·36
γ	0·439	5·36
δ	5·438	2·22
B	6·222	13·40
a	−16·075	−2·89
b	0·104	2·11
c	0·308	2·33
d	0·144	6·40

one. The hypothesis of a unitary scale elasticity cannot be rejected, however. The sum of the elasticities of both types of labour inputs corresponds on average to the share of labour income in value added. The coefficient of working hours, γ, is statistically significant (t-values: 5·36), is different from the coefficient for full-time jobs, and satisfies the condition for an interior solution. Also, the coefficient δ is significantly different from one, implying that non-direct labour costs play an important role in optimizing behaviour.[17]

More revealing than the above parameter estimates for the effects of changes in exogenous variables on labour demand are the respective elasticities calculated at the sample mean. Table 12 contains these elasticities. First, we notice that the elasticity of demand for jobs with respect to output is approximately one and with respect to the user costs of capital 0·12. Second, overtime hours react quite sensitively to changes in the negotiated wage rate, the degree of unionization and the overtime premium, R_0. An upward shift in the overtime premium by 10 per cent—by increasing the constant term a—will induce a reduction of overtime work by 36 per cent. On the other hand, an increase in the negotiated wage rate by the same percentage will stimulate overtime work by 26 per cent. A decline in negotiated hours also causes more overtime work; however, it reduces total working hours almost by the same percentage. With respect to jobs, a decrease in normal hours—as demanded recently by unions, for example—appears to be quite favourable because of a positive impact on the number of jobs by the same percentage. On the other hand, increasing the negotiated wage rate will lower the demand for jobs, its impact on total working hours being comparatively small, however. As is well-known (e.g. Hart, 1984), the sign of the effect of overtime premium on working hours and jobs is theoretically ambiguous. According to our estimates, an increase in R_0 will reduce total working hours (by a minor percentage) but will also reduce the demand for jobs. The latter effect may be explained as follows. Increases in w imply higher wage costs for hours *and* jobs, by equation (7), and induce substitution in favour of capital. But we should stress that calculations of elasticities are biased, owing to the approximation of wage costs per worker by the effective wage rate. In the theoretical model the elasticity of w with respect to R_0 is weighted by $[w(h-\bar{h})/\{\overline{wh}+w(h-\bar{h})\}]<1$, and the elasticity of h with respect to R_0 by $[wh/\{\overline{wh}+w(h-\bar{h})\}]>1$ (for $h>\bar{h}$). Owing to the approximation of wage costs by the effective wage rate, both weights are set equal to one, thus overstating the negative impact of the elasticity of the wage rate with respect to R_0. Inserting plausible values for those weights, however,

TABLE 12

ELASTICITIES

Endogenous variables	Exogenous variables					
	R_0^{a}	$\bar{w}$	$\bar{h}$	z	y	r
(1) $h-\bar{h}$	−3·59	2·63	−0·40	−11·04		
(2) h	−0·04	0·03	0·99	−0·12		
(3) L	−0·10	−0·54	−1·09	−0·16	1·01	0·12
(4) w	0·15	0·77	−0·002	0·45		

[a] $R_0 = \hat{a} + \hat{d}t$ evaluated at sample means.

may result in a positive elasticity of jobs with respect to R_0 but with a rather small magnitude. Finally, we might mention that a 1 per cent increase in the negotiated wage rate will reduce total man-hours Nh by 0·5 per cent, and a 1 per cent increase in the overtime premium will reduce man-hours by 0·14 per cent. A reduction of 1 per cent in negotiated hours $\bar{h}$ leads to a decline in man-hours of only 0.1 per cent.

Needless to say, these results indicate tendencies and should not serve as policy recommendations *per se*. The list of our caveats is rather long: the problem of a correct specification of the production function, especially the neglect of raw material inputs and the assumption of a putty-putty technology; the treatment of labour as an homogeneous factor; the use of unionization as an exogenous variable; and, not least, structural shifts in the product mix owing to exogenous shocks. Moreover, indivisibilities as well as uncertainty with respect to the nature of demand shifts may be still another source of overtime work not dealt with explicitly here.

In spite of these deficiencies, we think that the results indicate the importance of a separate treatment of both dimensions of labour input for labour market policy and shed some light on some important causes of the rise in unemployment in Germany:

—the negative impact of the negotiated wage rate on employment;
—the role of insufficient product demand; and
—the higher degree of unionization, especially in the early 1970s.

IV. Summary: Causes of the Rise in Unemployment

In this conclusion we attempt to bring together the main results of the previous sections. While a precise accounting of the contribution made by the various factors to the rise in unemployment seems to us to be too ambitious, some general findings are less tentative.

One reason for the observed and expected future rise in unemployment can be found on the supply side of the labour market. Both the number of (young) persons entering the labour market and labour force participation rates (of married women) have increased substantially: in 1983 about 500,000 more persons were in the labour force, and the participation rate of married women was 6 percentage points higher compared with 1972. Owing to the baby boom in the 1960s, the tremendous inflow of young entrants will not fade away until the end of the 1980s.

On the demand side, we observe between 1973 and 1983 a net decline of 1·7 million employed persons for the whole economy, with the bulk attributable to the manufacturing sector. In contrast, employment in the service and government sectors increased. Our paper finds no convincing evidence that structural factors are a major reason for the rise in German unemployment. There are, of course, regional and occupational mismatches between labour demand and supply, and probably some unemployed people lowered their search intensity while being supported by the unemployment insurance system. But it is hard to see that this should be responsible for a higher (natural) rate of unemployment. More promising candidates for an explanation of the observed shift of the NAIRU 1975/83 are exogenous supply shocks such as the spurt in raw material prices and, moreover, the deterioration of the capital stock reinforced by the fall in investment.

In addition, these developments were caused by movements in real-unit labour costs (of about 6 and −13 per cent in the manufacturing and service sector, respectively, in the same time period). On the other hand, despite a 6 per cent decline in these costs over 1982–83, employment in the manufacturing sector continued to fall. Our findings, and those obtained in other studies, suggest that in recent years demand factors are looming larger in accounting for the doubling of the unemployment rate since the late 1970s.

Moreover, even in periods of a severe recession, the German economy operates with a considerable amount of overtime work. This phenomenon necessitates a separate treatment of both dimensions of labor demand. Our conclusion is that, not only did higher labour costs and lower product demand reduce the demand for men relative to hours, but this was also caused by institutional regulations which sometimes make it extremely difficult and expensive to dismiss employees. In any case, a careful distinction between types of labour costs and their impact on different dimensions of labour demand seems to be more appropriate than the usual claim that real wages are too high.

ACKNOWLEDGMENTS

This is a revised and shortened version of the paper presented at the Conference. A more detailed version of Section I is available on request by the authors. We are grateful to Charles Bean, Richard Layard, John Martin and the participants of the Conference, and regret not being able to take into account all their valuable comments. We thank T. Kempf, W. Pohlmeier and H. Seitz, at the University of Mannheim, and D. Brauner, C. Müller and P. Pintz, at the University of Stuttgart, for able research assistance.

NOTES

1. For details see Franz (1982).
2. A still further increase is accounted for in January/February 1985.
3. Note that these figures are census data. In contrast to unemployment figures published by the labour office, they include unemployed persons not registered at the labour office.
4. This concerns mainly the reduction of the labour force caused by persons aged 65 and over (−0·6 million persons between 1970 and 1983). They no longer registered themselves as unemployed (and consequently were not included in labour force statistics) when their claim to unemployment benefits was cancelled legally.
5. At this time total outflows of teenagers and adults aged 25 and over consisted of 15·1 and 26·4 per cent, respectively, of persons who have been unemployed six months and more.
6. Statistics report three wage groups for workers and five salary groups for salaried employees, where I is the highest pay in both groups. The wage groups displayed in Table 8 cover the major part of persons in each group j.
7. *Arbeitslosengeld* is roughly two-thirds of previously earned labour income and is granted for a limited time period, depending on how long contributions have been paid. *Arbeitslosenhilfe* is less than 60 per cent of previously earned income and is granted for an unlimited time period to persons without wealth of their families). For details see König and Franz (1978).
8. Lack of space prevents us from giving the estimates of the transition probabilities. They are available on request.
9. For this argument see Gordon in a comment on Franz (1983).
10. This statement is subject to the criticism of McCloskey (1985).
11. For a more elaborate approach see Artus (1985).
12. Instruments used are capacity utilization rate (four lags), value added deflator (four lags), price of raw material imports (four lags), interest rate (four lags).
13. We neglect material input M as a separate factor. Assuming that relative price changes of raw materials mainly influence capital input, we elaborated on a nested production function $Y = F(K^*, N, h)$ and $K^* = G(K, M)$. While this specification did not substantially alter

244   FRANZ and KÖNIG

parameter estimates of labour inputs, the estimate of α in (10) is quite sensitive with respect to the definition of raw materials. In view of these results, we exclude raw materials.
14. Formally, this aspect could be introduced by defining 'normal' labour input of jobs, $\bar{N}$, but empirically, the determination of this variable raises diffcult problems.
15. In fact, owing to the approximation used for the overtime premium in the empirical analysis, the restriction tested is stronger because the last term in the second bracket is ignored.
16. The inclusion of lags for N in (12) separately did not improve the results. Both lag parameters turned out to be small and insignificant.
17. Intuitively, the magnitude of δ may seem quite large, but one has to remember that other factors of production not explicitly taken into account in the production function may be captured by this estimate.

REFERENCES

ARTUS, J. R. (1985). An empirical evaluation of the disequilibrium real wage rate hypothesis. *International Monetary Fund Staff Papers*, **31**, 249–302.

BRASCHE, U., BÜCHTEMANN, C. F., JESCHEK, W. and MÜLLER, W. (1984). Auswirkungen des Strukturwandels auf den Arbeitsmarkt, Anforderungen des Strukturwandels auf das Beschäftigungssystem. Deutsches Institut für Wirtschaftsforschung, *Beiträge zur Strukturforschung*, **80**.

COE, D. T. and GAGLIARDI, F. (1985). Nominal wage determination in ten OECD economies. OECD Economics and Statistics Department, Working Paper no. 19 (March 1985). Paris: OECD.

CRAMER, U. and WERNER, H. (1984). Causes and consequences of high turnover among young people on the German labour market. In *The Nature of Youth Unemployment. An Analysis for Policy Makers*, pp. 113–140. Paris: OECD.

EVANS, J. M., FRANZ, W. and MARTIN, J. P. (1984). Youth labour market dynamics and unemployment: an overview. In *The Nature of Youth Employment. An Analysis for Policy Makers*, pp. 7–28. Paris: OECD.

FRANZ, W. (1982). *Youth Unemployment in the Federal Republic of Germany: Theory, Empirical Results, and Policy Implications. An Economic Analysis*. Tübingen: Mohr (Siebeck).

—— (1983). The past decade's natural rate and the dynamics of German unemployment: a case against demand policy? *European Economic Review*, **21**, 51–76.

—— (1985a). An economic analysis of female work participation, education and fertility: theory and empirical evidence for the Federal Republic of Germany. *Journal of Labor Economics*, **3**, S218–S234.

—— (1985b). Challenges to the German economy 1973–1983: supply shocks, investment slowdown, inflation variability, and the underutilization of labor. *Zeitschrift für Wirtschafts- und Sozialwissenschaften*, **105**.

GIERSCH, H. (1983). Arbeit, Lohn und Produktivität. *Probleme und Perspektiven der gegenwärtigen Wirtschaftspolitik*. Mannheim: Bibliographisches Institut.

GORDON, R. J. (1982). Inflation, flexible exchange rates, and the natural rate of unemployment. In M. N. Baily (ed.), *Workers, Jobs, and Inflation*, pp. 89–152, Washington: Brookings Institution.

HART, R. A. (1984). *The Economics of Non-Wage Labor Costs*. London: Allen and Unwin.

KIRKPATRICK, G. (1982). Real factor prices and German manufacturing employment: a time series analysis 1960(1)–1979(4). *Weltwirtschaftliches Archiv*, **118**, 79–103.

KÖNIG, H. (1976). Neoklassische Investitionstheorie und Investorenverhalten in der Bundesrepublik Deutschland. *Jahrbücher für Nationalökonomie und Statistik*, **190**, 316–48.

—— (1978). Zur Dauer der Arbeitslosigkeit: Ein Markov-Modell. *Kyklos*, **31**, 36–52.

—— and FRANZ, W. (1978). Unemployment compensation and the rate of unemployment in the Federal Republic of Germany. In H. G. Grubel and M. A. Walker (eds), *Unemployment Insurance. Global Evidence of its Effects on Unemployment*, pp. 236–66. Vancouver: Fraser Institute.

LEHMENT, H. (1982). Der Einfluß der Lohnpolitik auf Produktion, Preise und Beschäftigung in der Bundesrepublik Deutschland seit 1973. *Kieler Diskussionsbeiträge*, no. 82.

McCLOSKEY, D. N. (1985). The loss function has been mislaid: the rhetoric of significance tests. *American Economtc Review* (Papers and Proceedings), **75**, 201–5.

ROTH, J. (1982). Mehr Beschäftigung durch Reallohnzurückhaltung. *Kieler Diskussionsbeiträge*, no. 85.

Aggregate Unemployment in Italy, 1960–1983

By F. MODIGLIANI

Massachusetts Institute of Technology

F. PADOA SCHIOPPA and N. ROSSI

Libera Università Internazionale degli Studi Sociali, Rome

INTRODUCTION

When compared with other countries' experiences, the Italian performance on the unemployment front is interesting in many respects. As indicated in Table 1, the Italian unemployment rate has been consistently above that of major Western countries since the 1960s. The differential in unemployment rates tended to decrease between the second half of the 1960s and the first half of the 1970s because the initial rise in unemployment following the oil shock was less pronounced in Italy than in most other countries. Since that time the rise in unemployment has been pretty universal and steady, but Italian unemployment has risen somewhat faster than the average; thus the differential with the OECD has grown from 1 percentage point to over 2 by the early 1980s, though the EEC as a whole has performed even worse.

In assessing these trends, one should keep in mind that unemployment, as well as many other Italian statistics, is subject to an unusual margin of error, reflecting in part the large role played by the 'underground' economy.

Furthermore, as for other countries, the aggregate Italian unemployment rate hides substantial differences in unemployment rates for different groups of people in society (see Section I below). Though extremely important, such

TABLE 1

UNEMPLOYMENT RATES IN MAJOR COUNTRIES, 1966–1983
(percentages)

	1966–70	1971–75	1976–80	1981–83
Italy	4·7	4·9	7·4	10·5
United States	3·8	6·0	6·7	8·8
Japan	1·2	1·4	2·1	2·4
Canada	4·6	6·2	7·7	10·1
France	2·2	3·0	5·3	7·8
Germany	1·1	1·5	3·4	6·2
Netherlands	1·1	4·5	5·5	11·2
Belgium	2·4	3·2	7·9	13·0
Spain	2·5	3·0	7·3	15·8
United Kingdom	3·0	3·8	6·2	12·0
Seven major countries	2·8	4·0	5·3	7·6
EEC	2·7	3·4	5·6	9·0
OECD	2·7	3·9	5·3	7·9

Source: OECD, *Historical Statistics*, and Data Appendix at end of this book.

differences among demographic and social groups are outside the scope of
this paper. Instead, we focus on the aggregate unemployment rate in an attempt
to shed some light on its basic determinants.

To accomplish this task, the main characteristics of the Italian labour
market are first briefly reviewed (Section II). In particular, the relevance of
the institutional setting in which labour negotiations have taken place in the
last 20 years is assessed. In Section III a structural, highly aggregated
macroeconomic model is developed and its main implications explored. The
model (which owes much to Modigliani and Padoa Schioppa, 1978, and to
Dréze and Modigliani, 1981) is set in a framework of monopolistic competition
and explicitly allows for the openness of the Italian economy. The parameters
of the model are estimated and its performance tested in Sections IV and V.
In these sections a certain number of simulation experiments are also carried
out to investigate the nature of Italian unemployment. Finally, the main
conclusions of the paper are summarized in Section VI.

A distinguishing feature of our model is that it does not purport to account
explicitly for the determinants of aggregate demand. This variable is instead
taken as 'exogenous' on the premise that the observed aggregate demand
reflected, by and large, what was wanted by the authorities, given the constraints
imposed by the structure and openness of the economy.

We propose instead to use the model to pursue three issues: (1) What are
the forces, domestic and external, that seem to have shaped the behaviour of
the unemployment rate and in particular its striking rise in the last decade?
(2) How would alternative demand and supply policies have affected unemployment and the trade balance? and (3) What can be learned from this
exercise as to possible policies for dealing with the twin problem facing Italy
in recent years, namely, high unemployment and a large trade deficit?

I. THE FACTS

Though the purpose of this paper is to understand the movements of the
aggregate unemployment rate, a brief inspection of the trends, structure and
dynamics of unemployment is an obvious starting point. We shall mainly cover
the period 1960–83. This is a choice dictated upon us by data availability. In
fact, even for this period reliable annual series are impossible to obtain for
some variables.

As a first reference, Figure 1 presents the *official* time series of labour force
and employed persons. The unemployment rate fluctuated around a 4–5 per
cent level throughout the 1960s and the early 1970s but has steadily increased
since then, reaching 9·7 per cent in 1983. The labour force, decreasing in the
early 1960s and roughly constant till the early 1970s, shows a substantial
acceleration in the decade 1974–83, increasing at an average rate of 1 per cent
per annum. The increasing labour force, together with constant employment
from 1980 onward, accounts for the rise in unemployment.

On the labour force side, the 1·8 million person (male and female) decrease
in the period 1960–72 is due mainly to the longer schooling of postwar
adolescents and to earlier retirement by the elderly. The 3·9 million increase
in subsequent years can be attributed mostly to the higher participation rate
of women, the participation rate of men remaining fairly constant. For Italian

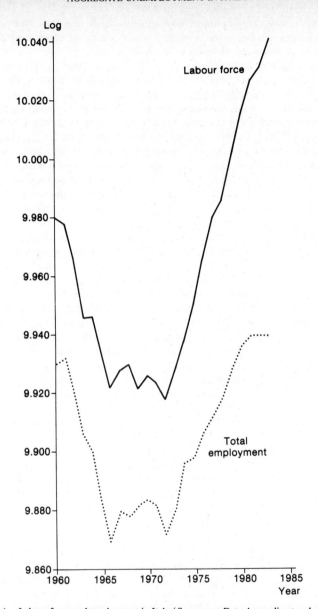

FIGURE 1.   Labour force and employment in Italy (*Source*: see Data Appendix at end of book).

residents the participation rate of females sharply increased from 19·4 per
cent in 1974 to 27·3 per cent in 1983 while the corresponding rate for males
moved slowly, from 52·8 per cent in 1974 to 54·6 per cent in 1983. Furthermore,
the increased participation of women in the labour force concerned mainly
females aged 25–39, while participation rates of teenagers and elderly women
exhibited a much flatter profile.

Labour force participation rates are, of course, only one dimension of labour supply. However, the outright absence of reliable information prevents us from discussing the question of hours supplied.

Reverting now to labour demand, as Figure 1 shows, total employment steadily declined from 1960 to 1966; it remained fairly constant throughout the late 1960s and the early 1970s and finally increased in the late 1970s, remaining approximately constant thereafter. However, this pattern is the result of opposite forces. On the one hand, employment in industry (excluding construction) steadily increased up to the mid-1970s, remaining constant in the late 1970s and then falling in the early 1980s. On the other hand, in private services and agriculture the trend is respectively upward and downward, though average rates of growth differ markedly in different subperiods. As a result, the share of industrial employment, which had been growing consistently until 1976–77, reaching almost 30 per cent, declined thereafter, falling to 26·5 per cent in 1983.

Interestingly, the recent Italian debate has concentrated almost exclusively on industrial employment. In the light of the above figures, we feel that such concern (though justified on several obvious grounds such as data availability and quality) can be misplaced when analysing aggregate unemployment. At the same time, the reader should take into account the heterogeneous behaviour of the various sectors of the economy when evaluating the results of the following sections.

Official unemployment figures implicitly shown in Figure 1 tell, only part of the whole story, however. Additional important information is given by the adjustment applied to official unemployment figures to take account of the so-called Wage Supplementation Fund (Cassa Integrazione Guadagni). Established in 1941, this fund was originally aimed at subsidizing employees in short-term surplus because of cyclical fluctuations. In practice, employers were therefore able temporarily to lay off workers while formally retaining them as employed.

In the early 1970s, the Wage Supplementation Fund was substantially amended and the public fund was allowed also to subsidize redundancies arising from causes other than cyclical fluctuations, mainly of a structural nature. In such cases the subsidy was meant to last possibly more than a year, with a legal replacement ratio equal to 80 per cent or more. Though not working, subsidized workers are counted as employees by the National Accounts. Therefore official figures overestimate employment.

The extent of such overestimation is shown in Figure 2, where the official and adjusted unemployment rates are reported.[1] Owing to the negligible importance of the Wage Supplementation Fund, adjusted and official rates coincide in the 1960s. However, from 1971 onward they tend to diverge substantially. In fact, when adjusted, total employment declines substantially in the early 1980s instead of remaining constant.

The pattern of unemployment shown by adjusted figures calls, among other things, for a closer inspection of the movements in labour cost. Figure 3 provides some evidence with respect to the private sector of the economy. It shows the real labour cost (gross wage paid to the worker, inclusive of contributions to social security and other compulsory schemes, relative to the value added deflator), the consumption wage (net-of-direct-taxes, take-home

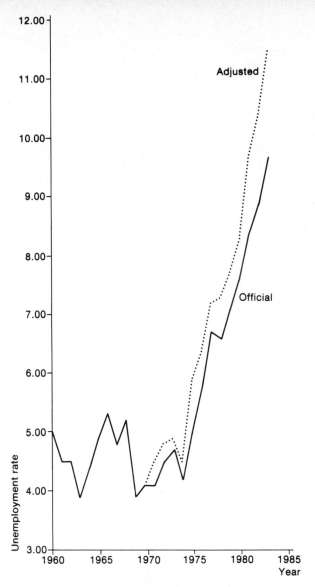

FIGURE 2.   Official and adjusted unemployment rates (*Source*: see Data Appendix at end of book).

pay received by the worker relative to the consumer price index[2]) and the real labour cost per unit of output.

Clearly, real labour costs have increased substantially in the period under consideration, at an average rate of 5·4 per cent per annum. Much of this increase was offset by productivity improvements, since real labour cost per unit of output only shows a relatively mild increase, mostly concentrated in

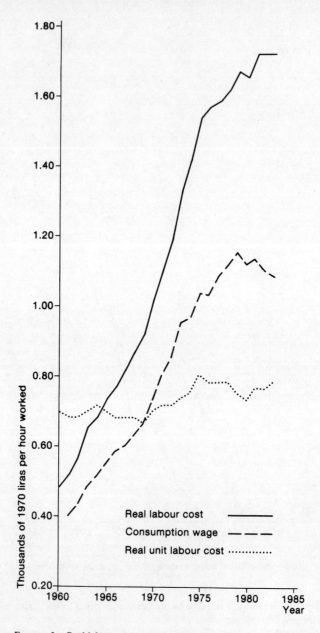

FIGURE 3. Real labour cost, consumption wage and real unit labour cost.

the first half of the 1970s. (It should be kept in mind, however, that there is no generally valid ground for supposing that labour should absorb the growth in productivity, except under quite restrictive conditions—see Dornbusch *et al.*, 1983.) At the same time, as is apparent from the figure, the rise in real labour costs was only partly reflected in a rise in real take-home pay. The explanation is to be found in a large rise in the tax wedge, including, in particular, direct taxes and social security contributions, at least through the mid-1970s.[3] For the period as a whole, the total increase amounts to nearly 25 per cent.

Of course, time series of aggregate real-unit labour costs provide only partial information. Differences by sector and by skill are concealed. As far as the latter is concerned, consistent information is not available for the whole 1960–83 period. However, a recent survey makes it possible to reach some conclusions for the late 1970s and early 1980s.[4] Since 1976, the wage gap between skilled and unskilled workers has been considerably reduced (from 30 to 18 per cent in the Metal Sector). As we shall see later on, the indexation system operating in Italy has to be held responsible for such a result. However, the interesting point is that wage differentials by skill appear to have shrunk much less than one might have expected on the basis of the escalator mechanism and widely publicized national contracts, thanks to sectoral and firm wage bargaining, as well as of individual wage concessions reflected in wage drift.

Having reviewed the major aspects of labour supply and demand patterns, we turn now to a brief examination of the unemployment pool. An inspection of the age and sex structure of unemployment reveals internationally familiar patterns. Females at any age suffer more from unemployment than males. People without work experience face greater difficulties in securing a job, as do those who possess lower educational qualifications. Irrespective of sex, young adults and the elderly are more severely hit by unemployment than persons in the middle of their life-cycles. Moreover, the rise in unemployment of the last decade appears to have exacerbated these tendencies.

However, such figures are of limited interest if they are not supplemented by some information on the duration of unemployment. As of 1983, long-term unemployment (i.e. 12 months or more) is estimated to account for 42 per cent of total unemployment in Italy. This compares with 37 per cent in 1980, 23 per cent in 1975, 19·7 per cent in 1970, and 17 per cent in 1965. Moreover, such proportions are consistently higher for females and first-time job-seekers. In other words, in the last decade we seem to have been witnessing the emergence of a class of 'permanently' unemployed.

II. INSTITUTIONAL CHARACTERISTICS OF THE ITALIAN LABOUR MARKET

The role of institutions in the Italian labour market is generally assumed to be too pervasive to be neglected, as well as too complex to be formally understood (with some noteworthy exceptions like Modigliani and Tarantelli, 1973, 1977; Modigliani and Padoa Schioppa, 1978, and, more recently, Spinelli, 1980; Bodo, 1981; Visco, 1984; Malcomson and Sartor, 1984).

Escalator clauses, the timing and extension of wage bargaining agreements, internal wage structure, employment and unemployment protection legislation, and severance rules are among the pillars of the Italian labour market. In this section we shall summarize some of these institutional arrangements and the nature of Italian labour relations. In particular, we intend to suggest that much of the prevailing institutional practices are best seen in terms of the implied rigidities.

Labour relations and institutional arrangements have undergone substantial changes in the period examined. In particular, at the cost of some simplification, we may conveniently divide labour relations history into three periods: the 1960s the 1970s, and the 1980s.

Up to 1970, protective laws concerned particular segments of the working population, those considered the weakest (i.e. women, teenagers, people of retirement age). Moreover, in much of the same decade, trade union activity remained around what might be considered 'physiological' levels (see the Data Appendix at the end of the book).

The events of 1969 ('Autunno caldo') and the wage bargaining agreements that went into effect in 1970 mark instead the beginning of a new regime in the process of wage determination and are widely believed to have had a profound influence on the whole system of labour relations. Trade union activity, as measured by the number of strikes and the average hours of strike per worker, rose to unprecedented levels. A high degree of labour protection showed up formally and informally while pervasive conflicts about income distribution slowed down the adjustment processes in the labour market.

In particular, the Maternity Act of 30 December 1971 (no. 1204), which was (probably mistakenly) intended to increase the equality of opportunity, needs to be mentioned in this respect, along with a set of new laws concerning the whole of the labour force (e.g. the Workers Act of 20 May 1970, no. 300, known as 'Statuto dei lavoratori'), which were passed in a turbulent social environment and imposed severe constraints on firm's behaviour.

The main constraints regarded hiring and firing conditions, with the consequence that job separation and job-finding rates quickly dropped while trade union membership rose to unprecedented levels. Moreover, in the same decade absenteism became a union's means of class warfare, sometimes coupled with, sometimes preferred to, the 'traditional' strike. In 1980, however, white-collar unrest ('marcia dei quarantamila') appeared to moderate previous tendencies.

To understand this phenomenon better, some remarks on the effects of the escalator clauses, operating in Italy since the Second World War are needed. From January 1957 until January 1975, such clauses provided a mechanism of nominal wage increases approximately proportional to consumer price increases. Thereafter, the system was substantially amended: wages and salary earnings were increased by an absolute amount in each quarter rather than in proportion to earnings. Furthermore, in the second half of the 1970s the escalator clauses were extended so as to cover pension schemes and severance payments.

As a consequence, as mentioned in the previous section, wage differentials were progressively squeezed, thus leading to a growing uneasiness among skilled workers. Interestingly, firms and unions eventually used local bargaining agreements in order to counteract the trends arising from the institutional environment and the country-wide collective bargaining agreements. Non-automatic components of wage and salary earnings thus played a relevant role in counteracting, at least partially, the equalizing effects of the indexation system (both across time and across workers). Bargaining at the sectoral and firm level in coincidence with general bargaining agreements was particularly important in this respect (e.g., 1973, 1976, 1979). However, the same component was far from negligible in between periods of national bargaining. The same can be said for the wage drift component.

In the light of this, the attention given in the Italian debate to the national bargaining system and to the escalator clauses appears somewhat misplaced.[5] Nevertheless, their influence on the functioning of the labour market and on the general Italian macroeconomic performance has been profound and certainly hardly overstated (see Modigliani and Padoa Schioppa, 1978). We feel, however, that in the 1970s *de facto* indexation has been larger than, and qualitatively different from, *de jure* indexation: local wage bargaining and drift have substantially raised the non-automatic components of the wage structure while increasing wage rigidity at a time when the degree of protection from escalator clauses was declining, owing to the rising rate of inflation.

Reverting to historical developments, from 1980 onwards labour mobility increased again, owing partly to amendments to the above legislation but mostly to changes in the mode of its application. In the same light, one can understand the massive resort, briefly mentioned above, to the Wage Supplementation Fund (Cassa Integrazione Guadagni) in the last decade and especially in the early 1980s. On the one hand, an 80 per cent legal replacement ratio for 'temporary' layoffs presumably prompted unions to press for higher real wages, especially because 'temporary' layoffs could well last more than a year. On the other hand, the fact that employers' contributions to this fund were not based on experience rating induced both firms and unions to use such a public institution as a soft landing into otherwise socially unacceptable unemployment. In particular, the latter element appears as an important component of the recovered flexibility of the 1980s. Notice, moreover, that the rising intermediation of the public sector in the labour market is not limited to the support of 'temporary' layoffs or of layoffs in general. Active participation in private collective bargaining and large tax wedges are two other relevant features, especially of the most recent period.

III. The Basic Model and its Implications

In this section we set out the model of firm and union behaviour that underlies the empirical analysis undertaken in Section IV.

We view the Italian economy as characterized by monopolistic competition with a large number of identical firms each facing the same input prices and downward-sloping demand curves. Each firm's technology is described by a constant return CES production function defined over labour (N), intermediate inputs (M) and capital (K).[6] Technical progress (A) is assumed to take the Harrod-neutral labour-augmenting form.

Firms control the demand for inputs and set the price. Under the previous set of assumptions, the demand for labour and intermediate inputs will be given by

(1) $N/Y = \lambda (WT_1/P)^{-\sigma} A^{(\sigma-1)}$

(2) $M/Y = \mu (P_M/P)^{-\sigma}$

where Y is aggregate output, W is the pre-tax wage rate, $(T_1 - 1)$ is the social security contribution tax rate levied on the firm, P is the firm's product price, P_M is the price of intermediate inputs, and σ is the (constant) elasticity of substitution ($\sigma > 0$). The constant terms λ and μ are functions of technological parameters and the price elasticity of demand. Notice that at the firm level M also includes domestically produced productive inputs; however, these cancel out in the process of aggregation, so that at the aggregate level M can be thought of as net imports of productive inputs. This implies that Y should be seen as the amount of output available to satisfy final domestic demand for domestic products, Y^d (consumption expenditure plus gross capital formation less imports of final goods) and foreign demand for domestic products (i.e., exports of final goods and services).

As far as prices are concerned, we suppose that firms are able to partition the market for their output between two non-communicating sub-markets defined by the buyers' location (i.e., domestic and foreign buyers). We assume that demand in the export and import markets can be approximated by the following constant elasticity homothetic form:

(3) $X / Y^* = \varepsilon (P_X / P^*)^{\eta_X}$

(4) $IM / Y^d = \nu (P_{IM} / P_d)^{\eta_d}$

where X is exports, IM is imports of final goods and services, P_d is the price on the domestic market and an asterisk denotes a foreign variable. Hence the aggregate demand for domestic output, $Y^d = Y - IM$, is given by

(5) $Y^d / Y = [1 + \nu (P_{IM} / P_d)^{\eta_d}]^{-1}$.

The price in each market is supposed to take the form of a mark-up on long-run minimum achievable averages cost AC, given technology and factor prices, but with the mark-up depending on prices of competitors in each market. Thus,

(6) $P_d = \phi_d AC$

with $\phi_d = \phi_0^d (P_{IM} / AC)^{\phi_1}$

(7) $P_X = \phi_X AC$

with $\phi_X = \phi_0^X (P^* / AC)^{\phi_2}$.

Note that this formulation is equally consistent with the oligopolistic mark-up theory of Sylos Labini and Bain; cf. Modigliani (1958).

In (6) and (7) AC is a well-defined highly nonlinear function of factor prices. In fact, it is the unit cost function associated with the CES technology. To avoid nonlinearities we approximate AC as follows:

(8) $A\tilde{C} = (WT_1 / A)^{\theta_L} P_K^{\theta_K} P_M^{(1 - \theta_L - \theta_K)} \approx AC$.

Taken together, (2), (3), (4) and (7) define the country's total net trade in real and nominal terms.

Reverting now to wage formation, we imagine that, in the bargain struck between unions and firms, the former set nominal wages on the basis of their point expectations of the consumer price level, with the intention of achieving a certain real wage which takes into account their knowledge of the firm's employment function, (1); employers retain the right to manage and thus control employment.

The main objections to this approach, which is common to much of the literature on this field,[7] are well known: first, the wage–employment bargain is not on the contract curve; second, firms appear to be passive in the wage bargain, whereas their interest in the wage outcome is self-evident; third, unions appear to take a partial equilibrium approach, in so far as they ignore the feedback of wage-setting on the consumer price level and capital formation.

These objections do not seem to be overriding in the Italian context as described in the previous section. In particular, we know that the Italian institutional setting allows bargaining to take place at three different levels: national, sectoral and firm. Given that the last one has played an increasingly relevant role in supplementing and amending the general framework of national collective bargaining, we believe that a partial equilibrium approach is not inappropriate. Of course, while at the firm level the consumer price level or the general rate of unemployment can be taken as given, in the aggregate the same variables become endogenous.

The unions are assumed to be interested in both after-tax real wages and employment, and to maximize a simple objective function of the Cobb–Douglas form subject to the firm's labour demand.

The aggregate wage outcome equation can then be shown to take the following form:[8]

(9) $(W/PA) = \omega T_1^{-1}(1 - R\sigma)^{1/(1-\sigma)}$

with $R = \alpha(u - \bar{u})$ $(\alpha > 0)$. Here R is the ratio between the employment and the real-wage elasticities in the union's objective function (sometimes called the 'proportional technical rate of substitution'). We suggest that R is a function of the aggregate unemployment rate, u, net of frictional component $\bar{u}$. Thus, in the bargain at the firm level, the aggregate unemployment rate represents outside workers' opportunities.

The full model therefore comprises the labour demand equation (1), the imports of intermediate inputs equation (2), the exports equation (3), the imports of final goods and services equation (4), the domestic price equation (6), the export price equation (7), the approximation for average costs (8) and the real-wage equation (9), together with definitions for the nominal trade balance (NE) and the unemployment rate:

(10) $NE = XP_X - IMP_{IM} - MP_M$

(11) $u = (L - N - N^P)/L$

where L is labour supply and N^P is employment in the public sector. For simplicity we also approximate the price on the domestic market P_d by P and domestic demand Y^d by Y to obtain

(4') $IM/Y = \nu(P_{IM}/P)^{\eta_d}$

(6') $P/\tilde{A}C = \phi(P_{IM}/\tilde{A}C)^{(1-\beta)}$.

The essential parameters and exogenous variables of the model are: the proportional technical rate of substitution in the union's function; the elasticity of substitution in the production function; technical progress; the frictional rate of unemployment; the fiscal instruments (social security, indirect tax rates, employment in the public sector); labour supply; world commodity prices in liras; price elasticities in the domestic market and in all the components of net trade.

In order to lay bare the basic logical structure of our model and its implications with respect to the determinants of unemployment and wages, let us denote by C labour costs in efficiency units, or

(12) $C = WT_1/PA$,

and by $\bar{L}$ the labour supply net of frictional unemployment and of public labour demand:

(13) $\bar{L} = L - N^P - \bar{u}L$.

Then the labour demand, wage and price equations can be written as

(14) $N = \lambda Y C^{-\sigma}/A$

(15) $C = \omega[1 - \sigma\alpha\{(\bar{L} - N)/L\}]^{1/(1-\sigma)}$

and

(16) $P = C^{\beta\theta_L/(-\beta\theta_L)}B$

where

$$B = \phi^{1/(1-\beta\theta_L)} P_{IM}^{(1-\beta)/(1-\beta\theta_L)} P_K^{\beta\theta_K/(1-\beta\theta_L)} P_M^{\{\beta(1-\theta_L-\theta_K)\}/(1-\beta\theta_L)}.$$

It should be noted that the system (14)–(16) is substantially different from the standard formulation that has been used to describe closed economies. The major difference is in the wage equation (15), which typically takes the form of an expectations augmented Phillips curve:

(17) $\dot{W}/W = \dot{P}^e/P + \phi(\tilde{u}) + \gamma\dot{A}/A$

where $\tilde{u}$ is the deviation of unemployment from the 'natural' rate, and γ might be between 0 and 1.

In this formulation, the real wage, except possibly for transitory effects, is entirely determined by firms' pricing policy (which itself reflects the nature of market structures). The wage equation controls instead the dynamics of inflation. Labour behaviour is supposed to reflect not a specific real wage target but rather an adjustment process—real wage demands rise when $\tilde{u}$ is negative and falls when it is positive. This *tâtonnement* process eventually results in labour receiving whatever real wage is consistent with the firm's mark-up. Finally, employment is determined by aggregate demand (up to limits determined by labour supply and by inflationary pressures).

By contrast, according to our equation (15), workers, and, more specifically, the unions representing them, endeavour to achieve a target real wage, or, more precisely, the real wage adjusted for productivity. This target, however, is sensitive to the prevailing rate of unemployment (especially of the short-term unemployed). But, how can labour secure the real wage it wants in the face of the firm's ability to enforce their mark-up, through pricing? The answer, of course, is that in an open economy it is possible for labour to set the real wage, and at the same time for firms to enforce their mark-up policy, because the variable cost includes not only labour but also imported materials, and because the desired mark-up on average cost is limited also by foreign competition in both the domestic and the foreign market.

The wage demand does, however, affect unemployment, since, for given aggregate demand, employment, and hence unemployment, depend on the real wage. Thus, for given output, both the real wage and unemployment are determined by the intersection of (14) and (15)—which thus form a closed subsystem. From (15) we can infer that, at around full employment, the real wage rate responds directly to the level of activity:

$$(18) \qquad \frac{1}{C}\frac{dC}{du} = -\sigma\alpha/(1-\sigma).$$

Thus, as long as the elasticity of substitution σ is less than unity, as seems to be the case for the Italian economy (see the next section), the real wage will respond positively to the rate of employment (or inversely to the unemployment rate), keeping technological progress constant.

Thus, with $\sigma < 1$, a change in output will produce a less than proportional long-run change in employment, even though the production function exhibits constant returns to scale in the long run. This result is reminiscent of Okun's law, but is a long-run property reflecting the fact that, if a rise in demand (larger than productivity) reduces u, unions successfully press for higher real wages and a larger share of the product. Indeed, (14) implies that the labour share S_L is given by[9]

$$(19) \qquad S_L = \frac{WT_1N}{PY} = \lambda C^{1-\sigma}.$$

Hence, if $\sigma < 1$, S_L is an increasing function of the real labour cost per unit of efficiency, and hence of output. The higher real wage in turn will induce substitution against labour, reducing the expansion of employment below that of output.

In addition, the resulting higher real-unit labour cost will cause a rise in prices relative to world prices—cf. (16). By substituting the solution for P of (14), (15) and (16) into the five foreign trade equations completing the system, one can derive a 'reduced form' relating the net trade balance to aggregate demand Y. In this form, a rise in Y is seen to reduce the net trade balance through two mechanisms. The first is the conventional one, working by way of a rise in aggregate demand raising imports. The second works through a rise in employment, raising real wages, and hence the price of domestic product relative to foreign prices; this generates an increase in imports and a reduction of export volume and a deterioration of the trade balance (provided the Marshall–Lerner condition holds). The empirical estimates for Italy reviewed in the next section suggest that these effects through the trade balance are surprisingly powerful.

Our model could be readily 'closed' by endogenizing Y through an aggregate demand sector relating Y to variables already in our system and policy variables, which in turn could be endogenized through policy targets. However, for the reasons set forth in the Introduction, we choose instead to treat income as an exogenous 'policy' variable.

IV. EMPIRICAL EVIDENCE

As it stands, the reference model whose structure and main implications have been discussed in the previous section is still unsuitable for an empirical analysis: dynamic adjustments and exact definitions of variables are needed.

We shall discuss the latter point first. Our aim is to shed some light on the changes in aggregate unemployment that have occurred in Italy in the last 25 years.

We shall therefore consider the private sector of the economy as a whole, i.e. agriculture, fisheries and forestry, industrial and private services.

As far as dynamics go, given the limited amount of available information (annual data for 1960–83), the treatment is, unavoidably, somewhat *ad hoc.* We model adjustment processes mainly through partial adjustment or error correction mechanisms; but no rigorous attempt is made to specify the (deterministic and stochastic) dynamics of each equation, let alone the whole model.

The final specification of the model is given and briefly analysed below, while Table 2 presents the estimated parameters of the model, their asymptotic *t*-ratios along with some purely indicative single-equation summary statistics. Estimation was carried out by the asymptotically efficient nonlinear Three-Stage Least Squares method.

Beginning with the *wage equation,* let lower-case letters denote the (natural) logarithm of the corresponding variables (i.e. $a = \log A$). The final specification of the equation takes the following form:

$$(20) \quad \Delta w_t = \Delta \tilde{p}_t + \omega_0 + \omega_2 \Delta d73 + (\omega_3' + \omega_3'' + \omega_3''')$$
$$\times \{(L - N - N^P)/L - \omega_4 z_{1,t} - \omega_5 z_{2,t}\}$$
$$+ \omega_1 (w_{t-1} + t_{1,t-1} - \tilde{p}_{t-1} + t_{3,t-1} - \omega_6 a_{t-1}).$$

As compared with (9), (20) involves a number of modifications. First, technical progress is approximated by the trend of average hourly productivity of all employees (including the self-employed). In an endeavour to eliminate changes of a purely cyclical character and to take into account the significant slow-down in productivity since the early 1970s, we approximate A by the systematic part of the regression:

$$(21) \quad Y_t/(N_t H_t) = 0.9 + 1.3 \ln(t) + e_t.$$

Here N is the average number of persons working and H the average number of hours worked. While this approximation of Harrod-neutral productivity trends is certainly open to criticism, it seemed the most satisfactory in terms of fit and reasonable coefficient estimates in comparison with a number of alternatives, including broken linear and exponential trends. However, in the light of the measurement problems that undoubtedly exist, we allow ω_6 to be different from unity.

Second, dynamics are modelled by the error correction term in braces on the right-hand side. Third, the variable $\tilde{P}$ appears instead of P. Unfortunately, available data did not allow us to construct a reliable product price net of indirect taxes (i.e. P). Therefore we were forced to use a gross product price (i.e. $\tilde{P}$) and separately to take into account the effect of the indirect tax rate $(T_3 - 1)$. Fourth, a dummy variable for the 1973 observation ($d73$) takes account of what appears to be an error in the National Accounts figures (see Barbone,

TABLE 2

PARAMETER ESTIMATES, ASYMPTOTIC t-RATIOS AND
SINGLE-EQUATION SUMMARY STATISTICS

Wage equation
$\hat{\omega}_0 = 0.095$ (3.14) $\hat{\omega}_1 = -0.225$ (3.51) $\hat{\omega}_2 = 0.068$ (6.83)
$\hat{\omega}_3' = -2.91$ (3.87) $\hat{\omega}_3'' = -1.22$ (1.92) $\hat{\omega}_3''' = -1.84$ (3.29)
$\hat{\omega}_4 = 0.90$ (3.66) $\hat{\omega}_5 = 1.32$ (2.11) $\hat{\omega}_6 = 0.643$ (13.79)
s.e. = 0.0169   DW = 2.64
mean lag: 4.4 years

Product price equation
$\hat{\pi}_0 = 0.041$ (2.66) $\hat{\pi}_1 = 0.479$ (8.28) $\hat{\omega}_6 = 0.643$ (13.79)
$\hat{\beta} = 0.645$ (10.40) $\hat{\theta}_L = 0.872$ (20.05) $\hat{\theta}_K = 0.014$ (0.60)
s.e. = 0.061   DW = 1.68
mean lag: 1.1 years

Labour demand equation
$\hat{\lambda}_0 = -0.154$ (4.09) $\hat{\lambda}_1 = 0.163$ (4.15) $\hat{\sigma}_L = 0.346$ (3.02)
$\hat{\omega}_6 = 0.643$ (13.79)
s.e. = 0.0084   DW = 1.62
mean lag: 5.1 years

Net imports of productive inputs equation
$\hat{\mu}_0 = -1.973$ (5.95) $\hat{\mu}_1 = 3.834$ (6.04) $\hat{\mu}_2 = -0.576$ (5.47)
$\hat{\mu}_3 = -0.245$ (4.39) $\hat{\mu}_4 = -0.130$ (2.55) $\hat{\sigma}_M = 0.186$ (2.10)
s.e. = 0.0966   DW = 1.99

Imports of final goods and services equation
$\hat{v}_0 = -0.316$ (4.24) $\hat{v}_1 = 1.606$ (9.35) $\hat{v}_2 = -0.530$ (4.91)
$\hat{v}_3 = -0.154$ (4.57) $\hat{v}_4 = 0.128$ (8.08)
s.e. = 0.0267   DW = 1.95

Exports of final goods and services price deflator equation
$\hat{\chi}_0 = 0.160$ (1.90) $\hat{\chi}_1 = 0.365$ (5.08) $\hat{\chi}_2 = 0.413$ (2.99)
$\hat{\chi}_3 = 0.217$ (4.56) $\hat{\chi}_4 = 0.141$ (1.88)
s.e. = 0.061   DW = 2.05
mean lag: 4.5 years

Exports of final goods and services equation
$\hat{\varepsilon}_0 = 2.142$ (4.01) $\hat{\varepsilon}_1 = 0.630$ (4.10) $\hat{\varepsilon}_2 = -0.232$ (2.23)
$\hat{\varepsilon}_3 = 0.055$ (3.62) $\hat{\varepsilon}_4 = -0.480$ (4.39) $\hat{\varepsilon}_5 = -0.862$ (4.36)
s.e. = 0.0267   DW = 1.91
mean lag: 0.8 year

Notes:
(i) Parameter estimate/asymptotic standard error ratios in parentheses.
(ii) Sample period: 1961–83 yearly data.
(iii) Estimation method: nonlinear three-stage least squares.

Bodo and Visco, 1981, p. 483). Fifth, the coefficient of the unemployment rate takes different values in different subperiods; i.e. ω_3' and ω_3'' refer, respectively, to the subperiods 1961–73 and 1974–79, while ω_3''' refers to the remaining 1980–83 subperiod. As is well known (see, among others, Grubb, Jackman and Layard, 1983), ω_3 has a natural relationship with the concept of wage rigidity. Therefore we thought it interesting to assess empirically the validity of the proposition put forward in Section II about the varying degree of flexibility shown by the Italian labour market in the period under consideration.

Sixth, in (20), z_1 is an index of sectoral shifts taking place in the labour market, and should help explain movements in the frictional unemployment rate (see Lilien, 1982, but also Johnson and Layard, 1986). Needless to say, other variables were considered, along with z_1, for the same task (e.g. changes in the age and sex composition of the labour force, union membership, replacement ratios, industrial disputes), but z_1 was the only one to survive. Finally z_2 is the long-term unemployment rate (i.e. with duration greater than one year). There are reasons to believe that the long-term unemployed exert less pressure on wages than the short-term unemployed. Furthermore, the idea that Italian trade unions have consistently disregarded the weakest components of the labour force is widely accepted.

Notice that in (20), according to theory, price homogeneity is imposed.[10]

Reverting now to the *product price equation*, its final specification is as follows:

$$(22) \quad \Delta(\tilde{p}_t - t_{3,t}) = \pi_0 + \pi_1[\beta\{\theta_L(w_t + t_{1,t} - \omega_6 a_t) + \theta_K p_{K,t} + (1 - \theta_L - \theta_K)p_{m,t}\}$$
$$+ (1 - \beta)p_{im,t} - (\tilde{p}_{t-1} - t_{3,t-1})] - \Delta t_{3,t}.$$

Recalling that $\tilde{P}$ is a product price gross of indirect taxes, equation (22) is simply a repeat of equation (6) with a superimposed partial adjustment mechanism. The variable Δt_3 catches short-term effects of indirect taxation. Its unitary coefficient is tested and imposed.

A partial adjustment mechanism has been also adopted for the *labour demand equation*:

$$(23) \quad \Delta n_t = \lambda_0 + \lambda_1\{y_t - \sigma_L(w_t + t_{1,t} - \tilde{p}_t + t_{3,t}) + (\sigma_L - 1)\omega_6 a_t - n_{t-1}\}$$

where the unit elasticity with respect to output is tested and imposed. In (23), notice that the elasticity of substitution is not constrained to equal the corresponding elasticity of substitution appearing in the *net imports of productive inputs equation*, which, in turn, takes the following form:

$$(24) \quad \Delta m_t = \mu_0 + \mu_1 \Delta y_t + \mu_2\{m_{t-1} - y_{t-1} - \sigma_M(p_{m,t} - \tilde{p}_t)\}$$
$$+ \mu_3(d65 - d68) + \mu_4 \Delta d78$$

where p_m includes indirect taxes.

The fact that different values of the elasticity of substitution appear in the two input demand equations obviously contradicts the theoretical assumption put forward in Section III. However, it should be underlined that, though the empirical evidence would not imply a clear rejection of the hypothesis $\sigma_M = \sigma_L = \sigma$, we decided not to impose such restrictions in the light of the negligible value taken by σ in the restricted estimates as well as on the grounds that equation (24) seems to require further thought, as is suggested by the number of dummy variables introduced for which there is no really convincing explanation.

In equation (24), the long-run unit elasticity with respect to output is tested and imposed. The highly significant output change term presumably reflects accelerator effects associated with the demand for inventories of imported materials.

Next, we have the *imports of final goods and services equation*:

$$(25) \quad \Delta im_t = \nu_0 + \nu_1 \Delta y_t + \nu_2(p_{im,t} - \tilde{p}_t) + \nu_3(im_{t-1} - y_{t-1}) + \nu_4 \Delta d63.$$

As with the previous equation, the dynamics take the form of an error correction mechanism that ensures a long-run unit elasticity of the import demand with respect to output. Unfortunately, the estimate of the speed of adjustment—0·15—is too low to be entirely credible, though the acceleration term goes in the opposite direction.

Finally, we report the final specification for the *exports of final goods and services price and quantity equations*:

$$(26) \quad \Delta p_{x,t} = \chi_0 + \chi_1 \Delta p_t^* + \chi_2 \Delta(\tilde{p}_t - t_{3,t}) + (\chi_3 + \chi_4)(\tilde{p}_{t-1} - t_{3,t-1})$$
$$+ \chi_4 p_{t-1}^* - \chi_3 p_{x,t-1}$$

$$(27) \quad \Delta x_t = \varepsilon_0 + \varepsilon_1 \Delta y^* + \varepsilon_2 \Delta p_{x,t} + \varepsilon_3 \Delta d79 + \varepsilon_4 \{x_{t-1} - y_{t-1}^* - \varepsilon_5(p_{x,t-1} - p_{t-1}^*)\}.$$

Equation (26) corresponds to (7) but with some appreciable modifications. In fact, joint estimation of (7) and (8) proved to yield disappointing results, mainly because there was no way of disentangling the separate effects of average costs and world prices. In (7) we therefore approximated AC by P and hypothesize that P and P^* both have an impact effect on P_x, captured by the first two quite significant terms. However, the final adjustment is gradual, as indicated by the highly significant, but rather low, speed of adjustment coefficient, χ_3.

As far as (27) is concerned, once more the dynamics are modelled by an error correction mechanism. As for previous cases, the restriction of a unit elasticity with respect to world demand is tested and imposed.

The parameter estimates themselves are given in Table 2 and the associated long-run solution in Table 3. We note that the overall performance of the

TABLE 3

THE LONG-RUN MODEL

Wages
$$WT_1 T_3 / \tilde{P}A = 1·525 \ e^{-12·933(u-\bar{u})} \qquad (1961–73)$$
$$= 1·525 \ e^{-5·422(u-\bar{u})} \qquad (1974–79)$$
$$= 1·525 \ e^{-8·178(u-\bar{u})} \qquad (1980–83)$$

Product prices
$$\tilde{P} / \tilde{A}C \cdot T_3 = 1·089 (P_{IM} / \tilde{A}C)^{0·355}$$

Labour demand
$$N / Y = 0·389 \ (WT_1 T_3 / \tilde{P})^{-0·346} A^{-0·654}$$

Net imports of inputs
$$M / Y = 0·033 \ (P_M / \tilde{P})^{-0·186}$$

Imports of final goods and services
$$IM / Y = 0·128 \ (P_{IM} / \tilde{P})^{-3·442}$$

Export deflator
$$P_X T_3 / \tilde{P} = 2·09 \ (P^* T_3 / \tilde{P})^{0·65}$$

Exports of final goods and services
$$X / Y^* = 86·7 \ (P_X / P^*)^{-0·862}$$

Average costs
$$\tilde{A}C = (WT_1 / A)^{0·872} P_K^{0·014} P_M^{0·114}$$

Note:
The apparently unreasonable value taken by some of the constant terms reflects scale differences.

model appears to be quite satisfactory. All coefficients are quite well determined and sensible, with one exception: the weight of the user cost of capital in average cost, which turns out to be correctly signed but not significantly different from zero. This result should not be taken as an outright rejection of the theoretical framework outlined in Section III. As is well known, the construction of an accurate user cost of capital incorporating the extensive changes in the way capital has been taxed and subsidized is far from easy. This is particularly·true when one deals with the entire private sector. The other parameter estimates are, on the whole, broadly consistent with previous Italian research.

Figure 4 shows the pattern of the actual unemployment rate and of its fitted counterpart, as derived from a dynamic simulation of the estimated model. On the whole, the model appears to track the actual variable reasonably well.

As an overall check, a general mis-specification test statistic was also computed (Pudney, 1981, p. 423). This statistic is asymptotically chi-squared under the null hypothesis of correct specification, with degrees of freedom equal to the number of equations times the number of predetermined variables less the number of free parameters in the model. The value of this statistic is 145·8, which implies that the null hypothesis of correct specification cannot be rejected.

First, the idea of a rigid labour market outlined in Section II seems to receive support by our results. As the mean lags shown in Table 2 suggest, adjustment processes in the Italian labour market are very slow, especially on the demand side. Probably, written and unwritten rules of Italian labour relations are important determinants of this result.

Second, real labour costs have a non-negligible effect on employment, though it should be recognized that Italian demand appears to be less price-elastic than suggested by some European and non-European investigations. Third, as we should expect, adjustment processes are much faster on the price side, where the effect of competitors' behaviour is substantial. Fourth, though showing sensible long-run elasticities, domestic demand for imports seems to fluctuate much more than the level of domestic activity. Given a foreign demand for Italian exports as well behaved as the one reported in Tables 2 and 3, this produces the well-known association of booms with large foreign deficits.

Having estimated the model, we can now use it to explain the movements in unemployment. However, before doing so, a few remarks have to be made. First, the theoretical discussion and the empirical analysis have neglected entirely the question of whether expected variables instead of realization in one or more equations should appear. We are obviously aware of the fact that, for example, the union's objective function should be defined over expected real wages and employment more than over actual real wages and employment. In this respect the results reported in Table 2 should be regarded as preliminary. Second, the approximation used for the technology-coherent definition of minimum costs is certainly questionable. Third, we suspect that some of the adjustment coefficients are not time-invariant. Finally, in the wage equation, the role of secular determinants of unemployment is clearly an area where further work has to be done.

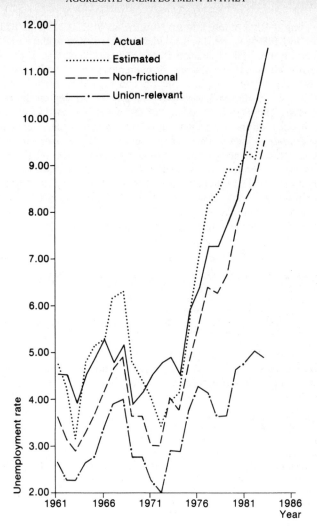

FIGURE 4. Actual and fitted (adjusted) unemployment rates (u), as derived from dynamic simulation of the estimated model; non-frictional unemployment rate ($u - \hat{\omega}_4 z_1$) and 'union-relevant' unemployment rate ($u - \hat{\omega}_4 z_1 - \hat{\omega}_5 z_2$).

Nevertheless, we would like to suggest that the implications of the present estimates can provide valuable insights in understanding recent developments. In particular, they can be used to investigate the forces that produced the observed unemployment. To this end, we can combine the long-run versions of our labour demand and wage functions to get[11]

$$(28) \quad u = \{-(\sigma\omega_0/\omega_1) - (\lambda_0/\lambda_1) - y + l - (N^P/N) + a$$
$$+ (\sigma\omega_3/\omega_1)\omega_4 z_1 + (\sigma\omega_3/\omega_1)\omega_5 z_2\}/\{(\sigma\omega_3/\omega_1) + 1\}.$$

Dividing up the sample into five subperiods (1961–65, 1966–70, 1971–75, 1976–79 and 1980–83), we then consider average values of the variables over these periods and look at changes from one period to the next.

The breakdown of the changes in unemployment over the last 20 years, based on (28), is presented in Table 4. Rows (1)–(6) report the effect of the change in each of the six 'exogenous' variables appearing on the right-hand side of (28). Row (7) gives the sum of those entries and thus measures the change in equilibrium unemployment corresponding to the actual changes in the exogenous variables. This change generally differs from the estimated change in actual unemployment (see Figure 4) reported in row (9) because of the presence of gradual adjustment—sometimes quite slow—which causes estimated (and actual) u to deviate from long-run equilibrium. The difference between rows (9) and (7) is reported in row (8) as 'transitory change'. Finally, the actual change in u is reported in row (10), which can be compared with (9) to infer the error of estimation of the model.

TABLE 4

BREAKDOWN OF THE CHANGE IN THE (ADJUSTED) UNEMPLOYMENT RATE,
1961–1983
(percentage points)

	1961–65 to 1966–70	1966–70 to 1971–75	1971–75 to 1976–79	1976–79 to 1980–83
(1) Structural shifts (z_1)	−0·41	0·57	−0·15	0·36
(2) Long-term unemployment (z_2)	—	0·10	1·06	1·22
(3) Demand (y)	−5·05	−3·84	−2·24	−1·71
(4) Labour force (l)	−0·52	0·11	0·96	0·84
(5) Public employment share (N^P/N)	−0·37	−0·55	−0·37	−0·22
(6) Labour-augmenting technical progress (a)	4·97	2·57	1·53	1·02
(7) Change in equilibrium unemployment (sum of rows (1)–(6))	−1·38	−1·04	0·79	1·51
(8) Transitory change	1·98	0·3	3·2	−0·4
(9) Estimated total change	0·6	−0·7	4·0	1·1
(10) Actual change	0·20	0·22	2·28	2·81

The table shows that the major sources of changing unemployment—aside from a steady but small erosion of the labour force available to the private sector through public employment—are aggregate demand, the labour force and productivity. However a 1 per cent rise in demand increases employment by much less than 1 per cent because of the positive response of real wages to lower unemployment; in fact, according to our estimates, the effect is in the order of only 0·2 per cent (though varying somewhat from period to period).

Between the first and the second half of the 1960s, there was an extraordinary expansion of long-term productivity which *per se* would have produced a rise in u of 5 percentage points, but its effect was more than offset by a declining labour force and, to a much greater extent, by a very large rise in demand (some 35 per cent). In the 1970s and 1980s the productivity effect tapered off. But at the same time labour force movements became unfavourable, and, more importantly, the growth in demand, though not negligible (somewhat over 10 per cent), in both the third and fourth subperiods was no longer adequate to offset the combination of productivity and labour force increase, partly because of the large unfavourable effect on employment of a rise in real wages. These various movements resulted in an increase of unemployment of some 5 percentage points between the late 1960s and the early 1980s, of which about half is estimated to be a rise in equilibrium unemployment.

V. SOME SIMULATION EXERCISES

The decomposition of the sources of unemployment changes referred to at the end of the previous section provides an essentially accounting interpretation of the recent growth in unemployment.

In this section we propose to rely on that interpretation, as well as on the structure of the model and our parameter estimates, to throw light on four issues:

1. Why has the growth of aggregate demand been so weak and inadequate to maintain full employment since the mid-1970s?
2. What would have been the consequences of an aggregate demand policy sufficiently expansive to maintain full employment after 1975? Would such a policy have been viable?
3. What kind of supply policy would have been necessary to maintain full employment and trade balance equilibrium?
4. What was the role of external forces, and particularly the weakening of world demand, in the recent observed rise in unemployment?

This analysis enables us to outline some policies that offer hope for a solution, or at least substantial relief, to the unemployment–balance of payments dilemma currently facing Italy.

The inadequate growth of aggregate demand

We suggest that the failure of aggregate demand to rise sufficiently to maintain a reasonable rate of unemployment after the mid-1970s can be traced primarily to the balance of payments constraint. Given the aggressive behaviour of unions, especially in the first half of the 1970s, and the structure of the economy, a policy of an appreciable and/or sustained excess of aggregate demand over the path actually followed would have promptly led to a quite large trade deficit which would have had disastrous consequences and in the end would have made the policy unenforceable. Indeed, such deficits could not have been financed with a fixed exchange rate. They would have led unavoidably to a floating exchange rate regime and to even further devaluation than actually occurred. This would not only increase inflation, but would also make it impossible to sustain a level of demand compatible with current account balance.

According to our model and parameter estimates, an attempt at reducing unemployment by expanding aggregate demand would result in a very large rise in the trade deficit per unit reduction in u. Because of the gradual adjustments, and other dynamic effects, the rise in the deficit is largest at the time of the expansion of demand and then declines somewhat if demand is kept at the new level—but it always remains large. The trade-off between u and net exports (NE) can best be understood by focusing on how a change in demand affects u on the one hand, and NE on the other. The effect on unemployment is the sum of the direct employment effect of higher output and the (unfavourable) indirect effect through higher wages. According to our estimates, the adjustments in the labour market are very slow. As a result, a 10 per cent rise in output is estimated to reduce u in the first year by only about 1·3 percentage points. At the same time, a 10 per cent rise in demand appears to have a large impact effect on trade deficit, increasing it by nearly 30 per cent of total trade ((exports + imports)/2)! This huge response, which has been noted before, can be traced primarily to the acceleration effect in the import equation—presumably owing to inventories. Thus, the trade-off between NE and u is strikingly unfavourable in the first year—a roughly 20 per cent deterioration of the balance for a 1 point reduction in u.

As the system has time to adjust more fully to the demand shock, one finds that, on the one hand, employment expands through the direct effect, but, on the other, the unfavourable indirect effect worsens. The first of these dominates, and so u tends to decline, but not by much. Simulations (see Table 5) suggest that after five years u might decline by $2\frac{1}{2}$ percentage points. Similarly, the net trade balance starts to improve but not by much, as the disappearance of the acceleration effect is counterbalanced partly by a rising wage–price effect, raising domestic relative to foreign prices, and by increasing elasticities of demand for imports and exports. Thus, after five years, we find the rise in net exports approaching some $2\frac{1}{4}$ times the rise in income. As a result, as equilibrium is approached, the trade-off between u and NE improves, but it still remains highly unfavourable, not much below a 10 per cent deterioration per 1 percentage point decline in u.

TABLE 5

PURE DEMAND POLICY AND IMPLICATIONS FOR TRADE BALANCE

		Adjustment Speed[a]			
		50% per year		25% per year	
	Full employment gap (1)	Output gap[b] (2)	Change in trade deficit (%)[c] (3)	Output gap[b] (4)	Change in trade deficit (%)[c] (5)
1976–79	5·9	24	50	17·1	36
1980–83	8·4	n.a.		24·4	54·6

Notes:
[a] Rate of absorption of non-frictional unemployment.
[b] Percentage change in real aggregate demand needed to reabsorb non-frictional unemployment given in column (1).
[c] Percent of total nominal trade (average of exports and imports).

The impossibility of pursuing full employment through aggregate demand policies

These conclusions are illustrated by the simulations reported in Table 5. The questions we ask are: (1) How much would one have to increase aggregate demand to absorb the estimated non-frictional unemployment, and (2) What effect would such an increase have on the net trade balance? To answer these questions we set unemployment at its frictional level and endogenize aggregate demand.

As already pointed out, the answers depend on how much time we allow for the system to adjust fully to the policy. In the table, we have chosen to report the percentage change in the *average* annual value of the relevant variables over a four-year period. This averaging also minimizes the effect of erratic year-to-year movements connected with shocks other than the original policy shock. Even with a four-year adjustment period, the results are appreciably affected by how fast the policy-maker endeavours to bring u to the target level—as noted, the more the time allowed, the more favourable is the trade-off. Accordingly, we show the results of two alternative simulations. In the first, reported in columns (2) and (3), the policy is designed to eliminate the excess unemployment at a rate of 50 per cent a year; in columns (4) and (5), the rate is half as large. Since unemployment first becomes a significant problem around 1975, the two simulations reported are for the four years, 1976–79 and 1980–83.

In the first period, our simulation (column (2)) indicates that a 50 per cent per year elimination of the non-frictional unemployment, estimated at some 6 per cent, would have required a level of output some 24 per cent higher, and would have resulted in a deterioration of the net balance of just about 50 per cent of the value of nominal trade! For the second period, with the excess unemployment estimated at $8\frac{1}{2}$ per cent, the simulation even failed to converge. Furthermore, by the end of the fourth year the system had not reached steady state; this is particularly true for real wages, which are still rising and in turn cause a rise in prices relative to foreign competition and a further substantial deterioration of net trade.

When the programmed absorption of unemployment is slower, the required expansion of demand and resulting deterioration in the trade balance is somewhat smaller and more sensible. Yet, the simulation for the second period suggests that even the more gradual approach requires an unrealistic expansion of demand, and an even more unsustainable trade deficit. Note in particular that the estimated rise in the deficit of 55 per cent would have come on top of an already large deficit—14 per cent on trade account and 7 per cent on current account. And, once more, further deterioration could be expected in later years.

Of course, one must allow for mis-specification and errors in the parameter estimates[12]. Still, these results make an impressive case for the propostion that the authorities had no choice but to follow a demand management policy similar to that realized, and that any attempt at maintaining full employment with pure aggregate demand policies could only have resulted in disastrous failure.

Full employment through supply policies

At the opposite extreme from a pure demand policy is a pure supply policy of real wage management. Column (1) of Table 6 presents our model's estimate

TABLE 6

PURE SUPPLY AND MIXED POLICIES TO REABSORB UNEMPLOYMENT

	A: Pure supply policy (demand constant)		B: Mixed supply and demand policies (zero trade deficit)	
	Real wage gaps[a] (1)	Changes in trade deficit[b] (2)	Base trade deficit[b] (3)	Real wage gap (4)
1976–79	31	−13·4	5·3	20
1980–83	39·4	−13·7	8·3	35

Notes:
[a] Percentage change in real wage needed to reabsorb unemployment, assuming that reabsorption is scheduled at 0·25 per cent per year.
[b] As a percentage of total nominal trade (average of exports and imports).

of the average reduction in real hourly wages that would have been required to eliminate non-frictional unemployment, in the absence of demand policies, in each of the two periods. The figures reported were obtained through a simulation in which the absorption of unemployment is scheduled to occur gradually—25 per cent per year (with a 50 per cent per year adjustment the simulation failed to converge).

Once again it appears that the reductions required in the real wage are staggering and unmanageable, even with a gradual programme.

Full employment through demand and supply policies

The results of column (1) may not be too relevant, however, because output is kept constant and, therefore, employment has to rise entirely through factor substitution. But this is not a sensible policy to pursue, since there are no valid grounds for targeting a constant level of demand. It would seem more appropriate, instead, to target the two final goals—namely, full employment and external balance. Now, one would expect that a policy of real-wage reduction, with output constant, in addition to expanding employment, would also reduce domestic relative to foreign prices—cf. equation (16)—thus improving the trade balance. The importance of this effect can be seen from column (2) of Table 6: the fall in wage of around 30 per cent results in an improvement in net exports amounting to 13–14 per cent of trade, in each of the two periods. That surplus makes it possible to expand demand to the point where the resulting additional imports absorb the surplus. The expansion of demand in turn permits an increase in employment, reducing the extent to which one must rely on real-wage cuts to achieve full employment. These inferences are confirmed by the entries of column (4), which show the wage reduction required to meet the target of full employment with balanced trade. For the first period the required reduction in real wage—20 per cent—is one-third lower and is of a magnitude perhaps not altogether unmanageable.

Unfortunately, for the more relevant current period the gain is much smaller and the required reduction remains over one-third. The reason why the required cut is so much larger in the last period is two-fold. The first and most obvious reason is that non-frictional unemployment in the second period is quite a bit larger—8·4 per cent versus 5·9 per cent in the first. The second reason is that the differential between columns (1) and (4) depends not on the *improvement* in the trade balance, which is recorded in column (2), but rather on the *amount* of trade surplus resulting from the wage cut, which is the sum of the improvement less the actual deficit present in the absence of the policy under consideration. That base deficit, reported in column (3), is seen to be substantially lower in the first period than in the second. Thus, the amount of surplus left for demand expansion is some 8 per cent of trade in the first period ($-5·3+13·4$) but only 5·4 per cent in the second.

Actually, the deterioration in the early 1980s compared with the late 1970s is even worse than appears from the table, as our figures tend to overestimate the needed wage cut in the first period and to underestimate it in the second period. First, in our simulation we had to rely on the base deficit generated by the dynamic simulation of the models. For the first period, this computed deficit turns out to be somewhat above actual (5·3 versus 3·7 per cent). Second, the measure of the target deficit relevant for policy should be the current account, not just the trade deficit, which we have used. In the first period, the difference between these measures is quite large, as the current account showed not a deficit but a hefty surplus averaging almost 8 per cent. These considerations suggest that, in the first period, the real-wage reduction needed for full employment might have been appreciably lower than the 20 per cent shown in row (1) of column (4).

On the other hand, for the second period, the estimated base deficit (8·3 per cent) *underestimates* the actual trade deficit (14·3 per cent) but happens to be fairly close to the more relevant current account deficit. Thus, for the second period the dark picture presented in Table 6 would not seem obviously biased.

The role of external forces

There remains an important question to be clarified before attempting to assess the outlook: namely, Why did the situation deteriorate so drastically in the last four years? The question is not merely why u has risen yet further—that we know can be traced back to a very low growth of demand, approaching zero since 1979. It is, rather, Why has there been such a deterioration in the cost of returning to a reasonable level of unemployment? This deterioration cannot be attributed to the circumstances that produced rising unemployment in the 1970s—real wages rising at a fast rate and outpacing output per man. Indeed, between 1978 and 1983 real wages are estimated to have grown only about $1\frac{1}{2}$ per cent per year, roughly the same as output per man-hour. Nor is this unexpected in the light of our wage equation. The cause of the deterioration must, instead, be sought in the country's inability to increase exports, despite stable or falling relative prices, at least until 1983. This inability, in turn, is a consequence of sluggish world demand. Thus, OECD imports grew by only $1\frac{1}{2}$ per cent per year from 1979 to 1982, and the growth in demand by Italy's EEC partners was even more sluggish.

We are thus led to the conclusion that up to 1979–80 the large rise of 2·5 per cent in u (or 2·3 per cent in adjusted u) was due, at least in part, to domestic developments and in particular to the aggressive wage policy. This view is supported by the consideration that unemployment in Italy in this period grew a bit faster than for the OECD as a whole and within the EEC was surpassed only by countries with similar problems, such as Belgium and the UK. But the further deterioration since 1979, despite the restraint in real wages, appears to reflect the dramatic slow-down in world demand. This interpretation is consistent with the observation that, in the last period, the growth of unemployment for Italy was *less* than for the EEC, and in fact was smaller than that of every country except France.

Some possible solutions

The considerations developed in the previous subsection suggest one possible remedy to Italy's unemployment problems—as well as everybody else's!—namely, a coordinated, substantial reflation of world demand, designed to reabsorb rapidly the high unemployment prevailing in all the EEC and most other countries. Yet, this remedy needs to be probed further.

Suppose, for the moment, that there were to occur—by agreement or by act of God—a rapid recovery of world demand, say by 10 per cent, followed by a return to the earlier trend. How much would that really help Italy? Surprisingly, the answer suggested by our model is, 'rather little', at least with existing institutions. To support this conclusion, let us consider first by how much such an expansion could be expected to lower u, keeping the trade balance constant. The increase in world demand, Y^*, would raise exports, which would permit raising aggregate demand to the point where imports rose as much as exports—and the rise in demand would finally raise the employment rate. As usual, the multiplier $d \log N / d \log Y^*$ depends on the length of time allowed for the response. It turns out that, because of slow responses, notably of exports to Y^* and employment to output, and a very fast response of imports through the accelerator mechanism, the impact response on u could be expected to be quite small—around $\frac{1}{2}$ percentage point.

With the passage of time, the effect would tend to rise, except for the fact that the decline of unemployment would tend to produce a rise in real wages. As noted earlier, this reduces the scope for an expansion of employment in two ways: (1) through factor substitution, and (2) by reducing net exports, other things equal. After a span of four or five years, the elasticity appears to settle down to around $\frac{1}{6}$, implying an effect on u of only $1\frac{2}{3}$ percentage points for a 10 per cent rise in Y^*! This reduction represents but one-fifth of estimated current non-frictional unemployment and is not even sufficient to undo the recent deterioration. In addition, the above calculation neglects the large initial deficit in the trade balance.

Thus, to solve the Italian employment and balance of payments problem, the expansion of world demand would have to be not 10 per cent but more nearly 50 per cent. But a growth of world demand within realistic limits could not offer a solution without an accompanying cut in real wages, though an expansion of Y^* would make it possible to contain such cuts below those indicated in Table 6. Simulations carried out for the period 1980–83, raising Y^* but maintaining the full employment and balance of trade constraint of Table 6, indicate that, with a 25 per cent per year adjustment, a 1 per cent increase in Y^* reduces the needed real-wage reduction by 0·6 per cent. Thus, even with, say, a 15 per cent rise in Y^*, there would still be a need for a real-wage reduction close to 25 per cent.

Some less gloomy alternatives

But after all this bad news, we would like to finish on a more hopeful tone by noting that our analysis points to the feasibility of less gruesome solutions relying simultaneously on demand *and* supply policies, combined with some changes in the institutional structure reflected in the parameters of our model.

To get an understanding of the nature of these policies and what they might achieve under favourable circumstances, consider the following scenario. (1) Labour agrees to hold the rise in real wages to the rate of productivity increase. (2) The many institutions that limit labour mobility, causing the extraordinary slow speed of adjustment in the labour market, are abolished, resulting in a more prompt adjustment of employment to variations in demand; and the lags in the demand for exports and imports are also somehow eliminated. It should be clear that under these conditions a 1 per cent rise in Y^* would increase exports by 1 per cent, which would permit demand to rise by 1 per cent, keeping net exports constant, which would result in a 1 per cent rise in employment and finally a corresponding fall in unemployment—and all this within a year!

In this case, a 10 per cent rise in Y^* might well prove nearly adequate to solve the Italian problem, since, as of 1983, non-frictional unemployment was just below 10 per cent and the current account was actually in surplus.

To be sure, this optimistic scenario could never be realized in practice—there is, for instance, no way to achieve instantaneous response in foreign markets, let alone in the management of aggregate demand, and employment could hardly adjust immediately. But this only means that the elimination of unemployment would require some time—something that would be desirable in any case for other reasons, such as avoiding overheating the economy by too rapid an expansion, especially since capacity has fallen behind in recent years.

It is none the less clear that the purely domestic aspects of the package—holding the line on real wages (in efficiency units) and dismantling legislation and practices limiting labour mobility—all of which are, in principle, feasible through agreements and legislation, would go a long way towards a rational solution of the current problems.

VI. Concluding Remarks

Through our survey of institutional development of the Italian labour market and our summary model, we have endeavoured to establish that the growth of unemployment beginning in the mid-1970s can be traced to an aggressive wage policy, pushing for a real-wage growth faster than underlying productivity growth (or for a rising share of output), inconsistent with full employment and balance of payments equilibrium. The inconsistency arises because real wages affect unemployment through two channels: via factor substitution, and via the level of demand compatible with sustainable net exports.

In the last three years, however, the problem has magnified because of stagnation in world demand. Accordingly, a solution to Italy's twin problems—high unemployment and external deficits—would require both a vigorous recovery in world demand and a set of internal measures including wage restraint and improved labour mobility. These measures in combination could, in our view, make a substantial rapid dent in a devastating economic and social problem.

ACKNOWLEDGMENTS

We would like to thank all the participants at the Conference, and in particular J. Muellbauer, for their helpful comments on a previous draft. Further stimulating comments were provided by the participants to the SADIBA Conference held in Perugia in March 1986. Skilful research assistance from G. De Santis, L. Felli, G. Leone and A. Mimmi, and financial support to F. Padoa Schioppa from the Italian National Research Council (grant no. 83.02388.53) are also gratefully acknowledged.

NOTES

1. Adjustment considers only the industrial sector excluding construction.
2. We use here an extremely rough estimate for the direct tax rate, i.e., the ratio of total direct taxes to total disposable income for the aggregate of taxpayers.
3. Actually, this is not strictly true, since the behaviour of the consumer price index depends also on the import prices of consumer goods.
4. We refer here to the survey undertaken since 1976 by the Confederation of Metal Industries (Federmeccanica). The survey covers approximately 3500 firms of different dimension, location, etc.
5. See Faustini (1976) Spaventa (1976, 1977); Filosa and Visco (1977a, 1977b); Baffi (1984); Guiso (1985).
6. The technology is not assumed to be separable so as to imply a value added aggregate. Such assumption seems to be rejected in the Italian context (see Heimler and Milana, 1984 p. 67).
7. A partial notable exception is McDonald and Solow (1981).
8. The form of equation (10) depends on $\sigma < 1$ (which is the Italian case). The wage outcome would be different if σ were bigger or equal to unity: on this point see Michel and Padoa Schioppa (1981).
9. Equation (19) indicates why, in the optimal long-run solution, if $\sigma < 1$, it makes no difference to set labour demand (14) as a function of the real labour cost per unit of efficiency or as a function of the real unit labour cost.
10. Evidence on the validity of restrictions applying to this and other equations, as well as on the role played by the Italian escalator clauses, is provided in a separate Appendix available on request from the authors.
11. We approximate u as follows: $u = l - n - (N^P/N)$.
12. Furthermore, it should be noted that all simulation results reported in the present section rely on the (dubious) assumption of invariant union behaviour (cf. equation 20).

REFERENCES

BAFFI, P. (1984). Sulla possibile definizione contrattuale di una fascia di flessibilità del salario reale. *Politica ed Economia*, **15**, 49-56.

BARBONE, L., BODO, G. and VISCO, I. (1981). Costi e profitti nell'industria in senso stretto: un'analisi su serie trimestrali, 1970-1980, Banca d'Italia. *Bollettino*, **36**, 465-510.

BODO, G. (1981). *Wage inflation in Italy.* Unpublished paper (mimeo).

DORNBUSCH, R., BASEVI, G., BLANCHARD, O., BUITER, W. and LAYARD, R. (1983). Macroeconomic prospects and policies for the European Community. *Economic Papers*, no. 12. Brussels: Commission of the European Communities, Directorate-General for Economic and Financial Affairs.

DRÈZE, J. H. and MODIGLIANI, F. (1981). The trade-off between real wages and employment in an open economy (Belgium). *European Economic Review*, **15**, 1-40.

FAUSTINI, G. (1976). Wage indexing and inflation in Italy, *Banca Nazionale del Lavoro, Quarterly Review*, **199**, 3-16.

FILOSA, R. and VISCO I. (1977a). L'unificazione del punto di contingenza e il grado di indicizzazione delle retribuzioni. *Moneta e Credito*, **117**, 55-83.

—— (1977b). Copertura delle retribuzioni e inflazione a tasso variabile. *Moneta e Credito*, 119, 327-37.

GRUBB, D., JACKMAN, R. and LAYARD, R. (1983). Wage rigidity and unemployment in OECD countries. *European Economic Review*, **21**, 11-39.

GUISO, L. (1985). Il dibattito sull'inflazione italiana negli ultimi quindici anni. *Contributi all'Analisi Economica.* Rome: Banca d'Italia.

HEIMLER, A. and MILANA, C. (1984). *Prezzi relativi, ristrutturazione e produttività.* Bologna: Il Mulino.

JOHNSON, G. E. and LAYARD, R. (1986). The natural rate of unemployment: explanation and policy. In O. Ashenfelter and R. Layard (eds), *Handbook in Labor Economics.* Amsterdam: North Holland.

LILIEN, D. (1982). Sectoral shifts and cyclical unemployment. *Journal of Political Economy*, **90**, 777-93.

MALCOMSON, J. and SARTOR, N. (1984). Tax push inflation in a unionized labour market. Working Paper no. 8406, Université Catholique de Louvain.

MCDONALD, I. M. and SOLOW, R. M. (1981). Wage bargaining and employment. *American Economic Review*, **71**, 896-908.

MICHEL, P. and PADOA SCHIOPPA, F. (1981). Union wage setting and factor substitution. Unpublished paper. Louvain-La-Neuve: CORE.

MODIGLIANI, F. (1958). New developments on the oligopoly front. *Journal of Political Economy*, **66**, 215-32.

—— and PADOA SCHIOPPA, T. (1978). The management of an open economy with 100% plus wage indexation. *Essays in International Finance*, no. 130, Princeton: Princeton University Press.

—— and TARANTELLI, E. (1973). A generalization of the Phillips curve for a developing country. *Review of Economic Studies*, **40**, 203-23.

—— (1977). Market forces, trade unions action and the Phillips Curve in Italy. *Banca Nazionale del Lavoro, Quarterly Review*, **120**, 3-36.

PUDNEY, S. E. (1981). Instrumental variable estimation of a characteristics model of demand. *Review of Economic Studies*, **58**, 417-33.

SPAVENTA, L. (1976). Salario protetto dal meccanismo di scala mobile a 'punto pieno', *Moneta e Credito*, **116**, 387-402.

—— (1977). Ancora sul grado di copertura del salario: un'estensione dell'analisi. *Moneta e Credito*, **116**, 217-27.

SPINELLI, F. (1980). The wage-push hypothesis: the Italian case. *Journal of Monetary Economics*, **6**, 493-507.

VISCO, I. (1984). *Inflation Expectations: The Use of Italian Survey Data in the Analysis of their Formation and Effects on Wage Changes*, Workshop on Price Dynamics and Economic Policy. Paris: OECD.

Trends in Unemployment, Wages and Productivity: The Case of Japan

Koichi Hamada and Yoshio Kurosaka

University of Tokyo and Musashi University

Introduction

Along with the high savings ratio, the functioning of the labour market is one of the most important factors behind the macroeconomic performance of the postwar Japan, which foreign observers have christened the 'miracle of the Rising Sun'.

In the first place, the nature of the Japanese labour market is important for the long-run trend of Japanese economic growth because labour, and its quality, are crucial factors for economic development. The high quality of a well disciplined workforce, as well as the migration of labour from rural to urban areas, has contributed much to the rapid growth of the Japanese economy.

Second, the nature of the labour market has influenced the pattern of Japanese business cycles by buffering demand fluctuations. The slow response of firms' demand for labour, combined with the fast response of the labour force participation ratio, has prevented a sharp increase in the unemployment rate during recessions. Relatively flexible nominal and real wages have also enabled the Japanese economy to adjust quite smoothly to supply shocks, notably after the second oil crisis.

In this paper we shall review trends in unemployment, wages and productivity in the postwar Japanese economy, and relate them to its macroeconomic performance. We shall also summarize the current literature concerning features of the labour market, evaluate quantitative estimates of trends in labour statistics, and explore future prospects.

I. The Japanese Labour Market

First, we should mention some basic figures and stylized facts concerning the Japanese labour market. Let us start from the supply side, that is, with population and the labour force.

1. The Japanese on average are now among the longest-living people. In 1983 the life expectancy at birth of males was 74·2 years, and that of females, 79·7. Although the present composition of the Japanese population is relatively young, this is changing rapidly. The proportion of the population over 65 years of age was only 9·7 per cent in 1983, but will exceed 14 per cent by the year 2000, and is expected to peak at 18·8 per cent in 2020. Japan will then have the highest proportion of its population over 65. (Incidentally, this will create a serious social security crisis in the future.)

TABLE 1

LABOUR PARTICIPATION RATIO, BY AGE GROUP, 1970–1983
(percentages)

	15-19	20-24	25-29	30-34	35-39	40-44	45-49	50-54	55-59	60-64	65-	All ages
Total												
1970	32·5	75·6	71·2	72·9	77·7	80·1	78·6	75·6	68·6	59·2	31·8	65·4
1980	17·9	69·8	72·7	73·0	77·9	80·8	80·5	77·4	68·9	55·9	26·3	63·3
1983	18·9	71·5	74·8	74·1	79·1	82·5	81·9	78·2	70·5	54·6	25·6	83·8
Male												
1970	31·4	80·7	97·1	97·8	97·8	97·5	97·0	95·8	91·2	81·5	49·4	81·8
1980	17·4	69·6	96·3	97·6	97·6	97·6	96·5	96·0	91·2	77·8	41·0	79·8
1983	19·1	71·0	96·5	97·5	97·9	97·5	97·1	95·8	91·3	74·9	38·9	79·4
Female												
1970	33·6	70·6	45·5	48·2	57·5	62·8	63·6	58·8	48·7	39·1	17·9	49·9
1980	18·5	70·0	49·2	48·2	58·0	64·1	64·1	59·3	50·5	38·8	15·5	47·6
1983	18·7	72·1	52·8	50·4	60·3	67·6	66·9	60·6	51·5	39·6	16·1	49·0

Source: Management and Coordination Agency, *Survey of Labour Force.*

2. The labour force participation ratio (see Table 1 and Figure 1) decreased between 1955 and 1975, but has remained stable, or risen slightly, since 1975. Cyclical movements in male and female participation ratios, which occasionally move in different directions, account for the flat or slightly upward pattern of the total figure.

In order to check the cyclical pattern of the participation ratio, we estimate the cyclical response of the total ratio as follows:

$$(1) \qquad R = 77 \cdot 803 - 1 \cdot 0468\,U - 1 \cdot 0436\,T + 0 \cdot 0218\,T^2$$
$$\qquad\qquad\quad (-2 \cdot 42) \quad (-6 \cdot 78) \qquad (4 \cdot 99)$$

$$\bar{R}^2 = 0 \cdot 86 \qquad \text{s.e.} = 0 \cdot 3818 \qquad \hat{\rho} = 0 \cdot 62$$

The estimation period is 1953–83 (annual data), and t-values are in parentheses. Here, R is the total labour participation ratio, U the unemployment rate and T a time trend. Thus, the participation ratio moves procyclically, showing a discouraged worker effect over business cycles.

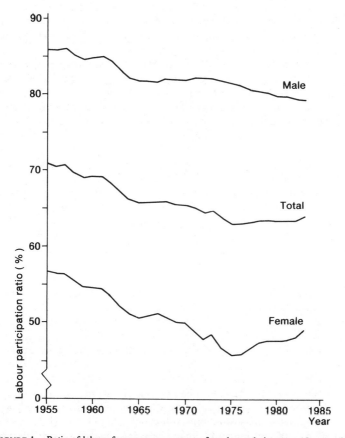

FIGURE 1.   Ratio of labour force as a percentage of total population over 15 years old.
Source: Management and Coordination Agency, *Survey of Labour Force.*

From our international perspective, a distinct feature of the Japanese labour market is that the labour force participation ratio of young people is much lower than in most countries (Sasajima, 1984). On the other hand, the participation ratio for people over 55 is higher, and for those who are above 60 much higher, then the corresponding figures in other countries. This feature reflects partly the Japanese educational system, and partly the social attitude towards work. Young people are under strong pressure to stay on at school and to study for a university degree or further education certificate. Older people often do not feel sufficiently supported by their pensions, and also prefer to stay in social contact through employment, although most of those who are hired 'for life' by large modern firms are transferred, to the firms' subsidiaries or to related small and medium-size firms when they reach the age of 55–60.

3. The unemployment rate in Japan is low compared with other industrial countries. The first three columns of Table 2 indicate annual unemployment rates, which hardly need to be smoothed by taking moving averages. Japanese unemployment rates moved from 1·1 to 2·7 per cent during the postwar years, and show a slight upward trend in recent years.[1] Since these low unemployment figures are probably the most remarkable feature of the Japanese labour market, the reasons for this phenomenon will be discussed in further detail in the next section.

We should point out here, however, that low unemployment is a distinct feature of the Japanese economy only after the 1970s—during the 1960s unemployment rates in most industrial countries, for example West Germany, were also quite low. Also, we should note that unemployment rates have a long-run upward trend in the past 15 years. Table 3 shows the rates of unemployment by age and sex. The unemployment rate is high for both the young and the aged; the relative contribution of youth unemployment is small because the labour participation ratio for youth is low, though the social cost of youth unemployment is not necessarily negligible (Tachibanaki, 1984). In spite of the low overall unemployment rates, the burden of unemployment is distributed unevenly across different age–sex groups.

4. Working hours of Japanese workers are quite long by international standards. Table 4 gives an international comparison of working hours. The number of hours worked per week in Japan are much longer than those in other countries but only since the middle of the 1970s. While working hours declined quite sharply in most countries after the first oil crisis, they went up in Japan during the five years between 1975 and 1980.[2] Only one-quarter of Japanese workers enjoy less than a five-day week and another quarter work a six-day week. The remainder work between five and six days a week (Sasajima, 1984). Banks are closed, for example, the second Saturday of each month. Moreover, workers take only a part (about 50–60 per cent) of their paid holidays.

One cannot attribute this phenomenon simply to a weakness in union bargaining power. It is due, at least in part, to living conditions, where the population density in terms of habitable land is extremely high. The high cost of housing and limited space for recreational activities make some workers prefer increased income to increased leisure. Koshiro

TABLE 2

RATE OF UNEMPLOYMENT AND JOB-OFFERED-JOB-WANTED RATIO, 1953–1984

	Unemployment rate (%)			
	Overall	Male	Female	JOJW ratio
1953	1·9	1·9	1·9	—
1954	2·3	2·4	2·1	—
1955	2·5	2·6	2·3	—
1956	2·3	2·3	2·3	—
1957	1·9	1·8	2·0	—
1958	2·1	2·2	1·9	—
1959	2·2	2·3	2·0	—
1960	1·7	1·6	1·7	—
1961	1·4	1·4	1·6	—
1962	1·3	1·2	1·5	—
1963	1·3	1·2	1·3	0·70
1964	1·1	1·1	1·3	0·79
1965	1·2	1·1	1·3	0·64
1966	1·3	1·3	1·4	0·73
1967	1·3	1·2	1·4	2·00
1968	1·2	1·2	1·1	1·12
1969	1·1	1·2	1·1	1·30
1970	1·1	1·2	1·0	1·41
1971	1·2	1·3	1·1	1·12
1972	1·4	1·5	1·3	1·16
1973	1·3	1·3	1·2	1·76
1974	1·4	1·4	1·3	1·20
1975	1·9	2·0	1·7	0·61
1976	2·0	2·2	1·7	0·64
1977	2·0	2·1	1·8	0·56
1978	2·2	2·4	2·0	0·71
1979	2·1	2·2	2·0	0·75
1979	2·1	2·2	2·0	0·75
1980	2·0	2·0	2·0	0·75
1981	2·2	2·3	2·1	0·68
1982	2·4	2·4	2·3	0·61
1983	2·6	2·7	2·6	0·60
1984	2·7	—	—	0·65

Sources; Management and Coordination Agency, *Survey of Labour Force*; Ministry of Labour, *Monthly Bulletin of Occupational Stability.*

(1983) and Koga *et al.* (1974) report that the marginal rate of substitution between income and leisure of Japensese workers indicates a stronger— and probably forced—preference for income than US workers have.

In addition, days lost through disputes are declining rapidly (see Data Appendix at end of volume). Per worker, less than one-hundreth of a day was lost through disputes in 1984. Thus, one of the reasons for good Japanese economic performance seems to be the eagerness, albeit sometimes enforced, of Japanese workers to work for long hours and their disinclination to strike.

TABLE 3

RATE OF UNEMPLOYMENT, BY AGE GROUP, 1976–1983
(percentages)

	Age group								Overall rate
	15–19	20–24	25–29	30–34	35–39	40–54	55–64	65–	
Total									
1976	3·9	2·9	2·3	1·5	1·3	1·4	2·6	1·6	2·0
1980	4·0	3·2	2·5	1·9	1·3	1·3	2·9	1·4	2·0
1983	6·1	4·0	3·0	2·5	2·1	1·8	3·7	1·6	2·6
Male									
1976	5·1	3·0	2·3	1·6	1·4	1·6	3·7	2·3	2·2
1980	5·4	3·5	2·0	1·7	1·3	1·3	3·9	2·1	2·0
1983	7·1	3·8	2·5	2·1	1·9	1·8	5·0	2·6	2·7
Female									
1976	2·7	2·7	2·8	2·0	1·2	1·1	0·9	0·0	1·7
1980	2·7	3·2	3·5	2·3	1·8	1·3	1·1	0·0	2·0
1983	5·1	4·2	3·8	3·0	2·4	1·8	1·7	0·9	2·6

TABLE 4

INTERNATIONAL COMPARISON OF WORKING HOURS PER WEEK,
MANUFACTURING INDUSTRIES, 1955–1983

	Japan	USA	UK	W. Germany	France
1955	45·7	40·7	48·7	48·8	44·9
1960	47·8	39·7	47·4	45·6	45·7
1965	44·3	41·2	46·1	44·1	45·6
1970	43·3	39·8	44·9	43·8	44·8
1975	41·2	37·4	39·8	36·2	40·1
1980	43·5	37·3	39·6	37·2	39·1
1983	43·4	37·5	40·4	36·1	37·4

Sources: Japan; Ministry of Labour, Monthly Bulletin of Labour Statistics; other countries: ILO Yearbook of Labour Statistics, UN Monthly Bulletin of Statistics, OECD Main Economic Indicators

5. Table 5 shows that the share of labour normally declines in the upward phase of business cycles, while it rises in the downward phase. The manufacturing sector data, in the second and third columns of the table, tell us that labour productivity declines relative to real wages in recessions, which implies an anti-cyclical movement of real wages, in efficiency terms, over business cycles. However, this regular pattern was disturbed during 1971–75. The share of labour kept increasing despite the boom; real wages increased more rapidly than labour productivity.

Thus, wages in Japan are often said to be flexible, reflecting demand and supply conditions in the labour market, and to accommodate productivity changes or external shocks, such as the terms-of-trade deterioration in the case of oil crises (e.g. Gordon, 1982). A simple comparison of variability in the rate of increase in wages (see Table 6)

TABLE 5

THE SHARE OF LABOUR, ANNUAL RATES OF INCREASE IN REAL WAGES AND LABOUR PRODUCTIVITY OVER BUSINESS CYCLES, 1952–1983

	Share of labour	Growth of:		
		Real wages (mfg)	Productivity (mfg)	Productivity (whole economy)
1952	0·79	10·4	—	—
1953	0·80	6·8	—	—
1954	0·77	−0·1	—	4·2
1955	0·79	3·6	—	4·5
1956	0·78	9·5	13·8	2·2
1957	0·73	1·9	7·3	5·6
1958	0·75	0	0	6·0
1959	0·74	7·4	12·2	6·5
1060	0·69	5·2	12·9	9·9
1961	0·69	4·2	10·7	14·9
1962	0·71	3·2	3·5	8·3
1063	0·72	3·2	10·0	10·5
1964	0·71	5·7	12·2	12·4
1965	0·73	2·5	3·5	5·5
1965	0·77	2·5	3·5	6·1
1966	0·74	7·1	12·9	7·9
1967	0·72	8·5	16·2	8·5
1968	0·71	10·3	13·6	11·5
1969	0·70	12·0	13·7	13·2
1970	0·68	8·0	10·4	10·3
1971	0·72	7·3	4·6	5·8
1972	0·72	11·1	11·0	9·7
1973	0·74	12·5	17·1	6·3
1974	0·78	1·5	−0·3	4·7
1975	0·79	0	−3·8	5·2
1976	0·79	2·8	12·0	1·0
1977	0·79	1·3	5·0	3·5
1978	0·77	3·1	7·9	3·2
1979	0·77	2·5	11·8	2·7
1980	0·75	−0·6	8·9	4·0
1981	0·75	1·3	3·5	3·7
1982	0·75	1·2	1·6	2·8
1983	0·76	1·6	4·5	1·1

Note: Reference dates for the cycle: peaks occurred at January 1954, June 1957, December 1961, October 1964, July 1970, November 1973, January 1977, February 1980. Troughs occurred at November 1954, June 1958, October 1962, October 1965, December 1971, March 1975, October 1977 and February 1983.

Sources: Economic Planning Agency, National Income Statistics, Indicators of Japanese Economy; Ministry of Labour, Monthly Bulletin of Labour Statistics; Japan Productivity Centre, Index of Labour Productivity in the Manufacturing Sector per Man-day.

TABLE 6

INTERNATIONAL COMPARISON OF WAGE FLEXIBILITY, MANUFACTURING
INDUSTRIES

Nominal Wages

	Year	Average (%)	Stand. dev.	Coefficient of variation
Japan	1951–83	11·1	6·7	0·60
	1951–73	11·8	5·8	0·49
	1974–83	9·3	8·0	0·86
USA	1951–83	5·7	2·3	0·40
UK	1951–83	9·9	5·2	0·52
W. Germany	1951–83	7·8	3·0	0·38
France	1953–82	10·9	4·1	0·37
Italy	1951–74	9·3	6·8	0·73

Real Wages

	Year	Average (%)	Stand. dev.	Coefficient of variation
Japan	1951–83	5·1	4·6	0·90
	1951–73	6·7	4·3	0·64
	1974–83	1·3	1·9	1·46
USA	1951–83	1·2	2·1	1·75
UK	1051–83	2·4	2·9	1·20
W. Germany	1951–83	4·3	2·5	0·58
France	1953–82	4·7	2·6	0·55
Italy	1951–74	4·4	4·1	0·93

Source: as for Table 4.

seems to indicate that the Japanese economy possessed both nominal
and real-wage flexibility in terms of these two measures of variation.
This tendency was strengthened particularly after 1974.

If we follow historical developments, however, the story is not so
simple. After the first oil crisis, Japanese nominal wages and labour's
share both increased to a great extent. This is, in a sense, due to a
coincidental misfortune of the Japanese economy. At the time of the
Shunto (the spring labour offensive), the Japanese did not realize that
the terms-of-trade deterioration arising from the oil crisis would be so
permanent, and that it would mean such serious damage to real purchas-
ing power for years to come. Firms were making enormous profits, and
the labour market was in a state of excess demand. The job-offered–job-
wanted ratio was close to 1·8—resulting from expansionary fiscal
(associated with Prime Minister Tanaka's 'archipelago plan' for
remodelling Japan) and monetary policy (to prevent the appreciation
of the yen). Management responded to increased union demands by
raising standard nominal wages in the Shunto by 32·9 per cent in 1974,
and this triggered the stagflation which then required a long, painful

process of employment adjustment. As Table 5 indicates, the share of labour declined throughout the adjustment process.

By the time the second oil crisis hit the Japanese economy in 1979, Japanese workers had learnt the lesson that aggresive wage demands would create quite serious unemployment problems. They chose a modest wage policy, though one could say that they had lost the political energy necessary to raise the share of wage income in total value added. Although in 1985 the high profits attained by firms encouraged workers to demand slightly higher wage hikes than in preceding years, a conformist attitude by labour unions continues to predominate in labour negotiations. This attitude is often cited as 'incomes policy—the Japanese version'.

6. Labour and its quality are important factors in promoting economic growth. Kosai and Toshida (1981) conducted a factor decomposition analysis, originated by Solow (1957), of economic growth with respect to every five-year period (1955-79). They report that the component of growth attributable to labour is between -0.2 and 2 per cent. This calculation shows that the growth rate of labour productivity is in the range of 4.0-10.1 per cent, and that it dropped sharply after 1970. In contrast to the analysis of Solow (1957) for US data, however, they attribute growth more to the rise in the capital-labour ratio than to technical progress.

Subdividing these levels, we see from Table 5 that the trend of labour productivity dropped sharply after 1974, and that cyclical responses became weaker. Incidentally, the rather high responsiveness of labour productivity over business cycles throughout the whole period partly explains the larger value of Okun's coefficient in the Japnese economy (Hamada and Kurosaka, 1984). During the process of continued rapid economic growth, firms were probably induced to hold workers, despite temporary demand reductions, because they expected a quick recovery; that is, the expected rate of return on hoarding workers exceeded its cost. After the first oil crisis, the relative cost benefit structure apparently changed, reflecting the less optimistic outlook for future growth.

II. Why Are Japanese Unemployment Rates So Low?

In this section we shall discuss further the low rate of unemployment that has attracted the attention of economists outside Japan. First, there are statistical problems concerning international comparisons of the unemployment rate, the definition of which differs across countries. Since comparison involves many intricate problems, we can give here only a rough summary of the issues. (For a full systematic account see Taira, 1983, and Sorrentino, 1984.)

Among many differences in definitions and survey methods, the following points deserve special attention:

1. The armed forces are included in the labour force in Japan, while in the United States they were excluded from the labour force until the end of 1982.

2. Unpaid family workers who work less than 15 hours are included in the labour force in Japan, while they are excluded from the labour force in the United States.
3. Those who are waiting to start jobs within 30 days are counted as unemployed in the United States, while they are not in the labour force in Japan.
4. Those who are laid off and waiting to be recalled are counted as unemployed in the United States, while those who suspend their work temporarily are counted as employed in Japan.
5. In the United States people who actively searched for jobs during the previous *four weeks* are classified as unemployed, while in Japan only those who search for jobs during the reference week (the last week of the month) are counted as unemployed.

The last component may have a substantial impact on the magnitude of unemployment. Shiraishi (1982) estimated the Japanese unemployment rate on a US basis, using the 'Special Survey of the Labour Force' which gives more structural information than the regular monthly survey on which the official unemployment rate is based. However, he found an unemployment rate for 1980 that is only 0·2 per cent larger than the officially published rate.

Taira (1983) and Yashiro (1982) question the validity of the requirement, imposed by Shiraishi, that only workers who can start work immediately may be counted as unemployed. Both authors claim that this requirement excludes discouraged female workers and students from being classified as unemployed. They also include in the category of unemployed those workers who are awaiting the results of job search activities made more than five weeks earlier. According to Taira's calculation, the unemployment rate for male workers is increased by 0·5-0·8 per cent during 1977-80, and the unemployment rate for female workers doubles or triples, depending on the year. Similar figures are obtained by Yashiro for 1980.

Sorrentino (1984), of the US Bureau of Labor Statistics (BLS), argues that Taira's estimates are overstated. March, when the 'Special Survey' is conducted, is a special month in Japan when graduates from high schools and colleges are waiting to begin new jobs in April. (See Nagayama, 1984, who also makes this point.) Sorrentino also argues that those persons who are employed, but not at work, should be counted as employed, whereas Taira considered them as 'temporarily laid off' and included them in the unemployment estimates. The reason is that, because of the difference in labour customs, those who have jobs but are not at work still receive their wages and do not seek other jobs. They are certainly a symptom of labour underutilization, but they are still formally employed. Excluding new graduates from the labour force, and counting the above types of 'layoff' as employed, Sorrentino obtains figures similar to those estimated by Shiraishi (1982).

The first three columns of Table 7 show the published data and different estimates by Taira and Sorrentino. Sorrentino's argument is quite convincing, though the differences reflect not only measurement problems but also a philosophical difference in judging unemployment (cf. Taira, 1984). It is worth noting, however, that her method also gives a large upward adjustment of the unemployment rate for female workers. It is thus true, as Taira (1983) empha-

TABLE 7

ADJUSTED JAPANESE UNEMPLOYMENT RATES, 1977–1980

	Total			Men		Women	
	Official rates	Taira method	BLS[a] method	Official rates	BLS[a] method	Official rates	BLS[a] method
1977	2·4	4·2	2·8	2·4	2·0	2·3	4·3
1978	2·6	4·7	3·0	2·7	2·2	2·4	4·3
1979	2·5	4·5	2·7	2·5	1·9	2·4	4·1
1980	2·2	3·8	2·3	2·2	1·7	2·3	3·3

[a] US Bureau of Labor Statistics.
Source: Sorrentino (1984, pp. 19 and 25).

sizes, that the main burden of employment adjustment is on the female population. The reason why male unemployment is reduced in Sorrentino's estimate is that she excluded from the unemployed those who were not actively searching for jobs in the previous four weeks.

In another study, Ito (1984) made an attempt to adjust US unemployment figures to the Japanese standard, on the alleged ground that US data contain more structural information. The differences in layoff practice, and in the buffer functions of the agricultural and self-employed sectors, account for a significant part of the divergence of unemployment rates. In particular, the low incidence of teenage unemployment in Japan explains between 20 and 25 per cent of the difference.

This discussion leads us to the second topic of this section, namely, the reasons for Japan's low unemployment rates. In addition to the shock-absorbing function of the agricultural and self-employed sectors, and the low rate of teenage unemployment, we note the following factors.

1. One factor arises on the demand side. Because of the permanent employment system, modern and large firms seldom fire or lay off regular employees under 55 years of age, unless the firm is in serious trouble. The employment of workers in declining industries was partially supported by government subsidies, mainly during 1975–79.[3] Workers are flexibly transferred to other jobs within the firm, or to other firms, such as the main firm's subsidiaries. Thus, the sluggishness of employment adjustment explains part of the low rate of unemployment.

2. On the other hand, working hours are quite flexible, especially since the 1970s. (It has been suggested that flexible working hours may account for one-half of Okun's coefficient in recent periods—Hamada and Kurosaka, 1984.) Recently, Higuchi and Seike (1985) have shown that during the recession of 1974–75, following the first oil crisis, employment in the United States declined *pari passu* with GNP but without much movement in working hours, while in Japan both working hours and employment declined, albeit not so drastically.

3. On the supply side, the labour force participation ratio changes in such a way that the labour force moves in the same direction as employment. There is a peripheral group of workers who are encouraged by recessions to exit

from the labour force. Female workers, in particular, used to retire from the labour force in periods of recession. Between 1973 and 1974, the number of female workers in Japan declined by about half a million, while those unemployed increased by only 20,000. Using the flow data on employment status from the 'Labour Force Survey', Higuchi and Seike (1985) successfully traced changes in the attitude of female workers. In 1975, 75 per cent of male and 96 per cent of female workers who left jobs left the labour force. In 1982 the corresponding figures were 68 and 90 per cent. Thus the discouraged worker effect seems to be declining. The negative correlation of the labour supply of married women to the income of the main wage-earner of the household is clearly observed (Douglas, 1934; Arisawa, 1956). This is the mechanism underlying the shift of labour participation ratios and the recent slight upward trend of the unemployment rate.

4. The unemployment insurance system was amended in 1975 in such a way that not only the duration of previous employment but also the age of a recipient now affects the length of the period for which he can receive benefits. Shimada *et al.* (1981) show that the duration of unemployment is influenced by the provision of the unemployment insurance system and the changes in requirements for recipients in 1975. Therefore, the relatively more strict conditions for eligibility for insurance payments might be one of the factors behind Japan's low unemployment rate.

III. INSTITUTIONAL CHARACTERISTICS OF THE JAPANESE LABOUR MARKET

The OECD Report (1972) on manpower policy in Japan mentioned three pillars or 'sacred treasures' of the Japanese labour market: lifetime employment, a seniority (*nenko*) wage system, and enterprise unions. A book edited by Shirai (1983) includes many chapters with rich explanatory descriptions of these characteristics. Here we shall take up some of the issues that may help in understanding unemployment statistics as well as wage behaviour.

At one extreme, there is a simplistic view which exaggerates the distinct feature of the Japanese labour market and corporate system. In his pioneering analysis of Japanese factories, Abegglen (1958) suggested that the Japanese practice of lifetime employment and a seniority wage system arose from the Japanese cultural heritage. 'As the result of the differences between Japan and the West in pre-industrial and social organization, the present organization of the factory would differ in systematic ways in the two types of societies.' (p. 8). In spite of Abegglen's careful analysis and considered statements, this thesis was popularized and oversimplified by subsequent authors, as follows. The cultural tradition of families and villages has made it possible for company employees to behave just like family members of a firm. They are paid wages not according to their short-run efficiency, but according to their hierarchical order in the corporation. Enterprise unions are naturally cooperative to the mnagement. Thus, wage increases are moderate and losses of working time arising from strikes are small.

Later, many economists (e.g. Dore, 1973; Koike, 1977) made the following counter-argument to this culturalistic view. First, the customs of lifetime employment and the seniority wage system apply to only part of the Japanese workforce, that is, to those who are regularly employed in large firms in modernized sectors. They do not apply to employees who work for small and medium-size companies, or to temporary workers in large companies. Moreover, most employees in large companies, except for those who are promoted to executive level, are secure in their employment only until the mandatory retirement age of between 55 and 60. The high labour participation ratio in the older age groups, and accordingly the high rate of employment for those who are above 55, are a result of their secondary employment in small and medium-size enterprises, or in subsidiaries or related firms of large companies. In sum, the coverage of lifetime employment and the seniority wage system is not as extensive as is commonly believed.

Second, as Dore finds, and as Koike develops in his extensive writings (e.g. Koike, 1977, 1983, 1984), the wage profile throughout a white-collar worker's career is not so different from the correspondng patterns in the United States or Europe. The steepness of profiles is a matter of degree rather than of qualitative difference among countries. Koike emphasizes the fact that in the United States 'seniority' plays the crucial role in the case of layoffs. Instead of being laid off, Japanese blue-collar workers are assigned different kinds of jobs within the firm, thereby accumulating firm-specific skills. Koike calls this 'the white-collarization' of blue-collar workers.

Third, neither of these customs developed until the interwar period. Moreover, even among large firms, they became prevalent only after the postwar period. Odaka (1984) carefully traces the path through which the shortage of skilled workers in the interwar period made it necessary for firms to adopt the lifetime employment system and a wage scale according to seniority. Thus, lifetime employment and the seniority wage system can be explained by human capital theory as well.

During the interwar period, when skilled workers became scarce, there was an incentive for firms to develop firm-specific skills among their employees in order to retain them. Employees can be encouraged to stay with the same firm by pay scales that rise with the duration of employment and that differ from the instantaneous marginal productivity of labour (Kuratani, 1973; Hashimoto, 1979). The adoption of the seniority wage system was reinforced during the Second World War when wage controls, built on seniority-based wage scales, were enforced nationwide.

These arguments seem quite reasonable. We believe, however, that one cannot completely neglect cultural and social factors. Economic rationality alone does not explain the rather paternalistic employment patterns of Japanese firms. Singing a company song every morning, driving exclusively the car of one's own firm, drinking beer of the brand produced by a member of a firm group and having the company president or executives play a ceremonial role as go-between in weddings, for example, do not arise simply as the rational choice of employers and employees. According to Confucius, one must be faithful first to one's own family, then to one's local community, and then to one's nation. This sort of group ethic, emphasizing the family as an important unit, facilitated the maintenance of permanent employment and a seniority wage system in the postwar period (cf. Morishima, 1982). In fact, many executives find the Abegglen thesis very congenial, and they encourage new employees to behave like family members in the company. At the very least, the family principle has been utlized as an ideology to strengthen employees' morale.

Enterprise unions are a uniquely Japanese phenomenon, though Koike (1977) notes that local unions in the United States have some similarity. (See the Data Appendix for statistics on unions and their membership.) It was only after the Second World War, following the establishment of three basic labour laws during the occupation period, that union activities were legalized and became active. Although at first there were several attempts to create craft unions, most active Japanese unions eventually became enterprise unions. In the meantime, after several unsuccessful militant strikes during the 1950s, enterprise unions began to adopt more moderate strategies. Yet they did not generally become 'company unions', but kept a certain degree of independence and negotiated reasonably hard (e.g. Shirai, 1983b).

The reason why Japanese unions are organized on an enterprise basis is not obvious. The influence of wartime control may count. In any case, enterprise unions were the most natural form of organization that workers could assemble during the short period that encouraged the labour movement at the onset of the occupation. As Shirai describes, enterprise unions were the result of spontaneous reactions that workers took under the existing historical constraints. At the same time, the unions have their own rationale, and their formation is strongly conditioned by the existence of lifetime employment and of the human capital formation of firm-specific skills.

We pause for a moment to explain here what 'Shunto' means. Shunto, the spring labour offensive, is the process of nationwide wage negotiations headed by some key sectors, including both private and public sectors. It was started in 1954 by five Sohyo (General Council of Trade Unions) unions, was later joined by other organizations, and now embraces about 10 million workers. In the almost simultaneous wage negotiation process for leading industries (consisting of the iron and steel, motor car, electrical machinery and shipbuilding industries), the wage pattern is set for the fiscal year. Macroeconomic variables, such as productivity and consumer price increases, are taken into account. In spite of the existence of many enterprise unions, a pattern of wage-setting is formed on a nationwide scale. This acts as a frame of reference for individual unions in firm-by-firm negotiations in which they determine their own wages and the semi-annual bonus payments.

IV. WAGE AND EMPLOYMENT EQUATIONS

Before our discussion of wage equations, we must explain another indicator of labour market conditions, the job-offered–job-wanted ratio (henceforth JOJW), i.e., the ratio of jobs offered to jobs demanded through public employment security offices (PESOs). The proportion of employment contracts that are actually mediated through the arbitration activities of PESOs is rather small; however, since the JOJW numerator (jobs offered) is responsive to business fluctuations, this ratio varies more than the unemployment rate. As we shall see below, the unemployment rate is often replaced by the JOJW ratio because it gives a better fit in estimated Phillips curves, although we must note that unemployment figures are statistically more reliable because of the

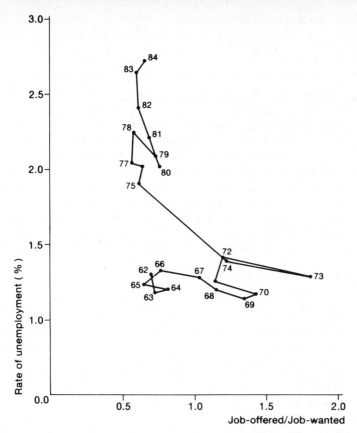

FIGURE 2.   The relationship between the JOJW ratio and the unemployment rate in Japan.
Source: Management and Coordination Agency *Survey of Labour Force*; Ministry of Labour *Monthly Bulletin of Occupational Stability*

homogeneity of data collected by a multi-stage sampling method. The relationship between JOJW and unemployment is depicted in Figure 2.

There is a large body of literature describing attempts to estimate the Phillips relationship, from the pioneering work of Watanabe (1966), who used the ratio of unemployment insurance recipients to total employees as an indicator of labour market conditions, to the most recent attempt by Shimada, Hosokawa and Seike (1982). (For a careful survey of literature, see Ueda and Yoshikawa, 1984; Toyoda, 1979.)

Following the line similar to Shimada, Hosokawa and Seike (1982), we estimated a variety of Philips curves from 1963 to 1984. In general, we found that the JOJW ratio performed better as a measure of excess demand in the labour market than the unemployment rate, and that models explaining the growth of regular earnings were more stable than those with the growth of total cash earnings (inclusive of bonus payments, etc.) as the dependent variable. A typical result is:

(2) $\Delta W / W$ = constant + seasonals

$$+ 6 \cdot 546 \log V + 0 \cdot 897 (\Delta P / P)_{-1} + 0 \cdot 05 \pi + 6 \cdot 843 \theta$$
$$(6 \cdot 76) \qquad (18 \cdot 01) \qquad\qquad (1 \cdot 74) \quad (5 \cdot 89)$$

sample period: 1962 (II)-1984(I); $\bar{R}^2 = 0 \cdot 88$; s.e. = $2 \cdot 06$; DW = $1 \cdot 99$

where $\Delta W / W$ = rate of growth of regular earnings
$\qquad\quad V$ = JOJW ratio
$\qquad\Delta P / P$ = rate of consumer price inflation
$\qquad\quad \pi$ = real profits (corporate profits/GNP deflator)
$\qquad\quad \theta$ = terms of trade (export deflator/import deflator)
and t-values are in parentheses. We note:

1. The rate of increase of the consumer price index (CPI) has high explanatory power, although the coefficient is somewhat less than unity. According to this estimation, the Friedman (1968)–Phelps (1967) model of the
   augmented Phillips curve applies only in a modified form. However,
   we may add that Shimpo (1979) and Toyoda (1982), using the Carlson-
   Parkin method of constructing price expectations, report results with
   the coefficient for expected inflation close to unity.
2. The coefficient of real profit as an explanatory variable shows the
   expected sign but is only barely significant. Therefore, our estimation
   per se does not necessarily support the hypothesis that Japan is a
   profit-share economy (Weitzman, 1984). More careful analysis at a
   disaggregated level is necessary to resolve the question of whether, and
   how, the Japanese economy is a profit-share economy.
3. The coefficient of the terms-of-trade variable is positive and significant
   at the 5 per cent level. This shows that labour unions and management
   negotiate in such a way that a deterioration in the terms of trade leads
   to reduced pressure for wage increases. This may be one explanation
   of why the Japanese economy survived the oil crisis without a large
   increase in unemployment.

We also attempted to identify the effect of labour unions. Because the
unionization rate is available only annually, we used only the JOJW ratio and
the rate of CPI inflation in addition to the ratio of organized workers, μ. The
estimated equation is:

(3) $\Delta W / W = -23 \cdot 5 + 6 \cdot 978 \log V + 0 \cdot 609 (\Delta P / P) + 0 \cdot 97 \mu$
$\qquad\qquad (2 \cdot 79)(5 \cdot 92) \qquad\quad (9 \cdot 09) \qquad\qquad (3 \cdot 80)$

sample period: 1963–84; $\bar{R}^2 = 0 \cdot 90$; s.e. = $1 \cdot 21$; $\hat{\rho} = 0 \cdot 53$

This gives some support to the hypothesis that an increase in the unionization
rate tends to increase wages. The recent declining trend in the ratio may
account for moderate wage behaviour in Japan.

In international perspective, the effect of labour demand conditions is
relatively strong and stable in Japan. For example, Grubb *et al.* (1983) report
that the degree of response of wages to unemployment rate fluctuations in
Japan is about five times as large as in France, more than ten times as large
as in Germany, and even larger when compared with the UK or the United
States, where the coefficient is insignificant. They deduce from their estimation

that the degree of real-wage flexibility in Japan is equalled only by Switzerland, and that the degree of nominal wage flexibility in Japan is also one of the highest (see also Sachs, 1979). These flexibilities are, of course, due partly to the insensitive statistical movement in unemployment rates, and also to the fact that the labour force participation ratio exhibits a strong discouraged worker effect and plays the role of buffering demand fluctuations and dampening upward movements in the unemployment rate.

However, Japan ranks only third in flexibility in terms of the output gap as opposed to the unemployment gap. This is a reflection of rigid movements in unemployment. Thus we probably have to refrain from overstating the flexibility of wages until further investigation is made on real-wage flexibility.

We now ask what the natural rate of unemployment is. Yoshida and Endoh (1982) used the relationship between the unemployment rate and the JOJW ratio, and decomposed the variation in the unemployment rate into two components, one part to be explained by the supply and demand conditions in the labour market, which they believe is reflected by the JOJW ratio, and the other part to be explained by a time trend which indicates structural changes in the labour market. According to them, the natural rate of unemployment rose from 1·2–1·4 per cent in 1967 to 2·2–2·4 per cent in 1982. If the time trend is important, however, one should ask what economic forces change these relationships (Ueda and Yoshikawa, 1984).

Following the attempt by Fujimoto (1984), we regressed the unemployment rate U on the JOJW ratio and variables indicating demographic changes. In the following equations τ_1 is the ratio of the age group 15–24 years in the population, τ_2 is the ratio of people above 55 years, and τ_3 the ratio of employment in tertiary industries. We obtained;

(4a) $\log U = -3\cdot09 - 0\cdot296\log V + 0\cdot009\tau_1 + 0\cdot065\tau_3$
          (3·0) (7·52)   (0·60)   (4·80)

sample period: 1963–84; $\bar{R}^2 = 0\cdot96$; s.e. $= 0\cdot04$; $\hat{\rho} = 0\cdot23$

(4b) $\log U = -2\cdot47 - 0\cdot294\log V + 0\cdot0005\tau_2 + 0\cdot057\tau_3$
          (15·0   (7·18)   (0·09)   (13·73)

sample period; 1963–84; $\bar{R}^2 = 0\cdot96$; s.e. $= 0\cdot04$; $\hat{\rho} = 0\cdot22$

One can see that the age ratios are not significant. The relative increase in employment in tertiary industries gives an upward trend in unemployment. The hypothetical natural rate of unemployment can then be calculated by substituting unity for the value of V. Figure 3 plots, along with the measured unemployment rate, the natural unemployment rate computed from equation (4a). The thin shading indicates excess unemployment; the thick excess employment.

We now consider whether labour demand responded more flexibly to business conditions in recent years. Previous authors have obtained contradictory answers depending on estimation methods (Muramatsu, 1983, Shimada *et al*, 1981). We start by assuming a constant elasticity of substitution (CES) production function:

(5) $Y = A\{\delta L^{-\rho} + (1-\delta)K^{-\rho}\}^{-1/\rho}$

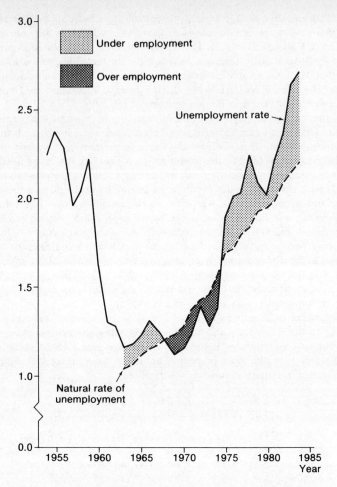

FIGURE 3.   Unemployment *v.* the natural unemployment rate, Japan, 1953–1984

Profit maximization under perfect competition implies that optimal employment N^* is given by

(6) $N^* = Y/(WA^\rho/\delta P)^{1/(1+\rho)}$

where $1/(1+\rho)$ is the elasticity of substitution. If we assume a partial adjustment mechanism with adjustment speed $\lambda\,(0<\lambda<1)$, we obtain

(7) $\log(N/N_{-1}) = \{\lambda/(1+\rho)\}\log(\delta/A^\rho) + \lambda\log(Y/N_{-1})$

$$-\{\lambda/(1+\rho)\}\log(W/P).$$

To allow for a change in the speed of adjustment after the first oil price shock, we include a dummy D with the value of zero up to the end of 1973 and unity thereafter. This is also interacted with the output and real-wage terms. We obtain (for manufacturing):

(8) $\log(N/N_{-1}) = \text{constant} + \text{seasonals} - 0\cdot004\text{D} + 0\cdot11 \log(Y/N_{-1})$
$$(1\cdot34) \quad (7\cdot35)$$
$$-0\cdot069D \log(Y/N_{-1}) - 0\cdot109 \log(W/P) + 0\cdot088D \log(W/P)$$
$$(3\cdot54) \qquad\qquad (8\cdot72) \qquad\qquad (4\cdot41)$$

sample period; 1960(I)–1984(III); $\bar{R}^2 = 0\cdot88$; s.e. $= 0\cdot007$; DW $= 2\cdot11$

These results seem to indicate that the adjustment speed declined after the first oil crisis. This conforms to the result of Shimada *et al.* and contradicts that of Muramatsu. The adjustment was in the direction of decreasing employment after the oil crisis, so that the cost of adjustment might have been higher. The elasticity of substitution declined from 0·99 to 0·512 as a result of the first oil crisis. We also tried using man-hours as the dependent variable, but the results were less satisfactory.

Finally, we need to assess briefly the effect of the Shunto. Since the Shunto normally determines the overall pattern of wage increase starting in the second quarter, the estimation of wage equations on quarterly data is questionable. As the staggered wage contract in the United States recovers the efficacy of monetary policy even under rational expectations, the wage determination process through Shunto will make monetary policy effective at most within a year under rational expectations. A limited case for discretionary policy can be made (Taniuchi, 1982; Grossman and Haraf, 1983).

Finally, the incidence of labour disputes has fallen in recent years. Ono (1973) shows that labour unions succeed in raising wages by resorting to industrial action. The recent demilitization of labour unions could be a significant factor in explaining the moderation of wage increases.

VI. CONCLUDING REMARKS

This paper could be subtitled 'The 'non-rise' of unemployment in Japan'. The output loss associated with this low and slow-moving unemployment is substantial, but probably the social burden of unemployment in Japan is relatively light, if not as light as the low figures themselves may indicate.

We did not build a complete formal model to explain the low rate of unemployment. The rough sketch of our theoretical structure is as follows. The low level of unemployment is the result of interaction between demand and supply in the labour market. On the demand side, firms are slow to respond to demand fluctuations, and, according to our employment equations, slower to respond after the first oil crisis, probably because the adjustment is in the downward direction. On the supply side, the discouraged worker effect on female labour supply shrank the labour force considerably (This effect is weakening.) These effects have reinforced each other to produce very rigid figures of unemployment rates. Our wage equations also show that Japanese wages are quite responsive to both nominal and real shocks. Real shocks, such as energy crises, are absorbed in the Shunto process, where now quite meek labour unions negotiate with management. This has facilitated the moderation of inflation in Japan without significantly increasing unemployment, even though substantial output losses were hidden behind the small movements in unemployment. These characteristics derive from the institutional and social environment, the development of the internal labour market or specific human capital in an enterprise, and social attitudes to the role of women in society.

Can we, then, attribute these institutional characteristics to the cultural or idiosyncratic nature of Japanese society? Or do they constitute a new 'organiz-ation- (rather than market) oriented' model of economy to which other societies may converge (Dore, 1973; Koike, 1984)? This is a difficult question.

Economic development is a process of human adaptation to the environ-ment—not only to the natural environment, but also to the historical environ-ment, which constitutes the initial conditions of any society. Economic rational-ity towards institutional improvement may prevail in the long run, but historical preconditions give constraints on the process of adaptation, and political leadership may be needed as a kind of catalyst.

Japan is a densely populated country, originally based on agriculture, where homogeneous and harmonius behaviour has high pay-offs. Family- and village-oriented behaviour has developed, we believe, as a natural response to the climate and environment. Firm-oriented working habits, cooperation between management and unions, labourers' eagerness to work hard and long, moderation in wage demands—all of these factors have facilitated the smooth functioning of the Japanese labour market and improved Japan's macroeconomic performance. Sometimes workers are solicited to work harder and longer because their choices are informally constrained, either by social customs, limitation of alternative personnel, or limitation of public facilities for the enjoyment of leisure. Behind these harmonious and homogeneous behaviour patterns, the sacrifice of individual preference, as well as sacrifices arising from the semi-discriminatory treatment of women, may be concealed. Still, Japanese workers spend long hours commuting to work and long hours at the factory, demand moderate wage increases, and are loyal to their company.

Probably they behave so because they know the alternatives accurately and calculate the payoff well. But if, by any chance, they behave like this because they have not yet tasted the forbidden fruit of more individual life-styles, what then will follow? As Japanese workers become more leisure-oriented, more individualistic, more consumer-oriented and less chauvinistic, the Japanese macroeconomic performance will become less satisfactory to economic policy-makers. Workers may enjoy life more, and in the short run the increased demand relative to supply may even help to reduce Japan's trade surplus!

ACKNOWLEDGMENTS

We are indebted to Professor Atsushi Seike of Keio University and Sushil Wadhwani of the London School of Economics for their valuable comments, to Ms Hisako Kurihara for her computational assistance, and to Ms Frances McCall for her help in improving the English style of our earlier version.

NOTES

1. Starting in late 1982, there is an upward drift in the unemployment rate, reflecting the fact that the sample size has been increased and changed to better reflect the composition of various labour categories. Since there are no panel data to enable us to trace the exact effect of the changes in the survey method, it is hard to tell why the Japanese unemployment rate jumped a few decimal points at that point.

2. Dr John Martin informs us that this tendency is even more conspicuous if we compare average annual hours worked per person employed. In 1983 the hours are 2097 for Japan, 1693

for the United States, 1682 for West Germany, 1570 for France and 1504 for the UK (OECD, 1983, Table 14, p. 34).

3. We remember a scene on television where employees in a depressed firm are being taught geometry by other employees. This may be due to the encouragement effect of the subsidies. However, these subsidies have disappeared completely now. For an evaluation of these adjustment measures, see Seike (1985).

REFERENCES

ABEGGLEN, JAMES C. (1958). *The Japanese Factory: Aspects of Its Social Organization.* Glencoe, Ill.: Free Press.

ARISAWA, HIROMI (1956). Wage differentials and the economic structure (in Japanese). In I. Nakayama (ed.), *Chingin Kihon Chosa.* Tokyo; Toyo Keizai.

DORE, RONALD P. (1973). British factory-Japanese factory: the origins of national diversity in industrial relations. Berkeley, Cal.: University of California Press.

DOUGLAS, P. H. (1934). *The Theory of Wages.* New York: Macmillan.

FRIEDMAN, MILTON (1968). The role of monetary policy. *American Economic Review,* **58,** 1-17.

FUJIMOTO, ICHIRO (1984). Towards the estimation of natural unemployment rates by wage equations (in Japanese). *Economy, Society and Policy,* no. 150, 120-125.

GORDON, R. J. (1982). Why US wage and employment behaviour differs from that in Britain and Japan. *Economic Journal,* **92,** 13-44.

GROSSMAN, H. and HARAF W. (1983). Shunto, rational expectations, and output growth in Japan. NBER Working Paper no. 1144 (July).

GRUBB, D., JACKMAN, R. and LAYARD, R. (1983). Wage rigidity and unemployment in OECD countries. *European Economic Review,* **21,** 11-40.

HAMADA, KOICHI and KUROSAKA, YOSHIO (1984). The relationship between production and unemployment in Japan: Okun's Law in comparative perspective. *European Economic Review,* **25,** 71-94.

HASHIMOTO, MASANORI (1979). Bonus payments, on-the-job training, and lifetime employment in Japan. *Journal of Political Economy,* **87,** 1086-1104.

HIGUCHI, YOSHIO and SEIKE, ATSUSHI (1985). Labour mobility and their economic causes in Japan (in Japanese). Paper presented at Zushi Conference, March 1985.

ITO, TAKATOSHI (1984). Why is the unemployment rate so much lower in Japan than in the US? Discussion Paper no. 198 (January), Center for Economic Research, Department of Economics, University of Minnesota.

KOGA, MAKOTO et al. (1974). Factors determining hours of work and the impact of shorter hours on output (in Japanese). *Keizai Bunseki,* no. 47, 1-65.

KOIKE, KAZUO (1977). *Trade Unions On the Shop Floor: A Comparative Study on Industrial Relations In the U.S. and Japan* (in Japanese). Tokyo: Toyo Keizai Shimposha.

—— (1983). Internal labor markets: workers in large. Chapter 2 of Shirai (1983a).

—— (ed.) (1984). *Unemployment in Modern Society* (in Japanese). Tokyo: Dobunkan.

KOSAI, YUTAKA and TOSHIDA, SEI-ICHI (1981). *Economic Growth* (in Japanese). Tokyo: Nihon Keizai Shimbunsha.

KOSHIRO, KAZUTOSHI (1980). Wage determination under the second oil crisis (in Japanese). *Nihon Rodo Kyokai Zasshi,* no. 254, 2-13.

—— (1983). Development of collective bargaining in postwar Japan. Chapter 9 in Shirai (1983a).

KURATANI, MASATOSHI (1973). A theory of training, earnings and employment: an application to Japan. PhD thesis, Columbia University.

MORISHIMA, MICHIO (1982). *Why Has Japan 'Succeeded'?* Cambridge: Cambridge University Press.

MURAMATSU, KURAMITSU (1983). *An Analysis of the Japanese labour market—From the Viewpoint of 'Internal Labour'* (in Japanese). Tokyo: Hakuto Shobo.

NAGAYAMA, SADANORI (1984). Is the Rate of Unemployment in Japan Too Low? (in Japanese). *Nihon Rodo Kyokai Zasshi,* no. 299, 9-17.

NAKAMURA, JIRO (1981). A quantitative study on the male and female labour market in macroeconometric models (in Japanese). *Economic Studies Quarterly,* **32,** 201-15.

ODAKA, KONOSUKE (1984). *An Analysis of Labour Market—The Development of the Dual Structure the Japanese Style* (in Japanese). Tokyo: Iwanami Shoten.

OECD (1972). *Reviews of Manpower and Social Policies, Manpower Policy in Japan.* Paris: OECD.

OECD (1983). *Employment Outlook,* September.

ONO, AKIRA (1973). *Wage Determination In Postwar Japan* (in Japanese). Tokyo: Toyo Keizai Shimposha.

PHELPS, EDMUND S. (1967). Phillips curve, expectations of inflation and optimal unemployment over time. *Economica*, **34**, 254–81.

SACHS, JEFFREY D. (1979). Wages, Profits and macroeconomic adjustment: a comparative study. *Brookings Papers on Economics Activity*, no. 2, 269–319.

SASAJIMA, YOSHIO (1984). *Employment and Unemployment in Japan, the US, and Europe—A Comparative Analysis of Labour Market* (in Japanese). Tokyo: Toyo Keizai Shimposha.

SEIKE, ATSUSHI (1985). Employment in the Japanese labor market. *Keio Business Review*, **22**, 25–57.

SHIMADA, HARUO et al. (1981). *Studies in the Organization of the Labour Market* (in Japanese). Research Series no. 37, Institute for Economic Research, Economic Planning Agency, Tokyo.

SHIMADA, HARUO, HOSOKAWA, TOYOAKI and SEIKE ATSUSHI (1982). Analyses of the wage and employment adjustment process (in Japanese). *Keizai Bunseki* (Institute for Economic Research, Economic Planning Agency), no. 84, 1–106.

SHIMADA, HARUO, and YOSHIO HIGUCHI, (1985). An analysis of trends in female labour force participation in Japan. *Journal of Labor Economics*, **3**, S355–74.

SHIMPO, SEIJI (1979). *An Analysis of the Contemporary Japanese Economy; Studies in Stagflation* (in Japanese). Tokyo: Toyo Keizai Shimposha.

SHINKAI, YOICHI (1980). Spillovers in wage determination: Japanese evidence. *Review of Economics and Statistics*, **62**, 288–93.

SHIRAI, TAISHIRO (ed.) (1983a). *Contemporary Industrial Relations in Japan*. Madison: University of Wisconsin Press.

SHIRAI, TAISHIRO (1983b). A theory of enterprise unionism. Chapter 5 in Shirai (1983a).

SHIRAISHI, EIJI (1982). International comparison of unemployment concepts, focusing on Japan and US (in Japanese). *Rodo Tokei Chosa Geppo*, **34**, 13–20.

SOLOW, ROBERT M. (1957). Technical progress and productivity change. *Review of Economics and Statistics*, **39**, 312–20.

SORRENTINO, CONSTANCE (1984). Japan's low unemployment; an in-depth analysis. *Monthly Labour Review*, **107**, 18–27.

TACHIBANAKI, TOSHIAKI (1984). *On the youth unemployment problem* (in Japanese). *Nihon Rodo Kyokai Zasshi*, No. 307, 12–22.

TAIRA, KOJI (1983). Japan's low unemployment: economic miracle or statistical artifact? *Monthly Labour Review*, **106**, 3–10.

—— (1984). On 'Rocho' unemployment, difficulty in fact findings and difference in philosophies (in Japanese). *Nihon Rodo Kyokai Zasshi*, no. 307, 2–11.

TANIUCHI, MITSURU (1982). Prior monetary expectation and output determination. PhD dissertation, Brown University.

TOYODA, TOSHIHISA (1979). The relationship between inflation and unemployment in Japan (in Japanese). *Kikan Gendai Keizai*, no. 36, 60–70.

—— (1982). Inflation and unemployment. Chapter 9 in Hiroshi Niida et al. (eds), *The Japanese Economy: A Text* (in Japanese). Tokyo: Yuhikaku.

UEDA, KAZUO and YOSHIKAWA, HIROSHI (1984). A macroeconomic analysis of the labour market (in Japanese). *Kikan Gendai Keizai*, no. 57, 62–77.

YASHIRO, NAOHIRO (1982). *An Economic Analysis of Women Workers—Another Subtle Revolution* (in Japanese). Tokyo: Toyo Keizai Shimposha.

YOSHIDA, KAZUO and EDOH, HIROSHI (1982). Changes in the unemployment structure after the oil crisis (in Japanese). *Kikan Gendai Keizai*, no. 51, 35–47.

WATANABE, TSUNEHIKO (1966). Price changes and the rate of changes of money wage earnings in Japan, 1955–1962. *Quarterly Journal of Economics*, **80**, 31–47.

WEITZMAN, MARTIN L. (1984). *The Share Economy*. Cambridge, Mass.: Harvard University Press.

Unemployment in the Netherlands, 1960–1983

By Wim Driehuis

University of Amsterdam

Introduction

The unemployment rate in the Netherlands has risen enormously, from about 1 per cent during the first half of the 1960s to about 15 per cent in 1984. In Figure 1 the stepwise development of the unemployment rate can be observed. The more than doubling of unemployment since 1980 is the result of an accelerated growth in the size of the labour force and a strong decrease in employment, particularly in the market sector (Figure 2). The most important explanatory factor for this decrease is the substantial decline in the rate of capital formation, which, in its turn, is related to a weak growth in output and a strong profit squeeze.

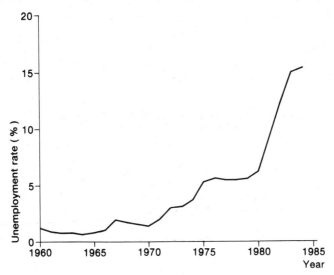

FIGURE 1. Unemployment in the Netherlands, 1960–1984.
Source: Data Appendix at end of volume.

In exploring the strong rise in unemployment we shall develop a small model, with the help of which a decomposition of this increase is made. The model is presented and explained in analytical terms in Section I. Section II deals with its empirical content. The results of the decomposition procedure are given in Section III, and Section IV contains the conclusions.

I. Analytical Framework

The model consists of two blocks, one for the commodity market and one for the labour market.[1] The size of the model is kept small in order to allow a

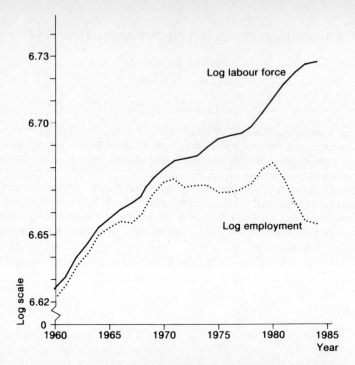

FIGURE 2.   Log labour force and log employment, the Netherlands, 1960–1984.
Source: Data Appendix at end of volume.

manageable decomposition of the rise in unemployment. The model consists partly of quasi-reduced-form equations which have been developed and estimated in existing research on the Dutch economy. The commodity market has a sectoral differentiation according to the capital intensity of production. The supply side of the most capital-intensive sector is modelled with the help of a clay–clay vintage specification.

The demand side of the commodity market is represented by a quasi-reduced-form expenditure equation for an open economy. Unless otherwise stated, lower-case letters denote logrithms and an overdot denotes a time derivative or a first difference, as appropriate.

(1) $\dot{y} = \zeta_1 \dot{y}^* - \zeta_2(\dot{p}_f + \dot{e}_f - \dot{p}_f^*) + \zeta_3 FP + \zeta_4 MP - \zeta_5 CC + \zeta_6.$

Determinants of production in the market sector (Y) are world demand (Y^*), price competitiveness measured by the difference between (logarithms of) the export price (P_f) (own currency), the effective exchange rate on the export market (E_f), and the export price of competitors (foreign currency) (P_f^*). Furthermore, we postulate an impact of fiscal policy (FP) and wealth effects which include effects of monetary policy (MP). Finally, we leave open the possibility that constraints on the commodity market (CC) prevent full adjustment of domestic output to external factors and/or policy measures.

The supply side of the commodity market has a moderate sectoral differentiation. The determinants of productive capacity of sector 1, the collection of industries that is capital-intensive, are different from those in sector 2, which is the collection of labour-intensive industries (excluding the public sector). Sector 1 consists of the manufacturing industries plus capital-intensive service industries, such as transport, storage and communication. The building industry plus labour-intensive service industries make up sector 2. The agricultural and energy industries are, as sector 3, treated as exogenous.

Productive capacity in sector 1 depends on installed equipment, the relationship with output being determined for each vintage of equipment by a capital-output ratio. Disembodied capital-augmenting technical progress lowers the capital coefficient. Vintages may become obsolete for technical and for economic reasons. Furthermore, machine time, which is supposed to be equal to labour time, has an impact on capacity output. In this way we have

$$Y^c_{1t} = \frac{H_t^{\delta_1}}{\kappa_0} e^{\varepsilon t} \int_{t-V_t}^{t} I_1(\nu) \, e^{-\pi(t-\nu)} \, d\nu, \qquad \begin{matrix} 0 < \delta_1 < 1 \\[4pt] 0 < \pi < 1 \\[4pt] 0 < \varepsilon < 1 \end{matrix}$$

where Y^c_1 = productive capacity of sector 1
  H = index of labour time
  V = age of the oldest vintage of equipment in existence
  $I_1(\nu)$ = gross investment in equipment of vintage ν in sector 1;
      $\nu = t - V, \ldots, t$
  κ_0 = capital coefficient in year $t = 0$
  π = rate of scrapping of equipment owing to technical obsolescence
  ε = rate of disembodied capital-augmenting technical progress
  δ_1 = elasticity of capacity with respect to labour time in sector 1

Assuming a steady growth path, we find, after taking logarithms and differentiation with respect to time (for the derivation see de Ridder, 1977 and van den Noord, 1984) the following equation for capacity growth in sector 1:

$$(2) \qquad \dot{y}^c_1 = \frac{1}{\kappa_0} j_1 + \theta(\dot{V} - 1) + \delta_1 \dot{h} + \varepsilon - \pi \qquad\qquad 0 < \theta < 1$$

where

  θ = share of the oldest vintage in existence in total stock of equipment
  $j_1 = e^{\varepsilon t} H^{\delta_1}(I_1/Y^c_1)$ = share of gross investment in equipment in productive capacity of sector 1, in efficiency units

Note that the time index t is deleted and that $\dot{V}$ represents changes in the economic obsolescence of capital through changes in the replacement of equipment.[2]

Productive capacity of sector 2 is assumed not to be determined by capital but by labour:

$$(3) \qquad \dot{y}^c_2 = \dot{l}_2 + \dot{s}^c_2$$

where Y^c_2 = productive capacity of sector 2
  L_2 = labour available for sector 2
  S^c_2 = structural labour productivity in sector 2

Finally, productive capacity in the agricultural and energy sector (Y^c_3) is assumed to be restricted by natural circumstances and is therefore exogenous.

The total rate of capacity growth is thus found to be

$$(4) \qquad \dot{y}^c = \lambda_1 \left\{ \frac{1}{\kappa_0} j_1 + \theta(\dot{V}-1) + \delta_1 \dot{h} + \varepsilon - \pi \right\} + \lambda_2 (\dot{s}_2^c + \dot{l}_2) + \lambda_3 \dot{y}_3^c$$

where λ_i $(i = 1, 2, 3)$ represent the share of production of sector 1, 2 and 3 in total production of the market sector.

Combining total production and capacity growth yields the following definition for changes in the rate of capacity utilization (Q):

$$(5) \qquad \dot{q} = \dot{y} - \dot{y}^c.$$

Equation (6) is a reduced-form export price equation, in which an unknown wage equation has been solved. In addition to import prices (foreign currency) (P_m) and the effective exchange rate on the import market (E_m), we include a negative impact of the growth of labour productivity. Because of a possible negative trade-off between nominal wage increases and excess supply on the labour market, the rate of unemployment (u) occurs as a potential explanatory variable as well. Finally, owing to severe centralized income policies in the Netherlands in the past, we hypothesize an impact of wage policy (WP):

$$(6) \qquad \dot{p}_f = \tau_1 (\dot{p}_m - \dot{e}_m) - \tau_2 \dot{s} - \tau_3 u - \tau_4 WP + \tau_5.$$

This equation makes it necessary to look for the determinants of labour productivity growth. For that purpose, we consider first the determinants of employment under full capacity utilization, which we call potential employment, or jobs. The starting point is the following specification for the creation of jobs in sector 1 (see van den Noord, 1984):

$$N_{1t}^c = H_t^{\delta_1 - \gamma_1} \frac{\alpha_t}{\kappa_0} e^{\varepsilon t} \int_{t-V_t}^{t} I_1(\nu) e^{-(\pi-\mu)(t-\nu)} \, d\nu \qquad \begin{matrix} 0 < \mu < 1 \\ 0 < \gamma_1 < 1 \end{matrix}$$

where N_1^c = potential employment (jobs) in sector 1
$\qquad \mu$ = rate of embodied labour-augmenting technical progress
$\qquad \alpha_t$ = labour coefficient
$\qquad \gamma_1$ = elasticity of jobs with respect to labour time in sector 1
with $\alpha_t = \alpha_0 \exp\left(-\mu t - \int_0^t \chi_1(\nu) \, d\nu\right)$, where α_0 is the reciprocal of potential labour productivity in year $t = 0$ and χ_1 is the rate of disembodied labour-augmenting technical progress in sector 1.

The creation of jobs in sector 1 is dependent on the stock of equipment, where each vintage has its own labour requirements, owing to embodied labour-augmenting technical progress. Using Verdoorn's law (Verdoorn, 1952), we postulate disembodied technical progress to be dependent on the rate of growth of productive capacity:

$$(7) \qquad \chi_1 = \rho \dot{y}_1^c \qquad\qquad\qquad\qquad 0 < \rho < 1.$$

After taking logarithms and differentiating with respect to time, we find

$$(8) \qquad \dot{n}_1^c = \frac{\psi}{\kappa_0} j_1 + \eta(\dot{V}-1) + (\delta_1 - \gamma_1)\dot{h} - \rho \dot{y}_1^c + \varepsilon - \pi$$

where ψ is the ratio of the labour coefficient of the best practice vintage to the labour coefficient of the average-practice vintage (for details see van den

Noord, 1984). The most important determinant of jobs in sector 1 is capacity growth, which depends primarily on the rate of capital formation. Furthermore, we see that economic obsolescence of equipment reduces the number of jobs. A shortening of machine (labour) time also diminishes job creation if $\delta_1 > \gamma_1$. A similar effect results from disembodied labour-augmenting technical progress, whereas capital-augmenting technical progress stimulates job creation.

Combining equations (2) and (8) yields the following specification for potential labour productivity growth in sector 1:

$$(9) \quad \dot{s}_1^c = (\dot{y}_1^c - \dot{n}_1^c) = \left(\frac{1-\psi}{\kappa_0}\right)j_1 - (\eta - \theta)(\dot{V} - 1) + \gamma_1 \dot{h} + \rho \dot{y}_1^c \qquad \eta > \theta.$$

For potential labour productivity growth in sector 2, we assume that

$$(10) \quad \dot{s}_2^c = \chi_2 + \gamma_2 \dot{h} + \xi(\dot{w} - \dot{p}).$$

In addition to disembodied labour-augmenting technical progress (χ_2), we postulate labour productivity growth in labour-intensive industries to be dependent on working time and real labour costs, i.e. on overall nominal labour costs (W) in relation to the price deflator of production (P).

Labour productivity growth in sector 3 is assumed to be influenced by disembodied labour-augmenting technical progress and working hours only:

$$(11) \quad \dot{s}_3^c = \chi_3 + \gamma_3 \dot{h}.$$

Total potential labour productivity growth is then equal to a weighted average of sectoral productivity growth rates:

$$(12) \quad \dot{s}^c = \lambda_1 \left\{ \frac{1-\psi}{\kappa_0} j_1 - (\eta - \theta)(\dot{V} - 1) + \gamma_1 \dot{h} + \rho \dot{y}_1^c \right\}$$
$$+ \lambda_2 \{\chi_2 + \gamma_2 \dot{h} + \xi(\dot{w} - \dot{p})\} + \lambda_3(\chi_3 + \gamma_3 \dot{h}).$$

Actual labour productivity growth is equal to potential labour productivity growth corrected for change in the degree of capacity utilization:

$$(13) \quad \dot{s} = \dot{s}^c + \beta \dot{q} \qquad 0 < \beta < 1.$$

Note that the coefficient β incorporates the influence of labour hoarding.

Next, we need the condition under which firms in sector 1 decide to replace vintages of equipment. If we assume profit maximization under imperfect competition (for details see Malcolmson, 1975), the replacement decision involves a comparison of wage costs plus capital costs on new equipment, with wage costs on old equipment, all per unit of capacity:

$$W_t H_t^{-\gamma_1} \alpha_t + P_{kt} H_t^{-\delta_1} \kappa_0 \, e^{-\varepsilon t} = W_t H_t^{-\gamma_1} \alpha_t (e^{\mu V_t})$$

where the user cost of capital, P_k, is defined as

$$P_k = r P_I A / (1 - e^{-rd})$$

where r = interest rate
P_I = price of new machines
A = impact of investment subsidies
d = depreciation period

After differentiation of this condition with respect to time and substitution of the function for α_t, we find for changes in the economic lifetime of equipment,

$$(14) \quad \dot{V} = \frac{1}{1+C_t} \left\{ \frac{-(\dot{w}-\dot{p}_k)-(\delta_1-\gamma_1)\dot{h}+\rho\dot{y}_1^c-\varepsilon}{\mu} + 1 \right\}$$

where C_t = ratio of labour costs to capital costs of the newest vintage; i.e.,

$$C_t = \frac{W_t\alpha_0 \, e^{-(\mu+x_1)t}H_t^{-\gamma_1}}{P_{kt}\kappa_0 \, e^{-\varepsilon t}H_t^{-\delta_1}}.$$

Finally, we explain the share of investment in production in sector 1 by a simple specification in which the production growth rate is used as a proxy for the desired rate of capacity growth. In addition, we hypothesize an impact of the profit rate after taxes. Assuming a constant profit tax rate, we arrive at

$$(15) \quad \dot{j}_1 = \varphi_1 \dot{y}_1 + \varphi_2 \{ \Pi_0 (1 + \dot{s} - \dot{w} + \dot{p}_y - \dot{a}) \}$$

where Π_0 is the after-tax profit share in the value of production in a base year.

We leave the commodity market to deal with the labour market. The relevant equations are

$$(16) \quad \dot{n}^c = \dot{y}^c - \dot{s}^c$$

$$(17) \quad \dot{n} = \dot{y} - \dot{s}$$

$$(18) \quad U = U_i + \{ L - \min(L, N^c) \} + \{ \min(L, N^c) - U_i - N \}.$$

Equations (16) and (17) refer to relative changes in potential employment (jobs) and actual employment as determined by the respective output and labour productivity variables. Finally, equation (18) distinguishes three types of unemployment: arising from labour market imperfections (U_i); arising from a shortage of jobs ($L - \min(L, N^c)$); and arising from cyclical factors ($\min(L, N^c) - U_i - N$, where L denotes the supply of labour).

Note that the term representing the impact of labour market imperfections includes both frictional unemployment and unemployment arising from mismatches on the labour market. This type of unemployment is an indication of the extent to which constraints on the labour market are important. Cyclical unemployment is related to cyclical fluctuations in output. A shortage of jobs may arise because of an acceleration of labour supply in combination with:

—a deceleration of capital formation (a fall in the share of investment in output), particularly in sector 1;
—an acceleration of real wages in sector 2;
—changes in production technology;
—changes in the organization of production (mergers, etc.).

In order to illustrate the working of the model, we do not consider circumstances that lead to temporary changes in production and employment at a given number of jobs, thus leading to cyclical unemployment. Rather, we consider a permanent fall in world demand in a situation where the possibility of a substantial downward wage (and price) adjustment arising from excess labour supply is absent. Initially, lower expenditure growth leads to a downward revision of desired capacity growth and thus to a lower share of investment in output. As a consequence, labour productivity is growing less, which drives export prices up, or profit margins down, which has a further negative impact on production, capacity, etc. The model thus reflects a chain of quantity adjustments on the commodity market which spills over to the labour market where structural unemployment may arise when the number of jobs falls short of the size of the labour force. The only way to check this downward spiral in commodity and labour quantities is to take compensating policy measures in the commodity market, such as expansionary fiscal and monetary policies and/or incomes policies, so as to check price increases (van Eyk, 1983).

In the above description the situation on the commodity market dominates the situation on the labour market. However, things may be different when excess supply on the labour market has a strong feedback, via wages, on prices, thus mitigating the initial fall in production growth, or even reversing it. In this case expansionary policy measures may frustrate the endogenous adjustment process which starts on the labour market and may also bring the commodity market into equilibrium. Obviously, in both situations constraints on the commodity and/or labour market limit the degree to which either quantity adjustments or price adjustments can be effective.,

II. Empirical Results

In this section we present empirical results for the equations discussed in the previous section. The quasi-reduced-form equation for production growth was estimated for the period 1951-77 (Driehuis, 1984). In addition to the double reweighted volume of exports of competitor countries, as a proxy for the growth of the relevant world market, there is a distributed lag on export prices. Fiscal policy is represented by changes in public expenditures and taxes (both including social security) as a percentage of national income. Interestingly, changes in the tax burden take a longer time to influence production growth than changes in public expenditures. Note that the negative impact of any effective shifting forward of taxes on production growth is included in the coefficient of the tax variable. Furthermore, relative changes in the money supply (M) as a percentage of national income have a significant impact on output growth with a lag of one year.

The production equation reads as follows (t-values in brackets):

$$(19) \quad \dot{y} = 0\cdot476\dot{y}^* - 0\cdot760(\dot{p}_f - \dot{p}_f^* + \dot{e}_f) + 0\cdot116(\dot{m} - \dot{z})_{-1}$$
$$\quad\quad\quad (6\cdot5) \quad\quad (2\cdot3) \quad\quad\quad\quad\quad (2\cdot2)$$

$$\quad + 0\cdot365(\dot{G}/Z_{-1}) - 0\cdot411(\dot{T}/Z_{-1}) - 0\cdot014CC + 0\cdot013$$
$$\quad (2\cdot4) \quad\quad\quad\quad (2\cdot2) \quad\quad\quad\quad (-) \quad\quad\quad (1\cdot2)$$

$$\text{sample period: 1951-77; } \bar{R}^2 = 0\cdot75; \, DW = 2\cdot22$$

where Z = nominal national income
  G = public expenditures, current prices
  T = taxes, current prices
  CC = dummy variable representing constraints on the commodity
      market (=0 before 1973 and =1 afterwards)
  $\bar{x} = 0\cdot4x_{-1} + 0\cdot3x_{-2} + 0\cdot2x_{-3} + 0\cdot1x_{-4}(x = p_f, p_f^*, e_f)$

Equation (19) was found by constrained maximum likelihood estimation. A few explanatory remarks are in order. Rather then attempt the difficult task of deflating public expenditures and taxes by appropriate price indices, I have

chosen to divide these variables by nominal national income. Note, furthermore, that the coefficients of public expenditure and the tax burden do not
differ significantly. This is in line with studies that suggest that balanced budget
policies do not seem to have a positive impact on production growth owing
to a severe process of shifting forward the tax burden. The impact of the Dutch
welfare state on production growth is thus clearly incorporated in equation (19).

Estimation of the output equation showed systematic residuals after 1973
which persisted when the equation was extrapolated until 1983. Although it
cannot be completely ruled out that the aggregative character of the output
equation is partly responsible for these residuals, further investigation has
made it clear that, after 1973, the price elasticity of exports in absolute terms
had declined substantially (Driehuis, 1984). In other words, the improvement
in price competitiveness that has taken place since 1977 has not resulted in
the usual extra export and output growth. The reasons for this phenomenon
are not clear, and I am not aware of any systematic study of it. Since export
prices are double reweighted, the reduced responsiveness of exports cannot
be attributed to changes in the geographical composition of exports. Rather,
one is inclined to blame inadequate supply following the sharp fall in the
share of investment in output, the considerable changes in energy markets,
and technological backwardness (WRR, 1980). For lack of anything better, I
have incorporated this feature into equation (19) by including a dummy
variable (CC), the coefficient of which was found by an iterative estimation
procedure (see Driehuis, 1984). The strong implication of this is that, according
to equation (19), the level of production in 1983 could have been almost 20
per cent higher without commodity market constraints.

The reduced-form export price equation reads

$$(20) \qquad \dot{p}_f = 0{\cdot}795(\dot{p}_m - \dot{e}_m) - 0{\cdot}290\dot{s}_{-1\frac{1}{2}} - 0{\cdot}006\,WP + 0{\cdot}018$$
$$\qquad\qquad\quad (39{\cdot}9) \qquad\qquad\quad (2{\cdot}5) \qquad (2{\cdot}1) \qquad\quad (3{\cdot}1)$$

$$\text{sample period 1951--83; } \bar{R}^2 = 0{\cdot}98; \; DW = 2{\cdot}01$$

where $WP = 1$ in 1951–63, 1971, 1974, 1976 and 1980
$\qquad\quad\; = -1$ in 1972, 1975, 1977 and 1982
$\qquad\quad\; = 0$ in other years

Because of the high coefficient of import prices, it seems likely that this variable
also represents the impact on Dutch export prices of competitors' export prices,
since Dutch exporting firms are partly price-takers on world markets. It is
interesting to note the impact of labour productivity growth, with a lag of one
and a half years, on export prices. This seems to be an important channel
through which firms have an influence on the market share and profitability
of their exports.

Less astonishing is the absence of the rate of unemployment because of
strongly centralized wage formation (see Driehuis, 1975). A recent OECD
study estimates a wage equation for the Netherlands where a small impact of
the unemployment rate on the percentage change in wages is found (Coe and
Gagliardi, 1985).[3] Combining their result with existing structural export price
equations yields a reduced-form export price function that is similar to equation
(20). Furthermore, we have tested whether wage policies have had a moderating
impact on inflation. The result is positive for the years 1951–63, where different

forms of central wage policy were continuously in practice. It is negative for the years 1971, 1974, 1976, 1980 and 1981, when incidental interventions in wage formation took place, but were followed by compensating wage increases in the following year.

To the two equations just mentioned we have to add a number of simple definitional equations in order to carry out the decomposition procedure in the next section. First, we have two equations linking the national income price deflator and the public expenditure price deflator to the endogenous price variable in the model, the export price of goods:

$$(21) \qquad \dot{p} = \phi_1 \dot{p}_f$$

$$(22) \qquad \dot{p}_g = \phi_2 \dot{p}_f.$$

Next, there is an equation for nominal national income:

$$(23) \qquad \dot{z} = (1 - \phi_3)\dot{y} + \phi_3 \dot{y}_g + \dot{p}$$

where Y_g = public production

ϕ_3 = share of public production in national production

Finally, we have a definition for the public burden:

$$(24) \qquad \dot{T}/Z_{-1} = \omega_1 \dot{g} - \omega_2 \dot{d}$$

where $\omega_1 = G/Z_{-1}$

$\omega_2 = D/Z_{-1}$

D = the public deficit

Equation (24) implies that the public deficit is considered the ultimate fiscal policy instrument.

In order to find values for parameters of the equations concerning production capacity, jobs and employment, especially for sector 1, a complicated estimation procedure has to be used. It is necessary to fix a few coefficients in advance, such as δ_1, γ_1 and π, while the value of ε has to be determined in an iterative procedure. Estimation results are available for sector 1 as a whole (Driehuis et al., 1979), for four subsectors (Driehuis and van den Noord, 1980) and for ten branches of industry (van den Noord, 1984). Table 1 presents the averages of the estimation results obtained for ten branches of industry, which are almost identical to results found in the more aggregative studies.

In addition, we have derived, from estimation results for five branches of industry in sector 2, the following equation:

$$(25) \qquad \dot{s}_2 = 0 \cdot 3(\dot{w} + \dot{p}) + 0 \cdot 5\dot{h} + 0 \cdot 02$$

where we have used overall real labour costs as a proxy for real labour costs in the labour-intensive sector.

TABLE 1

AVERAGE OF ESTIMATED PARAMETERS
IN EQUATIONS (2), (8) AND (13)

$\psi = 0 \cdot 790$	$\pi = 0 \cdot 020$
$\kappa_0 = 1 \cdot 600$	$\eta = 0 \cdot 074$
$\delta_1 = 0 \cdot 750$	$\theta = 0 \cdot 064$
$\gamma_1 = 0 \cdot 500$	$\rho = 0 \cdot 342$
$\varepsilon = 0 \cdot 010$	$\beta = 0 \cdot 257$
$\mu = 0 \cdot 037$	

Finally, the equation explaining the share of investment in production capacity (in efficiency units) reads

(26) $j_1 = 1 \cdot 22 \phi_4 \dot{\bar{y}} + 1 \cdot 275 \{0 \cdot 130(1 + \dot{k} - \dot{w} + \dot{p} - \dot{a})\}$

where $\bar{y}_t = 0 \cdot 2 y_t + 0 \cdot 3 y_{t-1} + 0 \cdot 3 y_{t-2} + 0 \cdot 2 y_{t-3}$; Π_0 is estimated to be $0 \cdot 130$ in 1956; and ϕ_4 is a parameter linking production growth in sector 1 to total production growth.

III. Decomposition

Using equations (21)-(24) and Table 2, we can construct Table 3, which is a decomposition of the determinants of production growth for four periods: 1960-66, 1967-73, 1974-79, and 1980-83. It should be noted that the fourth period is in fact too short and that its data are partly preliminary.

Table 2 shows the most characteristic forces behind the development of the Netherlands economy during the years 1960-83. It shows the fall in the

TABLE 2

DATA AND PARAMETERS USED FOR THE DECOMPOSITION
PROCEDURE

	1960–66	1967–73	1974–79	1980–83
Data (averages)				
$\dot{y}^*$	0·085	0·089	0·044	0·013
$\dot{p}_f^*$	0·020	0·049	0·124	0·092
$\dot{p}_m$	0·007	0·037	0·129	0·062
$\dot{e}_f$	0·008	0·016	0·042	0·005
$\dot{e}_m$	0·006	0·012	0·033	−0·016
$\dot{d}$	0·233	0·050	0·704	0·042
$\dot{p}_e$	0·051	0·046	0·036	0·033
$\dot{m}$	0·070	0·119	0·108	0·063
$\dot{w}$	0·081	0·122	0·102	0·051
$\dot{p}$	0·040	0·063	0·064	0·037
$\dot{p}_k$	0·046	0·058	0·044	0·070
$\dot{a}$	0·015	0·014	−0·031	−0·002
$\dot{h}$	−0·008	−0·009	−0·007	−0·002
WP	0·570	0	0	0
CC	0	0	1	1·430
$\dot{l}$	0·013	0·008	0·007	0·013
j_1	0·257	0·243	0·197	0·170
Parameters				
ϕ_1	6	3·5	1	0·4
ϕ_2	4	2·4	0·5	0·3
ϕ_3	0·10	0·12	0·14	0·14
ω_1	0·37	0·51	0·60	0·69
ω_2	0·037	0·035	0·049	0·108
χ_1	0·023	0·021	0·010	0·008
χ_2	0·020	0·020	0·020	0·020
χ_3	0·090	0·133	0·052	0·020
C	2·240	2·120	2·380	2·100
λ_1	0·429	0·401	0·328	0·273
λ_2	0·425	0·462	0·523	0·560
λ_3	0·146	0·137	0·149	0·167

growth rate of world trade after 1973, reweighted according to the geographic and product orientation of Dutch exports, as well as the acceleration of world inflation up to 1979 and its deceleration thereafter. The effective appreciation in the guilder was particularly strong during the third period. The difference between the effective appreciation on export markets and on import markets is significant. The latter even turned out to be an effective depreciation in the fourth period.

As concerns economic policy, there are three important trends: the first is the strong increase in the public deficit in the 1970s; the second is the slowing down of the growth rate of the volume of public expenditure of goods and services; and the third is the fall in the terms of exchange between market (export) goods and public goods (ϕ_2). These facts together imply a substantial increase in the public burden as a percentage of national income.

The most important determinant of production growth in the Netherlands is the volume of world trade, but the impact of domestic variables is not unimportant either (see Table 3). One of these variables is labour productivity growth, which slowed down remarkably. Economic policy has continuously played a significant role, although the policy mix was changing over time. Monetary and fiscal policy were stimulating during the years 1967–79 but restrictive afterwards. Exchange rate developments have played a significant negative role after 1973. Furthermore, since then the Netherlands economy has been under severe supply-determined constraints on commodity markets.

TABLE 3

DETERMINANTS OF PRODUCTION GROWTH, THE NETHERLANDS, 1960–1983
(averages)

	1960–66 (%)	1967–73 (%)	1974–79 (%)	1980–83 (%)
Foreign impact (total)	4·5	3·4	2·2	3·6
World trade	4·0	4·2	2·1	0·6
World inflation	0·5	−0·8	0·1	3·0
Domestic impact (total)	0·8	2·2	0·5	−4·1
Economic policy (total)	1·4	1·4	1·8	−0·6
of which:				
fiscal policy	0·2	0	1·3	0·1
monetary policy	0·8	1·4	1·3	0·7
exchange rate policy	0	0	−0·8	−1·4
wage policy	0·4	0	0	0
Other domestic factors	−0·6	0·8	0·3	−1·5
of which:				
labour productivity	1·9	1·9	0·7	0·3
Constraints commodity market	0	0	−1·4	−2·0
Production growth[a]	5·3	5·6	2·7	−0·5

[a] Production growth refers to gross value added in enterprises in constant prices.

It will be clear that the labour market situation suffered considerably from the bad performance of the commodity market. In order to make that clear, we first study the determinants of labour productivity growth on the basis of the relevant labour productivity equations. Actual labour productivity growth is dominated by fundamental or potential labour productivity growth (see equation (12)). Fluctuations in prodution also play a part via the rate of capacity utilization. However, there is a high degree of labour hoarding, because firing of workers is difficult and time-consuming in the Netherlands.

The main determinants of potential labour productivity growth (Table 4) are the rate of capital accumulation and the rate of disembodied labour-augmenting technical progress.[4] The installation of new capital goods wherein new production techniques are embodied is of utmost importance in order for an open economy to maintain its international market share and to control the profitability in industries exposed to foreign competition (Driehuis, 1981). The share of investment in output has fallen steadily in the Netherlands owing to the necessity for firms to adjust their capacity growth to the decline in expenditure growth and to a squeeze in the after-tax profit share, which in its turn was related mainly to the excess of the rise of real wages costs over labour productivity growth. The slowing down of the growth rate of productive capacity in sector 1 also reduced productivity growth through dynamic economies of scale (Verdoorn's Law). It is furthermore of importance to note that the development of relative factor prices—or, more accurately, the development of real labour costs in comparison with real capital costs—has stimulated the replacement of equipment in sector 1 so that potential labour productivity growth was stimulated in this way. After 1979 this process moderated because relative factor prices developed in such a way that rationalization investments were reduced. In sector 2, real wage costs rather than relative real factor prices play a part in the rise in labour productivity. Although labour productivity growth is much lower here than in capital-intensive industries, rising real labour costs have caused an acceleration of potential labour productivity growth in sector 2, at least up to 1980. Finally, there was a negative influence of the shortening of working hours on the growth of labour productivity.

Combination of the decomposition results for production growth (Table 3) and labour productivity growth (Table 4) enable us to make a decomposition of the development of employment in the market sector (Table 5).

TABLE 4

DETERMINANTS OF LABOUR PRODUCTIVITY GROWTH,
THE NETHERLANDS, 1960–1983
(averages)

	1960–66 (%)	1967–73 (%)	1974–79 (%)	1980–83 (%)
Impact of disembodied labour-augmenting technical progress	1·3	2·2	1·7	1·3
working hours	−0·6	−0·7	−0·5	−0·1
real-labour costs	0·6	0·8	0·6	0
real-capital costs	−0·1	−0·2	−0·3	0·1
production	2·9	2·9	1·3	−0·2
other factors	0·2	0·4	0·1	0·2
Labour productivity growth	4·3	5·4	2·7	1·3

Employment growth in each period is less than in the preceding one. The positive influence of external factors is evident. Economic policy measures have also contributed to employment growth, but in the last period it was reducing employment in the market sector. Other factors depressing employment were the constraints on the commodity market from 1973 onwards, disembodied labour-augmenting technical progress, and relative factor prices, although the impact of the last two were clearly weakening.

TABLE 5

DETERMINANTS OF EMPLOYMENT GROWTH,
THE NETHERLANDS, 1960–1983
(averages)

	1960–66 (%)	1967–73 (%)	1974–79 (%)	1980–83 (%)
Impact of				
external factors	2·2	1·8	1·1	2·5
economic policy	0·4	0·7	1·1	−0·4
constraints commodity market	0	0	−0·7	−1·0
real-labour costs	−0·5	−0·7	−0·5	0
real-capital costs	0·1	0·2	0·3	−0·1
disembodied labour-augmenting technical progress	−1·2	−1·9	−1·5	−1·1
shortening working hours	0·5	0·6	0·4	0·1
other factors	−0·9	−0·5	−0·2	−1·9
Employment market sector	0·6	0·2	0	−1·8

Finally, we attempt to make an estimate of the relative importance of the three types of unemployment. Once a starting year is chosen, equations (4) and (12) enable us to calculate a time series for jobs. Comparison with a time series for the labour supply, in which discouraged-worker and additional-worker effects are included, yields an estimate of the shortage of jobs (if any). This gives an idea of Marxian or classical unemployment (Malinvaud, 1977, 1980).

According to equation (18), we must also make an estimate of unemployment arising from labour market imperfections (including frictional unemployment). From a great number of studies it becomes clear that, after 1967, unemployment arising from labour market imperfections started to rise, and not in the Netherlands alone (Driehuis, 1978, den Broeder et al., 1984; Muysken, 1985). However, views differ with respect to the importance of this phenomenon. All studies agree about a level of 65,000–70,000 unemployed arising from labour market imperfections in the beginning of the 1960s, but they yield diverging estimates for recent years. Here we shall assume the most pessimistic views on the functioning of the Dutch labour market, as incorporated in studies by Muysken (1985) and den Broeder et al. (1984), which imply that this type of unemployment rose from about 65,000 in 1960 to about 150,000 in 1983. Among the reasons for this phenomenon, increased selectivity of both workers and employers facilitated by the welfare state rank high; but increased

variability of production growth, regional problems and demographic factors
are also very important.

On the basis of all the information mentioned, we arrive at the conclusion
(see Table 6) that since 1973 an increasing shortage of jobs has arisen in the
Netherlands. This shortage is due mainly to the decline in capital formation
in sector 1 and to a fall in output growth in sector 2 arising from reduced
(consumer) demand.

TABLE 6

DETERMINANTS OF RISE IN UNEMPLOYMENT IN THE NETHERLANDS,
1960–1983
(averages)

	1960–66 ('000)	1967–74 ('000)	1974–79 ('000)	1980–83 ('000)
Labour Supply	57	37	35	68
Employment in:				
market sector	56	10	−2	−69
public sector	6	12	15	7
Unemployment	−5	15	22	130
arising from				
labour market imperfections	1	3	6	9
shortage of jobs	0	0	31	57
business cycle	−6	12	−15	64

In addition, we can observe increasing unemployment arising from labour
market imperfections. However, this type of unemployment is far less important
than that arising from a shortage of jobs. After 1980 cyclical unemployment
is also of significance. A rough estimate suggests that, out of an unemployment
total of 800,000 in 1983, 20 per cent is due to labour market imperfections, 55
per cent is due to a shortage of jobs, and 25 per cent is the consequence of
cyclical movements in production. However, it is not impossible that labour
hoarding has decreased during the last recession so that the real amount of
cyclical unemployment may be lower than our calculations suggests.

IV. CONCLUSIONS

On the basis of existing empirical work on the commodity market and the
labour market, we have undertaken a breakdown of the factors determining
the rise in unemployment in the Netherlands during the period 1960–83. The
conclusions are as follows.

Until 1967 unemployment was frictional, i.e. arising from normal labour
market imperfections, and cyclical. After 1967 mismatches on the labour
markets increased because of greater selectivity of both workers and employers.
Frictional unemployment was rising as well, owing to increased cyclical instability in the commodity market. After 1974 a new important component of

unemployment can be observed because of an increased shortage of jobs. An accelerating labour supply, as well as a declining number of jobs in the market sector, caused this shortage. Behind the decline in the number of jobs are sectorally differentiated factors, such as the fall in the rate of capital accumulation in capital-intensive industries and the slowing down of production growth in labour-intensive industries.

The falling rate of investment was in its turn caused by the squeeze in after-tax profits and a slowing down of production growth, which cannot be explained by world trade and world inflation. Two additional factors seem to be responsible for the weak performance of output growth in the Netherlands: supply constraints on the commodity market, and restrictive economic policies, particularly since 1979.

No equilibrating price mechanism on the commodity or labour market was observed that could have reversed the downward spiral in economic quantities such as production and employment. Even if favourable movements in relative factor prices had occurred, expansionary economic policy measures would have been indispensable for the creation of a more favourable labour market situation. Although labour market imperfections play a part, their role in the rise of unemployment is strongly exaggerated in public discussions. Much more important and urgent is the removal of mismatches on the commodity market.

ACKNOWLEDGMENTS

I wish to thank Tammo Oegema and Corine Sips for their research assistance, Rick van der Ploeg for his comments during the conference, and the editors of this special volume for their suggestions for improving the first draft of this paper.

NOTES

1. This model is called JELKA II and succeeds JELKA I (Driehuis, 1984), which only modelled the demand side of the commodity market.

2. In equation (2) $\dot{V}$ is reduced by unity, because when the economic lifetime of equipment is constant ($\dot{V} = 0$) at given factor prices, a constant fraction of productive capacity is scrapped because of economic obsolescence.

3. This equation reads (estimation period 1969–82)

$$\dot{w} = 0 \cdot 94\dot{p} - 2 \cdot 24 \log u + 4 \cdot 92$$
$$\quad (3.5) \quad (5 \cdot 6) \qquad (4 \cdot 3)$$

$$\bar{R}^2 = 0 \cdot 63; \ DW = 2 \cdot 03; \ \text{s.e.e.} = 1 \cdot 17.$$

4. It will be clear that row 1 in Table 4 also reflects the change in the sectoral composition of output. The declining impact of disembodied labour-augmenting technical progress is therefore also the result of the fall in the share of the capital-intensive sector, the decline in production of natural gas, and the rise in the share of labour-intensive production.

REFERENCES

BROEDER, G. DEN, HEIJKE, J. A. M. and KONING, J. DE (1984). *Friction between Supply and Demand on the Netherlands Labour Market.* NEI paper no 2.

COE, D. T. and GAGLIARDI, F. (1985). *Nominal Wage Determination in the OECD Economics,* OECD Working Paper no. 19. Paris: OECD.

DRIEHUIS, W. (1975). Inflation, wage bargaining, wage policy and production structure: theory and empirical results for the Netherlands. *De Economist,* **123**, 638–79.

—— (1978). Labour market imbalances and structural unemployment. *Kyklos,* **31**, 638–61.

DRIEHUIS, W. (1981). Employment and technical progress in open economies. In Z. Hornstein et al., *The Economics of the Labour Market*, pp. 187-211. London: HMSO.

—— (1984). Dertig jaar economische ontwikkeling en economische politiek in Nederland. In H. den Hartog and J. Weitenberg (eds), *Toegepaste Economie: Grenzen en Mogelijkheden*, pp. 243-70. The Hague: Central Planbureau.

—— (1985). Arbeidsmarktrigiditeiten als Macro economisch Probleem. In *Praedviezen over de Flexibilisering van de Arbeidsmarkt*. OSA. The Hague: Staatsuitgeverij.

—— HEINEKEN, K. A. and SAVORNIN LOHMAN, A. F. DE (1979). Werkgelegenheid in kapitaal-gebruikende bedrijfstakken. In J. J. Klant *et al.* (eds), *Samenleving en Onderzoek*, pp. 147-82. Leiden: Stenfert Kroese.

—— and NOORD, P. J. VAN DEN (1980). *Produktie, Werkgelegenheid, Betalingsbalans en Sector-structuur in Nederland, 1960-1985*. Voorstudies en Achtergronden. The Hague: WRR.

EYK, C. VAN (1983). Possible policy implications of modern underemployment equilibrium theory. *De Economist*, **131**, 344-72.

MALINVAUD, E. (1977). *The Theory of Unemployment Reconsidered.* Oxford: Basil Blackwell.

—— (1980). *Profitability and Unemployment.* Cambridge: Cambridge University Press.

MALCOLMSON, J. M. (1975). Replacement and the rental value of capital equipment subject to obsolescence. *Journal of Economic Theory*, **10**, 24-41.

MUYSKEN, J. (1985). *Full capacity employment, unemployment and labour hoarding.* In D. Bosworth and D. F. Heathfield (eds), *Measuring Capacity and Factor Utilization.* London: Macmillan.

NOORD, P. J. VAN DEN (1984). *De Groei van de Arbeidsproduktiviteit in Nederland.* Amsterdam: SEO.

—— (1982). De Ontwikkeling van de Arbeidsproduktiviteit in Nederland, 1963-1980. *Maandschrift Economie*, **46**, 395-411

RIDDER, P. B. DE (1971). *Een Jaargangenmodel met Vaste Technische coëfficiënten en in Kapitaal Geincorporeerde Arbeidsbesparende Technische Vooruitgang.* CPB Occasional Paper no. 14. Den Haag: CPB.

VERDOORN, P. J. (1952). Welke zijn de achtergronden en vooruitzichten van de economische integratie in Europa en welke gevolgen zal deze integratie hebben met name voor de welvaart in Nederland? *Prae-adviezen van de Vereniging voor de Staathuishoudkunde*, pp. 48-132.

WRR (1980). *Industry in the Netherlands: its Place and Future.* The Hague: WRR.

Spanish Industrial Unemployment: Some Explanatory Factors

By J. J. Dolado and J. L. Malo de Molina

Bank of Spain

and A. Zabalza

Ministry of Economy and Finance and University of Valencia

Introduction

The high level of unemployment is probably the worst feature of the recent evolution of the Spanish economy. In 1970 the overall unemployment rate stood at 1 per cent of the civilian labour force; in 1984 it is estimated to have gone over the 20 per cent level. This is a substantial increase which has no parallel in any European country. Between 1970 and 1983 the average unemployment rate in the EEC rose by 8·6 percentage points, while the increase in Spain over the same period was of 17 points.

There is wide agreement among Spanish economists that these figures may be overstating the actual extent of the problem. The incidence of the underground economy and of fraudulent practices in unemployment registration may be wider than in most EEC countries. Nevertheless, we believe that, even taking into account these measurement difficulties, there has been a genuine worsening of the employment situation in Spain relative to that in other Western economies.

The purpose of this paper is to review the evidence of the last 20 years about the main variables that influence the Spanish labour market, and to attempt a preliminary explanation of the increase in unemployment. For the latter task we use the analytical framework recently developed by Layard and Nickell (1984a), and concentrate on those institutional factors that may have influenced the level of unemployment consistent with non-accelerating inflation (NAIRU).

The next section of the paper describes the key facts that we are trying to explain. Section II presents the analytical framework that we use, and discusses its theoretical foundations. These are dealt with very briefly, since they are fully explained in Layard and Nickell (1984a). Here we concentrate mostly on the empirical specification and on the description of the variables. The econometric results are presented in Section III and the explanation of the unemployment increase is given in Section IV. The final section summarizes our findings.

I. The Facts

Spain's overall economic performance was outstanding during the second half of the 1960s and the beginning of the 1970s, but afterwards has deteriorated substantially. Figure 1 shows the growth of GDP, the rate of inflation and the rate of unemployment during the last 20 years. The behaviour of GDP resembles that of other European countries, although the rates of growth during the first ten years of the period were much higher in Spain than elsewhere in Europe.

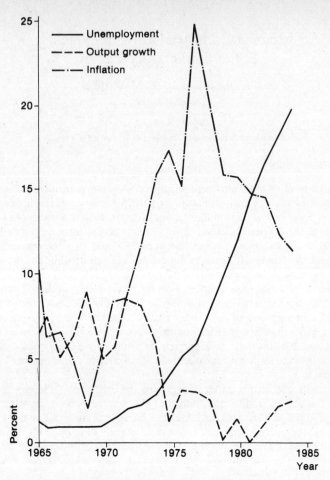

FIGURE 1.   GDP growth, inflation and unemployment. 'Unemployment' refers to the overall unemployment rate of the civilian labour force; 'inflation', to the rate of growth of CPI; and 'output growth', to the rate of growth of GDP.
Sources: National Accounts and Bank of Spain.

The fall of this rate in 1975 roughly coincides with the general slowdown in economic activity that followed the first increase in the price of oil. The effects of the crisis on GDP are reflected in a decrease of almost 5 points in its average rate of growth. Although real output has managed to keep on growing even in the worst years of the crisis, it has doubtless experienced a severe reduction relative to its potential level. (Before 1974, real output was growing on average at more than 8 per cent per year.) Inflation has in general run at levels well above those of other European countries, and has proved difficult to curb in the last years of the period, even with widespread unemployment and with very low levels of output growth. Clearly, the worst feature of Spain's recent economic performance has been unemployment, which has grown to levels that ten years ago would have seemed unthinkable. We turn now to a more detailed look at this rate, which is going to be the main object of our analysis in this paper.

Figure 2 shows the evolution of employment and of the labour force. From 1964 until 1973, both labour force and employment increase consistently and practically in the same manner, with a gap between them of about 2 percentage points. After 1973, however, while the labour force stays more or less constant, employment falls very rapidly, showing in 1984 a gap of about 20 percentage points with respect to the labour force.

Figure 3 shows again the evolution of the overall unemployment rate since 1964, and gives details of how the agricultural, industrial, building and service sectors have contributed to this rate.[1] Until 1970 the overall rate was practically stable, around the 1 per cent level. From that year onwards it began to show a moderate increase, reaching 2·7 per cent of the labour force in 1974. Since then the rise has accelerated dramatically, particularly after 1977, and in the fourth quarter of 1984 the unemployment rate was 21·7 per cent, more than 12 times the rate 20 years earlier.

FIGURE 2. Total labour force and employment (logs).
Source: Bank of Spain.

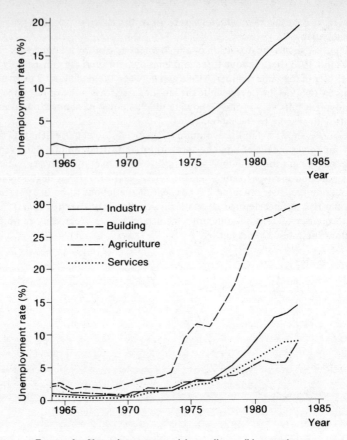

FIGURE 3.   Unemployment rates: (a) overall rate; (b) sectoral rates.
Source: Bank of Spain.

The sectoral rates shown in Figure 3(b) give some idea of the unemployment structure by sector. There was a clear lead in the building sector, where unemployment began to increase markedly in 1975. In the other sectors the change in the trend did not appear until after 1977, but since then, with the exception of agriculture, unemployment has risen consistently rapidly in all sectors. There is some deceleration in the rate of growth during the last two or three years. This deceleration hardly shows in the overall rate, but this is due to the substantial increase of unemployed school-leavers that has taken place towards the end of the period considered, and which is not taken into account in the sectoral rates.

The Spanish occupational structure has experienced substantial changes during the last 20 years. The share of building and industry in overall employment has remained more or less constant. That of agriculture, on the other hand, has gone down dramatically, the fall being completely absorbed by services. In 1964, agricultural employment represented 36·5 per cent of total employment, while employment in services was 31 per cent. In 1984 the shares were 17·6 and 49·0 per cent, respectively. This is, by any standard, a major structural change, which differentiates Spain from other European countries, and which could have had an influence on the overall unemployment rate.

We will abstract somewhat from these structural changes by concentrating our attention on the industrial sector. This is a choice forced upon us by data availability. Even for industry, it is impossible to go back before 1964 and to obtain reliable annual series of most of the variables of interest. For other sectors, the poor quality of the data, if not its outright absence, prevent any statistical analysis with even a minimum hope of rigour.[2] By concentrating on the industrial sector we will also be able to compare some of our estimates with other results that have been obtained by independent research, and thus will be able to evaluate more confidently the meaning of our findings.[3]

The cost of labour has increased substantially in Spanish industry, and this could be one of the reasons behind the huge rise in unemployment. Figure 4 shows the evolution of four measures related to the price of labour. There has been an impressive rise in the real cost of labour faced by employers. In 1984 it had more than trebled with respect to 1964. Social contributions paid by employers have also increased markedly, as is shown by the widening gap between the product wage and the real labour cost. In 1984 the average employer contribution in industry was 26 per cent of gross pay, whereas in 1964 it was only 15 per cent.

Since employee contributions represent a small fraction of gross pay, and since indirect taxes have been roughly constant over the period, the evolution of the real wage, also shown in Figure 4, is very similar to that of the product wage. On the other hand, the consumption wage, which subtracts income taxes from pay and is the closest approximation to what workers can potentially devote to consumption, has increased much less than the real wage, the difference representing the evolution of income taxes.[4] While in 1983 the real wage was 3·46 times higher than in 1964, the consumption wage was only 3·24 times higher.

Spanish industry has undergone an important process of modernization during the period considered, and it could be argued that most of the increases in labour costs documented above are simply reflecting productivity improvements. This is to some extent true, but we believe that, even after taking that into account, labour has recently become a much more expensive factor than it was before. A rough way of accounting for productivity improvements is to consider how real labour costs per unit of output have grown.[5] From 1970 until 1982 these increased by 41·6 per cent in Spain, while in Italy (the EEC country with the highest rise) the corresponding index was only 17·5 per cent higher. In other EEC countries the increase was much smaller, and in Denmark and the Netherlands it was even negative. We thus conclude that, in comparison with other countries, Spanish industrial labour has become much more expensive than it was in the 1960s, although this must to a certain extent be due to the relatively low level at which these labour costs started.

While the increase in labour costs is clearly endogenous to the labour market, the increase in the relative price of imported materials that also took place during this period is to a large extent exogenous. Figure 5 presents the evolution of this relative price during the period, which clearly charts very closely the incidence of the two oil price crises. There are three well differentiated periods. First, there is the period 1964–73, in which input prices were

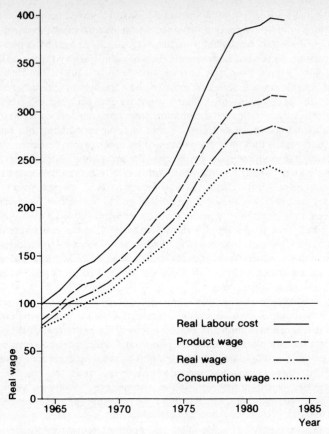

FIGURE 4.   Real cost of labour, product, real and consumption wages. The 'product wage' is defined as W/P. 'Real labour cost' is defined as $W(1+t_1)/P$, where W is gross pay, P is product price and t_1 is employer's contribution to social security. The 'real wage' is defined as $\{W(1-t_4)/P(1+t_3)\}$, where t_4 is employee's contribution to social security and t_3, indirect taxes. 'Consumption wage' is defined as $\{W(1-t_4)(1-t_2)/P(1+t_3)\}$ where t_2 is income tax.
Source: Bank of Spain.

more or less constant. Second, there is the period that begins with the first oil price rise, which in Spain shows up with a big increase in relative input prices, particularly in 1974, and with some translation of this rise into output prices in the following five years. Despite this rise in output prices, in 1979 the relative price of materials was 21·5 per cent higher than in 1973. Third is the period from 1980 until now, which is dominated by the second oil price shock, and which has meant an increase in relative prices of an additional 66·1 per cent between 1983 and 1979. Overall, in 1983 relative input prices were 100·3 per cent higher than in 1964.

These huge changes in the relative price of labour and other inputs may have also produced a process of accelerated economic obsolescence of capital, which shows up most forcefully in industry. Some estimates of the stock of capital for that sector show that, while between 1964 and 1973 it grew at an

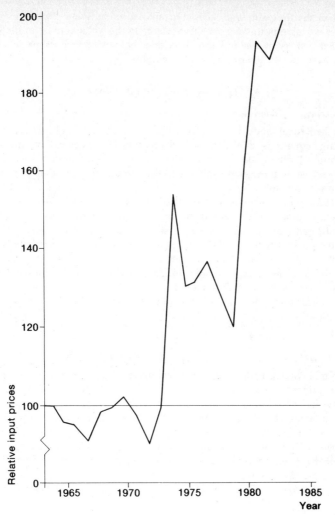

FIGURE 5. Relative imported input prices (price of imported inputs relative to product price). *Source*: Bank of Spain.

average annual rate of 4·5 per cent, between 1974 and 1978 this rate of growth went down to 3·6 per cent, and between 1979 and 1982 to 1·9 per cent. Thus, the squeezed or even negative profit margins experienced by firms may have had serious and durable consequences both on the level of installed capacity and on its potential growth.

We therefore see that the period under analysis has been characterized by substantial increases in two relative prices: the relative price of labour and the relative price of materials.[6] The second has been quite widespread in Europe, but the severity of the first is a rather singular Spanish phenomenon. Both increases could, in principle, have affected labour demand and thus could explain the dramatic upsurge of unemployment in Spain. In the rest of the paper we attempt to consider these factors in the wider context of the labour market and try to evaluate the effect that they, or other possible influences, may have had on the evolution of unemployment.

II. ANALYTICAL FRAMEWORK

Theoretical considerations

The theoretical model is taken from Layard and Nickell (1984a) and consists of three equations: a labour demand equation, a wage equation, and a price equation. Probably the best way to go about the description of this model is to start first with the employment and wage equations, and then to introduce the price equation.

The labour demand and wage equations together form a fairly conventional structural model of the labour market. The main innovations introduced by Layard and Nickell, which we also take into account in our empirical work, are the possibility that cyclical aggregate demand factors enter directly in the employment equation, the specification in level terms of the wage equation, and the much more explicit and detailed consideration of labour demand and supply factors in the wage equation.[7]

In logarithms, the basic structure of these two equations can be represented as follows:

$$(1) \qquad n = -\alpha(w-p) - \beta(p_m - p) + \gamma D + \lambda k + Z$$

$$(2) \qquad (w-p^e) = -\delta(l-n) - \eta(p_m - p) + \rho D + \mu(k-l) + Y.$$

Employment, n, depends negatively on real wages $(w-p)$ and on relative input prices $(p_m - p)$,[8] and positively on a cyclical aggregate demand factor, D. Demand for labour is defined for a given stock of capital, k, and, under certain assumptions, in the long-run it will grow as this stock grows. Finally, Z is a demand shift variable, and all Greek letters are positive parameters. Equation (1) is therefore a fairly standard labour demand equation, in which output has been substituted out, and in which possible direct aggregate demand effects are taken into account.[9]

Real wages, defined in terms of the expected price level, are in turn determined by both demand factors—$(p_m - p)$, D and k—and supply factors—l and Y—where l is the size of the labour force and Y a supply shift variable. Factors that raise demand will raise real wages, and factors that raise supply will depress real wages. However, the equation should be interpreted not as a reduced form but as a structural form, at least when other variables suggested by wage bargaining models, such as outside labour opportunities—which here we proxy by $(l-n)$—also enter the model.

Writing the wage equation with actual real wages on the left-hand side (LHS) and introducing price shocks $(p^e - p)$ in the shift factor Y, we have that equations (1) and (2) determine real wages and employment (or unemployment), given all the other variables in the model. The resulting employment equation is:

$$(3) \qquad n = (l + \alpha\delta)^{-1} \{ \alpha(\delta + \mu)l + (\lambda - \alpha\mu)k - (\beta - \alpha\eta)(p_m - p) + (\gamma - \alpha\rho)D$$
$$+ (Z - \alpha Y) \}.$$

Equation (3) makes unemployment dependent on aggregate demand besides other, as yet unspecified, demand and supply factors. This is unsatisfactory because, to the extent that aggregate demand can be controlled by the government, unemployment could be reduced at will, by simply increasing D.[10] It is therefore more sensible to think of (3) as a relationship that gives pairs of values of n and D that are consistent with labour market equilibrium, but which in itself cannot determine the equilibrium level of employment. For that, we need another equation to explain cyclical demand.

Within the context of this model, the only other channel through which demand can exert an influence is the pricing decisions of the imperfectly competitive firms assumed above. The mark-up of prices on costs is determined by cyclical demand, by relative import prices, by the capital–labour ratio and by expectational errors, which in the empirical model below are represented by second-differences on wages.[11] Ignoring these expectational errors, the basic structure of this equation is the following:

$$(4) \qquad (p - w) = \sigma D + \phi(p_m - p) - \tau(k - l) + X$$

where X reflects other variables affecting the pricing decision.

Now, (4) and (1)—the labour demand function—also form a sub-model with two equations and three unknowns; the real wage, employment and cyclical demand. And, as previously, we can also eliminate real wages and this time interpret the resulting relationship as giving pairs of values of n and D that are consistent with product market equilibrium:

$$(5) \qquad n = (\alpha\sigma + \gamma)D + (\alpha\phi - \beta)(p_m - p) + (\lambda - \alpha\tau)k + \alpha\tau l + (\alpha X + Z).$$

For any given level of demand, prices will be determined according to (4) so that demand is satisfied and inflation is constant. But determining prices as a mark-up on costs means implictly also determining the real wage. And this real wage may not be consistent with labour market equilibrium, in the sense that the level of employment that follows may differ from the level of employment given by expression (3). Simultaneous labour and product market equilibrium can be obtained only when both (3) and (5) are satisfied. These form a system of two equations in the two unknowns n and D. Any level of demand above the equilibrium D given by (3) and (5) will increase employment but at the expense of increasing inflation. Setting $p = p^e$ and $w = w^e$, the level of n corresponding to equilibrium D gives the non-accelerating inflation level of employment and, for a given labour force, the non-accelerating inflation rate of unemployment.[12]

Empirical specification

In the following section we present the results of estimating equations (1), (2) and (4) using Spanish data for the industrial sector. Here we want to describe the empirical specification of these equations and the additional variables determining the shift factors Z, Y and X.

Labour demand equation. Employment, n, refers to male and female full-time employment in the Spanish industrial sector. We ignore hours worked owing to lack of adequate data on this variable for the whole period considered.

The relative price of labour is defined as *real labour cost*; that is, average gross weekly pay plus employer's social security contributions,[13] relative to output price. In logarithms, if gross pay is denoted by w, output price by p

and employer's contributions by t_1, real labour cost is defined as $(w + t_1 - p)$. Again, owing to lack of reliable data on hours, we could not define this variable in terms of hourly earnings.

Relative input prices, $(p_m - p)$, are an index of prices of imported materials relative to output price. Given that in this paper we are considering only the industrial sector, it might have been appropriate to include also an index of intermediate goods from other sectors of the economy. Data limitations prevented us from constructing such index, but, given the relative size of the other two sectors that could have contributed inputs to industry (building and agriculture), we doubt that this omission has any significant effect on our results.

We tried several variables to proxy *cyclical demand*, but in the end the only ones that exerted a significant effect were an index of *competitiveness* (the real exchange rate) (e) and an *after-tax real interest rate* (r).[14] Among the variables initially tried, but which proved to be insignificant, were an index of *world trade* (deviations from trend) and a battery of *adjusted and unadjusted deficits* (as a proportion of GDP). We corrected the deficit both for inflation and for the cycle, and we carried out these corrections using several methods, but could never obtain any significant result.

The stock of capital is taken from Dolado and Malo de Molina (1984),[15] and in the shift factor Z we consider two additional variables; *labour-augmenting technical progress* (a) and a measure of *firing costs* (c). Technical progress is defined as in Layard and Nickell (1984b), and the logarithm of the series is smoothed by a trend. We also impose the restriction (accepted by the data) that the elasticity of employment with respect to this variable ought to be equal to the absolute value of the real wage elasticity minus one. The measure of firing costs is defined as the ratio of average redundancy payments to wages, and is included to take into account the increasing relaxation in employment protection legislation that has recently taken place in Spain. Although this definition captures fairly well the actual cost of firing that (on average) employers have had to face when reducing their labour force, it is somewhat unsatisfactory because it depends on unemployment, and this introduces an endogeneity problem. As unemployment has become widespread, redundancy has affected workers with long periods of tenure. And the result of this is that, despite the increasing firing facilities given by the legislation, average redundancy payments as a percentage of wages have grown since 1977. We adjust for this endogeneity problem by defining the redundancy pay for an employee of a given tenure.

Wage equation. The dependent variable of the wage equation is the *real labour cost.* Note that in principle the appropriate price variable in this equation is the expected price of consumption. This expected price can be substituted by the actual consumption price by including a term $(p^{ec} - p^c)$ on the RHS of the equation, where p^{ec} is the expected consumption price. Also, if we want to define the variable in terms of output prices, as we do in equation (2), we must include *indirect taxes* (t_3) on the RHS of the equation.

Given that we are considering only the industrial sector, we face an additional problem. To be consistent with the employment equation, the price variable must be defined as the price of industrial output, which clearly is only one component of the price of consumption. We took this into account by including in the RHS of the equation also the price of consumption relative to the price of industrial output; but this variable, as well as the expectational error term considered above, was never significant.[16]

The *labour force* is obtained by adding employment, as defined above, to unemployed people in industry.

The shift factor Y includes the following variables.

(1) *Taxes.* In addition to *indirect taxes* as a proportion of GDP at market prices (t_3), and *employer's social security* contributions as a proportion of wages (t_1), which have been discussed above, we also include *labour income tax* and *employee social security contributions* as a proportion of wages (t_2). As pointed out in Section I, these have increased substantially in the recent past and may have played an important role in collective bargaining, exerting some upward pressure on gross wages.

(2) *Firing costs.* The reduction that redundancy payments for given tenure have experienced in Spain could also have had a positive influence on gross pay.

(3) *Replacement ratio.* The larger unemployment benefits are, relative to wages, the smaller is the amount of labour supplied and, *ceteris paribus*, the higher the real wage. We tested for this possible influence on wages by including the average replacement ratio, but, as with redundancy payments, this measure is somewhat affected by endogeneity. With the number of unemployed people, unemployed duration has also increased during the period. Thus, since the amount of the benefit paid decreases with duration, the existence of more long-term unemployed people has meant that the average replacement ratio has tended to fall—and this despite a consistent improvement of unemployment benefits. So in the empirical analysis we try an adjusted replacement ratio, which corrects for this effect by holding constant the unemployment duration over the period.

(4) *Mismatch.* Unemployment arising from a mismatch between demand and supply should not exert any restraining influence on wages. So, one way of taking this into account is to include a measure of mismatch in the wage equation, which should appear with a positive sign. Mismatch is proxied by the absolute change in the proportion of manufacturing over total employment, and to some extent should capture the effect that the structural change of Spanish industry documented above may have had on industrial wages.

(5) *Union pressure.* This is a difficult variable to define for Spain. During the Franco regime all workers were compulsorily unionized, but this meant little for the real effect unions could have on wages. Also, strikes were forbidden, and there is no reliable record of the number and extent of industrial disputes, although they are known to have grown in importance towards the end of that regime. On the other hand, it is widely acknowledged that unions had a decisive influence on wages during the transition between the previous regime and the present constitutional monarchy, and that subsequently this influence has been greatly mitigated by the existence of regular and wide-ranging incomes policies.

We tried several definitions of this variable. Excluding days lost on strike, for lack of data, or union membership, for lack of meaning of this indicator, we were left with the alternative of modelling this variable on the basis of incomes policies. The problem here is that the previous regime can be characterized by a constant application of an incomes policy of some sort, and that during the present regime incomes policies have also played an important and almost permanent role. After experimenting with several alternatives, which included using information on the agreed ceilings on wage growth, we opted for a simple 1-0 dummy, which took the value 0 until 1973, the year of the death of Franco's prime minister, Mr Carrero-Blanco; 1 from 1973 until 1977, the year in which the Moncloa Pact was signed between government, opposition and unions; and again 0 since then.

We believe that this definition captures well the period during which the pressure of unions on wages was at its highest. Before 1974 political control of unions was too great to allow them any influence. The death of Mr Carrero-Blanco in 1973 is accepted to have really signalled the end of the Franco regime, and the signature of the Moncloa Pact in 1977 marked the beginning of a series of agreements on incomes policies which have since been an almost continuous feature of Spanish economic life.

(6) *Other variables.* Since *labour-augmenting technical progress* has been included in the employment equation, it must also be considered in the wage equation, where it can have a positive or a negative effect. This variable should in principle fulfil the same neutrality condition as capital, but the data rejected this restriction.

We would have liked also to include variables proxying *changes in the intensity of search*, but data on vacancies do not exist in Spain, so it was impossible to test whether the relationship between unemployment and vacancies has remained stable over the period or has changed. We tried lagged values of the unemployment rate to see whether there is any significant 'discouraged worker' effect when unemployment rises rapidly, but the results were always negative.[17]

Price equation. Practically all variables that enter into the price equation have already been defined. Demand and relative input prices should have a positive effect on the price mark-up, and productivity a negative effect. We include technical progress, which should also reduce the price mark-up for given levels of the other variables. Finally, the expectational error term is measured by a *second-difference on nominal labour costs,* which we expect to have a negative influence on the mark-up. The faster labour costs grow, the more likely it is that expected wages have fallen short of actual wages, and that the mark-up has been fixed below the optimal level.

III. Empirical Results

Employment equation

Table 1 presents the results of estimating equation (1) on annual data on the industrial sector for the period 1964-83. The 20 observations available prevent us from attempting to estimate any complex dynamic structure for the equation or from carrying out proper stability tests.[18] Thus the results should be taken with care and interpreted as preliminary until more data become available. However, it is interesting to note that the estimates obtained for this equation are similar to those reported in Dolado and Malo de Molina (1984), with quarterly data, similar to those obtained by Raymond (1983) with annual data, and quite consistent with both economic theory and findings based on data from other countries (Layard and Nickell, 1984b).

TABLE 1

EMPLOYMENT EQUATION
Dependent variable, n

Independent variables	Coefficients	t-ratios
n_{-1}	0·896	14·3
$(w + t_1 - p)^*$	0·276	2·2
$(w + t_1 - p)_{-1}$	−0·373	2·6
$(p_m - p)^*$	0·0386	2·2
$(p_m - p)_{-1}$	−0·0677	4·1
c^*	—	—
a	−0·007	$\{x_L^2(1) = 2·3\}$
k	0·104	$\{x_L^2(1) = 3·0\}$
D^*	0·073	2·7
RHO		−0·38 (3·2)
s		0·009
DW		2·22
R^2		0·99
$x_{iv}^2(\cdot)$		4·5 (4)
wage elasticity		−0·935
Other input price elasticity		−0·280
Technical progress elasticity		−0·065

Notes:
1. Estimates are obtained by IV
2. The demand variable is $D = e - 1·95r$
3. RHO is the AR(1) coefficient using Fair's instruments plus some additional instruments; s is the standard error of the regression; R^2 is the coefficient of determination; DW is the Durbin–Watson statistic; $x_L^2(\cdot)$ test for the corresponding linear restriction, $x_{iv}^2(\cdot)$ test for the validity of the instruments.
4. The t-ratios correspond to White's heteroscedasticity-consistent t-ratios.
5. (*) denotes instrumented variables. The instruments used were Fair's instruments, the tax wedge and lagged labour force—in total, 10 instruments.

The estimated long-run wage elasticity is found to be −0·94, which is similar to the elasticity of −1·2 obtained by Dolado and Malo de Molina (1984) with quarterly data. Real input prices have an overall negative influence on employment in both equations, which suggests that in the long run the output effect of relative price changes dominates over the substitution effect. The net effect, however—an elasticity of −0·28—is much smaller than that exerted by wages.

To investigate possible direct demand effects, we first tried several variables on their own, and then, for efficiency, we ran the chosen linear combination as one single variable which we call D. Proceeding like this, in addition to overcoming some multicollinearity problems, also allows us to have a synthetic definition of demand effects for later use in the other equations.[19] Deviations from world trade and several measures of the public sector deficit did not exert any effect on employment.[20] In the end, the two variables selected were the real exchange rate and the after-tax real interest rate.

The elasticity of technical progress is imposed to be the absolute value of the wage elasticity minus one, and this, which is consistent with the hypothesis of labour-augmenting technical progress, is easily accepted by the data. The unit long-run elasticity of the stock of capital—that is, the assumption of constant returns to scale—is also imposed and is also roughly accepted by the data.[21]

Among other factors that could affect employment, we tried the firing cost variable defined above. Since its effect was very insignificant, Table 1 omits this variable from the equation.

Wage equation

Table 2 shows the results of estimating equation (2). As mentioned above, we tried a measure of price surprises in the form of a second-difference of consumption prices, but this was never significant and is therefore not included in the equation. Since on the LHS of the equation we consider the price of industrial output, and since the real wage over which workers bargain ought to be defined in terms of overall consumption, we also tried a variable measuring the price of consumption relative to the price of industrial output (see n. 16 at end of paper), but again, this was not significant and is excluded from the equation.[22] A final variable that was not significant, and is omitted from the equation, is the relative price of inputs. Thus, given the effect of this variable in the employment equation, the neutrality restriction relating to this variable (see n. 12) is not accepted by the data.

The rate of unemployment exerts an important and very significant restraining influence on real wages.

Taxes play an important role in wage determination. Owing to multicollinearity, we could not discriminate between the indvidual effect of different

TABLE 2

REAL WAGE EQUATION

Dependent variable $(w + t_1 - p)$

Independent variables	Coefficients	t-ratios
U_{-1}	$-3 \cdot 018$	$4 \cdot 2$
$(mm + mm_{-1})^*$	$0 \cdot 021$	$1 \cdot 8$
$(t_1 + t_2 + t_3)^*$	1	$\{x_L^2(1) = 1 \cdot 8\}$
rr^*	$0 \cdot 445$	$3 \cdot 7$
c^*	$0 \cdot 445$	$3 \cdot 7$
UP	$0 \cdot 065$	$3 \cdot 4$
a^*	$0 \cdot 024$	$2 \cdot 4$
t	$0 \cdot 069$	$5 \cdot 2$
$(k - l)^*$	$1 \cdot 070$	$\{x_L^2(1) = 2 \cdot 8\}$
RHO		—
s		$0 \cdot 019$
DW		$2 \cdot 28$
R^2		$0 \cdot 99$
$\chi_{iv}^2(\cdot)$		$6 \cdot 23 \, (5)$

Notes:
1, 3 and 4 As for Table 1.
2. (*) denotes instrumented variables. The instruments used were the exogenous plus lagged endogenous variables, lagged demand, lagged real government expenditure, and lagged real world trade—in total, 12 instruments.

types of taxes, but we found that the sum of direct and indirect taxes (the tax wedge between the product and the consumption wage) had a positive and significant effect on real wages. The results suggest that taxes are fully borne by firms, as the restriction that the coefficient on the tax wedge should be unity is easily accepted by the data.

Among the supply variables tried, we found that the mismatch index, the replacement ratio, firing costs and the index of union pressure all exerted a positive effect on real wages.[23]

The coefficient on the capital–labour ratio is imposed to be the inverse of the absolute value of the wage elasticity in the labour demand equation, and this neutrality restriction is accepted by the data. The data, however, reject the neutrality condition for technical progress, although this takes the expected positive sign in the wage equation. Thus, long-run unemployment is estimated to be dependent on technical progress. This result, for Spain and for the period considered, should not be taken as totally unexpected. The index of technical progress has changed quite dramatically during these years, and it would have been quite remarkable that a period of such rapid change could have captured the long-run neutrality property that we believe technical progress should have. Finally, we included a time trend which was also significant and positive, thus suggesting that productivity changes may have not been fully captured by the included variables.

Price equation

Table 3 shows the results of estimating equation (4). Econometrically speaking, the price equation is the one that performs best out of the three considered. All variables take the expected sign, all are well determined, and the dynamic

TABLE 3

PRICE EQUATION

Dependent variable $(p - w - t_1)$

Independent variables	Coefficients	t-ratios
$(p_{-1} - w - t_1)$	0·406	5·4
$(p_{-2} - w - t_1)$	0·334	10·0
$\Delta^2(w + t_1)$	−0·145	2·9
D_{-1}	0·331	2·7
$(p_m - p)^*$	0·096	7·9
a^*	−0·033	2·2
$(k - l)$	−0·278	$\{x_L^2(1) = 3 \cdot 1\}$
RHO		—
s		0·0064
DW		2·31
R^2		0·99
$x_{iv}^2(\cdot)$		4·78 (5)

Notes:
1, 2, 3 and 4. As for Table 1.
2. (*) denotes instrumented variables. The instruments used were a constant, lags of prices, nominal labour cost, price of other inputs, lags of capital–labour ratio, real exchange rate, real interest rate, technical progress, government expenditure and mismatch—in total, 12 instruments.

structure of the equation is very robust to specification changes. Perhaps the most interesting result is that relative input prices exert a substantial effect on the price mark-up, despite the fact that we have not been able to detect any input price influence in the wage determination process. Another interesting finding is the slowness with which increases in wages are passed into prices. The short-run wage elasticities are around 0·12 with median lags of around one year. The specific form of the lagged dependent variables results from the imposition of a unitary long-run elasticity with respect to wages in an original specification where the dependent variable was p. The unit elasticity was easily accepted in the long run, but it was rejected in the short run.

IV. Explaining Spanish Industrial Unemployment

Actual unemployment

We first want to see to what extent these estimates explain the actual evolution of unemployment. That is, we want to evaluate how each of the variables considered, together with the level of cyclical demand, has contributed to the unemployment growth experienced during the last 20 years. Expression (3) above, expressed in terms of unemployment, answers precisely this question, and this (following Layard and Nickell, 1984a) is the accounting framework that we use in this section.

The nature of the model estimated in this paper does not allow us much precision about the dynamic structure of causes and effects. So we limit ourselves to explaining changes between averages of fairly large periods. We choose these periods according to the different regimes that can be identified in the explanatory variables. Probably, as far as recent economic history is concerned, the most representative of these is the relative price of imported inputs, which, as a result of the oil price crises, has gone through very clearly identifiable stages. As discussed in Section I (see Figure 5), there are three well differentiated periods as far as this variable is concerned: a first period of price stability (1964–73); a second period which is dominated by the initial increase in the price of oil (1974–79); and a third period, which begins with the second big increase in the price of oil and is continuing (1980–84). Given the small sample size available, we have preferred a slightly different distribution in order to make more equal the number of years in each subperiod and still keep the oil price shocks in two different subperiods. So the first subperiod runs from 1965 to 1971, while the second and third subperiods cover the years 1972–78 and 1979–83, respectively. Then we assume that changes between the averages of these periods explain changes between the unemployment averages of the corresponding periods with a one-year lead; that is, 1966–72, 1973–79 and 1980–84.[24]

Substituting the estimates obtained into equation (3), we arrive at the following expression:

$$u = 0·244(t_1 + t_2 + t_3) + 0·079rr + 0·079c + 0·017UP + 0·010mm$$

$$+ 0·073(p_m - p) + 0·023a - 0·184D + 0·017 \text{ time} + \text{constant}.$$

In Table 4 we show the actual changes that the explanatory variables have experienced between the three selected periods. It is interesting to note the

TABLE 4

ACTUAL CHANGES OF EXPLANATORY VARIABLES
(logarithmic differences)

Explanatory variables	$\dfrac{1972\text{–}78}{1965\text{–}71}$	$\dfrac{1979\text{–}83}{1972\text{–}78}$
$(t_1 + t_2 + t_3)$	0·047	0·105
rr	0·055	0·070
c	0	−0·180
UP	0·710	−0·710
mm	−0·150	−0·040
$(p_m - p)$	0·280	0·315
a	0·526	0·170
D	0·231	−0·205

Note: $(p_m - p)$ has been corrected for real exchange rate changes.

very large increase in taxes. The tax wedge rose almost 5 percentage points between the first two periods and more than 10 points between the second and third, and most of this rise was due to employer contributions to social security and to labour income taxes. Changes in demand are also quite different depending on the period considered. During the first oil price crisis there was an expansion of demand, but during the second shock demand was a clear contractionary factor. The two changes in relative input prices show that the impact of the first oil price rise was smaller than that of the second. Finally, the data clearly suggest that technical improvements have taken place during the 20 years considered, but that the rate of modernization was higher between the first two periods than between the second and third.

Table 5 presents the contribution of each of the variables to unemployment growth. Looking first at the growth experienced between the first and second

TABLE 5

CONTRIBUTION OF EXPLANATORY VARIABLES TO THE
GROWTH OF UNEMPLOYMENT
(percentage points)

Explanatory variables	$\dfrac{1966\text{–}72}{1973\text{–}79}$ (1)	$\dfrac{1973\text{–}79}{1980\text{–}84}$ (2)
$(t_1 + t_2 + t_3)$	1·15	2·56
rr	0·44	0·55
c	0	−1·42
UP	1·21	−1·21
mm	−0·15	−0·04
$(p_m - p)$	2·04	2·30
a	1·21	0·39
D	−4·25	3·77
Time	1·19	1·02
Explained change	2·84	7·92
Actual change	2·52	8·00

periods (column (1)), we see that, for an observed increase of 2·52 percentage points, the model explains an increase of 2·84 points. The main contributors to unemployment during this first comparison were, in this order, the real price of materials, technical progress, union pressure, and the tax wedge. Time also contributed with 1·2 points, and may be capturing unmeasured productivity effects. These factors alone would have meant an increase in unemployment of almost 7 percentage points. However, between the two periods considered aggregate demand acted as a clear expansionary factor and this cut unemployment by more than 4 percentage points, leaving the net increase at about 3 percentage points.[25]

In column (2) of Table 5 we repeat the exercise for the period between the two oil price shocks. Here, out of an increase of unemployment of 8 percentage points, the model explains 7·9 points. With the exception of union pressure, all the factors that contributed positively to unemployment growth in the first comparison continue to exert an influence in the same direction in this second comparison. Among these, the tax wedge is now the most important contributor, followed by the relative price of materials, time, the replacement ratio, and technical change. The main differences with respect to the first comparison are the effect of demand, which now acts as a contractionary factor and adds 3·8 points to unemployment, and the effect of firing costs, which during this period have decreased and help to lower unemployment by 1·4 points. Overall, we find that the much higher growth of unemployment during this period is explained, on the one hand, by the negative effect that material prices and taxes have had on employment and, on the other, by the contractionary influence of demand.

So far we have looked at the factors that explain actual unemployment. But an even more interesting question is how actual unemployment compares with equilibrium unemployment, as this can give us an idea of the policy options and their consequences for inflation.

Equilibrium unemployment

The contributions shown in Table 5 have been calculated conditional on cyclical demand. This level of demand will in general be different from that associated with non-accelerating inflation. What we want to do now is to substitute out demand for the factors that explain their equilibrium level, and to see how the non-accelerating inflation unemployment rate (NAIRU) has evolved during the period. That is, we want to evaluate, on the basis of the estimates shown in Tables 1–3, the equilibrium unemployment level that comes out of the solution of equations (3) and (5). Our estimates imply:

$$(6) \quad u = 0·273t + 0·088rr + 0·088c + 0·019UP + 0·011mm + 0·088(p_m - p)$$
$$+ 0·005a + 0·019 \text{ time} + \text{constant.}$$

Expression (6) can now be used to calculate equilibrium unemployment. To get a sensible baseline it is assumed that equilibrium unemployment can be identified with the average unemployment rate of the period 1965–72, when inflation was roughly constant. Then for subsequent periods the corresponding level can be found using (6).

Table 6 shows the results of this exercise, which we identify as NAIRU (I). It also presents alternative estimates which are obtained by adding to

TABLE 6

NAIRU ESTIMATES

(percentages)

Unemployment rate	1966–72	1973–79	1980–84
Actual rate	0·90	3·42	11·42
NAIRU (I)	0·90	6·99	11·27
NAIRU (II)	0·90	7·31	11·35

Note: NAIRU (I) uses expression (6) to determine the increment over the baseline. NAIRU (II) adds to NAIRU (I) the discrepancy between the explained and the actual change in the unemployment rate in Table 5.

NAIRU (I) the part of the growth of actual unemployment that the model cannot explain. That is, we assume that the unexplained gap in Table 6 is all due to omitted factors which would affect the equilibrium rate. We call this new estimate NAIRU (II).

During the period 1973–79, the actual rate was well below the NAIRU. This means that, with the proviso explained in n. 25, the success of the expansionary demand policy that took place during this period in keeping the unemployment rate low (see column (1) of Table 5) must have been achieved at the expense of accelerating prices. This is in fact corroborated by the data, which show that over this period inflation was both high and increasing. The last period, on the other hand, is characterized by a much higher NAIRU, and by an actual rate that is more or less around the level of the NAIRU. For this situation, the model predicts that prices should not have accelerated, and this is roughly what we find. In fact, inflation has tended to decrease, although the decreasing trend is to a very large extent determined by the substantial reductions in inflation achieved in the last two years.[26]

Given that, at the moment, the actual unemployment rate appears to be about the same level as the NAIRU, our results suggest that achieving a reduction in unemployment through an expansion of demand will be difficult without endangering the present performance on inflation. A safer course of action would involve policies directed at reducing the present level of the NAIRU.

Our findings indicate that more effective incomes policies could go some way towards this objective. A lower level of taxation could also reduce the NAIRU, but this would have to be implemented together with a reduction in public expenditure; otherwise the public deficit would increase, and we have not been able to show that this would have any positive effect on employment.[27] Other types of measures that could reduce unemployment are those directed at increasing the flexibility of the labour market. The reduction in firing costs seems already to have exerted some beneficial effects in the last few years, and the fall in the extent of mismatch between supply and demand could also have helped to reduce unemployment. Finally, if the present tendency towards lower relative input prices is maintained, this should contribute significantly to lowering the equilibrium unemployment level, and thus should allow more scope for growth without inflation.

V. CONCLUSIONS

This paper has reviewed the evidence of the last 20 years about the main variables that influence the Spanish labour market, and has attempted an explanation of the substantial increase in unemployment that has occurred during the period.

Our findings suggest that, as compared with the period 1966–72, the main factors behind the rise of unemployment during the first oil crisis (roughly, during the period 1973–79) were the real price of materials, technical progress, union pressure, and taxes. But against this we must count the effect of demand, whose expansion meant a reduction of unemployment. The second oil crisis (roughly, the period 1980–84) has meant a further and much larger increase in unemployment. Tax and real materials price increases again played an important role, but this time the problem has been aggravated by the contractionary pressure of cyclical demand.

We have also been able to identify the unemployment rate consistent with non-accelerating prices. During the first oil crisis actual unemployment is found to be well below the NAIRU, while during the second oil crisis actual and equilibrium unemployment are about the same. This casts some doubt about the effectiveness of expansionary demand policies. Given the present situation, reductions in unemployment through demand expansion should be difficult to achieve without rising inflation.

The model suggests that the policies most suited to reducing unemployment without increasing inflation are those directed at lowering the present level of the NAIRU. This can be achieved by more effective incomes policies, lower taxation, and a greater degree of labour market flexibility. Our estimates indicate that the maintenance of the decreasing trend in the real price of materials could also be an important factor in a future reduction of the NAIRU.

It is important to recall that these results have been obtained with data that are not as abundant and reliable as we would have liked. Although they conform with what we would expect from economic theory, and although they are quite consistent with findings obtained by researchers in other countries, until better data become available we believe they should be viewed with more reserve than that normally accorded to this type of research.

ACKNOWLEDGMENTS

We are grateful to C. Bean, R. Layard, S. Nickell, C. Pissarides and J. Viñals for their helpful suggestions on a previous draft of this paper.

NOTES

1. The Data Appendix gives a detailed definition of each variable and the sources used.
2. An attempt to investigate the overall unemployment rate would also have to deal with the substantial migration flows that have existed during these 20 years. During the 1960s there was a large net outflow of workers to the rest of Europe, which by the late 1970s had turned into a net inflow. This clearly has a bearing on the definition of the labour force, but again, the poor quality of the data is bound to make any adjustment on this account extremely tentative.
3. On the other hand, it is evident that the concept of unemployment in a given sector is much more loose than that for the whole economy. In particular, as we have pointed out above, school-leavers (whatever the length of time that they have been unemployed) are excluded from the industrial unemployment rate.
4. Obviously this is a rough approximation, since it neglects the foreign component of consumption goods.

5. The relevant concept here is that of 'normal productivity'. By using observed productivity we do not correct for increases arising from adjustments in employment and for the accelerated obsolescence and scrapping of capital and installed capacity (see Rojo, 1981, and Viñals, 1984, for a detailed discussion of these biases).

6. A much more detailed analysis of these and other labour-market-related data can be found in Malo de Molina (1983).

7. The introduction of cyclical demand factors, when output prices are already present in the equation, is justified on the basis of firm behaviour in an imperfect competitive market.

8. As far as relative input prices are concerned, it is assumed that the output effect dominates the substitution effect, and thus that an increase in relative input prices leads to a long-run fall in employment.

9. See Symons (1984) and Layard and Symons (1984) for a successful empirical estimation for Britain of a labour demand relationship specified only on relative prices. Dolado and Malo de Molina (1984) also obtain satisfactory results with this type of specification using quarterly Spanish data for the manufacturing sector.

10. We are assuming that the direct effect of demand on employment outweighs the indirect effect via wages.

11. This rough approximation is based upon the fact that both prices and wages, in their univariate time series representations, do not diverge from random walks in rates of growth, and therefore $p^e - p = -\Delta^2 p$.

12. Labour force, stock of capital and input price neutrality in (3) require that $\mu = 1/\alpha$, $\lambda - \alpha\mu = 0$, and $\beta - \alpha = 0$, respectively. Input price, stock of capital and labour force neutrality in (5) imply $\alpha\phi - \beta = 0$; $\lambda - \alpha\tau = 0$ and $\alpha\tau = 1$. These restrictions will all be tested with the data in the empirical work below.

13. Apart from these, there are no other significant employer taxes on labour.

14. The first variable reflects the fact that we are dealing with an open economy where demand fluctuations are a function of the degree of competitiveness and therefore should be included in D. The second variable is a candidate to pick up monetary and fiscal stance. (In fact, when deviations of real money balances from trend and adjusted measures of the budget deficit were introduced, together with the real interest rate, a high degree of collinearity was present among the three variables.) Since, in an era of floating exchange rates, both competitiveness and real interest rates tend to be correlated, they have been estimated in a synthetic way.

15. The procedure to measure the capital stock takes into account a variable depreciation rate to capture the economic obsolescence experienced by installed capacity. Ignoring this could lead to overestimation of the capital stock and also, given that this is taken as exogenous, to biased results (see Artus, 1984).

16. If P is the price of industrial output, P^{ec} is the expected price of consumption and P^c the actual price of consumption, then $W/P^{ec} = (W/P)(P/P^c)(P^c/P^{ec})$. Passing the last two parentheses to the RHS of the equation gives the specification discussed in the text.

17. We also tried to approximate vacancies by the inverse of the unemployment rate, given that vacancy and unemployment rates appear empirically to be related in a hyperbolic fashion; but the results always failed to support the combined specification.

18. Usual Chow tests are not valid when using an IV estimation method (see Pagan and Hall, 1984). In order to use an appropriate Wald test, we need to estimate the equation over the full period, including dummy variables and instruments consisting of vectors of zeros for the first period and actual data for the second. Since the maximum number of instruments was 12 in all the estimated equations, it was impossible to compute the tests given the available sample. None the less, estimating the equations until 1980 and using Chow tests, there was no sign of serious instability in any of the equations.

19. In theory, the variable proxying cyclical demand deviations should be the same in all three equations.

20. The contemporaneous effect of both variables was always negative and non-significant, while the lagged values gave the correct signs but very low t-ratios, implying in addition a synthetic variable which was also non-significant.

21. From Gallant and Jorgenson (1979), we use the following test statistic in order to test linear restrictions in the IV framework:

$$x_L^2(q) = \frac{T-k}{\sigma_u^2}(\sigma_u^2 R_u^2 - \sigma_R^2 R_R^2)$$

where σ_u^2 and R_u^2 denote the variance estimate and coefficient of determination from the unrestricted equation; and σ_R^2 and R_R^2 denote similar statistics for the restricted equation.

22. This inability to capture the unanticipated inflation term is in fact a serious problem, as pointed out in Nickell and Andrews (1983), since this term might proxy demand shocks. If we have not represented these adequately, they will be relegated to the error term, invalidating most of the current dated instruments related to aggregate demand. In order to deal with this problem we have used only lagged instruments in the equation, except for the capital stock.

23. For efficiency, the coefficients on the replacement ratio and firing costs, which are very similar, were restricted to be the same. The data accept this restriction.

24. This procedure, which is also used in Layard and Nickell (1984a), is an approximate way of representing the estimated dynamic structure of the model, which, as can be seen in Tables 1–3, and depending on the variable considered, varies between zero and two lags.

25. We must note that, for the estimates obtained here, it is not quite correct to attribute changes in unemployment arising from changes in the variable D to pure demand factors. Neither the real exchange rate nor the real interest rate are exogenous factors, and one of the variables that to some extent could be taken as being under the control of the government—the public deficit—proved not to exert any significant effect.

26. In 1980 inflation was 15·5 per cent and in 1982 it was 14·4 per cent. In 1983 it went down by 2·2 points to 12·2 per cent, and in 1984 by 3·2 points to 9·0 per cent.

27. Similar results are reached by Mauleón and Pérez (1984), who tackle the consequences of recent high budget deficits in terms of its 'crowding-out' effects.

REFERENCES

ARTUS, J. (1984). The disequilibrium real wage rate hypothesis; an empirical evaluation. *IMF Staff Papers*, **31**, 249–302.

DOLADO, J. and MALO DE MOLINA, J. L. (1984). Un estudio econométrico de la demanda de trabajo en la industria. Unpublished paper, Bank of Spain, Research Department, D.P. 12/84.

GALLANT, A. and JORGENSON, D. (1979). Statistical inference for a system of simultaneous, non-linear, implicit equations in the context of instrumental variables estimation. *Journal of Econometrics*, **11**, 275–302.

LAYARD, R. and NICKELL, S. (1984a). The causes of British unemployment. Unpublished paper, London School of Economics Centre for Labour Economics, W.P. 642.

—— (1984b). Unemployment and real wages in Europe, Japan and the US. Unpublished paper, London School of Economics Centre for Labour Economics, W.P. 677.

LAYARD, R. and SYMONS J. (1984). Neoclassical demand for labour functions for six major economies. *Economic Journal*, **94**, 788–99.

MALO DE MOLINA, J. L. (1983). Rigidez o flexibilidad en el mercado de trabajo. La experiencia Española durante la crisis. *Estudios Económicos*, **34**, 1–61.

MAULEÓN, I. and PÉREZ, J. (1984). Interest rate determinants and consequences for macroeconomic performance in Spain. Unpublished paper, Bank of Spain, Research Department, W.P. 8420.

NICKELL, S. and ANDREWS, M. (1983). Unions, real wages and employment in Britain, 1951–79. *Oxford Economic Papers*, **35**, 507–530.

PAGAN, A. and HALL, A. (1983). Testing residuals. *Econometric Review*, **5**, 159–218.

RAYMOND, J. L. (1983). Una nota sobre demanda de empleo, niveles de actividad económica y salarios reales. *Papeles de Economía*, **15**, 276–281.

ROJO, L. A. (1981). Desempleo y factores reales. *Papeles de Economía*, **8**, 124–136.

SYMONS, J. (1984). The demand for labour in British manufacturing. Unpublished paper, London School of Economics, Centre for Labour Economics, D.P. 91.

VIÑALS, J. (1984). Medición de la productividad del trabajo y clases de paro. *Investigaciones Económicas*, **25**, 19–30.

—— (1985). El déficit público y sus efectos macroeconómicos. Unpublished paper, Bank of Spain, Research Department (mimeo).

Data Appendices

AUSTRIA

	U	$\log L$	$\log N$	$\log Y$	V	CU	$\log \dfrac{W(1+t_1)}{P}$
1964	0·271	7·795	7·768	6·085	0·168	85	−0·945
1965	0·268	7·803	7·775	6·114	0·176	86	−0·893
1966	0·251	7·803	7·778	6·164	0·192	86	−0·835
1967	0·266	7·793	7·766	6·192	0·137	83	−0·768
1968	0·294	7·787	7·758	6·233	0·118	85	−0·739
1969	0·277	7·793	7·765	6·286	0·144	88	−0·693
1970	0·239	7·802	7·779	6·348	0·190	89	−0·643
1971	0·207	7·827	7·806	6·398	0·228	88	−0·568
1972	0·192	7·848	7·829	6·458	0·247	88	−0·524
1973	0·156	7·882	7·866	6·506	0·253	86	−0·481
1974	0·153	7·900	7·885	6·545	0·217	86	−0·440
1975	0·204	7·905	7·885	6·541	0·117	81	−0·351
1976	0·201	7·916	7·896	6·586	0·109	81	−0·307
1977	0·183	7·933	7·915	6·628	0·117	81	−0·272
1978	0·208	7·943	7·922	6·634	0·107	81	−0·237
1979	0·200	7·984	7·928	6·680	0·113	83	−0·218
1980	0·187	7·952	7·933	6·709	0·131	83	−0·184
1981	0·242	7·961	7·937	6·708	0·091	83	−0·161
1982	0·367	7·963	7·925	6·718	0·062	80	−0·176
1983	0·445	7·959	7·914	6·739	0·056	79	−0·157
1984	0·454	7·964	7·917	6·760	0·063	81	−0·157

	$\log (K/L)$	$\Delta \log W$	$\Delta \log P$	UP	t_1	t_2	t_3
1964	−0·170			65·13	0·154	0·159	0·137
1965	−0·150	0·103	0·054	64·78	0·158	0·172	0·137
1966	−0·120	0·094	0·036	64·65	0·157	0·181	0·141
1967	−0·081	0·099	0·034	64·10	0·160	0·181	0·139
1968	−0·047	0·057	0·031	64·72	0·163	0·177	0·146
1969	−0·023	0·078	0·035	64·35	0·167	0·193	0·145
1970	−0·000	0·102	0·053	63·63	0·168	0·204	0·147
1971	0·014	0·136	0·060	62·18	0·167	0·204	0·149
1972	0·035	0·118	0·073	61·37	0·165	0·208	0·156
1973	0·042	0·124	0·077	59·79	0·161	0·203	0·162
1974	0·064	0·130	0·091	59·48	0·164	0·212	0·152
1975	0·093	0·144	0·063	59·76	0·173	0·199	0·141
1976	0·117	0·097	0·055	59·74	0·175	0·210	0·136
1977	0·136	0·083	0·051	59·15	0·178	0·224	0·141
1978	0·157	0·072	0·051	59·06	0·195	0·257	0·134
1979	0·184	0·057	0·041	59·18	0·198	0·260	0·135
1980	0·212	0·080	0·050	59·56	0·203	0·269	0·133
1981	0·232	0·081	0·061	58·51	0·207	0·278	0·135
1982	0·255	0·046	0·065	59·47	0·213	0·275	0·132
1983	0·280	0·051	0·037	59·49	0·219	0·282	0·133
1984	0·297	0·042	0·046		0·219	0·285	0·143

	H	TH	$\log A$	$\log N^*$	$\Delta \log PC$	$\Delta \log HPR$	LU
1964	2229·2					−0·182	
1965	2192·5				0·0455	−0·144	
1966	2195·2	2185·2	4·707	7·749	0·0229	−0·097	
1967	2172·9	2185·2	4·800	7·738	0·0392	−0·047	
1968	2188·6	2185·2	4·890	7·750	0·0248	−0·006	
1969	2184·7	2185·2	4·985	7·770	0·0353	0·042	
1970	2127·3	2123·5	5·098	7·827	0·0447	0·117	
1971	2090·8	2101·7	5·218	7·846	0·0485	0·157	0·228
1972	2064·7	2070·8	5·343	7·889	0·0626	0·207	0·219
1973	2064·7	2059·7	5·460	7·910	0·0639	0·217	0·207
1974	2070·0	2059·7	5·594	7·917	0·0952	0·235	0·264
1975	1997·0	1997·4	5·708	7·899	0·0763	0·267	0·199
1976	1970·9	1975·4	5·825	7·922	0·0629	0·314	0·234
1977	1965·7	1944·9	5·919	7·951	0·0526	0·341	0·210
1978	1960·5	1944·5	6·004	7·926	0·0418	0·341	0·190
1979	1960·5	1944·2	6·085	7·947	0·0427	0·381	0·194
1980	1939·6	1943·8	6·168	7·948	0·0625	0·416	0·194
1981	1918·8	1943·4	6·246	7·920	0·0719	0·422	0·161
1982	1934·4	1943·0	6·327	7·914	0·0621	0·436	0·196
1983	1929·2	1942·6	6·404	7·910	0·0310	0·471	0·258
1984	1942·7	1942·2	6·484	7·911	0·0547	0·481	0·283

List of variables

U	Rate of unemployment
L	Labour supply (employees plus unemployed)
N	Total number of employees, annual average
Y	Gross domestic product
V	Vacancy rate
CU	Capacity utilization
W	Gross hourly wages per employee, excluding employers' contribution to social security
P	Deflator of gross domestic product
K	Aggregate capital stock, at 1976 prices
t_1	Employers' contribution to social security as a proportion of wages and salaries
t_2	Workers' tax rate, including social security contributions
t_3	Indirect tax rate
UP	Union power; trade union membership (percentage of employees)
H	Hours of work per employee
TH	Trend value of hours of work per employee
A	Index of labour-augmented technical progress; three-year backward moving average
N^*	Desired employment emerging from the labour demand equation; see Table 2 in the text
PC	Deflator of private consumption
HPR	GDP per man-hour
LU	Percentage of unemployed who have been unemployed for over six months
t	Time trend

BELGIUM

The data are annual time series convering the period 1953–82. If not otherwise indicated, the series come from the MARIBEL Data Bank constructed by the Belgian Planning Office.

	UR	log LS	log LT	log YT	log VS	DUC	log WH/P	log KA/LS
1953	8·04060	1·31098	1·22715	6·78008	2·56125		4·36363	5·60837
1954	6·99617	1·30435	1·23182	6·82023	2·51276		4·38540	5·66632
1955	5·79042	1·29973	1·24008	6·86706	3·35829		4·43269	5·72610
1956	4·71522	1·29956	1·25126	6·89398	3·32370		4·46291	5·78568
1957	3·85778	1·30210	1·26276	6·91361	3·23884		4·52570	5·82712
1958	5·84812	1·29984	1·23958	6·91084	2·25612		4·55796	5·86272
1959	6·50527	1·28537	1·21810	6·94041	1·72669		4·59057	5·92022
1960	5·00181	1·28307	1·23176	6·99251	2·64546		4·61371	5·97287
1961	3·97636	1·28429	1·24371	7·04035	3·25721		4·66137	6·03006
1962	3·42480	1·29429	1·25944	7·09251	3·30487		4·70351	6·08645
1963	3·36710	1·29229	1·25803	7·13480	3·53736	81·30	4·75054	6·14929
1964	2·46191	1·29662	1·27169	7·20189	3·25902	83·80	4·82551	6·20369
1965	3·07636	1·29937	1·26813	7·23761	2·80808	81·87	4·87545	6·25563
1966	3·05839	1·30185	1·27079	7·26584	2·71158	82·27	4·93879	6·31739
1967	3·94967	1·30513	1·26483	7·30463	2·09013	78·27	4·99512	6·37611
1968	4·26814	1·30825	1·26463	7·34461	2·16585	78·97	5·02785	6·42746
1969	3·55346	1·31871	1·28253	7·40360	3·18672	86·00	5·06523	6·47278
1970	3·03891	1·32917	1·29831	7·46280	3·39746	86·27	5·14221	6·52201
1971	3·28906	1·33960	1·30615	7·50327	2·70511	83·67	5·21535	6·57245
1972	3·73853	1·34422	1·30612	7·55627	2·20915	82·70	5·30638	6·62423
1973	3·82085	1·35810	1·31914	7·61660	2·74148	84·70	5·37112	6·66210
1974	4·31306	1·37539	1·33130	7·66037	2·90570	83·27	5·45611	6·69598
1975	7·50164	1·38354	1·30556	7·63992	1·43818	72·23	5·57045	6·73135
1976	8·47584	1·39265	1·30408	7·69484	1·49178	75·13	5·62191	6·75911
1977	9·82973	1·40116	1·29769	7·70202	1·39252	73·07	5·66303	6·78322
1978	10·55616	1·40801	1·29645	7·73428	1·49335	73·25	5·69051	6·80729
1979	10·96395	1·42377	1·30765	7·75687	1·82729	77·25	5·72257	6·82320
1980	11·94510	1·43019	1·30298	7·79194	1·98389	76·20	5·77785	6·85310
1981	14·32945	1·43267	1·27801	7·78273	1·56381	75·10	5·83137	6·87889
1982	15·94589	1·44234	1·26863	7·79465	1·49918	76·05	5·83477	6·89605

	log *IPC*	Δ log *WH*	Δ log *P*	log U_p	*T*1	*T*2	*T*3	*DUR*
1953	3·94606			5·40668	0·09860	0·12906	0·05434	
1954	3·95045	0·02762	0·00584	5·47890	0·09890	0·12139	0·05253	
1955	3·96249	0·05440	0·00711	6·26137	0·10246	0·12634	0·05770	
1956	3·94288	0·06546	0·03524	6·19443	0·10379	0·12630	0·05045	
1957	3·87936	0·10064	0·03785	7·55669	0·11036	0·13311	0·05997	64·72
1958	3·88461	0·04245	0·01019	5·01086	0·10926	0·12981	0·06000	71·87
1959	3·89791	0·03158	−0·00104	6·24104	0·10662	0·13530	0·05987	49·66
1960	3·89446	0·02860	0·00547	5·14927	0·11125	0·13023	0·06014	64·00
1961	3·87739	0·05272	0·00505	3·83667	0·11787	0·13714	0·06637	50·75
1962	3·88236	0·05764	0·01550	4·89055	0·11693	0·14533	0·06872	55·78
1963	3·86846	0·07605	0·02903	4·78001	0·12531	0·14708	0·06942	56·53
1964	3·84654	0·12137	0·04639	5·33325	0·13093	0·14530	0·07166	47·84
1965	3·83171	0·10185	0·05191	3·47380	0·13730	0·15258	0·07217	31·82
1966	3·80441	0·09599	0·03265	5·50679	0·13990	0·16292	0·08354	35·77
1967	3·77500	0·08404	0·02771	4·43232	0·14052	0·16957	0·08657	32·61
1968	3·78841	0·06389	0·03116	5·12867	0·14150	0·18246	0·08757	46·83
1969	3·78730	0·08444	0·04706	4·30735	0·14373	0·18857	0·08839	33·24
1970	3·76747	0·12556	0·04858	6·48446	0·15303	0·20224	0·08839	35·36
1971	3·70559	0·12535	0·05221	6·32472	0·15739	0·20813	0·08919	37·35
1972	3·74191	0·15965	0·06862	5·09122	0·16089	0·21564	0·82280	32·66
1973	3·90759	0·13628	0·07154	5·99667	0·16217	0·22657	0·08101	44·55
1974	3·78498	0·19921	0·11422	5·54531	0·15985	0·24542	0·08365	47·05
1975	3·73895	0·23821	0·12388	5·60908	0·16717	0·27733	0·07641	42·75
1976	3·68667	0·12062	0·06916	6·02095	0·16223	0·27166	0·08427	59·64
1977	3·61526	0·11054	0·06941	5·72256	0·16613	0·29424	0·08491	65·50
1978	3·66646	0·06749	0·04002	6·15752	0·16062	0·31142	0·08834	69·00
1979	3·72246	0·07736	0·04530	5·68407	0·16131	0·32009	0·08809	71·78
1980	3·83745	0·08906	0·03378	4·66070	0·16056	0·31562	0·08638	70·59
1981	3·89966	0·10279	0·04928	5·47812	0·15386	0·32078	0·09173	69·99
1982	3·87803	0·06842	0·06502	5·41946	0·14510	0·34911	0·08979	73·56

	DUL	log W/V	log C/T	log D/I	log PC	log MT	log FD	log PM	log PF
1953	81·77054	5·39932	6·47368	6·55837	-0·80926	5·19929	6·87080	-0·53028	-0·92383
1954	83·12750	5·44419	6·50373	6·59064	-0·79316	5·32015	6·93379	-0·56741	-0·91375
1955	83·82182	5·44866	6·54812	6·64143	-0·79419	5·42028	6·98797	-0·56085	-0·91604
1956	84·62270	5·45016	6·56982	6·66063	-0·76345	5·55159	7·04319	-0·53776	-0·88347
1957	88·98209	5·45469	6·58820	6·66612	-0·71904	5·56825	7·05832	-0·50583	-0·83803
1958	79·40160	5·47761	6·60113	6·70354	-0·72335	5·52467	7·04231	-0·57593	-0·83787
1959	78·04346	5·54274	6·63005	6·72119	-0·70711	5·63247	7·10001	-0·59343	-0·83537
1960	85·98001	5·57570	6·66922	6·76964	-0·70053	5·75193	7·16315	-0·58902	-0·83159
1961	88·37239	5·60236	6·69825	6·80613	-0·68629	5·81179	7·22651	-0·56139	-0·82815
1962	89·08740	5·61169	6·73812	6·85319	-0·66904	5·84531	7·27252	-0·54435	-0·80610
1963	85·73256	5·65361	6·77930	6·89807	-0·64310	5·89155	7·31392	-0·48733	-0·77629
1964	92·50603	5·71585	6·80593	6·95932	-0·60293	6·00754	7·39610	-0·45659	-0·73977
1965	89·64320	5·76757	6·84548	7·00444	-0·55224	6·07847	7·43439	-0·44501	-0·69151
1966	89·97382	5·79392	6·86957	7·03078	-0·51341	6·15600	7·47188	-0·41208	-0·67028
1967	87·05145	5·81764	6·90687	7·06257	-0·48963	6·18439	7·50874	-0·40564	-0·64707
1968	88·70403	5·86771	6·95312	7·11659	-0·46466	6·28988	7·56720	-0·39107	-0·62562
1969	90·22395	5·90283	7·00010	7·17447	-0·43326	6·42679	7·64863	-0·35368	-0·59392
1970	91·39880	5·88869	7·04022	7·23702	-0·39774	6·49248	7·70812	-0·30712	-0·54180
1971	82·25768	5·91463	7·08649	7·27712	-0·34609	6·54170	7·75012	-0·27996	-0·48398
1972	90·09161	6·00357	7·14426	7·33391	-0·28896	6·61753	7·81193	-0·26371	-0·42321
1973	90·83342	6·05523	7·21017	7·38783	-0·22096	6·81326	7·90664	-0·20485	-0·35416
1974	88·91956	6·04881	7·24672	7·43083	-0·10967	6·91095	7·96821	-0·05142	-0·22858
1975	77·62975	6·09006	7·25884	7·45922	0·00000	6·81175	7·90744	0·00000	-0·11299
1976	84·12320	6·15580	7·30794	7·50107	0·08169	6·93038	7·98931	0·06220	-0·04096
1977	80·88490	6·17209	7·32173	7·50919	0·14859	7·08748	8·02210	0·09493	0·02439
1978	81·01419	6·19921	7·34955	7·52412	0·19324	7·12752	8·06011	0·11566	0·06671
1979	81·22845	6·20267	7·38441	7·55748	0·23284	7·21560	8·10429	0·18790	0·10796
1980	78·16812	6·23019	7·41481	7·58774	0·28747	7·24457	8·12726	0·26634	0·16530
1981	73·92728	6·26038	7·41317	7·59999	0·35671	7·23889	8·11044	0·35845	0·22429
1982	76·79924	6·27630	7·42648	7·57334	0·43483	7·25624	8·12723	0·47091	0·29842

DATA APPENDICES

	log W	log WN	log P	log PI	log LP	log YP	log YD	log MD	RED
1953	4·25826	4·06025	−0·86617	−0·86921					
1954	4·28915	4·09978	−0·86033	−0·88010					
1955	4·34494	4·14723	−0·85322	−0·84587	1·26328	6·88719	6·86190	5·44194	1·01080
1956	4·39351	4·19395	−0·81798	−0·78901	1·27508	6·92257	6·90501	5·50821	1·01656
1957	4·45951	4·24698	−0·78013	−0·73736	1·28758	6·95895	6·92412	5·52687	1·00760
1958	4·49359	4·28461	−0·76994	−0·72296	1·28841	6·98662	6·90660	5·54145	1·00022
1959	4·52171	4·30853	−0·77097	−0·74334	1·27508	7·00857	6·94010	5·63360	1·00087
1960	4·56360	4·35303	−0·76551	−0·72770	1·26948	7·03959	7·00466	5·70873	1·01397
1961	4·60303	4·38084	−0·76045	−0·71852	1·27369	7·08048	7·05020	5·77740	1·01514
1962	4·67591	4·44301	−0·74495	−0·68143	1·28813	7·12906	7·09706	5·82930	1·01622
1963	4·76022	4·51919	−0·71593	−0·64342	1·29692	7·17498	7·14007	5·87305	1·01585
1964	4·87040	4·62792	−0·66953	−0·59339	1·30101	7·22141	7·21157	5·97488	1·03596
1965	4·94847	4·69306	−0·61763	−0·56013	1·30644	7·27140	7·25042	6·03649	1·02779
1966	5·03336	4·76204	−0·58498	−0·53715	1·31614	7·32351	7·28434	6·09769	1·02124
1967	5·10157	4·82080	−0·55727	−0·51242	1·32920	7·37702	7·31178	6·16213	1·01116
1968	5·16957	4·87288	−0·52610	−0·50205	1·33289	7·42366	7·36139	6·24007	1·01616
1969	5·24526	4·93904	−0·47904	−0·46369	1·33500	7·46830	7·43392	6·34149	1·03347
1970	5·34142	5·01047	−0·43046	−0·36231	1·35403	7·52225	7·48957	6·41821	1·03884
1971	5·45175	5·10796	−0·37825	−0·32853	1·37169	7·57523	7·52437	6·48432	1·02982
1972	5·57785	5·22176	−0·30963	−0·28612	1·36788	7·61641	7·56777	6·58750	1·02787
1973	5·69720	5·32513	−0·23810	−0·23843	1·36226	7·65727	7·65405	6·72418	1·05611
1974	5·86404	5·46525	−0·12368	−0·10200	1·37372	7·70766	7·70432	6·81106	1·05550
1975	6·03040	5·58195	0·00000	0·00000	1·38053	7·74214	7·65224	6·78296	1·00765
1976	6·16107	5·72356	0·06916	0·06074	1·37422	7·76830	7·69173	6·93702	1·01141
1977	6·25840	5·78523	0·13857	0·11301	1·37245	7·79513	7·73159	7·03040	1·01826
1978	6·32335	5·82905	0·17859	0·14393	1·37067	7·82077	7·74289	7·11153	1·01244
1979	6·39371	5·88515	0·22389	0·18380	1·37372	7·84683	7·77427	7·18497	1·01668
1980	6·47378	5·97065	0·25767	0·20741	1·37447	7·87099	7·80516	7·22131	1·01791
1981	6·54578	6·03939	0·30695	0·24759	1·36609	7·88669	7·79894	7·21034	1·01023
1982	6·61353	6·07094	0·37196	0·31220	1·35067	7·89371	7·80309	7·24163	1·01035

Symbols

UR	Unemployment rate $= 100 * (LS - LT)/LS$
LS	Labour force (millions of workers) $= LT +$ unemployment (including partial unemployment and unemployed occupied by public sector; homogeneous series constructed by Schuttringer and Tollet at the Belgian Planning Office)
LT	Total employment (millions of workers), excluding the partially unemployed and the unemployed employed by public sector
YT	GDP at factor cost (1975 Bfr billions)
VS	Vacancies (thousands of workers, annual average) (*Source*: IRES, Université Catholique de Louvain)
DUC	Degree of utilization of production capacities (*Source*: Banque Nationale de Belgique)
WH	Labour cost per hour in the private sector (Bfrs per hour)
P	GDP deflator (factor cost)
KA	Capital stock, excluding dwellings (1975 Bfr billions) (*Source*: Bureau du Plan., note (84) TdB/3445/4389)
IPC	Index of price competitiveness: world export prices (excluding energy) in Bfrs (at the Bfr/$ current exchange rate), relative to domestic final demand prices net of indirect taxes.
U_p	Number of working days lost owing to strikes, per 1000 employees (*Source*: INS, Bruxelles, and Y. Leruth, Mémoire de Licence et Maîtrise en Sciences Economiques)
T1	Employers' employment tax (employers' social security contributions relative to employees' gross income)
T2	Workers' tax rate (direct taxes + social security contributions)
T3	Indirect tax rate
DUR	Duration of unemployment = % of unemployed for over six months (category: fully unemployed of normal aptitude) (*Source*: ONEM and IRES, Université Catholique de Louvain)
DUL	Degree of utilization of labour $= 100 * \{1 = 10 * \text{(partial unemployment)}/LT\}$. (*Source*: INS and MARIBEL)
W/V	Labour cost per employee relative to the price of investment goods (Bfr thousands)
CT	Private consumption at constant prices (1975 Bfr billions)
DI	Households' real disposable income (1975 Bfr billions)
PC	Private consumption price index.
MT	Imports of goods and services, excluding energy (1975 Bfr billions)
FD	Private consumption + investment + exports of goods (excluding energy) at constant prices (1975 Bfr billions)
PM	Price index of imported goods and services (excluding energy); beginning of the period, data reconstructed by assuming same rate of growth as total imports
PF	Price index of domestic final demand, net of taxes
W	Wage cost per employee in the private sector (Bfr thousands per year)
WN	Net wage per employee in the private sector (Bfr thousands per year)
PI	Price index of gross fixed capital formation in the private sector
LP	Estimated potential employment level (millions of workers)
YP	Estimated potential output level (1975 Bfr billions)
YD	Estimated demand for domestic goods (1975 Bfr billions) $= YT + MT - MD$
MD	Estimated structural demand for non-energy imports (1975 Bfr billions)
RED	Estimated rate of excess demand
Time	1 = 1953, 30 = 1982.

FRANCE

	U	l	nt	nb	yt	yb	dd
1963	2·07	9·917	9·896	9·725	13·198	13·062	12·033
1964	1·86	9·926	9·907	9·739	13·262	13·130	12·131
1965	2·05	9·931	9·910	9·742	13·308	13·180	12·213
1966	2·08	9·938	9·918	9·747	13·359	13·236	12·272
1967	2·37	9·944	9·920	9·748	13·405	13·283	12·330
1968	2·61	9·944	9·917	9·742	13·447	13·324	12·373
1969	2·26	9·955	9·932	9·757	13·514	13·396	12·430
1970	2·43	9·971	9·946	9·769	13·570	13·455	12·474
1971	2·67	9·978	9·951	9·772	13·623	13·510	12·527
1972	2·77	9·985	9·957	9·777	13·680	13·571	12·584
1973	2·65	9·997	9·970	9·790	13·732	13·627	12·654
1974	2·83	10·008	9·979	9·798	13·764	13·661	12·694
1975	4·08	10·013	9·971	9·785	13·766	13·661	12·794
1976	4·39	10·023	9·978	9·789	13·816	13·710	12·831
1977	4·90	10·037	9·986	9·795	13·846	13·742	12·867
1978	5·23	10·044	9·990	9·796	13·883	13·780	12·930
1979	5·91	10·052	9·991	9·795	13·916	13·815	12·976
1980	6·30	10·057	9·991	9·794	13·926	13·825	12·995
1981	7·37	10·063	9·986	9·783	13·931	13·829	13·028
1982	8·10	10·072	9·987	9·780	13·949	13·847	13·074
1983	8·30	10·069	9·982	9·769	13·956	13·855	13·088
1984	9·76	10·075	9·972	9·754	13·969	13·870	13·098

	wd	k	z_1	ω	w	$k-nt$	φ	π
1963	3·965	13·464	84·8	4·208	2·010	3·567	0·908	5·8
1964	4·047	13·515	84·3	4·178	2·063	3·607	0·869	4·2
1965	4·129	13·565	82·7	4·142	2·109	3·654	0·855	2·8
1966	4·207	13·619	83·7	4·178	2·146	3·701	0·841	2·5
1967	4·243	13·672	82·9	4·225	2·191	3·751	0·829	1·4
1968	4·371	13·725	83·5	4·601	2·260	3·807	0·953	3·6
1969	4·496	13·784	86·5	4·605	2·311	3·851	1·017	3·9
1970	4·605	13·843	86·1	4·605	2·370	3·896	1·000	2·4
1971	4·662	13·903	85·8	4·732	2·436	3·952	0·992	4·0
1972	4·760	13·963	86·1	4·807	2·486	4·006	0·994	4·8
1973	4·912	14·022	88·1	4·953	2·549	4·052	1·030	6·3
1974	5·005	14·076	85·4	5·050	2·623	4·096	1·066	3·9
1975	4·993	14·119	78·8	5·288	2·689	4·148	1·087	6·1
1976	5·107	14·165	82·9	5·079	2·741	4·186	1·083	4·0
1977	5·163	14·207	83·6	4·982	2·787	4·221	1·081	3·0
1978	5·236	14·249	83·4	5·043	2·823	4·258	1·085	3·8
1979	5·306	14·289	84·6	5·135	2·856	4·298	1·077	4·4
1980	5·363	14·332	84·8	5·096	2·886	4·340	1·078	1·1
1981	5·370	14·368	82·1	5·020	2·918	4·382	1·109	−1·2
1982	5·370	14·402	82·2	5·128	2·978	4·415	1·129	−3·6
1983	5·385	14·432	82·0	5·097	3·005	4·449	1·141	−1·6
1984	5·462	14·458	82·0	4·968	3·017	4·485	1·162	−2·4

	γ	$\dot{w}$	$\dot{p}$	t_1	t_2	t_3
1963	78·06	9·66	6·21	24·18	5·53	18·19
1964	78·70	9·10	4·06	24·18	5·74	18·49
1965	79·40	6·32	2·69	24·71	5·91	18·28
1966	83·36	6·25	2·85	24·65	6·14	18·35
1967	83·82	6·58	3·13	25·30	6·36	17·77
1968	81·25	10·71	4·16	24·75	6·48	17·50
1969	88·77	10·80	6·36	22·72	6·87	18·07
1970	100·00	11·43	5·47	22·21	6·55	16·78
1971	102·57	11·80	5·60	22·31	6·58	16·60
1972	100·15	10·93	6·00	22·29	6·81	16·67
1973	95·27	13·37	7·49	22·44	6·92	16·49
1974	101·39	17·01	10·55	22·60	7·09	16·11
1975	90·48	16·76	12·57	24·15	7·58	15·98
1976	90·67	14·02	9·40	24·58	8·25	16·62
1977	97·10	12·28	8·60	25·14	8·84	15·75
1978	97·01	11·98	9·04	25·56	8·94	16·16
1979	93·67	12·43	9·91	26·01	10·35	16·82
1980	90·97	14·04	11·51	26·16	11·34	16·87
1981	91·10	14·07	11·15	26·13	10·97	16·83
1982	93·82	16·90	11·90	26·73	11·71	17·11
1983	96·61	10·51	9·09	27·53	12·45	17·09
1984	97·10	7·84	7·01	27·74	13·44	17·44

List of variables

All figures are annual averages. All logarithms are natural logarithms.

U Unemployment rate. Number of unemployed (ILO definition), divided by labour force. In per cent: Regularly published in *Rapport sur les Comptes de la Nation*, INSEE, or 'Banque de données DMS', INSEE. (The series was recently revised).

l log labour force, in thousands, same source as above.

nt log of total employment, in thousands, same source as above.

nb log of employment in non-financial non-governmental activities ('emploi dans les branches marchandes'), in thousands, same source as above.

yt log of gross domestic product, at 1970 prices, in millions francs, same source.

yb log of output in non-financial non-governmental activities ('PIB marchand'), at 1970 prices, in millions francs, same source.

dd log of domestic autonomous demand, at 1970 prices, defined as government demand for goods and services, *plus* gross domestic investment by households and large public corporations ('Grandes Entreprises Nationales'), *plus* social transfers received by households, in millions francs. Figures come from *Comptes de la Nation*.

wd log of world demand addressed to France (weights are shares in French exports). (Index base 100 in 1970). INSEE series.

k log of productive capital stock, at 1970 prices, in millions francs, INSEE series.

z_1 rate of capacity utilization in industry, computed from answers to INSEE business survey (per cent). Banque de données DMS.

ω log of relative cost of labour with respect to capital. (Index base 100 in 1970). INSEE series.

w log of real labour cost: hourly labour cost in non-financial non-governmental activities, in 1970 francs, deflated by price of value added in these activities ('PIB marchand'). 'Banque de données DMS', INSEE.

$k - nt$ log capital/employment ratio. Difference between the two previously defined series.

φ ratio between the minimum wage and the average wage rate. Index base 1 in 1970. 'Banque de données DMS', INSEE.

π profitability: measure computed in Malinvaud (1983), which is the difference between an inflation-corrected net profit rate and a real interest rate, in per cent.

γ index of competitiveness, defined as ratio of unit labour cost abroad over unit labour cost in France corrected by exchange rates changes, base 100 in 1970. 'Banque de données DMS', INSEE.

$\dot{w}$ rate of increase of the hourly wage rate in non-financial non-governmental activities, in per cent. 'Banque de données DMS', INSEE.

$\dot{p}$ rate of increase of the price of value added in non-financial non-governmental activities, in per cent. 'Banque de données DMS', INSEE.

t_1 employers' labour tax and social security contribution rate in non-financial non-governmental activities, as per cent of total labour cost. 'Banque de données DMS', INSEE.

t_2 workers' social security contribution: compulsory social security contributions of wage earners and self employed, divided by gross wages received *plus* gross operating surplus of non-corporate firms (in non-financial non-governmental activities), per cent. 'Banque de données DMS', INSEE.

t_3 indirect tax rate, per cent of total value added. 'Banque de données DMS', INSEE.

GERMANY

	Capacity utilization rates (%) (1)	Vacancies (000) (2)	Unem- ployment rate (%) (3)	Total employed persons (000) (4)	Manufacturing sector		
					Capital Stock (million DM) (5)	Employed persons (6)	Employ- ment- capital ratio (7)
1970	100·0	795	0·7	26,560			
1971	98·3	648	0·8	26,721			
1972	97·8	546	1·1	26,661	599,183	8,627,962	14·400
1973	98·4	572	1·2	26,849	622,065	8,663,522	13·927
1974	96·0	315	2·6	26,497	639,521	8,434,318	13·189
1975	92·1	236	4·7	25,746	652,292	7,887,735	12·092
1976	95·2	235	4·6	25,530	663,030	7,698,499	11·611
1977	96·1	231	4·5	25,490	673,860	7,631,789	11·326
1978	97·1	246	4·3	25,644	683,956	7,583,826	11·088
1979	99·2	304	3·8	25,986	694,277	7,606,927	10·957
1980	98·8	308	3·8	26,251	707,028	7,659,343	10·833
1981	96·7	208	5·5	26,048	719,615	7,488,720	10·407
1982	94·5	105	7·5	25,572	729,090	7,225,854	9·911
1983	94·6[a]	76	9·1	25,126	736,501	6,926,939	9·405
1984	94·8[a]	89	9·1	25,000[a]		6,663,000	

[a] Preliminary.
[b] 1984 (I) and (II).

Notes:
Column
(1)	Capacity utilization rate = (actual GNP/potential GNP) × 100
(2), (3)	As registered at the labour offices; averages per year
(4)	Includes self-employed persons
(5)–(7)	Manufacturing industry and mining
(8)	Labour cost per man-hour divided by GNP deflator
(9)	Lost days arising from strikes as a fraction of total worked days, per million workers
(11)	Gross labour income, including employers' contribution to social security times (1 + indirect tax rate), divided by net take-home pay
(12), (13)	Defined as

$$\Sigma \left| \frac{U_i}{U} - \frac{V_i}{V} \right|$$

where U = unemployed, V = vacancies, $i = 1, \ldots, 141$ (regions, col. (12)) and $i = 1, \ldots, 327$ (occupations, col. (13)).

(14)	Percentage of unemployed who have been unemployed for over six months

Real labour cost (DM) (8)	Industrial disputes (per million workers) (9)	Trade union membership (%) (10)	Measure of tax wedge (11)	Regional mismatch (12)	Occupational mismatch (13)	Duration of unemployment (%) (14)
11·90	0·01317	35·93	1·67			23·9
12·45	0·36366	36·01	1·71			22·7
13·18	0·00928	36·49	1·72			26·1
14·07	0·07881	36·83	1·79			26·7
14·91	0·14961	38·36	1·82			24·5
15·37	0·01005	39·28	1·83			36·8
15·76	0·07765	39·94	1·89	0·359	0·730	40·8
16·46	0·00347	40·06	1·91	0·381	0·701	40·4
16·91	0·62599	40·95	1·91	0·443	0·707	41·4
17·39	0·06986	40·77	1·92	0·457	0·705	39·9
17·90	0·01834	40·38	1·96	0·438	0·721	36·2
18·25	0·00842	40·98	1·97	0·455	0·713	38·1
18·18	0·00221	41·31	2·00	0·456	0·703	46·4
18·22	0·00608	41·59	2·03	0·422	0·610	54·1
17·74[b]			2·05[b]			55·2

Sources:

Column	
(1), (10)	Sachverständigenrat zur Begutachtung der gesamtwirtschaftlichen Entwicklung, Jahresgutachten 1982–1984
(2), (3), (12), (13)	Bundesanstalt für Arbelt, Amtliche Nachrichten der Bundesanstalt für Arbeit, current volumes
(4), (8), (10)	Deutsches Institut für Wirtschaftsforschung, Sozialprodukt und Einkommenskreislauf, Vierteljährliche Volkswirtschaftliche Gesamtrechnung für die Bundesrepublik Deutschland, A 11
(5), (6) (12), (13), (14)	E. Baumgart, R. Mehl und J. Schintke (1984), Produktionsvolumen und-potential, Produktionsfaktoren des Bergbaus und des Verarbeitenden Gewerbes in der Bundesrepublik Deutschland, Deutsches Institut für Wirtschaftsforschung, Statistische Kennziffern 26. Folge 1972–1983, p. 41 (col. 4) und p. 18 (col. 5). Employment data for 1984 means 1984 (III), taken from Sachverständigenrat zur Begutachtun der Gesamtwirtschaftlichen Entwicklung, Jahresgutachten 1984/85, Table 43. Note that definition of manufacturing sector in this table differs from that in Tables 4 and 5
(9), (10), (11)	Statistisches Bundesamt, Statistische Jahrbucher 1970–1984

ITALY

	u^*	u	L	N	N	N^P	GDP	Y
1960	0·04976	0·04976	21,599	20,524·2	18,423·5	2100·7	36,093	32,117·55
1961	0·04502	0·04502	21,535	20,565·49	18,420·09	2145·4	39,055	35,185·24
1962	0·04494	0·04494	21,306	20,348·59	18,140·5	2208·1	41,478	37,866·63
1963	0·03932	0·03932	20,852	20,032·0	17,775·7	2256·3	43,805	40,445·71
1964	0·04442	0·04442	20,870	19,942·9	17,644·0	2298·9	45,030	41,244·68
1965	0·04889	0·04889	20,612	19,604·19	17,267·09	2337·1	46,502	42,201·00
1966	0·05273	0·05273	20,367	19,293·0	16,907·3	2385·7	49,285	45,005·77
1967	0·04803	0·04803	20,507	19,522·09	17,085·39	2436·7	52,823	48,739·51
1968	0·05186	0·05186	20,555	19,489·0	16,998·4	2490·7	56,280	51,805·34
1969	0·03885	0·03885	20,369	19,577·0	17,039·6	2538·1	59,712	55,704·34
1970	0·04052	0·0414	20,436	19,608·0	16,987·5	2602·5	62,883	59,069·00
1971	0·04112	0·04457	20,404	19,565·0	16,785·7	2708·8	63,916	59,383·14
1972	0·04519	0·04765	20,293	19,376·0	16,502·2	2823·9	65,963	61,395·80
1973	0·047	0·0487	20,490	19,527·0	16,558·4	2933·8	70,601	66,052·63
1974	0·04176	0·04451	20,714	19,849·0	16,742·8	3049·3	73,525	68,532·88
1975	0·05008	0·0586	20,946	19,897·0	16,556·1	3162·4	70,851	64,882·22
1976	0·05826	0·06408	21,285	20,045·0	16,700·89	3220·2	75,011	69,420·88
1977	0·06734	0·07246	21,607	20,152·0	16,762·5	3278·9	76,435	70,552·50
1978	0·06595	0·07277	21,730	20,297·0	16,809·9	3338·8	78,488	72,392·06
1979	0·07147	0·07709	22,075	20,497·3	16,970·3	3403·0	82,337	77,256·50
1980	0·07639	0·08296	22,372	20,662·9	17,076·1	3440·0	85,558	80,803·58
1981	0·08404	0·09719	22,665	20,760·2	16,950·2	3512·0	85,707	79,806·88
1982	0·08872	0·10371	22,746	20,728·0	16,827·1	3560·0	85,334	79,520·44
1983	0·09664	0·11477	22,982	20,761·0	16,730·4	3614·0	84,326	77,924·19

	CU	k	W	C'	P_K	$\tilde{P}$	JFR	JSR
1960	0·881	0·52809	0·26931	0·58125		0·68204		
1961	0·9	0·47797	0·29097	0·62561	0·42106	0·69241		
1962	0·912	0·4265	0·33375	0·69315	0·50799	0·72186		
1963	0·921	0·3801	0·3975	0·78175	0·546	0·77029		
1964	0·869	0·35436	0·45976	0·84676	0·54078	0·81811		
1965	0·852	0·33224	0·50839	0·89277	0·50116	0·84641	323·15	342·58
1966	0·874	0·31094	0·5456	0·93239	0·67906	0·86615	462·30	329·71
1967	0·899	0·29766	0·58199	0·99353	0·7842	0·8874	387·79	344·39
1968	0·911	0·27895	0·61899	1·04845	0·78756	0·89872	407·41	352·83
1969	0·907	0·26336	0·67449	1·10188	0·82761	0·93393	434·08	371·32
1970	0·93	0·24668	0·77589	1·21747	0·99999	0·99923	355·28	322·84
1971	0·888	0·23032	0·89076	1·3106	0·77124	1·06388	376·25	400·91
1972	0·881	0·21509	1·00818	1·3906	0·69828	1·12572	363·74	345·68
1973	0·922	0·20382	1·25796	1·51229	1·00459	1·26974	371·11	334·73
1974	0·932	0·19488	1·56055	1·52413	0·88498	1·56824	209·24	206·82
1975	0·828	0·18633	1·96924	1·61492	0·50576	1·84835	140·54	169·22
1976	0·909	0·18153	2·36367	1·6495	2·06674	2·18813	173·40	174·03
1977	0·898	0·17644	2·95932	1·69471	3·15567	2·56421	142·41	164·20
1978	0·889	0·17196	3·45683	1·74759	3·12555	2·88888	114·86	134·04
1979	0·919	0·16818	4·11527	1·77424	5·14238	3·34219	143·45	144·70
1980	0·946	0·16268	4·9087	1·74259	6·43587	4·07637	126·56	155·11
1981	0·906	0·15582	5·95706	1·78074	9·85501	4·81823	101·03	156·26
1982	0·868	0·15066	6·92827	1·7933	11·62208	5·59577	88·97	
1983	0·806	0·14699	7·98463	1·89005	11·17249	6·36451		

	T_1-1	T_2-1	T_3-1	H	UR	SR	z_1	z_2
1960	0·32543		0·11061	2·22835		0·25642		0·01033
1961	0·33594	0·04388	0·11436	2·20933		0·22323	0·00998	0·00791
1962	0·35196	0·04793	0·10891	2·17304		0·6189	0·01507	0·00678
1963	0·37061	0·04733	0·10527	2·15249		0·41921	0·01146	0·00464
1964	0·36062	0·05555	0·10741	2·11239		0·51867	0·01389	0·00442
1965	0·34182	0·05743	0·10771	2·04267		0·24456	0·01438	0·00612
1966	0·34051	0·05724	0·10419	2·09359		0·5254	0·0124	0·0059
1967	0·36527	0·05351	0·1096	2·10279		0·25715	0·00209	0·00566
1968	0·3819	0·05932	0·10157	2·10579		0·5801	0·00398	0·00602
1969	0·39087	0·05944	0·09695	2·08632	33·5	1·22222	0·00266	0·0064
1970	0·43115	0·05095	0·09555	2·07535	37·0	0·53849	0·00601	0·00628
1971	0·43265	0·05335	0·09261	2·02941	39·3	0·50026	0·01612	0·00569
1972	0·43626	0·05682	0·0811	1·99095	41·3	0·70363	0·02	0·00694
1973	0·42064	0·05515	0·06856	1·96873	42·8	1·15139	0·00975	0·00824
1974	0·44052	0·05783	0·06326	1·94263	45·8	1·3872	0·00759	0·00648
1975	0·45125	0·05913	0·04446	1·92201	47·60001	1·66665	0·01227	0·00763
1976	0·45556	0·06913	0·04908	1·93211	50·0	0·73381	0·01051	0·00896
1977	0·39115	0·07857	0·05555	1·92012	50·0	1·694	0·00995	0·01684
1978	0·38514	0·09021	0·05439	1·90191	50·0	0·88775	0·01184	0·01928
1979	0·37572	0·09065	0·04741	1·86962	49·60001	1·55273	0·01233	0·02224
1980	0·37349	0·10742	0·05361	1·92017	49·60001	1·46162	0·00683	0·02347
1981	0·36935	0·11715	0·05182	1·92352	47·89999	0·87244	0·01669	0·02612
1982	0·37917	0·12773	0·05019	1·93069	46·60001	1·07374	0·01883	0·028
1983	0·40692	0·14465	0·07081	1·92525	45·5	0·6567	0·02204	0·035

	M	IM	X	NE	Y*	P_M	P_{IM}	P_X	P^*
1960	915·56	1547·33	2058·88	426·00	101·32	1·23458	0·89798	1·01696	0·27435
1961	1076·24	1865·04	2549·28	399·00	105·12	1·12389	0·86643	0·95184	0·27534
1962	1498·63	2105·07	3005·7	584·00	115·74	0·92116	0·92348	0·91176	0·27435
1963	1896·71	2776·36	3337·07	1219·00	125·9	0·83239	0·96345	0·90939	0·27975
1964	1493·68	2620·86	3711·54	417·00	142·02	0·85485	0·98171	0·9249	0·28364
1965	1188·00	2648·65	4342·64	−338·00	154·61	0·89242	0·98773	0·9244	0·28907
1966	1516·77	2999·08	4908·85	−116·00	171·43	0·94593	0·99208	0·92203	0·29558
1967	1878·51	3444·43	5440·95	126·01	181·3	0·93391	0·998	0·93107	0·2975
1968	1607·35	3796·58	6256·92	−505·99	206·68	0·95642	0·98649	0·9251	0·29411
1969	2290·35	4573·29	7287·63	−185·00	235·83	0·91861	0·99045	0·93564	0·306
1970	2775·00	5510·00	7838·99	446·00	255·35	0·98357	0·98872	0·98626	0·321
1971	2256·14	5935·28	8212·42	93·00	271·94	1·04457	1·05108	1·03528	0·3331
1972	2521·81	6639·7	9195·51	267·00	303·58	1·02293	1·12708	1·06532	0·34498
1973	2884·63	7467·78	9592·41	2859·00	340·02	1·44159	1·3547	1·19011	0·4149
1974	2607·91	7617·34	10407·25	6182·00	356·47	3·49619	1·6857	1·51589	0·57951
1975	1649·22	7202·96	10826·18	1519·00	326·95	4·06319	1·88497	1·73279	0·6488
1976	2399·9	8002·91	12366·8	3958·00	371·89	4·77264	2·29427	2·09082	0·8306
1977	2155·5	7993·73	13198·23	891·00	391·06	5·53205	2·75368	2·50379	0·95093
1978	2003·06	8778·52	14409·59	1536·98	417·82	5·98241	2·89567	2·70235	1·03315
1979	3144·56	9788·91	16179·47	1905·01	455·05	6·01895	3·27553	3·03383	1·17444
1980	3468·62	11023·04	15422·65	15716·01	479·6	8·38588	3·82104	3·59801	1·36364
1981	2293·88	10897·33	16126·2	14056·08	478·92	15·06087	4·50998	4·31834	1·75117
1982	2506·48	11236·69	16487·17	13218·05	478·02	14·55867	5·12676	4·90569	2·00128
1983	1905·19	12462·32	17775·52	7258·03	506·06	15·84904	6·08812	5·55875	2·17524

Data sources and definitions

u^*	official unemployment rate (units) (*ISTAT ASL*)
u	'adjusted' unemployment rate (units). Includes dependent workers supported by the Wage Supplementation Fund. Adjustment relates only to the industrial sector (*BI RA*)
L	labour force (thousands of units, yearly averages). Figures include unemployed previously in employment, first job-seekers, other persons seeking employment (students, housewives, etc.) (*ISTAT ASL*)
N^*	domestic (dependent and independent) total employment (thousands of units) (*ISTAT ACN, ISTAT CI*)
N	'adjusted' domestic (dependent and independent) employment in the private sector (thousands of units). Does not include dependent workers supported by the Wage Supplementation Fund. Adjustment relates only to the industrial sector (*ISTAT ACN, ISTAT CI, BI RA*)
N^P	employment in the public sector (thousands of units) (*ISTAT ACN, ISTAT CI*)
GDP	gross domestic product (1970 L billions) (*ISTAT ACN, ISTAT CI*)
Y	'extended value added' of the private sector (1970 L billions). Defined as value added of the private sector plus net imports of productive inputs. All variables at market prices (*ISTAT ACN, ISTAT CI, ISCO*)
CU	capacity utilization rate in industry excluding construction (*BI RA*)
k	employment–capital ratio in the private sector. For employment see N; for capital stock, our calculations largely based on *RS*
W	hourly pre-tax wages and salaries per dependent worker (L thousands) (*ISTAT ACN, ISTAT CI, PA*)
C'	$WT_1 T_3 / \tilde{P}$
P_K	user cost of capital, defined as usual. Does not include tax and other incentives, but *does* include a measure of capital gains
$\tilde{P}$	implicit deflator of Y
$T_1 - 1$	tax rate on employment borne by the firm in the private sector. Includes actual and imputed contributions to social security (*ISTAT ACN, ISTAT CI*)
$T_2 - 1$	income tax rate, calculated as income taxes off disposable income (*ISTAT ACN, ISTAT CI*)
$T_3 - 1$	net indirect tax rate (indirect taxes less subsidies) in the private sector (*ISTAT ACN, ISTAT CI*)
H	average hours worked by (dependent and independent) workers in the private sector (in thousands) (*PA*)
UR	trade union members as a percentage of total employment. Figures refer to the three major unions (CGIL, CISL, UIL) (*CER*)
SR	workers involved in industrial conflicts divided by industrial employees (*ISTAT ACN, ISTAT CI, ISTAT BM*)
z_1	change in non-agricultural employment structure. Defined as the sum of the changes (in absolute values) of the proportions of non-agricultural employment employed in industry, excluding construction, construction industry, private services, public services (*ISTAT ACN, ISTAT CI*)
z_2	high-duration (more than one-year) unemployment (as a fraction of the labour force) (*ISTAT ASL*)
M	net imports of productive inputs (1970 L billions) (*ISCO*)
IM	imports of final goods and services (1970 L billions) (*ISCO*)
X	exports of final goods and services (1970 L billions) (*ISCO*)
NE	$P_M M + P_{IM} IM - P_X X$

Y^*	OECD total imports in 1970 dollars (OECD)
P_M	implicit deflator of M
P_{IM}	implicit deflator of IM
P_X	implicit deflator of X
P^*	industrial countries export unit value (L) (*IMF IFS, BI RA*)
JFR	job-finding rate in industry excluding construction, computed as the number of newly hired employee out of existing operatives (*RSL*)
JSR	job separation rate in industry excluding construction, computed as the number of separations out of existing operatives (*RSL*)
d_j	dummy variable ($=1$ in year j, 0 elsewhere)

Abbreviations for sources

ISTAT ACN	Istituto Centrale di Statistica, Annuario di Contabilità Nazionale
ISTAT CI	Istituto Centrale di Statistica, Collana di Informazioni
ISTAT BM	Istituto Centrale di Statistica, Bollettino Mensile
ISTAT ASL	Istituto Centrale di Statistica, Annuario di Statistiche del Lavoro
BI RA	Banca d'Italia, Relazione annuale
ISCO	Istituto di Studi sulla Congiuntura
CER	Centro Europa Ricerche, Rapporto no. 4, 1984
PA	P. Antonello, Investimenti in macchine e prodotto per ore lavorate nell'economia italiana, LUISS, *Quaderni ISE*, no. 12, 1984
RS	G. Rosa and V. Siesto, *Il capitale fisso industriale*. Bologna: Il Mulino, 1985
RSL	Rassegna di Statistiche del Lavoro

The Netherlands

	Unemployment rate[a]	Log labour force[a]	Log employment[a]
1960	0·012	6·627	6·621
1961	0·009	6·631	6·628
1962	0·008	6·640	6·636
1963	0·008	6·646	6·642
1964	0·007	6·653	6·650
1965	0·008	6·657	6·653
1966	0·010	6·661	6·656
1967	0·019	6·664	6·655
1968	0·017	6·667	6·659
1969	0·015	6·675	6·668
1970	0·014	6·679	6·673
1971	0·019	6·683	6·675
1972	0·030	6·684	6·671
1973	0·031	6·685	6·672
1974	0·037	6·689	6·672
1975	0·053	6·693	6·669
1976	0·056	6·694	6·669
1977	0·055	6·695	6·670
1978	0·055	6·698	6·673
1979	0·056	6·704	6·679
1980	0·063	6·710	6·682
1981	0·092	6·717	6·675
1982	0·124	6·722	6·665
1983	0·150	6·726	6·656
1984	0·154	6·727	6·655

All notes appear to end of Netherlands data.

	Growth in real national income[a]	Growth in real production by firms[a]
1960	0·075	0·099
1961	0·039	0·035
1962	0·040	0·044
1963	0·046	0·043
1964	0·088	0·099
1965	0·059	0·059
1966	0·022	0·028
1967	0·058	0·060
1968	0·071	0·070
1969	0·062	0·067
1970	0·051	0·062
1971	0·035	0·039
1972	0·048	0·041
1973	0·052	0·049
1974	0·006	0·042
1975	−0·011	−0·006
1976	0·057	0·054
1977	0·024	0·022
1978	0·021	0·025
1979	0·009	0·025
1980	−0·007	0·007
1981	−0·013	−0·011
1982	−0·008	−0·021
1983	0·010	0·007
1984	0·035	0·025

All notes appear to end of Netherlands data.

	Vacancy rate[b]	Capacity utilization rate[c]	Growth in real-wage cost[d]
1960	0·022	0·917	0·043
1961	0·028	0·902	0·056
1962	0·028	0·886	0·034
1963	0·027	0·871	0·054
1964	0·029	0·906	0·086
1965	0·028	0·903	0·061
1966	0·025	0·873	0·058
1967	0·015	0·855	0·056
1968	0·017	0·861	0·052
1969	0·027	0·881	0·076
1970	0·027	0·896	0·103
1971	0·023	0·865	0·032
1972	0·013	0·844	0·044
1973	0·014	0·880	0·074
1974	0·014	0·989	0·077
1975	0·010	0·850	0·033
1976	0·010	0·913	0·023
1977	0·011	0·916	0·022
1978	0·013	0·925	0·021
1979	0·013	0·938	0·026
1980	0·011	0·926	0·000
1981	0·004	0·908	−0·018
1982	0·002	0·864	0·003
1983	0·002		0·020
1984	0·003		−0·056

All notes appear at end of Netherlands data.

	Competitiveness[e]	Wage inflation[a]	Price inflation[a]
1960	−0·026	0·082	0·039
1961	0·012	0·072	0·016
1962	0·000	0·059	0·025
1963	0·015	0·090	0·036
1964	0·000	0·149	0·063
1965	0·008	0·111	0·050
1966	−0·018	0·110	0·052
1967	−0·008	0·088	0·032
1968	0·002	0·089	0·037
1969	−0·016	0·134	0·058
1970	−0·006	0·130	0·027
1971	−0·002	0·137	0·105
1972	−0·002	0·123	0·079
1973	−0·059	0·158	0·084
1974	−0·004	0·157	0·080
1975	0·038	0·126	0·093
1976	0·010	0·109	0·086
1977	0·036	0·087	0·065
1978	−0·031	0·072	0·051
1979	−0·030	0·062	0·036
1980	−0·027	0·059	0·059
1981	−0·019	0·043	0·061
1982	0·033	0·061	0·064
1983	0	0·040	0·020
1984	−0·010	0·005	0·061

All notes appear to end of Netherlands data.

	Unionists relative to employees[f]	Workers involved in industrial conflicts[g]
1960		0·028
1961		0·003
1962		0·001
1963		0·009
1964		0·003
1965		0·007
1966	0·32	0·004
1967	0·32	0·005
1968	0·31	0·001
1969	0·31	0·004
1970	0·36	0·016
1971	0·37	0·011
1972	0·38	0·006
1973	0·38	0·017
1974	0·40	0·001
1975	0·40	0·000
1976	0·40	0·005
1977	0·41	0·013
1978	0·40	0·003
1979	0·40	0·011
1980	0·39	0·007
1981	0·38	0·003
1982	0·37	0·022
1983	0·32	0·003
1984		

All notes appear at end of Netherlands data.

	Employers' employment tax rate[h]	Workers' tax rate[k]	Indirect tax rate[m]
1960	0·135	0·220	0·109
1961	0·127	0·230	0·111
1962	0·134	0·229	0·110
1963	0·148	0·240	0·111
1964	0·152	0·248	0·110
1965	0·151	0·257	0·111
1966	0·166	0·276	0·115
1967	0·175	0·288	0·104
1968	0·188	0·298	0·105
1969	0·192	0·306	0·101
1970	0·193	0·311	0·117
1971	0·199	0·326	0·120
1972	0·202	0·333	0·124
1973	0·216	0·346	0·122
1974	0·221	0·360	0·116
1975	0·222	0·363	0·119
1976	0·225	0·357	0·121
1977	0·220	0·343	0·129
1978	0·219	0·344	0·133
1979	0·223	0·350	0·132
1980	0·225	0·354	0·133
1981	0·225	0·348	0·130
1982	0·220	0·346	0·128
1983	0·231	0·363	0·132
1984			

All notes appear to end of Netherlands data.

	User cost of capital[c]
1960	0·031
1961	0·027
1962	0·003
1963	0·028
1964	0·082
1965	0·061
1966	0·090
1967	0·008
1968	0·018
1969	0·125
1970	0·132
1971	0·093
1972	0·028
1973	0·009
1974	0·119
1975	0·113
1976	0·053
1977	−0·009
1978	−0·058
1979	0·044
1980	0·142
1981	0·141
1982	0·060
1983	
1984	

Notes
[a] *Source*: Central Planning Bureau, *Central Economic Plans 1978, 1979 and 1985*; new definition from 1969 onwards
[b] *Source*: Central Bureau of Statistics, *Maandschrift*
[c] Own computation
[d] *Source*: see note (a); wage inflation minus price inflation
[e] *Source*: see note (a); Δ ln export price minus Δ ln foreign competitors' price (guilders; double reweighted from 1970 onwards); energy excluded after 1972; a negative change indicates an improvement of competitiveness
[f] *Source*: see note (b); until 1969, only members of the three most important unions
[g] *Source*: ILO, *Yearbook of Labour Statistics*, and Central Planning Bureau, *Central Economic Plan*; relative to employees in employment
[h] *Source*: Central Bureau of Statistics, *National Accounts*; social security contributions relative to wages plus salaries plus social security contributions
[k] *Source*: see note (h); household direct taxes plus household social security premiums relative to total household income minus non-household social security contributions
[m] *Source*: see notes (a) and (h).

JAPAN

	Unemployment rate (%)	Log labour force (10,000 persons)	Log employment (10,000 persons)	Log real GDP (billion yen)	JOJW ratio (ratio)	Capacity utilization (index)
1953	1·85	8·29	7·41			
1954	2·25	8·30	7·44			
1955	2·38	8·34	7·48			
1956	2·29	8·35	7·55			
1957	1·96	8·38	7·62			
1958	2·04	8·38	7·66			
1959	2·23	8·39	7·71			(101·6)
1960	1·62	8·41	7·77			(106·4)
1961	1·30	8·42	7·81			(107·6)
1962	1·28	8·41	7·86			(100·8)
1963	1·16	8·44	7·89		0·70	(101·3)
1964	1·18	8·45	7·92		0·79	(106·1)
1965	1·22	8·47	7·96	11·14	0·64	(100·0)
1966	1·31	8·49	8·00	11·24	0·73	(106·5)
1967	1·26	8·51	8·02	11·34	1·00	(115·7)
1968	1·18	8·52	8·05	11·46	1·12	112·2 (117·5)
1969	1·12	8·53	8·07	11·58	1·30	112·8
1970	1·15	8·54	8·10	11·67	1·41	110·0
1971	1·23	8·55	8·13	11·72	1·12	103·7
1972	1·39	8·55	8·15	11·80	1·16	104·4
1973	1·27	8·58	8·19	11·89	1·76	108·4
1974	1·38	8·57	8·19	11·88	1·20	99·2
1975	1·89	8·57	8·20	11·90	0·61	84·6
1976	2·01	8·59	8·21	11·95	0·64	91·6
1977	2·03	8·60	8·23	12·00	0·56	90·9
1978	2·24	8·61	8·24	12·05	0·71	94·3
1979	2·08	8·62	8·26	12·10	0·75	99·9
1980	2·01	8·63	8·28	12·15	0·75	100·0
1981	2·21	8·64	8·30	12·19	0·68	95·4
1982	2·36	8·66	8·31	12·22	0·61	92·6
1983	2·64	8·68	8·34	12·25	0·60	94·1
1984	2·71	8·68	8·35		0·65	102·0

	Log labour cost per hour relative to producer prices (yen per man-hour)	Log capital–employment ratio (yen per man)	Log competi-tiveness (ratio)	Wage inflation (log hourly wages) (yen per hour)	Price inflation (log GDP deflator) (index)	Unionists as % of employees (%)
1953	(2·75)		(0·29)	4·28		36·3
1954	(2·78)		(0·29)	4·43		35·5
1955	(2·80)		(0·29)	4·49		35·6
1956	(2·79)		(0·33)	4·52		33·5
1957	(2·79)		(0·30)	4·61		33·6
1958	(2·86)		(0·33)	4·67		32·7
1959	(2·87)		(0·40)	4·66		32·1
1960	(2·90)		0·83 (0·42)	4·78		32·2
1961	(2·96)		0·95	4·88		34·5
1962	(3·07)		0·79	5·00		34·7
1963	(3·16)		0·78	5·11		34·7
1964	(3·24)		0·79	5·23		35·0
1965	3·81 (3·31)		0·80	5·31	3·85	34·8
1966	3·85	14·74	0·78	5·42	3·90	34·2
1967	3·91	14·81	0·79	5·53	3·96	34·1
1968	4·00	14·91	0·79	5·66	4·01	34·4
1969	4·16	15·02	0·79	5·82	4·05	35·2
1970	4·20	15·12	0·80	6·00	4·13	35·4
1971	4·31	15·21	0·79	6·15	4·18	34·8
1972	4·40	15·31	0·80	6·30	4·23	34·3
1973	4·48	15·37	0·71	6·51	4·34	33·1
1974	4·56	15·45	0·48	6·78	4·53	33·9
1975	4·66	15·52	0·37	6·93	4·60	34·4
1976	4·69	15·57	0·31	7·05	4·61	33·7
1977	4·73	15·62	0·31	7·13	4·72	33·2
1978	4·75	15·67	0·43	7·20	4·76	32·6
1979	4·77	15·71	0·28	7·24	4·79	31·6
1980	4·81	15·75	0·00	7·31	4·82	30·8
1981	4·85	15·80	−0·004	7·37	4·84	30·8
1982	4·87	15·84	−0·04	7·41	4·86	30·5
1983	4·89	15·87	−0·02	7·43	4·87	29·7
1984			0·01	7·50		29·1

	Industrial conflicts[a]	Employers' employment tax rate[b]	Workers' tax rates[b]	Indirect tax rate	Duration of unemployment	Log employed (including self-employment)
	(hours per man)	(%)	(%)	(%)	(%)	(10,000 persons)
1953	0·25	(1·62)	(8·27)	(14·7)		8·27
1954	0·22	(1·70)	(8·13)	(13·8)		8·28
1955	0·19	(1·82)	(7·82)	(14·0)		8·31
1956	0·23	(1·91)	(7·80)	(13·9)		8·33
1957	0·27	(1·91)	(7·17)	(14·5)		8·36
1958	0·28	(1·95)	(7·05)	(14·2)		8·36
1959	0·26	(1·99)	(6·66)	(15·0)		8·37
1960	0·20	(2·01)	(7·12)	(15·4)		8·39
1961	0·24	(2·08)	(7·70)	(16·3)		8·41
1962	0·20	(2·16)	(8·31)	(15·1)		8·42
1963	0·10	(2·45)	(8·73)	(14·4)		8·43
1964	0·11	(2·54)	(9·07)	(13·9)		8·44
1965	0·19	2·73 (2·82)	9·24 (9·47)	12·5 (13·4)		8·46
1966	0·09	2·84	9·37	12·3		8·48
1967	0·05	2·86	9·53	12·5		8·50
1968	0·09	2·87	9·80	13·0		8·51
1969	0·11	2·87	9·98	12·7		8·52
1970	0·11	2·96	10·5	13·5		8·53
1971	0·17	3·23	11·2	13·2	24·5	8·54
1972	0·14	3·34	11·3	13·0	19·1	8·54
1973	0·12	3·25	11·5	13·0		8·56
1974	0·26	3·67	11·8	12·7	15·7	8·56
1975	0·21	4·43	12·2	11·5		8·56
1976	0·08	4·37	12·2	11·4		8·56
1977	0·04	4·72	12·8	12·1	27·5	8·58
1978	0·03	4·79	12·7	12·0	31·2	8·59
1979	0·02	4·84	14·0	12·7	37·7	8·60
1980	0·02	5·12	14·3	12·8	35·4	8·61
1981	0·01	5·57	15·2	13·1	30·2	8·62
1982	0·01	5·77	15·5	13·1	31·2	8·63
1983	0·01	5·77	15·8	12·7	32·3	8·65
1984	0·00				35·6	8·65

Notes:
[a] Workers involved in industrial conflicts as percentage of employees in employment
[b] Includes social security contributions

Data sources and calculation methods

(1) *Unemployment rate*: Management and Coordination Agency, *Survey of Labour Force.*

(2) *Labour force*: as in (1).

(3) *Employment* (excluding self-employed): as in (1).

(4) *Real GDP*: Economic Planning Agency, *Annual Bulletin of National Income Statistics*, 1975 constant prices.

(5) *Job-offered–job-wanted ratio*: Ministry of Labour, *Bulletin of Occupational Stability.* Vacancy rate cannot be singled out because of data inconsistency between unemployment rate and JOJW ratio.

(6) *Capacity utilization*: Ministry of International Trade and Industry, *International Trade and Industry Statistics*, 1968–84; average = 100 (1984). Figures in parentheses are based on average = 100 (1965).

(7) *Labour cost per hour relative to producer price*: Economic Planning Agency, *Annual Bulletin of National Income Statistics*; Ministry of Labour, *Monthly Bulletin of Labour Statistics*; Management and Coordination Agency, *Survey of Labour Force.* Employees' income: average monthly hours worked per regular worker (whole industry including service industry since 1970) × 12 × GNP deflator × total number of employees. Figures in parentheses are based on old SNA data.

(8) *Capital–employment ratio*: Economic Planning Agency, *Capital Stock Statistics of Private Firms*; Management and Coordination Agency, *Survey of Labour Force.* Capital stock is on installment basis.

(9) *Competitiveness*: Bank of Japan, *Annual Bulletin of Wholesale Price Index*, export prices divided by import prices. Figures in parentheses are based on average = 100 (1975); others on average = 100 (1980).

(10) *Wage inflation*: Ministry of Labour, *Monthly Bulletin of Labour Statistics*; total cash earnings of regular workers, average monthly hours worked per regular worker.

(11) *Price inflation*: as in (4).

(12) *Unionists as percentage of employees*; Ministry of Labour, *Basic Survey of Trade Unions*; Management and Coordination Agency, *Survey of Labour Force.*

(13) *Workers involved in industrial conflicts as percentage of employees*: Employment Ministry of Labour, *Survey of Industrial Dispute Statistics*; Management and Coordination Agency, *Survey of Labour Force.*

(14) *Employers' employment tax rate* (including social security contributions): as in (4). Employers' social security contributions: employees' income + firms' income. Figures in parentheses are based on old SNA data.

(15) *Workers' tax rate* (including social security contributions): as in (4). Household's sector data: Direct taxes + social security contributions; total receipts.

(16) *Indirect tax rate*: as in (4); indirect taxes; private final consumption expenditure.

(17) *Duration of unemployment*: the percentage of unemployed who have been unemployed for over six months; Ministry of Labour, *Special Survey of Labour Force.* Survey data are based on figures in March 1972, 1974, 1977, 1978, 1979, 1980, 1981, 1982; February 1983, 1984; and October 1971, not on yearly average figures.

(18) *Numbers employed* (including self-employed): as in (1).

SPAIN

	$\log N$	$\log\{w(1+t_l/P)\}$	$\log(P_m/P)$	$\log K$	$\log L$	u	cu	$\log(P^*e/P)$	LKL	mm
1964	4·559	4·064	4·584	4·362	4·561	0·01	0·835	4·468	4·406	2·00
1965	4·525	4·178	4·544	4·385	4·526	0·009	0·832	4·456	4·463	3·85
1966	4·545	4·296	4·530	4·420	4·544	0·006	0·83	4·462	4·481	1·62
1967	4·578	4·396	4·494	4·465	4·576	0·006	0·80	4·477	4·493	2·71
1968	4·577	4·438	4·570	4·505	4·577	0·007	0·805	4·589	4·533	0·77
1969	4·604	4·518	4·578	4·549	4·603	0·006	0·837	4·599	4·550	2·31
1970	4·605	4·605	4·605	4·605	4·650	0·008	0·837	4·605	4·605	0·07
1971	4·628	4·684	4·565	4·662	4·628	0·007	0·823	4·616	4·639	1·99
1972	4·656	4·783	4·486	4·704	4·663	0·015	0·868	4·590	4·646	1·27
1973	4·688	4·867	4·577	4·764	4·697	0·016	0·888	4·582	4·671	0·77
1974	4·721	4·931	5·024	4·806	4·731	0·018	0·840	4·563	4·680	2·02
1975	4·735	5·044	4·893	4·854	4·757	0·029	0·795	4·563	4·703	3·63
1976	4·741	5·155	4·869	4·889	4·765	0·031	0·815	4·580	4·728	1·89
1977	4·747	5·250	4·905	4·918	4·770	0·030	0·828	4·596	4·754	1·55
1978	4·733	5·321	4·842	4·944	4·770	0·043	0·800	4·574	4·779	0·17
1979	4·701	5·394	4·772	4·965	4·750	0·055	0·798	4·445	4·821	0·61
1980	4·668	5·406	5·103	4·985	4·737	0·073	0·788	4·472	4·853	0·47
1981	4·626	5·419	5·254	5·004	4·720	0·096	0·788	4·542	4·889	1·35
1982	4·569	5·438	5·229	5·019	4·690	0·121	0·80	4·564	4·934	4·37
1983	4·548	5·437	5·279	5·034	4·684	0·134	0·788	4·664	4·955	1·47

	t_1	$t_2 = (t_2' + t_4)$	t_3	$\Delta \log W$	$\Delta \log P$	$\Delta \log P^c$	$\log Y$	$\log GDP$
1964	0·151	0·091	0·065				4·062	4·236
1965	0·149	0·085	0·068	0·154	0·037	0·123	4·172	4·292
1966	0·144	0·096	0·072	0·154	0·031	0·060	4·270	4·364
1967	0·156	0·117	0·071	0·123	0·034	0·063	4·323	4·412
1968	0·160	0·110	0·067	0·072	0·034	0·048	4·400	4·472
1969	0·165	0·108	0·072	0·105	0·030	0·021	4·527	4·557
1970	0·165	0·109	0·071	0·128	0·041	0·055	4·605	4·605
1971	0·173	0·110	0·066	0·124	0·052	0·079	4·665	4·659
1972	0·175	0·114	0·067	0·150	0·054	0·079	4·802	4·741
1973	0·175	0·123	0·071	0·164	0·080	0·108	4·904	4·819
1974	0·176	0·115	0·060	0·228	0·164	0·146	4·964	4·877
1975	0·195	0·123	0·056	0·240	0·144	0·156	4·958	4·890
1976	0·209	0·127	0·053	0·249	0·150	0·139	4·925	4·922
1977	0·211	0·136	0·053	0·260	0·175	0·232	5·037	4·952
1978	0·235	0·141	0·043	0·226	0·166	0·180	5·057	4·977
1979	0·242	0·168	0·044	0·202	0·139	0·146	5·056	4·979
1980	0·251	0·183	0·044	0·145	0·136	0·145	5·060	4·993
1981	0·253	0·184	0·052	0·133	0·126	0·136	5·065	4·990
1982	0·252	0·190	0·055	0·133	0·112	0·135	5·058	5·002
1983	0·260	0·203	0·060	0·119	0·123	0·115	5·088	5·023

Notes:

(i) All variables, except u, cu, mm, t_1, t_2, t_3 $\Delta \log W$, $\Delta \log P$ and $\Delta \log P_c$, are expressed as indices with base 1970 = 100.

(ii) The notation of the variables is the standard one. Some of cases that may raise doubts are:

cu = capacity utilization

LKL = log capital-labour ratio

t_2' = income tax average rate

t_4 = employees' contributions to social security

P = GDP deflator

P^c = retail price index

Y = industrial output

Definitions

n	$\log N$; N = total number of employees in industry (annual average) (*BE*) (elaborated from *GTE* and *EPA*).
u	total unemployment rate in industry (annual average), excluding 'school-leavers' (*BE*) (elaborated from *GTE* and *EPA*).
l	$\log L$; L = total workforce in industry; defined as $l = u + n$.
w	$\log W$; W = average monthly earnings per employee (*BE*) (elaborated from *ES*).
t_1	employer's mandatory contributions to social security; defined as the ratio of the average contribution per employee to the average wage in industry (*CN*).
p	$\log P$; P = industrial output index; elaborated from the industrial component of the wholesale price index and the index of industrial prices (*BE*).
p^c	$\log P^c$; P^c = index of consumer prices (*BE*).
p_m	$\log P_m$; P_m = index of industrial import prices; elaborated as a weighted average of an index of domestic prices and the indices of unit value of imports of raw materials and semi-elaborated goods in industry (*BE*).
k	$\log K$; K = capital stock; elaborated through the integration of flows of 'total gross domestic fixed capital formation' of the non-financial firms, as defined by the CN (see Dolado and Malo de Molina, 1984) (*BE*).
Y	$\log Y$; Y = index of value added in industry (CN).
a	$\log A$; A = index of labour-augmenting technical progress. This is computed as follows. Starting from a value added production function.

$$Y = F(NA, K),$$

by taking logs and differencing, we find that

$$\Delta y = (1 - v_k)(\Delta n + \Delta a) + v_k \Delta k$$

where v_k is the share of capital. Thus we have

$$\Delta a = (1 - v_k)^{-1}\{\Delta y - (1 - v_k)\Delta n - v_k \Delta k\}.$$

Then the variable is integrated taking an initial value. Since the production function refers to potential value added and we have used actual value added, the index might be underestimated. In order to somehow correct for this deficiency and to iron out cyclical components, the fitted values from a quadratic have been used.

rr	replacement ratio; defined as the ratio of unemployment subsidies per unemployed person to average earnings per employee (*BEL*). Owing to its potential endogeneity, the following adjusted version was computed. An expected measure for an individual who has a probability of 0·5 of having a complete unemployment spell of 6 months or less, a probability of 0·3 of being employed between 6 and 12 months, a probability of 0·1 of unemployment between 12 and 18 months, and finally, a probability of 0·1 of being unemployed for longer than 18 months. The corresponding legal replacement ratios have been 0·8 for the first spell until 1965, an additional 0·7 for the second spell between 1966 and 1975, an additional 0·6 for the third spell between 1976 and 1980, and an additional 0·5 for the fourth spell beyond 1980.
c	an index of firing costs; defined as the ratio of average redundancy payments as agreed by the Labour Court to average earnings per employee (*BEL*). This variable was adjusted as follows. For a given individual with a duration of 5 years of employment in a firm, the redundancy payments, when fired, accounted for 100 per cent of his (her) annual earnings until 1979 and 90, 75, 75 and 70 per cent in 1980, 1981, 1982 and 1983, respectively.
mm	an index of mismatch; defined as the absolute change in the proportion of 'Total employees in industry (annual average)' relative to 'Total employees (annual average)' (*GTE* and *EPA*).
t_2	labour income taxes; defined as the average rate of income tax that a single worker with the same real wage throughout the period would pay, plus the rate of employee's contributions to social security (*MEH*).

t_3 indirect taxes; defined as the ratio of total indirect taxes net of subsidies to GDP at factor costs (CN).

e $\log E$; E = real exchange rate; defined as the ratio of an index of export prices of industrial countries in pesetas to an index of industrial prices (BE).

r after-tax real interest rate; defined as $(1 - \tau)R - \Delta p_{+1}$ where τ is the corporate tax rate, R is the interest rate on bank credits between one and three years, and p is as above (BE). This variable was always instrumented to take account of the measurement error induced by using Δp_{+1} as opposed to Δp_{+1}^e.

wt $\log WT$; WT = index of world trade; defined as a quantum index of exports by industrial countries and LDC non-oil-exporting countries. The actual series used in the paper are the deviations of that index in logs from a third-degree polynomial in time (IFS).

m $\log M$; M = M3 nominal holdings (billions) (BE).

AD adjusted budget deficit as a proportion of GDP. The cyclically adjusted deficit has been taken from Viñals (1985).

Abbreviations for sources

BE   *Boletín Estadístico* (Bank of Spain)
BEL   *Boletín de Estadísticas Laborales*
CN   *Contabilidad Nacional*
EPA   *Encuesta de Población Activa*
ES   *Encuesta de Salarios*
GTE   *Grupo de Trabajo del Ministerio de Economía*
IFS   *International Financial Statistics*
MEH   *Ministerio Economía y Hacienda*

DATA APPENDICES

United Kingdom

	$\log N$	$\log K$	$\log(W/\bar{P})$	ν	AD	$\log(P^*/\bar{P})$	WT
1950							
1951							
1952							
1953	9·927	5·426	4·173	0·236	0·097	−0·556	
1954	9·944	5·452	4·220	0·232	0·089	−0·591	−0·013
1955	9·958	5·477	4·254	0·243	0·082	−0·628	−0·005
1956	9·970	5·502	4·292	0·229	0·080	−0·604	0·044
1957	9·974	5·528	4·292	0·227	0·079	−0·626	0·028
1958	9·966	5·553	4·326	0·209	0·067	−0·651	−0·055
1959	9·972	5·580	4·350	0·211	0·075	−0·661	−0·038
1960	9·994	5·618	4·408	0·226	0·083	−0·674	0·031
1961	10·009	5·651	4·443	0·211	0·080	−0·700	0·001
1962	10·019	5·682	4·467	0·205	0·074	−0·728	−0·010
1963	10·022	5·715	4·487	0·205	0·079	−0·728	0·019
1964	10·035	5·749	4·518	0·213	0·088	−0·756	0·011
1965	10·047	5·790	4·569	0·203	0·085	−0·775	0·013
1966	10·054	5·825	4·633	0·197	0·085	−0·771	0·004
1967	10·035	5·867	4·643	0·203	0·093	−0·816	−0·049
1968	10·028	5·908	4·672	0·224	0·087	−0·696	−0·004
1969	10·027	5·951	4·706	0·220	0·065	−0·697	0·011
1970	10·020	5·989	4·801	0·225	0·062	−0·715	0·005
1971	10·004	6·026	4·842	0·220	0·068	−0·765	−0·003
1972	10·004	6·061	4·909	0·223	0·083	−0·795	0·001
1973	10·028	6·097	4·935	0·267	0·095	−0·715	0·046
1974	10·034	6·130	4·913	0·336	0·097	−0·674	0·031
1975	10·031	6·160	4·973	0·282	0·092	−0·717	−0·074
1976	10·023	6·190	4·944	0·300	0·086	−0·649	−0·009
1977	10·026	6·217	4·910	0·299	0·073	−0·667	−0·015
1978	10·033	6·244	4·966	0·278	0·079	−0·713	−0·002
1979	10·049	6·269	5·010	0·285	0·077	−0·796	0·036
1980	10·041	6·295	5·037	0·258	0·069	−0·941	0·023
1981	9·992	6·312	5·052	0·247	0·059	−0·945	−0·026
1982	9·971	6·330	5·072	0·270	0·053	−0·896	−0·101
1983	9·955	6·346	5·075	0·247	0·062	−0·854	−0·165

	$\log A$	U	$\log L$	MM	ρ	$\log Y^P$ (smoothed)	$\log(U_p)$
1950							
1951							
1952							
1953		0·017	9·944	0·107	40·500	−0·030	−2·408
1954	0·010	0·014	9·958	0·160	37·800	0·034	−2·659
1955	0·021	0·011	9·969	0·487	37·500	0·067	−2·408
1956	0·037	0·012	9·982	0·161	37·700	0·096	−1·966
1957	0·053	0·016	9·990	0·275	36·200	0·127	−1·832
1958	0·067	0·022	9·988	0·244	40·100	0·142	−1·897
1959	0·084	0·024	9·996	0·535	40·600	0·164	−2·040
1960	0·107	0·018	10·012	0·359	42·000	0·196	−1·833
1961	0·132	0·017	10·026	0·065	42·000	0·226	−1·772
1962	0·157	0·023	10·042	0·729	42·400	0·254	−1·661
1963	0·187	0·028	10·050	0·668	43·900	0·285	−1·897
1964	0·218	0·020	10·055	0·159	43·000	0·317	−1·832
1965	0·246	0·017	10·064	0·061	47·500	0·351	−1·661
1966	0·276	0·018	10·072	0·181	48·200	0·381	−1·772
1967	0·309	0·030	10·065	0·586	52·600	0·410	−1·772
1968	0·344	0·033	10·061	0·534	51·700	0·442	−1·619
1969	0·375	0·033	10·060	0·031	50·800	0·470	−1·561
1970	0·407	0·036	10·056	0·487	51·200	0·496	−1·347
1971	0·441	0·047	10·051	0·999	50·600	0·524	−1·347
1972	0·471	0·051	10·055	1·270	47·000	0·552	−1·171
1973	0·501	0·036	10·064	0·603	46·600	0·587	−1·171
1974	0·524	0·036	10·070	0·311	47·200	0·613	−1·386
1975	0·545	0·055	10·086	1·542	49·200	0·640	−1·171
1976	0·560	0·071	10·094	0·793	50·000	0·664	−1·204
1977	0·577	0·074	10·100	0·095	51·300	0·687	−1·139
1978	0·591	0·072	10·105	0·432	49·800	0·701	−1·273
1979	0·612	0·067	10·116	0·518	46·000	0·722	−1·238
1980	0·627	0·087	10·128	1·012	45·800	0·740	−0·892
1981	0·641	0·137	10·129	1·807	50·300	0·745	−0·832
1982	0·659	0·160	10·131	1·076	53·500	0·756	−0·842
1983	0·681	0·167	10·122	0·986	54·400	0·766	−0·846

	t_1	t_2	t_3	V	log POP	log G
1950	4·503					
1951	4·498					
1952	4·505					
1953	4·503	0·086	0·029	0·044	10·426	9·561
1954	4·506	0·086	0·025	0·051	10·426	9·507
1955	4·507	0·090	0·027	0·062	10·427	9·494
1956	4·507	0·093	0·029	0·053	10·426	9·523
1957	4·505	0·098	0·026	0·041	10·427	9·521
1958	4·512	0·110	0·019	0·030	10·429	9·491
1959	4·512	0·108	0·015	0·035	10·434	9·534
1960	4·510	0·110	0·010	0·046	10·440	9·568
1961	4·509	0·116	0·010	0·045	10·446	9·618
1962	4·513	0·123	0·015	0·031	10·459	9·658
1963	4·516	0·122	0·014	0·030	10·461	9·691
1964	4·511	0·127	0·020	0·046	10·465	9·756
1965	4·517	0·141	0·030	0·054	10·462	9·803
1966	4·545	0·152	0·036	0·052	10·463	9·856
1967	4·551	0·153	0·037	0·036	10·462	9·941
1968	4·556	0·167	0·048	0·040	10·464	9·981
1969	4·563	0·175	0·067	0·042	10·463	9·986
1970	4·568	0·186	0·063	0·040	10·462	10·021
1971	4·568	0·188	0·048	0·026	10·462	10·034
1972	4·571	0·178	0·027	0·029	10·462	10·051
1973	4·583	0·186	0·019	0·056	10·464	10·142
1974	4·579	0·209	0·002	0·051	10·465	10·195
1975	4·605	0·237	0·000	0·026	10·466	10·245
1976	4·619	0·245	0·006	0·021	10·469	10·251
1977	4·634	0·233	0·022	0·025	10·473	10·192
1978	4·641	0·223	0·016	0·031	10·477	10·181
1979	4·648	0·213	0·032	0·032	10·482	10·202
1980	4·646	0·220	0·040	0·019	10·485	10·252
1981	4·648	0·238	0·046	0·013	10·493	10·236
1982	4·642	0·243	0·057	0·015	10·161	10·248
1983	4·633	0·244	0·047	0·020	10·160	10·294

	$\log(P_m/\bar{P})$	σ(Model 1)	$\log(K/L)$	B/Y^P	OIL	τ
1950			−4·573			0·285
1951			−4·556			0·321
1952			−4·536			0·295
1953			−4·518			0·301
1954	0·028	0·355	−4·506	6·500		0·252
1955	0·230	0·245	−4·492	−7·990		0·256
1956	0·206	0·304	−4·480	9·952		0·245
1957	0·170	0·256	−4·463	10·543		0·232
1958	0·077	0·019	−4·435	15·584		0·175
1959	0·058	0·111	−4·416	7·078		0·171
1960	0·044	0·249	−4·394	−8·871		0·162
1961	−0·005	0·159	−4·374	1·710		0·123
1962	−0·040	0·059	−4·360	5·382		0·097
1963	−0·026	0·137	−4·334	4·085		0·105
1964	−0·029	0·203	−4·306	−10·719		0·098
1965	−0·065	0·149	−4·274	−0·836		0·048
1966	−0·087	0·144	−4·247	3·403		0·136
1967	−0·118	0·133	−4·198	−6·642		0·104
1968	−0·051	0·241	−4·153	−5·545		0·083
1969	−0·061	0·011	−4·109	10·745		0·046
1970	−0·092	−0·040	−4·067	15·981		0·044
1971	−0·130	−0·035	−4·025	19·446		0·022
1972	−0·158	0·098	−3·994	3·484		0·002
1973	−0·014	0·356	−3·968	−13·230		0·021
1974	0·161	0·405	−3·940	−38·977		0·092
1975	0·080	0·198	−3·925	−14·327	0·017	−0·191
1976	0·132	0·270	−3·904	−6·672	0·120	−0·133
1977	0·150	0·099	−3·883	0·363	0·372	0·010
1978	0·100	0·137	−3·861	6·917	0·492	0·038
1979	0·079	0·074	−3·847	−2·673	0·720	−0·025
1980	0·067	−0·169	−3·833	15·765	0·727	0·128
1981	0·050	−0·336	−3·817	28·407	0·685	0·042
1982	0·077	−0·424	−3·801	18·774	0·671	0·091
1983	0·105	−0·357	−3·776	9·678	0·704	0·156

Data sources and definitions

Abbreviations

AAS	*Annual Abstract of Statistics*
BB	'*Blue Book*', National Income and Expenditure (yearly).
BEQB	*Bank of England Quarterly Bulletin*
BESA 70	*Bank of England Statistical Abstract*, 1970
BESA 75	*Bank of England Statistical Abstract*, 1975 (*BESA* only published twice)
BLSHA	*British Labour Statistics, Historical Abstract*, 1886–1968
DEG	*Department of Employment Gazette* (monthly)
ETAS	*Economic Trends Annual Supplement*
ET	*Economic Trends* (monthly)
FS	*Financial Statistics* (monthly)
MDS	*Monthly Digest of Statistics*
NIER	*National Institute Economic Review*
YB	British Labour Statistics *Year Book*, 1969–1976 (published eight times, between 1969 and 1976)

(Data relate to UK unless otherwise stated.)

Definitions

N   Employees in employment, males and females, mid-year, Great Britain (*ETAS*).

K   Capital stock. The series used is 'gross capital stock at 1975 replacement cost', in £ billion. Data are available yearly from 1958 onward in successive issues of the *BB*, at various base years (which were easily 'spliced' together). Before 1958 only the 1954, 1951 and 1948 observations were published. Data were interpolated using real investment data, namely 'total gross domestic fixed capital formation', £ million at 1975 prices, using the usual technique involving the estimation of a decay parameter $\hat{\delta}$ from the postulated relationship,

$$K_n = \sum_{i=1}^{n} (1-\delta)^{n-i} I_i + (1-\delta)^n K_0$$

where K_n, K_0 are end of period and beginning of period capital stocks, and I_i is investment. The missing K's are calculated recursively by setting $n=1$ each time, and using $\hat{\delta}$. The investment series is published in *ETAS*.

(W/P)   The real product wage. W is a labour cost variable equal to $\bar{W}(1+t_1)$. $\bar{W}$ is the pre-tax wage calculated as follows. We first take E and H, the average weekly earnings and average weekly hours of full-time male manual workers (21 years and over), at October in each year, for all industries covered; and N^h, the average normal weekly hours of male manual workers, for all industries and services. Given an overtime premium of 0·3, we now compute $\bar{W}$ as the hourly earnings if the individual works 45 hours per week. Thus

$$\bar{W} = \frac{E\{N^h + 1\cdot3(45 - N^h)\}}{45\{N^h + 1\cdot3(H - N^h)\}}$$

All data for E, H and N^h are published in *BLSHA*, *YB* and the latest issue of *DEG*.

ν   Ratio of imports to GDP.

AD   Adjusted public sector deficit as a percentage of potential GDP. We calculate the weighted, cyclically adjusted deficit by the method described in *NIER* 3/85, but with the following alterations: (1) the weights used on current expenditures and capital expenditures are reduced to 0·82 and 0·77 to capture the impact effects of these items on home demand; (2) instead of debt interest, we use 0·02 × volume of public sector debt outstanding (*AAS*) as an adjustment for the inflation tax.

$P^*/\bar{P}$ This is a measure of competitiveness. P^* is the unit value index of world manufacturing exports from the *UN Monthly Digest of Statistics*. This is converted from dollars to pounds using the $/£ exchange range (*ETAS*).

WT   This measures the deviation of world trade from trend. The world trade measure is the log of the quantum index of world exports (*WE*) from the *UN Monthly Digest of Statistics*. The actual variable consists of the residuals from the regression

$$\log(WE) = 1\cdot53 + 0\cdot50t - 0\cdot057t^2 + 0\cdot0033t^3 - 0\cdot000086t^4$$
$$\quad\quad\; (2\cdot5) \quad (2\cdot5) \quad\;\; (2\cdot7) \quad\quad (2\cdot7)$$

$$+ 0\cdot000000081t^5.$$
$$(2\cdot7)$$

A   Index of labour-augmenting technical progress. This is computed via the formula

$$\Delta \log A_t = \frac{1}{(1-\nu_{Kt})}\{\Delta \log Y_t - (1-\nu_{Kt})\Delta \log N_t - \nu_{Kt}\Delta \log K_t\}$$

Y_t is GDP at factor cost (*ETAS*) and the weights are defined using the variables 'compensation of employees' and 'operating surplus' which are rows 17 and 18 in the UK table of *National Accounts of OECD Countries* (Paris, 1981). The series used in the annual estimation procedure corresponds to a five-year moving average of the 'A' index.

U   Male unemployment rate. The series used is 'males wholly unemployed as a percentage of the number of employees (employed and unemployed) at the appropriate mid-year, for the UK'. The numbers unemployed exclude 'temporarily stopped' but include school-leavers. The data are published in BLSHA, the YB, and finally DEG. We consider the male rate to be the most accurate available measure of the aggregate unemployment rate (including unregistered women). The data refer to the pre-1982 definition of the male unemployment rate; more recent data have been appropriately adjusted.

L   Labour force, defined by $\log L = U + \log N$. (Note that $\log L - \log N = -\log N/L = -\log\{1-(L-N)/L\} = L - N/L = U$.) This definition of the labour force is consistent with the view expressed under U above.

MM   An index of mismatch. This is the absolute change in the proportion of 'employees in employment, males and females, in index of production industries at each mid-year, Great Britain', to 'total employees in employment, males and females at each mid-year, Great Britain' (BLSHA, YB, DEG).

ρ The replacement ratio. This variable is measured as a weighted average of different family types using the following proportions: single householder 0·35, married couple with no children 0·12, with one child 0·11, with two children 0·16 and with three children 0·12. The components of this weighted average are calculated from Table 6·4a of the DHSS Abstract of Statistics for Index of Retail Prices, Average Earnings, Social Security Benefits and Contributions (1983). This gives for each family type, data on supplementary benefits, plus rent addition and on net income for a one-earner family on average earnings. We compute annual income on benefit and relate it to mid-year earnings.

Y^P Potential GDP, constructed from the equation

$$\Delta \log Y_t^P = (1 - \nu_{Kt})\Delta \log L_t + \nu_{Kt}\Delta \log K_t + (1 - \nu_{Kt})\Delta \log A_t$$

where L refers to the labour force.

U_p Our measure of union power is the log of the union/non-union mark-up (UM). The procedure by which this variable was estimated is described in Layard, Metcalf and Nickell (1978, Table 5).* Cross-section regressions have been estimated for each year, 1953–83. The modified series is plotted in Figure 3 of the text alongside series derived from DEG on strike activity and union membership.

t_1 The 'employment tax' borne by the firm. This series is calculated by taking the ratio of two indices, the 'total labour costs per unit of output for the whole economy', 1975 = 100, and 'wages and salaries per unit of output for the whole economy', 1975 = 100. However, it is an index based at 1975 = 100. Thus the only way to obtain an approximation to t_{1t} is to take logs ($\log k(1 + t_{1t}) = \log k + t_{1t}$) and let $\log k$ be absorbed by the regression constant. The former series is published in BLSHA (Table 203), YB 1976 (Table 55) and the latest issue of DEG; the latter series is in ETAS.

t_2 Income tax rate, computed as follows:

$$t_2 = (DT + SS)/HCR.$$

where DT is direct taxes on household income, SS is households' contributions to social security schemes, and HCR is households' current receipts minus employer contributions to social security schemes. All three series are from OECD National Accounts.

t_3 The indirect tax rate. The log of the ratio of the GDP deflator at market prices (1975 = 100) to the GDP deflator at factor cost (1975 = 100) yields t_3 + constant (ETAS).

V   Vacancy rate. This is defined by $V = (V' \times 10^3)/\lambda N$, where V' = registered vacancies (DEG),

         λ = a correction factor

* See Reference list at end of paper.

$$= \tfrac{1}{2} \left\{ \left(\frac{\text{outflow of registered vacancies}}{\text{engagements}} \right) \right.$$

$$\left. + \left(\frac{\text{inflow of registered vacancies}}{\text{separations}} \right) \right\}.$$

λ is discussed in Jackman *et al.* (1984).

POP	Working population (*DEG*).
G	Real government expenditure. *G* is calculated from 'general government expenditure on goods and services', in £ million, which is divided by the GDP at factor cost deflator. The GDP factor cost deflator was used because the equivalent series at constant prices do not exist (*ETAS*).
P_m	Import price index for the UK (*ETAS*).
P	A value-added price index. We define it by

$$(1+\nu) \log \bar{P} = \log P + \nu \log P_m$$

where $\bar{P}$ is a gross output price index, P_m is an import price index and ν is the share of imports in value added.

$\bar{P}$	The output price index. $\bar{P}$ is defined as the *TFE* deflator at market prices (*BB*) divided by $(1+NT3)$ where *NT3* is the indirect tax rate relevant to the *TFE* deflator. This is defined as $NT3 = FCA/(TFE - FCA)$ where *TFE* = total final expenditure at market prices (*ETAS*); *FCA* = factor cost adjustment which is expenditure taxes (*ETAS*) − selective employment tax (*BB*) − national insurance surcharge (*BB*) − subsidies (*ETAS*).
IPD	Incomes policy dummy. The variable is unity in 1976 and 1977, zero otherwise.
RI	Post-tax real interest rate. This is defined as $(1 - \tau_{ct})R_t - \Delta \log P_{t+1}$ where τ_c is the corporate tax rate, R_t is the Treasury bill rate and P_t is as above (*FS*). This variable is always instrumented to take account of the measurement error induced by using $\Delta \log P_{t+1}$ as opposed to $\Delta \log P^e_{t+1}$.
B/Y^p	Total current balance of trade (exports − imports) (*ETAS*) divided by Y^p (potential GDP).
OIL	Real output of oil:

$$OIL = \frac{\text{crude oil output (barrels)} \times \text{price of crude oil (per barrel)}}{\bar{P}}.$$

The data on crude oil output and the relevant price per barrel are found in the Annual Report of the British National Oil Corporation.

τ	The effective average corporate tax rate defined for the whole economy, following the procedure proposed by King (1975) and Beath (1979). The effective tax liability is described by

$$T = t(\Pi - D) + t_d \phi - \Sigma$$

where Π is gross trading profits, Δ is tax deductions, ϕ is gross dividends, Σ is investment grants, t is the corporate tax rate and t_d is personal tax rate on dividend income. The component series were obtained on an annual basis from the following sources:

Π	Gross trading profits after deduction of stock appreciation allowable for tax purposes, per companies and financial institutions (*ETAS*). (Stock appreciation was allowable against tax liability for 1975–83.)
ϕ	Dividends paid on ordinary shares by companies and financial institutions (*ETAS*). This series was adjusted for personal income tax post-1973, as prior to that data it was reported *gross* of tax payments.
Σ	Investment grants received by industrial and commercial companies (*BB*).
D	Interest payments by companies and financial institutions ('other' payments) (*ETAS*); capital consumption allowances are given by gross profits less net profits (*BB*).

The effective tax rate is given as the ratio of the annual tax liability series to gross trading profits. Following Beath (1979), the variable appears in the regressions as $(1 - \tau)^{-1}$. Negative liabilities were set equal to zero.

Author Index

Abegglen, J. C., 286, 287, 295
Abel, A., 50
Altonji, J., 191
Andrews, M. J., 164, 168, 333, 334
Antonelle, P., 352
Argy, V., 73
Arisawa, H., 286, 295
Arnolt, S. W. 86
Artus, J. R., 50, 51, 243, 244, 334
Artus, P., 206, 217
Ashenfelter, O., 21, 169, 171, 195, 273

Bachrach, C., 50
Backer, G. M., 62, 72, 74
Baffi, P., 272
Baily, M. N., 244
Bain, J. S., 254
Barbone, L., 258, 272
Barro, R. J., 15, 97
Basevi, G., 46, 50, 51, 251, 272
Baumgart, E., 346
Bauwens, L., 96, 118, 119
Bean, C. R., 1, 20, 86, 243, 332
Beath, J., 151, 168, 374
Beck, R., 191
Beckerman, W., 51
Bell, D. N. F., 164, 168
Benassy, J. P., 97
Berghe, C. Vanden, 96, 119
Blanchard, O., 46, 50, 51, 166, 168, 251, 272
Blundell, R., 217
Bodo, G., 251, 259, 272
Bourguignon, F., 217
Boutillier, M., 206, 217
Brasche, V., 229, 244
Brauner, D., 243
Bruno, M., 6, 8, 13, 14, 16, 17, 21, 33, 50, 51, 144, 146, 194, 216, 217
Buchtemann, C. F., 229, 244
Buiter, W. H., 21, 46, 50, 51, 251, 272
Bureau of Labour Statistics, 194, 195
Burtless, G., 186, 195
Butkiewicz, J. C., 169
Buttler, F., 87

Caffet, J. P., 216
Cameron, D. R., 16, 21
Card, D., 171, 195
Carlin, W., 137, 168
Catinat, M., 206, 217

Caves, R. E., 73
Cette, G., 201, 217
Chamberlin, E. H., 29
Chan-Lee, J. H., 43, 51
Chouraqui, J. C., 202, 217
Christl, J., 77, 86
Clark, K. B., 211, 217
Coe, D. T., 32, 34, 237, 244, 304, 311
Cramer, U., 229, 244

D'Alcantara, G., 95, 96, 118, 119
Davies, D., 169
Dawkins, P., 73
De Santis, G., 272
Dolado, J. J., 3, 313, 322, 324, 325, 333, 334, 366
Domberger, S., 168
Dore, R. P., 286, 287, 294, 295
Dornbusch, R., 46, 50, 51, 57, 58, 72, 73, 251, 272
Douglas, P. H., 286, 295
Drèze, J. H., 15, 89, 198, 246, 272
Driehuis, W., 297, 303, 304, 305, 308, 309, 311, 312
Dubois, P., 201, 216, 217
Dunlop, J. T., 5, 21

Edoh, H., 291, 296
Ermann, K., 227
Evans, J. M., 224, 244
Eyk, C., 303, 312

Faustini, G., 272
Felli, L., 272
Feroldi, M., 214, 216, 217
Filosa, R., 272
Fischer, G., 78, 86
Fischer, S., 57, 58, 72, 73
Fisher, P. G., 164, 168
Fitoussi, J. P., 119
Flanagan, R. J., 75, 86
Fortin, P., 191
Franz, W., 86, 219, 222, 224, 235, 236, 243, 244
Friedman, M., 15, 30, 290, 295
Fujimoto, J., 291, 295

Gagliardi, F., 32, 34, 237, 244, 304, 311
Gallant, A., 33, 334
Geary, P. T., 195

Gerald, M., 96, 119
Gerlach, K., 87
Giersch, H., 224, 237, 244
Gordon, R. J., 50, 51, 146, 168, 235, 243, 244, 280, 295
Gregory, R. J., 16, 53, 62, 63, 64, 72, 73, 85, 86
Grossman, H., 15, 97, 293, 295
Grubb, D., 1, 20, 21, 80, 86, 128, 169, 259, 272, 290, 295
Grubel, H. G., 244
Guiso, L., 272, 273

Haberler, G., 75, 86
Hall, A., 333, 334
Hall, R. E., 63, 73
Hamada, K., 275, 283, 285, 295
Haraf, W., 293, 295
Harper, I., 72, 73
Hart, P. E., 169
Hart, R. A., 241, 244
Hartog, H. den, 312
Hashimoto, M., 287, 295
Heimler, A., 272, 273
Heineken, K. A., 305, 312
Heijke, J. A. M., 309, 311
Henry, B., 169
Highuchi, Y., 285, 286, 295, 296
Ho, V., 72
Hornstein, Z., 312
Hosokawa, T., 289, 296
Hughes, B., 72, 73

Isaac, J. E., 73
Ito, T., 285, 295

Jackman, R.A., 5, 21, 80, 86, 124, 125, 128, 139, 167, 169, 259, 272, 290, 295
Jenkinson, T., 51
Jeschek, W., 229, 244
Johnson, G., 5, 21, 123, 128, 138, 139, 169, 273
Joly, P., 201, 217
Jonson, P. D., 73
Jorgenson, D., 333, 334

Kempf, T., 243
Kendall, M. G., 18, 19, 21, 22
Kennan, J., 195
King, M., 169, 374
Kirby, M., 57, 58, 71, 72, 73
Kirkpatrick, G., 237, 244
Klant, J. J., 312
Koford, K. J., 169
Koga, M., 279, 295
Koike, K., 286, 287, 288, 294, 295
Kokkelenberg, E. C., 187, 195
Kong, P., 166

Konig, H., 219, 233, 238
Koning, J. de, 309, 311
Kosai, Y., 283, 295
Koshiro, K., 278, 295
Kranse, L. B., 73
Krelle, W., 169
Kunst, R., 79, 86
Kuratani, M., 287, 295
Kurosaka, Y., 275, 283, 285, 295
Kurihara, H., 294

Lambert, J. P., 96, 98, 100, 119
Lancaster, T., 165, 169
Layard, P. R. G., 1, 3, 5, 6, 7, 15, 21, 22, 46, 50, 51, 80, 83, 86, 87, 121, 123, 124, 125, 128, 138, 139, 147, 148, 160, 166, 167, 168, 169, 195, 243, 251, 259, 260, 272, 273, 290, 295, 313, 320, 322, 324, 328, 332, 333, 334, 373
Lehment, H., 237, 244
Leone, G., 272
Leroy, R., 95, 119
Leruth, Y., 119
Lilien, D., 260, 273
Lipschitz, L., 50, 51
Lollivier, S., 217
Lucas, R. E., 15

Magnus, J., 20
Mahar, K. D., 73
Malcolmson, J., 251, 273, 301, 312
Malgrange, P., 169
Malinvaud, E., 15, 24, 25, 34, 51, 75, 86, 97, 100, 119, 197, 202, 204, 207, 216, 217, 309, 312, 344
Malo de Molina, J. L., 3, 313, 322, 324, 325, 333, 334, 366
Marc, N., 217
Marchand, O., 217
Martin, J. P., 206, 217, 224, 243, 244, 294
Mauleon, I., 334
Maurer, J., 80, 86
Maurice, J., 206, 217
Mazodier, P., 216
McCall, F., 294
McCallum, J., 16, 21, 22, 50, 51, 191
McCloskey, D. N., 243, 244
McDonald, I., 20, 22, 272, 273
Meade, J., 75, 86
Mehl, R., 346
Mehta, F., 119
Mendis, L., 85, 86
Meraud, J., 217
Metcalf, D., 167, 169, 373
Meunier, F., 214, 216, 217
Michel, P., 272, 273
Milana, C., 272, 273
Miller, J. B., 169

Mills, G., 169
Mimmi, A., 272
Minford, P., 152, 165, 168, 169
Mitchell, D., 57, 73
Modigliani, F., 3, 245, 246, 251, 253, 254, 272, 273
Moran, P. A. P., 21, 22
Morishima, M., 287, 295
Muellbauer, J., 85, 86, 100, 119, 272
Muet, P. A., 169, 206, 217
Muller, C., 243
Muller, W., 229, 244
Muramatsu, K., 291, 293, 295
Murfin, A., 166
Muysken, J., 309, 312

Nagayama, S., 284, 295
Nakamura, J., 295
Narendranathan, W., 165, 169, 211, 217
Neusser, K., 83, 86
Nevile, J., 73
Newell, A., 6, 21, 22, 81, 83, 86
Nickell, S. J., 1, 3, 6, 7, 15, 21, 22, 46, 51, 86, 121, 135, 139, 147, 148, 160, 165, 166, 167, 168, 169, 211, 217, 313, 320, 322, 324, 328, 333, 334, 373
Niida, H. H., 296
Noord, P. J. Van den, 299, 300, 301, 305, 312

Odaka, K., 287, 295
OECD, 206, 212, 217, 295
Oegema, T., 311
Okun, A., 63, 73
Olson, M., 75, 86
Ono, A., 293, 296
Oswald, A., 139, 169

Padoa Schioppa, F., 3, 245, 272, 273
Padoa Schioppa, T., 246, 251, 253, 273
Pagan, A. R., 21, 22, 72, 73, 333, 334
Peel, M., 169
Pencavel, J. J., 5, 22, 139, 169
Perez, J., 334
Phelps, E. S., 290, 296
Phipps, A. J., 57, 72, 73
Pichelmann, K., 75, 76, 80, 86, 87
Pintz, P., 243
Pissarides, C., 5, 21, 124, 125, 139, 167, 332
Ploeg, F. Van der, 311
Pohlmeier, W., 243
Price, R. W. R., 202, 217
Pudney, S. E., 153, 169, 262, 273
Puig, J. P., 216, 217
Purvis, D., 191

Raoul, E., 201, 217
Raymond, J. L., 324, 334
Riboud, M., 217
Richardson, C. J., 62, 73, 74
Riddel, W. C., 184, 195
de Ridder, P. B., 299, 312
Rojo, L. A., 333, 334
Rosa, G., 352
Rossi, N., 3, 245
Roth, J., 237, 244

Sachs, J., 6, 8, 14, 16, 17, 21, 50, 51, 52, 216, 217, 291, 296
Sargan, J. D., 169
Sartor, N., 251
Sasajima, H., 278, 296
Savornin Lohman, A. F. de, 305, 312
Sawyer, M., 168, 169
Schadler, S. M., 50, 51
Schinthe, J., 346
Seike, A., 285, 286, 289, 294, 295, 296
Seitz, H., 243
Shapiro, C., 5, 22, 139, 169
Sheehan, P., 62, 74
Shimada, H., 286, 289, 291, 293, 296
Shimpo, S., 290, 296
Shinkai, Y., 296
Shirai, T., 286, 288, 295, 296
Shiraishi, E., 284, 296
Shorrocks, A., 169
Siesto, V., 352
Simes, R. M., 62, 73, 74
Sips, C., 311
Smith, R. E., 62, 63, 72, 73
Sneessens, H. R., 15, 50, 52, 89, 98, 119, 198
Sockell, D. R., 87, 195
Solow, R. M., 3, 20, 22, 23, 63, 74, 272, 273, 283, 296
Sonnet, A., 119
Sorrentino, C., 283, 284, 285, 296
Soskice, D., 137, 168
Soskje, D. W., 75, 86
Spaventa, L., 272, 273
Spinelli, F., 251, 273
Sprague, A., 169
Stern, J., 156, 169, 211, 217
Stewart, M., 167, 169
Stiassny, A., 83, 85, 87
Stiglitz, J. E., 5, 22, 139, 169
Stricker, P., 62, 74
Summers, L. H., 211
Sutch, H., 43, 51
Swidinsky, R., 183, 191
Sylos Labini, P., 254
Symons, J. S. V., 6, 21, 22, 81, 83, 86, 87, 161, 169, 195, 333, 334

Tachibanachi, T., 278, 296
Taira, K., 283, 284, 296
Taniuchi, M., 293, 296
Tarantelli, E., 16, 22, 251, 273
Thelot, C., 216
Thompson, G. L., 73
Toshida, S., 283, 295
Toyoda, T., 289, 290, 296
Trivedi, P. K., 62, 72, 74
Turnbull, P., 139, 169

Ueda, K., 51, 52, 289, 291, 296
Ulman, L., 75, 86

Verdoorn, P. J., 300, 312
Villa, P., 206, 217
Vinals, J., 332, 333, 334, 367
Visco, I., 251, 258, 272, 273

Wadhwani, S., 294
Wagner, M., 75, 77, 78, 79, 86, 87

Walker, M. A., 244
Wallis, K. F., 164, 168
Watanabe, T., 289, 296
Weiss, A., 5, 22
Weitenberg, J., 312
Weitzman, M. L., 290, 296
Werner, H., 229, 244
Whitely, J. D., 164, 168
Whittaker, J. K., 169
Wibaut, S., 119
Wickens, M., 147, 169
Winckler, G., 79, 86
Wooden, M., 73
Worgotter, A., 83, 87
Wren-Lewis, S., 169

Yashiro, N., 284, 296
Yoshida, K., 291, 296
Yoshikawa, H., 51, 52, 289, 291, 296

Zabalza, A., 3, 313

Subject Index

Absenteeism, 252
aggregate demand, 2, 3, 4, 8, 14, 19, 29, 35, 36, 45–7, 96, 97, 121, 122, 131, 135, 136, 146, 164, 202, 242, 246, 254, 264–6, 298, 310, 320, 329, 332
aggregate supply, 35, 36, 45–7, 96, 133, 141, 298, 299, 303, 304, 306
aggregation, 104–07, 161
apprenticeship, 95
asymmetric information, 34
Australia, 1, 2, 9–11, 16, 17, 32, 53–74
Austria, 1, 2, 9, 11, 12, 16, 17, 31, 32, 75–87, 335, 336

Balance of payments, 93, 155, 202, 257, 265, 266, 290
bankruptcy, 97, 119
Belgium, 1, 2, 9, 11, 17, 38–41, 45–9, 89–119, 245, 270, 337–41
Beveridge curve, 72, 212
business cycle, 201, 275

Canada, 1, 2, 9, 11, 12, 16, 17, 33, 38–41, 43–8, 73, 171–95, 245
capacity constraints, 130, 166, 307
capacity utilization, 201, 207, 210
capital gap, 103–07, 114
capital markets, 119
Carrero Blanco, 324
competitiveness, 138, 140–2, 148, 202, 203, 206, 322
consumption, 90, 109, 110
corporatism, 16–19, 79, 86

Deflationary gap, 79
demand management, 103, 104, 107, 202, 267, 271
demand shocks, 144–6, 162, 164
demand-side, 117, 157, 164, 177
Denmark, 1, 2, 9, 11, 12, 17, 38–41, 45–9, 93, 94, 317
D'Estaing G., 215
discouraged worker effect, 2, 15, 77, 80, 277, 286, 293
disequilibrium models, 15, 16, 47, 89, 96, 204
dismissals, 118, 205, 252, 323
distributive gap, 102, 104–07, 114
dualism in labour markets, 211, 212, 287
dynamic models, 122, 154, 160–4, 258–65

Education, 22, 199

EEC, 1, 11, 13, 19, 35, 46, 49, 50, 89, 90, 92, 94, 97, 222, 245, 269, 270, 313, 317
effective demand, 117, 118
efficiency wages, 5, 34, 139
employment, 17, 54, 76, 91, 117, 133, 142–6, 172, 174–8, 189–91, 197, 219, 220, 246, 247
    determination, 111–13, 137, 141, 206, 207, 288–93, 302, 309, 324–6
    distribution by sector, 180, 181, 201, 223, 316
    see also labour demand
employment capital ratio, 81–3
employment equilibrium, 84, 86
employment protection legislation, 121, 122, 125, 165, 251
Europe, 16, 22, 25, 36–41, 47, 49–51, 86, 118, 146, 168, 169, 181, 199, 213, 217, 286, 296, 313, 314, 317, 319, 334
exchange rates, 49, 50, 78, 95, 173, 188, 189
export prices, 203, 304
exports, 89, 90, 96, 97, 192, 193, 254, 259, 261

Family allowances, 200
Finland, 1, 2, 9, 11, 17
fiscal policy, 3, 15, 79, 83, 86, 305
Flanders, 95
France, 1, 2, 9, 11, 17, 32, 38, 40–8, 50, 73, 94, 197–217, 245, 270, 290, 295, 342–4
Franco, 323, 324
frictional unemployment, 96, 209, 267, 302, 310
Friedman M., 214
full employment, 268

GDP, 54, 76, 89, 90, 175–8, 313, 314
Germany, 1, 2, 9, 11, 12, 16, 17, 31, 32, 38, 40, 41, 43, 44, 46–8, 51, 73, 94, 95, 219–44, 245, 290, 295, 345, 346
goods demand, 101–03, 202, 203, 206
    see also aggregate demand

Harris-Todaro theory, 211
hidden unemployment, 231
hiring, 95, 118, 205, 209, 212, 239, 252
hours of work, 76, 83, 90, 92, 199, 200, 219, 224, 226, 278, 285, 308

human capital, 15, 64, 222, 287
hysteresis effect, 15, 128

Imperfect competition, 3, 5, 121, 133
  see also normal cost pricing;
    monopolistic competition
implicit contracts, 64
import prices, 11, 13, 40, 42, 49, 122,
  128, 157, 165, 203, 317–19, 328
imports, 111, 254, 259–61
incomes policies, 53, 57, 68–71, 79, 95,
  158, 159, 166, 283, 323, 324, 332
income share of labour, 92–4, 257, 280–1
industrial unemployment, 317, 328–31
inflation, 49, 50, 54, 57, 60, 61, 76, 78,
  93, 105, 121, 158, 159, 216, 236, 307,
  311, 314, 331
insider-outsiders, see outside opportunities
interest rates, 95, 202, 216, 322
international policy coordination, 49, 50,
  213
investments, 37, 42–5, 90, 95, 96, 99,
  119, 201, 243, 297, 303, 308, 310, 311
Ireland, 1, 2, 9, 11, 12, 16, 17, 21
Italy, 1–3, 9–12, 17, 21, 25, 38–44, 46,
  73, 93, 94, 245–73, 317, 347–52

Japan, 1, 2, 9–12, 16, 17, 21, 22, 32,
  38–41, 43–8, 51, 86, 94, 168, 169,
  245, 275–96, 334, 360–3

Labour costs, 3, 97, 131, 133, 203, 206,
  208, 214, 225, 239, 240, 243, 248–51,
  262, 317
labour demand, 3, 9, 12, 26, 45, 46, 80–3,
  85, 95, 96, 112, 117, 121, 136, 137,
  141, 146, 147, 150, 151, 160, 161,
  200–09, 222–4, 237–42, 253, 256,
  259, 261, 271, 293, 320–2
labour force, 2, 76, 77, 128, 130, 174,
  197, 219, 220, 246–8, 264, 265, 284,
  315
  composition by industry, 180, 181
  demographic structure, 122, 123, 178,
    179, 198, 199, 220–2, 275, 276
labour hoarding, 107, 111, 283, 307
labour management, 204
labour market, 3, 76–8, 121, 139, 173,
  209–13, 251–3, 275–83, 286–8
  rigidity, 171, 181–8, 191, 332
  see also labour mobility
labour mobility, 209–11, 253, 271
labour productivity, 54, 76, 79, 92, 97,
  117, 128, 153, 166, 172, 201, 264,
  280, 281, 283, 301, 308, 317
labour shortages, 56, 63, 84, 171, 207
labour supply, 62, 63, 76, 77, 80, 85, 95,
  124, 128, 138, 199, 293
  see also labour force

labour surplus, 75
labour utilization rate, 63–7, 71, 72, 83,
  232, 237
layoffs, 97, 239, 248, 253, 284, 285
limited-duration contracts, 212

Manufacturing, 37, 42–6, 68–71, 90, 92,
  95–7, 118, 224, 242, 243
mark-up of prices on costs, 4, 5, 121,
  135–7, 143, 146, 254, 256, 257
mark-up of wages on prices, 121, 127,
  143, 146, 153
Marshall-Lerner Condition, 257
migrations, 77, 80, 83, 219, 222
minimum wages, 172, 173, 181–3, 191,
  205, 212, 215
misery index, 16
mismatch, 3, 62, 104, 106, 112, 114, 122,
  125, 126, 153, 158, 159, 165, 209,
  210, 212, 233, 235, 302, 309–11, 323
monetary policy, 3, 15, 293
money supply, 27, 48, 192, 193
monopolistic competition, 25, 26, 80, 246,
  253
monopoly union, 5

Natural rate of unemployment, 6, 15, 16,
  24, 30–3, 71, 121, 122, 139, 149, 157,
  158, 160, 166, 235–7, 256, 291, 292,
  313, 321, 330–2
Nash Equilibrium, 26, 34
Netherlands, 1, 2, 9, 11, 16, 17, 20, 38,
  41, 45, 46, 94, 95, 245, 297–312, 317,
  353–9
New Zealand, 1, 2, 9, 11, 17
nominal wages, 24–30, 54
non-accelerating inflation rate of
  unemployment, see natural rate of
  unemployment
non-inflationary rate of excess demand,
  103–06, 108, 114–16
non-inflationary rate of unemployment, 98,
  102–06, 108, 114–16, 118
normal cost pricing, 13, 14, 136, 142–6
North America, 168, 175
Norway, 1, 2, 9, 11, 12, 17, 38, 40, 41,
  45, 46

OECD, 1–3, 6, 7, 19–22, 31, 32, 34, 35,
  38, 40, 43, 44, 47, 50, 51, 71, 75, 81,
  82, 86, 90, 203, 244, 245, 269, 270,
  272, 280, 286, 295
oil production, 159
oil shocks, 2, 36, 39, 42, 75, 114, 214,
  216, 220, 222, 237, 245, 278, 280,
  282, 283, 293, 318, 328, 329, 332
Okun's Law, 257, 283, 285
OPEC, 222, 237

outside opportunities, 5, 16, 20, 34, 66, 80, 139, 140, 255, 320

Participation rates, 2, 76, 77, 99, 173, 174, 198–200, 220–2, 246, 247, 276–8, 285, 286
perfect competition, 13, 14, 121, 142–6
Phillips curve, 21, 30–3, 36, 53, 58, 60, 63, 64, 68, 71–3, 85, 139, 148, 214, 215, 235, 256, 288, 290
potential employment, 94, 95, 99, 117, 300, 302
potential output, 135
price determination, 4, 5, 26, 101, 114, 117, 121, 133, 135, 136, 141, 147, 151, 161, 162, 214, 256, 261, 305, 324, 327, 328
price expectation, 58, 60–2, 71, 135
production function, 37, 98–100, 133–6, 237
    CES, 37, 80, 96, 253, 254, 291
    Cobb-Douglas, 28, 38, 98, 207, 239
    Leontief, 99
productive capacity, 299–301
profits, 37, 42–5, 204, 216, 311 319
profit-sharing, 290
public deficit, 7, 76, 90, 92, 93, 131, 202, 307, 322
public employment, 166

Quantity theory of money, 26, 28
quits, 5, 139, 211

Rate of excess demand, 104–08, 116
rationing, 97–107, 117
real wages, 2, 3, 24–30, 54, 75, 76, 81–6, 94, 117, 118, 121, 122, 142, 144–6, 160–4, 215, 216, 271, 308, 317
    and business cycle, 280, 281
    and employment, 19, 189–91, 241, 242, 257, 271
relative wages, 34, 188, 189, 191, 252
repressed inflation, 98, 99, 104, 119
retirements, 80, 278

Scandinavia, 1, 16
seniority wage system, 286, 287
severance rules, 251
    see also dismissals
shortage of jobs, 302, 310, 311
simulations, 265
skills, 3, 123, 124, 211, 230, 251, 287, 288
social security, 121, 124, 125, 181, 275
Soviet block, 3
Spain, 1, 2, 3, 6, 245, 313–34, 364–7
stagflation, 213
strikes, 7, 252, 279

structural unemployment, 104, 105, 112, 114, 126, 165, 233, 235
substitution between factors, 39, 204, 257, 271
substitution between income and leisure, 279, 294
supply shocks, 36, 144–6, 162, 164
supply-side, 75, 117, 121, 140, 271
Sweden, 1, 2, 9–11, 17, 38–41, 43, 44
Switzerland, 1, 2, 9, 11, 12, 17, 291

Tanaka, 282
taxation, 11, 13, 128, 157–9, 165, 253, 323, 332
technical progress, 8, 166, 308, 324, 327, 332
    Harrod-Neutral, 39, 42, 253
    Hicks-Neutral, 51
Thatcher M., 86, 128
trade unions, 3, 75, 78, 79, 83–6, 122, 125–8, 157, 159, 165, 181, 219, 252, 260, 265, 286, 288, 293, 323
turnover, 125

Unemployment, 10, 24, 33, 34, 46–9, 53–6, 58–60, 62–7, 78–80, 83, 89–95, 115, 116, 121–4, 128, 146, 148–50, 155–7, 160–6, 175, 191, 213, 219–31, 263–5, 302, 310, 332
    Classical, 2, 30, 98, 99, 102–04, 118, 121, 144, 146, 216, 224, 309
    Keynesian, 2, 3, 98–102, 118, 121, 146
    definitional issues, 283–5
    demographic composition, 251
unemployment benefits, 3, 7, 54–6, 77, 124, 125, 139, 164, 165, 171, 172, 182, 184–6, 191, 200, 211, 233, 286
unemployment duration, 54–6, 65, 66, 77, 78, 123, 154, 211, 228–35, 251, 286
unemployment rates, 1, 2, 11, 54, 55, 64, 66, 67, 75, 76, 89–95, 105, 107, 121–5, 158, 160, 171–8, 197, 199, 212, 213, 220, 227–9, 245, 246, 262, 263, 278–80, 292, 293, 297, 313–16
unionization rate, 17, 19, 173, 182, 187, 188, 199, 241, 242, 290
United Kingdom, 1–3, 9, 11, 17, 22, 32, 38–41, 43, 44, 46–9, 51, 73, 86, 94, 121–69, 211, 245, 270, 290, 295, 333, 334, 368–74
United States, 1, 2, 8–12, 16, 17, 21, 22, 33, 35–41, 43–51, 73, 86, 94, 142, 169, 171–95, 199, 211, 245, 279, 285, 288, 290, 295, 296, 334

Vacancies, 5, 7, 62, 63, 83, 85, 122, 124, 125, 139, 154, 165, 212, 213, 222, 233, 288, 289
Verdoorn's Law, 300, 308

vintages, 299
voluntary unemployment, 231–3

Wage adjustment, 83–5, 99
wage bargaining, 5, 6, 16, 20, 24, 34, 80,
  83, 84, 137, 139, 142, 146, 159, 161,
  251–5, 282, 283, 288, 293
wage changes, 56, 58–60, 63–72, 92, 93,
  116, 173, 200, 214
wage determination, 4–6, 9, 10, 12,
  58–60, 63, 68, 69, 71, 79, 84, 85,
  101–03, 113, 117, 121, 138–41, 148,
  152–5, 160–4, 214, 254–6, 258–61,
  288–93, 304, 320, 322–4
wage-elasticity of labour demand, 118,
  137, 151, 160, 325

wage flexibility, 80, 83, 85, 86, 210, 215,
  216, 280, 282, 291
wage gap, 14, 37–42, 49, 144, 146
wage indexation, 25, 53, 57, 68, 70, 72,
  102, 215, 251–3
wage pressure variables, 121, 153, 154,
  164
wages policy, 53, 57, 68, 267, 269,
  304
wedge variables, 6, 10, 11, 128, 138
work effort, 5, 139
world demand, 208, 213, 269–71, 307,
  311, 322

Youth employment, 278